Investment Appraisal and Financing Decisions

The VNR Series in Accounting and Finance

Consulting Editor
John Perrin, Emeritus Professor of the University of Warwick and Price Waterhouse Fellow in Public Sector Accounting at the University of Exeter

J.M. Cope
Business Taxation: Policy and Practice

J.C. Drury
Management and Cost Accounting (2nd edn) (Also available: Students' Manual, Teachers' Manual)

C.R. Emmanuel and D.T. Otley
Accounting for Management Control (Also available: Solution Notes)

D. Henley *et al.*
Public Sector Accounting and Financial Control (2nd edn)

R.C. Laughlin and R.H. Gray
Financial Accounting: method and meaning (Also available: Teachers' Guide)

G.A. Lee
Modern Financial Accounting (4th edn) (Also available: Solutions Manual)

T.A. Lee
Income and Value Measurement (3rd edn)

T.A. Lee
Company Financial Reporting (2nd edn)

T.A. Lee
Cash Flow Accounting

S.P. Lumby
Investment Appraisal and Financing Decisions (3rd edn) (Also available: Teachers' Guide)

A.G. Puxty and J.C. Dodds
Financial Management: method and meaning (Also available: Teachers' Guide)

J.M. Samuels and F.M. Wilkes
Management of Company Finance (4th edn)

F.M. Wilkes and R.E. Brayshaw
Company Finance and its Management: Principles, Practice Problems and Solutions

R.M.S. Wilson and Wai Fong Chua
Managerial Accounting: method and meaning (Also available: Teachers' Guide)

Investment Appraisal and Financing Decisions

THIRD EDITION

Stephen Lumby

VNR
International

To Vanessa and Bertie

First published in 1981 as INVESTMENT APPRAISAL

Published by Van Nostrand Reinhold (International) Co. Ltd
Molly Millars Lane, Wokingham, Berkshire, England

Reprinted 1982, 1983
Second edition 1984
Reprinted 1985, 1986, 1987
Third edition 1988

Typeset in 10/11 pt Times New Roman by Times Graphics, Singapore

Printed and bound in Hong Kong

Lumby, Stephen
Investment appraisal and financing decisions.
1. Business firms. Financial management.
Decision making – Manuals
I. Title II. Lumby, Stephen. Investment appraisal and financing decisions
658.1'51

ISBN 0–278–00065–7

Contents

Preface

> There is a popular feeling that 'theory' is opposed to 'practice' and the merits lie with 'practice'. This is a false conclusion, based on a false supposition. If practice has long been successful and does not conform to theory, the theory is bad and in need of revision . . . The distinction should not be between theory and practice; it should be between good theory and bad theory, between good practice and bad practice . . . Practice is brick; theory is mortar. Both are essential and both must be good if we are to erect a worthy structure.
>
> D. Paarlberg, *Great Myths of Economics*

> . . .the description in plain language will be a criterion of the degree of understanding that has been reached.
>
> W. Heisenberg, *Physics and Philosophy*

This book takes the above two quotations as its starting point. The subject matter covered is basically concerned with the evaluation and financing of major long-term capital expenditure projects. As such, it is an area of vital importance because it represents the main way in which firms can enhance the wealth of their shareholders. Indeed, this importance is clearly reflected in the fact that the topics covered represent a standard element in most degree courses that are concerned with industrial and commercial decision making – as well as being a prominent element in professional accountancy examinations.

It is with all these groups of people in mind that this book has been written. However, it is hoped that practising financial decision-makers will also find its contents of interest, in that it may help to provoke thoughtful reflection on how their financial decisions are presently made.

The book's origins lie in my undergraduate lectures on corporate financial management, given at the London School of Economics from 1975 to 1985. However, I have added to these lectures, from my experience of teaching financial management to a wide range of other students, including those preparing for the final examinations of all three of the major professional accountancy bodies, and to engineers and economists.

In many ways this is not my book, but my students' book. It has been their searching questions that have forced me to think through the subject matter to greater depth; it has been their problems with understanding that have caused me to look for new ways of providing clear and full explanations, and it is their comments that have led me to introduce a greater element of realism into explanations of the theory.

This third edition represents a radical re-writing of most of the chapters. Extra examples, and more detailed examples, have been included in many places. A number of chapters have been split up and re-arranged to make them less demanding. A completely new chapter has been added, on the interesting subject of overseas capital investment. The readings have also been revised and updated, with particular attention being paid to trying to provide articles that are accessible to those readers without a doctorate in mathematics!

Each chapter now ends with a brief summary, a set of 'quickie questions' and two or three full length exam-style questions. The summaries are designed to give a general run-down of the topics covered in each particular chapter, and the 'quickie questions' are designed to test both recall and understanding. (The answers are tucked away towards the end of the book to reduce any temptation to cheat!)

The exam-style questions have been selected to try to cover the major elements of each chapter's subject matter. These questions are either of my own design, or have been culled from the recent examination papers of the various professional accountancy bodies. These examiners have collectively set some splendid questions in the past, and I am grateful to the accountancy bodies concerned for their kind permission to use them. Solutions to these questions have not been included here, but are contained in the *Teachers' Guide,* which is available from the publishers.

Overall, the main purpose behind this third revision is to try and increase further the 'user-friendliness' of the book and to expand its explanatory power. In this respect, I am very grateful to both the teachers and students who have been kind enough to make suggestions for improvements. I have incorporated many of their comments in this new edition. Of course, further comments are more than welcome.

As before, I should make it clear that this is not a cook-book of capital investment decision making, but is an attempt at a fairly detailed exposition of a normative theory of financial decision making. Therefore, examples that have used real-world data are there for the purposes of exposition, rather than to encourage the unthinking application of the theory to practical decision making. The aim is not to put forward theoretical solutions to practical problems, but to promote more thought and reflection on how decisions are actually made and, maybe, how they can be improved.

As far as possible, the presentation has been argued in descriptive and graphical terms, rather than using a strict mathematical analysis. The reasons for this are two-fold. First, a mathematical treatment often excludes a great many potential enquirers and reduces the subject matter to a degree of terseness that makes unrealistic demands upon the concentration of readers. Second, a mathematical treatment, although often elegant, can sometimes fail to make clear the full significance of important conclusions. However, it has been impossible to exclude mathematics completely – indeed it would have been counterproductive to do so in certain areas – but its complexity has been kept to an absolute minimum.

Finally, if this third edition does prove to be an improvement on what has gone before, much credit must be given to the sunshine of Portugal where most of the re-writing was undertaken. Blue skies, blue sea and a warm sun make splendid conditions for writing and the thought of lunch to come on the beach speeds the task along! Some of the names given to companies used in examples give a clue to the afternoon's beach!

As always thanks go to the people at VNR – this time Stephen Wellings drew the short straw, but made a splendid job of gently prompting my progress. Thanks also go to Vanessa for readily agreeing to sunbathe through the mornings alone. Most of all, thanks go to my students as they are the ones who make teaching so enjoyable.

1
Introduction

Chapter Contents

AN OVERVIEW

This book covers an area of managerial economics which is relatively new in terms of degree and professional examination courses: the theory of business financial decisions. It is concerned with how management within companies[1]* *should* make[2] financial decisions,[3] and so it can be called a normative theory because it sets out to establish a standard or norm. But such a theory cannot hope to succeed in its task if it is developed in isolation from what actually does happen in practice, and so we shall also examine how financial decisions *are* made, in order to guide the development of the normative theory.

The value base

However, it is important to realize that financial decisions are no different in their fundamental aspects from other decisions of a non-financial nature, be they in industry or commerce or elsewhere, such as marketing decisions or even international diplomacy decisions. In essence, *all* decisions are based on the concept of the comparison of alternatives, and it is in this sense that the theory of financial decisions

*Notes are to be found at the end of each chapter. In general they are intended to assist understanding and so the reader is requested not to neglect them.

really has its roots in valuation theory, because all the alternatives in any decision-making situation have to be valued in order to be compared. Therefore, although we can say that all types of decisions involve the same fundamental process, each is given its own unique characteristics by the valuation basis which it employs.

The financial decision theory developed in this book is founded on the valuation basis of capitalism[4] and the idea of the free market economy. It is important that this is specified from the outset, as a different valuation basis is likely to produce a different overall theory of financial decisions. However, many parts of our financial theory will be applicable to other types of economic organization, and the reader may wish to consider and reflect upon the implications of our theory for more social value bases, such as those which might be appropriate to the public sector and, in particular, public enterprises.

The 'model' approach

The theory will be developed by examining the three major areas of financial decisions:

1. The capital investment decision.
2. The financing and capital structure decision.
3. The dividend decision.

In the course of this development a considerable number of abstractions from and simplifications of the 'real world' will be made, in order to distil the difficulties and focus attention on areas of major importance.

Thus we are going to take a 'modelling' approach, but we must be careful not to fall into the trap of oversimplifying the real world and, in so doing, leaving out important and relevant factors which should properly be included. This is particularly important because we are developing a normative theory and are therefore attempting to give advice on how financial decisions should be taken. If we work with oversimplified models and the theory is followed in practice, the quality of financial decisions made in business may deteriorate rather than improve.

Therefore the difficulties caused by taxation, inflation and capital scarcity will all be taken into account, as will the concept of risk and the fact that the future is uncertain.[5] All these real world realities will be added layer by layer, and so we shall begin with a model which, although a poor reflection of the real world, provides a logically sound framework upon which to build.

A warning

As a final point, the reader should be constantly aware that the theory of financial decisions which is presented here is neither in a state of general detailed agreement, nor does it yet provide complete solutions to many of the important problems of financial decision making. In order to reflect this state of affairs, we shall examine the causes and evidence of these controversies and point out the irrationalities, ambiguities and inconsistencies that necessarily accompany the development of any theory that aspires to real world application.

THE DECISION PROCESS

In order to examine the decision process and to answer the question: 'How do we make a decision?', we have first to discuss the circumstances in which a decision needs to be made. We can specify two necessary conditions for a decision situation: the existence of alternatives and the existence of an objective or goal.

The first necessary condition

The existence of alternatives is necessary for, if there are no alternatives amongst which to choose, then there is no need for a decision. This condition can be specified further in that not only must alternatives exist, but they must be seen to exist by the potential decision maker. There are two points of interest here.

First, notice that we talk of a decision *situation* and of a *potential* decision maker. This is because the mere existence of perceived alternatives does not necessarily mean that a decision will be made. For instance, the potential decision maker may well procrastinate, and therefore the passage of time takes him (or her) out of a decision situation and into a situation where there is only one possible course of action and no alternatives are available. (Death is the ultimate example of the passage of time removing a decision situation from an individual.)

The second point of interest is that we are *not* specifying that all possible alternatives are perceived (if they were, we could call this an optimal decision situation), because we are examining how decisions are made, given a decision situation exists; whether the decision is optimal or non-optimal is of no concern at present.

The second necessary condition

The second necessary condition for a decision situation arises from the fact that the actual process of 'making a decision' is liable to cause the decision maker to expend both time and effort. Rationally he will be unwilling to do so unless he expects that some of the perceived alternatives will be preferred to others in relation to attaining the desired objective. Thus the existence of an objective is the second necessary condition; without it, there will be no purpose in making a decision.[6]

Valuation of alternatives

Together, these two necessary conditions give the rationale for making decisions: if the decision maker does not perceive alternatives or see no reason to choose between the alternatives if they are perceived, then no decision will be made (expect one of a totally arbitrary kind, as in note 6). But once these conditions do exist, a decision cannot actually be made until values are placed upon the alternatives. In fact, we can assert that the *only* reason why any alternative course of action is ever evaluated is in order to make a decision about it; therefore, the valuation method used must be related to the objective involved in making the decision and the way in which that objective is expressed.

For example, if our objective were to drive from A to B in the shortest possible time, then we should value the alternative routes from A to B by a common value criterion which was related to our objective of time, and choose whichever route took the shortest time. Suppose there were three alternative routes and one we valued by time, one by distance and one by scenic beauty. We obviously could not make a decision because the alternatives have different measures or yardsticks of value and so cannot be compared. Alternatively, if all three routes were measured in terms of scenic beauty, we should again be unable to make a decision even though we could compare the routes – because the basis of the comparison is not the one which gives the rationale for the decision: the value base of the objective, which in this example is 'time'.[7]

Therefore, any decision making process consists of these three components: a series of perceived alternatives, an expectation that these alternatives are not all equally desirable in terms of attaining an objective held by the decision maker, and a common value base related to the decision objective. So it is with all financial decisions made in business.

FINANCIAL DECISION MAKING

This book focuses attention on only two of the three components that we have identified in the decision process and examines how they relate to the making of financial decisions: the expectation that the perceived alternatives are not all equally desirable in terms of attaining a specific objective, and the common value base that is related to this objective and is used to compare the alternatives.

The remaining component of the decision process is the series of perceived alternatives. We shall not be examining it in the main body of the text as it is primarily a condition for the decision *situation,* and we are concentrating on the actual decision making, assuming that the decision situation already exists. However, this omission does not mean that the 'search process' (as it is called) for alternatives is unimportant. It is in fact extremely important. If this search process is not efficient in seeking out alternatives, then there is a grave danger that the decision itself will not be optimal because the 'most preferred' alternative may go unperceived.

The decision objective

Turning to the two decision process components that we shall examine in detail, we immediately become involved in value judgements, because the objective we use for financial decision making, and the consequent value base, will completely determine the decision reached on which alternative is selected. Therefore, what objective are we going to use and what valuation base are we going to set up for our theory of financial decisions?

We stated earlier that the fundamental value judgement upon which this theory is based is capitalism. So it is a theory that is essentially (but by no means exclusively) applicable to companies operating in largely unregulated, competitive economies. In such economies, companies exist for one overriding purpose: in order to benefit their owners.[8] Certainly it may be said that companies provide a source of employment for local populations, that they supply the needs of a particular market or even that they are the vanguard in technological advance, but the fact still remains that the fundamental rationale for their existence must be to bring benefit to their owners.

This rationale for existence undoubtedly holds true for the great majority of privately owned [9] companies (and also, to some extent, for the nationalized industries although their rationale for existence can be more complex[10]). Therefore, management's objective in making financial decisions should be to further the very reason for the company's existence, of benefiting the owners, i.e., the shareholders. If that is to be their decision objective, what is the value base to be used for the comparison of alternatives?

To answer this question, we have to examine the decision objective more closely. It is obvious from what we have already said that not only should company managements make financial decisions so as to benefit the shareholders but they should also strive to maximize that benefit, otherwise shareholders will be interested in replacing them with a set of decision makers who will do this. Therefore, what is meant by the term *maximizing owners' or shareholders' benefit*?

Maximizing shareholder wealth

We are going to assume that maximizing benefit means maximizing wealth. Although there is nothing surprising about this, we have to be careful here because we are going to assume that maximizing the increase in the owners' wealth is the *only* way in which management decisions can benefit owners.

This is a slight simplification of the real world because it is quite possible for shareholders to gain benefit from a company other than by increases in wealth. For example, shareholders of the Rolls Royce company may gain benefit from ownership in terms of pride in owning part of Britain's 'Industrial Heritage'. However, this is a comparatively minor point and we shall proceed on the relatively sound assumption that increase in wealth is the sole source of benefit from company ownership.

What about firms selling military arms to countries with repugnant policies, or firms causing pollution to land, air or water resources? Do these types of activity enter into consideration of our decision objective? On the basis of our underlying assumption about the nature of the economy, our answer must be that they should not, because if these activities were thought to be truly undesirable, governments would legislate to constrain companies' decision-choice alternatives so as to exclude them (as in many cases they do). Company decision makers should only need to perceive and analyse the decision alternatives in terms of maximizing the owners' wealth.

Under the market economies of western countries, we develop a theory of financial decisions for privately owned firms in this way because of the workings of the market system for company capital. Ordinary share capital, the substance of ownership, is normally provided through supply and demand markets (e.g., stock exchanges), which means that potential shareholders will wish to own companies that are expected to provide them with the greatest possible increase in wealth (i.e., shareholders have to make financial decisions in much the same way as management, choosing between alternative ownership opportunities), and existing shareholders will change their ownership allegiances if they see other companies providing greater increases to their owners' wealth than they are receiving. (An important concept here, and one we have yet to deal with, is that the future is uncertain and so any decision amongst alternatives usually has a risk attached to it: the risk that the alternative chosen may not turn out as expected. Some alternatives are riskier than others and so shareholders will really want to own companies that they expect will give them the greatest possible increase in wealth, *for a given level of risk.* This concept we shall consider much more fully later.)

Therefore, if a company in its financial decision process starts consistently to take into account factors other than that of maximizing shareholder wealth, the whole rationale for the company's existence – so far as shareholders are concerned – is cast into doubt and they are likely to take their investment funds elsewhere. In the extreme case, company law provides the opportunity for shareholders to replace a company's decision makers if enough of them believe that decisions are not being taken in their best interests.

Defining wealth

However, we still cannot determine the value base for financial decision making until we have 'wealth', because the purpose of the value base is to act as a common denominator with which to make the alternative courses of action directly comparable and to see which one leads furthest towards the decision objective. As the objective of financial decisions is assumed to be to 'maximize the increase in owners' wealth', let us define 'wealth' and so determine the value base.

Wealth can be defined as purchasing power or, to put it in more straightforward terms, money or cash.[11] Thus company management's objective becomes the maximization of shareholders' purchasing power, which can be achieved by maximizing the amount of cash paid out to shareholders in the form of dividends. But which dividend should a company's management try to maximize, this year's, next year's or what?

The point here is that it would be a relatively easy task for a company to maximize a single year's dividend, simply by selling up all the assets and paying a final liquidation dividend! (We are ignoring the niceties of company law here, but the point still remains.) Obviously this is not what is meant by our decision objective of maximizing dividends, and the trouble arises through the omission of the time dimension. When fully defined, including the time dimension, the objective of a company's financial decision makers becomes the maximizing of the *flow* of dividends to shareholders *over or through time.*

The role of accounting profit

Now there are two points of fundamental importance that arise from the development of this decision objective. Firstly, the word 'profit' has not been mentioned and the emphasis has been laid on wealth defined as *cash.* Secondly, the introduction of time means that decisions must be analysed not only in terms of immediate cash gains and losses, but also in terms of *future* gains and losses.

These two points are interlinked. Profit, when used in a business sense, is a concept developed by accountants in order to assist them with their auditing and reporting functions, performed on behalf of shareholders.

The external accountant or auditor has an unenviable task. His job is to divide up what is a *continuous* process – the change in a company's worth over time – into discrete periods of time. These discrete periods of time are referred to as the *accounting year.* It is the accountant's task to try to measure what has been the change in the company's worth during that time period in order to report back to the shareholders – the company's owners – on how successful their management have been in increasing shareholders' wealth.

In order to assist in this very difficult task, the accountant has developed a highly specialized and specific measuring-rod, based on a whole series of principles and conventions (such as the accruals concept and the prudence principle), which is termed Accounting Profit. Thus accounting profit is, very clearly, a reporting concept.

In contrast, financial decisions are basically *economic* or *resource allocation* decisions. Management have to decide whether they should allocate the firm's scarce resources (land, labour, machinery, etc.) to a particular project. The economic 'unit of account' is cash, not accounting profit, because it is cash which gives power to command resources (i.e. resources are purchased with cash, not profit). Thus to use the accounting profit concept in financial decision making would be to use an entirely inappropriate concept – a concept specially developed for reporting the *outcome* of decisions and not developed for helping to take the actual decision itself.

However, we cannot discard the accounting profit concept completely. To do so would be rather like a sports team whose policy is that they do not mind whether they win or lose, so long as in playing they give maximum entertainment to their supporters. This is fine, and it is probably the correct attitude; but often it is on winning and losing that the success of the team is ultimately judged and therefore that part of the game cannot be ignored. So it is with accounting profit. The company's financial decision makers should have as their major concern the maximization of the flow of cash through time to the shareholders, but they should always do so with an eye to reported profit. Profitability, as expressed in annual published accounts, forms a major criterion by which shareholders and prospective shareholders judge a company's success and, as we shall see later, it is important that people do form correct judgements about a company's performance.

A further reason why the effects of financial decisions on reported profits cannot be completely ignored is provided by the fact that the level of retained profit, in company law, can form a very substantial maximum barrier to an annual dividend payment. Thus a company that wishes to maximize its dividend flow must ensure that its dividend payout intentions are legally within the confines of company law.

Therefore, with the exception of these two provisos, we can say that the financial decision theory developed here is built on an analytical framework that is largely devoid of the accounting profit concept, although it would be correct to assume that, in the longer run, good company cash flows will result in good reported profits.

The time dimension

Turning to the second point of importance in our decision objective, the introduction of the time dimension, we have already noted that the arbitrary time segmentation of a continuous flow process has been the cause of major problems for the accounting profit concept, but to see the true significance of the introduction of this factor we have to return to our discussion on value.

An asset (such as a machine or a share in a company) is valued on the basis of the gains, or losses, that the owner receives. Furthermore, these gains and losses do not refer to just a single time period, but to the whole period of future time for which the asset will exist. (This concept is sometimes referred to as the asset's *earning power.*)

Let us consider an asset of company ownership: an ordinary share. Ordinary shares are traded (i.e., bought and sold) in supply and demand markets and so its market valuation represents an equilibrium value, a value at which demand for the share by people who wish to buy it equates with the supply of the share by people who wish to sell it. But what process actually gives a share its equilibrium price, what makes prospective purchasers wish to buy it at that price and what makes prospective sellers wish to sell it at that price? Let us examine the prospective purchaser's reasons.

Suppose an ordinary share of XYZ plc has a stock market price of 150p.[12] A prospective owner of that share would only be willing to buy it if he thought it was worth 150p. In other words, he would expect that the gains to be received from ownership would have a value of at least 150p.

These *gains of ownership* consist of two elements: the stream of dividends received for as long as he owns the share and the selling price received when the share is sold (and so ownership relinquished) at some future point in time. However, it is important to note that this future selling price of the XYZ share is itself based on the value the succeeding owner puts on the benefits that he in turn expects to receive from ownership – the dividend flow received and the selling price that he will receive upon selling the share at some future point in time. So the process goes on *ad infinitum.* Therefore, although there are two benefits of ownership, the dividends received and the future selling price, this latter benefit is itself determined by the flow of dividends expected to be generated by the share subsequent to its sale.

Given this argument, our theory will assume that shares derive their (equilibrium) stock market price on the basis of the sum of the dividend flow that they will produce through time. (As the future is uncertain it is more correct to talk of valuation based on the *expected* dividend flow, but we shall return to this later.) Thus the greater the future dividend flow, the more highly are the shares valued. Therefore if our financial decision makers are taking decisions so as maximize dividend flow through time, then via the direct link between dividend flow and a share's market price, this action will result in the *maximization of the market value of the company's shares.* It is this that we shall take as being the operational objective of financial management decision making.[13]

The objective hierarchy

So let us summarize our assumed hierarchy of decision objectives:

1 Decisions are taken by companies so as to maximize owners' wealth.
2 Owners' wealth can be maximized through maximizing owners' purchasing power.
3 Purchasing power can be maximized through maximizing the amount of cash the company pays out to shareholders in the form of dividends.
4 With the introduction of the time dimension the objective becomes the maximizing of the value of the dividend flow through time to the shareholders.
5 The maximization of the value of the dividend flow through time maximizes the stock market's valuation of the company's ordinary share capital.

However, it is important to realize that although it is this 'fifth level' of objective we shall use in developing the theory of financial decision making, it is really only a *surrogate* objective for the fundamental, underlying objective, of maximizing shareholders' wealth.

A fundamental assumption

As a final point, let us state the assumptions about the shareholder which have been implied in the analysis. It was earlier argued that the maximization of shareholders' wealth had to be the fundamental decision objective because of the nature of the capital markets. However, the validity of this assertion depends entirely upon the assumption that shareholders perceive wealth in the way we have postulated and that in this perception they are rational. In essence this means that we have assumed that shareholders see wealth as the receipt of cash flows through time and that they will always prefer a greater to lesser cash flow. These appear reasonably safe assumptions, but we shall consider situations where they may not hold when we look later at dividend policies.

MAXIMIZING VERSUS SATISFICING

Principal–agent relationship

A company's management (or, more strictly speaking, its directors) are in a principal–agent relationship with the owners. The shareholders are the principals and the management are employed as agents to take decisions on their behalf.

The major problem facing any principal is that of control: how to control the agent so as to ensure that the agent always acts in the best interests of the principal. The problem arises out of the fact that there may well be a conflict between the private objectives of agents and the objectives that their principal wishes them to pursue.

Therefore, shareholders will wish management to take financial (and non-financial) decisions so as to maximize the worth of the company's shares. However, management will have their own, personal objectives which may well conflict with those of their shareholders. These objectives will be mainly concerned with three things: their pay, their 'perks' (or non-monetary rewards such as holiday entitlements, working conditions, company cars, etc.) and their job security.[14]

In such circumstances, it is sometimes argued that managers will become satisficers rather than maximizers of shareholder wealth. This means that they will do sufficient to keep shareholders reasonably satisfied in terms of increasing their wealth, and at the same time put their remaining efforts into the pursuit of their own personal objectives.

This point is important because, as was mentioned earlier, if management really have as their objective the satisficing rather than the maximizing of shareholders' wealth, then our normative theory of financial decision making would change. However, we will argue that although satisficing behaviour may well exist in the short term, it is unlikely to do so in the medium to long term – particularly in stock exchange quoted companies.

There are two principal reasons for this argument:

1 The competitive market for the shareholders' funds.
2 The competitive market for management jobs.

In a stock exchange quoted company, shareholders can monitor their management's performance through their company's share-price performance, relative to that of similar companies. If one set of management is only satisficing, whilst the management of a similar company is striving to maximize shareholder wealth, then this fact can be expected to be reflected in the respective share price performance of the two companies (because of the resulting lower flow of dividends). Under such circumstances the satisficing company's management are likely to suffer adverse criticism in the financial press and their shareholders are likely to 'vote with their feet' – selling their shares and buying into the maximizing company. The resulting selling pressure on the company's shares is likely to depress their market price and, unless the situation is corrected fairly rapidly, market forces – perhaps in the form of an 'unwelcome' takeover bid – will lead to a change in management.[15] Thus the competitive market for shareholders' funds can help to ensure adherence to the maximizing objective.

In addition, one way for a manager to pursue his own objectives in terms of pay and perks is through job promotion. Given that most managers perceive that promotion can be gained through doing a job well, then it follows that in a competitive market for managerial jobs – as exists within a company – individual maximizing managers will look to advance their own personal objectives by replacing satisficing managers. Thus a satisficing manager runs the risk of being displaced by an ambitious maximizing manager.

It is, therefore, for both these reasons that we argue for maximizing behaviour by management in the medium to long term. However, it should be noted that unquoted company shareholders do not have the 'protection' of relative share-price performance comparisons. Nevertheless, in such cases there is likely to be a much less clear-cut divorce between ownership and control and hence a much greater congruence between manager and shareholder objectives.

Goal convergence

This brief discussion about the possibility of conflicting objectives between managers and shareholders does lead to considerations as to how management's own personal goals can be made to accord with shareholders' objectives. The obvious approach is to link managerial rewards to the attainment of shareholders' goals through incentive payments.

However, if possible, the incentive scheme should not be through reported profitability – for all the reasons that profit as a decision-making concept was rejected earlier. Ideally, the incentive should either be linked to the company's relative share price performance or be in terms of share options.[16]

The problem with all such schemes is to design them so that the incentive element is a significant part of management's overall remuneration package (in other words, the gain from trying to maximize the worth of the shares must exceed any likely gain through satisficing activities). At the same time, such schemes run a danger of over-rewarding management and thereby resulting in a net loss of wealth to shareholders.

THE BROADER PICTURE

The role of financial management

Before moving on to look more closely at the theory and practice of financial decision making, it is important to see the place of financial decision making within the overall financial management function. This book is not concerned about the whole spectrum of financial management, but it is concerned with what are probably the most fundamental elements within that spectrum and, as such, they have important implications for the other elements.

Essentially, the financial management function can be divided up into five principal areas:

1 *Translating* the company's business plan into a financial plan.
2 *Evaluating* the financial plan to ensure its validity, given the company's objective as far as shareholder wealth maximization is concerned.
3 Ensuring that sufficient *finance* is made available in order to undertake the planned activities.
4 *Controlling* the plan's implementation.
5 *Reporting* the outcome of the business plan's implementation to all interested parties.

Therefore, the starting point is where the company – either formally or informally – draws up a business plan. This would normally be done in non-financial terms: sales targets, percentage market shares, capacity levels and manpower levels, etc. These plans would then have to be examined and analysed (and modified if need be), to ensure that their financial implications are satisfactory and that they will help to increase shareholder wealth.

In addition to evaluating the financial feasibility of the business plan, financial management has also to ensure that the company has adequate financial resources at its command to enable it to undertake the plan. If those resources do not already exist within the company, then arrangements have to be made to raise additional finance from the financial markets.

The business plan is then implemented and controlled, typically through standard costing, budget setting and variance analysis. Finally, the outcome of all this activity has to be reported to the company's own management in the form of management accounts, and to its shareholders in the form of financial accounts (i.e. the profit and loss account, balance sheet and funds flow statement). In addition, financial reports to other interested parties such as the employees, the company's bankers and the tax authorities may also be required.

Organization of the finance function

Figure 1.1 is of a typical organizational chart for the finance function of a large company. From it can be seen how these different elements of financial management are normally split up between the three major participants: the finance director, the chief accountant and the treasurer.

The main responsibilities of the finance director are as follows:

1 The setting of the company's broad financial strategy.
2 Decisions on major capital expenditure on new assets and the acquisition of other companies.
3 Interpretation and implications of macro and micro economic financial developments for the company.

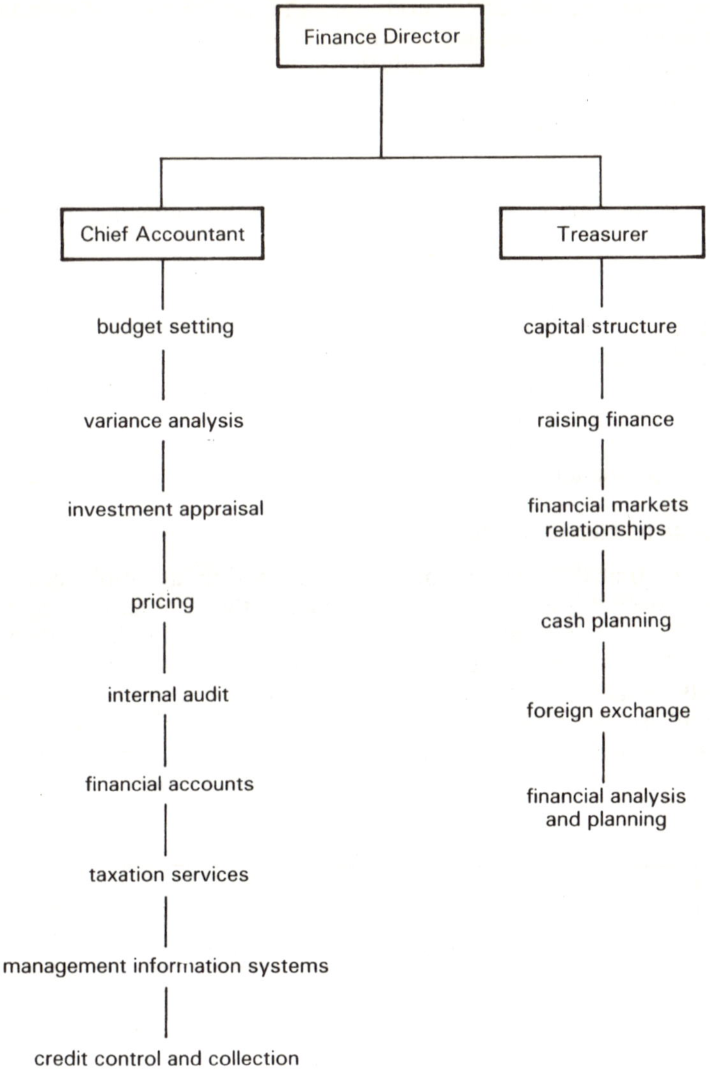

Figure 1.1

4 Implications for the company of Government economic and fiscal (tax) legislation and proposals.
5 The dividend decision.

The Chief Accountant is responsible for the following tasks:

1 Preparation of financial reports to all internal and external user groups including: management, employees, shareholders, bankers, other creditors and tax authorities.

2 Installation, maintenance, updating and review of the company's management information system.
3 Preparation and control of budgets.
4 Pricing policies.
5 Capital investment appraisals.
6 Management of working capital.

The Treasurer's main responsibilities concern the following six areas:

1 The establishment and maintenance of good relationships with shareholders and financial institutions.
2 Ensuring that sufficient finance, and credit facilities, are available to meet all foreseeable contingencies.
3 The issue of securities and investment of surplus cash.
4 Cashier and payroll activities.
5 Management of the company's exposure to foreign exchange risk.
6 Corporate financial planning.

The firm in the economy

There are basically two major groupings within a simple economic system: households and firms. 'Households' is the term used by economists to refer to individuals within the economy (like you, the reader) who own the physical resources such as land, property, machinery, raw materials or labour. Households then transfer these resources to firms who then use them to produce outputs (which can be anything from cornflakes to theatre tickets) that people want. This process is seen by the innermost pair of arrows in Figure 1.2. It is known as the *real*

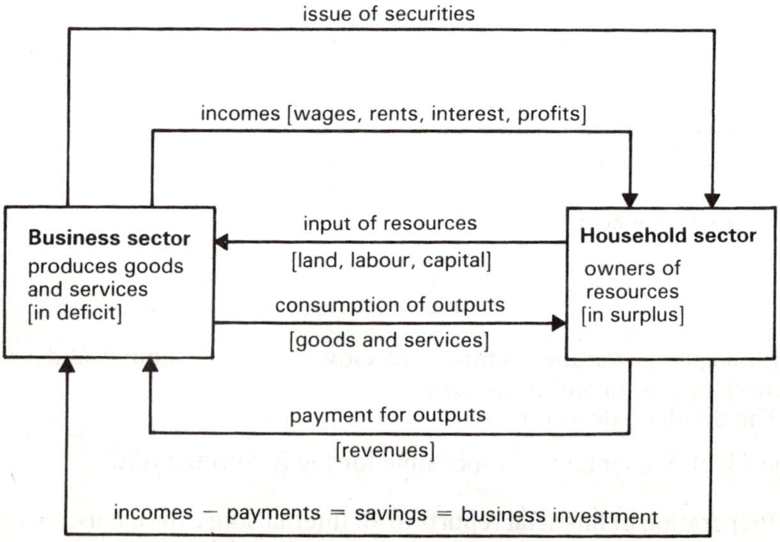

Figure 1.2 Simple Two-Sector Economy

sub-system in the economy's *flow of funds* as it deals with the flow of real or physical inputs (resources) and outputs (goods and services) in the economy.

Firms pay households for their resources with money in the form of wages, rents and prices. In turn, households pay for the outputs of firms also by using money. Thus there is a secondary pair of arrows in Figure 1.2 which is referred to as the *monetary* sub-system as it relates to the flow of cash between households and firms.

The money that households receive from firms in payment for their resources is known as their *income.* The money households pay to firms in order to buy the outputs of firms is their *expenditure.* Households generally have an excess of income over expenditure, known as *savings.* Similarly, the households' income represents the firms' *costs* and the households' expenditure represents the firms' *revenues.*

In aggregate, within an economy, the household sector usually has a surplus (of income over expenditure) while the firm sector is in deficit (i.e. it requires additional cash). Therefore households lend their savings to firms and, in return, firms pay out interest and dividends to households. This flow is represented by the outermost pair of arrows on Figure 1.2 – the *financial* sub-system.

Obviously, what has been described here is a very simplistic analysis and a more complete picture of the flow of funds within the economy would involve at least three other sectors: the Government, the financial intermediaries (of which more later) and overseas economies. However, our purpose for the moment is sufficiently served by this very simple illustration.

Liquidity

Within this simple illustration of the flow of funds in an economy, there lies a problem. Generally speaking, households dislike lending their savings to firms *unless* they have the ability to get their money back again quickly and easily, if they so wish (because some unforeseen need to spend their savings on goods and services has arisen). In other words, households only like to invest their savings if they have a considerable degree of *liquidity.*

On the other hand, firms want to be able to keep the money that they borrow from households for lengthy periods of time because they will often want to invest it in long-term or permanent assets such as machinery or buildings. It would be no good a firm borrowing £1m from households one week, and then the households asking for their money back the next week (because some unforeseen circumstances have arisen) if, in the meantime, the firm has bought a new factory with the money. Thus the problem is that there is a mis-match between firms and households in their liquidity requirements. Because of their *liquidity preference,* households generally want only to lend short term, but firms want to borrow medium-to-long term.

Within the economy, this problem is surmounted in two ways: by the existence of *financial intermediaries* (such as banks), and *financial markets* (such as the stock market). Both financial intermediaries and financial markets stand between the firms and the households in order to solve the mis-match in liquidity requirements.

Taking a bank as the best-known example of a financial intermediary, the role they play can be simply illustrated as follows. Suppose a household has £1,000 of savings. They want to invest those savings but they also require to be able to recall their money (liquidate their investment) if an unforeseen need for it arises. Instead of lending the money directly to a firm, which is likely to want to keep the money medium-to-long term, and will not want (or be able) to offer the household the facility of returning the money at short notice, the household lends the £1,000 to a bank. In other words, the money is placed on bank deposit. The bank undertakes to repay the contents of the deposit account to the household at any time, but then promptly lends £900 of the £1,000 to a firm. The loan to the firm may be for, say, a 5-year term. The result of this is that the household has the required liquidity for its savings and the firm has got its required *illiquidity*.

But what happens if, shortly after the loan is made to the firm, the household demands their money back? The bank has only got £100 of the original £1,000. It is here that the bank takes advantage of being able to pool the savings of many households. Knowing that it is unlikely that *all* the households who have placed money on deposit will simultaneously want their money back, the bank tries to keep sufficient *liquid resources* (the £100 kept back would be part of these) available to be able to satisfy those households who do actually want to liquidate the investment of their savings.

This mis-match of liquidity requirements between households and firms is also reconciled through the existence of capital markets like the stock exchange. Basically the stock exchange provides a market place where medium-to-long term securities (debentures and shares) issued by firms to households can be sold (or liquidated).

For example, the household which wanted to invest £1,000 of its savings could, instead of going through a financial intermediary, invest the money in the firm *directly*. In return the firm might issue £1,000 worth of share certificates. If a stock market did not exist, a household would be extremely reluctant to take this course of action because ordinary shares form part of the firm's permanent capital and are unlikely ever to be repaid unless the firm is itself wound-up. Thus the household's investment would be completely illiquid.

However, the problem is overcome through the existence of stock markets. If the firm's shares are *quoted* on the stock market, it means that there are institutions known as *market makers* whose function is always to be prepared to buy (and sell) shares in the firms from households. Thus if our household who has invested £1,000 in the shares of the firm wishes to liquidate the investment because unforeseen cirumstances have arisen where the money is needed, they can simply sell their shares – not back to the company, but on the stock market (to the market maker) – and so liquidate their investment.

Risk

There is, of course, an important difference between the two examples used of the household with £1,000 of savings. When the bank deposit account is liquidated, the household will recover the *precise* amount placed on deposit – £1,000 – (plus any interest that has accrued). However, when the £1,000 investment in the company's shares is liquidated, just how much money will be recovered – it could be more or less than £1,000 – is uncertain because the market maker sets a price based on supply and demand considerations. Thus the household suffers a degree of uncertainty in the latter case which is avoided in the former.

This problem of risk – that is, uncertainty of outcome – will play a major role in the development of the theory of financial decision making. In many ways it is what financial decision making is all about. Householders (i.e. investors) dislike risk, they are *risk averse,* and will only be willing to take on risk if they can be expected to be rewarded for so doing. This reward comes in the form of the expected level of return. Thus much of financial decision making is concerned with the risk and return trade-off – is the expected return worth the risk involved?

For this reason, the household in our example would expect to get a higher return on his savings invested in shares (coming in the form of dividends plus a possible capital gain on subsequent sale) than when they were placed on bank deposit (coming in the form of interest). In fact, the capital markets provide a whole spectrum of different risk (and expected return) investments in which households can place their savings. However, the nature of this risk and the determinants of the reward structure will be returned to at a later point.

SUMMARY

This chapter has covered the following major points:

- The decision process consists of three elements:
  - ☐ A series of perceived alternatives.
  - ☐ An expectation that these alternatives are not all equally desirable in terms of attaining an objective held by the decision maker.
  - ☐ A common value base, related to the objective, by which the alternatives may be compared.
- As far as financial management is concerned, it is assumed that the objective of financial management decision making is the maximization of shareholder wealth. This is normally translated to mean maximizing the current worth of the company's shares.
- Given that shareholder wealth is seen in terms of an ability to consume goods and services and that it is cash which provides consumption power, so share value can be maximized by maximizing the sum of the expected stream of dividends through time generated by the share.
- Accounting profit is essentially an inappropriate concept within the

context of financial management decision making because it is a *reporting* device, not a decision making device. Finance decisions are economic or resource allocation decisions and the economic unit of account is cash; hence decisions are evaluated in terms of their cash flow impact. However, the reported profit impact of financial decisions remains an important consideration in terms of the correct communication of managements' actions to shareholders and others.

- Financial managers are unlikely to be able to sustain satisficing rather than maximizing behaviour for more than the short run. This is because of the competitive market for shareholders' funds causing the shareholders of satisficing companies to switch to maximizing companies; and because of the competitive market for management jobs both with the firm and between firms.

- The role of financial management can be split into five broad elements:
  - ☐ The translation of the business plan into financial terms.
  - ☐ The financial evaluation of the plan.
  - ☐ The raising of finance for the plan.
  - ☐ The implementation and control of the plan.
  - ☐ The reporting to interested parties as to the financial outcome of the plan's implementation.

- The mis-match in liquidity requirements between households and firms can be resolved through the use of financial intermediaries and capital markets. However, there is a significant difference in the risk a household/investor is exposed to through each means and this is reflected in the expected returns on investment each provides the household.

The next stage

Having discussed in general terms the problem of choice in relation to financial decisions, we are now ready to examine closely the investment decision, which is the most fundamental of all the three decision areas covered by this book. But before doing so, it is perhaps prudent to emphasize at this point that although our analysis will appear to separate out the three decision areas – investment, financing and dividend – in practice they are inexorably interlinked. For example, the investment and dividend decisions may well be competing for the same cash resources within the company, the financing decision may be closely bound to what investment decision is made and vice versa, and the dividend decision is likely to have a direct bearing on the financing decision. It is only for the sake of clarity of exposition that these decisions have been artificially segregated, and each should really be seen as just another complex layer of the whole financial decision 'cake'; but, to continue the metaphor, it is the investment decision that forms the foundation layer.

NOTES

1 Be these either large stock exchange quoted companies such as ICI or Unilever, or small unquoted companies such as a local printing company or car rental company.

2 The terms decision 'making' and decision 'taking' can be used synonymously. However, the term decision 'making' will be used in this book because of its more positive emphasis on deliberate creative action.

3 We will carefully define just what financial decisions are, but for now this covers such things as a decision to invest in a new machine, to borow money from the bank or a decision to 'pass' (i.e. not pay) an annual dividend that shareholders were expecting.

4 There are many variants of capitalism (which in itself is just one type of economic system; for example, alternatives could include socialist, feudal and primitive communal economies) but its two general features are the private ownership of property and the allocation of the economy's resources (land, labour and machinery) through a supply and demand price mechanism.

5 Indeed, we shall also occasionally allude to the psychological processes behind firms' financial decisions, where conflicts of interest arise.

6 In a way, in specifying this second necessary condition, we are ignoring the situation where a decision *has* to be made even though this second condition does not exist. For instance, if you are out for a walk with no particular destination in mind and you come to a crossroads, a decision *has* to be taken on what direction to go, even though the second necessary condition is really unfulfilled. Such situations are of little interest as far as the decision *process* is concerned; we could call them indifference decisions.

7 For the present, we shall ignore the possibility of multiple objectives, although we shall touch upon it later. However we may observe that where multiple objectives exist in real life, one objective is often regarded (either implicitly or explicitly) as being of overriding importance, with the other objectives acting as constraining factors or considerations.

8 In abstract terms we can define a company as a collection of assets. The owners of the company have therefore pooled their funds to assemble such a collection and are logically only likely to do so in order to bring benefit (either directly or indirectly) to themselves.

9 The term 'privately owned companies' can be a source of confusion. It refers to all companies which are owned by individuals, either singly or collectively, whether or not they are 'publicly quoted' on a stock exchange or otherwise. Thus both public and private companies (in financial nomenclature) are privately owned companies.

10 See, for instance, Ivy Papps, *Government and Enterprise*, Hobart Paper No.61, Institute of Economic Affairs, 1975.

11 We shall be ignoring the effects of inflation until later.

12 This is obviously a simplification, as in practice each share has two equilibrium prices, a buying price and a selling price. The former will be the higher of the two, and the difference constitutes the market maker's 'turn'. However, for simplicity, we will ignore this complication and use a 'middle' value.

13 Of course, if the company's shares are not quoted on a stock exchange, then the objective simply reduces to the maximization of the value of the company's shares. This, however, still leaves the problem of how the shares are to be valued. In fact they should be valued on exactly the same basis as quoted shares: the future expected dividend flow. It is one of the great advantages of a stock market quotation that this value is 'automatically' and continuously provided for use both by management and by investors.

14 Job security refers here to the risky nature of a company's business. The more risky the company, the more likely it is to go bankrupt so causing the management to lose their jobs. Hence management may be concerned to reduce the company's exposure to risk and such action may not be in the shareholders' best interests. This point will be explored further at a later stage.

15 Changes in management, and hence changes in objectives, may come about through several ways. Shareholders, either behind the scenes or in the open at the company's Annual General Meeting, might force a change or, alternatively, a company's non-executive directors may be the responsbile catalyst for action to be taken.

16 A share option gives management the right to buy shares in the company, in the future, at a specified price. Therefore the greater the actual worth of the shares exceeds the option price, the greater is the gain to management. Hence management would have a personal interest in maximizing the worth of the company's shares.

FURTHER READING

1 Two articles which give an interesting overview of finance are: J. Fred Weston, 'New Themes in Finance', *Journal of Finance,* March 1974, and S.C. Myers, 'Finance Theory and Financial Strategy', *Midland Corporate Finance Journal*, Spring 1987.
2 For a discussion on conflicts between managers' and shareholders' objectives, see: G. Donaldson, 'Financial Goals: Management *vs.* Stockholders', *Harvard Business Review*, May-June 1963; C.M. Findley and G.A. Whitmore, 'Beyond Shareholder Wealth Maximisation', *Financial Management*, Winter 1974; N. Seitz, 'Shareholders Goals, Firm Goals and Firm Financing Decisions', *Financial Management*, Autumn 1982; and J.R. Grinyer, 'Alternatives to Maximisation of Shareholder Wealth', *Accounting and Business Research*, Autumn 1986.
3 The ideas of satisficing and of the principal-agent problem can be found in: H.A. Simon, 'Theories of Decision Making in Economics and Behavioural Science', *American Economic Review*, June 1959; M.C. Jensen and W.H. Meckling, 'Theory of the Firm: Managerial Behaviour, Agency Costs and Ownership Structure', *Journal of*

Financial Economics, October 1976; and E.F. Fama, 'Agency Problems and the Theory of the Firm', *Journal of Political Economy*, Spring 1980.

4 For a lengthy discussion of the search process (among other things) see: J. Grieve Smith, *Business Strategy*, Blackwell 1985.

5 Finally, for two thought-provoking articles, see: F.A. Hayek, 'The Corporation in a Democratic Society: in whose interests ought it and will it be run?' reprinted in H.I. Ansoff, *Business Strategy*, Penguin 1978; and J.J. Chrisman and A.B. Carroll, 'Corporate Responsibility – Reconciling Economic and Social Goals', *Slogan Management Review*, Winter 1984.

QUICKIE QUESTIONS

1 What are the three major areas of financial decisions?
2 What is the search process?
3 What is the fundamental objective of financial management decision making?
4 Why is accounting profit an inappropriate criterion for financial decision making?
5 How are shares valued?
6 What is the principal-agent problem?
7 What are the typical responsibilities of the chief accountant?
8 Sketch out the basic *flow of funds* diagram.
9 What role does the stock market play?
10 What is the assumed attitude to risk of investors?

PROBLEMS

1 What might be the objectives of financial management in a non-commercial organization such as a charity or a hospital?
2 How might you go about devising an incentive scheme for top management?
3 What is meant by the term 'a risky investment'? What makes some investments more or less risky than others?
4 What might be the financial management objectives of nationalized industries?

2
Traditional methods of investment appraisal

Chapter Contents

INTRODUCTION

In its simplest form, an investment decision can be defined as one which involves the firm in making a cash outlay with the aim of receiving, in return, future cash inflows. Numerous variations on this definition are possible, such as a cash outlay with the aim of reducing or saving further cash outlays, but these can all generally adapt to the initial definition with little trouble.[1]

Therefore decisions about buying a new machine, building a factory, extending a warehouse, improving a delivery service, instituting a staff training scheme or launching a new product line are all examples of the investment decisions that may be made by industry. In order to help in making such decisions, and to ensure that they are consistent with each other, a common method of appraisal is required which can be applied equally to the whole spectrum of investment decisions and which should, in terms of the decision structure so far outlined, help to decide whether any particular investment will assist the company in maximizing shareholder wealth (via share price maximization).

A warning

In looking for such an investment appraisal method we shall begin by examining two of the most widely used[2] methods, Payback and Return on Capital Employed, to see how well they fit in with our financial decision objective and value base. However, before doing so we should be clear that neither of these two methods nor any other method of investment appraisal can give a *definitive* decision. They cannot tell a company's financial decision maker to 'invest' or 'not invest', but can only act as a decision *guide*. This extremely important point will become obvious as we develop our theory, but it is all too easy to slip back into the erroneous (and sometimes comforting) belief that the techniques that we shall develop here will make decisions for us. They will not do this. All they will do is help to communicate information to the decision maker; but when the actual decision is finally made, it is based on a whole range of very diverse considerations which are beyond our present capabilities to encompass in 'overall' decision making formulae.[3]

There has sometimes been a considerable amount of resistance and resentment by financial management to the introduction of any new investment appraisal technique, based partially on the belief that with such methods their decision making function would be replaced by a formula, 'handle-turning' function. Such a belief is ill-founded, not only for the reason already given, but also because any investment appraisal will always consist of making forecasts/estimates/guesses about the investment's future performance, and it is upon these forecasts that the appraisal techniques are applied. However, the future, almost without exception, is uncertain and so any investment appraisal technique can give only investment *advice* based on these forecasts and not a definitive decision. Such techniques can never replace managerial judgement, but they can help to make that judgement more sound.

THE PAYBACK METHOD

Let us start by looking at the first of these two traditional methods of investment appraisal: the payback method.[4] This is one of the most tried and trusted of all methods and its name neatly describes its operation, referring to how quickly the incremental benefits that accrue to a company from an investment project 'payback' the initial capital invested – the benefits being normally defined in terms of after-tax cash flows.

The payback method can be used as a guide to investment decision making in two ways. When faced with a straight accept-or-reject decision it can provide a rule where projects are only accepted if they payback the initial investment outlay within a certain predetermined time. In addition, the payback method can provide a rule when a comparison is required of the relative desirability of several mutually exclusive investments.[5] In such cases projects can be ranked in terms of 'speed of payback', with the fastest paying-back project being the most favoured and the slowest paying-back project the least favoured. Thus the project which paid back quickest would be chosen for investment.

Given below are examples of the payback method operating in both decision making situations. With Project A, assuming that the criterion for project acceptance is a four-year (maximum) payback, then we can see that it should be accepted because it pays back the initial outlay of £4000 within this time period:

Project A

Year[6]	*Cash flow*
0	−£4,000
1	+£1,000
2	+£1,000
3	+£2,000 payback period
4	+£3,000
5	+£1,000

If Projects B and C are mutually exclusive, Project C has the faster 'speed of payback' and so is the preferred investment. B pays back within three years (i.e., $2\frac{3}{5}$ years: years 1 and 2 cash flow plus three fifths of year 3 cash flow), whereas C pays back in two years exactly:

Project B

Year	*Cash flow*
0	−£10,000
1	+£ 3,000
2	+£ 4,000
3	+£ 5,000
4	+£ 6,000

Project C

Year	*Cash flow*
0	−£12,500
1	+£ 5,000
2	+£ 7,500
3	+£ 1,000
4	+£ 1,000
5	+£ 1,000

Working capital

Most projects not only involve an expenditure on capital equipment, but also on *working capital.* For example, suppose a company was considering investing in a sausage-making machine. Not only would the company have to incur the capital expenditure on the machine itself, but they would also have to invest in working capital: raw material stocks, finished goods stocks and debtors. However, the point to be recognized is that, at the end of the project's life, although the capital equipment will only have (at best) a scrap value, the working capital should be recovered *in full.* This is because, at the end of the project's life, the firm can run down its stocks of raw materials and finished goods and, hopefully, all outstanding debtors will pay up.

The following question then arises: should working capital be included as part of the project's outlay and so be included in the payback calculation? Example 2.1 illustrates such a situation. The correct answer to the dilemma that arises in Example 2.1 is that in payback calculations *only*, working capital should be excluded from the analysis, and so the advice given by payback is to accept the sausage machine project[7].

The logic behind the approach of excluding working capital is as follows. Payback is concerned about how long it will take the project to

Example 2.1
Ajax plc is considering the purchase of a sausage machine. The machine would cost £12,000, have an expected life of 5 years and a zero scrap value (net of disposal costs) at the end of that time. In addition, an expenditure of £8,000 on working capital will be required throughout its life. The firm's management accountants have estimated the net, after-tax, operating cash flows of the project as follows:

Year	*Operating Cash Flow*
	£
1	+6,000
2	+6,000
3	+6,000
4	+4,000
5	+3,000

Ajax evaluates investment opportunities using a 3-year maximum payback criterion.

The problem here is what set of cash flows should be evaluated using packback: Alternative 1 or 2?

Alternative 1

Year	*Capital Expenditure*	*Working Capital*	*Operating Cash Flow*
	£	£	£
0	−12,000	−8,000	
1			+6,000
2			+6,000
3			+6,000
4			+4,000
5		+8,000	+3,000

Alternative 2

Year	*Capital Expenditure*	*Operating Cash Flow*
	£	£
0	−12,000	
1		+6,000
2		+6,000
3		+6,000
4		+4,000
5		+3,000

If working capital is taken into account, the project should be rejected as it takes more than 3 years to recover the total initial outlay of £20,000. But if working capital is excluded from the analysis, the project is acceptable as it has a two-year payback.

reach its break-even point where at least the outlay has been recovered. Management are interested in this point because they recognize the uncertainties that surround any estimate of a project's future cash flow. Thus the more quickly a project achieves payback, the less risky is that project in the eyes of many managements. As a project's working capital is likely to be recovered whenever the project comes to the end of its life (i.e. working capital is automatically paid-back), it is excluded from the analysis of the break-even point.

Advantages of payback

As can be seen from the two initial illustrations, payback is quick and simple to calculate (once the project's cash flow forecasts have been made) and is likely to be readily understood by management. This is one of its greatest advantages as an appraisal technique, but it has other advantages in addition.

A second advantage is that it is thought by many managements to automatically select the less risky project in mutually exclusive decision situations. The point has already been mentioned that one of the most difficult tasks in investment appraisal is the forecasting of future project cash flows. In this respect, generally speaking, the further ahead in time is the cash flow estimate, the less reliable is that estimate. Therefore by emphasizing 'speed of return' and selecting the project, from a series of alternatives, that pays back quickest, the appraisal method is – almost by definition – choosing the least risky project in that it chooses the one which reaches break-even most quickly. However, this is a complex point and we shall return to it later when the problem of risk is more fully discussed.

A further advantage of payback, and one that is connected to what has been said previously, is that it saves management the trouble of having to forecast cash flows over the *whole* of a project's life. Given that the forecasting process is difficult, and the further ahead in time the forecast has to be made the greater the difficulty, the fact that project cash flows need not be forecasted beyond the maximum payback criterion (by which time the project either is or is not acceptable) is an obvious advantage. For instance, in Example 2.1, although the sausage machine was thought to have had a five year life, there really was no need to forecast its cash flows beyond three years (the decision criterion) in order to evaluate it.

A final advantage of payback, that is seen by many managements, is that it is a convenient method to use in *capital rationing* situations. Capital rationing is a subject which we shall return to later, to look at in more detail; however, it basically refers to a situation where a company does not have unlimited capital expenditure funds. (Perhaps the limit has been imposed by the company itself in the form of an annual capital expenditure budget.) Example 2.2 illustrates the situation.

Example 2.2 shows how the capital rationing problem can be met by reducing the payback criterion and so reducing the number of acceptable projects. In addition the approach can also claim to have yet another advantage in that, in such a situation, it appears to accept the most 'sensible' projects. If capital is in short supply, it could be argued that the best projects to accept would be those which returned the expenditure rapidly – which is exactly what the payback method does.

The decision criterion

Nothing has so far been said about how the decision criterion is set. There are a number of possible methods that management might utilize. One

Example 2.2

Alpha plc has identified five independent[8] investment opportunities and wishes to evaluate their desirability. The company normally uses payback with a three-year criterion and has specified a maximum capital expenditure budget for the year of £200,000. The project's net after-tax cash flows are estimated as follows:

Project:	1	2	3	4	5
			(all cash flows in £000s)		
Year					
0	−100	−300	−100	−200	−250
1	+ 50	+100	+ 20	+ 50	+ 50
2	+ 50	+100	+ 80	+ 50	+100
3	+ 50	+100	+ 50	+100	+ 80
4		+ 80	+ 30	+ 50	+ 80
5		+ 50			

Using payback, Projects 1 to 4 are all acceptable as they each payback within the three-year criterion. Project 5 is unacceptable. However, Alpha has a problem. To undertake all four acceptable projects will require total expenditure of £700,000 and only £200,000 has been budgeted. How is the firm to 'ration-out' the available cash among the competing projects?

The solution is to reduce the payback criterion from three down to two years. Projects 2 and 4 are now undesirable, leaving just 1 and 3 which, between them, will utilize the available capital.

would simply be to base the criterion on past experience; for example if the firm's experience is that most successful projects have paid back within four years, then that time period might be set as a criterion. Alternatively, general 'industry practice' might be taken as the guideline.

One obvious, and very sensible, basis for setting the decision criterion would be forecasting ability. For example, if a firm believed that, realistically, it could not forecast project cash flows with sufficient accuracy beyond five years ahead, then five years might be set as the criterion. Here management would be recognizing their forecasting limitations and would be sensibly deciding not to evaluate a project on cash flow forecasts which might be seen more as guesses than estimates.

Disadvantages of payback

Having looked at the advantages – true or otherwise – claimed for the method, let us now turn to the disadvantages. The first is the problem of what is meant by the term 'investment outlay'. If we look at Projects D and E, just how should the investment outlay be defined in each case?

Project D		*Project E*	
Year	*Cash flow*	*Year*	*Cash flow*
0	−£10,000	0	−£5,000
1	+£ 5,000	1	+£1,000
2	+£ 5,000	2	−£5,000
3	+£ 5,000	3	+£3,000
4	−£ 2,000	4	+£3,000
		5	+£4,000

Is Project D's outlay £10,000 or £12,000? Is Project E's outlay £10,000 or £9,000? The point is that in each case we *can* come to a decision, say, Project D's outlay is £10,000 and E's is £9,000, but the decision rule as it stands is too ambiguous in its definition of terminology to give a definitive ruling.

The problem of ambiguity can also be seen in the definition of the *start* of the payback time period. In other words, from what point do we begin counting? Suppose that Project E will be accepted only if it pays back within three years. If this means that E must pay back its outlay by Year 3 – that is, three years after its commencement – clearly, it should not be accepted. On the other hand, if the payback criterion means that it should pay back within three years of the completion of its outlays – that is, by Year 5 – then it is acceptable. Once again, as it stands, the decision rule is too ambiguous to give a definitive ruling.

This ambiguity is an important problem. When any technique, designed as a decision making aid, is open to ambiguity in interpretation, then it is likely to be manipulated so as to lend backing for the *desired* decision, rather than the right decision. Any decision rule open to such misuse is dangerous and must be viewed with suspicion.

A further problem, and probably the most important one, arises from the fact that the decision is concentrated purely on the cash flows that arise *within* the payback period, and flows that arise outside this period are ignored. Projects F and G illustrate the problem that this can cause:

Project F		*Project G*	
Year	*Cash flow*	*Year*	*Cash flow*
0	−£100,000	0	−£100,000
1	+£ 10,000	1	+£ 50,000
2	+£ 20,000	2	+£ 50,000
3	+£ 40,000	3	+£ 10,000
4	+£ 80,000		
5	+£160,000		
6	+£320,000		

According to the payback rule, if the two projects are mutually exclusive, Project G is preferred because it pays back the more quickly. If the two projects are independent (i.e. either one or both could be accepted or rejected) and the company has a three-year payback period criterion, again Project G would be accepted and F rejected. In both situations, looking at the cash flows over the whole life of each project, we can see that the wisdom of the decision advice given by the payback method is open to some doubt.

The time value of money

A final problem with the payback method is that, in the format used above, it suffers from the fundamental drawback of failing to allow for the 'time value of money'.[9] However, this difficulty can easily be overcome by applying the method – not to ordinary cash flows – but to 'present value' cash flows. In such circumstances, the technique is usually referred to as *discounted payback.* The concept of the time value of money has a central place within financial decision theory and will be developed formally in the next two chapters. Nevertheless, it will be useful to introduce the idea briefly, at this point.

Essentially what is meant by the term 'the time value of money' is that a given sum of money has a different value depending upon when it occurs in time. The idea is not directly concerned with inflation or deflation (let us assume that neither exists, so that price levels are stable through time) but really concerns the fact that money can be invested so as to earn *interest.*

Suppose you were owed £100 and were given the choice of having your £100 returned to you either now or in one year's time (assume that if you choose £100 in a year's time the event is 'certain' – i.e., you are certain to be alive then and you are certain to be paid the money). Most people would instinctively take the £100 now – even if they did not need the money – and this would be the correct decision in terms of the time value of money.

The reason why £100 in a year's time has a smaller value than £100 now is because if you took the £100 *now* the money could be placed on deposit at (say) a 6% interest rate and so turn into £106 in one year's time. Therefore if the person who was in debt to you offered the choice of £100 now or £106 in one year's time (again both events are certain to occur), you would have no preference for either alternative. Thus we could say that the *present value* of £106 received in a year's time is £100 or that the *future value* of £100 now is £106 in a year's time, assuming a 6% interest rate.

This concept of the time value of money will be much more fully discussed when we talk about the discounted cash flow methods of investment appraisal in Chapter 4, but the point to be made here is that the payback method does not make any allowance for the time value of money, its emphasis on the speed of return being purely a consideration of project risk. For example, the payback method would be indifferent between Projects H and I whereas, as the reader may well discern, if allowance is made for the time value of money, Project I is preferable to Project H, as money received *nearer* in time is more valuable than money received *later* in time.

Project H		*Project I*	
Year	*Cash flow*	*Year*	*Cash flow*
0	−£4,000	0	−£4,000
1	+£ 500	1	+£3,000
2	+£ 500	2	+£ 500
3	+£3,000	3	+£ 500
4	+£ 500	4	+£ 500

A worked example of discounted payback will be shown when the time value of money concept has been more fully explored in Chapter 4.

In conclusion

Despite these criticisms it is still possible to say that, to a great extent, payback has been unfairly maligned in the literature on financial decisions. However it obviously has a robust ability to survive, because it remains the most popular of all appraisal methods. This popularity stems mainly from two of the reasons that we have already given, that of ease of comprehension and its apparent bias towards less risky projects. Indeed it can be strongly argued that the payback method does provide a very useful 'rule of thumb' check mechanism for the very many minor investment decisions that companies have to make, which are financially too small (either in relative or absolute terms) to justify the time and expense that would necessarily be incurred in using a complex, but more theoretically correct appraisal method.[10] Furthermore, as shall be seen at the end of Chapter 4, a particularly supportive case can be made for the *discounted payback* technique.

The real problem does not stem from the payback concept itself, but more from the way the method is *used* in the decision making process. Except in the case of very minor investment decisions, it should not really be used to give decision *advice* at all, but only to give *information* on the speed of return of the initial outlay, which may, or may not, be of relevance (depending upon the firm's liquidity) in the decision process. It cannot really be considered as an investment appraisal technique because of its major defect: its inability to report the expected return over the whole life of an investment, through its disregard of the investment's post-payback period flows. Using the payback method to choose between alternative investments or to set a minimum criterion for investment acceptance is really applying it to a task which is well beyond its ability to handle. At best, for large investments, it can act successfully only as an initial screening device before more powerful methods of appraisal are applied.[11]

THE RETURN ON CAPITAL EMPLOYED

The second traditional approach to investment appraisal is the return on capital employed (ROCE) which, like payback, has many different names (perhaps the most common is the Accounting Rate of Return) and a wide variety of different methods of computation. In its basic form, it is calculated as the ratio of the accounting profit generated by an investment project to the required capital outlay, expressed as a percentage. There are many variations in the way these two figures are actually calculated, but normal practice in its use for investment appraisal is to calculate profit after depreciation but before any allowance for taxation, and to include in capital employed any increases in working capital that would be required if the project were accepted.

Example 2.3

The Beta Company wished to evaluate an investment proposal using the ROCE technique. The project requires an initial capital expenditure of £10,000, together with £3,000 of working capital. The project will have a four-year life, at the end of which time the working capital will be fully recovered and the project will have a scrap value of £2,000.

The project's net pre-tax *cash* flows are as follows, and the company uses straight-line depreciation:

Year	*Net Cash Flow*
	£
1	+4,000
2	+6,000
3	+3,500
4	+1,500

In these circumstances (and lacking further information) 'profit' can be calculated as equal to cash flow *minus* depreciation. The annual depreciation charge would be:

$$\frac{£10{,}000 - £2{,}000}{4} = £2{,}000\text{/year, depreciation.}$$

			£
Annual Profit or (Loss): Year	1	4,000 − 2,000 =	2,000
	2	6,000 − 2,000 =	4,000
	3	3,500 − 2,000 =	1,500
	4	1,500 − 2,000 =	(500)
		Total profit =	£7,000

$$\text{Average annual profit} = \frac{£7{,}000}{4} = £1{,}750$$

The initial capital employed would equal £13,000 (capital expenditure plus working capital). The *average* capital employed would be calculated as:

$$\frac{\text{Capital Expenditure} - \text{Scrap Value}}{2} + \text{Scrap Value} + \text{Working Capital}$$

that is: $\frac{£10{,}000 - £2{,}000}{2} + £2{,}000 + £3{,}000 = £9{,}000$[12]

Hence: Return on Initial Capital Employed =

$$\frac{£1{,}750}{£13{,}000} = \underline{0{\cdot}135} \text{ (approx.) or } 13{\cdot}5\%$$

and: Return on Average Capital Employed =

$$\frac{£1{,}750}{£9{,}000} = \underline{0{\cdot}194} \text{ (approx.) or } 19{\cdot}4\%$$

There are two common ways of expressing the ROCE in practice. One is the ratio of the average annual profit generated over the life of the project, to its average capital value (i.e. the average capital employed). The other approach is to take the average annual profit as a ratio of the *initial* outlay. Example 2.3 illustrates these calculations.

The ROCE can be employed in the investment appraisal of both independent projects and mutually exclusive projects. First, a decision criterion is set in terms of a *minimum* acceptable level of ROCE. (The figure used here often reflects the firm's overall return on capital.) Then, for an independent project to be acceptable, its ROCE must at least equal the 'hurdle' or criterion return specified. In a situation of mutually exclusive projects, the best of the alternatives is the project with the highest ROCE. However, this 'best' project will only be accepted by the firm if it, too, meets the set criterion.

Advantages of ROCE

The ROCE investment appraisal technique is widely used in practice, although it is probably declining in popularity. It has three main advantages. The first is that by evaluating the project on the basis of a percentage rate of return it is using a concept with which all management are familiar. For example, being told that a project had a four-year payback would not immediately convey whether that was good or bad; but being told that a project is expected to produce a 35% return on capital would appear obviously desirable (given we know what is the going rate of return on, say, the overall company).

The second advantage is connected to the first. It is the fact that the method evaluates the project on the basis of its profitability which, many managements believe (despite comments in Chapter 1) should be the focus of the appraisal. Finally, a third advantage that exists is that of logic. Management's own performance is often evaluated by shareholders in terms of the company's *overall* return on capital employed. Therefore there does seem to be a certain logic in evaluating individual capital investment opportunities on a similar basis. (This line of thinking then often leads to the specification of the ROCE criterion being set equal to the company's actual or desired overall return on capital.)

Disadvantages of ROCE

To set against these advantages, there are a number of major disadvantages, the first of which is the ambiguous nature of the ROCE concept. There are so many variants that no general agreement exists on how capital employed should be calculated, on whether initial or average capital employed should be used or on how profit should be defined. As a result, the method lays itself open to abuse as a technique of investment appraisal by allowing the decision maker to select a definition of ROCE which best suits his prejudgement of a project's desirability.

Second, because the method measures a potential investment's worth in percentage terms it is unable – in an unadjusted form – to take into account the financial size of a project when alternatives are compared.

For example, suppose a company was considering whether to build a large factory, at a cost of £10m, or a small factory at a cost of £3m. If the large factory turned out to have an ROCE of 20% while the small factory's ROCE was 24%, then the latter investment would be the one chosen (assuming 24% exceeded the ROCE criterion). However, it is not at all certain that the small factory would be a wise decision. While the small factory would result in an aggregate profit of £720,000 (24% of £3m) the large factory would produce a profit of £2m for the firm.

However, these two criticisms are relatively insignificant when compared to two further difficulties. The first concerns the fact that accounting profit rather than cash flow is used as the basis of evaluation. As our earlier discussion in Chapter 1 showed, this is an entirely incorrect concept to use in a decision making context. Accounting profit is a *reporting* concept. A capital investment decision is an economic or resource allocation decision and the economic unit of account is cash, because it is cash which gives power over resources.

The other major criticism of the ROCE is that it also ignores the time value of money. Furthermore, unlike payback where *discounted payback* can be used, there is no way that the ROCE can be modified to take the time value of money into account.

However, despite these criticisms, the method is still widely applied to investment decisions in industry and it may be fair to say that, like payback, although there are many problems associated with its application, it may give acceptable decision advice when applied to relatively minor, short-run investment projects.

Nevertheless, there is survey evidence (for this, see Chapter 19) which does indicate a decline in the technique's popularity. There are perhaps two reasons for this, both of which arise from the high rates of inflation suffered by the economy in the late 1970s and early 1980s. The first is that high rates of inflation led to high interest rates and this high time value of money sharply brought home to management the importance of taking it into account in decision making. With interest rates of around 20% it becomes obvious that the *timing* of cash flows is important. A second reason for the ROCE's decline in popularity could be that the high rates of inflation – and the failure of the inflation accounting debate – taught management about the doubtful validity of the accounting profit number. Thus a method that uses accounting profit and ignores the time value of money has little to recommend it as a decision making tool.

In conclusion

Comparing these two 'traditional' investment appraisal techniques, each has its own advantages and disadvantages and it is not clear whether either is superior. Each has its own group of advocates and it is common to find both used in conjunction so as to produce a 'two-tier' decision rule, e.g. projects may be accepted only if (say) they payback within five years *and* have a minimum ROCE of 12%.

In the final analysis, our conclusion must be that, apart from the possible exception of the evaluation of relatively small, short-lived investments, neither method has sufficient advantages to offset its disadvantages, and particularly the failure of both normally to allow for the time value of money.[13] In the next chapter we shall start to examine investment appraisal methods that do attempt to make such an allowance.

SUMMARY

This chapter has covered the following major points:

- The two 'traditional' methods of capital investment appraisal – payback and the return on capital employed – were examined to see how they are calculated and how they are applied, both to individual project evaluation and to situations involving mutually exclusive projects.
- As far as payback was concerned, the technique was usually applied to a project's after-tax cash flows, but working capital was excluded entirely from the evaluation.
- Basically there were four advantages to payback:
  - ☐ Quick and simple.
  - ☐ Seen as automatically selecting the less 'risky' project from amongst alternatives.
  - ☐ Seen as helpful in capital rationing situations.
  - ☐ Saved management from having to forecast project cash flows beyond the criterion time period.
- Payback's main disadvantage was its failure to consider project cash flows *outside* the payback period. However, it was argued that, to some extent, this omission might be understandable where management felt that their forecasting ability was suspect beyond the criterion time period.
- The other disadvantage is payback's failure to account for the time value of money, but this can be taken into account through the use of discounted payback.
- The ROCE also had advantages:
  - ☐ It evaluated using the familiar percentage concept.
  - ☐ It evaluated projects on the basis of profitability.
  - ☐ Management's success or failure in taking financial decisions *in aggregate* is judged on the basis of the company's return on capital employed (amongst other things). Therefore it appears sensible that individual investment decisions should be taken on the same basis.
- However, to be set against these advantages were two major disadvantages: a failure to consider cash flow and a failure to take the time value of money into account.
- In sum, these two techniques may be suitable as initial screening devices, or to evaluate small, short-lived projects. However, they should not be used otherwise, with the possible exception of discounted payback.

NOTES

1 Although this point will be expanded upon later, it is worth specifying now that an investment's 'cost' can be defined as all cash outflows and/or reduced cash inflows through time that result (either directly or indirectly) from the investment decision. Similarly, an investment's 'benefit' can be described as all cash inflows and/or reduced outflows through time that result (directly or indirectly) from the investment decision. Thus all costs and benefits of an investment are defined in terms of being *incremental* to the firm, through time and expressed in cash terms.

2 Various empirical surveys both in the UK and the USA and elsewhere have shown that these two investment appraisal methods have widespread popular appeal. Their familiarity and directness will make the task of replacing them by superior appraisal techniques a difficult one.

3 Not least amongst these diverse considerations is the decision maker's own psychology; and one recent survey (Scapens, Sale and Tikkas, 1982, see Chapter 19) concludes that concern with an investment's financial viability is of almost secondary importance to whether or not it 'fits in' with the company's strategic plans.

4 There are a variety of names given to this method. Others include: payback period, pay-off period, capital recovery period, cash recovery factor.

5 The term 'mutually exclusive' when applied to investment projects is best explained by means of an example. Suppose a company requires a new warehouse and there are two possible sites under consideration, then the decision could be analysed in terms of two mutually exclusive investments: building the warehouse at Site A and building the warehouse at Site B. The projects are said to be mutually exclusive because only *one* new warehouse is required, so if it is built at Site A, the acceptance of this project excludes the other project from being chosen, and vice versa. More generally a pair of projects are mutually exclusive if the acceptance of one means that the other would not or could not be accepted. This definition can be extended to any number of alternative investment projects of which only one can be chosen.

6 It is important to note that throughout this book we shall use the following convention when dealing with all types of financial flows (e.g., profit, dividend, cash or tax flows): all flows will normally be assumed to occur instantaneously on *the last day of the year in which they arise.* Thus a cash flow in the second year of a project's life will be assumed to occur on the last day of the second year. The main exception to this rule is that a project's outlay (or cost) which arises in the first year of its life is assumed to occur on the first day of the year.

These rather unrealistic assumptions are made for arithmetical convenience but, in most circumstances, they do not affect the realism of our results in any substantial way. (See the Appendix to Chapter 4 on Compounding and Discounting.) Diagrammatically:

```
Year   0              1              2              3
       |______________|______________|______________|___________...
       : 1st year     : 2nd year     : 3rd year     : .............
```

Thus 'Year 0' (or t_0) refers to the start of the first year (i.e., 'now'). 'Year 1' refers to the *end* of the first year and – simultaneously – the start of the second year.

'Year 3' refers to the end of the 3rd year, and so on. References in the text to, for example, 'the second year' will refer to events that happen during the second year, whilst references to 'year 2' (or t_2) will refer to a financial flow that is assumed to arise at the end of the second year (or, the start of the third year).

7 However, it is important to notice that payback is the *only* appraisal technique which excludes working capital from the analysis.

8 Project independence can be defined as a situation where the expected financial flows that arise from a project will occur irrespective of any other project being or not being undertaken.

9 There do exist special cases where the ordinary payback decision rule effectively allows for the time value of money, but such situations are simply fortuitous and of little more than arithmetical interest.

10 This may be especially true of very small companies which may be lacking the resources and knowledge to undertake a more complex appraisal.

11 Even this is really open to doubt. Original writers on the topic such as Joel Dean and Ezra Solomon believed that payback could be used as a coarse screening device to pick out projects whose desirability (in terms of profitability) is so obvious as to remove the need for more refined appraisal. For similar reasons it is held that the method could also be used to reject 'obviously' highly unprofitable projects. There is little evidence to support this belief, neither has there been an operational definition of 'obvious' in this context.

12 The rationale for this calculation can be most easily seen with the help of a diagram:

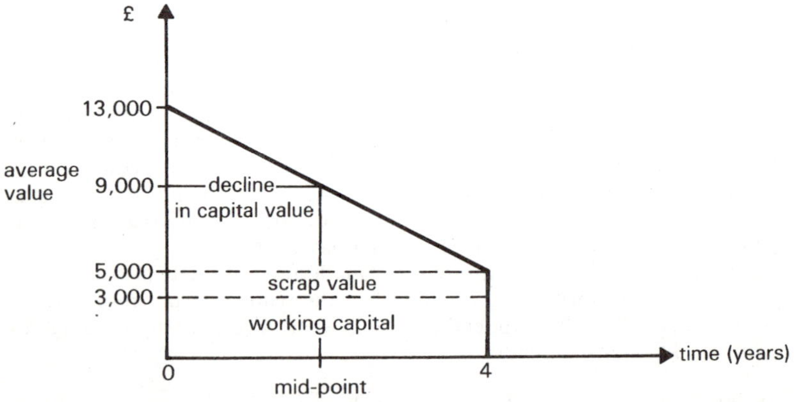

13 Even allowing for the discounted payback variant referred to earlier, payback still carries the major criticism of not considering a project's financial flows outside the payback period.

FURTHER READING

1 Most of the literature concerning payback and ROCE is fairly old, and the more up-to-date contributions have tended to contrast them with the DCF techniques which are to be discussed in Chapter 4. Nevertheless, an interesting starting point is the discussion in: D. Bodenhorn, 'On the problem of capital budgeting', *Journal of Finance*, December 1959.
2 Even older, but also of interest is: J. Dean, 'Measuring the Productivity of Capital', *Harvard Business Review*, Jan–Feb 1954; as is: E.A. Ravenscroft, 'Return on Investment: Fit the Method to your Needs', *Harvard Business Review*, Mar–Apr 1960.
3 Specifically on payback, see: M. J. Gordon, 'The Payoff Period and the Rate of Profit', *Journal of Business*, October 1955; A. Rappaport, 'The Discounted Payback Period', *Management Science*, Jul–Aug 1965; H. Levy, 'A Note on the Payback Method', *Journal of Financial and Quantitative Analysis*, December 1968; and M.H. Weingartner, 'Some New Views on the Payback Period and Capital Budgeting Decision', *Management Science*, August 1969.
4 Two interesting articles which discuss reasons for the continuing popularity of payback are: M. Statman, 'The Persistence of the Payback Method: A Principal-Agent Perspective', *Engineering Economist*, Winter 1982, and R.H. Pike, 'Owner Manager Conflict and the Role of the Payback Method', *Accounting and Business Research*, Winter 1985.
5 The ROCE method is generally recognized as being inadequate, but see: M.J. Mepham, 'A Reinstatement of the Accounting Rate of Return', *Accounting and Business Research*, Summer 1968.

QUICKIE QUESTIONS

1 What is the payback decision rule for mutually exclusive projects?
2 What is the payback of Project W:

Capital expenditure: £11,000	Net cash flow:	Yr 1	+4,000
Working capital: £4,000		Yr 2	+4,000
Scrap value: £1,000		Yr 3	+4,000
Life: 5 years		Yr 4	+3,000
		Yr 5	+2,000

3 What are the advantages of payback?
4 How is payback used in capital rationing situations?
5 How might the payback criterion be set?
6 What is 'discounted payback'?
7 What is the single most important criticism of payback?
8 Why does money have a 'time value'?
9 What is Project W's (see question 2) ARR/ROCE, assuming straight-line depreciation?
10 What are the main advantages of ARR/ROCE?
11 What are the two most serious disadvantages of the ARR/ROCE?

PROBLEMS

1 Gamma PLC is a diversified industrial conglomerate. Its head-office accounting staff are currently evaluating investment proposals put up by different divisions for approval.

The Electronics division have put forward a proposal to produce a new type of calculator which, because of rapid technological change, can only be expected to have a four-year life, once the production facilities have been set up during the first twelve months.

The Property division propose taking a four-year lease on a building which already has a tenant paying an annual rent.

The Mining division proposes to spend £1.5m developing a small copper mine. The mine would only have a three-year life. At the end of that time, the environmental damage the company had caused would need to be rectified at a cost of £0.75m.

The net cash flows of the projects (excluding working capital) are as follows (£000s):

Year	*Electronics*	*Property*	*Mining*
0	−1,000	−1,000	−1,500
1	−1,000	+ 200	+ 500
2	+ 800	+ 400	−1,000
3	+ 800	+ 400	+ 800
4	+ 800	+ 400	− 750
5	+ 800		

Gamma normally uses payback to evaluate projects with a decision criterion of three years.

Required:

(a) Calculate the payback of all three projects and determine the decision advice.

(b) If the Electronics and Property division projects were mutually exclusive, which project would you advise the company to accept? Think carefully before reaching a decision and then justify your decision.

(c) If the Property and Mining division projects were mutually exclusive, which project would you advise the company to accept? Again, think carefully and justify your decision.

(d) Comment on the company's use of the same decision criterion for projects from all three divisions. Would you think this wise?

2 Zeta PLC is a manufacturer and distributor of ice-cream. The management are presently considering a project which will require capital expenditure of £200,000, together with £50,000 of working capital. The capital equipment is expected to have a scrap value of £80,000 at the end of its four-year life and 80% of the working capital will also be recovered. (The remaining 20% of unrecovered working capital will consist of bad debts and spoilt stocks.)

The project's annual revenues and operating cash costs are estimated as follows (£000s):

Year	*Revenues*	*Operating Costs*
1	200	150
2	260	200
3	400	290
4	100	80

The company calculates depreciation on a straight-line basis. Normally projects are evaluated using both payback and the return on initial capital employed. The criterion used is 3 years for payback and 13% for the ROCE.

Required:

(a) Evaluate the project using the company's normal decision criteria. What advice would you give?

(b) The chairman, after receiving your advice, is puzzled over your treatment of working capital in the payback calculation. Explain to her your reasonings.

(c) The chairman also wondered whether the returns on *average* capital employed should be used instead of initial capital. What would your advice be and would the decision advice change? Think carefully before giving your answer; your promotion depends upon it!

(d) If Zeta decides to use only one appraisal technique, which would you advise – payback or ROCE/ARR – and why?

3
The single-period investment consumption decision model

Chapter Contents

INTRODUCTION TO THE MODEL

In the previous chapter two widely-used investment appraisal decision rules, payback and ROCE/ARR, were examined. One criticism of payback was that it ignored the time value of money – unless discounted payback was used. A similar criticism was made of the ROCE/ARR approach but, in addition, that was also criticised for evaluating projects on the basis of profit, not cash flow.

The other two main methods of capital investment appraisal are net present value (NPV) and the internal rate of return (IRR). These will be examined in detail in Chapter 4. However, in this chapter we take the opportunity to expand upon our initial discussion about the time value of money, and then look at how, in theory, capital investment decisions should be taken. This will then enable a judgement to be made as to how closely the four alternative investment appraisal techniques accord with the theoretically correct approach.

In order to look at the theory of investment decision making, we are going to develop a simple graphical analysis.[1] In no way does this analysis purport to represent the real world, but it will be useful in that it allows conclusions to be reached that do have real world validity.

The basic assumptions

So as to simplify the analysis and to lay bare the problem of investment decision making, we shall specify six assumptions about the real world environment within which investment decisions are made.

Assumption 1.
The decision maker is only concerned with making investment decisions over a one-year time horizon. Given this horizon, there are only two points of time that concern us – the start of the year or now (i.e. t_0 or Year 0) and the end of the year (i.e. t_1 or Year 1). Therefore all the available investment opportunities possess the general characteristic of requiring a *cash outlay* now, in return for a *cash inflow* at the end of the year. No investment cash flows extend beyond t_1.[2] (We will show later that this analysis can be easily expanded to cash flows that extend over many years).

Assumption 2.
The size and timing of any investment's cash outflow and subsequent cash inflow is known with certainty by the decision maker and so no risk is involved in the investment decision.[3]

Assumption 3.
Only 'physical' investment opportunities are available, i.e., investments involving the use of factors of production (land, labour and machinery) to produce a future return. This means that there is no 'capital market' where money can be lent or borrowed at a rate of interest.[4]

Assumption 4.
All investment projects are infinitely divisible; therefore fractions of projects may be undertaken, and they exhibit decreasing returns to scale.

Assumption 5.
All investment project cash flows are entirely independent of each other. Therefore the return produced at the end of the year from any investment now is fixed and known for certain and is unaffected by any other investment decision.

Assumption 6.

The person in receipt of the benefits from investment decisions is rational in that 'more cash' is always preferred to 'less cash' in any period.

These are the six major assumptions that we are going to make initially (although there are several other assumptions which we shall specify later as we develop the analysis), and obviously most of them are very unrealistic and in no way reflect the real world: investors are almost invariably faced with making decisions where the effects stretch over many periods; the future is largely unknown and so future cash flows cannot be certain; non-physical investments, such as placing money on deposit at a bank, are usually available to investors; investment projects are often indivisible and so must either be undertaken completely or not at all; many investment project cash flows depend upon what other investment decisions have or have not been made. However, such simplifying assumptions do provide a starting point for our analysis; we shall examine later the effect of replacing them with more realistic descriptions of the real world, but for the moment let us accept them.

The time value of money

We have already defined an investment decision by a company as one which involves the company in cash outlay (now) with the aim of receiving a (future) cash inflow in return. If we also make the simplistic but basically correct assumption that a company can do either of two things with any 'spare' cash[5] it has – pay it out to shareholders as a dividend[6] or retain it within the company and invest it – then if a company makes a decision to invest, it is in fact deciding not to pay that cash to shareholders now but instead to put it into a project with the aim of obtaining an increased amount of cash in the future, which can then be paid out as a dividend.

Therefore, a decision to invest by a company means that shareholders forego the opportunity of consumption *now* (i.e., a dividend now) with the aim of increasing *future* consumption (i.e., an enlarged dividend later). This is what investment decisions are all about: the delaying of current consumption in order to increase future consumption. (Or in non-economic terms, not spending money on consuming goods and services now, but investing the money instead so as to produce *more* money later which can then be spent on an increased quantity of goods and services.)

To look more closely at the investment decision, let us first consider the case of the single-owner firm (i.e., one in which the company has only one shareholder, who owns all the shares, and whose entire wealth is represented by the company), in which the owner is also the decision maker. In deciding to invest, the owner is forgoing some present consumption in order to increase future consumption and, in taking such action, he must also have decided that the future consumption so gained is somehow of greater value than the present consumption sacrificed in making the investment.

To make such investment decisions in a consistent manner, the owner requires a specific criterion that will enable him to judge whether or not any particular investment opportunity will produce sufficient compensation, in terms of increased future consumption, for having to reduce current consumption in order to make the investment.

Suppose our owner-manager requires a minimum of £1.20 back at the end of the year in order to persuade him to invest £1 now. Thus he requires compensation of 20p for every £1 of current consumption he foregoes. This requirement – which is a type of *exchange rate* of money between points in time and is, in fact, the owner's time value of money (TVM)[8] – can be expressed as a percentage:

$$\frac{£1.20}{£1.00} - 1 = 0{\cdot}20 \text{ or } \underline{20\%}$$

So an investment appraisal decision rule could be formulated in which a project is only undertaken if it produces at least a 20% return on capital. The owner-manager would not be willing to invest in a project which produced less than a 20% return, because 20% represents his time value of money.

It is important to realize that this time value of money is unlikely to remain a constant but will probably increase as more and more present consumption is sacrificed for investment so as to produce a greater amount of future consumption. That is to say, with each successive reduction in current consumption the owner is likely to demand a higher and higher minimum future return in order to persuade him to invest, because each additional £1 of current consumption forgone is likely to be of increasing value (in terms of the benefits received from consumption), and each additional £1 of future consumption gained is likely to be of decreasing value. This is an example of the economic concept of diminishing marginal utility.

THE BASIC GRAPHICAL ANALYSIS

The single-owner firm case

The one-period graphical analysis, made under our six assumptions, is shown in Figure 3.1. The curve AB is called the *phyical investment line*[9] (PIL) and is composed of all the physical investment opportunities available to the company at t_0, arranged in order of decreasing return.[10] Thus the most 'profitable' investments – in terms of greatest return – would be undertaken first by the firm.

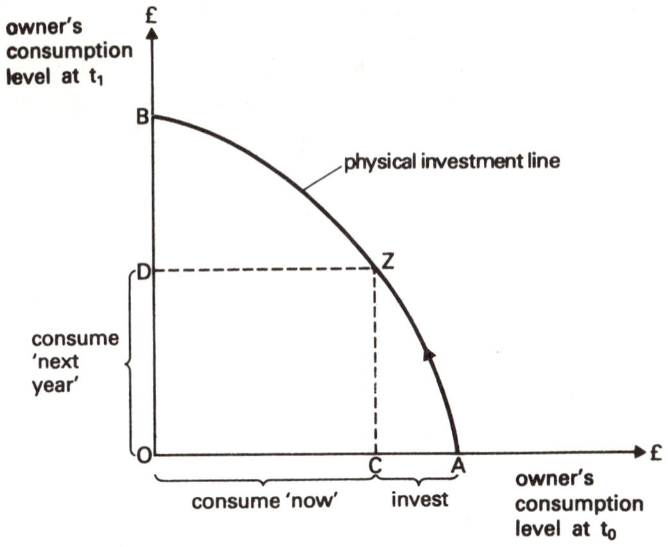

Figure 3.1

The physical investment line represents the complete range of maximum consumption combinations that the owner can obtain between the two points in time[11] by applying varying amounts of the company's existing resources to physical investment opportunities. Therefore as the owner gives up increasing amounts of current consumption in order to make physical investments, the company locates further and further up and around the physical investment line. (For instance if it locates at point A, no investment is undertaken and if it locates at point B, all possible physical investments are undertaken.)

Using Figure 3.1, OA represents the owner's total wealth now (i.e. at t_0) and can be regarded as the (unforced) liquidation value of the company. If all this wealth is consumed now and none is invested, then there will be zero wealth available for consumption next year (i.e. t_1). If only part of this year's wealth is consumed, say OC, and the rest, CA, invested, then the company locates itself at point Z on the physical investment line and this level of investment will produce OD available for consumption next year.

The return received by the company from the last (i.e., marginal) £1 of investment made at t_0 – the final piece of investment that brings the company to locate at point Z – can be found from the slope of the physical investment line at that point.[12] But besides being the return on the marginal investment, this slope also represents something else. The company has located at point Z because the owner must feel that *further* investment is not worth while. In other words, the gain in next year's consumption generated by a marginal increase in investment now, does not provide sufficient compensation for the further reduction in present consumption that would be necessary to finance the increased investment. Therefore the marginal return on investment being obtained at Z must be equal to the owner's time value of money (TVM).

If the marginal return at Z was greater than his TVM, the company would continue to invest, and if it was less than his TVM, the company would have stopped investing *before* reaching point Z, because the return gained from a move along the PIL from below Z to point Z would have been insufficient compensation for the present consumption that would have to be forgone to make the investment.

Introduction of indifference curves

We can derive this result better by asking the question: given that the physical investment line represents a whole series of infinitely divisible and independent opportunities for investment projects, arranged in decreasing order of rate of return, so that the investment with the greatest return is ranked (and undertaken) first and the one with the smallest return last, how does the company know when to stop investing? In order to answer this fully, we have to use another economic concept: the indifference curve.

It is assumed that the reader is familiar with the derivation and meaning of this term – it is explained in most basic economic textbooks. In rough terms, indifference curves are curves of constant utility or welfare, and when mapped on to our graph of consumption 'now' and consumption 'next year', and individual indifference curve indicates all possible combinations of consumption at the two points in time which give the same level of utility. The curves are convex to the origin, indicating that there is diminishing marginal utility attached to consumption at any single point of time, and each indifference curve, moving from left to right, gives the individual a higher overall level of utility.

Their place here concerns the fact that the set of indifference curves belonging to the company's owner can be mapped on the Figure 3.1 graph, as shown in Figure 3.2, and can be used to indicate at what point the company should stop investing; it is that point on the physical investment line which enables the owner to achieve his highest indifference curve, that is, his highest level of utility. This is found at the point of tangency between an indifference curve and the physical investment line. In terms of Figure 3.2, the company invests CA 'now' because the two time-point pattern of consumption that results for the owner – OC 'now' and OD 'next year' – places him on his highest possible indifference curve and so maximizes his welfare.

The point of tangency between the two curves represents a point where the slopes of each equate. As the slope of the indifference curve reflects an individual's marginal time value of money and the slope of the physical investment line represents the rate of return on the marginal project, then the point where the slopes of these two curves equate must be the point at which the owner's TVM equals the return on the marginal investment made by the company. Thus the investment decision rule is that the company continues to make physical investments until the return from

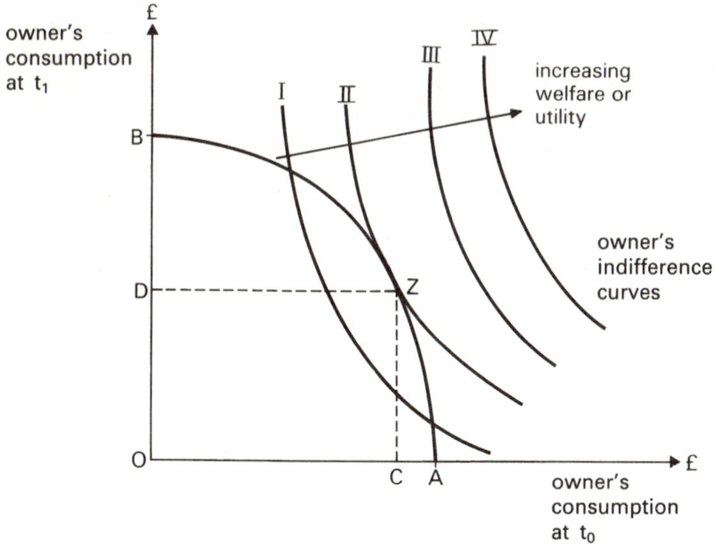

Figure 3.2

the marginal investment (i.e., the last one made) equals the owner's marginal time value of money. Any further investment will not produce the necessary return required and so will have the effect, in terms of our indifference curve analysis, of placing the owner on a lower indifference curve.[13]

INTRODUCTION OF CAPITAL MARKETS

From this simple analysis, under a series of restrictive assumptions about the real world, we have seen how investment decisions would be made and why money is said to possess a 'time value'. If we now make our analysis slightly more realistic by relaxing our third assumption so as to make available to the single-owner firm the opportunity of being able to lend and borrow money on a *capital market* at a rate of interest, we can then develop a second reason for money having a time value.

With the introduction of capital markets, the firm is faced with three possible courses of action at t_0: consumption, physical investment or capital market investment. Making the very important additional assumption that there is a *perfect* capital market[14] and therefore only one market rate of interest[15] (which is both the borrowing and lending rate), we can use the one-period graphical analysis to illustrate how the company makes investment decisions so as to allow the owner to distribute his consumption between the two points in time in such a way that he maximizes his welfare.

The financial market line

In terms of Figure 3.3, suppose the single-owner firm has amount OG available for consumption at t_0 and OH available at t_1. The capital market can be represented by a straight line, AE, which passes through point F, the co-ordinate of the existing consumption distribution. The slope of this line[16] is given by $-(1 + r)$, where r is the perfect capital market rate of interest, and the line is termed the financial investment line (FIL).

This line shows the range of capital market transactions available to the single-owner firm, given the existing distribution of cash resources of OG now (i.e., t_0) and OH next year (i.e., t_1). A move *down* the financial investment line from F to (say) point L means that the firm borrows GM on the capital market now – so increasing consumption at t_0 from OG to OM – and repays (capital plus interest) HN next year – so reducing consumption at t_1 from OH to ON. Notice that the maximum that can be borrowed now is amount GA; if the firm attempts to borrow more than this, there will not be sufficient resources available next year to repay the capital and accrued interest.

A move *up* the financial investment line to (say) point I means that the firm is lending JG on the capital market so as to reduce consumption now (to OJ) and to increase consumption next year (to OK). Again notice that a maximum of OG can be lent now – reducing current consumption to zero – and this results in having OE available for consumption next year.

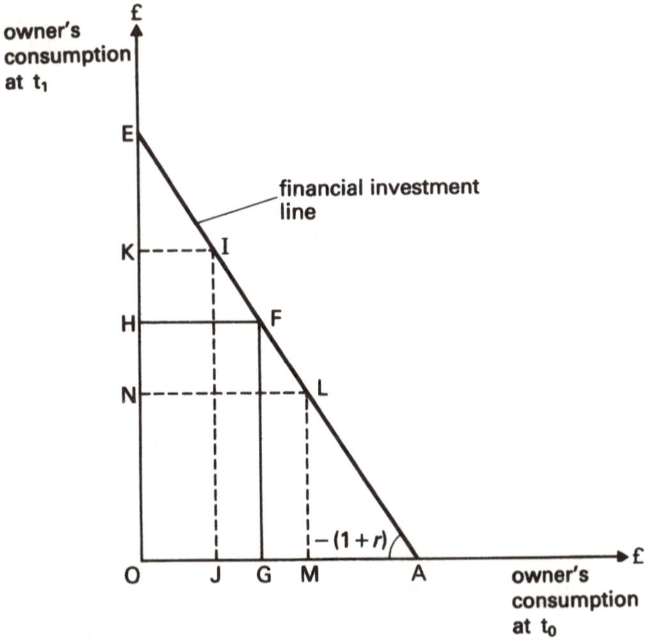

Figure 3.3

The separation theorem

Having seen how the financial investment line works, we can now combine the physical and financial investment lines on a single graph. This allows us to examine how both physical investment decisions *and* capital market borrowing or lending decisions are made in conjunction with each other, in order to allow the owner to achieve his highest possible indifference curve and so optimize his consumption spread over the period and maximize his utility.

However, up to this point we have taken as our decision making entity the single-owner firm, where the investment decision maker and the owner were one and the same person. Introducing the possibility of using the capital market allows us to analyse the investment decision process not only in the single-owner case, but also in the much more important situation where there are *many* owners (i.e., shareholders) and they are separate from the investment decision makers (i.e., management). This is the Separation Theorem.[17]

The capital investment decision rule now becomes: the company (i.e., managers) undertakes physical investments until the return from the marginal physical investment equates with the perfect capital market interest rate/rate of return. This level of physical investment results in some particular dividend flow, at t_0 and t_1, to the shareholders. The shareholders then make financial investment decisions (by either borrowing or lending on the capital market) until their individual marginal time values of money equate with the capital market rate of interest. Such action will result in them achieving their highest possible indifference curves by producing a distribution of consumption over the period, which maximizes their individual levels of utility.

Graphical derivation of the decision rule

We can see how these *separation theorem* decision rules are derived and why they help to maximize the shareholder's utility by examining Figure 3.4. Here the financial investment line is superimposed on the Figure 3.1 situation. Let us assume for the moment that although ownership is separate from management, the company has only one shareholder.

The current liquidation value of the company is OA. In the *absence* of a capital market we know that the company management will invest amount AC, and so make physical investments up to point Z on the physical investment line. This represents the point of tangency between the physical investment line and the owner's indifference curve (UT_1), and therefore, at this point the return from the marginal investment (derived from the slope of the physical investment line) equates with the shareholder's time value of money (given by the slope of the indifference curve tangential to point Z). Thus in our one-period world, the shareholder would receive a 'dividend' of OC now and OD next year. This distribution of consumption over the period places him on his highest attainable indifference curve: UT_1, and so maximizes his utility.

With the introduction of a capital market, the company's management now invest amount QA, so as to undertake physical investments up to the point where the return on the marginal physical investment equates with the capital market interest rate/rate of return (derived from the slope of the financial investment line). This occurs at point P where the financial investment line is tangent to the physical investment line. Thus the shareholder now receives a different dividend distribution: OQ now and OR next year. The company has undertaken physical investments up to point P because this has the effect of placing the shareholder on the highest possible *financial investment line* (VW).

Unlike the situation where capital market opportunities did not exist, the shareholder now does *not* have to accept the pattern of dividend distribution given by the company for consumption. Instead, he can borrow or lend on the capital market (i.e., move down or up VW from point P) so as to adjust his received dividend flow to suit whatever consumption pattern is preferred.

This preferred pattern is given by the point on the financial investment line which is tangent to one of his indifference curves, because this indifference curve will be the highest attainable. Thus the shareholder either lends or borrows on the capital market until his marginal time value of money (derived from the slope of the indifference curve) equates with the perfect capital market rate of interest. In Figure 3.4 the shareholder achieves this point, S, by moving down the financial investment line and borrowing an amount QT to make a total of OT

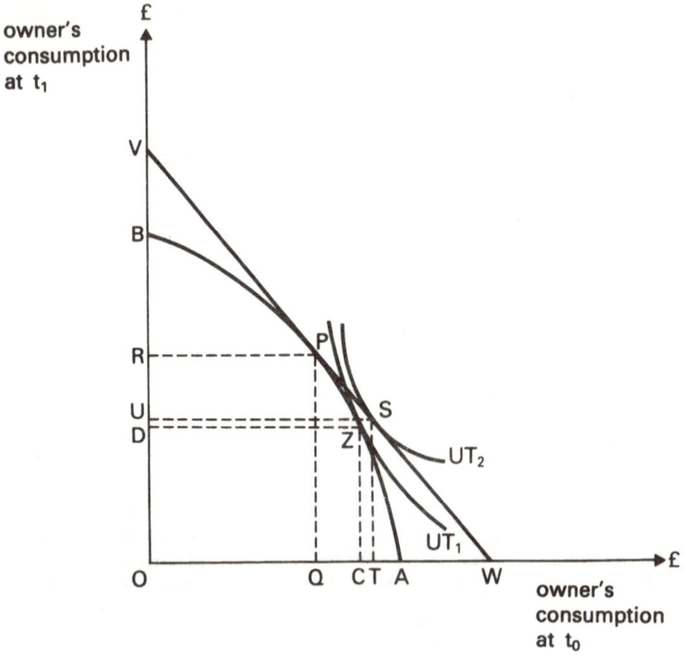

Figure 3.4

available for consumption 'now' and OU available for consumption 'next year'. (A dividend of OR is received from the company next year, but part of this RU, is used to repay the borrowed capital and accrued interest.)

Whether the shareholder lends or borrows or even omits to use the capital market at all depends solely upon the location of the point of tangency between the financial investment line and the shareholder's indifference curve, as Figure 3.5 shows. What Figure 3.4 illustrates is how, by taking advantage of both physical *and* financial investment opportunities, the shareholder can attain a higher indifference curve, UT_2 (and so increase his utility), than would have been possible from making physical investments alone. In fact this can unambiguously be seen occurring in Figure 3.4, because the shareholder has managed to increase his consumption in *both* periods through using the capital market: by amount CT 'now' and UD 'next year'.[18]

The multi-owner firm

The development of this separation theorem is extremely important. It results in a company's management making only *physical* investment decisions and leaving individual shareholders to adjust their received dividend pattern to fit their particular consumption requirements by using the capital market. In the owner-manager firm and in the situation where ownership and management are separate but there is only *one*

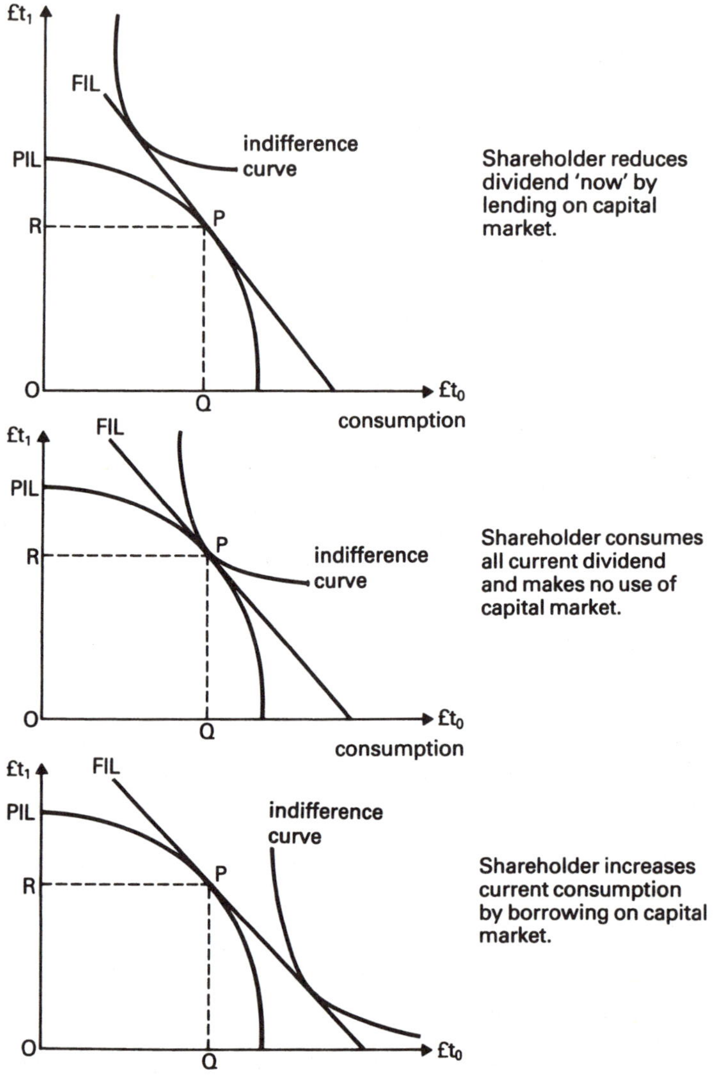

Figure 3.5

owner, it makes no difference to the analysis whether the individual owner/shareholder uses the capital market or the company uses the capital market on the owner's/shareholder's behalf (as long as, in the case where owner and management are separate, the managers are aware of the owner's marginal time value of money).

However, the crucial importance of the separation theorem comes when ownership is separated from management *and* there is more than one owner. Quite simply, different individuals have different time values of money, and so a company would be able to undertake the physical investment decisions but *not* the financial investment decisions, because there would be more than one marginal time value of money.[19] The use of the separation theorem avoids this problem by leaving the financial investment decisions to the individual shareholders.

Figure 3.6 shows a situation where a company is owned by two shareholders: one with 75% of the equity (Shareholder 1) and the other, 25% of the equity (Shareholder 2). The firm continues to make physical investments until the marginal return on investment equates with the market rate of interest, and then pays out the resulting dividends to each shareholder in proportion to his equity holding. In so doing, the company would still be ensuring that each individual shareholder is placed on the highest possible financial investment line. It is then up to the individual shareholder to make whatever decision is best, in the knowledge of his own set of indifference curves and time value of money, with regard to using the capital market in order to adjust his received dividend flow.

In the example shown in Figure 3.6, Shareholder 1 (75% holding) will use the capital market to borrow and so increases consumption 'now' at the expense of a reduced future consumption level. Shareholder 2 will use the capital market to lend, thereby reducing consumption 'now' but, in return, having an increased level of consumption 'next year'.

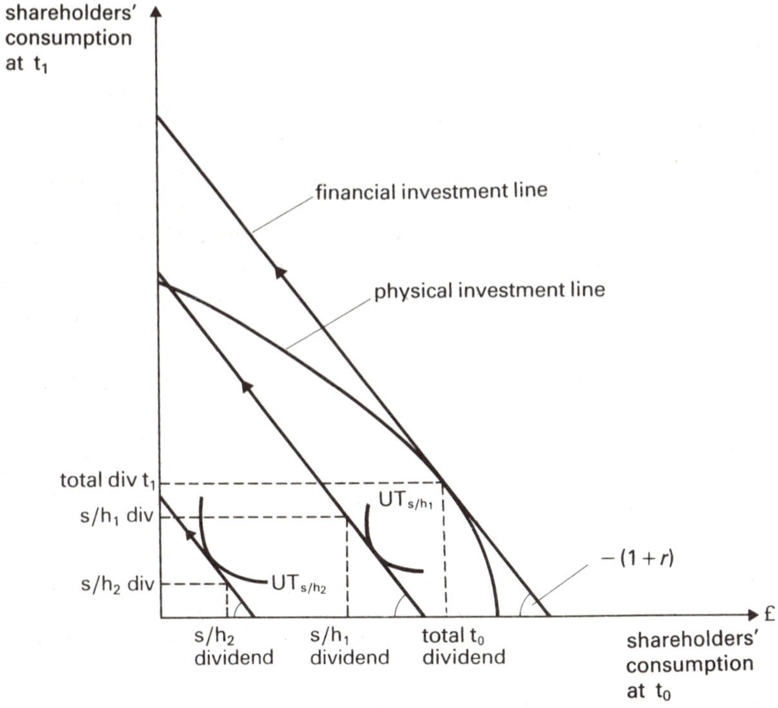

Figure 3.6

The conclusions of the basic model

This development of the single period investment–consumption model, as it is called, is important not only for illustrating how and why money has a time value, but also as acting as an introduction to financial decision making in general. In this respect, we stated that management's objective must be to try to maximize shareholders' wealth and this would be achieved through the maximization of the dividend flow through time. The separation theorem places this latter statement in a clearer light.

Management must make investment decisions so as to maximize the dividend flow to shareholders. But this is only the first stage of a two-stage process, because the individual shareholder then uses the capital market to adjust the timing of this dividend flow so that it accords with his desired pattern of consumption.

The conclusions of our one-period investment–consumption model *and the assumptions upon which it is based* are important and wide-ranging (as we shall see later). The model implies that we require a technique of investment appraisal which will ensure that companies undertake physical investment until the return from the marginal investment equates with the perfect capital market rate of return. In other words, companies should undertake capital investment projects as long as the return generated (from each one) is *not less* than the market rate of interest.

Introducing uncertainty

At this point, it should also be noted that, just as individuals have their own personal time value of money, so the capital market interest rate represents the economy's *average* time value of money. Therefore the capital investment decision rule for companies could be re-stated as: undertake capital investment projects as long as the rate of return generated from each one is not less than the *market's* time value of money. However, it should also be noted that this decision rule, as it stands, is set in a world of certainty. In an uncertain world, as we shall see, there is a whole range of different market interest rates. Therefore this decision rule will require some slight modification.

The problem of uncertainty will be developed fully in later chapters, but it will be helpful to introduce the basic idea at this stage. In a certain world, an investment's outcome is known with certainty by the decision maker. In an uncertain world, an investment's outcome is uncertain and hence is referred to as a *risky* investment. With such investments, decision makers are not entirely uninformed about the possible outcome in that they *expect* a particular outcome (or cash inflow) from an investment, but realize that the *actual* outcome may differ from what was expected. (Notice too, therefore, that risk is a two-way street. An investment's actual outcome may be either better or worse than what was expected.)

Generally speaking, investors dislike uncertainty of outcome. This does not mean that they are unwilling to take on a risky project. Instead it means that they require a reward for doing so and this reward is a higher level of expected return. Therefore, in an uncertain world, there is not just a single capital market interest rate/rate of return, but a whole series of different rates of return – one for each level of risk: the higher the risk, the higher the capital market rate of return.

As a result, in an uncertain world, our capital investment decision rule for companies now has to be modified. Projects should only be undertaken as long as they generate a rate of return which is not less than the capital market's rate of return *for a risk level equivalent to that of the project.*

Payback and ROCE

Clearly, the payback investment appraisal method does not meet the requirements of our decision rule that has been derived through this graphical analysis. The reason being that – even allowing for the fact that it can be adapted to allow for the time value of money – it uses *speed of return*, rather than rate of return, as its criterion of project desirability.

Equally unsuitable is the return on capital employed because, although it is a rate-of-return concept, it ignores the time value of money.[20] In the next chapter we shall turn to the discounted cash flow methods of investment appraisal and examine the extent to which they meet the requirements of our model.[21]

SUMMARY

This chapter dealt with the Hirshliefer single period investment-consumption model to examine what was required of a capital investment appraisal decision rule. The following were the main points covered:

- The model was developed initially under six basic assumptions:
  - ☐ single time period horizon;
  - ☐ certainty of investment outcome;
  - ☐ only physical investment opportunities;
  - ☐ investments exhibit infinite divisibility and diminishing returns to scale;
  - ☐ investments are all independent;
  - ☐ investors are rational.
- The concept of the investor's marginal time value of money was introduced, which would be likely to be an increasing function of the amount invested.
- The firm's physical investment line was introduced and it was seen that the slope of the function represented the marginal rate of return on investment projects at any point.
- As a result, firms would locate on the physical investment line at the point where the slope of the line (the marginal project rate of return) equated with the investor's own marginal time value of money.

- In terms of indifference curves, this optimal investment point occurs at the point of tangency between the PIL and the investor's indifference curve set: the slope of the indifference curve reflecting the investor's marginal time value of money.
- With the introduction of capital markets and the financial market line, the graphical analysis can now handle cases other than the single-owner firm. The decision rule is that the firm should invest in projects as long as their return is not less than the market rate of return – given by the slope of the FIL, which reflects society's average time value of money.
- This capital investment decision rule then allows each individual shareholder to adjust the received pattern of dividends/cash flow by using the capital market to locate on the highest possible indifference curve.
- This analysis is known as the Hirshliefer Separation Theorem in that the capital investment decision (made by managers) can be separated from the capital market decision (made by owners/investors/shareholders).
- Finally, the concept of risk was briefly examined. It was argued that, in an uncertain world, the investment decision rule that arose out of the Hirshliefer analysis had to be modified: the firm should accept projects as long as they were expected to produce a return that was not less than the capital market rate of return for that level of risk.

NOTES

1 This approach was first used by the American economist Irving Fisher (and hence has become known as Fisherian Analysis) in *The Theory of Interest* (New York, Macmillan, 1930). Its use was revived specifically in terms of financial decision theory of Jack Hirshleifer, 'On the Theory of Optimal Investment Decisions', *Journal of Political Economy*, August 1958.

2 Alternatively we could say that all investment opportunities have a life-span of just one period of time, t_0 to t_1.

3 In this assumption of no risk, we are also implicitly assuming that our investor will be alive to enjoy the fruits of his decisions.

4 We are also assuming here that the relative price levels of these factors of production are unchanging and so no 'holding gains' (in inflation accounting parlance) are possible.

5 Here we are using the term 'spare cash' in the sense of the residual cash resources of a company after allowing for the claims of all creditors.

6 In this simple case we are obviously ignoring the possible constraining influence of government legislation in respect of company dividends.

7 We can define a consistent criterion for investment decisions as one which

would produce the following decision: if Project A is preferred to Project B and Project B is preferred to Project C, then the decision criterion should result in Project A being preferred to Project C. If not, the criterion is not producing consistent decisions. Technically, the decision making must exhibit *transitivity*.

8 This time value of money could be either positive or negative. For instance, an individual could be willing to take 5p less 'next year' for every £1 invested 'now', so his exchange rate would be $95/100 - 1 = -0{\cdot}05$ or -5%. However, there is considerable evidence to suggest that TVMs are usually positive with the ultimate, although somewhat morbid, argument being the inevitability of death. So in a one-period case, in order to be persuaded to forgo £1 of consumption 'now', the owner will have to be offered £1 + 'next year', just to cover the risk that he may not be around next year to collect the return from the investment – he may be dead!

As an individual's time value of money is likely not to remain constant but to change with events, it is more correct to call any TVM a *marginal* time value of money.

9 The literature gives this curve a variety of names, e.g., investment opportunity line, productive opportunity line or time-exchange function.

10 As a result of this arrangement and of our assumption that all physical investment opportunities are infinitely divisible and display decreasing returns to scale, the physical investment line is likely to be generally smooth and concave to the origin.

11 The term 'maximum consumption combinations' is meant in the sense that with any given amount of current consumption, no higher consumption next year is possible with the company's existing resources and similarly, with any given amount of consumption next year, no higher level of current consumption is possible.

12 The return on the marginal investment – the marginal return – can properly be found from the first derivative of the function of the physical investment line. For illustration purposes it can be *very* roughly approximated by:

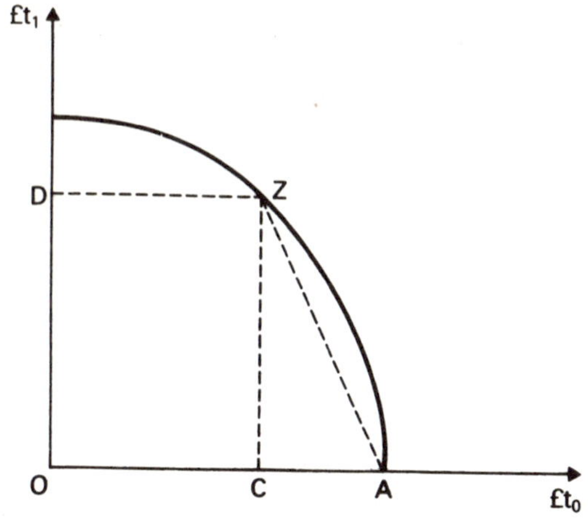

$$\frac{OD - CA}{CA} = \frac{OD}{CA} - \frac{CA}{CA} = \frac{OD}{CA} - 1$$

Therefore if the company has a total value now of £1,000 (OA) of which the owner consumes £600 (OC) and invests the remainder (CA) in order to produce £450 (OD) next year, we can obtain a rough approximation of the return on the marginal project (point Z) as:

$$\frac{450}{400} - 1 = 0{\cdot}125 = 12\tfrac{1}{2}\%$$

Graphically, we are finding the slope of the dotted line ZA. In fact this calculation of $12\frac{1}{2}$% does not provide the return on the marginal investment, but the *average* return on the *total* investment.

13 It is worth noting that under our present assumptions it makes no difference to our analysis whether or not the company represents the owner's *sole* source of consumption. However, we shall see later that when some of the assumptions are varied, this factor becomes one of importance.

14 The concept of a perfect capital market will prove extremely important to us, in later developments of the theory. For the time being we shall define it – under the assumption of a world of certainty – as a market where everyone can borrow or lend as much money as they wish (within their ability to repay) at a single rate of interest which is applicable to all, whether borrowing or lending. Additionally there are no transaction costs involved in using the market, no single investor or group of investors dominate the market and all information is freely available.

15 Up to this point, no mention has been made of taxation. It is easiest to assume that taxation does not exist, but it makes little difference to the analysis if tax is levied on gain as long as all investors face the same level of taxation and there is no differentiation between gain from physical and capital market investment. In such circumstances the return on investment referred to in the analysis is, of course, the after-tax return.

16 This term is negative because the line AE has a negative slope – it slopes *downwards* from left to right.

17 This is often referred to as the Hirshliefer Separation Theorem.

18 The reader must be careful not to be misled here. The test of being 'better off' or increasing utility is whether or not a higher indifference curve is reached. So we could just as easily get a situation where the shareholder achieves a higher indifference curve through using the capital markets but this results (say) in a decrease in consumption 'now' and an increase 'next year'. As a higher indifference curve has been reached the reduction in consumption 'now' *must* be more than offset (in the shareholder's mind) by the gain in consumption 'next year'.

19 It would be possible, although somewhat unlikely, for all of a company's shareholders to have an identical set of indifference curves/time value of money. In such cases the separation theorem would lose its importance.

20 In fact there do exist chance circumstances when ROCE will provide correct

investment appraisal advice, but such situations are likely to be highly artificial and of little practical significance.

21 It may be wise to correct here a mistaken impression that the reader could possibly gain from this presentation and development of the theory. Historically payback and ROCE were derived (largely) in ignorance of the single-period investment–consumption model. It is therefore not surprising that neither method meets the model's requirement for an investment appraisal technique. However, the two major discounted cash flow methods, which are to be discussed in the next chapter, were *not* developed in isolation from the model but arise out of the logic which lies behind the model's construction.

The reader should not hold the belief that it is just fortuitous that these later two methods of investment appraisal accord (as we shall see) with the model.

FURTHER READING

1 The basic reading for the ideas discussed in this chapter is: J. Hirshliefer, 'On the Theory of Optimal Investment Decisions', *Journal of Political Economy*, August 1958. The article is not easy reading, especially the second half, but is very much worthwhile.

2 Although the idea of risk has only been introduced very briefly at this stage, an accessible article to read would be: J. Hirshliefer, 'Risk, the Discount Rate and Investment Decision', *American Economic Review*, May 1961.

QUICKIE QUESTIONS

1 Why is an individual's personal time value of money likely to increase as more investment is undertaken?

2 What does the physical investment line represent?

3 What determines the slope of the physical investment line?

4 What is an indifference curve?

5 Given a single owner-manager firm, how does the firm decide on its level of capital investment?

6 If an owner wants to lend money at t_0, does he move up or down the financial investment line?

7 What is the two-part decision rule that arises out of the Hirshliefer separation theorem?

8 Define a risky capital investment.

9 Taking risk into consideration, what is the capital investment decision rule that managers should follow if they wish to maximize shareholder wealth?

10 What are the *four* main assumptions (remember, two were dropped at later stages in the analysis) of the single period investment-consumption model?

11 What is the generally assumed attitude of investors to risk?

12 If your personal marginal time value of money was less than the market interest rate, would you want to lend or borrow?

PROBLEM

1 Phonetic plc has £500 of cash resources available at t_0. It has identifed three investment projects, as follows:

Project	I	II	III
Outlay at t_0	100	200	200
Inflow at t_1	110	230	210

Assume that all projects exhibit *constant* returns to scale.

Required:

(a) Draw, to scale, the physical investment line facing the firm.

(b) Given that the market interest rate is 8% show, graphically, the firm's investment decisions and the resulting t_0 and t_1 cash flow to the owner.

(c) How might the investment decisions of the firm change if the market interest rate moved:

(i) to 4%;

(ii) to 12%;

(iii) to 10%?

(d) Given the market interest rate of 8%, before the firm can implement the investment plan given in your answer to part (b) an extra project is identified:

Project	IV
Outlay at t_0	250
Inflow at t_1	295

Show the new situation graphically. What is your revised investment decision advice to management?

4
The discounted cash flow approach

Chapter Contents

NET PRESENT VALUE

Having examined the two 'traditional' methods of capital investment appraisal, it is now time to turn to the other two main appraisal techniques. These two other techniques are known as the *discounted cash flow* (DCF) methods and are: *net present value* (NPV) and the *internal rate of return* (IRR). We shall start by first examining the net present value technique.

The NPV investment appraisal method works on the simple, but fundamental, principle that an investment is worthwhile undertaking if the money got out of the investment is *at least* equal to – if not greater than – the money put in. On this very commonsense principle, project A is worth investing in. For an outlay of £500, it produces a total cash inflow of £600. Thus it has a net value of + £100.

Project A

Year	*Cash Flow*	
0	−£500	
1	+£200	
2	+£200	
3	+£200	
	+£100	Net value

We can easily see that, with such a straightforward approach, the decision rule would be: accept all investments with a positive or zero net value (as they produce a return either equal to or greater than their cost), and reject all those with a negative net value.

However, let us take a totally different situation. Suppose you were made an offer: if you pay £500 now, you will immediately receive 200 French Francs, 200 Japanese Yen and 200 German Marks. How would you go about deciding whether the offer was worthwhile? What you certainly would *not* do is to say: I have to give up 500 pieces of paper and, in return, I'll get 200 + 200 + 200 = 600 pieces of paper. As I end up with 100 more pieces of paper, the deal is worthwhile! Instead, you would recognize that in order to evaluate the offer, you have to convert all the different currencies to a *common* currency, and *then* undertake the comparison.

Although it does not look as silly as that which was initially suggested with the currency offer, our suggested approach to evaluating Project A is *just* as silly. In the same way that money in different currencies cannot be compared directly, but first has to be converted to a common currency, money in the *same* currency (as in Project A), but which occurs *at different points in time* cannot be compared directly, but must first be converted to a common point of time. This is because of the *time value of money*.

Therefore the net present value investment appraisal decision rule basically takes the same approach as that used with Project A, but with one vital difference. That difference is that the time value of money is taken into account in assessing whether the investment has a positive or negative net value.

The discounting process

The time value of money is taken into account through the *discounting* process. The arithmetic of discounting is dealt with in an appendix to this chapter and the reader is advised to become familiar with its contents. However, it will help to explain the NPV technique if the basic concepts of discounting are developed here.

We have already seen from our initial discussion on the time value of money in Chapter 2 that, given the choice between £100 now, or £100 in 12 months' time, most people would *intuitively* take the £100 now. This is because the £100 could be placed on deposit at (say) 6% interest and so turn itself into £106 in 12 months' time. (And, being rational investors, £106 in 12 months' time will be preferred to only £100 in 12 months' time.) Therefore 6% – the interest rate – represents the time value of money.

The mathematics of this process works through the compound interest formula:

$$A(1 + r)^n$$

where A is the initial amount invested or deposited, r is the (annual) rate of interest and n is the number of years for which A is left deposited. In the example used above, these three letters (or 'variables') have the respective values of: £100, 0·06 and 1. So, £100 left on deposit for twelve months is turned into:

$$£100(1 + 0{\cdot}06)^1 = £100 + £6 = £106$$

Using this compound interest formula, but switching it around, we can also calculate that to receive £106 in twelve months' time, the amount to be invested now is:

$$\frac{£106}{(1 + 0{\cdot}06)} = £106\frac{1}{(1 + 0{\cdot}06)} = £100$$

Therefore £100 is the 'present value' of £106 received in twelve months' time and £106, the 'terminal value' of £100 deposited twelve months' previously, assuming a 6% interest rate in each case.

Similarly, £100 invested for two years at a 6% compound interest rate would turn into:

$$£100(1 + 0{\cdot}06)(1 + 0{\cdot}06) = £100(1 + 0{\cdot}06)^2 = £112{\cdot}36$$

and £112·36 received in two years' time is equal to:

$$\frac{£112{\cdot}36}{(1 + 0{\cdot}06)^2} = £112{\cdot}36\frac{1}{(1 + 0{\cdot}06)^2} = £100 \text{ now}$$

Thus the terminal value in two years' time of £100 invested now is £112·36, whilst the present value of £112·36 received in two years' time is £100. In each case we are assuming an annual compound interest rate of 6%.

In general terms: $A(1 + r)^n$ is the terminal value of an amount A that has been placed on deposit for n years at an annual compound interest rate of r. Similarly: $A[1/(1 + r)^n]$ is the *present value* of an amount A received in n years' time, where r is the annual compound interest rate.

In the calculation of the terminal value, an amount of money is being 'compounded' *forward* through time, whereas in the calculation of the present value, an amount of money is being 'discounted' *backwards* through time. To distinguish between these two processes, it is usual to refer to the compound interest rate, when used in the discounting process, as the *discount rate.* Also, usually a slightly easier notation is used for the present value expression: $A(1 + r)^{-n}$. Thus in the previous example, the present value of £112·36 received in two years' time, when the annual rate of discount was 6%, is given by:

$$\frac{£112{\cdot}36}{(1 + 0{\cdot}06)^2} \equiv £112{\cdot}36(1 + 0{\cdot}06)^{-2} = £112{\cdot}36 \times 0{\cdot}8900 = £100$$

A discounting example

The NPV method makes use of the idea of present values by expressing the project's cash flows in terms of its net *present* value, although the cash flows could just as easily be expressed in terms of net *terminal* values. It is really for no reason other than convention that *present* values are used.

To see how the NPV method works, let us return to Project A, but this time, instead of just netting out the cash inflows and outflows to produce a net value of + £100, we first of all convert (or 'discount') the cash flows to *present value* cash flows, in order to allow for the time value of money, and then net out the inflows and outflows. Thus with a discount rate of (say) 8%, the net present value of Project A is + £15·40:

Project A

Year	*Cash flow* ×	*Discounting factor*		=	*Present value cash flow*
0	−£500	× $(1 + 0{\cdot}08)^{0}$	= −£500 × 1	=	−£500·00
1	+£200	× $(1 + 0{\cdot}08)^{-1}$	= +£200 × 0·9259	=	+£185·18
2	+£200	× $(1 + 0{\cdot}08)^{-2}$	= +£200 × 0·8573	=	+£171·46
3	+£200	× $(1 + 0{\cdot}08)^{-3}$	= +£200 × 0·7938	=	+£158·76
				NPV	+£ 15·40

From this analysis we can see that Project A is worth undertaking because the cash outflows associated with it are exceeded by the cash inflows produced by it. The time value of money has been taken into account by the fact that all the cash flows of the project, for the purposes of comparison, are converted to values at one point in time: the present.

To emphasize this important point further, it is vital to understand that once the fact is accepted that money has a time value, then it follows that money at different points in time is not directly comparable: £1 now cannot be directly compared with £1 next year, and so the cash flows of a project that arise at different points through time all have to be converted to a value at one particular point in time. By convention, and because it has many practical advantages, the point in time normally chosen is the present.

Thus our original netting procedure with Project A which produced a net value of + £100 was nonsensical, because we were not comparing like with like, but were trying to compare directly the net money flows arising at different points in time without first converting them to a common point in time. The NPV approach tells us that in terms of present values (i.e., converting all the cash flows to money values *now*) Project A produces a return which is £15·40 in excess of the investment outlay (i.e., in present value terms the cash outflow is £500 and the total cash inflow is £515·40) and is therefore a worthwhile investment.

Project B

Year	*Cash flow*	× *Discounting factor*	=	*Present value cash flow*
0	−£1,000	× $(1 + 0{\cdot}08)^{0}$	=	−£1,000·00
1	+£ 100	× $(1 + 0{\cdot}08)^{-1}$	=	+£ 92·59
2	+£ 200	× $(1 + 0{\cdot}08)^{-2}$	=	+£ 171·46
3	+£ 200	× $(1 + 0{\cdot}08)^{-3}$	=	+£ 158·76
4	+£ 550	× $(1 + 0{\cdot}08)^{-4}$	=	+£ 404·25
Net value	+£ 50		NPV	−£ 172·94

As another example, evaluating Project B without taking into account the time value of money, the cash inflows exceed the cash outflows by £50 and so the project appears to be a worthwhile investment. However if we do take into account the time value of money by discounting the cash flows into present values at an 8% discount rate, then we can see that Project B is *not* a worthwhile investment because the cash outflow required exceeds the cash inflows produced, resulting in a negative net present value.

(Note that the discounting factors, such as $(1 + 0{\cdot}08)^{-3}$, can be calculated quite easily on any basic calculator that has a 'powers' function, i.e. x^y. In addition, a table of discounting factors for a variety of values of n and i is given on page 481. These tables can be used to find that $(1 + 0{\cdot}08)^{-3}$ equals 0·7938. In other words, the present value of £1 in three years' time at an 8% rate of discount is 79·38 pence. Therefore, £200 in three years' time has a present value of: £200 × 0·7938 = £158·76.)

The NPV decision rule

In general terms, we can express the net present value of an investment project as the sum of its net discounted future cash flows:

$$\sum_{t=0}^{n} \frac{A_t}{(1 + r)^t}$$

where A_t is the project's cash flow (either positive or negative) in time t (t takes on values from year 0 to year n, where n represents the point in time when the project comes to the end of its life) and r is the annual rate of discount or the time value of money (which is here assumed to remain a constant over the life of the project). If the expression has a zero or positive value, the company should invest in the project; if it has a negative value, it should not invest.[1] (This general mathematical expression for the net present value of an investment project is more fully explained in the appendix on compounding and discounting at the end of this chapter.)

Let us take a closer look at Project B to see why the NPV method tells us not to invest. Project B requires an outlay of £1,000 and would produce cash inflows for the four following years. However, if we did not invest £1,000 in B we could, presumably, put the money on deposit (i.e., lend the money on the capital market) at the going rate of interest of 8%. At the end of four years' time this would produce £1,000 × $(1 + 0{\cdot}08)^4$ = £1,360·50.

Suppose we *did* invest in Project B and as the generated cash inflows arose we placed them on deposit (at 8% compound interest). How much cash would we be able to accumulate by the end of four years (i.e., by the time the life of the project was completed)? This is shown below, where the £100 Project B produces in twelve months' time can be invested for three years, the £200 it produces in twenty-four months' time can be invested for two years, and so on:

Year	Project's cash inflow	Compounding × factor	Terminal value = (end of year 4)
1	+£100	$\times (1 + 0{\cdot}08)^3$	= +£ 125·97
2	+£200	$\times (1 + 0{\cdot}08)^2$	= +£ 233·28
3	+£200	$\times (1 + 0{\cdot}08)^1$	= +£ 216·00
4	+£550	$\times (1 + 0{\cdot}08)^0$	= +£ 550·00
		Total terminal value	= +£1,125·25

So putting the £1,000 on deposit for four years produces £1,360·50, whereas if we invest our £1,000 in Project B and place on deposit any cash flows that arise, at the end of four years this will produce only £1,125·25.

Therefore, looking at the two alternatives, the project is *not* the most desirable investment: we should be better off placing the £1,000 on deposit in the capital market. This is the basis of the advice given by the NPV appraisal method, because, the present value of £1,360·50 received in four years' time with an 8% discount rate is:

$$£1{,}360{\cdot}50\ (1 + 0{\cdot}08)^{-4} = £1{,}000$$

whilst the present value of £1,125·25 received in four years' time with an 8% discount rate is:

$$£1{,}125{\cdot}25\ (1 + 0{\cdot}08)^{-4} = £827{\cdot}06$$

The difference between these two sums (£1,000 – £827·06) is £172·94, which is the amount of Project B's negative net present value.

So we can see that the NPV method of investment appraisal evaluates projects by looking at the *alternative* to an investment in that project, that is, lending the money out on the capital market at the market rate of interest. It automatically carries out this comparison of alternatives through the decision rule: only invest in projects which produce zero or positive NPVs. As we have seen, the value of a project's NPV represents the increase or decrease (depending upon whether the NPV is positive or negative) in return that would arise from investing in the project rather than lending the money on the capital market at the market rate of interest, and it is this rate that is used as the discount rate.

Alternative interpretations of NPV

There are some equally valid, alternative interpretations of the meaning *behind* a project's net present value which might be helpful to examine in order to gain a deeper understanding. We will take another project as an example. Project C is expected to produce the following net cash flows:

Year	*Cash Flow*
0	−£100
1	+£ 30
2	+£ 40
3	+£ 50
4	+£ 20

Referring back to our brief discussion at the end of the previous chapter about risk, suppose that the capital market rate of return available from an investment of similar risk to Project C is 10%. Thus 10% is the relevant time value of money and so is the appropriate discount rate to use in an NPV analysis.

Project C's NPV is calculated as:

Year	*Cash Flow*		*Discount Factor*		*P.V. Cash Flow*
0	−£100	×	$(1 + 0{\cdot}10)^{0}$	=	−£100·00
1	+£ 30	×	$(1 + 0{\cdot}10)^{-1}$	=	+£ 27·27
2	+£ 40	×	$(1 + 0{\cdot}10)^{-2}$	=	+£ 33·06
3	+£ 50	×	$(1 + 0{\cdot}10)^{-3}$	=	+£ 37·57
4	+£ 20	×	$(1 + 0{\cdot}10)^{-4}$	=	+£ 13·66
					+£ 11·56 NPV

Project C has a positive NPV and therefore, according to the decision rule, is worthwhile undertaking. There are three obvious interpretations that can be made of this result:

1 An investment of £100 in Project C produces £11.56 more, in t_0 terms, than investing on the capital market. In this sense, the £11.56 is an *excess* return or a measure of *economic profit.* (This is our original interpretation.) ?

2 As Project C produces a positive NPV, it is generating a return which is greater than 10%, the discount rate used.

3 If £100 were borrowed at 10% interest, in order to undertake Project C, then the project would generate a sufficient cash flow to pay the interest, repay the loan *and* leave a surplus of £11.56 in present value terms.

Given these three interpretations, the logic of the NPV decision rule becomes even more obvious:

1 A negative NPV project is unacceptable because it indicates that the project makes a loss *relative* to a capital market investment (i.e. an opportunity loss).

2 A negative NPV project is unacceptable because it is producing a return less than that available for a similar level of risk on the capital market.

3 A negative NPV project is unacceptable as it would not generate sufficient cash flow to repay the financial cost of undertaking it.

Also notice, given these interpretations, that a zero NPV project would be *acceptable* – but we would not be overjoyed if we identified one.

Finally, there is a *fourth* interpretation of a project's NPV that can be made. In many ways, this is the most important interpretation and, how it arises will be seen in the next section when we return to the Hirshliefer analysis. Quite simply, a project's net present value indicates the increase in shareholders' wealth that it will generate if it is undertaken. Hence, the technique links *directly* into our fundamental objective of financial management decision making.

NPV AND THE INVESTMENT–CONSUMPTION MODEL

When looking at our single-period investment–consumption model, we saw that in order to act in the best interests of its owners, a company should move along the physical investment line until the return from the marginal investment becomes equal to the return given by the capital market (i.e., the market rate of interest). How does the NPV method of investment appraisal help us achieve this point ?

Returning to Project A, we saw that, using an 8% discount rate, the project had an NPV of + £15·40 whilst Project B had an NPV of −£172·94. On the basis of what we already understand about the net present value, we can also say – using the two examples above – that as Project A has a positive NPV when discounted at 8%, it must be producing a rate of return *greater* than 8%, and similarly, as Project B has a negative NPV when discounted at 8%, then it must be producing a rate of return of *less than* 8%.

Just what the exact rate of return is in each case we shall consider later, but looking at Project D, since it gives a zero NPV when discounted at 8% we can conclude that it has a rate of return *exactly equal* to 8%:

Project D

Year	*Cash flow*	× *Present value factor*	= *Present value cash flow*
0	−400	× $(1 + 0{\cdot}08)^{0}$	= −£400·00
1	+200	× $(1 + 0{\cdot}08)^{-1}$	= +£185·18
2	+100	× $(1 + 0{\cdot}08)^{-2}$	= +£ 85·73
3	+162·62	× $(1 + 0{\cdot}08)^{-3}$	= +£129·09
		NPV	£ 0

Therefore, if a company follows the NPV rule and invests in all physical investment opportunities available to it, that possess either zero or positive net present values, using the market rate of interest as the discount rate, it will automatically move along the physical investment line until a point of tangency is reached with the financial investment line.

If a company makes physical investments beyond this optimal point, these projects will have a rate of return which is less than the market rate of interest and therefore *negative* net present values. As long as investment decision makers within companies follow the NPV decision rule and *only* invest in projects with zero or positive NPVs, then the company is ensured of optimally locating on the physical investment line.

The graphical interpretation

In Figure 4.1, if management assess the company's total resources (i.e., the full, liquidated value of the company at time t_0) as OA and they have sought out all the investment alternatives available to them, expressed by the physical investment line AB, then using the NPV method of investment appraisal, they will invest in all projects with positive or zero NPVs when discounted at the market rate of interest.

This simple decision rule will lead to DA of the company's resources being put into productive investments at t_0 and the remainder, OD, being paid out to shareholders as dividends. This investment will result in a total dividend of OC being paid out at t_1. Shareholders can then adjust their individual dividends to fit their desired consumption pattern by lending or borrowing on the capital market. This two-stage process, with the company first making physical investment decisions and then the individual shareholder making financial investment decisions, will ensure that individual shareholders will achieve their highest possible indifference curves and hence maximize their level of utility.

We should also note that if the company does invest up to the optimal point P in Figure 4.1 (i.e., the point of tangency between the physical and financial investment lines), then the present value of the cash *inflows* generated by all the company's investment project undertakings is given by DE, the cash expenditure made on these investments is given by DA and so, by difference, AE represents the total *net* present value of the investment projects undertaken by the firm. (Alternatively, OE can be said to represent the present value of the sum of dividend OD at t_0 and dividend OC at t_1.)

From this we can see the derivation of that important fourth

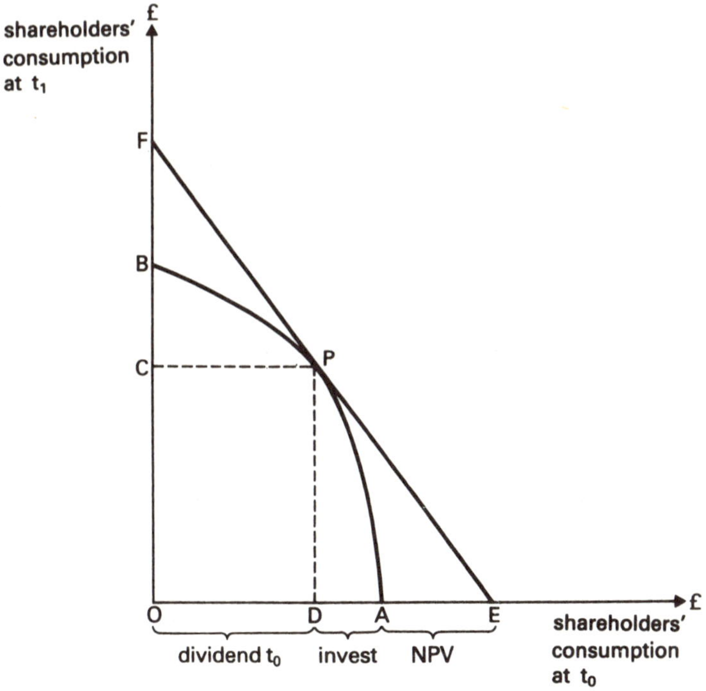

Figure 4.1

interpretation of the idea of net present value. Notice that with no investment undertaken, the total worth of the company's resources (in t_0 terms) is given by AO. If amount AD is invested to yield OC at t_1, then the worth of the company (again, in t_0 terms) increases to amount EO. Thus undertaking the investments required to locate at point P on the physical investment line, has resulted in an increase in the current worth of the company – in other words, in shareholders' wealth – of AE, which of course represents the total NPV of the investments undertaken. Therefore the net present value of a project represents the amount by which shareholders' wealth (measured in t_0 terms) will change as a result of accepting the project. (It thus becomes obvious why management should not accept *negative* NPV projects – they will cause shareholders' wealth to be reduced.)

In general, the single-period investment–consumption diagram can measure the NPV of a company's total physical investments as the distance between the point at which the physical investment line cuts the horizontal axis and where the financial investment line, passing through the point at which the firm has located on the physical investment line, also cuts the horizontal axis.[2] As can be seen from Figure 4.2, if a company either underinvests and locates at (say) point X, or overinvests and locates at (say) point Y, or optimally invests and locates at point Z on the physical investment line, in each case the total NPV earned by the company's investment decisions is given by the distance on the horizontal axis between the physical investment line and the financial invest-

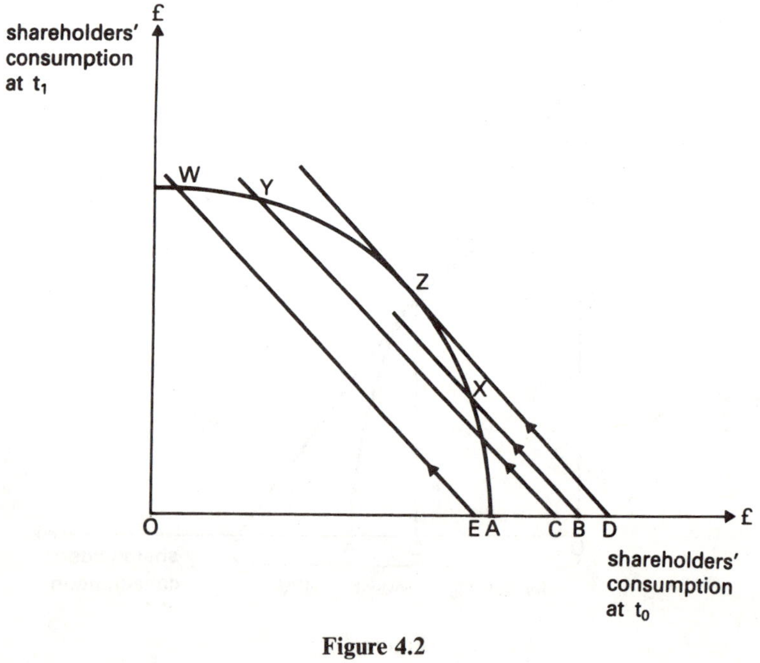

Figure 4.2

ment line passing through the location point: respectively AB, AC and AD.[3] Locating at the optimal point on the physical investment line (at the point of *tangency* with the market line) also maximizes NPV and so here is yet another surrogate for the financial decision making objective of maximizing shareholder wealth, that of maximizing total net present value.

One final point of interest from this graphical analysis is to use it to look at the effect of a change in the market rate of interest. A *fall* in the market rate of interest will cause the financial investment line to pivot anticlockwise and become flatter. This would then have the effect of moving the point of tangency (and hence the optimal physical investment point) higher up the physical investment line, thus increasing the amount of investment that a company must undertake to reach its point of optimality. This is just as we would expect, as is the case where the market rate of interest rises and the reverse effect is observed.

(The reader no doubt has noticed how the analysis has slipped in and out of the assumption of a single period time horizon. The assumption was made in the Hirschliefer analysis in order to allow a graphical/two-dimensional presentation. However, the conclusions drawn can be quite simply applied to a multi-time period example, such as that of project D.)

INTERNAL RATE OF RETURN

Before looking more carefully at this analysis and specifically at the implicit and explicit assumptions that lie behind the NPV method, let us turn to the second major discounted cash flow investment appraisal technique, the internal rate of return (IRR) or yield.[4] As we shall see later on in the discussion, the IRR has some very great theoretical and practical difficulties as a method of investment appraisal, and indeed it may be questioned whether it is truly a method of appraisal at all, or just an arithmetic result.

The IRR model

To discover what the IRR is, let us return briefly to our discussion of NPV. We stated that if a project had a positive NPV at a certain discount rate (say) 10%, this meant, amongst other things, that the project's return was actually greater than 10%, whilst if the project had a negative NPV then its return was less than the discount rate, and if it had a zero NPV, then its return was equal to the discount rate.

The IRR of a project can be defined as the rate of discount which, when applied to the project's cash flows, produces a zero NPV (hence the method could be seen as just an arithmetic result of the NPV method). In general terms, the IRR is the value for r which satisfies the expression:

$$\sum_{t=0}^{n} \frac{A}{(1+r)^t} = 0$$

For a very simple project such as E, where cash flows only extend over two periods, the internal rate of return is easy to calculate using simple algebra:

Project E

Year	*Cash Flow*
0	−£200
1	+£218

The IRR of Project E is equal to r, where:

$$-200 + \frac{218}{1 + r} = 0$$

Multiplying both sides by $(1 + r)$ gives:

$$-200\,(1 + r) + 218 = 0$$

and rearranging:

$$218 - 200 = 200\,r$$
$$18 = 200\,r$$
$$\frac{18}{200} = r \qquad = 0{\cdot}09 \quad \text{or} \quad \underline{9\%}$$

Thus if Project E's cash flows were discounted by 9% they would have a zero NPV:

Project E

Year	*Cash flow*	× 9% *Present value factor*	= *Present value cash flow*
0	−£200	× $(1 + 0{\cdot}09)^{0}$	= −£200
1	+£218	× $(1 + 0{\cdot}09)^{-1}$	= +£200
		NPV	£0

And with a slightly more complex project, with cash flows occurring at three points of time, t_0, t_1, and t_2, the IRR can still easily be found through the solution to a quadratic equation, as with Project F:

Project F

Year	*Cash flow*
0	−£100
1	+£60
2	+£55

IRR = r, where:

$$-100 + \frac{60}{1 + r} + \frac{55}{(1 + r)^2} = 0$$

Multiplying both sides by $(1 + r)^2$, we produce a quadratic equation in $1 + r$ that can be solved via the quadratic formula:

$$-100(1 + r)^2 + 60(1 + r) + 55 = 0$$

$$(1 + r) = \frac{-60 \pm \sqrt{60^2 - (4 \times -100 \times 55)}}{(2 \times -100)}$$

$$\underline{(1 + r) = +1{\cdot}10} \text{ or } \underline{(1 + r) = -0{\cdot}50}$$

This second (negative) result can be discarded as meaningless for our purposes, so that $1 + r = 1{\cdot}10$ and $r = 0{\cdot}10$ or 10%. This is the internal rate of return of Project F, and therefore if the project's cash flows were discounted at this rate they would have a zero NPV.

Estimating the IRR via linear interpolation

However, to find the IRR of projects whose cash flows extend over more than three points in time, we become involved with finding solutions to complex polynomial equations. There are many computer package programmes that will carry out this task, but a fairly good *approximation* of an investment project's IRR can be found through the mathematical technique called linear interpolation.

Returning to Project F, although we have found its IRR to be 10%, let us now estimate it by using the *linear interpolation* method.

If a whole series of different discount rates were applied to Project F's cash flow, the the resulting NPVs could be plotted out on a graph against the discount rate. Figure 4.3 illustrates the sort of result that might occur, termed the *NPV profile.* Notice that the project's IRR is given by the point where the NPV profile cuts the horizontal axis.

We will first deal with the *mechanics* of linear interpolation, and then examine its rationale. The approach used is to select a pair of discount rates so that one of them, when applied to the project's cash flow, produces a +NPV and the other produces a −NPV. From observing Figure 4.3, it can be seen that as the discount rate (the time value of money) gets larger, the positive NPV gets progressively smaller, passes through zero, and then becomes an increasingly large negative value. (This result is, of course, not surprising, knowing as much as we do about the time value of money concept.) Therefore a low and a high discount rate should be chosen to provide the required positive and negative NPVs.

Therefore using 4% and 20% discount rates (the extreme discount rate values given in the table on page 481) the NPV of project F can be calculated as:

$$\begin{array}{llrcr} 0 & - & 100\,(1{\cdot}04)^{0} & = & -100{\cdot}00 \\ 1 & + & 60\,(1{\cdot}04)^{-1} & = & +\ \ 57{\cdot}69 \\ 2 & + & 55\,(1{\cdot}04)^{-2} & = & \underline{+\ \ 50{\cdot}85} \\ & & \text{NPV} & = & \underline{+\ \ \ 8{\cdot}54} \end{array} \qquad \begin{array}{llrcr} 0 & - & 100\,(1{\cdot}20)^{0} & = & -100{\cdot}00 \\ 1 & + & 60\,(1{\cdot}20)^{-1} & = & +\ \ 50{\cdot}00 \\ 2 & + & 55\,(1{\cdot}20)^{-2} & = & \underline{+\ \ 38{\cdot}19} \\ & & \text{NPV} & = & \underline{+\ \ 11{\cdot}81} \end{array}$$

Given the IRR is that discount rate that produces a *zero* NPV, Project F's IRR must lie somewhere between 4% and 20%. As the IRR is more than 4%, *how much* more than 4% is estimated by taking the NPV at 4% as a proportion of the difference between the two NPVs calculated (0·42). That proportion is then taken of the difference between the two discount rates used (16%):

$$\text{IRR} = 4\% + \left[\frac{+8{\cdot}54}{+8{\cdot}54-(-11{\cdot}81)} \times (20\% - 4\%)\right]$$

$$\text{IRR} = 4\% + [0{\cdot}42 \times 16\%] = \underline{10{\cdot}72\%}$$

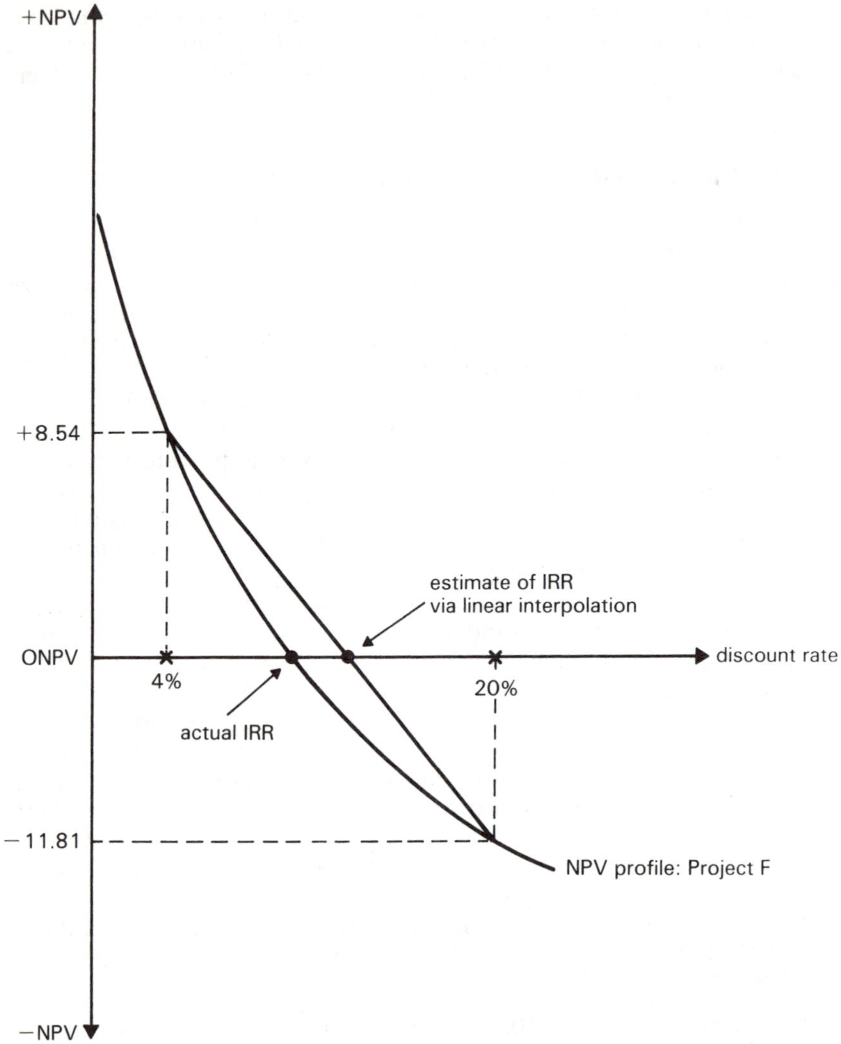

Figure 4.3 (not to scale)

Figure 4.3 shows the linear interpolation method diagrammatically. The IRR is only *estimated* because the NPV profile is being approximated by a straight line.

This 'bracketing' of discount rates around the true IRR so as to produce a positive and negative NPV is not strictly necessary, but it does make the approximation calculation easier. Furthermore, the narrower the bracketing around the actual IRR, the more accurate the estimate of the IRR. For example, using 8% and 12% discount rates, linear interpolation estimates project F's IRR as:

At 8% discount rate: +2·70 NPV
At 12% discount rate: −2·58 NPV

$$\text{IRR} = 8\% + \left[\frac{+2{\cdot}70}{+2{\cdot}70-(-2{\cdot}58)} \times (12\% - 8\%)\right] = 10{\cdot}04\%$$

A much closer result to the actual IRR. However, for most investment appraisal purposes, a highly accurate estimate of the IRR is not justified and an estimate with the accuracy of our initial calculation is usually more than sufficient.

The IRR decision rule

Having seen how to calculate a project's internal rate of return, how are we to use it for investment appraisal purposes? The decision rule is that only projects with an IRR greater than or equal to some predetermined 'cut-off' rate should be accepted. This cut-off rate is usually the market rate of interest (i.e., the discount rate that would have been used if an NPV analysis were undertaken instead). All other investment project opportunities should be rejected. Therefore Project F would be acceptable if the decision criterion has been set at 10%, or less.

The reasoning behind the IRR decision rule is similar to that behind NPV. The market interest rate reflects the *opportunity cost* of the capital involved. Thus to be acceptable, a project must generate a return at least equal to the return available elsewhere on the capital market.

IRR and the investment–consumption model

Again, just as the NPV method fitted into our single period investment–consumption model so too does the IRR method. We originally described the physical investment line as representing the whole series of infinitely divisible physical investment projects which were available to the company, arranged in order of decreasing rate of return. This rate of return can be viewed as the individual project's internal rate of return and can be derived (as we have already seen) from the slope of the physical investment lines.

In Figure 4.4 therefore, moving progressively along the line from point A to B, the slope gets less and less steep, indicating that the company initially invests in projects with high internal rates of return and then works its way through to projects with much smaller IRRs. Thus from the slope of the physical investment line at point C can be derived the IRR of the marginal physical investment represented by that point.

The IRR decision rule tells a company to invest in all projects with IRRs greater than or equal to the market rate of interest. Thus a company will move up and around its physical investment line until it reaches the point of tangency with the financial investment line. Up to this point, all investment projects that the company has undertaken will have IRRs

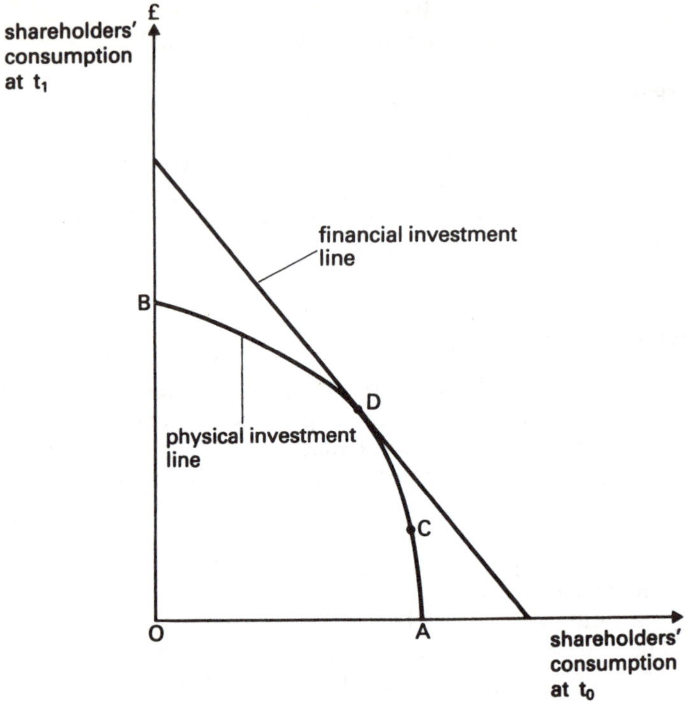

Figure 4.4

greater than the market rate of interest. At point D on Figure 4.4, the marginal project will have an IRR equal to the market interest rate, and it is at this point that the company will cease further investment, because the remaining investment opportunities will all have IRRs which are less than the market interest rate. Therefore, the internal rate of return investment appraisal rule, like the NPV rule, will ensure that a company locates at the optimal point on its physical investment line.

DISCOUNTED PAYBACK

Having examined the basic application of the two discounted cash flow techniques of capital investment appraisal, it is appropriate to return briefly to look at the discounted payback technique, which was referred to in Chapter 2. There it was stated that a major limitation of payback was that it did not take the time value of money into account. However, this criticism could be overcome through the use of discounted payback.

All that discounted payback does is to see how quickly a project takes to pay back its outlay in *present value* (rather than undiscounted), cash flow terms. Example 4.1 illustrates the approach.

Example 4.1
Phonate plc wishes to evaluate an investment opportunity using discounted payback, for which it uses a four-year decision criterion. For discounting purposes, the company uses a 10% discount rate which, it is judged, reflects the return available elsewhere in the capital market for a similar risk investment. The project, code-named G, has a five-year life and the following estimated cash flows:

Year	*Cash Flow* £
0	−250,000
1	+100,000
2	+100,000
3	+102,000
4	+ 50,000
5	+ 35,000

The discounted payback of Project G is calculated as follows:

Year	*Cash flow* £	×	*Discount factor*	=	*P.V. cash flow* £	
0	−250,000	×	1	=	−250,000	
1	+100,000	×	0·9091	=	+ 90,910	
2	+100,000	×	0·8264	=	+ 82,640	
3	+102,000	×	0·7513	=	+ 76,633	3 year payback
4	+ 50,000	×	0·6830	=	+ 34,150	
5	+ 35,000	×	0·6209	=	+ 21,731	

Project G has a discounted payback of approximately 3 years and so is acceptable, according to the company's decision criterion.

Truncated NPV

Discounted payback can be looked upon as a variation of the basic payback technique. However it is perhaps instructive to see it more as a variation on the NPV method.

In Example 4.1 the decision rule the company implied was: accept the project as long as its NPV is at least zero (if not positive) at the end of four years. If a project complies with this requirement then it does payback within the criterion. Thus discounted payback is no more than a *truncated* version of NPV. Instead of calculating the project's NPV over the *whole* of its life, the NPV is effectively calculated up to some specified cut-off point which, in this example, happened to be four years.

Discounted payback still suffers from the criticism made of standard payback – that of ignoring project cash flows that lie outside the payback time period. However, as before, the point should be made that setting this artificial time horizon on a project's life may be no more than making a realistic allowance for management's limited forecasting abilities.

Finally, despite the foregoing, it should be pointed out that the use of discounted payback will not necessarily lead to the firm's optimal physical investment line location. This is because some positive NPV projects may well be rejected because they do not generate that positive NPV sufficiently quickly. In addition, a further criticism will be made of discounted payback in the following chapter.

APPENDIX: COMPOUNDING AND DISCOUNTING

Tables A to F can be found on pp. 481–483.

1 Compound interest factors

The amount to which a sum of £1 accumulates when placed on deposit for N years at a constant annual rate of interest of i is given by:

$$(1 + i)^N$$

Thus, £500 placed on deposit for 6 years at an annual rate of interest of 12%, accumulates to:

$$£500\,(1{\cdot}12)^6 = £500 \times 1{\cdot}9738 = £986{\cdot}90$$

Similarly, if £200 is placed on deposit for 3 years at 10% and 2 years at 8%, then the accumulated sum at the end of 5 years is:

$$£200\,(1{\cdot}10)^3\,(1{\cdot}08)^2 = £200 \times 1{\cdot}3310 \times 1{\cdot}1664 = £310{\cdot}50$$

Table A provides compound interest factors for various values of N and i.

2 Present value factors

The value now (i.e., the present value) of £1 arising in N years' time when the rate of discount (interest) is i is given by:

$$1/(1 + i)^N \quad \text{or} \quad (1 + i)^{-N}$$

Thus, £500 arising in 6 years' time, when the annual rate of discount is 12%, has a present value of:

$$£500\,(1{\cdot}12)^{-6} = £500 \times 0{\cdot}5066 = £253{\cdot}30$$

Similarly, £200 arising in 5 years, where the annual rate of discount is 10% for 3 years and 8% for 2 years, has a present value of:

$$£200\,(1{\cdot}10)^{-3}\,(1{\cdot}08)^{-2} = £200 \times 0{\cdot}7513 \times 0{\cdot}8573 = £128{\cdot}82$$

Table B provides present value factors for various values of N and i.

3 Annuities

An annuity can be defined as a constant amount of cash which arises for a given number of consecutive years. Three main types of annuity can be specified:

(a) an annuity due, where the first sum arises immediately;
(b) an immediate annuity, where the first sum arises in one year's time;
(c) a deferred annuity, where the first sum arises in two or more years' time.

Examples of the cash flows of 4-year £100 annuities of each type are given below:

Year		0	1	2	3	4	5
(a)	Annuity Due	£100	£100	£100	£100		
(b)	Immediate Annuity		£100	£100	£100	£100	
(c)	One-Year Deferred Annuity			£100	£100	£100	£100

4 Present value of an annuity

The present value of an *immediate* annuity of £1 per year for N years, where the rate of discount is i, is given by:

$$\frac{1-(1+i)^{-N}}{i}, \text{ denoted as } A_{\overline{N}|i}$$

Thus the present value of a four-year £100 *immediate* annuity, where the rate of discount is 16%, is:

$$£100\,\frac{1-(1{\cdot}16)^{-4}}{0{\cdot}16} = £100\ A_{\overline{4}|0{\cdot}16} = £100 \times 2{\cdot}7982 = £279{\cdot}82$$

The present value of a four-year £100 annuity *due*, where the rate of discount is 16%, is:

$$£100 + £100\ A_{\overline{3}|0{\cdot}16} = £100 + (£100 \times 2{\cdot}2459) = £324{\cdot}59$$

Whereas the present value of a four-year £100 annuity, deferred for (say) two years (so that the first sum arises at year 3), at a rate of discount of 18%, is:

$$£100\ A_{\overline{4}|0{\cdot}18}\,(1{\cdot}18)^{-2} = £100 \times 2{\cdot}6901 \times 0{\cdot}7182 = £193{\cdot}20$$

Notice the precise function of the $A_{\overline{N}|i}$ factor. It gathers the annuity together and brings it to a point in time that is *one year earlier than the point of time when the first annuity amount* arises. For an *immediate* annuity, one year earlier than when the annuity commences is t_0. Thus $A_{\overline{N}|i}$ will provide the present value of an immediate annuity; but for a deferred annuity the $A_{\overline{N}|i}$ factor will have to be applied with an additional discount factor – as in the example above – to get it back to present value. Table C provides factors for the present values of £1 immediate annuities for various values of N and i.

5 Terminal value of an annuity

The amount to which an annuity of £1 per year for N years accumulates when the annual rate of interest is i takes the form of a geometric progression, which simplifies to:

$$\frac{(1+i)^N - 1}{i}, \text{ denoted as } S_{\overline{N|}i}$$

Thus the 'terminal value' of a four-year £100 immediate annuity (the amount to which it accumulates at the end of its life), where the rate of interest is 14%, is:

$$£100 \frac{(1{\cdot}14)^4 - 1}{0{\cdot}14} = £100\ S_{\overline{4|}0{\cdot}14} = £100 \times 4{\cdot}9211 = £429{\cdot}11$$

Table D provides terminal value of an annuity factors for various values of N and i.

6 Annual equivalent factors

The annual value of an *immediate* annuity which lasts for N years, where the prevailing rate of discount is i, and which has a present value of £1, is given by:

$$\frac{i}{1 - (1+i)^{-N}}, \text{ denoted as } A^{-1}_{\overline{N|}i}$$

In other words, the reciprocal of the $A_{\overline{N|}i}$ factor.

Thus the annual value of an immediate annuity which lasts for 5 years, where the rate of discount is 8%, and which has a present value of £2,000, is:

$$£2000 \frac{0{\cdot}08}{1 - (1{\cdot}08)^{-5}} = £2000 \times 0{\cdot}2505 = £501 \text{ per year}$$

If this was a five-year annuity, deferred for (say) 3 years, then its annual value would be:

$$£2000 A^{-1}_{\overline{5|}0{\cdot}08} (1{\cdot}08)^3 = £2000 \times 0{\cdot}2505 \times 1{\cdot}2597 = £631{\cdot}11$$

In other words, a £631·11 five-year annuity, deferred for three years, would have a present value of £2,000 if the annual rate of discount was 8%. Table E provides these factors for immediate annuities with a present value of £1, for various values of i and N.

7 Sinking fund factors

The annual value of an annuity which lasts for N years, where the prevailing rate of interest is i, and which has a terminal value of £1, is given by:

$$\frac{i}{(1+i)^N - 1}, \text{ denoted as } S^{-1}_{\overline{N|}i}$$

Thus the annual value of a four-year annuity which has a terminal value of £100, where the interest rate is 16%, is:

$$£100 \frac{0{\cdot}16}{(1{\cdot}16)^4 - 1} = £100 \times 0{\cdot}1974 = £19{\cdot}74 \text{ per year}$$

In other words, a four-year £19·74 annuity would have a terminal value of £100 when the annual interest rate is 16%. Hence, the annual amount of £19·74 would be known as the Sinking Fund. Table F provides sinking fund factors for annuities with terminal values of £1, for various values of i and N.

8 Perpetuities

An annuity that continues indefinitely is termed a perpetuity. As it never terminates it cannot have a terminal value. The present value of an *immediate* annuity of £1, which continues indefinitely, where the annual rate of discount is i, is given by:

$$\frac{1}{i}$$

Thus a perpetuity of £150 per year, where the rate of discount is 15%, is:

$$£150 \times \frac{1}{0{\cdot}15} = \frac{£150}{0{\cdot}15} = £1000$$

SUMMARY

This chapter has looked at the basic application of the two discounted cash flow (DCF) methods of investment appraisal. The main points covered were as follows:

- The fact that money has a time value (i.e. an opportunity cost in terms of a rate of interest) means that cash flows that arise at different points in time cannot be compared directly but must first be converted to a common point of time (usually, t_0, the present time).
- The NPV decision rule states:
  - ☐ Accept a project if its NPV $\geqslant 0$ (i.e. + or zero).
  - ☐ Reject a project if its NPV < 0 (i.e. −).
- Although a number of different (but correct) interpretations can be made about the meaning of NPV, the most important is that the magnitude of a project's NPV represents the increase in shareholder wealth that can be expected to come about through its acceptance.
- It was seen that the NPV decision rule (see above) would lead the company to locate at the optimal point on the physical investment line of the Hirshliefer analysis. It was from this analysis that the connection between NPV and shareholder wealth could be seen.
- The internal rate of return (IRR) of a project is that discount rate which, when applied to a project's cash flow, produces a zero NPV. It is therefore a simple arithmetic result.
- The IRR decision rule is:
  - ☐ Accept a project if its IRR $\geqslant$ decision criterion or 'hurdle rate'.
  - ☐ Reject if its IRR < decision criterion.

- Like NPV, use of the IRR decision rule will also lead to the company optimally locating on its physical investment line.
- Discounted payback, in which the speed of payback is computed in *present value* cash flow terms was seen to be simply a version of NPV with an artificially truncated project life.

NOTES

1 There is a widely advocated DCF method of investment appraisal (but not widely used), variously called the 'excess present value index', the 'profitability index', the 'discounted profitability index', or even the 'benefit–cost ratio'. This method arises directly out of the NPV method (and so gives equivalent decision advice) and can be defined as:

$$\frac{\text{Present value of project cash inflows}}{\text{Present value of project cash outflows}}$$

If the index is less than 1, the project should be rejected (equivalent to a negative NPV). If the index is greater than or equal to one, the project should be accepted. Thus in terms of Project B:

$$\text{Index} = \frac{827{\cdot}06}{1000{\cdot}00} = 0{\cdot}8271$$

and as the index (is less than) <1, Project B should be rejected.

2 To a limited extent a similar analysis can be performed on the vertical axis in terms of net *terminal* values (i.e. at t_1) rather than net present values. For instance, in the situation illustrated in Figure 4.1, OF represents the terminal value of the sum of dividend OD in t_0 and OC in t_1; OC represents the terminal value of the cash inflows generated from the company's investments; and CF represents the net terminal value of the investments undertaken.

3 Notice that if the company were to overinvest up to point W, the *total* net present value of its investment decision would be negative. In other words, the shareholders would have been better off if management had undertaken no investment at all, rather than overinvesting to such an extent. This analysis does serve to support management's general inclination to invest conservatively (i.e., a tendency to underinvest or invest less than the optimal amount). Under-optimal investment must always lead to an increase in shareholders' wealth, relative to their wealth if management undertook zero investment, as long as negative NPV projects are not undertaken. However, with overinvestment a situation like point W *is* possible where shareholders are actually *worse* off as a result of the company's investment decisions. In the real world, a management with poor appraisal ability may well do right to err on the side of conservatism rather than taking a very sanguine or cavalier attitude to investment decisions.

4 This method of investment appraisal has unfortunately suffered a confusing array of alternative names in the past, such as the 'marginal efficiency of capital', 'true yield' and even (to really add to the confusion) 'discounted cash flow'. Some of these alternatives still persist in the literature, but it is now most widely known as the 'internal rate of return'.

5 Strictly speaking this is not correct. The IRR of a project is its *average* rate of return, whilst under our assumptions of infinite project divisibility and diminishing returns, the IRR of each incremental piece of a project will be slightly lower than that of the previous increment. Hence the physical investment line is composed of the IRRs of each incremental investment in the projects that are available, rather than of the IRRs of each complete project that is available.

FURTHER READING

At this stage we are only mid-way through our evaluation of the two discounted cash flow investment appraisal techniques. Therefore many relevant articles will not yet be appropriate. However, a very interesting starting point are two articles which question the whole basis of the investment decision making developed here: P.F. King, 'Is the Emphasis of Capital Budgeting Theory Misplaced', *Journal of Business Finance and Accounting*, Spring 1975, and D. Cooper, 'Rationality and Investment Appraisal', *Accounting and Business Research*, Summer 1975. In addition, a further article which is of interest at this stage is: E.M. Lerner and A. Rappaport, 'Limit DCF in Capital Budgeting', *Harvard Business Review*, September–October 1968.

QUICKIE QUESTIONS (including questions on the appendix)

1 Using a 14% discount rate, what is the NPV of the following project?

Year	*Cash flow*
0	−1,000
1	+ 500
2	+ 600
3	+ 400

2 If a project costing £1,000 has an NPV of +£120 at a 10% discount rate, how would you interpret the NPV figure and what should be the investment advice?

3 Estimate what is the IRR of the following project:

Year	*Cash flow*
0	−500
1	+200
2	+300
3	+200

4 Using the project in question 3, what is its discounted payback, given a 10% discount rate.

5 In the real world where the outcomes of investment projects are uncertain, what should the NPV discount rate represent?

6 What is the connection between the NPV discount rate and the IRR hurdle rate?

7 Given a 10% discount rate, what is the present value of the following annuity:

Year	*Cash flow*
0	
1	+350
2	+350
3	+350
4	+350

8 What are the three main types of annuity?

9 A project costs £1,000 and produces a cash inflow of £100 per year for ever. What is its IRR?

10 Using annuity factors, what is the NPV of this project at a 16% discount rate?

Year	*Cash flow*
0	−1,000
1	+ 200
2	+ 200
3	+ 500
4	+ 500
5	+ 500

PROBLEMS

1 Trionym PLC is a manufacturer of confectionery, based in the West Midlands. It has recently merged with a sugar refiner, West Indian Sugar Supplies PLC (WISS). For some weeks, the accountants in the two companies have been discussing investment appraisal techniques. Trionym traditionally uses payback and the return on average capital employed while WISS has used NPV for a number of years.

The discussion on appraisal techniques has now reached a crisis as a decision is required on a proposal to invest £1·8m on a new chocolate-coating machine in order to move into the chocolate biscuit market. The financial details are as follows:

Outlay:	£1.8 million at t_0
Life:	10 years
Net cash flow:	Years 1–6 +£500,000/year
	Years 7–10 +£300,000/year
Scrap value:	Zero, net of dismantling costs

The company uses straight-line depreciation and has a target rate of return, for both ROCE and NPV of 18%, and a payback criterion of three years.

Required:

(a) Calculate the project's NPV.

(b) Calculate the ROCE in line with company practice.

(c) Calculate the project's payback.
(d) On the basis of your calculations, formulate your investment decision advice. Write a report to the Chairman which justifies your decision and mention any reservations which you might have.
(e) In order to try and resolve the conflict between the two managements you suggest that the company uses discounted payback as a compromise. Estimate the project's discounted payback and write a memo to the Chairman outlining its advantages and disadvantages.
(f) Comment critically on the company's existing decision criteria.

2 Congo Ltd is considering the selection of one of a pair of mutually exclusive investment projects. Both would involve purchase of machinery with a life of five years.

Project 1 would generate annual cash flows (receipts less payments) of £200,000; the machinery would cost £556,000 and have a scrap value of £56,000.

Project 2 would generate annual cash flows of £500,000; the machinery would cost £1,616,000 and have a scrap value of £301,000.

Congo uses the straight line method for providing depreciation. Its cost of capital is 15 per cent per annum. Assume that annual cash flows arise on the anniversaries of the initial outlay, that there will be no price changes over the project lives and that acceptance of one of the projects will not alter the required amount of working capital.

Required:

(a) Calculate for each project:
  (i) the accounting rate of return (ratio, over project life, of average accounting profit to average book value of investment) to nearest one per cent;
  (ii) the net present value;
  (iii) the internal rate of return (DCF yield) to nearest one per cent;
  (iv) the payback period to one decimal place.
(b) State which project you would select for acceptance, if either, giving reasons for your choice of criterion to guide the decision.

Ignore taxation.

3 Stadler is an ambitious young executive who has recently been appointed to the position of financial director of Paradis plc, a small listed company. Stadler regards this appointment as a temporary one, enabling him to gain experience before moving to a larger organization. His intention is to leave Paradis plc in three years, with its share price standing high. As a consequence, he is particularly concerned that the reported profits of Paradis plc should be as high as possible in his third and final year with the company.

Paradis plc has recently raised £350,000 from shareholders, and the directors are considering three ways of using these funds. Three projects (A, B and C) are being considered, each involving the immediate purchase of equipment costing £350,000. One project only can be undertaken and the equipment for each project will have a useful life equal to that of the project, with no scrap value. Stadler favours Project C because it is expected to show the highest accounting profit in the third year. However, he does not wish to reveal his real reasons for favouring Project C and so, in his report to the chairman, he recommends Project C because it shows the highest internal rate of return. The following summary is taken from his report:

	Net cash flows (£000)									*Internal rate*
	Years									*of return*
Project	0	1	2	3	4	5	6	7	8	%
A	−350	100	110	104	112	138	160	180	–	27·5
B	−350	40	100	210	260	160	–	–	–	26·4
C	−350	200	150	240	40	–	–	–	–	33·0

The chairman of the company is accustomed to projects being appraised in terms of payback and accounting rate of return, and he is consequently suspicious of the use of internal rate of return as a method of project selection. Accordingly, the chairman has asked for an independent report on the choice of project. The company's cost of capital is 20% and a policy of straight-line depreciation is used to write off the cost of equipment in the financial statements.

Required:

(a) Calculate the payback period for each project.
(b) Calculate the accounting rate of return for each project.
(c) Prepare a report for the chairman with supporting calculations indicating which project should be preferred by the ordinary shareholders of Paradis plc.
(d) Discuss the assumptions about the reactions of the stock market that are implicit in Stadler's choice of project C.

Ignore taxation.

5

Net present value and internal rate of return

Chapter Contents

NPV AND PROJECT INTERDEPENDENCE

In Chapter 2, when examining the payback and ROCE/ARR techniques, *two* investment decisions were dealt with:

1 decisions involving single, independent projects where a straightforward 'accept' or 'reject' decision was required;
2 decisions involving mutually exclusive projects, where a decision on the one best project from a series of alternative projects was required.

However, in Chapter 4, when examining the two discounted cash flow techniques of NPV and IRR, our discussion only covered the decision rule for single independent project decisions. In this chapter, we start by looking at the NPV and IRR decision rules when faced with mutually exclusive projects and other forms of project decision interdependence.

NPV and mutually exclusive projects

We have already seen from the single-period investment–consumption model that, in terms of net present value, the higher the aggregate NPV of a firm's investments, the higher will be the level of wealth achieved by its shareholders. Therefore, as far as deciding between mutually exclusive investment alternatives is concerned, the decision rule would appear to be quite straightforward in terms of using the NPV: accept whichever alternative project produces the greatest positive NPV because this will produce the greatest addition to the shareholders' wealth[1].

As an example, suppose a company has to make an investment decision concerning two mutually exclusive projects, A and B, whose cash flows and NPV calculations are set out below:

Project A

Year	*Cash flow*	×	*10% discount factor*		*Present value = cash flow*
0	−1500	×	1		= −1500
1	+ 500	×	0·9091		= + 454·55
2	+ 800	×	0·8264		= + 661·12
3	+1000	×	0·7513		+ 751·30
				NPV	+ 366·97

Project B

Year	*Cash flow*	×	*10% discount factor*		*Present value = cash flow*
0	*−1900*	×	*1*		= *−1900*
1	*+ 500*	×	*0·9091*		= + 454·55
2	+ 800	×	0·8264		= + 661·12
3	+1000	×	0·7513		= + 751·30
4	+ 700	×	0·6830		+ 478·10
				NPV	+ 445·07

Assuming that the appropriate discount rate is 10%, when the project cash flows are converted to present values, Project B is preferred to A because it has the larger positive NPV. It is important to realize that the appraisal method in such circumstances is *entirely unaffected* by the fact that these two projects have differing capital outlays and life-spans. The whole decision is based purely on the absolute size of the positive NPV.

The mutually exclusive investment decision can be made in this way because of two important assumptions underlying the analysis. When developing the single period investment–consumption model, a number of simplifying assumptions about the real world were specified. However, when we then moved on to examine the DCF investment appraisal techniques, many of these assumptions (such as a single time period and a world of certainty) were either implicitly or explicitly dropped. Nevertheless, there are two important assumptions that underlie the use of DCF techniques. They are:

1 A perfect capital market exists. Reference has already been made to this concept when the existence of a capital market was introduced in the Hirshleifer analysis in Chapter 3. A perfect capital market describes a market where investors can lend and borrow money and which has a number of particular characteristics. We will examine the concept in greater detail at a later stage but, for the present, all that is required is to specify that characteristic which is of particular importance as far as the DCF techniques are concerned. It is that

investors/companies will always be able to raise finance to undertake any project that they identify as having a non-negative NPV (or whose IRR meets the decision criterion hurdle rate). Therefore, decision makers will never find themselves in a position where they are unable to take on a positive NPV project because of lack of finance. In addition, we should add to this condition the assumption that the *cost* of the finance raised will always be at the going rate of return for investments of that particular risk level.

2 The discount rate used in an NPV analysis, or the hurdle rate used in an IRR analysis, correctly reflects the degree of risk involved in the project. The phrase 'reflects the degree of risk involved' refers to the fact that the discount rate should represent the return available elsewhere in the (perfect) capital market on a similar risk investment. Therefore notice how this assumption is, itself, dependent upon the first assumption.

As a result of these two assumptions the choice between Projects A and B can be made on the basis used. The fact that B is a more costly project than A is irrelevant, given the first assumption. Project B is preferred to A simply because it is capable of generating a cash flow that will pay back its outlay and its financing costs and leave an *economic profit,* in present value terms (a rise in shareholder wealth), of £445·07. Project A will also repay its outlay and its financing costs, but will only cause shareholder wealth to rise by £366·97.

Also, the fact that B is more expensive than A, and it has a longer life than A, *might* suggest that it is more risky. (Neither fact will *necessarily* make B more risky than A.) However, these differences can also be ignored in the decision analysis because of our second assumption. In other words the whole problem of riskiness is taken account of in the discount rate. The fact that both projects are being discounted at 10% implies that a judgement has been made that they are equally risky.

In this respect, if it was felt that two mutually exclusive projects were of *different* risk levels, then different discount rates should be used to evaluate each one. However, the decision – with its focus on maximizing the increase in shareholder wealth – would remain unchanged. Example 5.1 illustrates such a situation.

The point to notice about Example 5.1 is that the decision has been taken on the basis of what would be the resulting increase in shareholder wealth. The fact that the Amusement Park Development produces a return in excess of 18% (in fact its IRR is approximately 18·6%), whilst the Private Housing Development only produces a return in excess of 10% (its IRR is approximately 12·5%), is irrelevant. Rates of return cannot be compared in isolation, but *must* be looked at relative to the risk involved. In this example, given the risk involved, the Private Housing Development is the better project from the viewpoint of shareholder wealth.

Finally, the operation of this modified NPV rule for mutually exclusive projects requires an additional assumption in the face of unequal project lives (but not unequal investment outlays). This is that the mutually exclusive projects are 'isolated' investments in the sense that they do not

Example 5.1

Epitasis PLC is a small company engaged in house-building. The company is presently considering whether to purchase a piece of land that has come up for sale at a cost of £10 million. Two suggestions have been made for the use of the land. One is to construct a number of private houses for sale and the other is to construct and operate an amusement park.

The company's management accountants have made the following estimates of both projects' net cash flows (including the cost of the land):

Year	*Private House Development* £m	*Amusement Park* £m
0	−10	−10
1	− 5	− 8
2	+ 7	+ 4
3	+ 9	+ 6
4	+ 4	+ 8
5		+ 7
6		+ 9

The company uses NPV to evaluate projects and normally takes 10% as a discount rate, as this reflects the return available elsewhere on house-building investments. In the present situation this appears to be a suitable rate for the Private Housing Development, but not for the Amusement Park. After much research, the company has decided that the minimum required rate of return that they should expect on this more risky projects' is 18%.

On this basis, the project's NPVs were calculated:

Private Housing Development: + £0·733m.
Amusement Park Development: + £ 0·264m.

Therefore the company's decision was to purchase the land and undertake a private housing development.

form part of a replacement chain. In other words, it is assumed that the nature of the mutually exclusive projects is such that, whichever project is chosen, it will not be replaced when it reaches the end of its life. If this assumption does *not* hold, then we are involved with a different type of project interdependence which requires a more complex decision rule. This issue is treated separately when the Replacement Decision is examined.

Interlinked projects

Another type of project interdependence can arise when a project's cash flows are affected by investment decisions taken elsewhere. It would be highly unusual to find *any* project which had truly independent cash flows, as almost certainly the magnitude and timing of a project's cash flows will be affected to some extent by other investment decisions. However, this problem really arises out of uncertainty about the future, and will be examined later in that context.

The case of interdependence to be examined here is the simpler case in which the cash flows of an investment opportunity are directly affected by the company's decision regarding another investment project. For example, when two *non*-mutually exclusive projects, C and D, are appraised it is found that Project C has the following cash flows, which are independent of any other investment decisions made by the company:

Project C

Year	*Cash flow*	×	*10% discount factor*		=	*Present value cash flow*
0	−1000	×	1		=	−1000
1	+ 400	×	0·9091		=	+ 363·64
2	+ 500	×	0·8264		=	+ 413·20
3	+ 200	×	0·7513		=	+ 150·26
				NPV		− £72·90

When discounted by 10% (assumed to be the appropriate rate), Project C has a negative NPV of £72·90. Viewed in isolation, and following the NPV rule for independent projects, it would be rejected as an unsuitable investment.

Table 5.1

Project D

Year	*Cash flow 1*	×	*10% discount factor*		=	*Present value cash flow*
0	−2000	×	1		=	−2000
1	+ 500	×	0·9091		=	+ 454·55
2	+ 800	×	0·8264		=	+ 661·12
3	+1000	×	0·7513		=	+ 751·30
4	+1000	×	0·6830		=	+ 683·00
				NPV		+ 549·97

Year	*Cash flow 2*	×	*10% discount factor*		=	*Present value cash flow*
0	−2000	×	1		=	−2000
1	+ 500	×	0·9091		=	+ 454·55
2	+ 800	×	0·8264		=	+ 661·12
3	+1200	×	0·7513		=	+ 901·56
4	+ 600	×	0·6830		=	+ 409·80
				NPV		+ 427·03

However, suppose Project D, which is also under consideration, has *two* alternative sets of cash flows and NPVs, depending upon whether Project C is accepted by the company (cash flow 1) or rejected (cash flow 2).

(Table 5.1 provides the details.) The correct way to analyse this situation, within the assumptions made, is to treat the problem as *three* mutually exclusive investments: Project C, Project D, and Project C + D. Whichever alternative produces the largest positive NPV should be accepted. In this example:

Project C = − £72·90
Project D = + £427·03
Project C + D = − £72·90 + £549·97 = + £477·07

Thus the correct investment decision, in terms of maximizing shareholder wealth, is to accept Projects C and D jointly, because it is this alternative which produces the largest net present value.

IRR RULE AND INTERDEPENDENT PROJECTS

Introduction

We have seen that in the face of these two types of non-independent cash flow, the NPV investment decision rule can be fairly easily modified so as to produce the correct decision advice. In terms of the single-period investment–consumption model, these modified decision rules would ensure a company's attainment of the optimal point on the physical investment line and the consequent maximization of sharenolder wealth. But what modifications would have to be made to the IRR decision rule?

In a situation of mutually exclusive investment projects, a modification, apparently similar to that made to the NPV rule, is traditionally advocated: accept whichever project has the greatest IRR, as long as it exceeds the decision criterion/hurdle rate. Such an approach is incorrect, but it has been widely advocated because of a misunderstanding concerning the process involved in using both NPV and IRR as criteria for investment decisions.

We have already seen that when an individual project is evaluated by NPV, an 'automatic' comparison is made between the cash flows produced by the project and the cash flows that *would* have been produced (but were forgone, and so represent an opportunity cost under the assumption of a perfect capital market) if the project's outlay had been invested on the capital market for the period of the project's life-span. Therefore, the decision whether to accept or reject the project is not an absolute decision, but a *relative* one – relative to what the forgone alternative would yield. As a result, when faced with mutually exclusive investments, the choice between projects is carried out on the basis of this automatic comparison with the capital market. Whichever project performs best, relative to the capital market, is chosen – given that the chosen alternative out-performs the capital market alternative, i.e., has a positive NPV.

Incremental cash flows

We can approach this idea another way. Suppose we have a pair of mutually exclusive projects E and F which have the following cash flows, lives and present values when discounted at the appropriate market rate of return of 10%:

Project E

Year	*Cash flow*	×	*10% discount factor*		*Present value* = *cash flow*
0	−1500	×	1		= −1500
1	+ 550	×	0·9091		= + 500·00
2	+1400	×	0·8264		= +1156·96
				NPV	+ 156·96

Project F

Year	*Cash flow*	×	*10% discount factor*		*Present value* = *cash flow*
0	−1900	×	1		= −1900
1	+ 400	×	0·9091		= + 363·64
2	+ 800	×	0·8264		= + 661·12
3	+ 800	×	0·7513		= + 601·04
4	+ 700	×	0·6830		= + 478·10
				NPV	+ 203·90

Project F would be preferred to E as it has the larger, positive NPV.

Now, let us look at the present value of the extra, or *incremental*, cash flows that the firm would obtain from investing in project E, rather than F and vice versa. Table 5.2 lists these incremental cash flows and computes their NPVs.

Table 5.2

Year	*Project E c/f*	− *Project F c/f*	*Incremental* = *E − F c/f*	*10% PV* × *Factor*		*Present* = *value cash flow*
0	(−1500)	− (−1900)	= +400	× 1		= +400
1	(+ 550)	− (+ 400)	= +150	× 0·9091		= +136·36
2	(+1400)	− (+ 800)	= +600	× 0·8264		= +495·84
3		− (+ 800)	= −800	× 0·7513		= −601·04
4		− (+ 700)	= −700	× 0·6830		= −478·10
					NPV	− 46·94

Year	*Incremental F − E c/f*	*10% PV* × *Factor*		*Present* = *value cash flow*
0	−400	× 1		= −400
1	−150	× 0·9091		= −136·36
2	−600	× 0·8264		= −495·84
3	+800	× 0·7513		= +601·04
4	+700	× 0·6830		= +478·10
			NPV	+ 46·94

In our initial analysis of this decision problem, Project F was preferred to E. The incremental analysis of Table 5.2 helps to explain further the reason for the decision: if F is chosen in preference to E, this will produce an NPV which will be £46·94 greater than if E was preferred to F.

(Notice the NPV of Project F, less that of Project E, is: £203·90 − £156·96 = £46·94)

Therefore, F is chosen.

Use of the IRR

In the case of mutually exclusive investments, use of the IRR decision rule causes problems. Unlike the NPV calculation which automatically compares the project with the alternative capital market investment forgone, the IRR method makes the comparison on a somewhat different basis by using the decision rule: does the project yield a greater or lesser return than the capital market? But, in doing so, it does not give a consistently reliable indication of *how much* better or worse the project is, relative to the capital market investment alternative.

Thus the IRR decision rule is safe to apply to single, independent decision situations (when all that is required is an answer to the question: does the project produce a return better or worse than that of the capital market?), but it cannot reliably be used to judge between *alternative* projects. This is a rather subtle, but important point, and it requires some further explanation.

Using linear interpolation, the IRRs of the two projects, E and F can be estimated. For E the IRR is estimated at 17%, and for F at 15%. As E has the larger of the two IRRs and this is greater than the decision criterion hurdle rate (10%), the IRR decision rule would suggest that Project E is accepted and F rejected. However, to formulate decision advice on this basis is to forget that the IRR method only compares a project with the capital market alternative in the operation of the accept/reject decision rule. (Indeed the fact that this standard IRR decision rule gives unreliable decision advice is made obvious in this example, because the decision reached is the *opposite* of that reached by NPV.)

The IRR method can correctly advise in this case that both projects are worthwhile: Project E is worthwhile as it produces a return that is greater than that of the capital market, likewise with Project F. But it does not necessarily follow that E is *better* than F because it has an IRR of 17% as opposed to 15%. Indeed we know from operating the NPV decision rule that the advice is incorrect: F is a better investment than E; and selecting E will result in a £46·94 loss of NPV.

IRR and incremental cash flows

The correct approach to evaluating mutually exclusive investments using the IRR is to examine the incremental cash flows that arise between the alternatives. In order to clarify the problem and derive the correct IRR decision rule in such circumstances, we shall make use of a device which

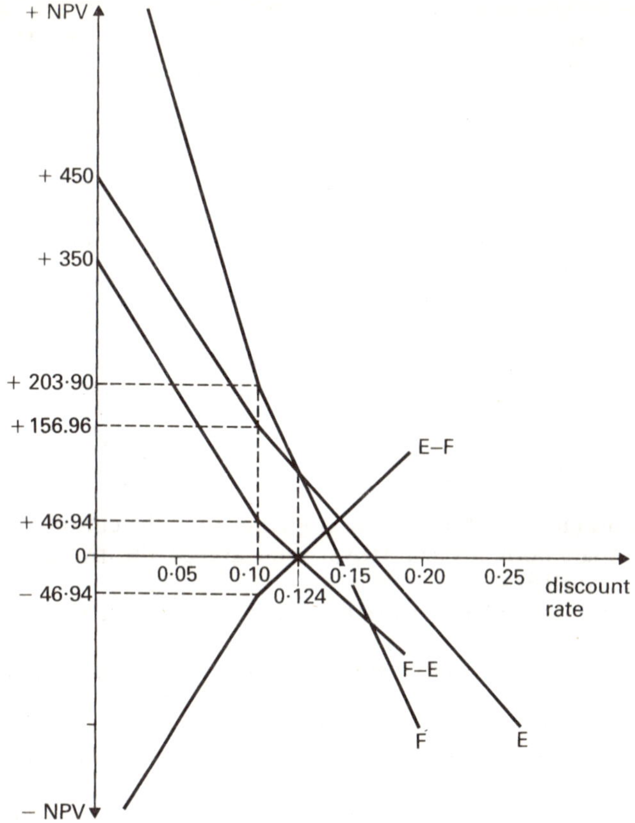

Figure 5.1

was used earlier to examine the IRR concept: the net present value profile.

Figure 5.1 graphs the NPV profiles of Projects E and F and both the differential cash flows (E − F, F − E). It is this figure that demonstrates one of the real problems of using the IRR as a decision criterion when choice amongst alternatives is involved.

Project E always has a higher IRR than F, whatever the rate of discount, and therefore, basing the choice between mutually exclusive investments on size of IRR, the decision is independent of the capital market rate of interest. In contrast, when the decision is based on the NPV rule, the choice of project changes as the discount rate/market rate of interest changes. It can be seen from Figure 5.1 that at rates of discount below 12·4%, Project F is preferred because it has the higher NPV; but at discount rates above 12·4%, Project E is preferred.

The intersection point of the two cash flow profiles is at a discount rate of 12·4% and so, at this rate, the decision would be indifferent between the two projects because they both produce the same NPV. Also notice that, as we would expect at that discount rate, the NPV of both differential cash flows is zero: both projects are equally acceptable, and the differential cash flows reflect this indifference.

On the basis of Figure 5.1, a number of firm conclusions can be made about the use of both methods in appraising mutually exclusive projects. The NPV can be used to give the correct decision advice with just a small (and commonsense) modification to the basic rule: accept whichever alternative has the highest positive NPV when discounted at the perfect capital market rate of interest. The use of the IRR involves a more complex decision rule. This complexity arises both from the fact that the IRRs of the differential cash flows have to be computed and (as can be seen from Figure 5.1) from the fact that the IRRs of both incremental cash flows are identical. The complete modified decision rule is as follows.

Calculate the IRRs of the two projects and the IRR of *either* of the differential cash flows, then:

1 If the differential cash flow IRR is *greater than* the cut-off rate, and
   (a) less than both project IRRs, then accept the project with the *smallest* IRR.
   (b) greater than both project IRRs, then accept the project with *highest* IRR.
2 If the differential cash flow IRR is *less than* the cut-off rate, and
   (a) the IRRs of one or both projects are higher than the cut-off rate, then accept the project with the *highest* IRR.
   (b) if neither project's IRR is greater than the cut-off rate, *reject* both.

In the example used therefore, using the NPV decision rule, Project F should be accepted because it has the highest positive NPV when discounted at 10% – the perfect capital market interest rate. The modified IRR decision rule also leads to the acceptance of F because the IRR of the differential cash flow (12·4%) is greater than the cut-off rate (10%) and less than the IRR of both projects (15% and 17%). Therefore, the project with the smallest IRR, F, is chosen.

A less complex, but somewhat incomplete decision rule can also be used in most cases:

1 If the IRR of the differential cash flow is less than the cut-off rate, accept the project with the largest IRR.
2 If the IRR of the differential cash flow is greater than the cut-off rate, accept the project with the smallest IRR.

In the example used above, as the IRR of the differential cash flow, at 12·4%, is greater than the 10% cut-off rate, then project F should be accepted as it has the smallest IRR – 15% as against 17% for Project E.

The conclusion that can be drawn from this example is that the IRR decision rule is excessively complex and unwieldly when compared against the NPV decision rule. What is more, the example used only two mutually exclusive projects. If faced with a choice between (say) a dozen alternatives, the NPV rule simply requires the calculation of each project's NPV and the project with the largest positive NPV is selected. With the IRR rule, the IRRs of *pairs* of the projects and their differential cash flow have to be calculated, making a choice between each pair of projects in turn, until an outright 'winner' is found – an extremely tedious operation.

A further example

Example 5.2 may help to clarify this approach to resolving the conflict that can occur between the advice given by the NPV decision rule and the advice given by the *standard* IRR decision rule for mutually exclusive decision situations.

Given Example 5.2, it should be made clear that it is very unlikely that any company actually uses this modified IRR decision rule in practice. To use it in this way implies a belief in the correctness of the NPV decision rule – because the modified IRR rule is designed always to give the same advice as NPV. But in that case it is both simpler and easier to use the NPV rule itself. Therefore Example 5.2 illustrates how it would be possible to use the IRR decision rule in mutually exclusive project situations so as to provide correct (i.e. shareholder wealth maximizing) decision advice.

The 'opportunity cost of cash' assumption

The fact that, in a decision choice involving mutually exclusive projects, selecting the project with the highest positive NPV will give a correct decision but selecting the project with the highest IRR will, *only by chance,* give the correct decision, has been explained on the basis that the IRR ranks projects in an order of preference which is independent of the capital market rate of return. But we have not really answered the question why, in the example used, does the NPV rule accept Project F and reject E? After all, Project E produces a higher return (17%) than F (15%). The reason lies in what is (somewhat misleadingly) called the *reinvestment assumption* of each decision rule. Perhaps a more apt description would be the *opportunity cost of capital* assumption.

The NPV decision rule assumes that project generated cash flows are reinvested to earn a rate of return equal to the discount rate used in the NPV analysis. (More strictly, remember, it is not so much a reinvestment rate of return, but an opportunity cost or benefit.) In contrast the IRR method assumes project generated cash flows are reinvested to earn a rate of return equal to the IRR of the project which generated those cash flows. Therefore using project E as an example:

Project E:	*Year*	*Cash flow* £	
	0	−1,500	NPV at a 10% discount
	1	+ 550	rate = + £156.96
	2	+1,400	
			IRR is approximately 17%

Example 5.2

Parabiotic PLC is involved in making a decision between a pair of mutually exclusive projects: X and Y. The cash flows of the two projects are as follows:

Year	*Project X* £000s	*Project Y* £000s
0	−1,000	−450
1	+ 400	+300
2	+ 600	+150
3	+ 187	+106

Given the risk involved, it is judged that 6% would be an appropriate NPV discount rate and IRR hurdle rate.

NPV calculation

Year	*Cash flow X*		*Discount factor*	
0	−1,000	×	1	= −1,000
1	+ 400	×	0·9434	= + 377·36
2	+ 600	×	0·8900	= + 534·00
3	+ 187	×	0·8396	= + 157·00
				+ 68·36 NPV

Year	*Cash flow Y*		*Discount factor*	
0	−450	×	1	= −450
1	+300	×	0·9434	= +283·02
2	+150	×	0·8900	= +133·50
3	+106	×	0·8396	= + 89·00
				+ 55·52 NPV

Using the NPV decision rule for mutually exclusive projects, Project X is preferred to Project Y as it has the largest positive NPV and so will give the greatest increase in shareholder wealth.

IRR calculation

Project X. At 6% it has an NPV of +68·36 NPV

At 20%:	−1,000 × 1	= −1,000
	+ 400 × 0·8333	= + 333·32
	+ 600 × 0·6944	= + 416·64
	+ 187 × 0·5787	= + 108·22
		− 141·82 NPV

Project Y. At 6% it has an NPV of +55·52 NPV

$$
\begin{aligned}
\text{At 20\%:}\quad & -450 \times 1 &&= -450 \\
& +300 \times 0{\cdot}8333 &&= +249{\cdot}99 \\
& +150 \times 0{\cdot}6944 &&= +104{\cdot}16 \\
& +106 \times 0{\cdot}5787 &&= +\ 61{\cdot}34 \\
& &&\overline{-\ 34{\cdot}51}\ \text{NPV}
\end{aligned}
$$

Linear interpolation can now be used to estimate the IRR of both projects:

$$\text{Project X: } 6\% + \left[\frac{68{\cdot}36}{68{\cdot}36 - (-141{\cdot}82)} \times (20\% - 6\%)\right] = 10{\cdot}5\% \text{ IRR}$$

$$\text{Project Y: } 6\% + \left[\frac{55{\cdot}52}{55{\cdot}52 - (-34{\cdot}51)} \times (20\% - 6\%)\right] = 14{\cdot}6\% \text{ IRR}$$

Using the *standard* IRR decision rule for mutually exclusive projects, Project Y is the better project as it has the higher IRR and should be accepted because its IRR exceeds the hurdle rate of return of 6%.

Therefore, in this case, we are getting a *conflict* between the advice given by NPV and the advice given by the IRR decision rule. However, if the *modified* IRR decision rule is used, we require to calculate the IRR of the differential cash flow: X minus Y.

Year	*Cash flow X*	–	*Cash flow Y*	=	*Differential cash flow*
0	−1,000	–	(−450)	=	−550
1	+ 400	–	(+300)	=	+100
2	+ 600	–	(+150)	=	+450
3	+ 187	–	(+106)	=	+ 81

$$
\begin{aligned}
\text{At a 4\% discount rate:}\quad & -550 \times 1 &&= -550 \\
& +100 \times 0{\cdot}9615 &&= +\ 96{\cdot}15 \\
& +450 \times 0{\cdot}9246 &&= +416{\cdot}07 \\
& +\ 81 \times 0{\cdot}8890 &&= +\ 72{\cdot}01 \\
& &&\overline{+\ 34{\cdot}23}\ \text{NPV}
\end{aligned}
$$

$$
\begin{aligned}
\text{At a 20\% discount rate:}\quad & -550 \times 1 &&= -550 \\
& +100 \times 0{\cdot}8333 &&= +\ 83{\cdot}33 \\
& +450 \times 0{\cdot}6944 &&= +312{\cdot}48 \\
& +\ 81 \times 0{\cdot}5787 &&= +\ 46{\cdot}87 \\
& &&\overline{-107{\cdot}32}\ \text{NPV}
\end{aligned}
$$

Again, using linear interpolation:

$$\text{Differential cash flow IRR}: 4\% + \left[\frac{34{\cdot}23}{34{\cdot}23 - (-107{\cdot}32)} \times (20\% - 4\%)\right] = 7{\cdot}9\%$$

Now, using the simplified, modified IRR decision rule for mutually exclusive projects: As the IRR of the differential cash flow is *greater than* the hurdle rate of 6%, Project X – the project with the smaller IRR – should be accepted. Notice that there is now no conflict with the advice given by NPV.

The NPV decision rule assumes that the £550 and £1400 cash flows generated at Years 1 and 2 respectively, can be reinvested to earn a 10% rate of return. The IRR method assumes they can be reinvested to earn a 17% rate of return.

This difference can be seen in the general forms of the two models. With the NPV model, the discount rate used is the market rate of interest:

$$\sum_{t=0}^{N} \frac{A_t}{(1+i)^t} = \text{NPV}$$

where A_t = project cash flow at time t.
i = market discount rate.
N = number of years of the project's life.

However, with the IRR model, the discount rate used is the project's own internal rate of return:

$$\sum_{t=0}^{N} \frac{A_t}{(1+r)^t} = 0 \qquad \text{where } r = \text{project's IRR.}$$

A simple example will help to illustrate the point. Suppose that the following project, G, is available, where the market rate of discount is 5%. The project has an NPV of +£12.39 and an IRR of 10%. What these results mean is shown in Example 5.3, where the re-investment assumptions can actually be seen to be in operation.

The IRR approach assumes that the project cash flows can yield a return equal to the IRR of the project that generated those cash flows. Now the important point is that investments yielding such returns may well be available to the company but, the flaw in the IRR's assumption is that these investments will be available *independently* of whether or not the company accepts the particular project under consideration. The NPV model accepts this argument, and takes as the opportunity cost of the project cash flows, the market rate of interest.

The market rate of interest is viewed as the opportunity cost because, even if a project's cash flow *is* used by a company to undertake an investment with a very high yield, if that cash flow were *not* available, the high-yielding investment could still be undertaken by using money borrowed from the capital market, *at the market rate of interest*. What the IRR model does is to credit some of the assumed profitability of those other investments to the project being appraised, by assuming that the opportunity cost of the project-generated cash flows is equal to the project's own IRR or yield.

Therefore, we can conclude that, given the presence of a perfect capital market, it is the NPV model and not the IRR model which makes the correct assumption about the opportunity cost of a project's cash flow. Hence it is the NPV decision rule that gives the correct decision advice. As a result, if we are to use the IRR, then we have to make use of the type of complex decision rule that was derived earlier. However there is no real *logic* to that type of rule, it simply ensures that the same decision is produced as that given by the (much simpler) NPV decision rule.

Finally, there is also a logical inconsistency in the IRR's reinvestment

Example 5.3

Project G:	*Year*	*Cash flow*	
	0	−173·55	At a 5% discount rate NPV = +12·39
	1	+100	
	2	+100	At a 5% hurdle rate IRR = 10%

The project's NPV is arrived at by calculating the sum of money that can be accumulated from the project by the end of its life (where intermediate cash flows are reinvested at 5%), and comparing this with the amount of money that could be accumulated by placing the project's outlay in a similar-risk capital market investment. £205 can be accumulated from the project and only £191·34 from the capital market investment. This difference of £13·66 in Year 2 terms has a present value of £12·39 – the project's NPV.

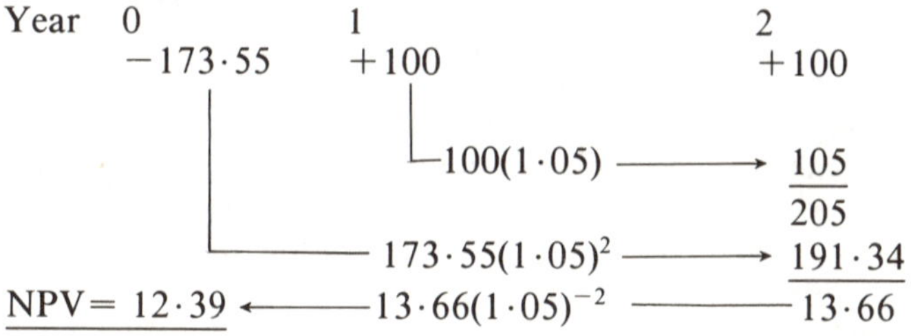

The project has an IRR of 10%. If it truly does produce a 10% return it must be capable of generating the same amount of cash by the end of its life that would be generated from investing the project's outlay to yield a 10% return. Investing £173·55 for two years at 10% generates £210. The only way that Project G can accumulate £210 by the end of its life is to assume that the intermediate cash flow (£100 at Year 1) can be reinvested to earn 10%.

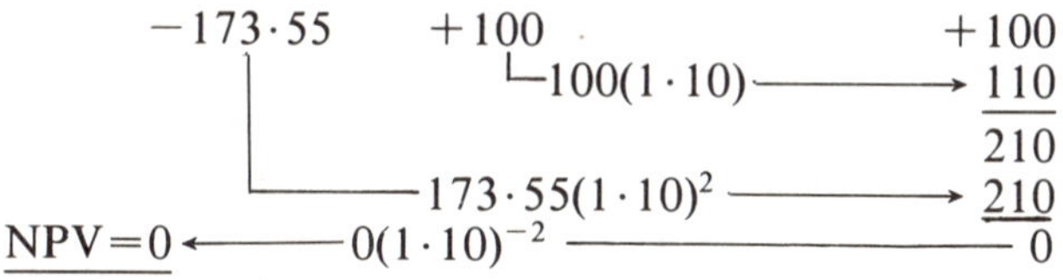

assumption. As an example of this take Projects H and I.

Project H	*Year*	*Cash flow*	*Project I*	*Year*	*Cash flow*
	0	−100		0	−150
	1	+ 30		1	+ 70
	2	+ 70		2	+ 70
	3	+ 19·80		3	+ 74·41

Project H has an IRR of 10%, while Project I has an IRR of 20%. Therefore the implicit assumption is that Project I's cash flows can be reinvested to earn 20%, but Project H's cash flows can only be reinvested to earn 10%. Therefore why, for example, can the £70 generated at Year 2 by Project I be reinvested at twice the rate as the same amount of cash, generated at precisely the same point in time, by Project H? There is a fault in the logic of the assumption. There is no logical reason why cash flows which arise at the same time from two different sources should be reinvested at different rates (i.e. have different *opportunity benefits*).

EXTENDING THE TIME HORIZON

Introduction

Having examined the case of mutually exclusive projects, let us now turn to another issue. This concerns the fact that the Hirshleifer's single period graphical analysis was undertaken under the assumption of a single period investment time horizon. Certainly since starting to examine the DCF methods of investment appraisal, examples have been used of projects which involve cash flows extending over more than one period. But what we must now ask is whether the assumption of a single period time horizon is simply an assumption of convenience which allows the model to be developed graphically.

In short, the answer to the question is that it is not. In a single-period world we have seen that both the NPV and IRR decision rules will give the same, correct decision advice (even if some fairly complex adjustments sometimes have to be made to the IRR rule). Both methods should enable a company to locate optimally on its physical investment line. However, problems can occur for the IRR decision rule once this two-dimensional world is left behind.

Average and marginal rates of return

As soon as the assumption of a single time period (t_0 to t_1) is explicitly relaxed, we get new support for the rationale of the NPV approach (to the detriment of IRR) and a new perspective from which to view the 'reinvestment' assumption. So far, in all the examples used, we have implicitly assumed that the capital market interest rate remains fixed over time. However, suppose a company is evaluating Project J, whose cash flows are given in Table 5.3. In this case, the annual market interest/discount rate is expected to be 10% over the coming year and 15% over the following year.

As far as the NPV decision rule is concerned, known fluctuations in the discount rate do not cause any problems. Project J has a positive NPV after its cash flows have been discounted by the appropriate market discount rate for each time period.

But what of the IRR decision rule? Project J should be accepted if its IRR is greater than the decision criterion/hurdle rate, but in this example, the IRR of J is *greater* than the market interest rate in one period, and *less* than the rate in the other period. In such circumstances, a

Table 5.3

Project J:	*Year*	*Cash flow*	*Discount factor*	
	0	−100	× 1	= −100
	1	+ 60	× $(1\cdot10)^{-1}$	= + 54·55
	2	+ 60	× $(1\cdot10)^{-1} \times (1\cdot15)^{-1}$	= + 47·43
			NPV	= + 1·98

The IRR of Project J is approximately 13%.

single figure IRR is just not valid for decision making purposes.

This is a very real problem with the IRR decision rule. Unless future market interest rates can be assumed to be, at least, approximately constant, the rule breaks down. What we are seeing in this example is that, although both DCF methods recognize that money has a time value and so cash flows that occur at different points of time cannot be directly compared, but first have to be converted to values at just one point of time via a weighting mechanism,[2] the IRR uses the *average* or long-run rate of return for weighting whilst the NPV uses the *marginal* or period-by-period rate of return.

Multiple IRRs

Another problem for the IRR decision rule, which arises out of the mathematics of its computation, comes to light when the investment time horizon is extended. The IRR of a project's cash flow is the root of a polynomial equation, the mathematics of which are explained in a note.[3] The problem is that any particular investment project may have more than one internal rate of return (i.e., there may be more than one rate of discount which will reduce the project's cash flow to a zero NPV), or it may not have any IRR at all. This important (and not uncommon) phenomenon can be examined in terms of the NPV profiles of projects on the basis that the IRR is given by the point at which the profile line cuts the graph's horizontal axis (along which the discount rate is measured).

To start with, we must define what have become known as 'conventional' and 'non-conventional' cash flows.[4] A conventional project cash flow is one where a cash outflow, or a series of cash outflows, is followed by a cash inflow or series of cash inflows. The essence of the definition is that in a conventional cash flow, there is only *one* change in sign (+, −) between the time periods. All three cash flows given below are therefore conventional:

	Year				
Project	0	1	2	3	4
K	−1000	+400	+ 500	+ 800	+ 50
L	−1000	−500	− 600	+1500	+2000
M	− 500	−600	+2000		

The one change of sign for Project K comes between year 0 and year 1, for Project L it comes between year 2 and year 3, and for Project M it comes between year 1 and year 2. In each project cash flow there is only one sign change. Such projects will only have one IRR each (there is an exception to this, to which we shall return), and so no problems arise for the IRR decision rule.

Non-conventional cash flows can therefore be defined as those which involve more than one change in sign, such as shown below:

	Year					
Project	0	1	2	3	4	
N	−100	+20	−50	+80	+170	3 changes of sign
P	−100	+60	+80	−20		2 changes of sign

Such projects are likely to have more than one IRR and, as a general 'rule of thumb', a project will have as many IRRs as its cash flow has changes in sign.

Non-conventional cash flows can make life very difficult for the IRR decision rule. For example, suppose that Project Q's NPV profile is illustrated in Figure 5.2. This project has three IRRs: 10%, 15% and 18%. In itself, this is not too disturbing if the cut-off rate is either less than 10% or greater than 18%, because the IRR rule still manages to give unambiguous (and operationally correct) decision advice. But if the cut-off rate is (say) 12%, the IRR decision can only give – at best – highly ambiguous advice (which may be incorrrect). In such circumstances, the NPV rule would have no difficulty in giving the correct advice: to reject the project because it has a negative NPV.

However, it can be shown that with most project cash flows that are likely to occur in practice, and where multiple IRRs occur, the variations in the project's NPV between the IRRs are usually very small, and the value of the NPV itself is likely to be close to zero. Therefore it follows that with a simple accept or reject decision, the problem of multiple IRRs is not too serious. If a project is accepted on the basis of (say) the majority of its IRRs being greater than the cut off/discount rate, whereas when evaluated using NPV it turns out to have a *negative* NPV, then the IRR-based decision would not be disastrous as the magnitude of the negative NPV would be likely to be relatively small. Nevertheless, the problem of multiple IRRs does remain to cause difficulties in the case of mutually

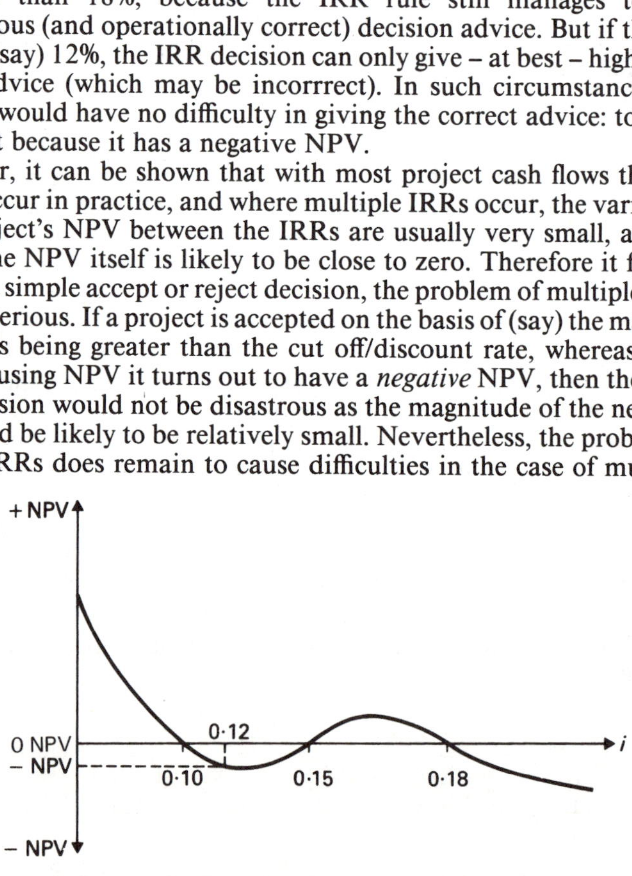

Figure 5.2

exclusive investment decisions. In such circumstances, the differential cash flow may well have multiple IRRs, which causes the decision rule to become non-operational.

Despite the foregoing argument concerning the practical unimportance of multiple IRRs, the conclusion reached must still be that the possible presence of multiple IRRs is yet one more factor to count against the use of that particular DCF technique. The argument that the IRR rule may give the wrong decision, but it will not be *very* wrong is not a persuasive one.

Extended yield method

One approach that is often suggested, and sometimes used in practice, to handle the problem of multiple IRRs, is the *extended yield* method. Project R is an example of a project which would cause difficulties for the IRR decision rule. The extended yield method solves the problem by eliminating the offending second change in sign. This is achieved by discounting the unwanted cash flow back to present value at the hurdle rate, and then netting the figure off against the Year 0 outlay. Table 5.4 illustrates the approach.

Table 5.4

A company wishes to evaluate Project R using the IRR decision rule with a 10% hurdle rate:

Year	*Cash flow*
0	−100
1	+ 50
2	+ 80
3	− 10

The Year 3 cash flow is discounted back to present value at 10%: $-10(1\cdot10)^{-3} = -7\cdot51$ and this figure is then netted off with the Year 0 cash flow to provide a *revised* cash flow for Project R:

Year	*Cash flow*
0	−107·51
1	+ 50
2	+ 80

At 4%, the project has an NPV of: +14·53
At 20%, the project has an NPV of: −10·29

Using linear interpolation, the IRR of Project R can be estimated as:

$$4\% + \left[\frac{14\cdot53}{14\cdot53-(-10\cdot29)} \times (20\% - 4\%)\right] = \underline{13\cdot4\%\ \text{IRR}}$$

However, it should be noted that the extended yield method only *gets around* the problem of multiple IRRs, it does not *solve* the problem.

Although a single IRR has been calculated for Project R, the point remains that in reality Project R has *two* IRRs (and neither is likely to be the 13·4% estimated).

Other problems with the IRR rule

Figure 5.3 illustrates another problematical situation for the IRR rule where there is only a single IRR for the project, but at no rate of discount does the project yield a positive NPV. If, in this example, the discount rate were 10%, the NPV rule would correctly reject the project. However, the IRR rule would accept it because its IRR (20%) is greater than the hurdle rate.

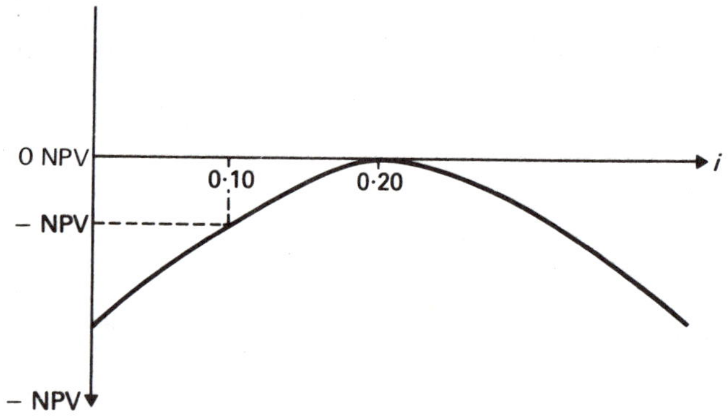

Figure 5.3

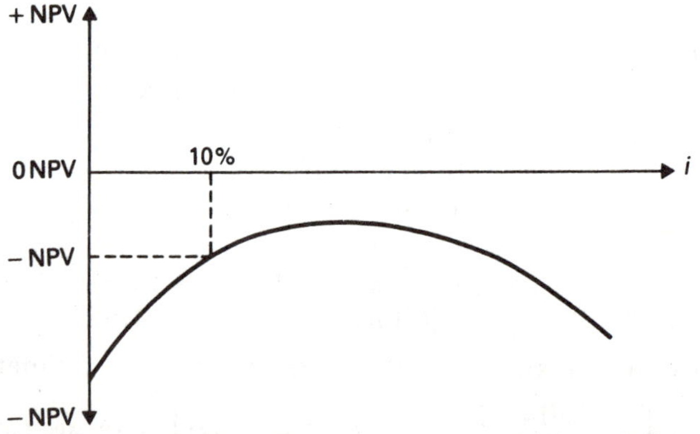

Figure 5.4

Figure 5.4 illustrate an NPV profile which causes the IRR decision rule to break down completely because no internal rate of return exists![5]

A further difficulty that arises out of the IRR approach is caused by the fact that it evaluates projects on the basis of a percentage rate of return. In other words it examines a project's return *relative* to its outlay, rather than in *absolute* terms as with NPV.

For example, suppose a company is evaluating a pair of mutually exclusive projects: a large factory or a small factory. The large factory has an outlay of £10m, the small factory has an outlay of £2m. Suppose the large factory has an IRR of 18% and the small factory 24%, and the hurdle rate is 15%. Therefore both alternatives are acceptable in their own right, but the standard IRR decision rule would accept the small factory as it produces the higher IRR. The problem is that the company would end up with a lot more 'profit' from an 18% return on £10m, than from a 24% return on only £2m. This is, of course, yet another reason for the possible existence of conflicting advice between NPV and the standard IRR decision rule.

In conclusion

The conclusion of this analysis appears strongly to favour the NPV decision rule for investment appraisal. At best the IRR method might be used as a support and as a communication device on the basis of management's familiarity with rates of return rather than net present values, for the decision advice given by the NPV rule.[6]

As a result of this conclusion, from now on, we shall be implicitly assuming that the NPV technique will be the approach that should be used by companies in investment appraisals. It is the only technique from amongst the four investigated that can be relied upon to give advice that will lead towards maximizing shareholder wealth.

THE REPLACEMENT CYCLE PROBLEM

Optimal replacement cycle

It was noted earlier that, when faced with a mutually exclusive investment decision, the NPV decision rule was to accept whichever project had the largest positive NPV. This decision rule was based on the assumption of a perfect capital market *and* on the assumption that the projects involved were 'one-offs'. In other words, they did not form part of a continuous replacement cycle.

However, where a project *does* form part of a continuous replacement cycle, the NPV decision rule needs to be modified. This situation is referred to as the *replacement cycle problem* and Example 5.4 illustrates the approach.

Example 5.4 (all figures in £000s)

Photolysis PLC uses a 10% discount rate for project appraisal. It is considering purchasing a machine which, when it comes to the end of its economic life, is expected to be replaced by an identical machine and so on, continuously. The machine has maximum life of three years but, as its productivity declines with age, it could be replaced after either just one or two years. The financial details are as follows:

Year	0	1	2	3
Outlay	−1,000			
Revenues		+900	+800	+700
Costs		−400	−350	−350
Scrap value		+650	+400	+150

The choice of when to replace this machine can be seen as a choice between three mutually exclusive alternatives, the cash flows and NPVs of which are as follows:

		Cash flows (£000s)			
Dispose of machine at end of:		0	1	2	3
First Year	Outlay	−1,000			
	Revenue		+ 900		
	Costs		− 400		
	Scrap		+ 650		
	Net cash flow	−1,000	+1,150		
Second Year	Outlay	−1,000			
	Revenue		+900	+800	
	Costs		−400	−350	
	Scrap			+400	
	Net cash flow	−1,000	+500	+850	
Third Year	Outlay	−1,000			
	Revenue		+900	+800	+700
	Costs		−400	−350	−350
	Scrap				+150
	Net cash flow	−1,000	+500	+450	+500

Disposal point

		NPV
Yr 1	$-1{,}000 \quad +1{,}150\,(1\cdot10)^{-1}$	$= +\ 45\cdot46$
Yr 2	$-1{,}000 \quad +500\,(1\cdot10)^{-1} + 850\,(1\cdot10)^{-2}$	$= +156\cdot99$
Yr 3	$-1{,}000 \quad +500\,(1\cdot10)^{-1} + 450\,(1\cdot10)^{-2} + 500\,(1\cdot10)^{-3}$	$= +202\cdot08$

If these were straightforward mutually exclusive projects then the decision could be based on whichever alternative has the largest positive NPV. However, the machine – whenever it is decided to replace it – will be replaced by an identical machine which will itself be replaced by another identical machine and so on. Therefore, purely on the basis of the NPVs alone, like is not being compared with like as each NPV is generated over a different span of time: one, two or three years.

In order to place the three alternatives on a comparable basis, the equivalent *annual* cash flow of each has to be computed:

Disposal point	*NPV* $\div A_{\overline{n}|0\cdot10}$	=	*Equivalent annual cash flow*
Yr 1	$+45\cdot46 \div A_{\overline{1}|0\cdot10}$	=	+50·00
Yr 2	$+156\cdot99 \div A_{\overline{2}|0\cdot10}$	=	+90·46
Yr 3	$+202\cdot08 \div A_{\overline{3}|0\cdot10}$	=	+81·26

In order to understand the meaning of the *equivalent annual cash flow* figures, let us take the two-year replacement option as an example. Quite simply, the cash flow of the machine over its two-year life has an NPV which is equivalent to that of a two-year immediate annuity of £90·46 per year:

Yr 0	*Yr 1*	*Yr 2*		
−1,000	+500	+850	=	+156·99 NPV
	+90·46	+90·46	=	+156·99 NPV

As a result, replacing the machine every two years is equivalent to a cash inflow of £90·46 at the end of every year:

Year	0	1	2	3	4	5	6 → ∞
1st machine	−1,000	+500	+850				
2nd machine			−1,000	+500	+850		
3rd machine					−1,000	+500	+850
etc etc							−1,000
Equivalent c/f		+90·46	+90·46	+90·46	+90·46	+90·46	+90·46

Therefore, the optimal replacement cycle of the machine can be decided on the basis of which replacement cycle gives the most favourable equivalent annual cash flow. In this example, it is: two-year replacement. Both one and three year replacement will result in a lower equivalent annual cash flow.

Repair versus replace

The repair versus replace decision is very common in practice. How long should the company continue to spend money on keeping an existing machine working, and when should they replace it with a new machine?

With this situation, it is important to realize that there are two decisions involved:

1 When should the *existing* machine be replaced?
2 What is the optimal replacement cycle of the *new* machine?

Furthermore, decision 2 *must* be made before decision 1 can be made. Example 5.5 continues on from Example 5.4 to illustrate the procedure.

Example 5.5 (all figures in £000s)

Photolysis PLC, referred to in Example 5.4, already have an *existing* machine doing the job of the new machine whose optimal replacement cycle has already been identified: 2-year replacement cycle. Therefore, the only remaining decision is: when should the company's existing machine be scrapped? The financial details are as follows:

Existing machine

Year	0	1	2
Scrap value	+250	+200	+ 50
Repair cost	−100	−250	
Revenue		+600	+600
Costs		−300	−340

On the basis of this information, the existing machine could be kept operational for a maximum of two years more. To be kept operational for the next twelve months requires £100,000 of repairs to be carried out now. To extend the machine's life up to the end of Year 2 would require a further £250,000 spent on repairs in twelve months' time. However, the repair costs in any particular year could be avoided by scrapping the machine in that year. The cash flows of the different options are as follows, based on the assumption that when scrapped, the existing machine will be replaced by the new machine (referred to in Example 5.4) which is itself replaced every two years and so locks the company into an equivalent annual cash flow of + £90·46:

Scrap the existing machine at:	Year	0	1	2	3
Year 0	Scrap value	+250			
	New machine		+90·46	+90·46	+90·46
	Net cash flow	+250	+90·46	+90·46	+90·46
Year 1	Scrap value		+200		
	Repair cost	−100			
	Revenue		+600		
	Costs		−300		
	New machine			+90·46	+90·46
	Net cash flow	−100	+500	+90·46	+90·46
Year 2	Scrap value			+ 50	
	Repair cost	−100	−250		
	Revenue		+600	+600	
	Costs		−300	−340	
	New machine				+90·46
	Net cash flow	−100	+ 50	+310	+90·46

The NPV of each of these perpetuity cash flows is:

Scrap at Year 0: $+250 + (90{\cdot}46 \div 0{\cdot}10) = + \underline{1154{\cdot}60 \text{ NPV}}$
Scrap at Year 1: $-100 + 500\ (1{\cdot}10)^{-1} + [90{\cdot}46 \div 0{\cdot}10]\ (1{\cdot}10)^{-1} = \underline{+1176{\cdot}92 \text{ NPV}}$
Scrap at Year 2: $-100 + 50\ (1{\cdot}10)^{-1} + 310\ (1{\cdot}10)^{-2} + [90{\cdot}46 \div 0{\cdot}10]\ (1{\cdot}10)^{-2} = \underline{+949{\cdot}20 \text{ NPV}}$

Therefore the best option for the company is to scrap the existing machine in 12 months' time (the largest NPV option) and replace it by the new machine, which itself is replaced every two years thereafter (see Example 5.4).

Finally, a major drawback of the repair or replace decision procedure should be pointed out. The drawback is the implicit assumption of unchanging technology. In other words, the assumption in the optimal replacement cycle that the new machine will be replaced by an *identical* machine, ad infinitum, is clearly unrealistic. Thus the technique's real-world usefulness should be seen with this limitation in mind.

SUMMARY

This chapter has looked at the application of the two DCF investment appraisal methods in a mutually exclusive projects decision situation. Arising out of this have come a number of difficulties with the IRR decision rule. The main points made are:

- The NPV decision rule for mutually exclusive decision situations is: accept whichever project has the largest, positive NPV. The logic behind this was obvious given the objective of shareholder wealth maximization and the meaning of NPV.
- The decision rule holds even when the alternative investments are of unequal magnitude, duration or risk, assuming a perfect capital market and the discount rate used properly reflects the return available elsewhere on the capital market from a similar-risk investment.
- The *standard* IRR decision rule for mutually exclusive investments is:
  - ☐ The 'best' project has the highest IRR.
  - ☐ Accept the best project if its IRR > hurdle rate.
- This standard IRR decision rule gives unreliable investment decision advice in situations of mutually exclusive projects: the problem arises from the arithmetic of the IRR and the fact that it assumes project generated cash flows will be reinvested to earn a rate of return equal to the IRR of the project generating those cash flows.
- The reinvestment assumption is, strictly speaking, an assumption about the opportunity cost of project generated cash flows. Given a perfect capital market, the assumption made by the IRR is incorrect – their opportunity cost equates with the capital market rate of return for

the risk level involved. The NPV method makes this, correct, assumption.

- The problem of the IRR can be resolved, in an artificial way, by a modified decision rule which, in its simplest form, states:
  - ☐ if IRR of the differential cash flow is > hurdle rate, accept the project with the smallest IRR;
  - ☐ if IRR of the differential cash flow is < hurdle rate, accept the project with the largest IRR.
- A further problem for the IRR arises out of the possible existence of multiple IRRs, when the decision rule then breaks down completely.
- The problem of multiple IRRs can be resolved, again in a purely artificial way, through the use of the extended yield technique. However, this was shown not to deal with the problem, merely to avoid it.
- The strong conclusion to the chapter is that, for several reasons, the IRR investment appraisal technique is – just like payback and ROCE/ARR – unsatisfactory. Therefore only NPV remains as an investment appraisal technique which will give consistently reliable advice which will lead to shareholder wealth maximization.
- Finally, a related area was examined: the repair or replace decision. This was seen to be a special case of mutually exclusive projects involving the use of the annuity discounting factors.

NOTES

1 This, of course, would be the decision rule for revenue generating projects. For purely cost generating projects (such as the installation of air conditioning equipment in a factory), the best project would be that which produces the *smallest negative NPV*.

2 The processess of discounting and compounding can be viewed simply as a method of assigning weights to cash flows.

3 The IRR calculation simply involves finding the roots of a polynomial equation of n terms (where n=the number of periods of the project's life). In general, the IRR equation of a project which lasts for n years will have n roots or solutions or IRRs. However, with a conventional type of cash flow, only one of these solutions is a *real* number and the rest will be imaginary (e.g. $\sqrt{-2}$), with mathematical, but no economic importance. However, a non-conventional project cash flow can produce a polynomial equation of a type which may have *several* real number roots, each one of which is an equally valid IRR. (Conventional and non-conventional cash flows are defined in the following paragraph in the main text.)

4 The use of these terms should not lead the reader into the all too easy substitution of 'usual' and 'unusual'. Non-conventional cash flows can be

extremely common in practice, as we shall discover when we examine the impact of taxation on investment appraisal.

5 The IRR is said not to exist only as a 'real' number, in such cases. It will exist, and so there will be roots to the polynomial, in terms of imaginary numbers. This mathematical result, however, has little relevance for our purposes.

6 Even this may be a disadvantage in that management may falsely believe that the IRR is essentially the same as the Accounting Rate of Return (ROCE), when in fact the two measures are totally distinct.

FURTHER READING

1 On the problem of the reinvestment assumptions, see: H. Bierman and S. Smidt, 'Capital Budgeting and the Problem of Reinvesting Cash Proceeds', *Journal of Business*, 1957; C.L. Dudley, 'A note on Reinvestment Assumptions in Choosing Between NPV and IRR', *Journal of Finance*, September 1972; and C.R. Beidleman, 'DCF Reinvestment Rates Assumptions', *Engineering Economist*, Winter 1984.
2 On more general problems with the IRR and NPV, see: R.A. Fawthrop, 'Underlying Problems in Discounted Cash Flow', *Accounting and Business Research*, Summer 1971, and B.A. Kolb, 'Problems and Pitfalls in Capital Budgeting', *Financial Analysts Journal*, November-December 1968.
3 Finally, the following articles examine other specific problems of using the IRR: D. Longbottom and L. Wiper, 'Necessary Conditions for the Existence of Multiple Rates in the use of the IRR', *Journal of Business Finance and Accounting*, Winter 1978; J.C.T. Mao, 'The IRR as a Ranking Criterion', *Engineering Economist*, Winter 1966; M. Sarnat and H. Levy, 'The Relationship of Rules of Thumb to the IRR', *Journal of Finance*, June 1969; and G.W. Emery, 'Some Guidelines for Evaluating Capital Investment Alternatives with Unequal Lives', *Financial Management*, Spring 1982.

QUICKIE QUESTIONS

1 Project A has an outlay of £1m and when using a discount rate of 10%, to reflect its risk, it has an NPV of + £20,000. Project B has an outlay of £10m and when discounted at 20%, to reflect its risk, has an NPV of + £15,000. If A and B are mutually exclusive, which project should the firm accept?
2 In question 1, what assumptions are you making in giving your answer?
3 What are the reinvestment assumptions of NPV and IRR, which is correct and under what circumstances?

4 Under what circumstances can multiple IRRs occur and what can be done to avoid the problem?

5 Project C has the following cash flows:

0	−100
1	+ 60
2	+ 80
3	− 20

What is its IRR, given a 10% hurdle rate?

6 Sketch out a diagram showing how the conflict between NPV and IRR can occur.

7 What is the simple version of the modified IRR decision rule?

PROBLEMS

1 Saucy Steamboats Ltd is currently evaluating a proposal to invest in a new in-shore rowing boat. Two possible types, A and B, have now been identified, each of which would have a five-year life and zero scrap value. Their costs and associated net revenues are:

Year	*Type A* £	*Type B* £
0	−1,000	−2,000
1	+ 350	+ 640
2	+ 350	+ 640
3	+ 350	+ 640
4	+ 350	+ 640
5	+ 350	+ 640

The appropriate discount rate is 10% per annum. Both alternatives can be considered marginal investments and acceptance of either one would leave the company's risk unchanged. The company operates in a perfect capital market. Ignore taxation and inflation.

Required:

(a) The managing director of Saucy Steamboats Ltd insists that the investment alternatives should be appraised using the internal rate of return. You are therefore required to appraise these projects *on that basis alone.* State the decision rule you use, making sure that it will produce the correct investment decision advice in terms of maximizing shareholders' wealth.

(b) Present a careful and detailed outline of the argument you might put forward to the managing director for using the net present value appraisal technique, rather than the internal rate of return, given the present conditions surrounding Saucy Steamboats Ltd.

Note that your answer to part (b) should *not* be confined to a discussion of the two investment opportunities under consideration in part (a). Assume that all cash flows arise on the last day of the year to which they relate, with the exception of the project outlays which occur at the start of the first year.

2 Mr Cowdrey runs a manufacturing business. He is considering whether to accept one of two mutually exclusive investment projects and, if so, which one to accept. Each project involves an immediate cash outlay of £100,000. Mr Cowdrey estimates that the net cash inflows from each project will be as follows:

	Project A	*Project B*
Net cash inflow at end of:	£	£
Year 1	60,000	10,000
Year 2	40,000	20,000
Year 3	30,000	110,000

Mr Cowdrey does not expect capital or any other resource to be in short supply during the next three years.

Required:

(a) Prepare a graph to show the functional relationship between net present value and the discount rate for the two projects (label the vertical axis 'net present value' and the horizontal axis 'discount rate').
(b) Use the graph to estimate the internal rate of return of each project.
(c) On the basis of the information given, advise Mr Cowdrey which project to accept if his discount rate is (i) 6%, (ii) 12%.
(d) Describe briefly any additional information you think would be useful to Mr Cowdrey in choosing between the two projects.
(e) Discuss the relative merits of net present value and internal rate of return as methods of investment appraisal.

Ignore taxation.

3 Charles Pooter (Investments) plc, are considering which, if any, of four independent projects to undertake. The forecast cash flows for each project are listed below; recepits arise at the end of each year.

		Net cash inflows		
Project	*Immediate outlay*	*Year 1*	*Year 2*	*Year 3*
1	−2,500	+1,000	+1,000	+1,000
2	−1,000	+ 100	+1,400	0
3	−1,000	+ 800	+ 600	0
4	−4,000	0	0	+5,000

The company faces a perfect capital market, in which the interest rate for the projects' risk level is 10%.

Required:

(a) Using the NPV decision rule, indicate which projects the company should accept. State clearly the reasons for your decisions.

(b) How would your conclusions in (a) differ if the projects were mutually exclusive?
(c) Estimate the IRRs of projects 2 and 3. Would it be valid to choose between projects 2 and 3 on the basis of their expected IRRs? If not, present revised calculations so that the internal rate of return method, and the method you have used in (a), lead to the same, unambiguous conclusions.
(d) In practice, the IRR method has been observed to be far more widely used than NPV. Suggest reasons for this relative popularity. Why might the supposed superiority of NPV be an illusion or an irrelevance in reality?

4 Demeter Ltd owns a machine of type DK which could be used in production for two more years at most. The machine originally cost £45,000 five years ago. Its realizable value is currently £8,000 (because a special opportunity for sale has arisen), but it would be zero at all subsequent times. If the machine were to be used for two more years, it would require a major overhaul at a cost of £9,000 at the end of one year.

A new model of the machine is now being marketed. It costs £40,000 and has a maximum life of ten years provided that special maintenance is undertaken at a cost of £10,000 after five years, and at a cost of £20,000 after eight years. The new model would have no realizable value at any time. Assume that no other new models are expected to become available in the foreseeable future, and that no changes are expected in costs or demand for output of the machine. Demeter's cost of capital is 15 per cent per annum.

Required:

Prepare calculations to show whether Demeter's existing machine should be replaced now or after one or two years.

6
Project appraisal cash flows

Chapter Contents

INVESTMENT APPRAISAL AND INFLATION

Up to this stage in the analysis, we have implicitly assumed, within our world of managerial investment decision making, that prices have been stable. That is not to say that we have excluded the possibility of any price changes, but that we have assumed that there are no *general* price movements within the economy, either upwards (inflation) or downwards (deflation). Indeed it was made clear when dealing with the concept of the time value of money that the concept, fundamentally, has nothing to do with inflation, and so inflation was assumed not to exist.

In this section we will now drop this assumption and examine how the existence of general price movements within an economy affect investment appraisal and decision making, and how appraisal techniques can be adapted, if need be, to cope with such circumstances. These effects will be examined mainly by analysing the inflation case, but the approach used and conclusions drawn will also apply, by analogy, to the case of deflation.

The problem of inflation

Inflation can be simply defined as a situation where prices in an economy are, in general, rising over time. Its expected (or unexpected) presence is likely to cause problems for the appraisal of investment opportunities in two main ways.

The first problem is that it will make the estimation of a project's expected cash flow more difficult. When a project is being appraised, management will have to provide estimates of its inputs and outputs. With inflation, the prices of these inputs and outputs are likely to change, and management will hence have to estimate the magnitude of these changes. In other words, management will have to estimate the expected future rates of inflation. Thus there is a forecasting problem caused by the presence of inflation.

The second problem is, in one sense, an extension of the first. Market interest rates, or rates of return, can be viewed as representing the price of money, and so interest rates – like other prices – can be expected to rise when there is general inflation within the economy. Thus management have the additional task of estimating the effects of inflation on the project appraisal discount rate.

'Real' and 'market' rates of interest

The effects of inflation on market interest rates can most easily be seen by way of an example. We know from the discussion about the concept of the time value of money that suppliers of investment capital make a trade-off between consumption now and consumption at some future point in time. Generally speaking, current consumption is preferred to future consumption and so, in order to be persuaded to forgo consumption now (and invest instead), investors have to be rewarded with the promise of increased consumption at a later point in time. Market interest rates reflect this time 'exchange rate' of consumption.

For the moment, suppose that within the economy there is no inflation. An investor, we are told, is willing to lend you £100 for a year as long as he receives £110 in twelve months' time. In other words, he is willing to give up £100 worth of consumption now, as long as he is rewarded with an extra 10% consumption in twelve months' time. Thus the 10% interest rate that he is demanding can be seen both in money terms – he wants an extra ten £1 coins – and in terms of consumption or purchasing power. However, it is this latter interpretation that is of fundamental concern to the investor – how much additional consumption he is to receive in the future for giving up current consumption. (Pound coins by themselves are of little use. What makes them desirable is that they give the power to consume; therefore consumption and consumption power – or purchasing power – is the point of importance.)

Now let us take a slightly different situation, with inflation expected to raise the general level of prices in the economy by 5% over the next twelve months. Our investor would still be willing to give up £100 worth of current consumption as long as he is rewarded with an extra 10% of *consumption* in twelve months' time. However, an extra £10 will now not be sufficient cash to buy this additional consumption because of the presence of inflation.

In order to consume, in twelve months' time, the *same* amount of consumption as that given up now, the investor will need £100 $(1+0{\cdot}05)$ $=$ £105, because of the rise in prices. But our investor has to be able to consume 10% *extra* in order to be persuaded to give up current consumption and so, in money terms, he will require £105 (1+0·10) = £115·50. This therefore represents a *money* interest rate of 15·5%: because of inflation, 15·5% extra cash is required to purchase 10% extra consumption.

It follows from this analysis that, in inflationary conditions, two interest rates can be identified – a money (or nominal) interest rate and a consumption (or purchasing power) interest rate. In the example above these were 15½% and 10%, respectively. We shall refer to the former rate as the 'market' interest rate (as it would be the rate quoted on the capital market) and the latter the 'real' interest rate. (It is real in the sense that it represents the market interest rate, *deflated*, to take out the effects of inflation.) Table 6.1 shows the general relationship, which is often referred to as the Fisher Effect, after the American economist who first developed it.

Table 6.1

$$\left(1 + \begin{array}{c}\text{Real}\\ \text{Interest}\\ \text{Rate}\end{array}\right)\left(1 + \begin{array}{c}\text{General}\\ \text{Rate of}\\ \text{Inflation}\end{array}\right) = \left(1 + \begin{array}{c}\text{Market}\\ \text{Interest}\\ \text{Rate}\end{array}\right)$$

Substituting in here the data from the example:

$$(1 + 0{\cdot}10)(1 + 0{\cdot}05) = (1 + 0{\cdot}155)$$

$$\text{Therefore, the real interest rate: } \frac{(1 + 0{\cdot}155)}{(1 + 0{\cdot}05)} - 1 = 0{\cdot}10 \text{ or } 10\%$$

$$\text{the market interest rate: } (1{\cdot}10)(1{\cdot}05) - 1 = 0{\cdot}155 \text{ or } 15{\cdot}5\%$$

$$\text{and the general inflation rate: } \frac{(1 + 0{\cdot}155)}{(1 + 0{\cdot}10)} - 1 = 0{\cdot}05 \text{ or } 5\%$$

Two possible approaches

The example used above shows that under inflationary conditions we can identify two possible interest or discount rates: the market interest rate and the real interest rate. Therefore the question that immediately arises is: which one should be used in an NPV investment appraisal analysis? The answer to this question is that either rate can be used, but they must each only be applied to an appropriate definition of the project cash flow. Specifically, we can state:

either (i) *Money* cash flows of the project can be discounted by the *market* interest rate to present value cash flows,

or (ii) *Money* cash flows of the project can be discounted by the rate of general inflation to *current general purchasing power* cash flows, and then these current general purchasing power cash flows can be discounted by the *real* interest rate to present value cash flows.

Either approach will generate exactly the same NPV for the project.

In these statements the term *money* cash flow can be defined as the physical quantity of money (i.e., pound coins) that the project will generate at any particular point in time; and the term *current general purchasing power* (CGPP) cash flow refers to the money cash flow, deflated by the general rate of inflation, so as to reflect the *current* general purchasing power of that future cash flow. A simple example 6.1 can clarify the definition and can also be used to show that these two alternative discounting approaches are entirely consistent with each other.

In Example 6.1 we should have expected the present values to be exactly the same for obvious reasons: in the first approach, the cash flow is being discounted by 15½%, whereas in the second approach the cash flow is being discounted by 10% and 5%. Thus in each alternative the cash flow is being discounted by the same amount because:

$$(1 + 0{\cdot}155) = (1 + 0{\cdot}10)\,(1 + 0{\cdot}05)$$

Therefore, it is for this reason that it was stated earlier that either the market discount rate or the real discount rate could be used in an investment appraisal analysis, *as long as each was applied to an appropriate definition of cash flow.*

The market discount rate is an interest rate expressed in money terms and so it is applied to the actual money cash flows that the project is expected to produce. The real discount rate is an interest rate expressed in consumption or purchasing power terms, and so it should be applied to the project cash flows that are similarly expressed; in other words it is applied to the money cash flows after they have had the inflationary element taken out. To illustrate this we can make use of the Year 2 cash flow from Example 6.1.

In Year 2 the project is expected to produce a physical cash flow of £600. Given an annual rate of general inflation of 5%, this money would buy the same 'basket of goods' that £544·20 would buy *today* (i.e. Year 0).

However, because of the time value of money of investors, £600 at Year 2 is not equivalent to £544·20 at Year 0. The present value of £600 at Year 2 (taking into account the time value of money, expressed in real terms, of 10%) is £449·73.

There are two further points to be noticed about this example. The first is that discounting the money cash flow by the general rate of inflation has nothing to do with the idea of the time value of money, it is simply a calculation to express the project cash flow – not in money terms, but in consumption/purchasing power terms. The idea of the time value of money is not taken into account until the discounting of these deflated cash flows by the *real* discount rate.

The second point to notice is that the project money cash flows are deflated (or discounted) by the general rate of inflation and *not* the specific rate of inflation that applies to a particular cash flow. For example, suppose that although the general rate of inflation (as given by changes in the RPI) is 14%, the rate of *wage* inflation is 20%. The actual money cash flow paid out in wages would be discounted by 14% and not

Example 6.1

Rhotacine PLC wishes to evaluate a project. The company has taken great care to estimate how future rates of inflation will affect the prices charged for the project's output (and hence its revenue), and how inflation will affect the costs incurred in generating those revenues. The project's actual (money) cash flows have been estimated as:

Year	*Cash flow*
0	−1,000
1	+ 800
2	+ 600

The company believes that a 15½% return is available elsewhere on the capital market for a similar risk project (i.e. the market rate of return) and that prices in general, as measured by the *retail price index* (RPI), will increase by 5% per year over the next two years.

i) Approach 1: Take the project's money cash flows and discount by the market rate of discount to NPV.

Year	*Cash flow*	×	*15½% discount*	=	*PV c/f*
0	−1,000	×	1	=	−1,000
1	+ 800	×	0·8658	=	+ 692·64
2	+ 600	×	0·7496	=	+ 449·76
					+ 142·40 NPV

ii) Approach 2: Take the project's money cash flows and discount by the RPI to CGPP cash flow. Then discount the CGPP cash flow by the real discount rate to NPV.

Year	*Cash flow*	×	*5% discount*	=	*CGPP c/f*
0	−1,000	×	1	=	−1,000
1	+ 800	×	0·9524	=	+ 761·92
2	+ 600	×	0·9070	=	+ 544·20

The *real* discount rate can be found from the Fisher Effect relationship:

$$\frac{(1 + 0{\cdot}155)}{(1 + 0{\cdot}05)} - 1 = \underline{0{\cdot}10} \text{ or } 10\%$$

Year	*CGPP c/f*	×	*10% discount*	=	*PV c/f*
0	−1,000	×	1	=	−1,000
1	+ 761·92	×	0·9091	=	+ 692·66
2	+ 544·20	×	0·8264	=	+ 449·73
					+ 142·39 NPV

Notice that the two NPVs are (virtually) identical. (The fact that they are not identical simply arises from rounding errors because only 4-figure discount factors were used.)

by 20%. This is because we wish to express the money cash flows of a project in terms of their ability to purchase a *general* range or collection of goods, and not their ability to purchase any one *particular* good.

A final example

The above analysis shows that the two possible approaches to project appraisal are exactly equivalent. Both start with the actual 'money' cash flows that the project is expected to produce and both result in an identical set of present value cash flows from which the net present value can be found.

Given this equivalence, it does not much matter which approach is used, although discounting the money cash flows by the market interest rate would appear more straightforward because it only involves a single set of discounting calculations and is the recommended approach to use. However, sometimes the easiest approach is to use a mixture of both, if there are some simplification benefits to be had through cancellations. Example 6.2 demonstrates the principle.

Example 6.2

Project A: Outlay: £1,000
Life: 30 years
Scrap value: £100
Net revenues: £120 per year in current (t_0) terms.
The net cash flow is expected to increase each year by 8%.
RPI: 6% per year.
Market discount rate: 14·48%.

It would be possible to set out the project's money cash flows and discount by 14·48% to present value. However, 14·48% is a rather awkward discounting number to use and 30 years of cash flows would be hard work! Therefore we could instead discount the money cash flows by a combination of RPI (6%) and the real discount rate.

Using the Fisher Effect:

$$\frac{1{\cdot}1448}{1{\cdot}06} - 1 = \underline{0{\cdot}08} \text{ or } 8\% = \text{real discount rate}$$

Therefore, the project's money cash flows can be expressed as:

Year	*Outlay*	*Scrap*	*Net revs.*
0	−1,000		
1			$+120\,(1{\cdot}08)^1$
2			$+120\,(1{\cdot}08)^2$
.			.
.			.
30		+100	$+120\,(1{\cdot}08)^{30}$

The outlay is already in present value terms and so does not require discounting. The scrap value can be discounted back either at 14·48% or at a combination of 6% and 8%:

Year 30: $+\ 100\,(1{\cdot}1448)^{-30} = +\ 100 \times 0{\cdot}0173 = \underline{+1{\cdot}73}$

or

Year 30: $+\ 100\,(1{\cdot}08)^{-30}(1{\cdot}06)^{-30} = +\ 100 \times 0{\cdot}0994 \times 0{\cdot}1741 = \underline{+1{\cdot}73}$

As far as the net revenue cash flows are concerned, it is convenient to discount them to present value using a combination of 8% and 6% in order to be able to simplify the calculation through cancellation:

Year	*Net revs.*	*Discount Factors*	
0			
1	$+120\,\cancel{(1{\cdot}08)^{1}}$	$\times\ \cancel{(1{\cdot}08)^{-1}}\,(1{\cdot}06)^{-1}$	$= +120\,(1{\cdot}06)^{-1}$
2	$+120\,\cancel{(1{\cdot}08)^{2}}$	$\times\ \cancel{(1{\cdot}08)^{-2}}\,(1{\cdot}06)^{-2}$	$= +120\,(1{\cdot}06)^{-2}$
·			·
·			·
·			·
30	$+120\,\cancel{(1{\cdot}08)^{30}}$	$\times\ \cancel{(1{\cdot}08)^{-30}}\,(1{\cdot}06)^{-30}$	$= +120\,(1{\cdot}06)^{-30}$

Therefore, we are left with a thirty-year annuity cash flow:

$$+120\,A_{\overline{30}|0{\cdot}06} = 120 \times 13{\cdot}7648 = \underline{+1651{\cdot}78}$$

Hence, the project's NPV is:

$$-1{,}000 + 1{\cdot}73 + 1651{\cdot}78 = \underline{\underline{+653{\cdot}51\ \text{NPV}}}$$

Inflation and the IRR rule

This discussion about allowing for inflation in investment appraisal has been conducted within the context of an NPV analysis. Nevertheless it is simple to transfer the conclusions into the context of an IRR calculation. Either the IRR of the money cash flows of the project can be compared against the hurdle rate of the market interest rate; or alternatively, the IRR of the project's current general purchasing power cash flows can be matched against the real interest rate. However, in order to be able to use the IRR successfully, it is important to remember that it is necessary to assume that either the market interest rate or the real interest rate will remain constant over the project's life.

INVESTMENT APPRAISAL AND TAXATION

Introduction

Taxation has an important role to play in investment appraisal as it can have a substantial impact on the desirability, or otherwise, of an investment opportunity. Furthermore, taxation considerations affect virtually every area of financial decision making both in a practical and in a theoretical context. Indeed, the complexity of the tax system and the fact that its application to individual financial decision making situations can sometimes be difficult to generalize means that it causes problems for the development of a realistic theory of financial decision making.

In this section we shall deal briefly with only a relatively simple aspect of taxation – its impact on investment project cash flows and their subsequent evaluation. However, in many of the later chapters we will be returning to examine some of the more complex problems that the presence of taxation poses for financial decision making.

The impact of tax

The theory of financial decision making is developed on the basis of an important underlying assumption: management are taking decisions so as to maximize the wealth of the shareholders. It therefore follows that in the appraisal of an investment project, what is of importance is the cash flows that will be generated by the project, *and that are available for shareholders.* In other words, as far as investment appraisal is concerned, we would wish to evaluate the *after tax cash flows* of a project.

In this analysis of the impact of tax on project appraisal, only a simplified version of the UK corporate tax system will be used. Furthermore it is assumed that the reader is aware – in outline – of this tax system but, for those who lack knowledge in this area, a brief appendix at the end of the chapter outlines the basic elements.

There are three ways in which the UK corporation tax regime impacts upon project appraisal:

(i) Tax relief is available on capital expenditure through the system of *writing-down allowances.*
(ii) A tax liability will arise on any *taxable profit* generated by the project.
(iii) There will also be a tax impact caused by how the project is financed. If it is financed with the help of debt capital, then there will be *tax relief* available on the interest payments. Alternatively, if the project is financed with shareholders' funds (i.e. equity capital), then dividends will be paid on the equity, which in turn will give rise to a liability for *advance corporation tax.*

With these three factors in mind, the approach taken to project appraisal is to evaluate the *after-tax project cash flows* using the *after-tax discount rate.* The after-tax project cash flows take into account effects (i) and (ii) above, and the after-tax discount rate takes into account effect (iii).

Financing cash flows

Up to this stage of our analysis of investment appraisal, very little has been said about how a project should be financed and the effect of the financing method on the project appraisal. This is how the position will remain until the capital structure/financing decision is discussed in detail in later chapters.

Example 6.3

Suppose a company wishes to acquire a machine which costs £1,000 and has a three-year life. The machine is expected to generate a net revenue (i.e. revenues less cash *operating* – not financing – costs) of £450 per year.

The company approaches its bank for a £1,000 three-year term loan in order to buy the machine. The bank agrees to the loan, after examining the riskiness of the proposed investment, and sets an interest rate of 10%. (Notice that this interest rate, like any rate of return, reflects the risk of the investment involved.)

Normally the company would then evaluate the NPV of the project, *ignoring* how it was to be financed and the cash flows (interest payments and loan re-payments) associated with the financing method. Using a 10% discount rate (as this reflects the project's risk – it is the return available elsewhere from a similar risk investment) the NPV is:

$$-1{,}000 + 450\,A_{3\urcorner 0\cdot 10} = \underline{\underline{+119\cdot 06\ \text{NPV}}}$$

However, it *could* be argued that this does not represent the true company cash flow as effectively the bank, not the company, buys the machine. Thus, from the company's standpoint the true cash flows associated with the project are:

Year	*0*	*1*	*2*	*3*
Interest		−100	−100	− 100
Loan repayment				−1000
Net revenue		+450	+450	+ 450
Net cash flow[1]	0	+350	+350	−650

However, when this cash flow is discounted to NPV at 10%, the result is *exactly* as before:

$$+350\,A_{2\urcorner 0\cdot 10} - 650\,(1\cdot 10)^{-3} = \underline{\underline{+119\cdot 06\ \text{NPV}}}\,^{2}$$

The reason for this is important: it is that the present value of the financing cash flow always equals the amount of the finance. Hence the present value of the bank loan cash flow equals the amount of the bank loan:

$$-100\,A_{3\urcorner 0\cdot 10} - 1{,}000\,(1\cdot 10)^{-3} = -1{,}000\ \text{PV}^{3}$$

Therefore, in the original NPV analysis of the project, the financing method is not *really* being ignored, because the project's outlay represents the present value of the financing cash flows.

Finally, care should be taken in not being misled by this simple example. The NPV analysis would have been undertaken in *exactly* the same way (with exactly the same + 119·06 NPV) if the project had been financed with (say) a £600 bank loan and £400 of retained earnings. The £1,000 NPV analysis outlay would implicitly represent the present value of *all* the financing cash flows, *however* the project was financed.

However, the basic philosophy of the approach of investment appraisal – and the NPV technique in particular – will be outlined now. This approach is that the financing method, and hence *all* the cash flows associated with the financing method, including interest payments, divided payments and loan re-payments, can be ignored. This is because, in effect, they are implicitly taken into account in the discount rate used in the NPV analysis. Example 6.3 attempts to show the underlying rationale to this advice using a very simple situation.

Example 6.3 shows why an NPV analysis can (apparently) ignore how a project is financed. The costs of finance are taken into account within the discount rate used. In a similar way – although this will not be explained in detail until a later chapter where the *cost* of *capital* is examined more fully – using an *after-tax* discount rate also takes into account the taxation impact on the financing cash flows.

Writing-down allowances

If a company spends money on capital equipment (such as a machine) the tax authorities do not usually allow that *whole* expense to be used to affect the tax liability in the year in which it is incurred. Instead, the expense – and so the tax relief – has to be spread over the project's life in accordance with a specific schedule. That schedule is the system of 25% writing-down allowances on the reducing balance of the project's worth.

Just how many tranches of writing-down allowance (WDA) the company will receive depends upon when the project is bought. In our simplified tax world, we can set up two alternative scenarios:

(i) Project is bought on the first day of the company's accounting year.
(ii) Project is bought on the last day of the *previous* accounting year.

In both cases the expenditure is effectively made at t_0, but it is made one *day* earlier in case (ii). One day makes no significant difference as far as an NPV discounting analysis is concerned, but it can make a significant difference as far as writing down allowances are concerned.

Therefore, in general, we can state that a project will have as many WDAs as there are years in its life in case (i) and there will be one *extra* WDA in case (ii). Furthermore, assuming that corporation tax is paid twelve months after year-end, in case (i) the *first* WDA tax relief is received by the firm in t_2; whilst in case (ii) the first WDA is received by the firm in t_1. (This therefore is the advantage of case (ii). By buying the machine one *day* earlier, the tax relief comes through one *year* earlier.) Table 6.2 shows the calculations.

'Profit' tax charge

In our world of a simplified UK tax system, a straightforward tax charge, at whatever is the going rate, can be made on the project's net operating cash flow. (Depreciation is, of course, not an allowable expense against tax as it is substituted by the WDA system and, in any case, it is not a *cash* flow.) This tax liability then will be offset, to some extent, by the WDA tax relief. Example 6.4 shows a fully-worked situation.

Table 6.2

A machine costs £1,000 and has a four-year life, at the end of which time it will be sold for £450 scrap. The corporation tax rate is 35%, payable 12 months in arrears and a system of 25% WDA, on the reducing balance is in operation. The WDA tax relief is as follows.

(i) *Machine is bought on first day of the accounting year*

			WDA		*Tax Relief*	*Timing*
Opening value	1,000	× 0·25 =	+250	× 0·35 =	+87·50	Yr 2
	250					
Yr 1 Written-down value	750	× 0·25 =	+187·50	× 0·35 =	+65·63	Yr 3
	187·50					
Yr 2 Written-down value	562·50	× 0·25 =	+140·63	× 0·35 =	+49·22	Yr 4
	140·63					
Yr 3 Written-down value	421·87 − 400 (↑ scrap value)	=	+ 21·87[4]	× 0·35 =	+ 7·65	Yr 5
	[1,000 − 400]	=	+600	× 0·35 =	+210·00 = Total tax relief	

(ii) *Machine is bought on last day of previous accounting year*

			WDA		*Tax Relief*	*Timing*
Opening value	1,000	× 0·25 =	+250	× 0·35 =	+ 87·50	Yr 1
	250					
Yr 0 Written-down value	750	× 0·25 =	+187·50	× 0·35 =	+ 65·63	Yr 2
	187·50					
Yr 1 Written-down value	562·50	× 0·25 =	+140·63	× 0·35 =	+ 49·22	Yr 3
	140·63					
Yr 2 Written-down value	421·87	× 0·25 =	+105·47	× 0·35 =	+ 36·91	Yr 4
	105·47					
Yr 3 Written-down value	316·40 − 400 (↑ scrap value)	=	− 83·60[5]	× 0·35 =	− 29·26	Yr 5
	[1,000 − 400]	=	+600	× 0·35 =	+210·00 = Total tax relief	

Example 6.4

Stanchion PLC is considering investing in a project which will require a capital expenditure outlay of £250,000. It will have a four-year life and, at the end of that time, the equipment used will be sold off for £100,000.

In addition, £38,000 of working capital will be required from the start of the project, and this figure will have to be increased to £50,000 at the end of the second year. All the working capital will be recovered at the end of the project's life.

The project is expected to generate annual revenues of £200,000 and incur annual cash operating costs of £80,000. The company believes that an after-tax discount rate of 10% would be appropriate.

The project would be bought on the last day of the company's financial year and would be financed with a three-year term loan of £250,000 at 3% over bank 'base rate'. Bank 'base rate' is currently 12%. The working capital would be financed out of Stanchion's own retained earnings.

Corporation tax is charged at 35%, payable 12 months after year-end. 25% writing-down allowances are available on capital expenditure. The company expects to have a substantial annual tax liability arising from other operations that it undertakes:

WDA Calculations (£000s)

		WDA		*Tax relief*	*Timing*
250	× 0·25 =	+62·5	× 0·35 =	+21·9	Yr 1
62·5					
187·5	× 0·25 =	+46·9	× 0·35 =	+16·4	Yr 2
46·9					
140·6	× 0·25 =	+35·1	× 0·35 =	+12·3	Yr 3
35·1					
105·5	× 0·25 =	+26·4	× 0·35 =	+ 9·2	Yr 4
26·4					
79·1	− 100 =	−20·9	× 0·35 =	− 7·3	Yr 5

Tax Charge on Project's Profits (£000s)

Annual revenues	200
less Annual costs	80
Taxable 'profit'	120
Tax at 35%	£42

NPV Calculation (£000s)

Year	*0*	*1*	*2*	*3*	*4*	*5*
Capital expenditure	−250					
Scrap value					+ 100	
WDA tax relief		+ 21·9	+ 16·4	+ 12·3	+ 9·2	− 7·3
Working capital	− 38		− 12		+ 50	
Revenues		+ 200	+ 200	+ 200	+ 200	
Costs		− 80	− 80	− 80	− 80	
Corporation tax			− 42	− 42	− 42	−42
Net Cash Flow	−288	+ 141·9	+ 82·4	+ 90·3	+ 237·2	−49·3
10% Discount Factor	× 1	× ·9091	× ·8264	× ·7513	× ·6830	× ·6209
PV Cash Flow	−288	+ 129·0	+ 68·1	+ 67·8	+ 162·0	− 30·6

NPV: +£108,300

Notes

1 Because of the company's substantial tax liability from other operations it is assumed that the company will be able to take the WDA tax relief that is available at Year 1. If not, this tax relief would have to be carried over to Year 2 when there would be a sufficient tax liability from the project to offset against the WDA relief.

2 At the end of Year 2 an *additional* £12,000 has to be spent on working capital to raise the total expenditure up to the required £50,000.

3 All financing cash flows have been ignored for the reasons outlined earlier in this section.

INVESTMENT APPRAISAL AND THE RELEVANT CASH FLOW

In an earlier chapter it was stated that in order properly to appraise an investment opportunity we have to appraise all the cash flows that arise either directly or indirectly as a result of the project. Some of the cost or benefit cash flows that arise as a result of undertaking a project are both obvious and easy to identify. For example, if a project consists of buying a machine, operating it and selling its output, there are some 'obvious' cash flows involved, such as the cost of the machine and the revenue generated from the sale of the output. However, the identification of cash flow costs and benefits that are relevant to a project's appraisal are not always obvious.

Guiding rules

A set of 'guiding rules' will be used to outline the most important points and then a comprehensive example will be used to illustrate their application.

Rule 1: All costs incurred (and revenues generated) *prior* to the investment appraisal decision should be excluded. They are *sunk costs* in that they are unaffected by the investment decision under appraisal.

As an example, suppose a company has spent £100,000 undertaking research (R and D) in order to develop a new product. They have now reached the stage where they need to take a decision on whether to invest in manufacturing facilities for the new product. In this investment appraisal, the £100,000 spent on R and D is a sunk cost and so is irrelevant to the decision to be made.

To see how misleading it could be to include the R and D expenditure, suppose the manufacturing equipment costs £500,000 and the product is expected to produce net revenues of £580,000. (For this simple example, we will ignore any discounting.) If the sunk costs were ignored the decision would be to 'accept', but if the sunk costs were included in the analysis, the decision would be to reject:

Sunk cost excluded		*Sunk cost included*	
Cost	: −£500,000	Cost	: −£500,000
Net revenues	: +£580,000	R and D expenses	: −£100,000
'Profit'	: +£ 80,000	Net revenues	: +£580,000
Decision	: Accept	'Loss'	: −£ 20,000
		Decision	: Reject

The point here is that if the company accepts the project, at least they have the £80,000 'profit' to offset the £100,000 spent on R and D. If they reject the project they are simply left with a £100,000 R and D expense.

Rule 2: Ignore depreciation charges. Depreciation is a non-cash flow and so does not enter into the NPV cash flow analysis.

Rule 3: Ignore all financing cash flows (e.g. interest charges, loan repayments, dividends, etc) and all their tax effects (e.g. interest tax relief and advance corporation tax (ACT)). This is because, as was seen in the previous section, these are all implicitly taken into account through the discounting process.[7]

Rule 4: Ignore all *non-incremental* cash flows. This is the more general case of Rule 1. What should be included in an NPV analysis are only those cash flows that arise because of the project. Any cash flow that would arise whether or not the project was undertaken should be excluded.

An example of Rule 4's application would be *allocated* fixed costs. If a company normally allocated a particular proportion of its fixed Head Office costs to any new project, as part of its budgeting/costing process, these should be excluded from the investment appraisal. They would be cash flows that are non-incremental to the investment decision in that the

Head Office costs would still be incurred whether or not the project was accepted.

Rule 5: This concerns the cost, to the project, of using resources (usually raw materials) that the firm already holds in stock. Here there are three possible 'costs':

(i) Original purchase price/historic cost.
(ii) Current replacment cost.
(iii) Resale value or disposal cost.

The first of these is *never* relevant. The historic cost of the raw material stock is a sunk cost. However, which of the other two costs is relevant depends upon the particular circumstances.

Where the resources held in stock are used elsewhere in the company, then the cost to the project of using them is their replacement cost. This is because if the resources are used on the project, then those stocks will have to be replaced. Hence the current replacement cost is the *opportunity cost*[8] of their use.

If the resources already held in stock have no other use in the company, than their use on the project, they will not be replaced. (Such a situation might arise through, say, the company using those particular resources in the past but no longer doing so, although some surplus stocks still remain.) Under these circumstances, if the stocks have a re-sale value then their re-sale value would be the (opportunity) cost to the project of their use. (The company, in using them on the project, foregoes the opportunity to sell them off.) If they only have a disposal cost, then their use on the project would *save* these costs. Hence the project would be credited with a benefit – or cash inflow – the saved disposal cost.

Rule 6: This concerns the use, by the project, of resources already in use with the company and where the company cannot obtain further supplies of those resources. In other words, this is the situation where the project utilizes 'scarce' or limited resources. The rule is that the cost of their use on the project is their *total* opportunity cost.

As an example, suppose that there is a shortage of well-qualified mining engineers. A mining company at present employs 100 mining engineers and they are all fully utilized undertaking various projects. The company is now considering the development of an additional mine which would require 5 mining engineers. Because of the shortage of such staff, they cannot recruit any more, and so, if they undertook the new mining project, the engineers would have to be taken away from their existing tasks elsewhere in the company.

Suppose that each engineer is currently contributing £80,000 per year to the company's profits (i.e. revenue generated, less the engineer's salary, less the material and incremental costs incurred, equals £80,000). This will be lost if the company re-deploys the engineer onto the new project: it would be the *internal* opportunity cost of using each engineer on the new project.

Thus the *total* cost of each engineer used on the new project would be the foregone contribution (the internal opportunity cost) *plus* the engineer's salary (the external opportunity cost or, the *market price* of the scarce resource).

An example

Some of these rules are now illustrated in Example 6.5.

Example 6.5

Radiometric PLC has been offered a contract to manufacture six special communication systems for the government. Manufacture would take a total of three years at a rate of two machines per year. Payment would be in two instalments: £350,000 at the start of manufacture and another £350,000 upon completion.

The company is now evaluating the contract to see if it is worthwhile undertaking, and its management accounting department have produced the following estimates about the resources required to produce the special communication systems:

1 *Materials*

Type of material	*Quantity per system* tons	*Amount in stock now* tons	*Original cost of stock per ton* £	*Current purchase price per ton* £	*Current realizable value per ton* £
Copper	20	60	700	1,000	800
Radium	10	20	500	750	See below

Copper is used regularly by the company on many contracts. Radium is used rarely and if the existing stock is not applied to this contract it will have to be disposed of immediately at a net cost of £100 per ton. Materials required for the contract must be purchased and paid for annually in advance. Replacement cost of copper and radium and the realizable value of copper are expected to increase at an annual compound rate of 20%.

2 *Labour*

Each of the six systems will require 3,000 hours of skilled electronic engineering and 5,000 hours of unskilled labour. Current wage rates are £4 per hour for skilled electronic engineers and £3 per hour for unskilled labour.

Radiometric expects to suffer a shortage of skilled electronic engineers during the first year so that acceptance of the contract would make it necessary for the firm to give up other work on which a contribution of £7 per hour would be earned. (The 'other work' would require no unskilled labour.)

Again, in the contract's first year only, the company expects to have 20,000 surplus unskilled labour hours. Radiometric has an agreement with the in-house trade union whereby it lays off employees for whom there is no work and pays them two-thirds of their normal wages during the lay-off period.

All wage rates are expected to increase at an annual compound rate of 15%.

3 *Overheads*
Overhead costs are currently allocated to contracts at a rate of £14 per skilled electronic engineer, calculated as follows:

	£
Fixed overheads (including equipment depreciation of £5)	11·00
Variable overheads	3·00
	£14·00

Special equipment will be required to undertake this contract, and will be purchased at a cost of £200,000 payable immediately. It will be sold once the contract is completed for £50,000. Both fixed and variable overheads are expected to increase in line with the Retail Price Index.

The special equipment will be financed with the first contract instalment paid by the government.

Radiometric have considerable experience in manufacturing this type of equipment and believe that a return of 20% would be available elsewhere on the capital market for a similar risk investment. The Retail Price Index is expected to increase by 15% per year over the life of the contract.

It can be assumed that all current prices will hold for the next 12 months, before increasing in line with inflation. Therefore the material costs incurred for the second year's production will be 20% higher than the current market prices. Also it can be assumed that all cash flows arise on the last day of the year to which they relate, unless otherwise stated. Taxation should be ignored for the purposes of this evaluation (to simplify the analysis).

Project Cash Flows (£000s)

Year	*0*	*1*	*2*	*3*
Revenues	+350			+350
Equipment cost	−200			
Scrap value				+ 50
Copper cost	− 40	− 48	− 57·6	
Radium cost	+ 2	− 18	− 21·6	
Elec. Engin. cost		− 66	− 27·6	− 31·7
Unskilled labour		− 10	− 34·5	− 39·7
Variable o/hs.		− 18	− 20·7	− 23·0
Net Cash Flow	+112	−160	−162	+305·6
20% discount factor	×1	×·8333	×·6944	×·5787
PV Cash Flow	+112	−133·3	−112·5	+176·8

Contract's NPV: +£43,000 Therefore it is worth undertaking.

Cont.

Data calculations

1 Materials.

Copper	Year 1:	Use 40 tons from stock. As this will have to be replaced, its cost is the current purchase price of £1,000 per ton.
	Year 2:	Buy in 40 tons at £1,000 (1.20) = £1,200 per ton.
	Year 3:	Buy in 40 tons at £1,000 $(1.20)^2$ = £1,440 per ton.
Radium	Year 1:	Use 20 tons from stock. This will *save* a disposal cost of £100 per ton. (Opportunity benefit).
	Year 2:	Buy in 20 tons at £750 (1.20) = £900 per ton.
	Year 3:	Buy in 20 tons at £750 $(1.20)^2$ = £1,080 per ton.

2 Labour: 6,000 hours of skilled engineers required per year.
10,000 hours of unskilled labour required per year.

Skilled	Year 1:	6000 hours taken from elsewhere in the company. Cost is wage rate plus lost contribution: £4 + £7 = £11 per hour.
	Year 2:	Hire 6,000 hours at £4 (1.15) = £4.60 per hour.
	Year 3:	Hire 6,000 hours at £4 $(1.15)^2$ = £5.29 per hour.
Unskilled	Year 1:	Utilize 10,000 hours of surplus labour. Cost is the *incremental* wages paid: £1 per hour.
	Year 2:	Hire 10,000 hours at £3 (1.15) = £3.45 per hour.
	Year 3:	Hire 10,000 hours at £3 $(1.15)^2$ = £3.97 per hour.

3 Overheads.

Fixed: Exclude as non-incremental.
Depreciation: Exclude as non-cash flow.

Variable	Year 1:	£3 per skilled labour hour.
	Year 2:	£3 (1.15) = £3.45 per skilled labour hour.
	Year 3:	£3 $(1.15)^2$ = £3.97 per skilled labour hour.

SUMMARY

Having concluded in the previous chapter that of the four basic investment appraisal techniques, only one – the NPV – was satisfactory, this chapter then turned to examine some of the possible problems that may be encountered with the application of NPV: inflation, taxation and relevant project cash flows. The main points made are as follows:

- Inflation is not the cause of the time value of money, but it does affect its value through the Fisher Effect relationship.

- The simplest approach to take in an investment appraisal in an inflationary environment is to discount a project's actual *money* cash flows by the market (or money) discount rate to NPV.
- *Real* cash flows should not be confused with cash flows in *current* terms. *Real* refers to expressing an actual money cash flow in current *general* purchasing power terms. This will only be the same as a cash flow in current terms if the latter is expected to inflate at the *general* rate of inflation.[9]
- With taxation, there are three impacts on project appraisal:
  - ☐ Tax relief on capital expenditure.
  - ☐ Tax charge on the project's profit.
  - ☐ Tax effects on the project's financing method: tax relief on debt interest and/or ACT liability caused by dividends.
- The approach to use is to evaluate the after-tax project cash flows with the after-tax discount rate. The after-tax project cash flows take account of the capital expenditure tax relief and the tax charge on the project's profit. The third tax impact is taken into account through the after-tax discount rate.
- As far as the relevant project cash flows are concerned, an investment appraisal should only include the *incremental* cash flows. This is the key concept. Any cash flows that have already occurred prior to the investment decision, or any subsequent cash flows that will occur whether or not the project is undertaken, are irrelevant.
- In addition, use has to be made of the opportunity cost concept to ensure that the *full* costs and benefits of undertaking the project are captured in the investment appraisal.

APPENDIX: THE UK CORPORATE TAX SYSTEM

This appendix briefly outlines the basics of the UK corporate tax system as it affects investment appraisal. In no way does it purport to represent a complete analysis. However, some familiarity with the tax regime is necessary in order to be able to appreciate how it is likely to impact on project appraisal.

1 Company 'profits' are taxed at a rate of 35% and the tax is paid approximately one year in arrears.
2 Profit can be defined as: revenues less allowable costs. Within these costs depreciation is not an allowable cost, not are dividend payments or working capital expenses. However, interest payments are an allowable cost. Most normal business expenses such as labour, materials and overhead costs are allowable against tax.
3 As a substitute for depreciation, writing down allowances are allowable costs. These are calculated annually at a rate of 25% of the reducing value of the capital expenditure. (Notice in the WDA calculations in example 6.4, the tax relief was taken into account *separately*. It could have been incorporated into the 'taxable profit' calculations.

4 If a company pays out a dividend, this has the effect of bringing forward part of the corporation tax payment. That part of the corporation tax liability that is bought forward for immediate payment is known as Advance Corporation Tax (ACT) and that which remains payable 12 months after year-end is known as Mainstream Corporation Tax.

The amount of ACT payable is determined by:

$$\text{Cash dividend paid} \times \frac{25}{100 - 25}$$

where 25 represents the 25% standard personal income tax rate. Therefore, for example:

		£
Revenues for year	:	10,000
less allowable costs	:	5,500
less WDA	:	1,200
equals: Taxable profit	:	3,300
Corporation tax at 35%	:	1,155
After-tax profit	:	2,145
Dividend paid	:	1,600
Retained profit	:	545

$$\text{ACT: £1,600} \times \frac{25}{100 - 25} = \text{£533·33}$$

Corporation tax liability	:	£1,155·00	
less ACT	:	£ 533·33	(payable immediately)
Mainstream corporation tax	:	£ 621·67	(payable in 12 months)

However, it should be remembered that, as far as investment appraisal is concerned, all financing cash flows and their tax effects are ignored.

Therefore, interest would not be included as an expense in computing the corporation tax liability for investment appraisal purposes and it would be assumed that the *entire* corporation tax liability would be paid 12 months after year-end. The interest tax relief and the ACT timing effect are taken into account in the use of the *after-tax* discount rate.

NOTES

1 Alternatively, the cash flows could be shown as:

Year	0	1	2	3
Loan from bank	+1,000			
Interest		−100	−100	−100
Loan repayment				−1,000
Capital expenditure	−1,000			
Net revenue		+450	+450	+450
Net cash flow	0	+350	+350	−650

but the net effect is the same.

2 Actually, using 4-figure discount tables the NPV is + 119·08, but the difference between the two NPVs is solely brought about through rounding error.
3 Again the two-pence difference is caused by rounding error in the discount factors used.

4 This value is referred to as the 'balancing allowance'.

5 This value is referred to as the 'balancing charge'.

6 Notice how tax produces a non-conventional cash flow and hence multiple IRRs.

7 There are two important possible exceptions to this rule. One is in a special investment appraisal situation: the *lease versus purchase* decision. The other is in the case of *overseas project appraisal.* Both topics will be covered at a later stage.

8 The concept of 'opportunity cost' is important in all forms of economic analysis. See the suggested reading.

9 An example might help to make this statement clear. Suppose the current wage rate is £5 per hour and we require 100 hours of labour at Year 2. Therefore the Year 2 labour cost in *current* terms is £500. This may or may not equal the Year 2 labour cost in *real* terms, depending upon the inflation rate of labour costs. If labour costs inflate at 10% per year and the RPI is also inflating at 10% per year, the current labour cost will equal the real cost. But if labour costs inflate up at a different rate to the RPI, then the two things are not equal:

(a) Labour inflates up at 10% per year.
RPI inflates up at 10% per year.
Actual Year 2 cash flow: £500 $(1{\cdot}10)^2$ = £605
Real Year 2 cash flow: £605 $(1{\cdot}10)^{-2}$ = £500
Current Year 2 labour cost = £500

(b) Labour inflates up at 15% per year.
RPI inflates up at 10% per year.
Actual Year 2 cash flow: £500 $(1{\cdot}15)^2$ = £661·25
Real Year 2 cash flow: £661·25 $(1{\cdot}10)^{-2}$ = £546·46
Current Year 2 labour cost = £500

FURTHER READING

1 A good overview article on the problem of inflation and capital investment appraisal is: N.J. Coulthurst, 'Accounting for Inflation in Capital Investment: State of the Art and Science', *Accounting and Business Research*, Winter 1986.
2 Other interesting articles include: B. Carsberg and A. Hope, 'Business Investment Decisions Under Inflation: Theory and Practice', *ICAEW* 1976; A. Rappaport and R.A. Taggart, 'Evaluation of Capital Expenditure Proposals Under Inflation', *Financial Management*, Spring 1982; M.K. Kim, 'Inflationary Effects in the Capital Investment Process', *Journal of Finance*, September 1979; and S–N. Chan, 'Capital Budgeting and Uncertain Inflation', *Journal of Economics and Business*, August 1984.

3 For an interesting introduction to the UK tax system in overview, see J.A. Kay and M.A. King, *The British Tax System*, Oxford University Press. Also of interest is L.D. Schall, 'Taxes, Inflation and Corporate Financial Policy', *Journal of Finance*, March 1984.
4 Finally, on the whole area of relevant cash flows and opportunity costs see: L. Amey, 'On Opportunity Costs and Decision Making', *Accountancy*, July 1961; J.R. Gould, 'Opportunity Costs: the London Tradition', in *Debits, Credits, Finance and Profits*, H.C. Edey and B.S. Yamey (eds.), Sweet and Maxwell 1974; and N.J. Coulthurst, 'The Application of the Incremental Principle in Capital Investment Project Evaluation', *Accounting and Business Research*, Autumn 1986.

QUICKIE QUESTIONS

1 If the market interest rate is 13% and the general rate of inflation is 4%, what is the real interest rate?
2 What approaches can be taken to an NPV investment appraisal in inflationary conditions?
3 What is a *real* cash flow?
4 Rent is paid each year. This year's rent has just been paid, it was £10,000. How much rent will need to be paid in 2 years' time if:
(a) the rent remains constant in real terms;
(b) the rent remains constant in money terms.

And, in each of the above cases, what is the PV of the Year 2 rent? Assume that the market discount rate is 15½% and the RPI is 5% per year.
5 A machine costs £500 and has a three-year life and a zero scrap value. It is bought on the first day of the accounting year. What are the amounts of WDA tax relief received if the corporation tax rate is 35%, paid 12 months in arrears, and the WDAs are calculated as 25% of the reducing balance?
6 A company owns a machine which is presently lying unused in the factory. The machine was bought 5 years ago at a cost of £60,000 and has now been depreciated down to a book value of £10,000. It could be sold now for £3,000. Alternatively it could be rented out for a year at £2,500. The company's chief engineer believes the machine will be totally obsolete in 12 months' time and would then have a scrap value of £800. The company is considering using the machine to undertake a one-year project. If it did, the machine's scrap value at the end of the year, net of dismantling costs, would be zero. Ignoring the time value of money, what is the cost of using the machine on the project?
7 What is the approach used to handling tax in investment appraisal?
8 Why should *allocated* fixed costs be excluded from project cash flows in an NPV analysis?
9 A company pays an annual rent of £20,000 for its factory of 10,000 m^2. All space is fully utilized and no more space is available for rent. Each square metre of space generates a contribution of £15. A project

is being considered that would require 150 m^2 of factory space. What would be the cost, to the project, of that space?

PROBLEMS

1 Sanglo Radios PLC is considering buying a machine to make printed circuit boards. The machine costs £1.2 m and will last for five years. Scrap value of these machines is £200,000. An investment of £150,000 in working capital will be needed initially. The accountant has prepared the following estimated annual trading account for the project:

	£
Sales	1,400,000
Materials	(300,000)
Labour	(500,000)
Depreciation	(200,000)
Allocated fixed overheads	(250,000)
Annual profit	£150,000

The machine would be financed with a four-year term loan from Barclays Bank at an interest rate of 3½% over base. Currently, the bank base rate is 8%. The interest payments attract tax relief.

The machine would be bought on the last day of the company's previous fiscal year and would attract a 25% writing down allowance. Corporation tax is payable at 35%, one year after year-end.

The company believes that 10% would be the minimum after tax return acceptable from a project with this level of risk and, if that return is achieved, then they will be able to increase dividends to shareholders by £50,000 a year over each of the next five years.

Required:
Calculate the project's net present value.

2 Sparrow Ltd is a construction company based in the South West of England. Mr and Mrs Hawk each own 50% of the company's issued share capital. The company's latest accounts show a balance sheet value for share capital and reserves of £250,000 and an annual turnover of £1.25 million.

The company has recently been offered two contracts, both of which would commence almost immediately and last for two years. Neither contract can be delayed. The prices offered are £700,000 for contract 1 and £680,000 for contract 2, payable in each case, at the contract's completion. The skilled labour force of Sparrow is committed during the coming year to the extent that sufficient skilled labour will be available to support only one of the two contracts. Due to a shortage in the area, the company will not be able to expand its skilled labour force in the foreseeable future. If necessary, Sparrow could subcontract one entire contract, but not both, to a nearby company, Kestrel Ltd, which is of a similar size to Sparrow. If one contract were subcontracted, all work would be undertaken by Kestrel subject to regular checks of progress and quality by Mr Hawk. Kestrel has quoted prices of £490,000 for contract 1 and £530,000 for contract 2, payable in either case by two equal instalments, half at the start of the contract and the remainder at the end of the first year.

Sparrow maintains a standard costing system and normally prices contracts on a cost-plus basis. Total cost is calculated by adding to direct costs 60% for overheads, this percentage being based on previous experience. A target price is then calculated by adding a 25% profit mark-up to total cost. Mrs Hawk has calculated the following target prices for the two contracts under consideration:

	Contract 1	*Contract 2*
	£	£
Materials: Special materials (at original cost)	50,000	–
Other materials (at standard cost)	200,000	240,000
Labour: Skilled (at standard cost)	80,000	80,000
Unskilled (at standard cost)	112,000	126,000
Direct costs	442,000	446,000
Overheads: 60% of direct costs	265,200	267,600
Total cost	707,200	713,600
Profit mark-up: 25% of total cost	176,800	178,400
Target price	£884,000	£892,000

The following additional information is available:

Materials: Contract 1 would require the immediate use of special materials which were purchased one year ago at a cost of £50,000 for a contract which was not completed because the customer went into liquidation. These special materials have a current purchase price of £60,000 and a current realizable value of £30,000. The company foresees no alternative use for these special materials. Usage of the other materials would be spread evenly between the two years of each contract's duration. These other materials are all used regularly by the company. Their standard costs reflect current purchase prices which are expected to continue at the present level for the next 12 months. In the following year, prices are expected to rise by 10%.

Labour: Skilled labour costs for each contract represent 8,000 hours each year for two years at a standard cost of £5 per hour. Unskilled labour hours required are 16,000 hours per annum for contract 1 and 18,000 hours per annum for contract 2, in each case at a standard cost of £3.50 per hour. Standard costs are based on current wage rates. Hourly wage costs for both skilled and unskilled labour are expected to increase by 5% in the current year and then by a further 10% in the following year.

Overheads: An analysis of the most recent accounts of Sparrow shows that total overheads may be categorized as follows:

Fixed administrative and office costs	60%
Depreciation of plant and equipment	30%
Costs which vary directly with direct costs	10%
	100%

Fixed administrative and office costs are expected to increase as a result of inflation by 5% in the current year, and by a further 10% in the following year.

Sparrow expects to have sufficient surplus plant and equipment capacity during the next two years for either contract 1 or contract 2.

Sparrow has a money cost of capital of 10% per annum in the current year. Mr Hawk expects this to increase to 15% per annum in the second year of the contract.

Assume that all payments will arise on the last day of the year to which they relate, except where otherwise stated.

Required:

Provide calculations, on the basis of the estimates given, showing whether Sparrow should accept either or both contracts and which one, if any, should be subcontracted to Kestrel.

3 Bailey PLC is developing a new product, the Oakman, to replace an established product, the Shepard, which the company has marketed successfully for a number of years. Production of the Shepard will cease in one year whether or not the Oakman is manufactured. Bailey PLC has recently spent £75,000 on research and development relating to the Oakman. Production of the Oakman can start in one year's time.

Demand for the Oakman is expected to be 5,000 units per annum for the first three years of production and 2,500 units per annum for the subsequent two years. The product's total life is expected to be five years.

Estimated unit revenues and costs for the Oakman, at current prices, are as follows:

	£	£
Selling price per unit		35·00
less Costs per units:		
Materials and other consumables	8·00	
Labour (see (a) below)	6·00	
Machine depreciation and overhaul (see (b) below)	12·50	
Other overheads (see (c) below)	9·00	
		35·50
Loss per unit		0·50

(a) Each Oakman requires two hours of labour, paid £3 per hour at current prices. The labour force required to produce Oakmans comprises six employees, who are at present employed to produce Shepards. If the Oakman is not produced, these employees will be made redundant when production of the Shepard ceases. If the Oakman is produced, three of the employees will be made redundant at the end of the third year of its life, when demand halves, but the company expects to be able to find work for the remaining three employees at the end of the Oakman's five year life. Any employee who is made redundant will receive a redundancy payment equivalent to 1,000 hours' wages, based on the most recent wage rate at the time of the redundancy.

(b) A special machine will be required to produce the Oakman. It will be purchased in one year's time (just before production begins). The current price of the machine is £190,000. It is expected to last for five years and to have no scrap or resale value at the end of that time. A major overhaul of the machine will be necessary at the end of the second year of its life. At current prices, the overhaul will cost £60,000. As the machine will not produce the same quantity of Oakmans each year, the directors of Bailey PLC have decided to spread its original cost and the cost of the overhaul equally between all Oakmans expected to be produced (i.e. 20,000 units). Hence the combined charge per unit for depreciation and overhaul is £12·50 ([£190,000 + £60,000] ÷ 20,000 units).

(c) Other overheads at current prices comprise variable overheads of £4·00 per unit and head office fixed costs of £5·00 per unit, allotted on the basis of labour time.

All wage rates are expected to increase at an annual compound rate of 15%. Selling price per unit and all costs other than labour are expected to increase in line with the Retail Price Index. The Retail Price Index is expected to increase in the future at an annual compound rate of 10%.

Corporation tax at 35% on net cash income is payable in full one year after the income arises. A 25% writing down allowance is available on the machine which will be bought on the first day of the company's accounting year. Bailey PLC has a money cost of capital, net of corporation tax, of 20% per annum.

Assume that all receipts and payments will arise on the last day of the year to which they relate. Assume also that all 'current prices' given above have been operative for one year and are due to change shortly. Subsequently all prices will change annually.

Required:

(a) Prepare calculations, with explanations, showing whether Bailey should undertake production of the Oakman.

(b) Discuss the particular investment appraisal problems created by the existence of high rates of inflation.

7
Capital market imperfections

Chapter Contents

CAPITAL RATIONING

In Chapter 3 we set up a single-period investment-consumption model to use as a guide to effective financial investment appraisal. The model was a crude and unrealistic simplification of the real world, but it was used so that the underlying principles of investment decisions could be examined without becoming embroiled in elaborate complications (such as the existence of taxation, inflation and an uncertain future). In addition, a time horizon of only one time period was used so that the conclusions could be presented graphically rather than algebraically.

We saw that neither payback nor ROCE/ARR were satisfactory investment appraisal rules in terms of the Hirshleifer analysis as they did not lead to the firm optimally locating onto the physical investment line. In contrast, both the DCF techniques – NPV and IRR – did lead the firm to locate optimally.

However, a closer examination of the IRR method uncovered a number of problems with its use and so, at the end of Chapter 5, we were able to conclude that the NPV decision rule was the only one of the four investment appraisal techniques which would consistently lead to investment decisions being taken that would help maximize shareholder wealth. Even so, the NPV decision rule required the assumption of a perfect capital market.

In this chapter we are going to examine what happens to the NPV decision rule when a perfect capital market doesn't exist. In particular, we are going to examine the case where the company may not be able to undertake all the positive NPV projects it has discovered because of a shortage of capital investment funds. This particular capital market imperfection is known as *capital rationing.*

Capital market borrowing

A great deal of attention, in both the applied and theoretical literature, has been paid to the problem of capital rationing but, even so, there is no general agreement on what precisely is meant by the term, and this has resulted in a great deal of confusion. In an effort to avoid adding to this, it is important that we explicitly state from the outset what we shall take to be the meaning of capital rationing.

From the viewpoint of the making of investment decisions by financial management within companies, capital rationing is a *managerial* problem. It is, most certainly, a theoretical problem for our decision making model but, more importantly, it is also a practical problem.

Up to this point, we have followed the NPV investment appraisal rule because it is most likely to indicate (in a practical sense) consistently good investment decisions. In its basic form the NPV decision rule is: accept all projects whose cash flows, when discounted by the market interest rate and then summated, have a positive or zero net present value. Such projects are acceptable because they yield a return that is either greater than (+ NPV), or at least equal to (0 NPV) the return that is available on the capital market for a similar risk investment (which is defined by the rate of discount used).

Therefore, in terms of opportunity cost, the discount rule can be viewed as the minimum return that management must earn from investing shareholders' money in physical investment opportunities. It represents the minimum acceptable rate of return because it is the return that shareholders themselves can earn by placing their money in *financial* investment opportunities (i.e., investing on the capital market). Hence management should not invest shareholders' money to earn a lower rate of return than can be obtained on the capital market.

Implicit in the NPV decision rule is the idea that as long as a company's management can find investment opportunities that yield at least the capital market return (i.e., they satisfy the NPV decision rule), then capital will be available to finance them. This is because investing borrowed funds in projects with non-negative NPVs ensures that the project will yield a return that will at least be sufficient to repay the borrowed capital plus interest. In terms of the single-period investment–consumption diagram, this implies that if a company identifies so many acceptable projects (i.e., + or 0 NPV) that the company's existing resources at t_0 provide insufficient investment capital to undertake them all, then *additional* finance can be borrowed from the capital market.

In Figure 7.1, OA represents the company's existing resources at t_0 and AB represents the physical investment line. The point of tangency between the physical and financial investment lines is at point C.

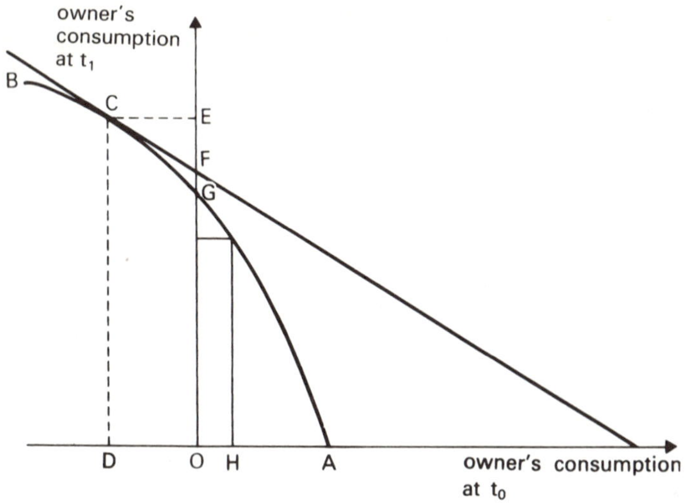

Figure 7.1

Therefore the company has identified acceptable projects that require a total investment outlay at t_0 of AD. As the company's existing resources only amount to OA, OD will have to be borrowed from the capital market.

The investment AD undertaken at t_0 will produce a cash inflow at t_1 of OE. The amount required to repay the loan, plus interest, is given by EF, leaving an amount OF for shareholders. Notice what the net result has been of borrowing on the capital market by the company. Without borrowing, the maximum amount of cash that could have been generated at t_1 would have been OG; but with borrowing (and hence undertaking additional physical investment), the company has been able to increase the t_1 cash flow available to the owner by the amount FG.

Capital rationing

The term 'capital rationing' refers to the situation where the implicit assumption within the NPV decision rule, that capital will always be available to finance acceptable projects, *does not hold.* For example, using the situation as found in Figure 7.1, suppose that the company could *not* raise OD on the capital market, then a situation of capital rationing would exist: acceptable projects requiring a total outlay of AD had been identified, but they cannot all be accepted because only OA of finance is available. Management have therefore to 'ration out' this limited amount of investment capital amongst the available projects.

It should be clear from the above that the existence of capital rationing need not only apply to externally raised funds. For example, not only may the company not be able to raise any capital market finance, but the shareholders (in the example used in Figure 7.1) may be unwilling to allow the company to invest the *whole* of OA. Suppose that for some reason the maximum that shareholders will allow to be applied to physical investments is AH. Then the company has an even tighter capital constraint than before: only AH of capital available, although they have identified acceptable projects which require a total of AD of capital.

It should be clear from the above that the existence of capital rationing represents a capital market imperfection: investment funds are no longer freely available at the market rate of return. The reasons why such capital rationing may occur in practice are many and varied, but in the context of our analysis they are only of passing interest. The point that we wish to examine is, given a situation of capital rationing, how does it affect the efficiency of the investment decision advice given by the NPV appraisal technique and can NPV be adapted to operate successfully in such situations?

Hard and soft capital rationing

Two types or classes of capital rationing are usually specified: 'hard' capital rationing (which has received the lion's share of attention in the literature but which is probably of little importance in practice, as far as investment decisions in companies are concerned), and 'soft' capital rationing.

Hard capital rationing describes the situation where forces external to the company, usually either the capital market itself or the government (which may or may not act through the capital market), will not supply unlimited amounts of investment capital to a company, even though the company has identified investment opportunities which would be able to produce the required return. Soft capital rationing arises from forces internal to a company, such as a capital budget, which limits the amount of capital available for investment. In certain situations and in certain cases, the distinction between hard and soft capital rationing and between the various different causes of hard rationing may be important for the analysis. Where they are, such a distinction shall be made, but for the moment we shall concentrate on the problems which capital rationing *per se* causes for investment appraisal.

An example

In a situation where capital rationing is non-existent (and hence we are assuming a perfect capital market), investment decision making involves a comparison between the investment funds being applied to the particular investment under consideration and their being applied to a similar risk capital market investment, because this latter alternative reflects the opportunity cost of undertaking the investment. With the introduction of capital rationing, choice is still involved, but the alternative to the application of capital to a proposed investment project is not *necessarily* the capital market investment, but may instead be another of the firm's investment projects.

In other words, the opportunity cost of undertaking a particular investment is now not necessarily reflected in the capital market rate of return, but may be a higher value, represented by the return yielded by another project which could not be undertaken by the company because the supply of capital is limited. An example can help illustrate the point.

Suppose a company has discovered two independent projects, A and B. Each requires £500 of investment capital, and Project A yields a return[1] of 12% whereas B yields a return of 15%. If the company's cost of capital were 10% and funds were unlimited, both projects would be accepted because both would have positive NPVs. The acceptance procedure, using the NPV method, would involve the comparison of the return given by each project *in turn* with the return available on the capital market.

However, if capital rationing exists, and the company's investment funds are limited to a *total* of £500, then a different decision process is required. The company must now choose, *not* between each project and the capital market return, but first between the two projects themselves and then, once it is decided which is the best project, compare its return with the alternative given by the capital market. Thus in a non-rationing situation the company would be making two decisions: accept/reject Project A, accept/reject Project B; whilst in a rationing situation they would be making one, two-stage decision: select Project A or B, then accept/reject the selected project.

SINGLE-PERIOD CAPITAL RATIONING

It appears at first sight that capital rationing involves little more than another type of the 'mutually exclusive projects' decision, which we dealt with earlier. In fact, as we shall see, the existence of capital rationing produces a much more difficult decision problem.

Most readers will be familiar with the idea of a budget as a means of planning and control[2] and so, for the sake of presenting a clear argument, we shall assume that for each decision period (say, a year), management have a capital budget within which to keep, i.e., total capital expenditure must not exceed some stated upper limit: the capital budget or (to avoid terminology confusion) the capital constraint. Therefore we shall assume a *soft* rationing situation, but the conclusions we derive will be equally applicable to hard rationing.

Let us begin with the most simple and straightforward capital rationing problem: a situation where capital is rationed at present (i.e., t_0) but will be freely available in the future – a rather unlikely situation in practice – or one where the collection of investment projects the company wishes to appraise involve capital outlays *only* in the current period (i.e., the capital outlay required for the project does not extend over more than one point in time). In addition, it is assumed that projects are infinitely divisible, so that fractions of projects may be undertaken, and that they exhibit constant returns scale.

In such a situation, only a slight modification to the standard NPV decision rule is required. Each investment opportunity should have its expected future cash flows discounted to net present value by the appropriate market discount rate. This NPV is then expressed as a ratio of the capital outlay which the project requires in the rationed time period, and is often termed the *benefit–cost ratio.*

All projects which have a positive or zero benefit–cost ratio would normally be accepted in a non-rationed situation. However, because capital rationing exists and a choice has to be made between the alternative projects, they should be ranked in order of decreasing benefit–cost ratio. Starting with the project with the largest (positive) ratio and working down the rankings, as many projects as possible (with positive or zero ratios) should be accepted, until all the available capital is allocated.

An example of benefit-cost ratios

The following example shows this decision method in operation. It assumes that capital rationing will only exist in the current time period (Year 0), all the projects are independent and divisible, and exhibit constant returns to scale and none can be delayed.

In a non-rationing situation all the projects in Table 7.1 would be accepted, except for Project F which has a negative NPV when discounted at the market interest rate. In order to undertake them all, the company would require a total of £460 of capital now (Year 0) and this would produce a total NPV of £283·09. Therefore acceptance of Projects A to E would cause shareholders' wealth to rise by £283·09.

Suppose that capital rationing exists at Year 0 (but not in Years 1 to 4) and as a result the company has only £300 of investment capital available. It therefore cannot undertake all of the five positive NPV projects. Which projects should be selected to be undertaken? Table 7.2 ranks the projects in decreasing order of benefit–cost ratio. (Note in particular, how project B's benefit–cost ratio is calculated. Although B requires two capital outlays, at Year 0 and Year 1, the ratio concerns the NPV and the outlay in the *rationed* time period only. Hence the denominator of the ratio is simply B's Year 0 outlay.)

The table shows that the £300 of available capital should be applied to Projects E, D, A and one third of Project B. This gives the company for its £300 capital outlay, a total positive NPV of £223·17, which is the maximum possible total NPV, given the capital expenditure constraint. Therefore, because investment capital is scarce shareholder wealth will only rise by £223·17 as a result of the investment decisions made, rather than by the possible total of £283·09. Thus, we can see that, as far as shareholders are concerned, there is a definite cost to capital rationing. In this case, because of the presence of capital rationing, shareholders'

Table 7.1

Year	*0*	*1*	*2*	*3*	*4*	*NPV when discounted at 10%*
A	−100	+20	+ 40	+ 60	+ 80	⇒ +50·96
B	−150	−50	+100	+100	+140	⇒ +57·94
C	− 60	+20	+ 40	+ 40	–	⇒ +21·29
D	−100	+60	+ 60	+100	–	⇒ +79·26
E	− 50	+20	+ 40	+ 60	+ 40	⇒ +73·64
F	−100	+30	+ 30	+ 30	+ 30	⇒ − 4·91

Table 7.2

Project	*NPV* / *Yr 0 Outlay*	=	*Benefit–cost Ratio*	*Ranking*
A	50·96/100	=	+0·51	3
B	57·94/150	=	+0·39	4
C	21·29/60	=	+0·35	5
D	79·26/100	=	+0·79	2
E	73·64/50	=	+1·47	1
F	−4·91/100	=	−0·05	6

Project	*Benefit–cost ranking*	*Outlay Yr 0*	
E	1	50	ACCEPT: E, D, A, $\frac{1}{3}$B
D	2	100	
A	3	100	
B	4	150	
C	5	60	
*F	—	100	

* Note that in this simple type of rationing situation, Project F would never be accepted because it has a negative benefit–cost ratio.

$$\text{Total NPV} = £73{\cdot}64 + £79{\cdot}26 + £50{\cdot}96 + \tfrac{1}{3}(£57{\cdot}94) = £223{\cdot}17$$

wealth will be approximately £60 below the value it would have otherwise attained.

However, given the situation specified, the process of selecting projects on the basis of their benefit–cost ratios ensures that the company will maximize the total amount of positive NPV gained from the available projects, assuming limited investment capital. This is because the terms in which the benefit–cost ratio focuses attention on the size of a project's NPV are not absolute but *relative* to the scarce resources required to undertake it. In other words, projects are ranked in order of preference, in terms of the NPV they produce, for every unit (i.e., £1) of the limited investment capital which they require. In the example used above, Project A is preferred to Project B (even though B has the larger total NPV) because it produces 51 p of (positive) NPV for every £1 of the scarce investment capital applied to its undertaking in Year 0, whereas Project B only produces 39 p of NPV per £1 of investment outlay.

A further example

Example 7.1 is divided up into two separate single-period capital rationing situations. In the first situation there is straightforward Year 0 rationing. However, it is in the second situation that a further element is added to the analysis. This shows that the standard NPV decision rule for independent projects: accept all non-negative NPV projects, breaks-down in capital rationing situations. This means not only will some positive NPV projects (like project B in Tables 7.1 and 7.2) *not* be accepted, but there may also be circumstances where it is advantageous to accept a *negative* NPV project.

Example 7.1

The management accounting department of Septillion PLC have identified six independent investment opportunities, code-named G to L. The Year 0 and Year 1 cash flows of these projects, together with their NPVs, are as follows:

	Year 0	*Year 1*	....	*NPV*
Project			(*£000s*)	
G	−100	−500	....	+25
H	−200	− 90	....	+36
I	−150	−220	....	+44
J	−300	−100	....	+30
K	− 50	+100	....	+10
L	−100	+ 80	....	−12

Therefore, under normal circumstances, Septillion PLC would accept Projects G to K, as they all have positive NPVs, and Project L would be rejected. However, to undertake Projects G to K, a total of £800,000 would be required at Year 0, and an additional £915,000 at Year 1. (Notice Project K does not require a further cash outlay at Year 1.)

In the first situation, Septillion's board of directors have stipulated that, although there will be no capital expenditure constraint at Year 1, the company is only willing to undertake £275,000 of capital expenditure at Year 0. Thus the company faces a single-time period capital rationing situation. In order to solve the problem, benefit–cost ratio rankings are used:

Project	*NPV*	÷	*Year 0 Outlay*	=	*Benefit-cost ratio*	*Rank*
G	+25	÷	100	=	+0·25	2
H	+36	÷	200	=	+0·18	4
I	+44	÷	150	=	+0·293	1
J	+30	÷	300	=	+0·10	5
K	+10	÷	50	=	+0·20	3
L	−12	÷	100	=	−0·12	—

			NPV
Investment decision:	275	available	
	150	invested in I, producing	: +44
	125	balance	
	100	invested in G, producing	: +25
	25	balance	
	25	invested in 50% of K, producing	: + 5
	—	all funds invested	
		Total NPV	+74

Thus the company should undertake Projects I and G, and 50% of K. This will generate a total positive NPV of £74,000, which will be the maximum possible, given the expenditure constraint.

The second situation is somewhat contrived, but serves to show an important point. Suppose that, instead of constraining capital expenditure at Year 0, the board of directors decide that there is *no* constraint on expenditure at Year 0, but a Year 1 there is only £290,000 of *external* finance available. However, this figure can be added to by any internally generated funds that arise from projects at Year 1.

Once again, the management face capital rationing and, although there is no constraint at Year 0, they must be careful at that time only to undertake projects for which there will be sufficient finance available at Year 1 for them to be continued. (It would be no good accepting every non-negative NPV project available at Year 0, only to find that many would subsequently have to be abandoned at Year 1 through insufficient finance.)

The revised set of benefit cost ratios are now:

Project	*NPV*	÷	*Year 1 Outlay*	=	*Benefit-cost ratio*	*Rank*
G	+25	÷	500	=	0·05	4
H	+36	÷	90	=	0·40	1
I	+44	÷	220	=	0·20	3
J	+30	÷	100	=	0·30	2
K	+10	÷	—			
L	−12	÷	—			

Obviously Septillion will undertake project K: it has a positive NPV and does not require any outlay in the rationed time-period. Furthermore, because it actually generates a cash *inflow* of £100,000 at Year 1, this amount can be added to the external funds available for capital expenditure. Thus the investment decision is:

	290	available	
plus	100	from investment in K, producing	: +10
	390	balance	
	90	invested in H, producing	: +36
	300	balance	
	100	invested in J, producing	: +30
	200	balance	
	200	invested in 91% of I, producing	: +40
	—	all funds invested	
		Total NPV	+116

However, this is not the end of the decision. Although the £390,000 of funds has been fully utilized it is possible to obtain additional funds at Year 1 by investing in Project L. The question is: does the additional *positive* NPV generated from investing Project L's Year 1 cash inflow compensate for the *negative* NPV arising from Project

Cont.

L directly? The answer lies in examining Project L's *cost–benefit* (rather than benefit–cost) ratio and comparing it with the benefit–cost ratio of the 'marginal' project.

Project L has a cost–benefit ratio of: $-12/+80 = -0{\cdot}15$. In other words, every £1 generated at Year 1 from investing in Project L has a cost of 12 pence of *negative* NPV.

The 'marginal' project in Septillion's investment decision is I, because it was into Project I that the last £1 of the available expenditure was spent. Project I can have a total of £220,000 invested in it at Year 1. So far, only £200,000 has been invested and so, if any *further* investment funds are available – up to a maximum of £20,000 – they too would be invested in I. The benefit gain from a further investment in I is given by its benefit–cost ratio of 0·20. In other words, every £1 extra invested in I generates an additional 20 pence of *positive* NPV.

From this comparison of Projects I and L, it can be seen that the benefit generated from a further investment in I *does* exceed the cost arising from the investment in L (i.e. $0{\cdot}2 > 0{\cdot}15$). Investing in the *whole* of L will produce £80,000 at Year 1, but as only a further £20,000 can be invested in I, for the moment, the decision will be to undertake just 25% of project L to produce the required cash flow:

		NPV
Invest in 25% L to yield 20, costing	:	−3
invest 20 in 9% of I, yielding	:	+4
Net *gain*		+1

Septillion has now undertaken the whole of Projects K, H, J *and* I, as well as 25% of L. On the benefit–cost ratio rankings, if any *more* investment funds were available, the next best project is G. Therefore is it worthwhile undertaking the remaining 75% of L – which would produce an extra £60,000 of funds at Year 1 – in order to invest in 12% of Project G ($60 \div 500$)?

Again comparison of the ratios indicates the answer: every £1 generated from L costs 12 pence of negative NPV; every £1 invested in Project G produces 5 pence of positive NPV. Therefore further investment in L in order to invest in Project G is *not* worthwhile. Thus the optimal investment decision is: undertake Projects K, H, J, I and 25% of L. This will yield a maximum total of positive NPV of: $10 + 36 + 30 + 44 - 3 = +£117{,}000$ NPV.

Divisibility assumption

The benefit–cost ranking approach to the situation of single-period capital rationing depends heavily on the assumption that investment projects are divisible (i.e., that fractions of projects can be undertaken, such as 25% of Project L in the example). Where this assumption does not hold, benefit–cost ratios do not work and instead, the investment selection decision has to be undertaken by examining the total NPV values of all the feasible alternative *combinations* of whole projects (where the term 'feasible' refers to the fact that the total outlay required to undertake the combination does not exceed the amount available). Therefore using as an example the situation as in Tables 7.1 and 7.2, if none of the investment projects were divisible, the combination of accepting Projects B, D and E would produce the greatest amount of NPV, keeping within the £300 capital expenditure limit.

Mutually exclusive investments

A variation on the infringement of the divisibility assumption occurs when mutually exclusive projects exist. Suppose the same example is again taken, but now it is assumed that Projects A and E are mutually exclusive. Therefore either one or the other or neither can be accepted, but both *cannot* be accepted. In order to obtain the optimum selection of projects we would proceed as we did originally, going down the list of projects ranked by their benefit–cost ratios until all the capital is utilized, but now this process has to be undertaken *twice* – once excluding Project A from the list and then again, but now excluding Project E from the list. Table 7.3 illustrates the process:

Table 7.3

Project	*Benefit–cost rank*	*Outlay*	
E	1	50	Accept E, D, B:
D	2	100	Total NPV = £210·84
B	3	150	
C	4	60	
Project	*Benefit–cost rank*	*Outlay*	
D	1	100	Accept D, A, $\frac{2}{3}$B:
A	2	100	Total NPV = £168·84
B	3	150	
C	4	60	

Preferred combination: Projects E, D and B.

Single-period rationing and the IRR

Before leaving the single-period rationing case, it is worth noting that the IRR investment appraisal technique cannot cope adequately with this situation. Ranking projects in terms of their IRRs is *not* the same as ranking via benefit–cost ratios. The reason why the IRR technique fails to adapt to capital rationing is because of the fact that the IRR is simply an absolute percentage rate of return, whereas what is required is a measure of project performance *relative* to the rational investment outlay. Hence this is just one more example of the limitations of the IRR technique.

MULTI-PERIOD CAPITAL RATIONING

Introduction

The problem of investment decision making in the face of capital rationing which extends over more than one period is both complex and, at present, not completely resolved. The complexity of the problem has not been helped by general confusion and differences in the literature over what is meant by the term capital rationing and by the range of differing assumptions that have been made, both explicitly and implicitly. The main source of confusion over capital rationing, as far as the theory of corporate investment decision making is concerned, has occurred through a failure to isolate the problem from general capital market theory. As a result, a number of paradoxical problems have arisen.

In attempting to outline a normative theory of investment decision making, we shall try to be both as practical and realistic as possible. In doing so, we will assume that hard (or external) capital rationing, both for individuals and companies, is likely to be only a relatively short-run phenomenon which may well arise, in practice, out of poor forward planning.[3] It is certainly true to say that unlimited amounts of investment capital are not immediately available to companies, because capital raising operations can take some time to arrange. Thus there can be a definite limit to capital supplies in the very short run. However, as long as a company plans its future operations carefully and well ahead of time, and its management appears competent, it is unlikely that it will be unable to raise the capital it requires for any planned project which is expected to be 'profitable', i.e., it is unlikely that it will run into any serious, externally imposed capital rationing. We are not assuming that hard capital rationing never occurs but that, in the majority of cases, for most of the time, it is an unlikely phenomenon.

Soft capital rationing

If we make the assumption that externally imposed constraints on the supply of capital to a company are unlikely to be anything but relatively short-term phenomena, we are left with the task of examining the effects of internally imposed or soft capital rationing on the investment decision making process. We can define soft capital rationing as a capital expenditure constraint which is imposed on a company by its own internal management rather than by external capital markets, and which limits the amount of capital investment funds available in any particular time period.

This capital limit will normally be imposed by a capital expenditure budget of which, in a well-managed company, there are likely to be two: a short-term capital budget for the immediate twelve months ahead and a medium-term capital budget which covers the next three to five years ahead.[4] Both budgets are likely to impose relatively inflexible capital constraints upon management.

When looking at how the NPV appraisal method could be adapted to deal with the single-period rationing problem, we saw that when the capital constraint was binding (i.e., there was insufficient capital available to invest in all projects with positive NPVs), companies would have to forgo undertaking some projects which they would have otherwise undertaken. Such a situation is understandable when imposed from outside the company, but it seems ludicrous when imposed from within the company. Why should a company wish to constrain itself in this way?

The reason is that companies require to plan for the future and to monitor, control and evaluate the implementation of these plans so that future planning and control can be further improved upon. A capital budget is just one part of these plans and of the controlling process. It requires the imposition of a ceiling on capital expenditure, because capital investment is not a simple operation but one which takes time and a range of resources.

For example, the decision to invest in a particular project does not consist simply of the evaluation and appraisal process. Capital may have to be raised for the project (an operation which cannot be carried out instantaneously), the company must have the trained manpower available to implement the project and monitor its performance (again, not an instantaneous process), and even the evaluation and decision procedure itself is likely to have its own manpower and resource constraints, as is the whole of the company's organizational structure. Thus, in order to plan carefully and to control efficiently, limits may quite properly have to be imposed – in the short and medium terms – on the level of capital investment expenditure that a company allows itself to undertake.[5]

The existence of capital budgets within companies is likely to mean that management is faced with the problem of decision making in a situation of multi-period capital rationing (i.e., where capital rationing extends over a number of future periods). In such circumstances, the simple benefit–cost ratio technique cannot be used to place investment opportunities in an order of preference. This is because, in the single-period rationing case, the problem was to allocate investment capital amongst competing projects in the face of a *single* constraint, in order to maximize the total amount of positive NPV gained. In the multi-period case, this allocation procedure has to be carried out simultaneously under more than one constraint, as each period's rationing forms a separate constraint. To assist in this simultaneous allocation problem, we employ the mathematical programming optimizing technique of linear programming (LP). It is assumed that the reader is familiar with the basic mechanics of this technique, which can be found in most introductory books on operational research methods. However, a brief outline of the technique is provided in an Appendix to this chapter.

The opportunity cost of capital dilemma

The presence of multi-period capital-rationing does not alter the objective of financial management decision making: the maximization of shareholder wealth. This, we know, can be achieved through making investment decisions so as to maximize the total amount of positive NPV generated. The NPV figure gains its significance from the fact that it represents the result of netting out project cash flows and comparing this net cash flow with the opportunity cost, which is embodied in the perfect capital market discount rate.

In examining how investment resources can be allocated to projects in a situation of multi-period capital rationing, we will assume that the *suppliers* of capital to a company do not themselves impose any form of capital rationing. It is self-imposed, rather than market imposed capital rationing. This assumption releases the analysis from one of the major difficulties of the multi-period rationing problem: the choice of discount rate.

We know that the discount rate used in the NPV calculation represents the opportunity cost of cash which, in a perfect capital market, is reflected in the market rate of interest. Once a perfect capital market no longer exists, then the market interest rate no longer necessarily reflects the opportunity cost of capital. In such circumstances, as we saw when looking at the single-period rationing problem, the opportunity cost of investment capital is represented by the return gained from the marginal project in the rationed period. Therefore, in a multi-period rationing situation, the appropriate discount rate for any period is given by the return on the marginal project in that particular period. This is the dilemma.

The company requires to know the opportunity cost of cash in each period to use as the discount rate, in order to make the correct selection. Each period's opportunity cost of cash is represented by the return on the marginal project in that particular period, but this marginal project can only be identified *after* the correct project selection has been made. In other words, in order to make the correct investment project selection, the opportunity cost of capital in each rationed period needs to be known, but this can only be known once the correct selection of projects has been made. Thus, we are firmly on the horns of a dilemma, unless we assume that the company faces a perfect capital market and it is the company alone which imposes capital rationing. In such circumstances, the market interest rate still represents the opportunity cost of capital to shareholders and so can be used as the discount rate to aid project selection. Hence the need to assume soft capital rationing.

The LP solution to capital rationing

An example is the best means of showing how, in multi-period capital rationing, linear programming can help to allocate scarce investment capital to projects so as to maximize the total amount of positive NPV.

A company has found the following independent investment opportunities (all figures in £000s):

	Year					
Project	*0*	*1*	*2*	*3*	*4*	*5*
A	−100	− 50	− 25	+100	+100	+100
B	− 50	− 70	+100	+100		
C		−100	− 30	+150	+200	
D	− 10	− 20	+ 50	−100	+100	+100

Project	*0*	*1*	*2*	*3*	*4*	*5*
E	−100	−100	+200	+100	+ 50	
F			−200	+300	+100	+100

We shall assume that none of these projects can have the timing of its cash flow brought forward or delayed and none can be undertaken more than once. Furthermore, we shall again assume that all projects exhibit constant returns to scale. Finally the perfect capital market rate of interest is 10% and this rate is expected to remain constant over the next five years, and can be assumed to reflect the capital suppliers' opportunity cost.

Calculating the NPVs of the projects, using a 10% discount rate, we can see that the company would normally undertake them all, because each has a positive NPV:

Project	*£ NPV*
A	+ 39·4
B	+ 44·1
C	+133·6
D	+ 68·4
E	+ 83·6
F	+190·5

but in order to do so would require the expenditure of £260,000, £340,000, £255,000 and £100,000 of investment capital in the next *four* time periods (Years 0–3) respectively.

Suppose that the company has an internally imposed capital constraint, such that external finance raised in any one period must not exceed £150,000. In addition, internally generated finance (from projects) *cannot* be used to increase the amount of capital expenditure. Clearly, in these circumstances the company cannot undertake all six projects, and so which should be selected to be undertaken and which should be rejected?

There are several ways in which this problem could be formulated into a linear programme, but each alternative formulation would produce a solution giving exactly the same selection of investment projects to undertake. One approach, which fits directly into our NPV approach, is to take as the LP's objective function the maximization of the total amount of NPV which the company can generate over the next five years, given the imposed constraints. Thus, taking a, b, c . . . f to represent the proportion of Projects A, B, C . . . F undertaken:

Objective function:

$$39{\cdot}4a + 44{\cdot}1b + 133{\cdot}6c + 68{\cdot}4d + 83{\cdot}6e + 190{\cdot}5f \quad \text{Max}$$

Constraints:

$$100a + 50b + 10d + 100e \leqslant 150 \text{ (Year 0)}$$
$$50a + 70b + 100c + 20d + 100e \leqslant 150 \text{ (Year 1)}$$
$$25a + 30c + 200f \leqslant 150 \text{ (Year 2)}$$
$$100d \leqslant 150 \text{ (Year 3)}$$
$$a, b, c, d, e, f \leqslant 1$$
$$a, b, c, d, e, f \geqslant 0$$

Solving this linear programme on a computer gave the following selection of projects: the whole of both Projects C and D should be undertaken, together with 0·3 of Project E and 0·6 of Project F; Projects A and B should not be undertaken.[6] This selection results in a total NPV of +£341,400 being generated, which is the maximum possible total sum, give the circumstances specified.[7]

The assumptions behind LP

In using linear programming to solve this type of capital rationing problem, there are a number of assumptions and limitations involved, one of which we have already touched upon: the specification of the rate of discount to be used. In addition, the technique assumes that all the relationships expressed in the model are linear (for example, all the projects are assumed to exhibit constant returns to scale) and that the variables are infinitely divisible. There is also an assumption that the project cash flows are known with certainty because, as yet, no way has been found of satisfactorily adjusting the technique to take account of risk.

The first of these three assumptions does not necessarily cause too much trouble because, where there are non-linear relationships involved, they can often be adequately described in the LP formulation as a number of linear approximations. Similarly, the second assumption also may not be too troublesome, especially if the LP is being applied to the solution of the capital rationing problem within a company operating in a process industry (e.g., oil or chemicals), because the output is (approximately) infinitely divisible. (Integer programming – another type of allocation technique – avoids this assumption, but in doing so involves a number of new, and often more difficult, problems.) However, what really is a serious practical drawback to the use of LP in capital rationing situations, is the inability of the technique to handle uncertainty. There have been some attempts to allow for uncertainty[8] but by and large they represent mathematical solutions to mathematical, rather than practical problems.

The dual values

In the example we used above, where the objective was to maximize the total amount of positive NPV generated, the solution involved the company undertaking the whole of Projects C and D, together with 30% of Project E and 60% of Project F. The reader will be able to confirm from the project cash flow information that this solution results in the utilization of only £40,000 of the £150,000 available for investment in Year 0 and of only £100,000 of the £150,000 available in Year 3. Therefore, although the company's capital expenditure is constrained in these two periods, the constraints are 'non-binding', i.e. they do not bind or constrain the company in its efforts to achieve its objective. For this reason, there is no *additional* opportunity cost of the cash used for capital expenditure in these two periods (i.e., there is no opportunity cost incurred in addition to that opportunity cost already allowed for in the discounting process used to convert the project cash flows to NPVs), because the company does not forgo any of its investment project opportunities as a result of these two constraints.

The situation is different in respect of the Year 1 and Year 2 capital expenditure constraints. In these periods, the linear programme's project selection results in the £150,000 available (in both Years 1 and 2) being *fully* utilized and therefore the constraints are said to be *binding*: their existence limits the company's freedom of action in pursuit of its objective of NPV maximization because it limits the amount of investment the company can undertake. As a result, there is an additional opportunity cost attached to the use of investment cash in each of these two periods.

These additional opportunity costs are represented by the 'dual' values produced by the linear programme. In the example used above, the LP solution produced the following dual values for the four capital expenditure constraints:

Year	*Dual value*
0	0
1	£0·837
2	£0·952
3	0

The dual values which are produced from a LP with a maximizing objective function represent the increase (decrease) in the total value of the objective function that would arise if a binding constraint were marginally – i.e., by one unit – slackened (tightened). Thus, in the example, the investment capital constraints result in the company achieving a total NPV value (i.e., the objective function value) of £341,400. If £150,001 were available for investment in Year 1 (keeping the £150,000 limit in force in each of the three other periods), then the value of the objective function would rise by £0·837 to £341,400·837.

In this very simple example, this increase in the objective function would be achieved by increasing the level of investment in Project E (the marginal project in Year 1) from 30% of E to 30·001%.[9] Also, because the use of LP assumes linear relationships, a *reduction* in the amount of capital available in Year 1 to £149,999 would result in the value of the objective function *falling* by £0·837.

A similar analysis can be made in terms of the Year 2 capital constraint dual value of £0·952, which is caused by a 0·0005% change in the level of investment in Project F. Because the capital constraints in Years 0 and 3 are non-binding, their dual values are both zero: a marginal change in either constraint will leave both the original project selection and the value of the objective function unaltered.

There are a number of points to be made here. The first is that the example used is a highly simplified one and the practical application of the use of LP to solve capital rationing problems is far more complex and problematical. We have only outlined the approach and specified the main theoretical difficulties. Second, if we accept that Projects E and F are the marginal projects in Years 1 and 2 respectively (i.e., investment levels in these two projects change in response to marginal changes in available investment capital in these two years), it is important to realize that the relative IRRs of these two projects do *not* produce their dual values, because the IRR represents a project's average return over the *whole* of its life, whilst the dual value refers to a project's marginal return in just the period specified.

A third point of importance is that dual values apply only to incremental/marginal changes in binding constraint values. To identify the effect of any non-marginal change – i.e., a substantial change – the LP has to be reformulated accordingly and re-solved. Finally, dual values apply only to *individual* marginal changes in binding constraints, i.e., they operate under a *ceteris paribus* assumption that all other variables in the formulation remain unchanged. Thus, in the example used, if an extra £1 of investment capital is available in Year 1 *and* 2, the resulting change in the value of the objective function is not necessarily the sum of the two individual dual values. Therefore we can see that dual values can be informative in that they represent part of the opportunity cost of investment capital, but their usefulness is relatively limited because of their marginal nature.

A more complex example

Example 7.2 deals with a more complex multi-period capital rationing problem.

Example 7.2

Butyrin Ltd is the subsidiary of a large holding company. It is formulating capital investment plans. The company has identified the following independent projects (all figures in £000s):

	Year			
Project	*0*	*1*	*2*	*3*
A	−100	− 50	− 60	+300
B	− 80	+ 40	+ 50	
C	−200	−100	+400	

The company judges that 10% is the correct discount rate to use, which produces the following NPVs:

Project	*NPV*
A	+30·35
B	− 2·36
C	+39·65

However, it finds itself in a capital rationing situation imposed upon it by its parent and there is only £170,000 available at Year 0 and £65,000 available at Year 1.

In addition, the following facts are relevant:

(i) Projects A and C each use a particular type of raw material which is in short supply. Project A requires 32 tons and Project C 17 tons. Butyrin can only purchase 25 tons in total.
(ii) Any surplus funds the company has can be placed on deposit from Year 0 to Year 1 at 8% interest. However, all surplus funds available at the end of any subsequent year must be returned to the parent company.
(iii) Butyrin's bank has indicated that it is willing to give a two-year term loan of any amount up to £120,000. Interest would be payable at each year end at 15%, and the loan would have to be repaid at Year 2.
(iv) The parent company will allow Butyrin to re-invest any project generated cash flows.

Before this problem can be formulated into an LP, points (ii) and (iii) above have first to be dealt with. Placing money on deposit can be viewed as a mini-project and so, like Projects A, B, and C, we need to calculate its NPV:

NPV of £1 placed on deposit

	Year 0	*Year 1*		
Cash flow	−1	+1·08		
10% Discount Factor	×1	×0·9091		
	−1	+0·98	=	−0·02 NPV

Similarly with the bank loan:

NPV of £1 bank loan

	Year 0	*Year 1*	*Year 2*		
Cash flow	+1	−0·15	−1·15		
10% Discount Factor	×1	×0·909	×0·8264		
	+1	−0·14	−0·95	=	−0·09 NPV

We are now ready to formulate the LP:

Let a equal the *proportion* of Project A undertaken.
Let b equal the *proportion* of Project B undertaken.
Let c equal the *proportion* of Project C undertaken.
Let d equal the *amount* of cash placed on deposit: Yr 0 to Yr 1.
Let L equal the *amount* of cash borrowed: Yr 0 to Yr 2.

The objective function is:

$$30{\cdot}35a - 2{\cdot}36b + 39{\cdot}65c - 0{\cdot}02d - 0{\cdot}09L \qquad \textit{Max.}$$

Notice that the *negative*, as well as the positive NPV variables are included. It should be left to the LP to decide the investment plan

Cont.

and, as we saw with single period capital rationing, *sometimes* negative NPV projects can be acceptable.

The set of capital expenditure constraints are:

$$\begin{aligned} 100a + 80b + 200c + d &\leqslant 170 + L \\ 50a + 100c + 0{\cdot}15L &\leqslant 65 + 406 + 1{\cdot}08d \\ L &\leqslant 120 \\ a, b, c &\leqslant 1 \end{aligned}$$

Notice that *only* the cash flows in the rational time period need be specified in the LP. Hence the LP doesn't need to know explicitly about the loan repayment because it occurs in Year 2 when there is not expected to be any capital expenditure constraint. The LP implicitly is aware of the *overall* effect of the loan because it knows what its NPV is.

Finally, there is the raw material constraint and the non-negativity conditions:

$$\begin{aligned} 32a + 17c &\leqslant 25 \\ a, b, c, d, L &\geqslant 0 \end{aligned}$$

With the raw material constraint there is no need to enquire, *when* will the constraint occur. Time is only important in the LP as far as money flows are concerned because of the differing capital expenditure constraints. Also, notice that the non-negativity conditions not only prevent negative projects, but they also prevent a negative deposit account and bank loan.

Therefore, the complete LP formulation, ready for solution via a computer package, is:

$$\begin{aligned} 30{\cdot}35a - 2{\cdot}36b + 39{\cdot}65c - 0{\cdot}02d - 0.09L & \qquad \textit{Max.} \\ 100a + 80b + 200c + d &\leqslant 170 + L \\ 50a + 100c + 0{\cdot}15L &\leqslant 65 + 406 + 1{\cdot}08d \\ L &\leqslant 120 \\ a, b, c &\leqslant 1 \\ 32a + 17c &\leqslant 25 \\ a, b, c, d, L &\geqslant 0 \end{aligned}$$

Two applications of dual values

Two examples of possible applications of dual values will serve to indicate their usefulness and will also help to demonstrate the different procedures required. The first example concerns the evaluation of an additional investment, and the second shows how to determine the value of additional sources of cash.

In order to do so, use will be made of our original multi-period example in this section, involving six independent projects (A to F), where the LP's solution to the multi-period capital rationing problem was:

Investment plan: Project A: reject
Project B: reject
Project C: undertake 100%

Project D: undertake 100%
Project E: undertake 30%
Project F: undertake 60%

Dual values: Cash at Year 0: —
Cash at Year 1: £0·837
Cash at Year 2: £0·952
Cash at Year 3: —

Suppose that, before the investment plan can be undertaken, a new project is identified: Project W. This project involves the following cash flows (all figures in £000s):

Year	*Cash flow*
0	−100
1	+ 20
2	+ 90

The dual values can be used to indicate either that the project is *not* worth considering or that it *is* worth considering and so the LP should be reformulated to include Project W's cash flows, and then re-solved.

If the original LP formulation dual values are to be used, the project's NPV has first to be determined and then the opportunity cost of its cash flows. If the *net* effect is positive the project *is* worth considering and the LP should be reformulated and re-solved. If the net effect is negative, the project can be discarded without further analysis. The calculations are shown as follows:

Year	*Cash flow*		*10% discount rate*		*PV cash flows*
0	−100	×	1	=	−100
1	+ 20	×	0·9091	=	+18·18
2	+ 90	×	0·8264	=	+74·38
				NPV =	£−7·44

Year	*Cash flow*		*Dual value*		*Opp. cost cash flow*
0	−100	×	0	=	0
1	+ 20	×	0·837	=	+ 16·74
2	+ 90	×	0·952	=	+ 85·68
	Net Opp. Cost				+102·42

Net Effect of Project:

NPV + Net Opp. Cost = −£7·44 + £102·42 = +£94·98

As the overall net effect of the project is positive, this indicates that the project is worthwhile considering further and the LP should be reformulated (now including Project W's cash flows) and re-solved. This analysis is in fact very similar to the analysis made in Chapter 6 when looking at relevant cash flows. There we saw that the cost of utilizing a scarce resource was equal to its *total* opportunity cost: the internal opportunity cost, plus the external opportunity cost (the market price of the resource).

That is exactly the approach use to evaluate Project W. The NPV analysis evaluates the project's use of cash in terms of the market 'price' of cash (the discount rate); and then the subsequent analysis evaluates the project in terms of its impact on the firm's capital rationing problem – the internal opportunity cost.

On this basis, therefore, Project W could have been evaluated directly on the total opportunity costs involved. Table 7.4 illustrates this approach.

Table 7.4

	10% Discount rate	+	*Dual value of cash*	=	*Total opportunity cost of cash*
Year 0	1	+	0	=	1
Year 1	0·9091	+	0·837	=	1·7461
Year 2	0·8264	+	0·952	=	1·7784
Year 3	0·7513	+	0	=	0·7513

Project W

Year	*Cash flow*		*Opportunity cost*		
0	−100	×	1	=	−100
1	+ 20	×	1·7461	=	+ 34·92
2	+ 90	×	1·7784	=	+160·06
					+ 94·98

Thus, if project W is accepted, it should enable the total NPV generated by the projects under consideration to be increased.

Turning now to a second example, suppose the company, having formulated its production plan from the original six available projects, is then offered an opportunity to borrow additional cash at Year 2 as long as it is repaid (with interest) at Year 3. What is the maximum interest rate that the company would be willing to pay to take out such a loan?

The maximum interest rate represents the point of indifference or *equality* between what would be *gained* (in terms of the objective function) by borrowing (say) £1 at Year 2 and what would be *lost* from the resulting repayment of capital plus interest at Year 3. Using the *total* opportunity cost figures calculated in Table 7.4 makes for a simple solution to the problem:

$$\pounds1 \times \begin{matrix}\text{opportunity cost of}\\ \text{cash at Year 2}\end{matrix} = \pounds1(1+i) \times \begin{matrix}\text{opportunity cost of}\\ \text{cash at Year 3}\end{matrix}$$

$$\pounds1 \times 1{\cdot}7784 = \pounds1(1+i) \times 0{\cdot}7513$$

$$1{\cdot}7784 = 0{\cdot}7513 + 0{\cdot}7513i$$

$$\frac{1{\cdot}7784 - 0{\cdot}7513}{0{\cdot}7513} = i = 1{\cdot}367 \text{ or } \underline{136{\cdot}7\%}$$

This very high rate of interest should not come as a surprise. The firm should be willing to pay such a rate of interest (at a maximum) for the sake of gaining extra cash in a time period when cash is constrained, and repaying in a time period when it is unconstrained.

LEND–BORROW INTEREST DIFFERENTIALS

Introduction

Up to this point in this chapter, we have been examining the investment decision in the face of one particular capital market imperfection, that of soft capital rationing. Let us now turn to examine another common imperfection: the existence of a gap between the borrowing and the lending interest rate, caused by the presence of market transaction costs, where the borrowing rate is somewhat higher than the lending rate. Perhaps the best way to lay bare the problem here is to make use of the single period investment–consumption diagram.

Identification of the opportunity cost

In the basic model we saw that, because of the so-called 'Separation Theorem', it made little difference to the appraisal of physical investment opportunities whether a company had one or several owners and, if it had several owners, whether their indifference curve sets were similar or dissimilar; in fact the company did not even require knowledge of its owners' indifference curve sets.

In the face of a perfect capital market, a company would invest in physical investment opportunities until the return from the marginal project equated with the market rate of interest (i.e., it would invest in all projects which had positive or zero NPVs). This investment decision rule determined the dividend flow pattern which the individual shareholder could adjust, if he wished, by using the capital market. The company used the market interest rate as the investment appraisal discount rate because it reflected the opportunity cost of cash to the shareholders.

Let us now start with the simple case of a single-owner company and a perfect capital market except that transaction costs result in the borrowing interest rate being higher than the lending interest rate. In such a case the separation theorem (i.e., separation between management investment decisions and shareholder consumption decisions) breaks down, as there is no longer a single opportunity cost of cash because there are now two market interest rates.

Figure 7.2 illustrates this situation with the steeper of the two financial investment lines (BC) representing the borrowing rate and the other (DF) representing the lending rate. In these circumstances the shareholder's indifference curve may be tangential at any point along the non-linear boundary BCDF. We can specify three separate cases:

1 If a point of tangency occurs on the BC segment then, at time t_0, the company should undertake physical investments up to point C, and

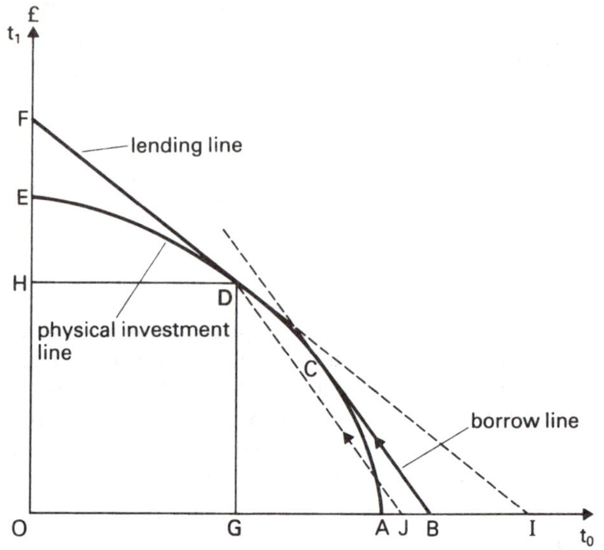

Figure 7.2

then the shareholder should add to his received dividend by borrowing on the capital market. For the company to locate itself correctly at point C on the physical investment line, the market *borrowing rate* should be used as the NPV discount rate because it would represent the opportunity cost of cash. The borrowing rate reflects the opportunity cost in these circumstances because the shape and location of the shareholder's indifference curve set is such that preference emphasis is placed on consumption at time t_0. Thus, if cash is to be invested rather than consumed at time t_0, the investment should earn a return at least equal to the borrowing rate, because the shareholder will be borrowing to replace (at least in part) the investment outlay undertaken.

2 If a point of tangency occurs along segment DF, then the company should locate itself at point D on the physical investment line and the shareholder should then lend out some part of his received dividend on the capital market. In this case, the company can ensure optimally locating at point D by undertaking all physical investments which produce positive or zero NPVs when discounted at the market *lending* rate. This rate represents the shareholder's opportunity cost of cash for reasons analogous to those cited in the previous case, except that his indifference curve set is now shaped so as to bias preference towards consumption at time t_1. Thus the company should undertake physical investments as long as they earn a return which is at least equal to that which the shareholder could earn by lending on the capital market.

3 If the point of tangency between the shareholder's indifference curve set and the boundary curve BCDF occurs along the segment CD, then

this also represents the optimal point of location for the company on its physical investment line. In such circumstances, the opportunity cost of cash is represented by the slope of the shareholder's indifference curve at the point of tangency (his *personal* time value of money) and it is also represented by the return on the marginal investment at the point of tangency on the physical investment line. Therefore, this is the rate of discount which the company should use in its investment appraisal, to ensure that it locates itself at the optimal point on the physical investment line.

In practical terms, the company's management is unlikely to be aware of the location of its shareholder's indifference curve set in relation to the boundary BCDF and so will not know whether to use the borrowing rate (case 1), the lending rate (case 2) or some intermediate rate between the borrowing and lending rates (case 3) as the investment appraisal discount rate. However, even if the company were aware of its single shareholder's indifference map and so could optimally locate on the physical investment line, in the more realistic case where there are several shareholders, their indifference curve sets are unlikely to be the same, which may well lead to a direct conflict over the value at which the discount rate should be set in order to reflect the opportunity cost of cash.

Quite simply, then, the real-world solution to the problem is indeterminate, and all that a company can hope to do is to use a single discount rate both consistently and publicly, so that it attracts shareholders whose opportunity cost of cash approximates to this rate.

Three further points

There are three further points worth noticing in this analysis. First, suppose that the company is aware of the indifference curve set of shareholders and, as a result, uses the lending rate for discounting and so locates at point D in Figure 7.2. The total net *present* value of the company's investments (given by AI) does not have any real meaning in the sense that the dividend flow produced of OG at t_0 and OH at t_1 cannot be converted by the shareholder into a cash flow of zero at t_1 and OI at t_0. Such a dividend flow can only have a present value of OJ.

This presents an interesting problem in terms of management's objective function, which we have stated as the maximization of the stock market's current valuation of the company. To do this – and assuming the stock market valuation is based on the present value summation of the future dividend flow – it could be argued that the company should use the borrowing rate as the discount rate, because this is the only meaningful way a 'present value' could be stated, but then in this example, maximization of the market value of the company's equity capital would not bring maximum benefit to the shareholders, in terms of assisting them to obtain the highest possible indifference curve.

A second point is that, given the company selects a discount rate between the market borrowing and lending rates (inclusively) and it makes an *incorrect* selection, the smaller the gap between the borrowing and lending rate, the less serious (in terms of lost utility) will be the mistake.

Finally it is interesting to speculate upon the situation of a company which was either totally ignorant of its shareholders' indifference curve sets or had shareholders with widely different indifference maps. In these circumstances, and still using a one-period analysis, the most conservative action for the company to take would be to use the borrowing rate for discounting when evaluating projects.

If that is the correct rate (i.e., case 1) then there is no problem. If either the lending rate or some intermediate rate is correct, then, although shareholders will not maximize their utility, the utility level achieved will *always* be higher than if the company did not undertake any investment at all. If either the lending rate or an intermediate rate is chosen to evaluate investment possibilities and this chosen rate proves to be incorrect, then shareholders *may* find themselves at a *lower* utility level than if the company had undertaken no investment at all, but instead had liquidated[10] itself at time t_0. Taking immediate corporate liquidation as the ultimate alternative, investing in projects with positive NPVs when discounted at the borrowing rate will always raise shareholder's utility level. The use of a discount rate above the borrowing rate may reduce the utility level to below that achieved through immediate liquidation.

In conclusion

We have seen that the presence of different lending and borrowing interest rates can cause an insurmountable difficulty to investment appraisal (or at least to the theory). However, if we can conclude that in the real world the difference between lending and borrowing rates is likely to be relatively small, then the problem does not disappear, but it does take on considerably less significance. In such circumstances the detrimental effect on the owners' wealth and utility is likely to be fairly small. We shall touch upon this problem once again at a later stage.

SUMMARY

Principally, this chapter has covered the capital rationing problem; but, in addition, another capital market imperfection, that of differential interest rates for lending and borrowing, has also been examined. The main points made are as follows:

- Capital rationing refers to a situation where a company cannot undertake all positive NPV projects it has identified because of a shortage of capital.
- Two different types of capital rationing situation can be identified, distinguished by the *source* of the capital expenditure constraint. Hard capital rationing occurs when the constraint is *externally* imposed on the firm by the capital market. Soft capital rationing occurs when the constraint is *internally* imposed on the firm, by its own management.

- In a situation of capital rationing the standard NPV decision rule for independent projects no longer holds and so has to be modified.
- In the single-period capital rationing situation, the NPV decision rule is replaced with a benefit-cost ratio analysis which evaluates the project's NPV *relative* to the required outlay in the rationed time period.
- In multi-period capital rationing, the optimal investment solution can only be obtained through solving the individual capital rationing constraints simultaneously via linear programming.
- The solution to a multi-period capital rationing LP not only provides advice on the capital investment decision (the LP's *primal* solution), but it also provides a *dual* solution. The dual solution indicates the (internal) opportunity cost of the scarce resources which, in this type of situation, is principally cash.
- The usefulness of the dual values is limited because of their marginal nature. However, they can be used to help evaluate some decisions that arise *after* the capital rationing LP has been solved.
- Finally the problem of differential lending and borrowing rates of interest was examined. It was concluded that, in such circumstances, the optimal investment decision is indeterminate beause of lack of knowledge as to which market interest rate (lend or borrow) should be used to evaluate projects. However, it was judged that, in the real world, the sub-optimal decisions that might arise as a result would be likely to have only a small impact on shareholder wealth.

NOTES

1 This return would be the project's IRR. For simplicity, we are abstracting from the problems which may arise in calculating or using an IRR.

2 If not, any book on Management Accounting will outline the basic principles. For example, see J. Sizer, *An Insight into Management Accounting*, Penguin Education, 1980.

3 We will shortly discuss the reason for making this assumption.

4 In addition, there may be a very much longer term capital budget which might stretch as far as 20–25 years ahead, depending upon the company and the industry in which it operates and upon the gestation period of its major capital investment projects.

5 It could be argued that even this internally imposed capital rationing is, in reality, produced by external – but not exclusively financial – maket inefficiencies, in that there is a time-lag between demand signals and the subsequent supply.

6 The primal solution reads: $a = 0$, $b = 0$, $c = 1$, $d = 1$, $e = 0{\cdot}3$, $f = 0{\cdot}6$.

7 If it *were* possible to relieve the capital expenditure constraint through the use of internally generated funds (from projects) then the LP formulation would have

to be revised and a different solution would result:

$$39{\cdot}4a + 44{\cdot}1b + 133{\cdot}6c + 68{\cdot}4d + 83{\cdot}6e + 190{\cdot}5f \qquad \textit{Max.}$$
$$100a + 50b + 10d + 100e \leqslant 150$$
$$50a + 70b + 100c + 20d + 100e \leqslant 150$$
$$25a + 30c + 200f \leqslant 150 + 100b + 50d + 200e$$
$$100d \leqslant 150 + 100a + 100b + 150c + 100e + 300f$$
$$a, b, c, d, e, f \leqslant 1$$
$$a, b, c, d, e, f \geqslant 0$$

8 By including 'chance' constraints into the LP formulation, whereby some level of cash flow must be provided by the solution, with a given level of probability.

9 Project E produces a total NPV of +£83,700, and 0·001% of this amount is £0·837, the dual value for Year 1. This information on how the dual value arises is supplied by the computer solution to the problem. In a more complex example the source of the dual value is likely to involve more than merely an adjustment to the level of investment in a single project.

10 We are assuming here that liquidation can be achieved without incurring costs.

APPENDIX: LINEAR PROGRAMMING

A company has identified two independent projects with the following cash flows:

Project	*Year 0*	*Year 1*	*Year 2*
A	−100	−50	+200
B	− 80	−60	+170

Assuming a discount rate of 10% correctly reflects the return available elsewhere on the capital market, their NPVs are approximately:

Project	*NPV*
A	+20
B	+ 6

However, to undertake both projects requires an outlay of 180 at Year 0 and 110 at Year 1. The company has imposed a capital expenditure constraint of 65 at Year 0 and 90 at Year 1. This problem can be formed into a *linear programme* (LP) in order to solve the investment decision where:

Let a equal the proportion of Project A undertaken
and let b equal the proportion of Project B undertaken.

a and b can take on values between 0 (where *none* of the project would be undertaken), and 1 (where the *whole* of the project would be undertaken). Thus if the solution turns out to be: $a = 0{\cdot}25$ and $b = 0{\cdot}80$, it means 25% of Project A should be undertaken and 80% of Project B.

Every LP consists of just *three* elements: an objective function, a set of constraints and a set of non-negativity conditions. Here, the objective is to make an investment decision (that is select values for a and b) in order to maximize the total NPV generated. Therefore, the objective function will be:

$$20a + 6b \quad \text{Max.}$$

where $20a$ is the amount of positive NPV generated from the investment in A (i.e., if $a = 0{\cdot}40$, then $20a$ equals: $20 \times 0{\cdot}40 = 8$; undertaking 40% of Project A produces a positive NPV of 8), and similarly with $6b$.

There are two constraints on the investment decision: the fact that capital is limited in Year 0 and in Year 1. The formulation of the Year 0 capital expenditure constraint would be:

$$100a + 80b \leqslant 65$$

where $100a$ is the capital invested in Project A at Year 0 (i.e., if $a = 0{\cdot}40$, then $100a$ equals: $100 \times 0{\cdot}40 = 40$; undertaking 40% of Project A will require a Year 0 outlay of 40), and similarly for Project B. Thus this constraint simply indicates: the amount of cash spent on undertaking Project A at Year 0 ($100a$), plus the cash spent on undertaking B at Year 0 ($80b$) must not exceed ($\leqslant$) the 65 of investment finance available at Year 0.

The Year 1 capital expenditure constraint is similarly:

$$50a + 60b \leqslant 90$$

In addition, to prevent the LP from suggesting that any project should be undertaken more than once, the values that can be placed on a and b are limited to a maximum of 1 (i.e., 100%). Therefore:

$$a, b \leqslant 1$$

The non-negativity condition is simply there to prevent nonsensical *negative* values being assigned to a and b:

$$a, b \geqslant 0$$

Thus the complete LP formulation is:

$$\begin{aligned} 20a + 6b &\quad \text{Max.} \\ 100a + 80b &\leqslant 65 \\ 50a + 60b &\leqslant 90 \\ a, b &\leqslant 1 \\ a, b &\geqslant 0 \end{aligned}$$

There are many computer packages available which will solve this LP. What is being solved is the values of a and b in a pair of simultaneous equations (the two constraints), so as to maximize the total NPV generated. The solution to this particular, *very* simple, problem is:

$$\begin{aligned} a &= 0{\cdot}65 \\ b &= 0 \end{aligned}$$

In other words, 65% of Project A should be undertaken and Project B should be rejected. This produces a total NPV of 13, the maximum possible amount, given the constraints.

FURTHER READING

1 For a good starting point on the literature of capital rationing, see J.H. Lorie, L.J. Savage, 'Three Problems in Rationing Capital', *Journal of Business*, October 1955, and H.R. Fogler, 'Ranking Techniques and Capital Budgeting', *Accounting Review*, January 1972.
2 For an approach equating with the Hirshleifer analysis, see F.D. Arditti, R.C. Grinold, H. Levy, 'The Investment-Consumption Decision under Capital Rationing', *Review of Economic Studies*, July 1973.
3 For application of LP to multi-period capital rationing, see two articles by K.N. Bhashar, 'Linear Programming and Capital Budgeting: a Reappraisal', *Journal of Business Finance and Accounting*, Autum 1976, and 'Linear Programming in Capital Budgeting: the Financing Problem', *Journal of Business Finance and Accounting*, Spring 1983.
4 However, perhaps the most thoughtful article of all on the subject is H.M. Weingartner, 'Capital Rationing: *n* Authors in Search of a Plot', *Journal of Finance*, December 1977; whilst also of interest is G.W. Trivol and W.R. McDaniel, 'Uncertainty, Capital Immobility and Capital Rationing in Investment Decision', *Journal of Business Finance and Accounting*, Summer 1987.

QUICKIE QUESTIONS

1 What are the two types or classes of capital rationing?
2 Why does capital rationing cause problems for the NPV decision rule?
3 Given these projects:

	t_0	t_1	....	NPV
A	−100	− 50	....	+60
B	−200	−200	....	+90
C	− 40	−150	....	+20
D	−100	+ 20	....	−10

If only 200 is available at t_0, which projects should be selected?
4 Given the projects in question 3, if only 240 of *external* capital was available at t_1 (no capital rationing at t_0), which projects should be selected?
5 Given these projects:

	t_0	....	NPV
A	−100	....	+40
B	−100	....	+30
C	−200	....	+50
D	−100	....	+10
E	− 50	....	+ 4

Only 300 is available at t_0 and Projects B and C are mutually exclusive. Which projects should the firm accept?

6 Given the projects:

	t_0	t_1	t_2	....	NPV
A	−100	−200	+50	....	+40
B	−150	+ 70	+70	....	−20
C	−200	−120	−30	....	+50

External capital is limited to 190 at t_0, 110 at t_1 and zero at t_2. Formulate the problem into an LP.

7 If a capital rationing LP produces the following dual values for cash:

t_0	1·86
t_1	0·73
t_2	0·64
t_3	1·21

A bank loan is available at t_1, repayable at t_2. What is the maximum rate of interest you would be willing to pay, given the firm uses a 10% discount rate for project appraisal?

8 Given the dual values in question 7, the firm now discovers an additional project:

Year	*Cash flow*
0	−100
1	+ 40
2	+ 90

What action should be taken?

PROBLEMS

1 Sporangium PLC is a large bakery company with other interests including ice-cream manufacture and specialized catering. For investment appraisal purposes, it uses a 15% rate of discount.

The management are considering the company's capital investment plans for the coming year. One project under consideration is the purchase of a fleet of delivery vans. Two alternative proposals have been put forward. One is to purchase a fleet of petrol-powered vans; the other is to purchase electrically-powered vans.

Investment in the petrol-powered fleet would yield an internal rate of return (IRR) of 25%, whilst the electrically-powered fleet would only yield a return of 20%. However, when the two alternatives are evaluated using net present value (NPV), the electrically-powered fleet has the larger positive NPV.

In addition to the above, the company has identified four other projects (all independent). Their outlays and NPVs are shown below:

Project	*Outlay (t_0)* £000s	*NPV* £000s
A	50	+ 60
B	80	+ 40
C	140	+ 84
D	80	+ 32
Petrol fleet	100	+ 80
Electrical fleet	170	+110.5

All projects require only a single outlay at t_0, except Project A which requires a further £70,000 one year late at t_1.

The company has only £290,000 available for capital investment projects at t_0. Capital is expected to be freely available from t_1 onwards. None of the above projects can have their starts delayed. All projects are divisible, exhibit constant returns to scale and have the same level of risk, which is the same as that of the projects already being undertaken by the company.

Required:
(a) Carefully explain the reasons for the conflict in the investment advice about the fleet of delivery vans. In the absence of capital rationing which vehicle fleet should be purchased and why?
(b) When faced with capital rationing which projects should the company undertake at t_0? Explain the reasons for your decision.
(c) How would your advice in (b) above be modified if the start of the delivery fleet project could be delayed until t_1? What would be the resulting gain in shareholder wealth?

2 Hyalophane PLC has identified the following investment projects:

Project	t_0 *Immediate outlay* (£000)	t_1 *Year 1* (£000)	t_2 *Year 2* (£000)
A	−100	−100	+302
B	− 50	−100	+218
C	−200	+100	+107
D	−100	− 50	+308
E	−200	− 50	+344

Required:
(a) The company faces a perfect capital market, where the appropriate discount rate is 10%. All projects are independent and divisible. Which projects should the firm accept?
(b) The company faces capital rationing at t_0. There is only £225,000 of finance available. None of the projects can be delayed. Which projects should the firm accept?
(c) The situation is as in (b) above, except that you are now informed

that Projects A and B are mutually exclusive. Which projects should now be accepted?

(d) All projects are now independent but indivisible. Which projects should be accepted? What will be the maximum NPV available to the company?

(e) All projects are independent and divisible. There is capital rationing at t_1 *only*. No project can be delayed or brought forward. There is only £150,000 of external finance available at t_1. Which projects should be accepted?

(f) Given the information as in (e) above, except that there is capital rationing at both t_0 (£225,000 available) and t_1 (£150,000 available). Formulate the linear programme to solve the problem, so as to maximize the total NPV generated.

(g) Suppose that the solution to the above linear programme produces the following dual values for cash:

t_0 0.92
t_1 0.84
t_2 0

If money can be transferred from t_0 to t_1 via a deposit account, under what circumstances would it be worthwhile?

(h) Given the circumstances in (g) above, what minimum rate of interest would be required to make the linear programme transfer cash from t_1 to t_2?

In all the above questions, none of the projects can be accepted more than once.

3 Raiders PLC is a private limited company which is financed entirely by ordinary shares. Its effective cost of capital, net of tax, is 10% per annum. The directors of Raiders are considering the company's capital investment programme for the next two years, and have reduced their initial list of projects to four. Details of the projects are as follows:

	Cash Flows (net of tax)					
Project	*Immediately*	*After one year*	*After two years*	*After three years*	*Net present value (at 10%)*	Internal *rate of return (to nearest 1%)*
	£000	£000	£000	£000	£000	
A	−400	+ 50	+300	+350	+157·0	26%
B	−300	−200	+400	+400	+150·0	25%
C	−300	+150	+150	+150	+ 73·5	23%
D	0	−300	+250	+300	+159·5	50%

None of the projects can be delayed. All projects are divisible; outlays may be reduced by any proportion and net inflows will then be reduced in the same proportion. No project can be undertaken more than once. Raiders PLC is able to invest surplus funds in a bank deposit account yielding a return of 7% per annum, net of tax.

Required:

(a) Prepare calculations showing which projects Raiders should undertake if capital for immediate investment is limited to £500,000, but is expected to be available without limit at a cost of 10% per annum thereafter.

(b) Provide a linear programming formulation to assist the directors of Raiders PLC in choosing investment projects if capital available immediately is limited to £500,000, capital available after one year is limited to £300,000 and capital is available thereafter without limit at a cost of 10% per annum.

(c) Outline the limitations of the formulation you have provided in (b).

(d) Comment briefly on the view that in practice capital is rarely limited absolutely, provided that the borrower is willing to pay a sufficiently high price, and in consequence a technique for selecting investment projects which assumes that capital is limited absolutely, is of no use.

8
Risk and expected return

Chapter Contents

RISK AND RETURN

We have already introduced the concept of risk when examining the role of the discount rate in an NPV analysis. However, in this chapter, we start to take a much more careful look at risk, the problems it poses for investment decision making and how it can be taken into account.

Introduction to uncertainty

In other words we will begin to examine how investment appraisal can cope with the fact that the future is largely unknown and that decision making has to be carried out on the basis of *expectations*. That is, in an uncertain world, capital investment decisions have to be taken on the basis of *expected* project cash flows, which may or may not turn out to be the same as the cash flows that *actually* arise.

In a world where the future is uncertain, decision making involves taking a risk: the risk that the actual outcomes may differ from what was expected. In our analysis of the handling of uncertainty in financial decision making we shall use the two terms *risk* and *uncertainty* interchangeably. Although it is possible to distinguish between the two terms, there is little purpose in doing so for our present needs. Thus when reference is made to a risky investment decision, we are concerned with a situation where we are uncertain about what will be that investment's *actual* future outcome.

A simple approach

Our original approach to the problem of investment decision making in an uncertain world was to assert that investors are averse to uncertainty – in other words they dislike risk. Therefore, in order to be persuaded to take on an investment for which the outcome is uncertain, they have to be offered the expectation of a higher return[1] from the investment as a *reward*, or as *compensation* for taking on the risk involved. Further, it followed that the greater the degree of uncertainty surrounding an investment's outcome, the greater would have to be the level of expected return in order to make the investment attractive to investors.

In such a world as outlined above, the perfect capital market would not display just a single rate of interest, but a whole continuum of interest rates – one for each level of risk: the higher the risk, the higher the interest rate. We could therefore adapt the NPV appraisal technique by using as the discount rate for any particular project's appraisal, the perfect capital market discount rate which related to that particular project's level of risk.

In such a way the discount rate would still correctly reflect the opportunity cost of undertaking the investment: the investment should only be undertaken if it produces a return that is at least equal to the return that could be obtained on the capital market, *for a similar level of risk*. (The IRR appraisal technique could be similarly adapted. The perfect capital market interest rate appropriate for the project's level of risk would be used at the hurdle/cut-off rate).

However, this simple analysis – although fundamentally and conceptually correct – does beg two rather problematical questions: how are we to identify the degree of risk associated with a particular investment project and, given that we can measure a project's risk level, how are we then to identify the corresponding perfect capital market interest rate? These two questions will form the basis for much of the following discussion.

A caution

The impact of uncertainty has a fundamental and pervasive impact on the whole of financial decision making. It is often useful to assume away its existence in order to clarify the basic analysis of investment decision making; however, if our theory is to have any real-world validity then we must come to grips with the problems it poses.

In the introduction to this book it was pointed out that the theory of financial decision making is still under development and many areas of the theory contain considerable controversy. In fact, we know relatively little about how financial decisions should be made, or indeed, how they are made and there are many more unanswered questions than answered questions.

However, when we look at the research work that is currently being undertaken, we find that a very substantial proportion is concerned with the presence of risk in decision making, because it is our lack of understanding about risk – its nature, measurement and investors' attitude towards it – that causes the greatest number of problems and unanswered questions.

Given the situation as outlined above, we must treat our analysis of uncertainty with considerable caution. Generally speaking it is believed that the analysis that we shall develop does move in the right direction – it is relatively sound – but the conclusions reached can only be tentative and can be expected to alter over time as our understanding improves.

THE EXPECTED UTILITY MODEL

We are concerned with the construction of a theory of financial decision making by a company's management on behalf of its shareholders. Given the fact that management will have to take decisions about investment proposals whose outcomes are uncertain, it is important that we should be aware of how the individual shareholders would themselves come to a decision in such circumstances. Therefore we require a model that adequately reflects the risk attitudes of shareholders: how they perceive risk and how they react to its presence. Unlike our theory of financial decisions, which is a normative theory outlining how management *should* make financial decisions, the model of shareholders' risk attitudes needs to be a *positive* model – it should try to reflect their *actual* attitudes rather than what should be their attitudes. It is only in this way that we will be able to construct successfully a normative theory of managerial financial decision making based on shareholders' actual desires. To this end we have to make some carefully specified assumptions about shareholders and investors generally.

Investors' behaviour axioms

Stated succinctly, we shall assume that when faced with making risky financial decisions, individual shareholders or investors act *rationally* and *consistently*. More specifically, we can formulate four basic axioms[2] regarding the behaviour of investors when making decisions:

1 Investors are able to choose between alternatives by ranking them, in some order of merit, i.e. they are capable of actually coming to a decision.
2 Any such ranking of alternatives is 'transitive', i.e. if alternative A is preferred to B and alternative B is preferred to C, then alternative A *must* be preferred to C.
3 Investors do not differentiate between alternatives which have the same degree of risk, i.e. their choice is dispassionate in that it is based solely upon consideration of the risk involved rather than on the nature of alternatives available.
4 Investors are able to specify for any investment whose returns are uncertain, an exactly equivalent alternative which would be just as preferable but which would involve a *certain* return, i.e. for any gamble investors are able to specify a *certainty equivalent*.[3]

These four axioms of investors' decision-making behaviour can be used to construct an expression or function of utility. This utility function[4] can then be used as the basis of a model of investors' risk attitudes which will enable us to explore the way in which individuals make decisions about risky alternatives, on the assumption that they do so in order to maximize their own expected utility index.

Given below is an example which goes through the process by which an individual's utility function may be derived. Although this process may appear rather unrealistic, it is perfectly practical as long as the individual's decisions are both consistent and rational, in line with the four axioms stated above.

Utility function construction

Suppose that we inform an individual that a project will be made available to him and that we wish to know the maximum amount he would be willing to pay to be allowed to undertake it. There are just two possible outcomes[5] from this project: one is a gain of £5,000 (+ £5,000) and the other is a loss of £2,000 (−£2,000).

In order to construct the utility function we need a measure or index of utility. This measure is completely arbitrary, but for convenience we shall assign the utility index number of 1 to the + £5,000 outcome and 0 to the −£2,000 outcome[6]:

Outcome	Utility function index
+£5,000	1
−£2,000	0

Alternatively this could be written as:

$$U(+£5{,}000) = 1 \qquad U(-£2{,}000) = 0$$

If the probability of an outcome of +£5000 is p and of −£2000 is $(1-p)$, then the expected utility of the project will be:

$$p \times U(+£5{,}000) + (1-p) \times U(-£2{,}000)$$

As $U(+£5{,}000) = 1$ and $U(-£2{,}000) = 0$, then the expected utility of the project reduces to:

$$p \times 1 + (1-p) \times 0 = p$$

From axiom 4 we assume that for any project with a risky outcome, an investor can specify an equivalent certain alternative: the certainty equivalent or (*C-E*). This represents the maximum sum an investor would be willing to pay to undertake the risky project. Using the example above, the utility of the certainty equivalent can be specified:

$$U(C\text{-}E) = pU(+£5{,}000) + (1-p)\,U(-£2{,}000)$$
$$U(C\text{-}E) = p \times 1 + (1-p) \times 0 = p$$

We are now in a position to construct a utility function for a specific individual investor. However, before doing so, it is important to emphasize that the utility function we shall construct will be unique to this particular (hypothetical) investor. Different investors are likely to have different utility functions because they are based on each individual's *personal* attitude to risk.

The approach that we shall use is to ask the individual to state the maximum (certain) price he would be willing to pay to be allowed to undertake the project, for a whole range of different probabilities attached to the two outcomes. For example, if we said that the probability of the project producing +£5,000 is 0·80 and the probability of producing −£2,000 is (1−0·80) = 0·20, then he may state that he would be willing to pay a maximum of (say) £2,000. This is the project's certainty-equivalent, and its utility index can be calculated as:

$$U(C\text{-}E) = pU(+£5{,}000) + (1-p)\,U(-£2{,}000)$$
$$U(+£2{,}000) = 0{\cdot}80 \times 1 + 0{\cdot}20 \times 0 = 0{\cdot}80$$

Again we might specify that the probability of the project producing +£5,000 was 0·40, and the investor may allocate this project a certainty equivalent of (say) −£500. In other words, with probabilities of 0·40 and 0·60 attached to the project's two possible outcomes of +£5,000 and −£2,000 respectively, the investor would have to be *paid* £500 to induce him to undertake the project.

The utility index of this certainty equivalent would be:

$$U(-£500) = 0{\cdot}40 \times 1 + 0{\cdot}60 \times 0 = 0{\cdot}40$$

This process could be carried on idefinitely, because there are an unlimited number of different pairs of probabilities (each adding up to unity) which can be attached to the project's two outcomes. Eventually we shall have gathered sufficient utility indices of certainty-equivalents to enable us to plot the individual's personal utility index. Figure 8.1 illustrates such a function.

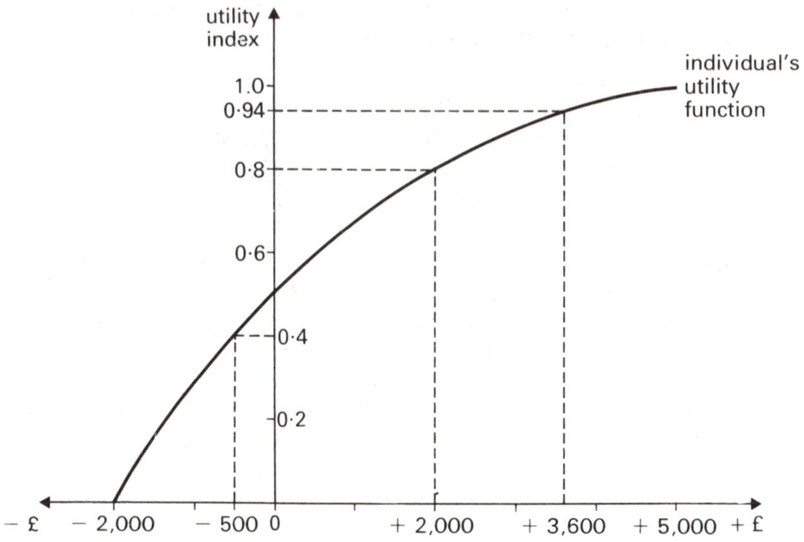

Figure 8.1

The shape of the utility function

The general shape of this utility function is of interest. Let us return to the first pair of probabilities attached to the project's outcome, where there was an 80% chance of an outcome of +£5,000 and a 20% chance of an outcome of −£2,000:

Project outcome	×Probability		
+£5,000	× 0·80	=	+£4,000
−£2,000	× 0·20	=	−£ 400
	Expected outcome	=	+£3,600

The project's expected outcome has a value of +£3,600, whereas our individual assigned it a certainty-equivalent of only +£2,000. That is, the expected utility of the project to the individual is *less than* the utility of the project's expected outcome or value. This can be written using the following notation:

$$E[U(\text{PROJ.})] < U[E(\text{PROJ.})]$$

In this particular case, the expected utility of the project is the utility of the certainty equivalent value assigned by the individual of +£2,000, and the utility of the project's expected value is the utility of +£3,600. Using the utility function in Figure 8.1 we can read off the following utility index values for these amounts:

$$\left.\begin{aligned} E[U(+£2{,}000)] &= 0{\cdot}80 \\ U[E(+£3{,}600)] &= 0{\cdot}94 \end{aligned}\right\} \; 0{\cdot}80 < 0{\cdot}94.$$

With the second pair of probabilities that we used for illustration where our investor assigned a certainty-equivalent of −£500:

Project outcome	×Probability		
+£5,000	× 0·40	=	+£2,000
−£2,000	× 0·60	=	−£1,200
	Expected outcome	=	+£ 800

We see that once again, the project's expected outcome of +£800 is higher than the certainty equivalent assigned of −£500.

We will find that this holds for all the probability combinations offered to our investor: he would assign a certainty-equivalent value which was below the project's expected value. This result is caused by the fact that the derived utility function is concave to the origin. If our individual always assigned a certainty-equivalent value which was *equal* to the project's expected value, the utility function would be a straight line, whilst if the individual assigned certainty-equivalent values consistently *greater* than the project's expected value, the utility function would be convex to the origin. Figure 8.2 illustrates these alternatives.

Because our individual consistently assigns certainty-equivalent values that are less than the project's corresponding expected value, he is termed

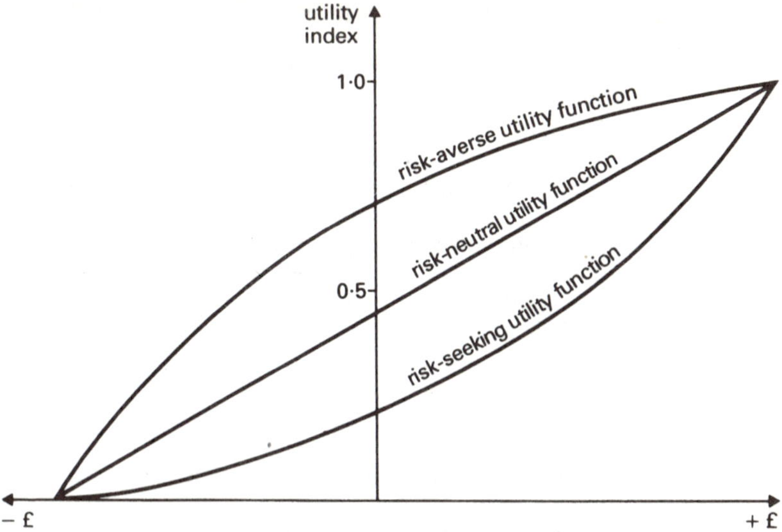

Figure 8.2

risk-averse. In other words he dislikes risk and shows this by being only willing to pay a sum of money to undertake the project (the *C-E*) which is less than the project's expected worth. The difference between the two figures is seen by the individual as the compensation he requires to bear the risk involved with the project. Thus when our individual indicated that £2,000 was the maximum he would pay to undertake a project with an expected value of +£3,600, the difference of £1,600 is the expected compensation required because of the risk involved.

Similarly, if an individual assigns certainty-equivalents *equal* to the project's expected value, he is termed *risk-neutral* in that he requires no compensation for undertaking a risky project. If the assigned certainty-equivalents are *greater* than the project's expected value, the investor is termed a *risk-seeker* because he is willing to pay a premium in order to be allowed to bear a risk.

Figure 8.2 illustrates the possible utility functions for these three categories of attitude to risk. It follows that the greater the aversion or attraction to risk, the more pronounced will be the concavity and convexity respectively of the utility functions, and vice versa.

Individual choice amongst risky investments

Once an individual's utility function has been constructed in this way, it can be used to indicate how he would choose between alternative risky projects on the assumption that he will attempt to achieve the greatest possible amount of utility, i.e., the individual selects whichever alternative is expected to produce the highest utility index value.

Suppose our individual, whose utility function is displayed in Figure 8.1, wishes to decide between two alternative investments: A and B. Once again we shall assume that the returns produced by both investments occur almost immediately after their required outlays so as to avoid the need for discounting.

The possible net returns from these two investments and their relevant probabilities are set out in Table 8.1, together with the calculation of the utility that the individual would expect to derive from each. From this table it can be seen that although investment A has the largest expected return, the individual would actually select investment B because it produces a higher level of expected utility: a utility index of 0·732 as opposed to 0·704. In other words, investment B is preferred because our risk-averse individual judges that it possesses a superior risk-expected return combination than does investment A.

The problem with this expected-utility model of investment decision making is that its practical usefulness is virtually zero because of its elaborate procedure. To derive an accurate representation of an individual's utility function is both difficult and time-consuming. In addition, an individual's attitude to risk can be expected to change over time as his personal attitudes and circumstances change, thus necessitating a periodic re-estimation of the function.

In addition, in terms of our normative theory of managerial financial decision making, the model presents another problem. Assuming that a company has several shareholders, the company's management would need to be aware of each individual's utility function. Even assuming that such a feat were possible, the utility functions of these individuals are likely to be different and there is no way in which they can sensibly be aggregated to assist managerial decision making. However, the expected utility model does provide a starting point for a more analytical approach to the problem of handling risk. In particular, of greatest interest is the fact that risk-averse investors generally are likely to have concave to the origin utility functions in the form of a quadratic equation: $U(x) = a + bx - cx^2$ as shown in Figure 8.1.

Table 8.1

Investment A Possible net return	× Prob.		*Investment B* Possible net return	× Prob.	
−£1,000	× 0·3 =	−£ 300	+£ 500	× 0·2 =	+£ 100
+£2,000	× 0·4 =	+£ 800	+£1,500	× 0·6 =	+£ 900
+£5,000	× 0·3 =	+£1,500	+£2,500	× 0·2 =	+£ 500
Expected return:		+£2,000	Expected return:		+£1,500

$E[U(\text{Inv. A})] = 0{\cdot}3U(-£1{,}000) + 0{\cdot}4U(+£2{,}000) + 0{\cdot}3U(+£5{,}000)$
$E[U(\text{Inv. B})] = 0{\cdot}2U(+£500) + 0{\cdot}6U(+£1{,}500) + 0{\cdot}2U(+£2{,}500)$

Using the utility function in Figure 8.1 to determine the utility index value:[7]

$$E[U(\text{Inv. A})] = (0{\cdot}3 \times 0{\cdot}28) + (0{\cdot}4 \times 0{\cdot}8) + (0{\cdot}3 \times 1) = \underline{\underline{0{\cdot}704}}$$

$$E[U(\text{Inv. B})] = (0{\cdot}2 \times 0{\cdot}59) + (0{\cdot}6 \times 0{\cdot}74) + (0{\cdot}2 \times 0{\cdot}85) = \underline{\underline{0{\cdot}732}}$$

As $E[U(\text{Inv. B})] > E[U(\text{Inv. A})]$ the individual will select investment B in order to maximize his utility.

THE APPROACH TO PORTFOLIO THEORY

Introduction

Accepting the fact that the operational usefulness of the expected utility model is severely limited, we must look elsewhere for a means of measuring an investment's risk. One particularly fruitful approach that can be seen as having its foundations in the expected utility model is that of portfolio theory. This theory was originally developed within the context of a risk-averse individual investor who was concerned with how to combine shareholdings in several different (stock-exchange) quoted companies in order to build an investment portfolio that would maximize the amount of expected return, given a specified level of risk. (Such a portfolio is termed 'efficient', and could also be defined as one that minimizes risk for a given level of expected return.)

Initially we shall outline the main characteristics of portfolio theory within the context of an investor constructing a share portfolio: but later we shall turn to examine the implications and validity of the theory for managerial financial decision making. However, to start with we need to define two terms: the *risk* and the *return* on an investment in the shares of a company.

Return on investment

We shall continue to avoid the problems that can arise through the discounting process by considering the return on a share over just a *single* time period. Therefore the return on an investment in the shares of a company takes on a very simple definition:

$$\text{Return} = \frac{(\text{Selling price}^{8} - \text{Purchase price}) + \text{Dividends received}}{\text{Purchase price}}$$

Thus the return is simply the amount of the capital gain (or capital loss) plus the dividends received while the share was held, expressed as a ratio of the original purchase price. For example, if a share was bought for 100 p and was sold for 114 p and during the time it was held a 3 p dividend was received, then the return on the share was:

$$\frac{(114 - 100\text{p}) + 3\text{p}}{100\text{p}} = \frac{14\text{p} + 3\text{p}}{100\text{p}} = 0{\cdot}17 \text{ or } 17\%$$

There are two things to note about this example. The first is that although the return is defined as a single-period return, it can be applied to *any* single time period: a week, a month, a year of whatever – because it is determined solely by the lapse of time between when the share was bought and when it was sold. However, because we are so used to dealing with *annual* rates of return, we will assume from now on that the period of time under consideration is that of a year.

The second point to note is that the example tells us a piece of history: what has been the return that was received on this investment. However, we are interested in decision making and so, although the *actual* achieved return on an investment is of interest in assessing decision making performance, we are really concerned with what *will be* the future return on an investment that can be expected.

Expected returns

If we are trying to calculate the return that we would be likely to receive from an investment, we need to estimate the future selling price and the dividends expected to be received while holding the share. In such an exercise it is unlikely that just a single estimate would be made, but instead a *range* of estimates, which might be determined by (say) general economic conditions.

For example if the current price of a share is 100 p and the following estimates are made:

Prevailing economic conditions	*Estimated selling price*	*Estimated dividends received*
Boom	128p	7p
Steady growth	117p	3p
Slump	105p	0p

then we estimate that the return will be 35% if the economy booms, 20% if it exhibits steady growth and only 5% if there is an economic slump. Although this information is of interest, it is of limited use for decision making purposes unless we have some idea about *how likely* each possible set of economic conditions is, and hence each possible investment outcome is. In other words, we need to apply some (subjective) probabilities to each outcome in order to produce a probability distribution of possible returns.

Suppose the following probability estimates are made:

Economic conditions	*Probability*	*Return on investment*
Boom	0·30	35%
Steady growth	0·40	20%
Slump	0·30	5%

This is obviously a very crude representation of a probability distribution as it only allows for three possible returns on the investment: 35%, 20% and 5%, and ignores the possibility of some intermediate return such as 18%. However such a degree of unsophistication is acceptable for our present purposes.

The probability distribution illustrated above is symmetrical in its range of possible returns and if constructed with greater complexity could be represented graphically such as in Figure 8.3.

The returns are symmetric in that they are evenly or regularly distributed around the most likely outcome. Such a distribution is termed as a Normal probability distribution and it can be fully described by just two *adjectives*: a measure of central tendency of the returns and a

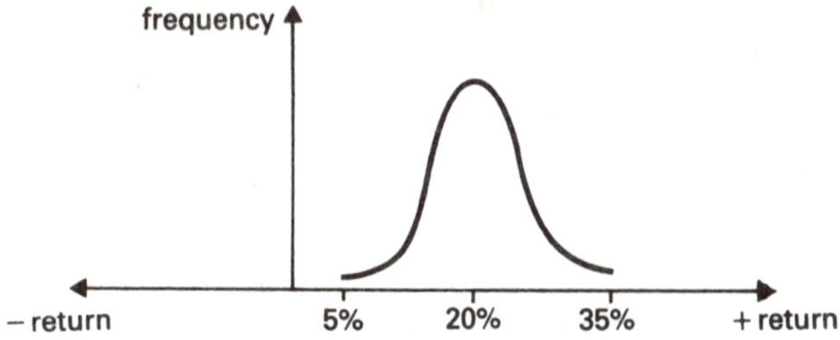

Figure 8.3

measure of the dispersion of the returns around the central tendency.

If the returns were not distributed symmetrically around the central tendency, as for example in Figure 8.4, then the distribution is said to be asymmetrical or skewed and so a third adjective is required: a measure of *skew*. For the moment, we shall assume that the returns on the investment are symmetrically distributed, but we shall return to the point at a later stage.

The measure of central tendency of returns we shall use is the *arithmetic mean* return (usually referred to as the expected return[9]) and the measure of dispersion, the *variance* (or the square root of the variance, the *standard deviation*).

The expected return, variance and standard deviation of returns are calculated in Table 8.2 using the data from the example, where the return is given by:

$$E(r) = \Sigma\, r_i\, p_i$$

and the variance is given by: $\sigma^2 = E(r^2) - E(r)^2$

$$= \Sigma r_i^2\, p_i - (\Sigma r_i p_i)^2$$

and the standard deviation is given by:

$$\sigma = \sqrt{\sigma^2}$$

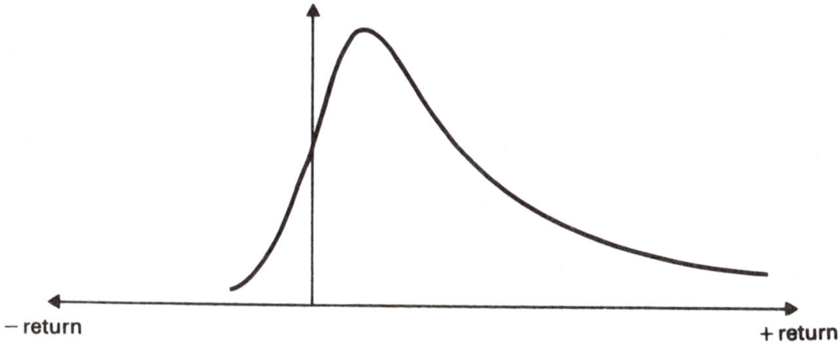

Figure 8.4

Table 8.2

Expected return

Return		*Probability*		
r_i		p_i		
35%	×	0·30	=	10·5%
20%	×	0·40	=	8·0%
5%	×	0·30	=	1·5%
		$E(r) = \Sigma r_i p_i$	=	20·0%

Variance of returns

$(Return)^2$		*Probability*		
r_i^2		p_i		$r_i^2 p_i$
1,225	×	0·30	=	367·5
400	×	0·40	=	160·0
25	×	0·30	=	7.5
		$E(r^2) = \Sigma r_i^2 p_i$	=	535

$$\sigma^2 = E(r^2) - E(r)^2 = 535 - 20^2 = 135$$

Standard deviation of returns

$$\sigma = \sqrt{\sigma^2} = \sqrt{135} \approx 11{\cdot}62\%$$

Summary[10] $E(r) = 20\%$; $\sigma^2 = 135$; $\sigma = 11{\cdot}62\%$

Risk

In the example used in Table 8.2, the investment under consideration is 'expected' to produce a return of 20%. That is, 20% represents the average or arithmetic mean return, but the actual return may turn out to be considerably better (up to 35%) or considerably worse (down to 5%) than the 20% expected. Thus the investment is risky: it involves some uncertainty in that there is scope for the actual return to be somewhat different from what is expected. We now require a means by which the risk of the investment can be measured or quantified; *how risky* is the investment?

If risk is defined as being concerned with the possibility that the actual outcome may be something other than expected, then one way of obtaining a measure of risk would be to use the *range* of possible outcomes. Thus in the example used above, the possible return ranged from 5% to 35%, and this 30% difference could be used as a measure of the risk involved. However, such a measure is rather crude and simplistic, as the following example shows.

Suppose a choice has to be made between two alternative investments, A and B, whose probability distribution of return is given below:

r_a	Probability	r_b	Probability
20%	0·30	20%	0·20
8%	0·40	8%	0·60
−4%	0·30	−4%	0·20

Both investments have an expected return of 8% and both have the same range of outcomes (24%), but are they equally risky? Having defined risk as being concerned with the possibility of actual outcomes differing from the expected outcomes, it would (correctly) appear to intuitive judgement that investment A was the more risky of the two alternatives as the extreme outcomes of A (20% and – 4%) have a greater probability of occurrence than the extreme outcomes of B. Conversely, the expected outcome of B has a greater probability of occurrence (0·60) than with A (0·40).

What we are looking for in a measure of risk is not the simple *range* of outcome, but how this range is *dispersed* around the expected outcome. Both the variance and the standard deviation provide acceptable measures of this dispersion, with the standard deviation being *especially* useful as it provides a measure in the same units as the expected return.[11]

Thus we can conclude that the risk of an investment can be measured by the variance or standard deviation of possible returns around the expected return: the greater the dispersion, the greater the risk, the greater the variance or standard deviation and vice versa; and where there is *no* dispersion of possible returns, then the expected return is a *certain* return, there is *no* risk and both variance and standard deviation give a measure of zero.

Therefore returning to the example used in Table 8.2, the return expected from the investment is 20% and its risk can be indicated by the standard deviation of 11·62% or by the variance of 135. With the later example of the two investments A and B, we concluded that A intuitively appeared to be more risky than B. The standard deviation of returns for A is 9·3% and for B 7·6%, which confirms A as the riskier investment as it has the larger standard deviation.

Further, if we continue to assume that the possible returns on an investment are symmetrically distributed around the expected return, then quoting the risk of an investment by means of its standard deviation can be converted into an intuitively more meaningful measure by using the properties of the area under the normal curve.[12]

Thus if an investment has an expected return of 10% and a standard deviation of returns of 7%, then it can be said that:

1 There is a 65% chance (approximately) that the *actual* return will lie somewhere between 17% and 3% (i.e., 10% ± 7%), and
2 There is a 95% chance (approximately) that the actual return will be somewhere between 24% and − 4% (i.e., 10% ± 2 × 7%).

Therefore, the greater the standard deviation, the greater the dispersion of possible return around what is the expected return.

Downside risk

One factor in the above discussion that may strike the reader as rather strange is that investment risk is defined as both the possibility of the investment doing worse than expected *and* the possibility of it doing better than expected. This does not seem to fit in precisely with out initial assertion that investors are risk-averse – that they dislike risk and require a reward or compensation for taking it on. This would tend to suggest that risk is really concerned with the chance that the investment's outcome will be *worse* than expected.

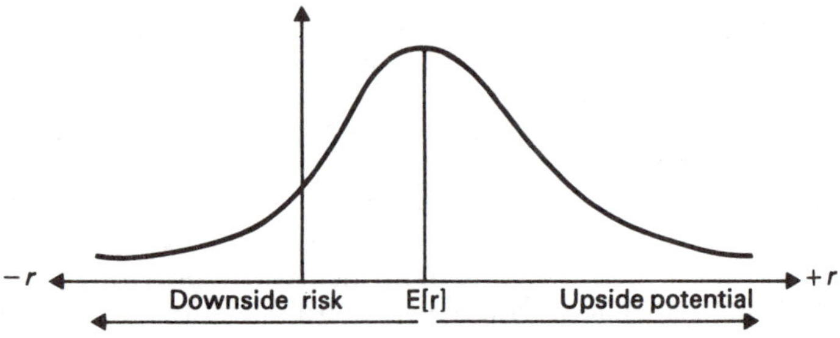

Figure 8.5

In one sense, this is quite correct. A risk averse investor is concerned with the chance of the investment performing below expectation and this is often referred to as the *downside risk* of the investment. However, part of the reward for holding this risk is the chance that the investment's performance might exceed expectation: the *upside potential* of the investment; therefore both elements are of interest to the investor and are illustrated in Figure 8.5.

The distinction between the two elements of investment performance variability is important if the distribution of returns is *asymmetrical.* With a symmetrical distribution, the expected return divides the probability distribution into two identical halves. Thus standard deviation (or variance) measures both upside potential and downside risk equally well.

Where the distribution is skewed, the standard deviation measure describes neither type of investment risk adequately, but produces a measure of dispersion which is an unhelpful average of the two risk types. In these circumstances, what is required is a specific measure of the dispersion of each risk type and this can be provided by a statistic called the *semi-variance*, which measures the dispersion of each half of the distribution individually. However, use of the semi-variance tends to complicate several of the calculations involved and therefore for the sake of convenience – if nothing else – we will assume symmetrically distributed returns and so continue to make use of the standard deviation and variance.

Risk and expected utility

The above analysis contained what could be called a casual justification for measuring investment risk by the standard deviation or variance of returns. However, it is possible to give a more analytical justification for these risk measures.

Our analysis of the expected utility model allowed us to conclude that risk-averse investors would be expected to have a utility function of the general form:

$$U(x) = a + bx - cx^2$$

and therefore, in terms of the utility an investor could expect to obtain from the return on an investment in the shares of a company, we can express the utility function as:

$$E[U(r)] = a + bE(r) - cE(r^2)$$

In other words the expected utility of the investment is determined by the distribution of the possible returns [which produce values for $E(r)$ and $E(r^2)$] and by the investor's personal attitude towards risk (which determines the values for the constants a, b, c).[13]

Given the definition of variance that we have used:

$$\sigma^2 = E(r^2) - E(r)^2$$

then the third term of our general utility function can be re-expressed as:

$$-cE(r^2) = -c[\sigma^2 + E(r)^2]$$

and multiplying this out, the general utility function can be re-expressed as:

$$E[U(r)] = a + bE(r) - c\sigma^2 + cE(r)^2$$

The advantage of undertaking this bit of algebraic manipulation is that we can now see that the expected utility produced by an investment is determined by the three risk-attitude constants (a, b, c), and two of the characteristics of the probability distribution of the investment's return: the expected return [$E(r)$ and $E(r)^2$] and the variance of returns (σ^2).

We know that if an investment's return is certain, then the variance has a value of zero, whereas if the investment's actual return is uncertain, the variance will have a positive value. However, because the constant attached to the measure of variance (c) in the utility function is negative for the risk-averse investor (it is this that causes the utility function to be concave to the origin), a *positive* variance results in a *reduction* in the value of the utility expected from the investment.

Thus the more uncertain the actual return on the investment, the greater will be the value of the variance and the less will be the utility expected from the investment by the investor. This is exactly what we would expect for a risk-averse investor: the more risky the investment, the less attractive is the investment, and hence the lower is the utility it is expected to provide.

Required assumptions

This analysis provides us with a much more carefully reasoned justification for using variance or standard deviation as a measure of investment risk. However, at least one of two alternative conditions must hold true for this analysis to be held to have real world validity.

The first is that the variance is acceptable as a measure of risk as long as the probability distribution of possible returns is symmetrical. If it is strongly *asymmetrical* then we know that the arithmetic mean and variance no longer provide a complete description as a measure of skew would also be required. Furthermore, neither the standard deviation nor variance would then provide an adequate measure of downside risk.

Alternatively, the conclusion only holds if investors' utility functions do follow the quadratic form developed earlier and are therefore *solely* determined by the expected return and variance of return variables. If utility functions of investors have a more complex form than that of a simple quadratic (and assuming returns are asymmetrically distributed) it follows that any measure of risk is also likely to be more complex.

The practical validity of these two alternative assumptions is troublesome. As an example, there is evidence to suggest that investors' utility curves may exhibit both convexity and concavity – i.e., they may be risk seekers or risk-averse, depending upon the size of the investment under consideration. However, perhaps the question of skew in investment returns poses the greater problems.

Intuition tells us that investment returns *must be* skewed: the maximum downside risk on an investment in a limited liability company is − 100%, but the upside potential return can quite easily exceed that percentage. Further, there is some evidence to suggest that investors *are* interested in skew and do recognise that skewed returns can exist. However, we shall continue our analysis on the assumption that variance (or standard deviation) of return is an adequate measure of risk, based on the reasoning that even if returns are skewed, the amount of skew is likely to be relatively small, and so will not be too much at odds with the assumption of symmetry.

Limitation of the analysis

Our analysis up to this point remains extremely limited as far as investment decision making is concerned. Assuming an investor is interested in maximizing expected utility and is risk-averse, then if a choice has to be made between two investments with identical expected returns, we can state that the alternative with the smaller amount of risk (either standard deviation or variance) will be preferred. Alternatively, given a choice between two investments with an identical amount of risk, the investor will prefer whichever has the highest expected return. Thus A is preferred to B and C is preferred to D:

$$\text{Choice 1:} \quad \begin{cases} E(r_A) = E(r_B) \\ \sigma_A < \sigma_B \end{cases}$$

$$\text{Choice 2:} \quad \begin{cases} E(r_C) > E(r_D) \\ \sigma_C = \sigma_D \end{cases}$$

However, the decision here is extremely limited. Certainly, we can conclude that A should be *preferred* to B, but we cannot say whether or not the investor will actually *choose* to undertake A, i.e., we cannot tell whether A gives a sufficiently large expected return to provide adequate compensation for the risk involved.

Furthermore, once we move away from this rather special choice situation, we cannot even make a preference statement: we cannot reach any conclusion as to which of the following pair of alternatives would be preferred:

$$\text{Choice 3:} \quad \begin{cases} E(r_E) > E(r_F) \\ \sigma_E > \sigma_F \end{cases}$$

For a possible solution to these decision problems, we now have to turn to have a look at portfolio theory. In addition, thinking back to the two questions that were posed at the start of this chapter: 'how are we to identify the degree of risk associated with a particular capital investment project?', and 'how can we identify the corresponding capital market interest rate that is appropriate for that level of risk?', it would appear that the analysis outlined above goes some way to providing an answer to the former, but not to the latter. We shall not comment further on these two questions at this stage, but wait until our understanding of the risk and expected return relationship has been further developed.

SUMMARY

This chapter has started to take a closer look at the relationship between risk and return in investment decision making. In particular, it considers how the risk and expected return of an investment might be measured. The main points covered are as follows:

- Four axioms of investor behaviour are specified:
  - ☐ Choice is possible.
  - ☐ Choice is transitive.
  - ☐ Choice is dispassionate.
  - ☐ Certainty-equivalents can be specified for any *gamble* situation.
- Given these axioms, then it is possible to construct a utility function for a risk averse investor of the general form: $U(x) = a + bx - cx^2$, where the constants a, b and c reflect the investor's own personal risk attitude.
- With such a utility function, when faced with an investment the following relationship holds: the expected utility of the investment will be *less than* the utility of the investment's expected outcome. The difference is the required reward for risk-taking.
- As far as stock exchange investment is concerned, the expected return on a share can be measured as its *arithmetic mean* return and the risk of the share can be measured either as its *variance* or – more conveniently – its *standard deviation* of returns.
- However, standard deviation (or variance), whilst fitting in with the utility function concept of risk, is only a satisfactory measure of risk if either investment returns are symmetrically distributed around the expected return, or if investors' utility functions actually follow the quadratic form specified:

$$E\,[U(r)] = a + bE(r) - cr^2 + cE(r)^2$$

- Finally, the analysis developed so far is highly limited. It can allow *choice* to be made either between projects of equal risk, or between projects of equal expected return. It does not allow choice between projects where there is neither equal risk nor expected return. Nor does it allow decision making on any investment's *absolute* desirability (i.e. accept or reject), but just on *relative* desirability (when compared with another project).

NOTES

1 'Higher', that is, than what they would have received if the investment's outcome was known *for certain*. They would get a higher return as a reward for taking on the risk involved.

2 An axiom can be defined as a statement which is generally accepted without any need for proof or verification.

3 For example, suppose an investor is offered an investment which has a 60% chance of producing £5,000 and a 40% chance of producing only £1,000. We are assuming that the investor will be able to specify a *certain* sum of money which would be equally acceptable as this uncertain investment. This sum might be £3,000. Thus £3,000 is said to be the certainty-equivalent of the above uncertain investment: the investor would be indifferent between receiving £3,000 for certain or receiving £5,000 with a 60% probability and £1,000 with a 40% probability.

4 We have already come across the idea of utility or indifference curves in the development and use of the single-period investment–consumption model.

5 We will assume that the project's outcome will occur almost immediately and so avoid – at this stage – the need to consider discounting.

6 Quite literally *any* utility index numbers could be used; for instance we could give +£5,000 an index of 75 and −£2,000 an index of 36 if we wished. The advantage of assigning index numbers of 1 and 0 to these two outcome extremes is simply that it eases the arithmetic.

7 The Figure given in the text is not detailed sufficiently for the reader to obtain these values. However, they were obtained from the utility index as shown.

8 To calculate the return on a share, you do not need to have actually *sold* the share. You may continue to hold the share and simply wish to know what return you have made to date. In such circumstances the 'selling price' would be replaced by the 'current market price'.

9 Note that the word 'expected' is now being used in a technical sense, meaning the arithmetic mean.

10 Notice that the standard deviation can be expressed as a percentage, just as can the expected return. However the variance involves a 'squaring-up' of the data and so cannot be viewed as a percentage, but simply as an uncategorized measure of dispersion.

11 The standard deviation is stated in rates of return whilst the variance represents 'rates of return squared'. Because it is easier to discuss risk as a percentage rate of return, rather than a rate of return squared, the standard deviation is now commonly used to measure risk. However, it is sometimes mathematically more convenient to measure risk by variance. Either definition of risk is conceptually valid since they are mathematically equivalent. The two measures *cannot* be used interchangeably, but they do give consistent rankings of risk.

12 Any introductory text book on inferential statistics will discuss these properties in detail.

13 The '*c*' constant is negative to ensure that the utility function is that of a risk-averse individual and hence concave to the origin.

FURTHER READING

1 Utility theory is not a simple area, but for an easy introduction see: R.O. Swalm, 'Utility Theory – Insights into Risk Taking', *Harvard Business Review*, November–December 1966.
2 For an example of an actual attempt to construct utility functions, see: C.J. Grayson, 'The Use of Statistical Techniques in Capital Budgeting', in *Financial Research and Management Decisions*, ed. A. Robichek, John Wiley 1967.
3 Finally, for a more complete discussion on utility functions, see Chapter 11 of J.C. Francis and S.H. Archer, *Portfolio Analysis* (2nd edition), Prentice-Hall 1979.

QUICKIE QUESTIONS

1 If the NPV discount rate should reflect the return available elsewhere in the capital market for an investment of similar risk to the project being appraised, what two *practical* problems arise?
2 What is meant by the term transitive with regards to ranking alternatives?
3 What is a certainty-equivalent?
4 If an investment has two outcomes: + £10,000 and − £5,000 and an investor indicates that £3,500 is the certainty-equivalent of a 60% chance of a +£10,000 outcome, what is the utility measure of £3,500 on a 0 to 1 scale?
5 If a utility function is concave to the origin, what risk attitude does this indicate?
6 What would the utility function of a risk-neutral investor look like?
7 For a risk-averse investor what is the relationship between an investment's expected outcome and its certainty-equivalent?
8 Define the return on a share.
9 Given the following information, what is the expected return and risk of an investment in the following shares?

Economic Conditions	*Probability*	*Investment Return*
Strong growth	0.20	+40%
Weak growth	0.60	+15%
Economic decline	0.20	−10%

10 What is down-side risk?

PROBLEM

1 An investor carefully considers a number of gambles and decides that he is indifferent between a certain income of £2,500 p.a. and each of the following possibilities:

(i) A 60% chance of receiving £4,500 p.a. + a 40% chance of receiving £500 p.a.
(ii) A 75% chance of receiving £1,600 p.a. + a 25% chance of receiving £4,500 p.a.
(iii) A 55% chance of receiving £1,600 p.a. + a 45% chance of receiving £3,500 p.a.
(iv) A 75% chance of receiving £2,000 p.a. + a 25% chance of receiving £3,500 p.a.
(v) A 50% chance of receiving £2,000 p.a. + a 50% chance of receiving £3,000 p.a.
(vi) An 85% chance of receiving £2,000 p.a. + a 15% chance of receiving £4,000 p.a.

The investor has an occupation which gives him an income of £1,000 p.a. which he regards as certain. He is now considering which of the two alternative *additional* activities he should undertake:

(1) Offers a 50% chance each of an income of £1,500 p.a. and £2,000 p.a.
(2) Offers a 50% chance each of an income of £1,000 p.a. and £2,500 p.a.

Assume that he will accept one of these opportunities and that he has no borrowing and investment opportunities available; the utility function measures the utility derived from the present contemplation of an income of the specified amount in any year.

Required:
(a) Sketch a utility function for the investor. What does this function indicate about his attitude towards risk?
(b) Use utility analysis to indicate which new opportunity he should accept.
(c) Calculate the variance of each possible income stream available to the investor.
(d) Comment briefly on the implications for the usefulness of variance calculations in analysing decisions subject to uncertainty.

9
Portfolio theory

Chapter Contents

TWO-ASSET PORTFOLIOS

Portfolio theory – as its name implies – is concerned with the construction of investment portfolios. Essentially it is based on a statistical result: if several probability distributions are combined and their arithmetic means and variances are known, together with the degree to which their returns co-vary, then the arithmetic mean and variance of the resulting *combined* probability distribution can be specified.

Therefore if the shares of several different companies are combined into an investment portfolio and the expected returns, variances of returns and covariances of returns are known for each company's shares, then the expected return and variance of the investment portfolio can be determined.

However the importance of portfolio theory does not lie so much in this statistical result, but in an observation that arises out of this result. This observation is that although the expected return of the investment portfolio is simply a weighted average of the expected returns on the individual investments that go to make up the portfolio, the risk of the portfolio (measured by its standard deviation of returns) is *less than* the weighted average risk of the individual constituent investments.[1] In other words, the statistical result upon which portfolio theory is founded supports the wisdom of the old adage of 'not keeping all your (investment) eggs in one basket' – that risk can be reduced through diversification.

Risk and expected return

Suppose that an individual investor has a sum of money with which he wishes to construct an investment portfolio by buying the ordinary shares of different companies. In order to keep the arithmetic simple, we shall initially assume that he is going to purchase the shares of just *two* companies – therefore he is constructing what can be termed a *two-asset risky portfolio*. Later on we will see how the approach used can be directly expanded to involve portfolios that consist of shareholdings in many companies.

Let the two companies whose shares comprise the individual's investment portfolio be called A and B, respectively. The individual uses a proportion, x, of his investment funds to buy shares in company A, and the remainder of his funds $(1 - x)$ is used to buy shares in company B. The statistical result that is the foundation of portfolio theory allows us to determine the expected return, $E(r_p)$ and variance of return, σ_p^2, of the resulting investment portfolio:

$$E(r_p) = xE(r_A) + (1 - x)E(r_B)$$
$$\sigma_p^2 = x^2\sigma_A^2 + (1 - x)^2\sigma_B^2 + 2x(1 - x)\,\text{Cov}\,(r_A, r_B)$$

For the moment it will be more convenient for us to deal with portfolio risk in terms of the standard deviation of returns, σ, and so the second expression becomes:

$$\sigma_p = \sqrt{[x^2\sigma_A^2 + (1 - x)^2\sigma_B^2 + 2x(1 - x)\,\text{Cov}\,(r_A, r_B)]}$$

The covariance

We are familiar with all the notation used in these expressions, except for $\text{Cov}\,(r_A, r_B)$. This notation represents the measure of the covariance between the returns on the shares in A and in B. In other words, the covariance examines the degree to which the variability of the returns on the shares of both companies tend to move together.

This covariance can either be positive or negative and can also be either weaker or stronger. Positive covariability indicates that the returns on the two shares will tend to vary together in the same direction (i.e. if, in a particular time period, the return produced by the shares in company A is above what was expected, then there will be a tendency to find that the return on the shares in B is similarly above expectations), whereas negative covariability indicates that the returns will tend to move in opposite directions.

In addition, the greater the strength of covariability (say, positive covariability) then the stronger will be the tendency for the variability in returns between the two companies to move in unison. It helps to explain the meaning of the covariance if its components are examined. We can express the covariability of returns as follows:

$$\text{Cov}\,(r_A, r_B) = \sigma_A\sigma_B\rho_{AB}$$

In other words, the covariance of returns in A and B represents the product of the risks of A and B (measured by the standard deviation of returns) and the correlation coefficient, between the returns in A and in B.[2]

The correlation coefficient expresses the strength of the linear relationship between the two variables – in this case the returns of the shares of A and B – and can take on any value between +1 and −1. A correlation coefficient of +1 indicates perfect positive correlation, such that the returns of the two shares will vary in perfect lock-step; whereas a correlation coefficient of −1 indicates perfect negative correlation. In this case the returns on the two shares will move in perfect *negative* lock-step. A positive correlation coefficient, but one which is less than +1, indicates that there is a *tendency* for the returns on the two shares to move together; and a negative correlation coefficient, but one which is less than 0 but greater than −1, indicates that there is a tendency for the returns to move in opposite directions.

The further away the correlation coefficient is from +1 or −1 (and hence the closer it is to zero) the weaker is the general tendency indicated by the sign of the correlation – or the greater is the tendency for the share return movements to be unrelated or *uncorrelated.* It is, of course, the sign attached to the correlation coefficient that determines the sign of the covariance.

The covariance calculation

This may be a good stage at which to provide a simple example of the calculations required to determine the covariance. Suppose the shares of two companies C and D have the following probability distributions:

State of Economy	*Probability*	*Returns on C*	*Returns on D*
Boom	0·2	24%	5%
Steady Growth	0·6	12%	30%
Slump	0·2	0%	−5%

Then their expected returns and standard deviation of returns can be calculated as:

$$E(r_C) = 12\% \qquad E(r_D) = 18\%$$
$$\sigma_C = 7{\cdot}59\% \qquad \sigma_D = 17{\cdot}15\%$$

and the covariance of returns is given by:

$$\Sigma\,[r_C - E(r_C)]\,[r_D - E(r_D)]\ \text{Pr.}$$

that is:

$$\begin{aligned}
(24\% - 12\%) \times (5\% - 18\%) \times 0{\cdot}2 &= -31{\cdot}2\\
(12\% - 12\%) \times (30\% - 18\%) \times 0{\cdot}6 &= 0\\
(0\% - 12\%) \times (-5\% - 18\%) \times 0{\cdot}2 &= +55{\cdot}2\\
\text{Cov}\,(r_C, r_D) &= +24{\cdot}0
\end{aligned}$$

Given that $\text{Cov}\,(r_C, r_D) = \sigma_C\sigma_D\rho_{C,D}$, then

$$\rho_{C,D} = \frac{\text{Cov}\,(r_C, r_D)}{\sigma_C\sigma_D} = \frac{+\,24}{7{\cdot}59 \times 17{\cdot}15} = +\,0{\cdot}184$$

This is a relatively low, positive correlation. It indicates that although the returns on the shares in the two companies *tend* to vary in the same direction, the tendency is rather weak.

Given the above information, if an investor was to construct a two-asset portfolio consisting of shares in companies C and D, such that 75% of his funds were placed in the shares of C (i.e. $x = 0{\cdot}75$) and the remainder of his funds placed in D (i.e. $1 - x = 0{\cdot}25$), then the resulting portfolio would have an expected return $[E(r_p)]$ and risk (σ_p) as follows:

$$E(r_p) = (0{\cdot}75 \times 12\%) + (0{\cdot}25 \times 18\%) = \underline{\underline{13{\cdot}5\%}}$$

$$\sigma_p = \sqrt{[(0{\cdot}75^2 \times 7{\cdot}59\%^2) + (0{\cdot}25^2 \times 17{\cdot}15\%^2) + (2 \times 0{\cdot}75 \times 0{\cdot}25 \times 24{\cdot}0)]}$$
$$\sigma_p = \sqrt{(32{\cdot}40 + 18{\cdot}38 + 9{\cdot}0)} = \sqrt{59{\cdot}78} = \underline{\underline{7{\cdot}73\%}}$$

THE RISK-REDUCTION EFFECT

Returning to the expressions for the risk and expected return of a two-asset portfolio, but now expanding the covariance term in the risk expression, we can examine the cause of the risk-reduction effect of investment diversification:

$$E(r_p) = xE(r_A) + (1 - x)E(r_B)$$
$$\sigma_p = \sqrt{[x^2\sigma_A^2 + (1 - x)^2\sigma_B^2 + 2x(1 - x)\,\sigma_A\sigma_B\rho_{AB}]}$$

The first of these two expressions does not give cause for much excitement. It simply shows that the portfolio's expected return is an average of the expected returns on the two component investments $[E(r_A)$ and $E(r_B)]$, weighted by their respective importance (by value) in the overall portfolio. This is just as we would have thought; however, the second expression is of considerably greater interest. This interest is caused by the last element in the expression – the correlation coefficient of returns – which can take on any value between $+1$ and -1 (including zero).

The third term in the expression for portfolio risk: $2x(1 - x)\,\sigma_A\sigma_B\rho_{AB}$ is at its largest value[3] when the correlation coefficient is $+1$. The further away the correlation coefficient is from $+1$, the smaller is the value of this third term and hence the smaller is its contribution to the portfolio's risk. (In fact when the correlation coefficient becomes negative, the term actually makes a *negative* contribution to risk, which reaches a maximum when the returns are perfectly negatively correlated, i.e., -1.)

It is this third term (and in particular the correlation coefficient it contains) that is the cause of the risk-reduction effect of investment diversification. Measuring portfolio risk as the standard deviation of returns, we can say that the portfolio risk is a weighted average of the risk of the component investments (just as with the expected return) but *only* if the returns on the shares in the two companies are perfectly positively correlated (i.e. $\rho_{AB} = +1$). If the correlation coefficient is *less than* $+1$ (as will normally be the case) then the risk of the portfolio is *less than* a weighted average of the risk of the individual investment components. The further away the correlation coefficient is from $+1$, the greater will be the risk reduction effect.

An example

An example will help to clarify matters at this point. This is shown in Table 9.1.

Table 9.1

An investor wishes to construct a portfolio which consists of placing 60% of his available funds into the shares of company E and the other 40% is placed in the shares of company F.

Companies E and F have the following expected returns and risk:

$$E(r_E) = 30\% \qquad E(r_F) = 10\%$$
$$\sigma_E = 12\% \qquad \sigma_F = 3\%$$

The expected return on the investor's portfolio will be a weighted average of the expected returns on the portfolio's component investments:

$$E(r_p) = (0{\cdot}60 \times 30\%) + (0{\cdot}40 \times 10\%) = \underline{\underline{22\%}}$$

But what of the portfolio's *risk*? That will depend upon the correlation coefficient between the returns on the shares of the two companies. If the correlation coefficient is: + 1 then there will be *no* risk-reduction effect and the portfolio's risk:

$$\sigma_p = \sqrt{[(0{\cdot}6^2 \times 12\%^2) + (0{\cdot}4^2 \times 3\%^2) + (2 \times 0{\cdot}6 \times 0{\cdot}4 \times 12\% \times 3\% \times +1)]} = \underline{8{\cdot}4\%}$$

is simply a weighted average of the risk of the portfolio's components:

$$\sigma_p = (0{\cdot}6 \times 12\%) + (0{\cdot}4 \times 3\%) = \underline{8{\cdot}4\%}$$

However, the further away the correlation coefficient is from + 1, the greater will be the amount of risk eliminated through the *diversification* effect. To illustrate this effect, three examples will be used:

(i) If $\rho_{E,F} = +0{\cdot}5$, then $\sigma_p = 7{\cdot}9\%$
(ii) If $\rho_{E,F} = 0$, then $\sigma_p = 7{\cdot}3\%$
(iii) If $\rho_{E,F} = -1$, then $\sigma_p = 6{\cdot}0\%$

From Table 9.1 it can be seen how portfolio risk, but *not* portfolio expected return, is progressively reduced as the correlation coefficient moves further and further away from perfect positive correlation (i.e. $\rho = +1$).

A diagrammatic example

This further example is designed to graphically illustrate the points made above and also to show how the portfolio risk and return can also be varied by varying the proportions of the investment funds placed in each risky asset.

Suppose that the ordinary shares of the two companies (G and H) with which the investor has chosen to construct his portfolio, exhibit the following characteristics:

From the foregoing analysis, we know that the expected return and risk of any portfolio made up of the shares in these two companies depends not only on the above information, but also on the proportions of the available funds invested in each company's shares [i.e., x and $(1 - x)$] and the correlation coefficient of the probability distributions of the returns from each company's shares (i.e., ρ_{GH}).

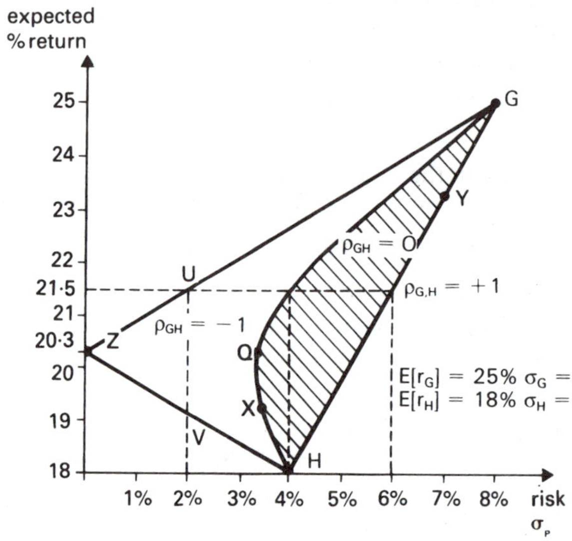

Figure 9.1

Company G	*Company H*
$E(r_G) = 25\%$	$E(r_H) = 18\%$
$\sigma_G = 8\%$	$\sigma_H = 4\%$

Figure 9.1 illustrates the range of possible portfolio risk and expected return that the investor could obtain by varying the proportions of his funds between the two companies, in three particular cases: when the correlation coefficient of returns has a value of +1, 0 and −1. For example, if the investor chose to construct a portfolio that consisted of splitting his investment funds equally between the shares of the two companies [i.e., $x = 0{\cdot}50$ and $(1 - x) = 0{\cdot}50$], then the expected return on the portfolio will be:

$$E(r_p) = (0{\cdot}50 \times 25\%) + (0{\cdot}50 \times 18\%) = 21{\cdot}5\%$$

However, the risk of this portfolio varies, depending upon the value of the correlation coefficient[4]:

ρ_{GH}	σ_p
+ 1	6%
0	4%
− 1	2%

Once again we see that portfolio risk is maximized where the two components are perfectly positively correlated and minimized where they are perfectly negatively correlated. For correlation coefficients between these two extremes, then portfolio risk will be less than 6%, but more than 2% (e.g., when $\rho_{GH} = 0$, the $\sigma_p = 4\%$).

Portfolio risk (and simultaneously, expected return) can also be varied by varying the proportions of investment funds placed in the two shares. Assuming that $\rho_{GH} = +1$, then we know that splitting the investment funds evenly between G and H produces a risk of 6% and an expected return of 21.5%; but *any* of the risk-expected return combinations that lie along the straight line GYH in Figure 9.1 could be obtained, simply by varying the proportions of G and H held.

At one extreme the portfolio would consist only of shares in G, then $E(r_p) = E(r_G) = 25\%$ and $\sigma_p = \sigma_G = 8\%$. At the other extreme the portfolio could consist solely of H, when the risk and expected return would be 4% and 18%, respectively. Alternatively any intermediate portfolio could be constructed such as Y which consists of 75% of funds being placed in G and the remainder in H. This portfolio has a risk and expected return of 7% and $23\frac{1}{4}\%$, respectively.

Notice that where G and H are perfectly positively correlated, all the possible portfolio risk-expected return combinations that are available [through varying x and $(1 - x)$] lie along a *straight* line. In order words both the expected return *and* the risk of the portfolios constructed are simple weighted averages.

In contrast, the risk-expected return portfolio combinations for all other correlation coefficient values (i.e., except for $\rho = +1$) lie along *non-linear* lines, with the non-linearity becoming more pronounced as the correlation coefficient moves further away from +1. Indeed the non-linearity is a graphical representation of the risk elimination effect.

Thus the curved line GXH represents all the possible portfolio combinations available by varying the proportion of G and H when the correlation coefficient is zero. For example, portfolio X consists of 80% of portfolio funds in H and the balance in G. The expected return is 19·4% (the same as it would have been if $\rho_{GH} = +1$) but the risk is only 3·58% (whereas it would have been 4·8% if $\rho_{GH} = +1$). The degree of curvature of GXH signifies the degree of risk reduction possible in the circumstances given.

The third example represented diagrammatically in Figure 9.1 is where the two risky assets display perfect *negative* correlation. Here the 'dog-legged' line GUZVH reflects all the possible portfolio combinations that would be available by varying the investment proportions. One unique feature about this set of circumstances is that, as can be seen from the diagram, it is now possible to construct a portfolio with *zero* risk. This is portfolio Z. The exact make-up of this portfolio can be found by solving for x in the expression[5]:

$$\sigma_p = x \times 8\% - (1 - x) \times 4\% = 0$$

In this case the solution is $x = 0{\cdot}33$. In other words, if one-third of the portfolio funds were placed in the shares of G and the rest in H, then the risk of the portfolio would be zero and the expected return (which would in fact be a *certain* return as no risk is involved), would be:

$$E(r_p) = (0{\cdot}33 \times 25\%) + (0{\cdot}66 \times 18\%) = 20{\cdot}13\%$$

However, it should be noted that the ability to reduce risk to *zero* in this way is a characteristic *only* of risky portfolios which consist of perfectly negatively correlated components. Where the correlation coefficient between portfolio components is greater than -1 (but less than $+1$), risk *reduction* is possible, but *total* risk elimination is impossible.

In practice the ordinary shares of most companies exhibit correlation coefficients (with shares in other companies) with values greater than zero but less than $+1$, thereby limiting the degree of risk reduction possible through portfolio manipulation. The shaded area on Figure 9.1 therefore gives the likely risk-return combinations that might be possible in practice with a two-component portfolio consisting of ordinary shares in companies G and H.

Dominance

Continuing with the example where the two portfolio components are perfectly negatively correlated, we can use it to illustrate the fact that, under some circumstances, there will be portfolios available to investors that will be seen as being unambiguously undesirable.

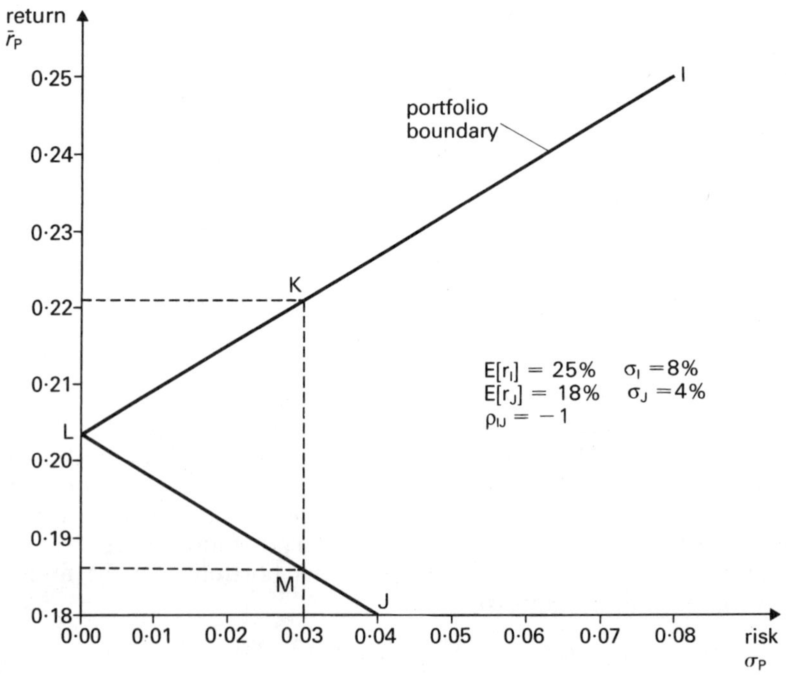

Figure 9.2

Suppose an investor wishes to construct an investment portfolio consisting of shares in I and J, when I and J are perfectly negatively correlated. In Figure 9.2 the line IKLMJ can be termed the *portfolio boundary* because it represents all possible portfolios constructed with the shares of the two companies, given the correlation coefficient.

From Figure 9.2 we can see that a rational risk-averse investor would not chose *any* portfolio lying along the lower part of the IKLMJ *dog-leg*, i.e., between L and J. The reason for this is that there will always be a *better* portfolio lying along the upper part of IKLMJ, where 'better' is defined in terms of a portfolio giving a higher expected return for the same amount of risk.

For example, our investor is always going to prefer portfolio K to portfolio M. Both involve the same amount of risk, but K is expected to produce a substantially higher return: K is said to *dominate* M. In fact all the portfolios lying along the lower part of the *dog-leg* are dominated by portfolios lying along the upper part. The portfolios that lie along the boundary between points I and L are therefore termed *efficient* in that each represents the maximum expected return for a given level of risk.

Returning to the previous figure, Figure 9.1, along the portfolio boundary for which the correlation coefficient is zero, portfolios lying between points G and Q are similarly *efficient* and those lying between points Q and H, *inefficient*.

MULTI-ASSET PORTFOLIOS

A three-asset portfolio

So far, we have considered two-component portfolios only. However, the analysis can be quite easily extended to portfolios containing many components (e.g. the ordinary shares of many different companies), although the calculations become much more lengthy. The risk (measured by variance) and the expected return of a portfolio consisting of N different components can be calculated from the expressions given below, where x_i represents the proportion of funds invested in component i:

$$E(r_p) = \sum_{i=1}^{N} x_i E(r_i)$$

$$\sigma_p^2 = \sum_{i=1}^{N} \sum_{j=1}^{N} x_i x_j \sigma_i \sigma_j \rho_{ij}$$

It is the calculation of the portfolio variance that is particularly time-consuming because it is calculated as the sum of the weighted variance of all possible combinations of pairs of components. Table 9.2 illustrates the computations necessary for even just a simple three-component portfolio consisting of shares in companies N, P and Q, in the respective proportions: 20%, 70%, 10%. The resulting portfolio, termed Z, has an expected return of 26·2% and a standard deviation of return of 8·04%.

Table 9.2

Company	Portfolio Proportion	$E(r_i)$	σ_i	ρ_{ij}
N	0·20	20%	6%	N, N = +1 N, P = +0·7 N, Q = +0·4
P	0·70	30%	10%	P, N = +0·7 P, P = +1 P, Q = +0·8
Q	0·10	12%	2%	Q, N = +0·4 Q, P = +0·8 Q, Q = +1

$$E(r_p) = \sum_{i=n}^{q} x_i E(r_i)$$

$$= (0{\cdot}20 \times 20\%) + (0{\cdot}70 \times 30\%) + (0{\cdot}10 \times 12\%) = \underline{\underline{26{\cdot}2\%}}$$

$$\sigma_p^2 = \sum_{i=n}^{q} \sum_{j=n}^{q} x_i x_j \sigma_i \sigma_j \rho_{ij}$$

$$\left.\begin{array}{l} = 0{\cdot}20 \times 0{\cdot}20 \times 6\% \times 6\% \times 1 = 1{\cdot}44 \\ 0{\cdot}20 \times 0{\cdot}70 \times 6\% \times 10\% \times 0{\cdot}7 = 5{\cdot}88 \\ 0{\cdot}20 \times 0{\cdot}10 \times 6\% \times 2\% \times 0{\cdot}4 = 0{\cdot}096 \\ 0{\cdot}70 \times 0{\cdot}20 \times 10\% \times 6\% \times 0{\cdot}7 = 5{\cdot}88 \\ 0{\cdot}70 \times 0{\cdot}70 \times 10\% \times 10\% \times 1 = 49{\cdot}0 \\ 0{\cdot}70 \times 0{\cdot}10 \times 10\% \times 2\% \times 0{\cdot}8 = 1{\cdot}12 \\ 0{\cdot}10 \times 0{\cdot}20 \times 2\% \times 6\% \times 0{\cdot}4 = 0{\cdot}096 \\ 0{\cdot}10 \times 0{\cdot}70 \times 2\% \times 10\% \times 0{\cdot}8 = 1{\cdot}12 \\ 0{\cdot}10 \times 0{\cdot}10 \times 2\% \times 2\% \times 1 = \underline{0{\cdot}04} \end{array}\right\} +$$

$$\sigma_p^2 = \underline{\underline{64{\cdot}672}}$$

$$\sigma_p = \sqrt{\sigma_p^2} = \sqrt{64{\cdot}672} = \underline{\underline{8{\cdot}04\%}}$$

Therefore the portfolio (we shall term it portfolio Z), consisting of 20% of investment N, 70% of investment P and 10% of investment Q has the following characteristics:

Expected return = 26·2%
Risk = 8·04%

A graphical representation

Whereas all possible portfolios that can be constructed from just two assets (with a specified correlation coefficient) can be illustrated graphically as lying along a line (as in Figures 9.1 and 9.2), when dealing with multi-asset portfolios, all possible combinations are represented by an *area*.

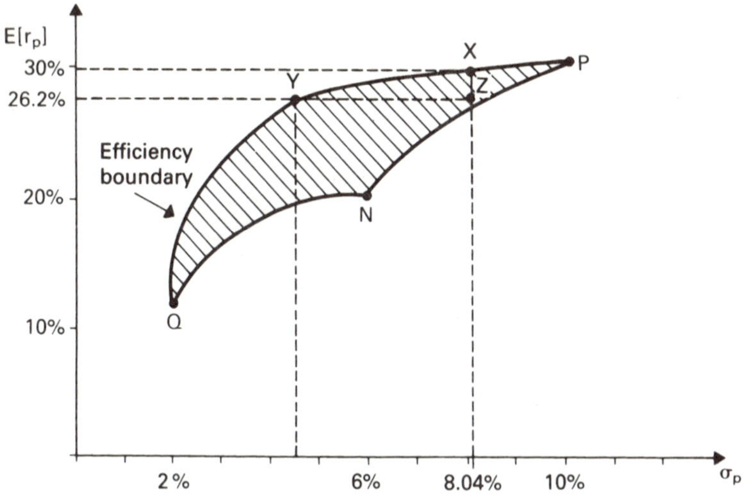

Figure 9.3

Figure 9.3 illustrates the area of possible portfolios that may be obtained from combining the shares of companies N, P and Q. Point Z represents the location of the portfolio actually constructed in Table 9.2.

From our previous discussion of dominance we know that, for risk-averse investors, the only portfolios of interest will be those lying along the north-west boundary of the portfolio area, PXYQ, the *efficient boundary*. These portfolios represent the greatest possible expected return for a given level of risk. Therefore a risk-averse investor would not be interested in holding portfolio Z: portfolio X would give a superior expected return for the same level of risk, whilst portfolio Y would give the same return for a much reduced level of risk. Indeed, all the portfolios lying along that part of the efficiency boundary between X and Y would be preferred to portfolio Z.[6]

An investor faced with holding a portfolio consisting of shares in the three companies N, P and Q would consider only the portfolios lying along the efficiency boundary and select the one which maximized his utility, given his own particular attitude to risk and return. In terms of indifference curves, the investor would select that portfolio which allowed him to obtain his highest possible indifference curve. Figure 9.4 illustrates this situation.

Considerations of practicality

Up to this point, although the analysis has been useful in identifying that it is the risk and expected-return characteristics of combinations of investments that is of importance, rather than the risk and expected return characteristics of single investments, the *practical* usefulness of the analysis is limited.

Individual investors themselves, never mind others who may be taking

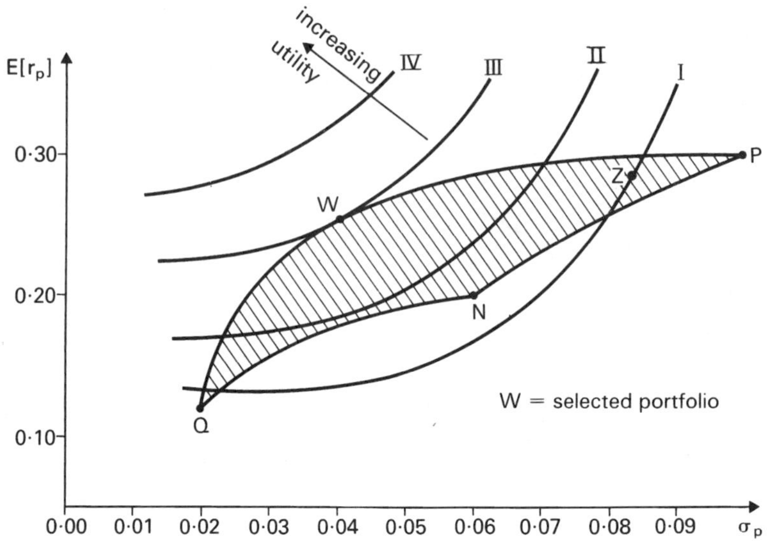

Figure 9.4

decisions on their behalf, are unlikely to be aware of the nature of their set of indifference curves. Thus in Figure 9.4, although in the circumstances given portfolio W would be optimal for the investor with that set of indifference curves (some of which are shown), in practice the investor can do little more than follow his own rather poorly formed 'judgement' as to the combination of the three investments which will produce the 'best' risk-return combination.

However, the main stumbling block to the practical application of the ideas we have developed so far is the vast numbers of calculations that would be needed to identify the efficiency boundary in practice. The example used above only involved the consideration of just three risky assets – and only looked at one possible portfolio – but we still saw that a substantial number of calculations were required as each possible combination of pairs of investments had to be considered. In the real world the investor faces a vast number of risky assets and so the data and computations necessary to identify the efficiency boundary become astronomical in number and, to all intents and purposes, totally impractical.

For example, the total amount of data required – in terms of expected returns, variances and covariances – is given by $N(N + 3)/2$, where N is the number of different shares. An investor facing the London Stock Exchange has over 7,200 securities from which to choose. In terms of portfolio theory, this would require almost 26 million calculations! Thus even if an investor was knowledgeable about his own set of indifference curves, it is unlikely that he would be able to identify the efficiency boundary, let alone the optimal portfolio lying along that boundary.

INTRODUCTION OF A RISK-FREE INVESTMENT

A two-asset portfolio

A move towards greater practical usefulness can be made if a *risk-free* investment is introduced into the analysis. With such an investment, the return is known for certain and exhibits no variability. Government bonds (or *stocks*), held to maturity are usually credited with being such an investment.[7]

To see the effect of introducing a risk-free investment we will start by examining the characteristics of a two-asset portfolio where one asset is a risk-free investment (e.g. government stock) and the other is a risky investment (e.g. the shares of company A). The risk-free return will be designated as r_F (it is no longer an *expected* return, but is now *certain*), and because its return is certain, its risk – measured by either the standard deviation (σ_F) or the variance (σ_F^2) – is zero.

The resulting portfolio has the following characteristics.

$$E(r_p) = xE(r_A) + (1 - x)r_F$$
$$\sigma_p^2 = x^2\sigma_A^2 + (1 + x)^2\sigma_F^2 + 2x(1 - x)\sigma_A\sigma_F\rho_{AF}$$

As the risk-free investment has a zero variance and standard deviation, the expression for portfolio risk reduces to:

$$\sigma_p^2 = x^2\sigma_A^2 \quad \text{or} \quad \sigma_p = \sqrt{(x^2\sigma_A^2)} = x\sigma_A$$

The risky-riskless boundary

Figure 9.5 illustrates the range of portfolio risks and expected returns that are possible from combining risky investment A, with an expected return of 18% and a standard deviation of 5%, with a risk-free investment producing a certain 8% return. The different portfolios that are available from combining the two investments lie along a straight line because, as the above expression for portfolio risk shows, when combining a risk-free and a risky investment, portfolio risk becomes a simple weighted average of the risk of the components.

To identify this particular type of portfolio boundary, we will term it the *risky-riskless* boundary. Portfolio P on this boundary consists of 75% of risky investment A and 25% of the risk-free investment. In other words, portfolio P is three-quarters the way up the boundary line between the risk-free asset (Government stock) and the risky asset (shares in company A). It produces the following characteristics:

$$E(r_p) = 0{\cdot}75 \times 18\% + 0{\cdot}25 \times 8\% = 15{\cdot}5\%$$
$$\sigma_p = 0{\cdot}75 \times 5\% = 3{\cdot}75\%$$

The slope of this boundary is particularly interesting. It is calculated as $[E(r_A) - r_F]/\sigma_A$ and gives the *additional* amount of expected return produced by the portfolio for each unit increase in its risk. Therefore in this example, every 1% increase in portfolio risk (σ_p) produces an extra $(18\% - 8\%)/5\% = 2\%$ of expected return.

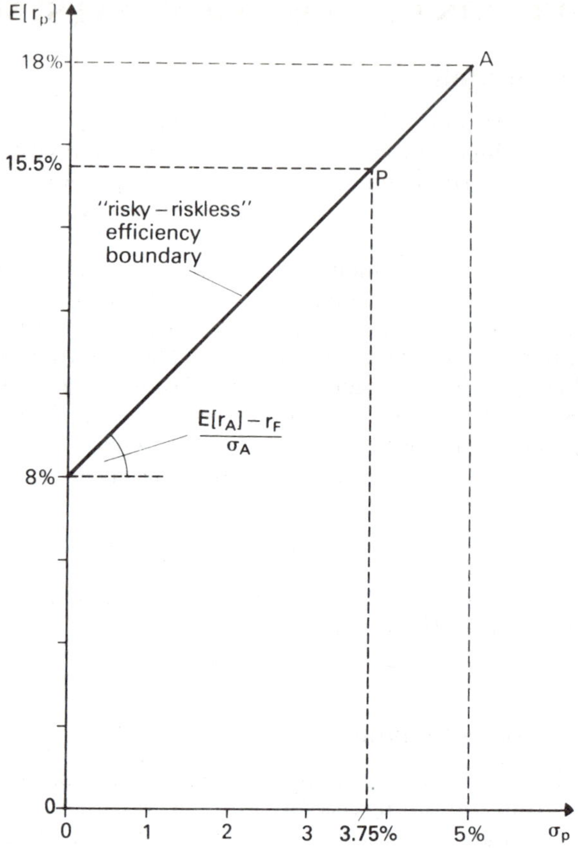

Figure 9.5

For example, if we wished to undertake a portfolio investment which involved taking on a risk of 4·75% (measured by standard deviation), then this should provide an expected return of 4·75 × 2% = 9·5% *in excess* of the risk-free return of 8%. Thus the total expected return from the portfolio would be 9·5% + 8% = 17·5%.

This can be seen to fit in with the portfolio risk and expected return expressions. If the portfolio is to display risk of 4.75%, then:

$$\sigma_p = x \times 5\% = 4{\cdot}75\%$$

This gives $x = 4{\cdot}75\% \div 5\% = 0{\cdot}95$
and $(1 - x) = 0{\cdot}05$
Therefore, $E(r_p) = 0{\cdot}95 \times 18\% + 0{\cdot}05 \times 8\% = 17{\cdot}5\%$

A riskless asset plus a risky portfolio

Extending this approach further, suppose that an investor is faced with a choice amongst many alternative risky investments (such as the London Stock Exchange). The shaded area in Figure 9.6 represents *all* possible

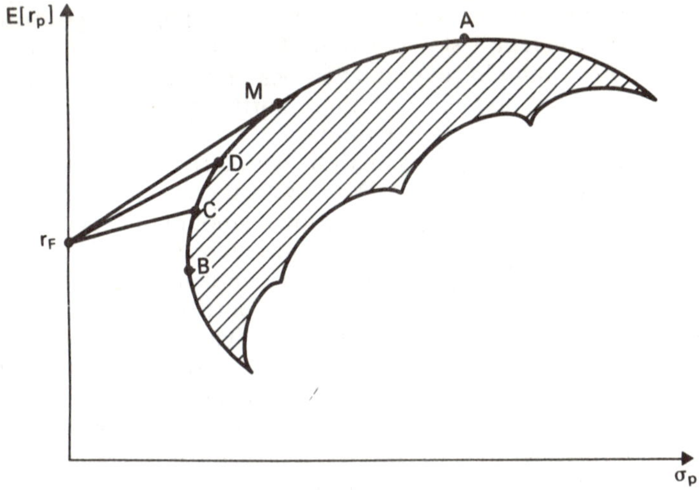

Figure 9.6

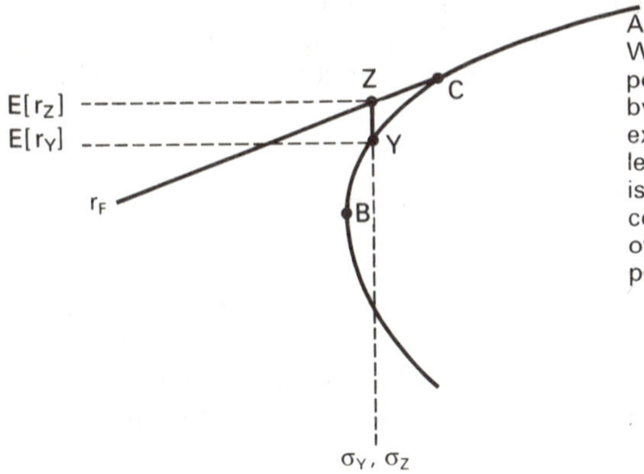

An example of dominance: What *was* an efficient risky portfolio Y is now dominated by Z which produces a higher expected return for the same level of risk. Portfolio Z is a two-asset portfolio consisting of a combination of Government stock and risky portfolio C.

Figure 9.7

risky investment portfolios open to him and AB represents the boundary of efficient portfolios[8] available.

If the possibility of undertaking a risk-free investment is introduced, we can now consider constructing another two-asset portfolio where one asset is risk-free and the other is risky. The difference between the situation here and that in the previous example is that now the risky asset is not a single investment (e.g., shares in a single company) but an investment in an *efficient portfolio of risky assets.*

Suppose such an investment was efficient risky portfolio C in Figure 9.6, then the two-asset portfolios available would lie along the line r_F, C. The point of interest to us here is that the introduction of this two-asset portfolio *dominates* part of the original efficiency boundary AB. Those portfolios lying along BC of the efficiency boundary are dominated by those lying along r_F, C. Figure 9.7 shows this situation in more detail.

Returning to Figure 9.6, it can be seen that combining government stock (r_F) with efficient risky portfolio C is not the *best* two-asset combination. For example government stock and portfolio D dominate all the r_F, C portfolios, as well as all those portfolios from B to D on the original risky portfolio efficiency boundary.

Another way of looking at this analysis is in terms of the slope of the risky-riskless efficiency boundary. We saw in the previous section that the slope of this boundary gave the additional amount of expected return (in excess of the risk-free return), for each unit increase in risk taken on. It therefore follows that it is in the investor's best interests to combine government stock with that efficient risky portfolio that creates the *steepest possible* risky-riskless boundary slope. This portfolio is found at the point of tangency of a line drawn from the risk-free return to the risky portfolio efficiency boundary: portfolio M in Figure 9.6.

Under these circumstances the original efficiency boundary AB has now been radically modified to AMr_F. An investor who wishes to locate somewhere along A to M has to specifically identify the particular portfolio of risky investments. However, an investor who wishes to locate along M to r_F will simply place a proportion of his investment funds in government stock and the remainder in risky portfolio M. Investors will no longer be interested in any portfolio lying along M to B as these are all dominated by portfolios lying along the risky-riskless boundary of M, r_F.

The possibility of borrowing

Buying government stock can be viewed as simply *lending* money to the government, and therefore the return on government stock, r_F, is the risk-free *lending* interest rate. In the previous section we saw how the original efficiency boundary was modified and extended by the introduction of a risk-free investment: lending at the risk-free interest rate. A complementary extension and modification can also be achieved by the introduction of the possibility that the investor can add to his investment funds by *borrowing.*

Assuming that investors can borrow unlimited amounts (given their ability to repay) at an interest rate of r_B, and assuming that both the interest payments and loan repayments are certain, then Figure 9.8 illustrates the modification and extension possible to the *original* boundary of efficient risky portfolios: the line AB. The revised efficiency boundary now becomes BNX, where X extends without limit (i.e., unlimited borrowing capacity).

For reasons similar to those of the previous analysis, portfolios lying along that part of the original efficiency boundary of A to N are no longer desirable as they are dominated by portfolios lying along NX. However the composition of the portfolios lying along NX are somewhat different to those lying along r_F M in Figure 9.6.

In Figure 9.6 the portfolios on the risky-riskless boundary were composed of investments split between risky portfolio M and risk-free government stock. In Figure 9.8, the investments lying along NX are constructed by the investor placing *all* his own investment funds into

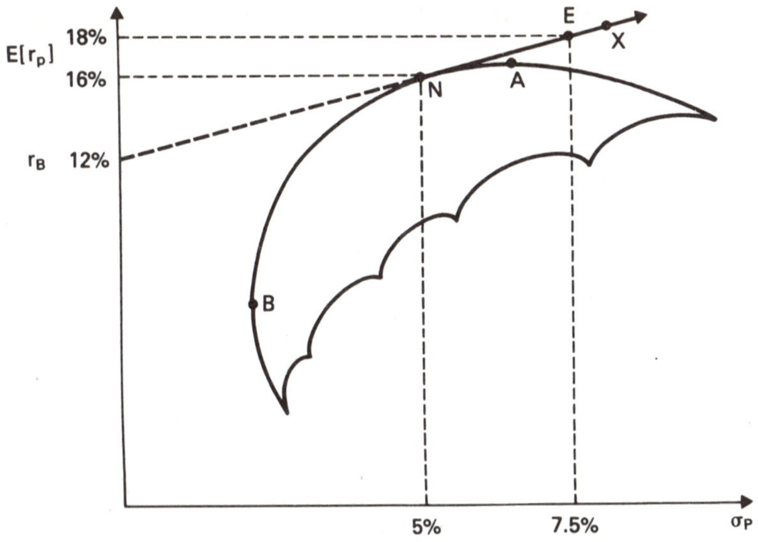

Figure 9.8

risky portfolio N, borrowing additional funds and placing these additional funds *also* in risky portfolio N. The greater the amount of money borrowed, relative to the investor's own funds, the further will his

Table 9.3

Suppose the following facts apply:

$$E(r_N) = 16\% \qquad r_B = 12\%$$
$$\sigma_N = 5\% \qquad \sigma_B = 0\%$$

If the investor has investment funds of £1,000 available, and he wished to increase his investment funds by 50% (0.50), by borrowings of £500, then the risk and expected return of the resulting portfolio E will be given by:

$$x = 1{\cdot}5 \qquad (1 - x) = -0{\cdot}5$$
$$E(r_E) = 1{\cdot}5 \times E(r_N) + (-0{\cdot}5) \times r_B$$
$$\sigma_E = 1{\cdot}5 \times \sigma_N$$
$$E(r_E) = (1{\cdot}5 \times 16\%) - (0{\cdot}5 \times 12\%) = \underline{\underline{18\%}}$$
$$\sigma_E = 1{\cdot}5 \times 5\% = \underline{\underline{7{\cdot}5\%}}$$

An alternative way of calculating the expected return would be as follows:

£1,500 invested in N at 16% = £240 expected annual return
less £500 borrowed at 12% = £ 60 annual interest
= £180 net expected annual return

An annual return of £180 on an outlay of £1000 of the investor's own cash represents a percentage return of 18% = $E(r_p)$

resulting investment portfolio be located *up* the line NX, towards (and beyond) X.

An example

An illustration of a portfolio lying along NX is shown in Table 9.3. Again, Figure 9.8 gives details.

Combined borrowing and lending possibilities

Figure 9.9 combines the possibility of borrowing money at an interest rate of r_B and the possibility of lending money at an interest rate of r_F, by buying government bonds, where $r_B \neq r_F$. The resulting efficiency boundary is now r_F, M, N, X. As this stands we have not advanced the practicality of portfolio theory to any great extent because we still have to rely on knowledge of the investor's set of indifference curves to identify which portfolio of risky assets is to be held and we still have the problem of identifying the composition of that risky portfolio. For example, Figure 9.9 shows the points of tangency between the indifference curves and efficiency boundary for three different investors: I, II and III.

Investor I will hold portfolio W, which consists of placing a proportion of his investment funds in government bonds and the balance in risky portfolio M. Investor II holds portfolio Y, which simply consists of placing all his investment funds in the collection of risky assets of which portfolio Y is composed. Finally, investor III holds portfolio Z, which consists of placing all his own investment funds in risky portfolio N, plus

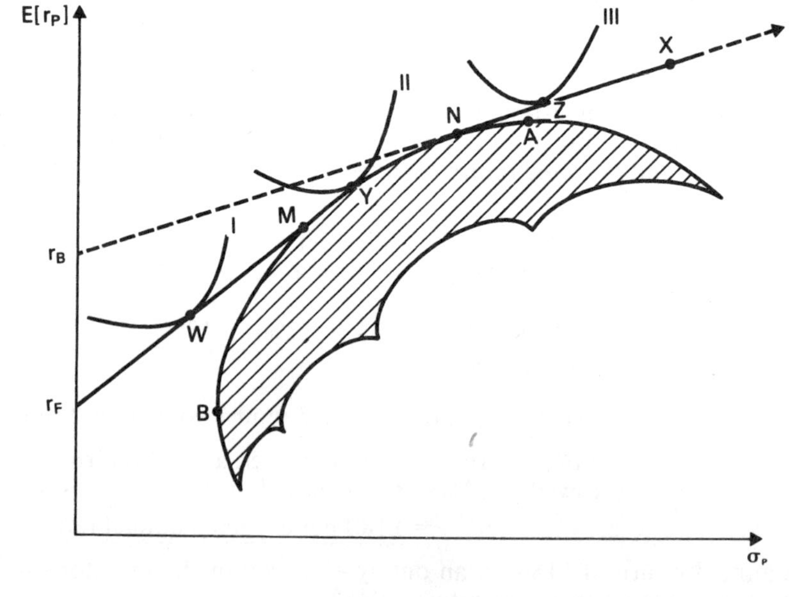

Figure 9.9

borrowing additional funds at a rate of interest of r_B and placing these funds also in portfolio N.

The situation displayed in this example is a slight improvement (in practical terms) when compared to the original situation where neither borrowing nor lending took place. We no longer have to identify the composition of the *complete* risky portfolio efficiency boundary of AB, but we still have to be able to identify a considerable proportion of this boundary. In terms of Figure 9.9, we still have to identify the set of risky portfolios lying between M and N.

THE CAPITAL MARKET LINE

From the above analysis, and from Figure 9.9, we can see that the only efficient portfolios which are composed *solely* of risky investments, lie along that part of the efficiency boundary represented by MN. It follows that the smaller is the gap between the borrowing (r_B) and lending (r_F) interest rates, then the smaller will be the segment of the *original* efficiency boudary of interest to investors.

Therefore, let us now assume that the individual can lend and borrow funds at the *same* risk-free interest rate (i.e., $r_B = r_F$). In such circumstances the efficiency boundary simply becomes the straight line drawn from r_F which is tangent to the original risky portfolio efficiency boundary. The efficiency boundary that arises out of this assumption of identical risk-free lending and borrowing rates leads to some very important conclusions and is termed the *Capital Market Line* (CML): it is illustrated in Figure 9.10.

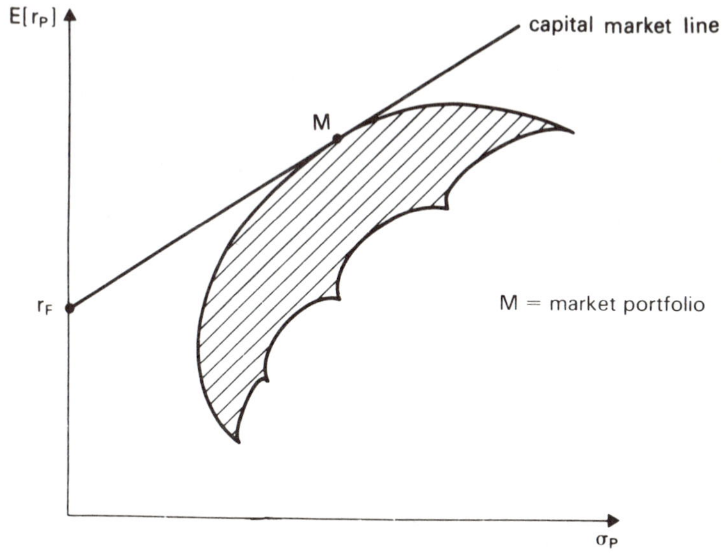

Figure 9.10

The Separation Theorem

Figure 9.10 shows that there is now *only one* collection or portfolio of purely *risky* assets that investors would be interested in holding. This is labelled portfolio M. Thus investors who wished to locate on the CML somewhere between r_B and M would invest a proportion[9] of their funds in that portfolio of risky assets represented by M, and the remainder of their funds would be placed in the risk-free security. Those investors who wished to locate on the CML above M would place all their own investment funds in the portfolio of risky assets M, borrow additional funds[10] at an interest of r_F and invest those additional funds also in M.

This case, where it is assumed that investors can lend and borrow unlimited amounts at the risk-free interest rate of r_F, is important because of the fact that in such circumstances *all* risk-averse investors will be interested in only *one* portfolio of risky investments: portfolio M in Figure 9.10. They will either put all their investment funds into this portfolio, or only part of their funds and lend the rest at the risk-free interest rate, or borrow additional funds and place all their own funds plus the borrowed funds into portfolio M. Therefore, whatever investment portfolio is constructed by an investor – in other words, wherever he choses to locate on the CML – he will only be interested in one collection or portfolio of purely risky assets. This will be portfolio M. As a result we are now in a position of being able to identify the portfolio of risky assets that an investor would wish to hold (i.e., M), without any knowledge of his set of indifference curves (except to assume that he is generally risk averse). This is the so-called Separation Theorem.[11] It has a significance similar to the separation theorem of the single-period investment–consumption model, in that decisions about investment in

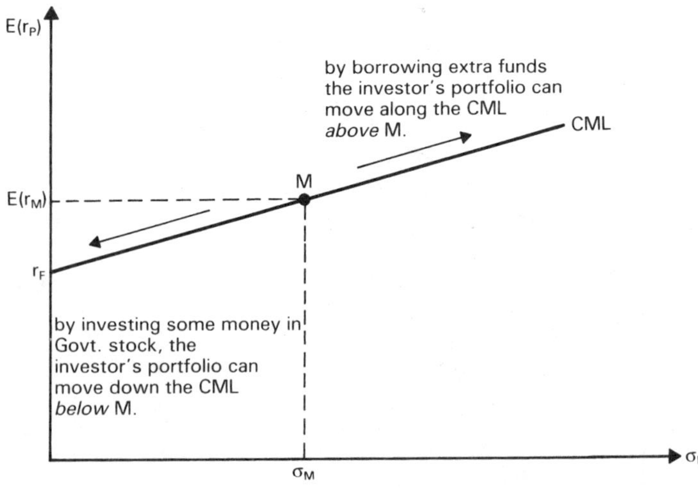

Figure 9.11

risky assets can be made on behalf of investors without the need for any knowledge about the *specific* characteristics of their indifference curves.

In other words we can distinguish between the individual investor's risk and expected return choice (i.e. where he decides to locate on the CML) and the choice of the optimal (share) portfolio. The optimal share portfolio is simply the market portfolio and the investors can adjust the riskiness of their own portfolio, *not* by changing the market portfolio, but by changing the level of lending or borrowing at the risk-free rate. Therefore investors with different risk preferences will *all* hold the same *risky* portfolio of shares (i.e. the market portfolio) but will have different proportions of borrowing or lending.

In addition, the introduction of the idea of the risky portfolio M helps to improve the practicality of portfolio theory for reasons other than just the separation theorem. We saw earlier that one of the main drawbacks of identifying the original risky-asset efficiency boundary was the astronomical number of calculations that would be required. The presence of the CML neatly gets around this difficulty, as long as the location of the CML can be determined. Given that the CML represents a linear function, its location can be determined with knowledge of just two points: the risk-free return and the expected return and risk of the risky portfolio, M. Identification of the former is relatively straight-forward whilst an acceptable proxy for the latter point – as we shall see in the following section – can be given by the expected return and risk of a general stock market index; for example, the Financial Times Stock Exchange (FTSE) index.

The market portfolio

If all investors display the characteristics we ascribed earlier to a single investor (general risk-aversion, rationality and consistency), then under the assumptions listed below, *all* investors will wish to invest some or all of their funds in portfolio M[12] of Figure 9.11. Further, as this will be the *only* combination or portfolio of risky investments that will be of interest to investors, and given that *someone* must hold each risky investment that is available, then it follows that risky portfolio M must contain *all the risky investments that are available.* That is to say, portfolio M must consist of shares in all the companies quoted on the stock exchange. Hence it is termed the *market portfolio.*

Therefore an investor who wishes to hold the market portfolio as part of his overall investment portfolio would (at least in theory) hold shares in *all* the companies quoted on the stock market, in amounts proportionate to their total market values. As an example, suppose that there were only three quoted companies: A, B and C and their total market values were £20m, £10m and £30m, respectively. An investor who wished to invest £1,800 in the market portfolio would buy £600 of shares in A, £300 of shares in B and £900 of shares in C.

The concept of the market portfolio produces a definition of equilibrium market prices. If the market portfolio contains the shares of all the quoted companies, then the market prices of those shares (and hence the return they are expected to produce) must be such that they are acceptable investments for inclusion in the market portfolio. In other words, share prices are at equilibrium when they produce an expected return that is just sufficient compensation for the risk that they involve.

It should also be noted that given the risk reduction effect of diversification, then the market portfolio represents the *ultimate* diversified portfolio: it represents that portfolio of risky assets in which all the risk that it is possible to eliminate, has been eliminated. However, the reader may understandably wish to question the practicality of the market portfolio concept. How can any investor seriously attempt to hold a risky portfolio that consists of shares in *all* quoted companies?

Fortunately, several studies have shown that by constructing a randomly selected portfolio of shares consisting only of between fifteen and twenty different securities (instead of the approximately 7,200 different securities that are quoted on the UK stock exchange) does result in the elimination of around 90% of the maximum amount of risk which it would be *possible* to eliminate through diversification. As a result it means that it is relatively easy to hold a portfolio of risky assets which closely resembles the market portfolio in terms of both risk and expected return. Figure 9.12 illustrates this relationship.

Figure 9.12 illustrates not only the risk elimination effect of diversification but also the fact that not *all* risk can be diversified away. There is an underlying rump on non-diversifiable risk. Various studies have shown that about 65% of total risk can, on average, be diversified away. The remaining 35% of total risk is *non-diversifiable.*

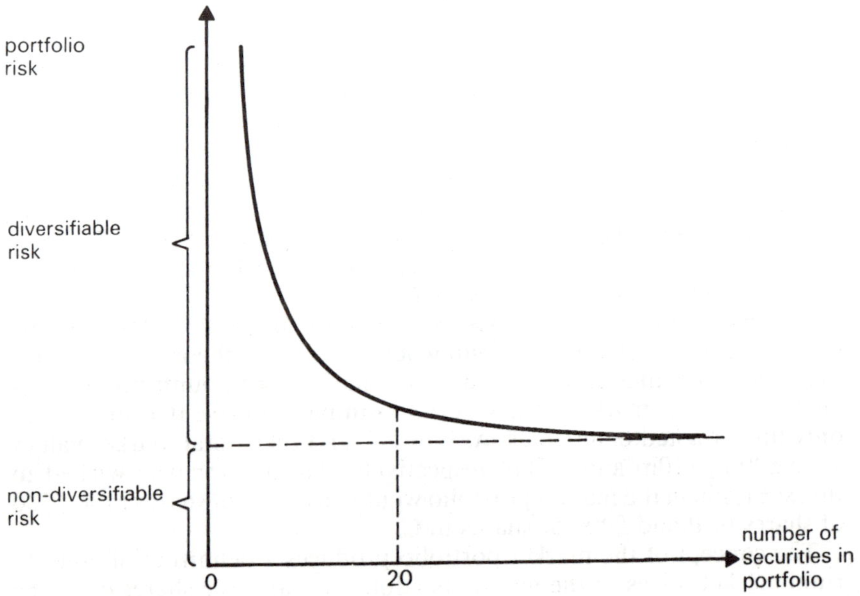

Figure 9.12

The assumptions

Many of the assumptions necessary for the conclusions reached in the foregoing analysis will be familiar, because they were used earlier in our development of a theory of financial decision making. There are six main assumptions in total:

1 The investor's objective is to maximize the utility of wealth.
2 Investors make choices on the basis of risk and return. Return is measured by the arithmetic mean return from a portfolio of assets, and risk is measured by the standard deviation or variance of those returns.
3 All investors can lend and borrow unlimited amounts of cash at the risk-free interest rate.
4 No taxation, transaction costs or other market imperfections.
5 All investors have the same knowledge and expectations about the future and have access to the complete range of investment opportunities. Investors are all price-takers and have free access to all relevant information.
6 All investors have the same decision making time horizon, i.e., the expected return on investments arises from expectations over the same time period.

These assumptions are important, but some of them are clearly unrealistic. However the lack of realism of the model's assumptions is an issue of secondary importance. The main issue surrounds the predictive ability of the model: does the model correctly predict the expected return on portfolios of a particular level of risk? If it has substantial predictive power, then the lack of realism of its assumptions is of little concern. We shall touch upon the model's predictive ability in the next chapter, but (generally speaking) it does seem to possess fairly good (but not perfect) predictive power. Further, when many of the above assumptions are relaxed we do find that the model appears to be remarkably robust and that its general conclusions continue to hold.

The market price of risk

The slope of the CML is of some interest. It can be calculated as:

$$[E(r_M) - r_F]/\sigma_M$$

where $E(r_M)$ and σ_M are the expected return and risk of the market portfolio and r_F is the risk free return.

The slope of the CML indicates the risk–expected return relationship of the whole capital market: in other words it indicates the reward that investors will get (in terms of an expected return *in excess* of the risk free return) for taking on risk. For this reason it is often referred to as the *market price of risk*.

As an example, suppose that the following values held:

$$E(r_M) = 16\%$$
$$\sigma_M = 3\%$$
$$r_F = 10\%$$

then the market price of risk would equal:

$$\frac{E(r_{\mathrm{M}}) - r_{\mathrm{F}}}{\sigma_{\mathrm{M}}} = \frac{16\% - 10\%}{3\%} = 2$$

Thus the CML would have a slope of + 2. This can be interpreted as indicating that for every 1% point of risk (standard deviation) taken on, the investor can expect to receive a return of 2% above the risk-free return. So, an investor willing to take on 4% of risk in his portfolio (i.e., $\sigma_p = 4\%$) could expect to receive (on the basis of the figures above) a return of:

$$10\% + (2 \times 4\%) = 18\%$$

That is to say, an investor who was willing to accept an investment risk of 4% could construct a portfolio yielding an expected return of 18%.

In general terms, the expected return from efficient portfolio '*j*' (where the term 'efficient' refers to a portfolio lying along the CML), is given by the expression for the CML function:

$$E(r_j) = r_{\mathrm{F}} + \frac{[E(r_{\mathrm{M}}) - r_{\mathrm{F}}]}{\sigma_{\mathrm{M}}} \sigma_j$$

or, more simply:

$$E(r_j) = r_{\mathrm{F}} + \lambda\sigma_j$$

where $\lambda = [E(r_{\mathrm{M}}) - r_{\mathrm{F}}]/\sigma_{\mathrm{M}}$ = the market price of risk.

Thus, the expected return on an efficient investment portfolio is equal to the risk-free return (r_{F}), plus the risk premium ($\lambda\sigma_j$). The premium reflects the portfolio's own risk (σ_j), together with the market's *risk attitude* or *risk–expected return trade-off* (λ).

Market portfolio risk

Finally, there are two inter-connected points about this analysis that are very important and should be understood clearly. The first is to notice that the market price of risk indicates the amount of additional return that can be expected for each 1% of 'market portfolio risk' taken on (σ_{M}).

We know that the market portfolio represents the ultimate diversified portfolio and hence, by definition, the risk it contains is the risk that cannot be eliminated through diversification. Therefore the market price of risk indicates the additional expected return (in excess of the risk free return) provided by the market to investors for each 1% of *non-diversifiable* risk taken on. The implied assumption here is that the market would not be willing to give investors any reward (in terms of expected return) for taking on risk that it is possible to eliminate through the diversification process. This is a conclusion of great importance and it will be expanded upon in the next chapter.

The second point is connected to the first. It is that the CML expression:

$$E(r_j) = r_{\mathrm{F}} + \lambda\sigma_j$$

gives the return that should be expected from an *efficient* investment portfolio. Thus it only applies to investment portfolios lying along the CML (a rational risk-averse investor would not be interested in any other portfolios). The point of importance here is that this analysis, and in particular the expression for the CML does *not* apply to *individual* investments (for example, it does not apply to the return we should expect from the shares of an individual company) – which could be termed *inefficient* investments – but only to *efficient* investments, i.e. efficient portfolios. Once again, this point will be picked up in the following chapter.

SUMMARY

This very brief analysis of portfolio theory can be summarized as follows:

- The expected return on a share can be measured by its arithmetic mean return and its risk can be measured by the standard deviation of returns.
- When investments are combined in a two-asset portfolio, the expected return on the portfolio is equal to a weighted average of the returns expected on the two component investments.
- However, the risk of the portfolio is less than a weighted average of the risk of the two component investments. This is the risk reduction or elimination effect of diversification.
- Portfolio risk can easily be reduced by investing in less risky investments; but, as a result, the portfolio expected return will also be reduced. However portfolio diversification can reduce portfolio risk *without* a consequent reduction in expected return: this is the true meaning of the risk reduction effect of diversification.
- From the two-asset portfolio analysis it follows that the greatest possible risk-reduction effect must be achievable with the greatest possible amount of diversification. This occurs when the portfolio includes investments in the shares of *all* quoted companies and is termed: the market portfolio.
- However, not *all* risk is capable of being diversified away and so the market portfolio does contain a significant element of risk. However risk which is capable of being diversified away will be eliminated from the market portfolio, leaving only non-diversifiable risk.
- The market portfolio, in terms of its risk-reduction characteristics can be fairly easily approximated by a portfolio of fifteen to twenty investments in different segments of the stock market. This is because the risk-reduction benefits of diversification arise fairly rapidly and most of the risk-reduction effect is achieved with only a relatively limited amount of diversification.
- Given that investors are rational and risk-averse, this means that they *like* expected return, but *dislike* risk. Thus investors will *only* be interested in holding one portfolio of shares (risky assets): the market

portfolio (or its more practical 20-investments equivalent). This is because it provides the minimum possible amount of risk for its given level of expected return.

- Investors can then adjust the risk of their own personal portfolios (σ_p) so that they hold more or less risk than the market portfolio (σ_M) by either borrowing or lending at the risk free rate of return, and so sliding their own personal investment portfolio up or down the CML from point M. See Figure 9.11.
- Therefore the equation of the CML indicates the return that can be expected by an investor from an *efficient portfolio*, which can be defined as one which is located on the CML.
- This return:

$$E(r_p) = r_F + \lambda\sigma_p$$

consists of two elements. The first is the return available on an investment with no risk at all (r_F). The second is the risk premium, ($\lambda\sigma_p$), the *additional* return available as a reward to investors for taking on risk.

- The risk premium itself consists of two elements: λ and σ_p. The first element, λ, is the market price of risk and represents the going rate of *reward* on the stock market (in terms of expected return) for taking on risk. The second element, σ_p, is the number of percentage points of risk taken on by the particular efficient portfolio chosen (j).
- Finally, it is important to realise that the *only* source of an efficient portfolio's risk (σ_p) is the market portfolio risk. The risk of the market portfolio is, by definition, *all* non-diversifiable and so the risk premium only relates to non-diversifiable risk.

NOTES

1 This is the case in all but the most exceptional circumstances, as will be seen later.

2 It is assumed that the reader is familiar with the statistical term: correlation coefficient. This is the term, often used in conjunction with two-variable linear regression analysis, that expresses the strength of the linear relationship between two variables. A fuller explanation than that given in the text will be found in any introductory book on general statistics.

3 That is, for any given set of values for x, σ_A and σ_B.

4 These values have been calculated from the portfolio risk and expected return expressions, but they could have been estimated from Figure 9.1.

5 This expression is a simplified version of the original expression for portfolio risk, which can be applied when the correlation coefficient is perfectly negative, i.e. $= \rho_p - 1$.

6 Indeed, any portfolio lying to the north-west of Z would be preferred, but the only portfolios that would not – in turn – be dominated themselves, are those lying along the boundary line.

7 These investments are held to be risk free as there is thought to be no chance of default either on the interest payments or on the redemption. (The reason for such a view is based on the fact that the Government can never 'run out' of money – if they do, then they can always print some more.) However, it is important to notice that this assumption only holds in the absence of inflation. If inflation is expected to be present then only the monetary return is certain, the *real* return remains uncertain.

8 The efficient portfolios lying along AB could be called efficient *risky* portfolios in that they are all portfolios that consist of risky investments – the shares of companies.

9 Just *what* proportion would depend upon where the investor wished to locate between r_F and M.

10 Just how much would be borrowed would depend upon how far up the CML, above M, the investor wished to locate.

11 In fact it is often referred to as the 'Tobin' Separation Theorem – after the author who developed the idea – in order to distinguish it from the Hirshleifer separation theorem that we dealt with in an earlier chapter.

12 With the exception of the investor who wishes to hold a totally risk-free portfolio. That investor would place all his investment funds in Government stock, in order to earn a certain return of r_F.

FURTHER READING

1 Many of the articles on portfolio theory are very mathematical and make difficult reading. However two important articles which are fairly straight-forward are: H.M. Markowitz, 'Portfolio Selection', *Journal of Finance*, March 1952, and W. F. Sharpe, 'A Simplified Model for Portfolio Analysis', *Management Science*, January 1963.
2 Three other good articles are W.H. Wagner and S. Lau, 'The Effects of Diversification on Risk', *Financial Analysts Journal*, November-December 1971; W.F. Sharpe, 'Risk Aversion in the Stock Market: Some Empirical Evidence', *Journal of Finance*, September 1965 and B.H. Solnik, 'Why not Diversify Internationally rather than Domestically?', *Financial Analysts Journal*, July–August 1974.

QUICKIE QUESTIONS

1 In a two-asset portfolio, what determines the degree of risk-reduction effect?

2 What is the expression for the risk of a two asset portfolio?
3 Given the following:

State of World	*Probability*	*Possible Return: A*	*Possible Return: B*
I	0·30	28%	35%
II	0·40	18%	15%
III	0·30	6%	20%

What is the correlation coefficient of returns between investments A and B?
4 Given the information in question 3, how would you construct a portfolio to produce an expected return of 20%?
5 What is the expression for the risk and expected returns of an *N*-asset portfolio?
6 What is an *efficient* portfolio?
7 What is the expression for the Capital Market Line?
8 If the risk free return (i.e. Government stock) was 10% and the expected return on the FTSE index was 16% (and risk measured by standard deviation was 3%), how would you construct an efficient portfolio to produce a 15% expected return and what would be its risk?
9 Given the information in question 8, and the fact that you have personal funds of £1,000 to invest, how would you construct a portfolio giving an expected return of 20%, and what would be its risk?
10 Define the market portfolio.

PROBLEMS

1 In Utopia, a very restrictive investment market exists. Investors are able to invest in four types of security (in any combination): A, B, C and X. Securities A, B and C are all risky investments and their current market derived expected (period) returns $E(r)$ and the standard deviation of these returns (σ) are given below:

Security	$E(r)$	σ
A	0·10	0·02
B	0·15	0·04
C	0·20	0·07

All are perfectly positively correlated with each other. Security X is a risk-free investment which yields a period return of 8%. Investors can also borrow unlimited amounts of cash at an interest rate of 8% per period. There is no taxation in Utopia.

Required:

(a) Draw to scale the area of possible risky portfolio. Draw the capital market line and identify the market portfolio.

(b) Calculate the market price of risk and explain what it represents.
(c) State briefly what conclusions you draw from your answer to (a) about the current state of the market for risky assets in Utopia.
(d) An investor in Utopia wishes to hold an efficient portfolio yielding a 10% expected period return. How would this portfolio be composed and what would its risk be?
(e) Show how an investor in Utopia might construct an efficient portfolio yielding a 20% expected period return.
(f) State the main assumptions underlying portfolio theory and indicate briefly why its conclusions may be of importance for investment decision making within individual companies.

2 Alpha PLC, a UK manufacturing company, wishes to diversify its operations internationally by establishing equal-sized subsidiaries in *two* other countries. Because of the company's trading relationships that exist, one should be in Europe and the other in the Far East.

Five countries have been considered and the forecasts of possible present values of net cash flows (excluding outlay) have been calculated using a 20% discount rate. In addition, the calculation of the expected net present value and the risk (measured by standard deviation of NPV) has also been completed. This data is given below:

Hong Kong (HK$m)		*Switzerland* (SFFm)		*Greece* (DRm)	
Prob.	PV	Prob.	PV	Prob.	PV
0·30	+3·8	0·35	+5·39	0·30	+620
0·40	+4·4	0·40	+5·80	0·50	+700
0·30	+4·9	0·25	+6·34	0·20	+730

Singapore (S$m)		*Austria* (AScm)	
Prob.	PV	Prob.	PV
0·30	+18·1	0·35	+100
0·40	+19·3	0·40	+125
0·30	+25·9	0·25	+ 84

The expected initial outlay in all cases is approximately £5·2m and all of the projects have an expected life of 5 years.

An investment analyst employed by Alpha has already started work on the decision and has calculated the expected NPV [*E*(NPV)] and the risk of the Austrian project:

AScm	£m	Outlay	£NPV	Prob.	
100 ÷ 20·8250	= 4·80 −	5·2	= −0·4	× 0·35	= −0·14
125 ÷ 20·8250	= 6·00 −	5·2	= +0·8	× 0·40	= +0·32
84 ÷ 20·8250	= 4·03 −	5·2	= −1·17	× 0·25	= −0·29
				E(NPV)	= £−0·11m

(£NPV)^2	Prob.	
0·16	× 0·35	= 0·06
0·64	× 0·40	= 0·26
1·37	× 0·25	= 0·34
	E(NPV)^2	= 0·66

$$\text{Risk} = \sqrt{0{\cdot}66 - (-0{\cdot}11)^2} = £0{\cdot}80\text{m}$$

The corporate finance department of Alpha PLC have estimated the following *average* exchange rates (number of units of overseas currency per £1) for the next five years:

HK$/£	:	12·7625
SFF/£	:	2·4400
DRm/£	:	225·7250
S$/£	:	3·4422
ASc/£	:	20·8250

They have also estimated the correlation coefficients of *E*NPV between the countries.

Hong Kong/Switzerland	:	−0·15
Hong Kong/Austria	:	+0·40
Switzerland/Greece	:	+0·60
Switzerland/Singapore	:	+0·30
Greece/Austria	:	+0·70
Singapore/Austria	:	+0·85

Required:

(a) The analyst looking at this investment decision has now left the firm. You are asked to complete the task by using the above information to advise the management of Alpha PLC in which two countries to locate its proposed subsidiaries. Alpha is concerned with both the profitability and the riskiness of its investments.

(b) Critically discuss the shortcomings of your analysis.

3 Europium PLC has been specially formed to undertake two investment opportunities. The risk and return characteristics of the two projects are shown below:

	A	B
expected return	12%	20%
risk	3%	7%

Europium plans to invest 80% of its available funds in Project A and 20% in B. The directors believe that the correlation co-efficient between the returns of the projects is + 0·1.

Required:

(i) calculate the returns from the proposed portfolio of Projects A and B;

(ii) calculate the risk of the portfolio;

(iii) comment on your calculations in part (ii) in the context of the risk reducing effects of diversification;

(iv) suppose the correlation coefficient between A and B was −1·0. How should Europium PLC invest its funds in order to obtain a *zero risk* portfolio.

10
The capital asset pricing model

THE SECURITY MARKET LINE

In the previous two chapters we started to analyse the financial decision making process in the face of uncertainty. We saw that on the basis of several assumptions concerning investors and their environment, investment decisions would be made on the criteria of expected return and the variability of return.

We then developed the idea of the CML which (if it can be held to apply in the real world) leads us to conclude that the capital markets display a linear risk–expected return relationship of the type:

$$E(r_j) = r_F + \lambda\sigma_j$$

Further, the analysis also indicated that this relationship is not based simply on the *total* risk of individual investments – in other words, the variability of their possible returns – but on just one part of that risk: the non-diversifiable risk. The market would not provide a reward (in terms of an increased expected return) for that part of an investment's risk that could be eliminated by holding it as part of a well diversified portfolio.

At this point it is worth recalling the purpose of our enquiry into the handling of uncertainty. We are concerned with building up a normative theory of managerial financial decision making: a theory about how company managements *should* make physical capital investment decisions on behalf of their shareholders. Therefore, although the analysis in the previous chapter was concerned with *investors* (rather than managers) making financial decisions, its relevance to our purpose is obvious. We are interested in how shareholders, as investors, take decisions in the light of uncertainty because of the guide-lines it can give us about how managers should take similar decisions on their behalf.

Our brief consideration of capital investment appraisal under conditions of uncertainty that was made right at the start of Chapter 8 led us to try to seek out two things: how to measure the risk of a capital investment project and how to identify the return that should be expected from it, given its level of risk. Although our development of portfolio theory will have given us some *clues* as to how both these questions should be answered, it has done no more than that, because it focused on the risk and expected return relationship of *collections* (or portfolios) of assets. Our concern is with the relationship as it applies to *individual* assets. It is this point that is tackled in the current chapter.

In particular, we are going to develop a share price valuation model. In other words, for the time being at least, we are going to continue to look at stock exchange investment decision making, but now in relation to investment in shares of *individual companies*, rather than *portfolios*. This share price valuation model is usually referred to as the *capital asset pricing model* (CAPM) and it arises directly out of the ideas and conclusions of portfolio theory.

However, it also involves the many unrealistic assumptions of our previous analysis. Nevertheless, the model is useful, in that it provides several significant insights into the major factors of share price determination, and so is of direct interest to decision makers within companies. Indeed, it is worthwhile remembering that the realism or otherwise of a model's assumptions is an irrelevant issue in considering its validity. What is important is the predictive power of the model. In other words, despite its (unrealistic) assumptions and simplifications of the real world, does it appear to capture the main elements of the relationship it seeks to portray? We shall conclude that although the CAPM is not a perfect and complete representation of the real world, it is reasonably adequate.

Derivation of the security market line

The CML function provides an expression for the return that can be expected from an efficient portfolio investment, i.e., an investment in the market portfolio, plus either lending or borrowing at the risk free rate of return. However, we can also use it to derive an expression for the expected return on an *inefficient* investment, such as a risky portfolio other than the market portfolio or, more importantly, an investment in the shares of a single company.

The expression for the expected return on an inefficient investment (e.g. on the shares of an individual company) is derived mathematically in an appendix to this chapter. What we shall do in this section is put forward a more reasoned argument.

We already know from our analysis of the risk and expected return of a two-asset portfolio that the risk is given by the expression:

$$\sigma_p = \sqrt{[x^2\,\sigma_A^2 + (1-x)^2\,\sigma_B^2 + 2x\,(1-x)\,\sigma_A\,\sigma_B\,\rho_{A,B}]}$$

and that the risk reduction effect of diversification is 'caused' by the correlation coefficient. The further away the correlation coefficient is from + 1, the greater is the risk reduction effect.

From this expression, we can see that portfolio risk is made up of three elements. The first element – given by the term $x^2\sigma_A^2$ – is the contribution that investment A makes *independently* to the portfolio. Similarly, the second element – $(1 - x)^2\sigma_B^2$ – is investment B's independent contribution to portfolio risk.

However, the third element – $2x\,(1 - x)\,\sigma_A\,\sigma_B\,\rho_{A,B}$ – is really composed of *two* identical parts:

$$x\,(1 - x)\sigma_A\sigma_B\rho_{A,B}$$

This represents the contribution made to the risk of the portfolio by the two investments *jointly*, and which is determined by their tendency to *co-vary* (i.e. $\rho_{A,B}$).

Because investment A co-varies with investment B in an *identical* fashion to how investment B co-varies with investment A, there are two identical parts to the third element. Within each part, the term $\sigma_A\sigma_B\rho_{A,B}$ – known as the *covariance* of returns between investments A and B – effectively represents the *non-diversifiable* risk that each investment contributes to the portfolio.

We saw that when the correlation coefficient was + 1, there was *no* risk reduction effect. This is because the *total* risk of each investment would be *all* non-diversifiable. Hence, when $\rho_{A,B} = +1$, the portfolio risk expression becomes:

$$\sigma_p = \sqrt{[x^2\,\sigma_A^2 + (1 - x)^2\,\sigma_B^2 + 2x(1 - x)\,\sigma_A\,\sigma_B]}$$

which simplifies[1] to:

$$\sigma_p = x\,\sigma_A + (1 - x)\,\sigma_B$$

That is, the portfolio risk is just a weighted average of the risk of the portfolio components.

However, when $\rho_{A,B} < +1$, then not *all* the total risk of each investment is non-diversifiable. Some of it can be diversified away and so:

$$\sigma_p < x\,\sigma_A + (1 - x)\,\sigma_B$$

which is the risk-reduction effect of diversification.

Furthermore, from our discussion of the capital market line, we derived the expression for the expected return from an efficient portfolio as:

$$E\,(r_p) = r_F + \lambda\sigma_p$$

where *all* the portfolio's risk – σ_p – consisted of non-diversifiable risk derived from the portfolio's holding of the market portfolio.

From this expression can be derived an expression for the return on an *inefficient* investment, such as the shares in company S:

$$E(r_S) = r_F + \lambda\sigma_S\rho_{S,M}$$

Indeed, this is the *general* expression for the expected return from *any* non-'efficient portfolio' investment and is termed the *security market line* – the SML.

The CML and the SML

An examination of the equation for the SML shows how closely related it is to the CML equation:

$$\text{CML:} \quad E[r_p] = r_F + \lambda\sigma_p$$
$$\text{SML:} \quad E[r_S] = r_F + \lambda\sigma_S\rho_{S,M}$$

In fact, in interpretation, they have *exactly* the same meaning.

The CML indicates that the return on an efficient portfolio consists of two elements. The first is the return available for holding an investment with no risk at all – r_F – and the second is the *additional* return that can be expected as a reward for holding the investment's risk – the *risk premium* – $\lambda\ \sigma_p$.

The risk premium is the product of the market price of risk (λ) and the risk taken on by the particular efficient portfolio[2] chosen (σ_p). The important point to remember here is that the risk taken on arises *purely* from the portfolio's holding in the market portfolio. As the riskiness of the market portfolio is all non-diversifiable (by definition – it is the ultimate diversified portfolio), thus the risk premium given by the market is *only for non-diversifiable risk.*

Turning to the SML expression we can see that, similar to the CML, the expected return on the shares in an individual company consists of two elements: the risk-free return and a risk premium. However, the risk premium is now not simply the product of the market price of risk (λ) and the investment's risk (σ_S), but is:

$$\lambda\sigma_S\rho_{S,M}$$

where $\sigma_S\rho_{S,M}$ is that part of investment S's total risk that contributes to the non-diversifiable risk of the market portfolio. In other words, $\sigma_S\rho_{S,M}$ represents the non-diversifiable risk of the shares in company S. Thus the risk premium is based, not on the total risk of investment S, but only on that part of total risk that cannot be diversified away – because the market provides a risk premium *only for non-diversifiable risk.* Example 10.1 puts some figures on this discussion to help clarify the point.

THE CAPM EXPRESSION

In the foregoing discussion we have seen that the expected return on any inefficient investment is determined only by its non-diversifiable risk. More technically, this risk is referred to as *systematic* risk. Similarly, the diversifiable risk is known as *unsystematic* risk.

The SML expression gives the return that an investor *should* expect from any inefficient investment, given its level of systematic risk. The relationship thus described is usually known as the *capital asset pricing*

Example 10.1

Suppose we are given the following information about the (total) risk of company S shares (σ_S) and the degree to which they are correlated with the expected return on the market portfolio ($\rho_{S,M}$):

$$\sigma_S = 8\%$$
$$\rho_{S,M} = +0{\cdot}70$$

Also, if $r_F = 10\%$
and $\lambda = 2$
then:

$$E(r_S) = 10\% + 2(8\% \times +0{\cdot}70)$$
$$E(r_S) = 10\% + 2 \times 5{\cdot}6\%$$
$$E(r_S) = 10\% + 11{\cdot}2\% = \underline{\underline{21{\cdot}2\%}}$$

Therefore, the risk premium of 11·2% is not based on S's *total* risk of 8%, but only on part of that risk 5·6%. This is because:

$$\begin{aligned} 8\% \times 0{\cdot}70 = 5{\cdot}6\% &= \text{Non-diversifiable risk of S} \\ \underline{2{\cdot}4\%} &= \text{Diversifiable risk of S} \\ 8{\cdot}0\% &= \text{Total risk of S} \end{aligned}$$

The market will only give a premium for non-diversifiable risk because S's *diversifiable risk* can be eliminated by holding the shares of S as part of a well-diversified (i.e. efficient) portfolio. Whether or not the investor in company S shares *does* actually hold them as part of a well diversified portfolio is irrelevant as far as the stock market is concerned. The stock market will not provide a risk premium for holding risk which can be easily eliminated through diversifying.

Thus if an investor *just* held company S shares, he would be holding a risk of 8%, but the return he could expect would only be based on a risk of 5·6%. So it can be seen how important it is to hold a well diversified portfolio for an investor to get the expected return deserved, given the risk taken on.

model or the CAPM. Thus, it would state that the return that should be expected on ICI shares (for example) is:

$$E[r_{ICI}] = r_F + \lambda \sigma_{ICI} \rho_{ICI,M}$$

That is to say, the return that should be expected from an investment in ICI shares is equal to the risk-free return, plus a risk premium. The risk premium is determined by the market price of (systematic) risk and the systematic risk level of ICI shares.

Interpreting systematic and unsystematic risk

The CAPM provides the relationship between an investment's systematic risk and its expected return. Therefore, given the general risk-aversion of the market, investments with high levels of systematic risk can be expected to provide a high return and vice versa.

On the other hand, it would be possible to have an investment with a relatively high amount of *total* risk, but only a low expected return: conversely, an investment with a low level of total risk might have a relatively high expected return. In each case, the actual level of expected return depends upon the degree of correlation concerned. The former case would hold where the correlation coefficient was low, whereas the latter case might hold where the correlation coefficient was strongly positive. Example 10.2 illustrates such a situation.

Because we will be interested in applying the CAPM to project investment appraisal, it is useful to consider the *source* or *cause* of systematic and unsystematic risk. Remembering that risk has to do with the variability of a share's return, and the return is, in turn, dependent upon movements in the market price (i.e., the capital gain or loss) and the level of dividends, then the determinants of risk are really the same as the determinants of share price movements and dividend levels.

This is an important area of the theory of financial decision making and we will return to analyse it in depth in a later chapter. However, for the moment we will simply (and very tentatively) conclude that both share price movements and dividends are determined by the level of a firm's cash flow[3]. (Indeed, we should not consider such a conclusion as being contentious, given our discussion in Chapter 1.) Therefore it follows that the *total* risk of a company is determined by the variability of its cash flow: the greater the variability, the greater the risk and vice versa.

Many factors affect the level, or variability, of a firm's cash flow over time. For example, the quality of its management, the state of its labour relations, the level of its advertising and the effectiveness of its research

Example 10.2

Given the following data concerning the stock market:

$r_F = 10\%$ $\lambda = 2$

Company C: $\sigma_C = 20\%$, $\rho_{C,M} = +0{\cdot}20$

Company D: $\sigma_D = 8\%$, $\rho_{D,M} = +0{\cdot}90$

Therefore, in terms of *total* risk, company C shares are significantly more risky than company D shares.

However: Systematic risk of company C: $20\% \times 0{\cdot}2 = 4\%$
Systematic risk of company D: $6\% \times 0{\cdot}9 = 7{\cdot}2\%$
Expected return on company C: $10\% + (2 \times 4\%) = 18\%$
Expected return on company D: $10\% + (2 \times 7{\cdot}2\%) = 24{\cdot}4\%$

Most of company C's risk is capable of being diversified away and so its expected return is relatively low, although its total risk is high. Conversely, most of company D's risk is systematic and so cannot be diversified away. As a result, although its total risk is relatively low, its expected return is relatively high.

and development efforts will all affect the level of cash flow. However, in addition, there are other more general factors that will also affect a firm's cash flow. Examples would include such things as the rate of growth of investment in the economy, the level of consumer demand, movements in exchange rates, rates of corporation tax and the level of interest rates.

All these factors can be roughly divided up into two groups. There are those factors that are *specific* or special to the company (such as the quality of its management and the effectiveness of its research and development); and there are the more general factors that affect *all* firms in the economy (to a greater or lesser extent) and not just the individual firm (e.g., the level of consumer demand). Roughly speaking, it is these former factors that are the determinants of *specific* or *unsystematic* risk, whereas the latter set of factors are the determinants of *market* or *systematic* risk.

The logic of this division of 'risk causes' is fairly easy to follow. Factors that are special or specific to an individual company will be 'washed out' or diversified away, when the shares are held as part of a well diversified portfolio. However, there is no such escape from the market-wide macro-economic type factors that affect all firms and hence cannot be eliminated by diversification.

For example, the effects of a period of bad labour relations in one firm is likely to be countered in a well diversified portfolio by another firm enjoying a period of peaceful labour relations: the one offsets the other. However, a high level of taxation or a rapid rise in interest rates will adversely affect *all* firms (although not to the same extent in each) and there is no offsetting effect.[4]

We shall return to the problem of identifying the sources of systematic risk at a later stage. However, it is worthwhile pointing out that, in practice, the identification of systematic and unsystematic risk factors is not as clear cut as the foregoing discussion might seem to imply. There is a considerable 'grey area' of boundary between the two sets of factors.

The determinants of the systematic risk level

Finally, this is an appropriate place to discuss what determines the degree to which a particular firm's shares are exposed to systematic risk. In other words, why do some companies have high systematic risk and other companies low systematic risk?

If systematic risk can be defined as the extent to which a company's cash flow is affected by macro-economic or non-company-specific factors, then there are likely to be two main determinants of that systematic risk exposure:

(i) The sensitivity of the company's revenues to the general level of economic activity in the economy and other macro-economic factors.

(ii) The proportion of fixed to variable costs (i.e. the degree of cost sensitivity).

In other words, what makes a company risky in systematic risk terms is the degree to which the company's revenues are determined by macroeconomic factors largely outside the control of its management.

This risk can then be either increased or reduced by the proportions of fixed and variable costs involved. A furniture retailing company might be seen as an example of high revenue sensitivity. If the economy is booming and wage levels are rising, people will start to have 'spare' money and their thoughts might turn to spending it by buying new furniture. However, if the economy is depressed and people are unemployed, even those with spare cash may prefer to save it for the uncertain future, rather than spend it on new furniture. Thus the furniture retailing company's revenue is volatile, being sensitive to general economic conditions and these general economic conditions cannot be diversified away in a portfolio.

On the other hand, a food retailer, such as a supermarket, might be taken as an example of a business with a low degree of revenue sensitivity. Generally speaking, in both good times and bad, the supermarket's revenue is likely to be little changed. In bad times people have still got to eat to live, while in good times spare cash might well be spent on other things (such as furniture), rather than increasing the consumption of food.

The proportion of fixed to variable costs includes both operating costs *and* financing costs (where fixed financing costs would consist of interest payments on loan capital and variable financing costs would consist of dividend payments on equity capital). This ratio of fixed to variable costs is particularly important in high revenue sensitive firms.

A high proportion of fixed costs in a firm with high revenue sensitivity will serve to *increase* that firm's already high level of systematic risk: a down-turn in the economy will bring about a down-turn in the firm's revenues, but the (fixed) costs will tend to remain the same. Similarly, a low proportion of fixed costs will help to reduce the level of systematic risk of a company with high revenue sensitivity.

In terms of a firm with low revenue sensitivity, the proportion of fixed to variable costs will make little difference to its riskiness. As its revenues are relatively stable, it should at all times be able to cover its costs, whether they are fixed or variable.

Given the foregoing, and assuming that managers – like investors – are risk averse, it should not surprise us to find that firms with high revenue sensitivity try to minimize the proportion of both fixed financing and fixed operating costs. On the other hand, the management of firms with low revenue sensitivity can afford to be more relaxed about such issues.

THE BETA VALUE

One difficulty that we have yet to mention concerns the practical application of the CAPM. The model will provide the return that should be expected from an individual risky investment. But how are we to identify the several variables that are required?

If the 'market price of risk' (λ) term is expanded, the CAPM expression becomes:

$$E(r_j) = r_F + \frac{[E(r_M) - r_F]}{\sigma_M} \sigma_j \rho_{jM}$$

Assuming that the values of r_F and $E(r_M)$ are relatively easy to identify (using the return on government stock and the expected return on the FTSE stock market index, respectively), there still remains the problem of identifying σ_M, σ_j and ρ_{jM}. These *could* be estimated individually by examining the historical variability of the returns on the market portfolio, the returns on the shares in company j and their correlation. However, fortunately, a much more straightforward estimation procedure exists (which we will examine shortly).

These three 'troublesome' elements (σ_M, σ_j and ρ_{jM}) are usually combined together and termed the *beta value of company j shares*, so that the CAPM is then re-expressed in the much neater form:

$$E(r_j) = r_F + [E(r_M) - r_F]\,\beta_j$$

where

$$\beta_j = \frac{\sigma_j \rho_{jM}}{\sigma_M}$$

Interpreting beta

The numerator of the beta value ($\sigma_j \rho_{jM}$) represents the systematic risk of company j, and the denominator (σ_M) represents the total risk of the market portfolio which (as we know) is *all* systematic risk. Hence the beta value of company j shares is an *index* of the amount of company j's systematic risk, *relative* to that of the market portfolio. Example 10.3 illustrates this point.

The beta value of a company's shares also indicates the degree of responsiveness of the expected return on the shares, relative to movements in the expected return on the market. Beta does *not* indicate the degree of total volatility that can be expected in an investment's return, but only indicates the extent to which expected return is likely to react to overall *market* movements. For example, if the expected return on the market portfolio rises or falls by (say) 10%, then the expected return on the share will react as follows:

$E(r)$ will tend to rise or fall by $>$ 10% if $\beta > 1$
$E(r)$ will tend to rise or fall by $<$ 10% if $\beta < 1$
$E(r)$ will tend to rise or fall by $\approx$ 10% if $\beta \approx 1$[5]

Beta can also be interpreted in terms of a share's risk premium. The beta value of a share indicates the relative magnitude of the change in the share's risk premium that will result from a change in the risk premium of the market portfolio. Example 10.4 provides some figures to illustrate this.

Example 10.3

Suppose we have the following data about company J and the market portfolio:

$$\left.\begin{aligned}\sigma_J &= 10\% \\ \rho_{J,M} &= +0{\cdot}70 \\ \sigma_M &= 5\%\end{aligned}\right\} \text{ Therefore, } \beta_J = \frac{10\% \times (+0{\cdot}70)}{5\%} = 1{\cdot}40$$

In other words, company J has a systematic risk of: 10% × (+ 0·70) = 7% and, as the market portfolio has only 5% of systematic risk, company J has 40% *more* systematic risk than the market portfolio:

$$\left(\frac{7\% - 5\%}{5\%}\right) = 0{\cdot}40 \text{ or } 40\%$$

Hence, company J's beta value of 1·40 indicates company J's systematic risk level *relative* to the average systematic risk level on the stock market (i.e. the risk of the market portfolio).

As further examples, a share with a beta of 2 would have *twice* as much systematic risk as the average, while a share with a beta of 0·67 would only have two-thirds the average level of systematic risk on the stock market.

Example 10.4

Given the following information:

$$\begin{aligned} r_F &= 10\% \\ E[r_M] &= 16\% \\ \beta_T &= 1{\cdot}50 \end{aligned}$$

Therefore the expected return on company T shares is:

$$E[r_T] = 10\% + [16\% - 10\%] \times 1{\cdot}50 = \underline{19\%}$$

Thus an investment in company T provides an expected *risk* premium of 9%. That is: 19% − 10%.

Suppose that the expected return on the market portfolio now increases by 2% to 18%. (Assume that r_F remains unchanged.) The risk premium on the market portfolio will then have risen by 2%, from 6% to 8%. However, company T's risk premium will tend to rise by 3%, because of its beta value: 2% × 1·50 = 3%. And so its overall expected return will become:

$$E[r_T] = 10\% + [18\% - 10\%] \times 1{\cdot}50 = \underline{22\%}$$

Conversely, a share whose beta value was only 0·50 would find its return only increasing by: 2% × 0·50 = 1% in such circumstances.

As a result, we can conclude that high beta shares (i.e., where $\beta > 1$) will tend to *outperform* the return on the market portfolio (the return on the FTSE index) and low beta shares (i.e., where $\beta < 1$) will tend to *underperform* the average return on the stock market. But, of course, this under or over performance comparison with the return on the market portfolio applies to both rises *and* falls in the return on the market portfolio. Therefore high beta shares can either be a good or a bad thing, depending on what is happening to the return on the FTSE index.

Finally, it is worthwhile making one point completely clear. The beta value can indicate the expected *change* in a share's return, relative to a *change* in the return on the market portfolio. What it cannot do is indicate the expected return on a share, relative to the expected return on the market portfolio. For this latter information, we also need to know the risk free return. For example, if a share has a beta of 1·4, then a *rise* of 10% in the expected return on the market portfolio would be expected to lead to a *rise* of 10% × 1·4 = 14% in the expected return on the share. However, if the expected return on the market portfolio is 18%, then we *cannot* say that the expected return from the share is 18% × 1·4 = 25·2%. This can only be found from using the CAPM itself:

$$E(r_j) = r_F + (18\% - r_F) \times 1{\cdot}4$$

Portfolio betas

Thinking back to the discussion in the previous chapter about the risk and expected returns of a two-asset portfolio, we saw that although the expected return was a weighted average of the expected returns of the two portfolio components, the risk of the portfolio was *less than* the weighted average of the risk of the components. This risk reduction was caused by the effects of diversification.

However, systematic risk, by definition, cannot be diversified away, and hence the *systematic* risk of a two asset portfolio[6] *is* a weighted average of the systematic risk of the component investments. As beta gives an index of relative systematic risk, we can conclude that the beta value of a portfolio (as well as the expected return) *is* a weighted average of the betas of its component investments.

Thus if we were to construct a three-asset portfolio as follows:

Asset	$E(r)$	β	Proportion of Invested funds
A	14·4%	1·6	0·60
B	12·8%	1·2	0·10
C	10·8%	0·7	0·30

Then:

$$E(r_p) = (14{\cdot}4\% \times 0{\cdot}6) + (12{\cdot}8\% \times 0{\cdot}1) + (10{\cdot}8\% \times 0{\cdot}3) = 13{\cdot}16\%$$
$$\text{and } \beta_p = (1{\cdot}6 \times 0{\cdot}6) + (1{\cdot}2 \times 0{\cdot}1) + (0{\cdot}7 \times 0{\cdot}3) = 1{\cdot}29$$

This is an important characteristic of beta and we shall return to it later.

The measurement of β

We also mentioned earlier that a share's beta value could possibly be estimated from its constituent components:

$$\beta_j = \frac{\sigma_j \rho_{jM}}{\sigma_M}$$

However, there are obvious difficulties in obtaining the required data. Fortunately, a much simpler surrogate method of estimating beta exists.

The beta value measures the degree to which the risk premium on the share varies as the average risk premium on the stock market varies. It is not surprising that this relationship can be observed directly in the stock market where share prices often move in line with the movement in the stock market index.

Given that the stock market index may well be regarded as some sort of indicator of the general state of the economy, then movements in a share's market price *relative* to movements in the stock market index could reasonably be taken to show how the share reacts to changes in the state of the economy. Therefore, the relationship could be used to measure the shares systematic risk or beta value.

If the *historical* return on the FTSE (acting as a surrogate for the market portfolio) is plotted on a scatter diagram, against the corresponding return on the shares of a particular company, then the points plotted will tend to scatter upwards to the right, indicating a *positive*[7] relationship between the two returns. This effect is illustrated in Figure 10.1. If a linear regression line[8] (a line of best fit) is then plotted through the scatter data, this will reflect the *average* relationship between the returns on the shares and the returns on the FTSE market index. This observed relationship is usually referred to as the *market model* and the linear regression line is known as the share's *characteristic line.*

The slope of the characteristic line indicates the volatility of the share's return (and hence its market price) relative to the return on the market portfolio (the FTSE). If the slope is *greater* than 45° (i.e. greater than 1), then the share's return will tend to be *more* volatile than the stock market index return. For example, if the index (or, more strictly speaking, the risk premium on the index) moves up by 10%, then the share's risk

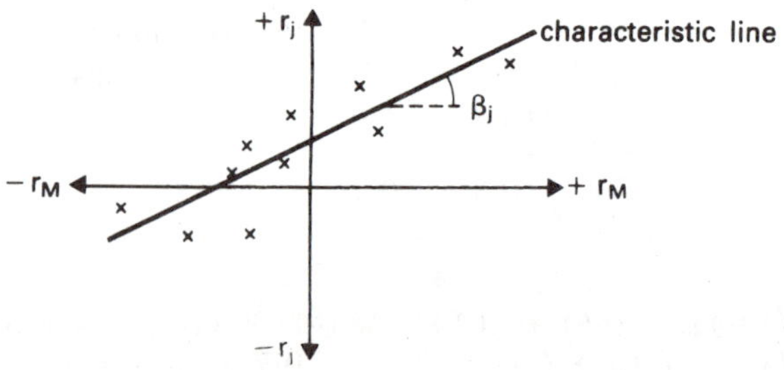

Figure 10.1

premium will move up by *more than* 10%. Conversely, if the market return falls by 10%, the share's return will fall by more than 10%.

Just as a share will tend to *out-perform* the stock market index (in both directions) when the slope of the characteristic line is greater than 1, the share will tend to *under-perform* the stock market index if the slope is *less* than 1. Thus a 10% rise in the market's return would be reflected in a rise of less than 10% in the share's return. Similarly, a 10% fall in the market would result in the share's return falling by less than 10%. Finally, if the characteristic line has a slope of 1, then the share's performance will tend to mirror the stock market index's performance.

This description of the share's behaviour, relative to the market portfolio's behaviour is, of course, directly comparable to our earlier discussion of the meaning of beta. For this reason, this is how beta values for shares are normally estimated: as the *slope* of the regression line.

The main problem with this approach is that, for decision making, we really require an estimate of what *will be* the company's beta value in the future, so that we can estimate what will be the expected return. However, the approach used for estimating beta looks at the *past*, or historical, relationship between the share and the stock market, not the future relationship.

Therefore, whether this method is a satisfactory approach to estimating beta depends upon a single issue: how stable are betas over time? If a company's beta value is found to change very little over time, then estimating the *future* beta on the basis of the *past* relationship may well be acceptable.

The beta value expresses the degree to which the company is exposed to systematic risk (relative to the market portfolio). Therefore it measures the degree to which the company's performance is affected by *macro-economic* forces in the economy (e.g. the rate of national economic growth, inflation levels, exchange rate movements, interest rates, etc.). Common sense would lead us to suppose that companies are unlikely to change their sensitivity to these factors *rapidly*, unless some major event (such as a large scale move into a new area of business) within the company takes place.

This is indeed what the evidence tends to show. Although there is some tendency over time for shares with high and low betas to move towards a beta of 1 (i.e. a general tendency for betas to regress towards the mean), generally speaking beta values are fairly stable and do not change substantially over relatively short (say, five years) periods of time.

Finally, as well as estimating beta from first principles, using the equation for beta:

$$\beta_A = \frac{\sigma_A \rho_{A,M}}{\sigma_M} \quad \text{or} \quad \beta_A = \frac{\text{Cov}\,[r_A, r_M]}{\sigma_M^2}$$

(notice that these two expressions are identical; if the covariance term is expanded, the expression reduces, through cancellation, to equal the first expression), and in addition to estimating beta through regression analysis, Example 10.5 shows how a 'rough and ready' approximation of beta might be generated quite simply.

Example 10.5

Given the following data, the beta value of company A shares could be estimated.

DATA:

	Company A		FTSE		
Year	*Average share price* p	*Dividend per share* p	*Average FTSE index*	*FTSE dividend yield*	*Return on Govt stock*
3 yrs ago	139	7	1300	3%	7%
2 yrs ago	147	$8\frac{1}{2}$	1495	5%	9%
1 yr ago	163	9	1520	$5\frac{1}{2}$%	8%
Current yr	185	10	1640	$5\frac{1}{2}$%	8%

Expected return on company A shares:

(i) Average percentage annual capital gain
Let g = average annual capital gain:

$$139\text{p}\,(1 + g)^3 = 185\text{p}$$

$$\therefore g = (185 \div 139)^{\frac{1}{3}} - 1 = 0{\cdot}10 \text{ or } 10\%$$

(ii) Average annual dividend yield

Year	Div. ÷ sh. price	=	Div. yield
3 yrs ago	7 ÷ 139	=	0·050
2 yrs ago	$8\frac{1}{2}$ ÷ 147	=	0·058
1 yr ago	9 ÷ 163	=	0·055
Current yr	10 ÷ 185	=	0·054
			0·217 ÷ 4 = 0·054 or 5·4%

Therefore the expected return on company A shares can be given as:

$$E[r_A] = \text{Av. ann. capital gain} + \text{Av. dividend yield}$$
$$E[r_A] = 10\% + 5{\cdot}4\% = \underline{\underline{15{\cdot}4\%}}$$

Expected return on the market portfolio (FTSE):

(i) Average annual percentage capital gain

Let g = average annual capital gain:

$$1300\,(1 + g)^3 = 1640$$

$$\therefore g = (1640 \div 1300)^{\frac{1}{3}} - 1 = 0{\cdot}08 \text{ or } \underline{8\%}$$

(ii) Average annual dividend yield

$$3\% + 5\% + 5\tfrac{1}{2}\% + 5\tfrac{1}{2}\% = 19\% \div 4 = 4{\cdot}75\%$$

Cont.

Therefore the expected return on the stock exchange index (FTSE) acting as a surrogate for the market portfolio is:

$$E[r_M] = 8\% + 4{\cdot}75\% = \underline{\underline{12{\cdot}75\%}}$$

Average annual risk-free return:

$$7\% + 9\% + 8\% + 8\% = 32\% \div 4 = \underline{\underline{8\%}}$$

Given the information gathered above:

$$E[r_A] = 15{\cdot}4\%$$
$$E[r_M] = 12{\cdot}75\%$$
$$r_F = 8\%$$

the CAPM can be used to estimate the beta value of company A shares:

$$E[r_A] = r_F + [E(r_M) - r_F]\,\beta_A$$
$$15{\cdot}4\% = 8\% + [12{\cdot}75\% - 8\%]\,\beta_A$$
$$\frac{15{\cdot}4\% - 8\%}{[12{\cdot}75\% - 8\%]} = \beta_A = \underline{\underline{1{\cdot}56}}$$

THE VALIDITY OF THE CAPM

The assumptions behind the CAPM

As has been seen, the capital asset pricing model is derived directly out of the conclusions of portfolio theory. In so doing, as with any model, a number of assumptions were made to simplify the real world. In particular, assumptions were made about investors, their attitudes and behaviour; and assumptions were also made about the capital market itself.

The main assumptions made are as follows:

Investors are: (i) rational
(ii) risk-averse
(iii) utility maximizers
(iv) interested in expected returns
and have (v) the same expectations about the uncertain future
(vi) a single-period investment time horizon

The capital market is perfect in which there are:
(i) no taxes
(ii) no transactions
(iii) no costs for information
and (iv) where investors can both lend *and* borrow at the risk-free rate of interest

Taking these factors individually, the reasons why each is required can be explained. Investors are said to be rational, risk-averse, utility maximizing individuals. That is, they always prefer more money to less, they dislike risk and they are always attempting to make themselves as 'well-off' as possible. In this latter respect, they perceive their 'well-offness' in terms of maximizing their expected returns from investments and they measure the riskiness of their investments through the standard deviation of returns. All these assumptions about investors are required so as to ensure that they will act in accordance with portfolio theory: wishing to hold an efficient investment portfolio, located somewhere on the capital market line.

The final two assumptions about investors are again made to concur with portfolio theory. First if investors did not generally share the same expectations about what the uncertain future holds (for example, if some investors were optimists whilst others were pessimists), a stable market in share prices and returns would not be possible. Secondly, as we know, portfolio theory and the CAPM are both built up on the definition of a single-period rate of return. This implies that decision making by investors is taken with only this limited time horizon in mind.

As far as the capital market is concerned, it is assumed to be perfect. This defines a capital market with a number of characteristics, of which the four listed are the most important. Taxes are assumed to be absent because their presence is likely to distort decision making.

If taxes could be applied in a perfectly balanced way so that all investors, at all times, were treated exactly the same, then no problems would occur. However, in reality, tax systems fail to do this and so they lead to distortions in investors' decision making behaviour.

The assumptions of no transaction costs is required in order to ensure a perfect market equilibrium in share prices. For example, suppose a share gave a return slightly *higher* than it should do, given its risk. In theory, investors (being utility maximizers) would perceive this and would want to buy the shares in order to take advantage. This buying pressure would force up the share price, and so *lower* the share's return. How long would investors continue to buy the shares, and by how much would the share price fall? The answer would be until equilibrium is restored: until the share's return was at the level it *should* be producing, given its risk.

The problem that transaction costs cause is that, if they exist, the share's slightly higher return may not be sufficient to make investors undertake the sort of transactions outlined in the previous paragraph. In other words the benefit of gaining a slightly higher return would be outweighed by the transaction costs (such as stockbrokers' commission) incurred in the share transaction. As a result, equilibrium would not be restored.

The assumption of freely available information is made to ensure that some investors are not excluded from information because they cannot afford to pay for it. If this were not the case, an equilibrium stock market would again not exist: there would not be a general market consensus about the value of all shares as some investors would possess information about them which others would not have.

Finally, there is the assumption that investors can lend and borrow at the risk-free rate of return. We saw in the development of portfolio theory just why this assumption is needed. It is necessary in order to construct a linear capital market line.

It should be clear to the reader that while some of these assumptions might be thought of as being reasonably realistic, others are quite clearly unrealistic and do not reflect the real world. However, as always with model building, the realism or otherwise of the assumptions is not that important. The important factor is the model's ability to predict what happens in the real world. It is this issue that we turn to now.

The empirical evidence

If the CAPM is plotted on a graph, as in Figure 10.2, then it can be used to indicate the expected return on any particular company's shares, given its systematic risk as measured by its beta value. But this then prompts the question: how accurate a reflection of the real world is the CAPM? The issue is not yet fully resolved, although it is probably safe to conclude that the CAPM is a *reasonably* good approximation of the real world.

This conclusion can first of all be argued purely from a point of logic. In Figure 10.2, suppose shares in company X – with a beta value of 0·5 – gave a return that fell *below* the return indicated by the CAPM line. Investors would not wish to buy or hold that company's shares because the expected return for a 0·5 beta investment indicated by the CAPM line could be easily achieved by investing 50% in the market portfolio and 50% in government stock. (Remember, a portfolio beta is a weighted average of its components.)

Company X shares could be said to be *over-priced*. Because their price is so high, they are expected to produce too low a return. As no investor would wish to buy or hold the shares of company X, the share price will fall (the stock market being a supply and demand market). How far will the share price fall? Until the expected return rises to the level indicated by the CAPM line. Only at that point will the share price reach equilibrium and investors will no longer want to sell.

A similar argument would apply to *under-priced* shares whose expected return (like Y in Figure 10.2) is located *above* the CAPM line. Thus, logically, we would expect the expected returns and beta values of all shares to map out along the CAPM line.

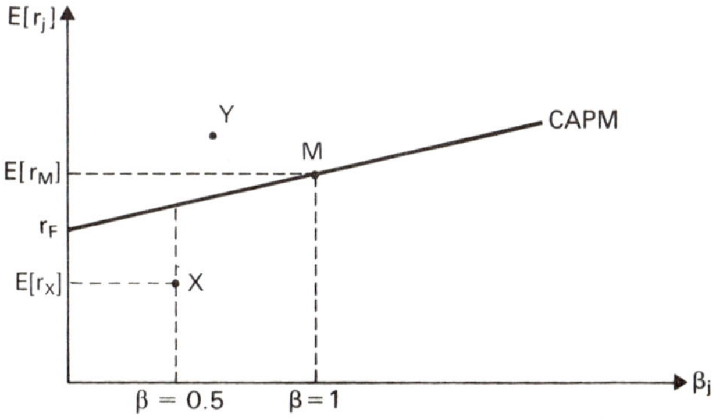

Figure 10.2

Empirically, one of the most famous studies to investigate this matter was by Black, Jensen and Scholes (1972) which indicated that a straight-line relationship, similar to Figure 10.2, did indeed exist between systematic risk and expected returns. However, a later article by Roll (1977) pointed out some methodological problems with such attempts to test for the CAPM relationship and the matter still remains in some doubt.

Not withstanding Roll's criticisms, other tests have been carried out which tend to show that the CAPM may not be a perfect representation of the real world. For example, Banz (1981) showed that small firms gave a slightly *higher* expected return than that indicated by the CAPM. (In other words, if you took two companies with the same beta value, but one was large whilst the other was small, the smaller company tended to give a slightly higher return than the larger company.)

Now this result may have arisen for reasons similar to the criticisms made by Roll, or it could be because the shares of small companies are much less frequently traded on the stock market than are the shares of large companies and traded in smaller quantities. (The market in small company shares is said to be sometimes illiquid.) Thus a buyer of a significant quantity of such shares may find he has to pay a premium over the market price and, similarly, a seller might have to sell at a discount.

Arbitrage pricing model

One of the great strengths of the CAPM is its simplicity. It says that the return that can be expected on the shares of a particular company is equal to the return available for holding no risk at all, plus a risk premium. This risk premium is simply determined by the level of the share's systematic (or non-diversifiable) risk *relative* to that of the average level of systematic risk on the stock market. Hence, the model is often referred to as a *single-index* model. The return is determined by a single factor: the share's beta value.

However, this strength may also be CAPM's weakness. In other words the model may be *too* simple and other factors may also determine return. For example, Banz's study could imply that firm *size* is also a determinant of expected return. Furthermore, it would be easy to think of other possible factors such as dividend policy or the firm's exposure to exchange rate movements which might also play a part in determining what return it should provide for investors.

In fact *multi-factor* asset pricing models have been developed of which the best known is the *arbitrage pricing model.* This model, developed by Ross, is derived in a completely different way from the CAPM. Nevertheless, it looks similar to the CAPM, except that it has got multiple *beta* factors.

The CAPM we have written as:

$$E[r_j] = r_F + [E(r_M) - r_F]\,\beta_j$$

If this is re-written as:

$$E[r_j] = r_F + \lambda_j\,\beta_j$$

where λ_j is the average risk premium on the stock market; then the arbitrage pricing theory (APT) model can be expressed as:

$$E[r_j] = r_F + \lambda_i \beta_i + \lambda_{ii} \beta_{ii} + \lambda_{iii} \beta_{iii} + \ldots.$$

where λ is the 'market price' for each risk factor and the β expresses the degree to which the shares are sensitive to that particular risk factor.

Arbitrage pricing theory is still at an early stage of its development and testing, and it really lies outside the scope of this book. However, early indications look quite promising and it may well be that, in the future, APT gains in importance. Nevertheless, we can also conclude with some certainty that although there may be other factors which contribute to determining the expected return on a share, by far the single most important factor looks to be the systematic risk of the CAPM model.

Thus the CAPM may not be perfect, but it does appear to given a reasonable approximation of the real world and it does have significant predictive ability. For example, high beta shares do tend to be more volatile and produce a higher expected return than low beta shares. In addition the model also gains strength from its logical reasonableness. It does seem to make sense logically. Therefore we can proceed with its use with a fair degree of confidence.

BETAS AND PROJECT INVESTMENT APPRAISAL

The project discount rate

The link between the CAPM and our quest for an NPV discount rate for project investment appraisal seems obvious. The CAPM can be used to generate the appropriate discount rate $[E(r_{\text{project}})]$ having taken into account the systematic risk of the project:

$$E(r_{\text{project}}) = r_F + [E(r_M) - r_F]\, \beta_{\text{project}}$$

However, there are two major difficulties: one conceptual and one practical.

The conceptual difficulty concerns the fact that the CAPM is a *single period return* model, whereas the discount rate required for an NPV calculation is obviously a multi-time period rate of return. As a result, strictly speaking, the CAPM-generated rate of return cannot be applied to an NPV calculation. One solution would be to derive a multi-time period capital asset pricing model and such models do exist. However, there are considerable difficulties involved with them which restricts their practical usefulness.

If it can be assumed that the risk-free return and the excess market return, i.e. $E(r_M) - r_F$, will remain approximately constant over the life of the project, then the single-period CAPM model *can* be used safely in a multi-time period analysis such as an NPV analysis. If such assumptions cannot be made with reasonable confidence – and one problem here is that the excess market return does show some degree of volatility over time – then at least we can try to allow for some of the multi time period effects. For example, the annual yield to redemption on government stock which has the same number of years to maturity as the life of the project can be taken as the estimate of the risk-free return. However, the basic problem of CAPM being a single-period model does remain.

Nevertheless, using the CAPM to provide an NPV discount rate is certainly a considerable improvement on estimating a discount rate on the basis of management's own subjective value judgement. The pragmatic solution is to conclude that, in the light of these circumstances, if a CAPM-generated expected rate of return is to be used as an NPV discount rate, it should only be used with caution. But, having stated that, the CAPM does at least provide a *framework* for analysing what should be a project's discount rate, and it is likely to provide an estimate which is of the correct order of magnitude, given the project's systematic risk. In short, the CAPM may not be the perfect way to estimate a project's discount rate – but it is the best way that we have available.

The project beta

The second difficulty concerns the identification of the project's beta value. Obviously this cannot be estimated in the way that a share's beta is estimated; nor would it be fruitful to consider trying to estimate a project beta through estimating the individual components of the beta value expression. One possible approach to solving the problem is to use the beta value of the *industry* within which the project could be classified, as a surrogate for the beta value of the project. The industry beta value would simply be an average (weighted by market value) of the beta values of the firms within that industry.[9] Thus, if the project under appraisal was a cement production facility, then the average beta value of the half dozen or so quoted companies in the cement industry could be taken as an estimate of the project's beta. However, some adjustments might have to be made to the beta value obtained in this way if it were thought that the project's systematic risk characteristics differed from those of the cement industry generally.

How should such adjustments be made? What happens if a project does not fall neatly within an industrial classification (or the classification is thought to be too wide to be appropriate)? The answer to both these questions is that we require a clearer idea of the identification of systematic risk.

We know that systematic risk refers to the degree of sensitivity to macro-economic changes. Thus to form a view about the systematic risk of a particular project, we need to examine the degree to which its cash flows – its revenue and cost flows – react to changes in the economy, such as changes in the business cycle or in rates of taxation. In other words, how closely tied are the project's cash inflows and outflows to macro-economic forces?

The greater the degree to which the cash *inflows* are tied (that is, the greater is their sensitivity to macro-economic changes), then the greater is their systematic risk and the greater should be the project's beta value. The reverse will apply to the project cash outflows; thus, if the cash outflows are also sensitive to macro-economic changes – i.e., the costs are variable rather than fixed – then this will tend to lower the degree of the project's systematic risk. Conversely, if most of a project's costs are fixed and do not vary with macro-economic changes, then this adds to the systematic risk.

A project whose cash *inflows* are highly sensitive to changes in macro-economic factors, but whose cash *outflows* are mostly fixed and therefore *not* sensitive to macro-economic changes, would be classified as a highly (systematic) risky project. The opposite would be a project with mainly variable costs and a revenue flow that was relatively insensitive to macro-economic changes.

Thus, if it is possible to identify a fairly narrow industrial classification within which a particular investment falls, then the beta value of that industry could be taken as an initial estimate of the project's beta. This can then be adjusted (on a necessarily subjective basis) to allow for the project's particular revenue and cost cash flow sensitivities, when they are thought to differ from the industry norm. In situations where a suitable industry classification does not exist, the relevant characteristics of the project's revenue and cost cash flows would have to be examined and an attempt made to match them to an industry (and its beta value) whose cash flows exhibit similar characteristics.

Finally, there is the situation where a stock-exchange quoted company is involved in the appraisal of a project that falls within the normal area of its business. Here the company's own beta value can provide the starting point, with adjustments being made to allow for the *atypical* aspects of the project's sensitivity to macro-economic factors. However, even in these circumstances, the *industry* beta (if possible) is likely to be a more satisfactory starting point than the individual company beta. This is because the individual company beta – estimated from the slope of the regression line through the historical market relationship – will contain some estimation error[10]. Using an industry beta, which is an average of individual company betas, helps to reduce substantially the amount of this error (in much the same way that unsystematic risk is reduced through diversification).

Two further points

The CAPM is a model for pricing capital assets, e.g., shares. We know from the previous chapter that in the single-period world of the CAPM, the return on a share is given by:

$$r_j = \frac{(P_j1 - P_j0) + \text{Divs}}{P_j0}$$

where P_j0 is the current price per share in company j and P_j1 is the end of period price per share. Suppose we take the simplest possible case and assume that no dividend is paid during the time that the share is held. In such circumstances:

$$r_j = \frac{P_j1 - P_j0}{P_j0}$$

From this, we can use the CAPM to determine what should be the current market price of the share:

$$\frac{E(P_j 1) - P_j 0}{P_j 0} = r_F + [E(r_M) - r_F]\,\beta_j$$

$$\frac{E(P_j 1)}{P_j 0} - \frac{P_j 0}{P_j 0} = r_F + [E(r_M) - r_F]\,\beta_j$$

Re-arranging:

$$P_j 0 = \frac{E(P_j 1)}{1 + r_F + [E(r_M) - r_F]\,\beta_j}$$

In this expression, the denominator can be thought of as a *risk-adjusted discount rate.* Therefore, the equilibrium current share price is equal to the expected future share price, discounted to present value using a risk-adjusted discount rate: in other words the discount rate reflects the (systematic) risk of the shares.

This way of looking at CAPM is useful in the context of the present section of this chapter because it shows CAPM as providing a risk-adjusted discount rate – albeit for just one time period. It was precisely this that we were seeking to use as a capital investment appraisal discount rate in the face of uncertainty.

The second point concerns taxation. The CAPM is developed in a world free from capital market imperfections, which includes no taxation. Thus if we are to apply the model to the real world where taxes exist, we must do so with some caution. We saw in an earlier chapter that, as far as capital investment appraisal was concerned, we required an after-tax discount rate to apply to the after-tax project cash flows. Thus if we were to try and allow for taxation in the CAPM model when using it to derive a project discount rate, we would use:

$$E(r_{\text{project}}) = r_{F_{AT}} + [E(r_M) - r_{F_{AT}}]\,\beta_{\text{project}}$$

where $r_{F_{AT}}$ was the after personal (income) tax return on government bonds.

This is not the end of our consideration either of the investment appraisal discount rate or the CAPM. We shall find that in the chapters that follow we will make repeated references to both topics.

SUMMARY

This chapter discussed how the CAPM is developed out of portfolio theory and examined its meaning and use. The main points made were as follows:

- The CML expression deals with the expected return on an efficient portfolio investment. From this can be derived the expected return on an *inefficient* investment: the expected return on the shares of an individual company. Such an expression is termed the capital asset pricing model.

- In the CAPM, the risk-premium is determined by the product of the market price of risk and the shares systematic risk level. This latter value is given by the product of the share's total risk (σ) and the degree to which the returns on the share are correlated to the returns on the market portfolio.
- Normally, in practice, a share's systematic risk is not measured in *absolute* terms, but in terms *relative* to the (systematic) risk of the market portfolio. This is indicated by the beta value.
- Shares with betas greater than one will have more systematic risk than the average level of systematic risk on the stock market (indicated by the risk of the market portfolio) and their share price behaviour will tend to be more volatile than the general stock market index.
- Shares with betas of less than one will have less systematic risk than the average and their share price behaviour will tend to under perform movements in the general market index.
- As high beta shares are more risky than average, they will be expected to produce a return higher than average. Low beta shares will similarly be expected to produce a return lower than average.
- Unsystematic, or diversifiable, risk is principally caused by company-specific factors (such as labour relations and management quality) which affect the performance of a company's cash flow. Such effects will be washed-out in a well-diversified portfolio.
- Systematic, or non-diversifiable, risk is principally caused by 'macro-economic' type factors which affect *all* firms in the stock market, to a greater or lesser extent. Such factors would include the rate of national economic growth and the level and volatility of exchange rates. The impact of these effects cannot be eradicated through diversification.
- A company's exposure to systematic risk is determined by the degree of its revenue sensitivity to these 'macro-economic' type effects and also by its cost sensitivity, that is, its ratio of fixed to variable costs. Most importantly, the greater the revenue sensitivity, the greater the degree of systematic risk.
- Beta can, in theory, be measured from first principles using the beta expression of covariance over market variance: Cov $[r_A, r_M] / \sigma_M^2$. However, it is usually estimated by the slope of the regression line of the relationship between the returns on the share and the returns on the market portfolio.
- Although the CAPM is developed under a set of rather unrealistic assumptions, the empirical evidence does tend to suggest that a positive, linear risk-return relationship, of the type described by the CAPM, does actually exist. Despite the theoretical problems that exist in the testing of the model, and despite the evidence which suggests that systematic risk is not the *sole* determinant of return, we can conclude that the CAPM does appear to capture the essence of the relationship between risk and return on the stock market.
- Finally, the use of CAPM to generate NPV discount rates for project appraisal was examined. A number of problems arise in this use of the

CAPM, not least of which are the facts that the CAPM is a single-period model and NPV is a multi-period analysis and that project betas have to be estimated on the basis of industry betas. However, this application of the CAPM will be further developed at a later stage.

APPENDIX: THE SECURITY MARKET LINE

Perhaps the simplest way of deriving an expression for the expected return on an inefficient investment is to examine the characteristics of a two-asset portfolio where one of the assets is an investment in the market portfolio and the other asset is an investment in the shares of a single company: company A. The risk and expected return characteristics of the resulting (inefficient) investment portfolio would be:

$$E(r_p) = xE(r_A) + (1 - x)\,E(r_M)$$
$$\sigma_p = \sqrt{\{x^2\sigma_A^2 + (1 - x)^2\,\sigma_M^2 + 2x(1 - x)\,\mathrm{Cov}[r_A, r_M]\}}$$

Suppose that Figure 1 illustrates the range of possible risk–expected return combinations AM, available from the two-asset portfolio. By the use of calculus, the slope of the line AM at point M can be identified and from this can be derived a general expression for the expected return on an inefficient investment (assuming market prices are in equilibrium).

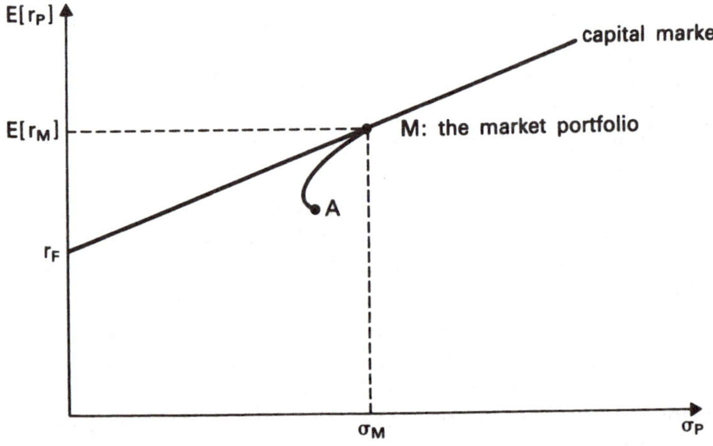

Figure 1

If the expected return of the portfolio is given by:

$$E(r_p) = xE(r_A) + (1 - x)\,E(r_M)$$

then the expected return from a marginal investment in the inefficient portfolio p can be found by differentiating $E(r_p)$ with respect to x:

$$\frac{dE(r_p)}{dx} = E(r_A) - E(r_M)$$

Similarly, the risk produced by a marginal investment in the inefficient portfolio p can be found by differentiating the expression for the portfolio's risk:

$$\frac{d\sigma_p}{dx} = \tfrac{1}{2}[x^2\sigma_A^2 + (1-x)^2\,\sigma_M^2 + 2x(1-x)\,\mathrm{Cov}(r_A, r_M)]^{-1/2}$$
$$\times\,[2x\sigma_A^2 - 2\sigma_M^2 + 2x\sigma_M^2 + 2\,\mathrm{Cov}(r_A, r_M) - 4x\,\mathrm{Cov}(r_A, r_M)]$$

At point M on the line AM, all the portfolio funds are invested in M and therefore the value of $x = 0$. This simplifies the expression for marginal risk:

$$\frac{d\sigma_p}{dx} = \tfrac{1}{2}[\sigma_M^2]^{-1/2} \times [(2\,\mathrm{Cov}(r_A, r_M) - 2\sigma_M^2]$$

which reduces further, to

$$\frac{d\sigma_p}{dx} = \frac{\mathrm{Cov}(r_A, r_M) - \sigma_M^2}{\sigma_M}$$

Given that the slope of the CML was $E(r_M) - r_F/\sigma_M$, then similarly, the slope of the line AM at point M is given by:

$$\frac{dE(r_p)}{dx} \Big/ \frac{d\sigma_p}{dx} \equiv \frac{dE(r_p)}{d\bar{x}} \times \frac{dx}{d\sigma_p} = \frac{dE(r_p)}{d\sigma_p}$$

that is:

$$\frac{\sigma_M[E(r_A) - E(r_M)]}{\mathrm{Cov}(r_A, r_M) - \sigma_M^2}$$

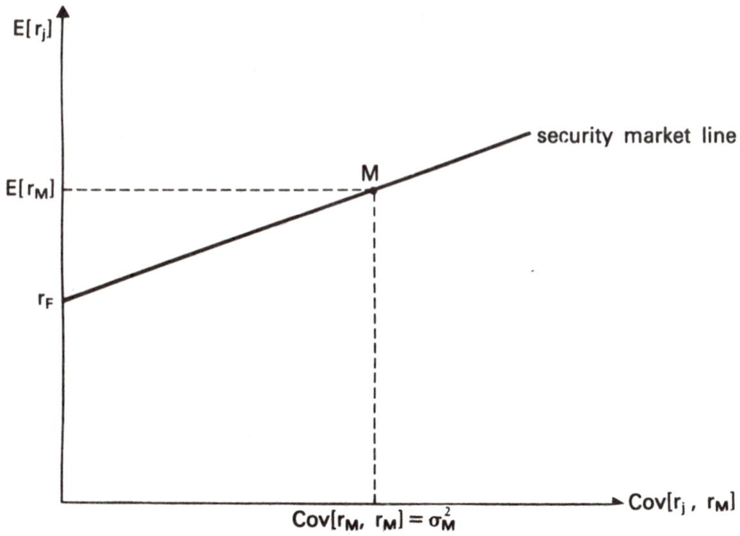

Figure 2

However, at point M the slope of the line AM must also equal the slope of the CML. Therefore at point M, the following relationship holds:

$$\frac{\sigma_M[E(r_A) - E(r_M)]}{\mathrm{Cov}(r_A, r_M) - \sigma_M^2} = \frac{E(r_M) - r_F}{\sigma_M}$$

This equality can then be re-arranged to provide an expression for the expected return on the shares of company A:

$$E(r_A) = r_F + \frac{E(r_M) - r_F}{\sigma_M^2} \times \mathrm{Cov}(r_A, r_M)$$

In fact this is the *general* expression for the return on *any* inefficient asset, and is termed the equation of the security market line (SML):

$$E(r_j) = r_F + \frac{E(r_M) - r_F}{\sigma_M^2} \times \mathrm{Cov}(r_j, r_M)$$

This is graphed in Figure 2. Examination of the SML function shows that it is a linear function (as was the CML function) of three variables: the risk free return (r_F), the market's risk–expected return trade-off $[E(r_M) - r_F/\sigma_M^2]$ and the covariance of returns between the market portfolio and the inefficient investment j $[\mathrm{Cov}(r_j, r_M)]$. In other words, the expected return from an investment in the inefficient asset j is equal to the risk free return, plus a risk premium:

$$\underbrace{r_F}_{\text{Risk-Free return}} + \underbrace{\frac{E(r_M) - r_F}{\sigma_M^2} \times \mathrm{Cov}(r_j, r_M)}_{\text{Risk premium}}$$

Expanding the covariance term and given the definition of λ, the market price of risk:

$$E[r_A] = r_F + \frac{E(r_M) - r_F}{\sigma_M^2} \sigma_M \sigma_A \rho_{A,M}$$

this expression simplifies to:

$$E[r_A] = r_F + \lambda \sigma_A \rho_{A,M}$$

NOTES

1 The portfolio risk expression – when $\rho_{A,B} = +1$ – can be given as:

$$\sigma_p = \sqrt{[x^2 \sigma_A^2 + (1 - x)^2 \sigma_B^2 + 2x(1 - x)\sigma_A \sigma_B]}$$

Remembering that: $(a + b)^2 = a^2 + b^2 + 2ab$

then: $\sigma_p = \sqrt{[x\sigma_A + (1 - x)\sigma_B]^2}$

and: $\sigma_p = x\sigma_A + (1 - x)\sigma_B$

2 That is, the risk taken on by the particular point the investor has chosen to locate his portfolio on the CML.

3 Perhaps a safer description at this stage would be to say that share price movements and dividends are determined by 'the fortunes of the company'.

4 Although it is not considered here, there may well be a possibility of eliminating some country-specific macro-economic factors by holding an *internationally* diversified portfolio.

5 The sign '$\approx$' means '*approximately* equal to'.

6 Or an *n* asset portfolio.

7 The relationship would be positive in a 'correlation coefficient' sense. In other words, the return on the shares in the individual company will tend to move in the *same* direction as the return on the FTSE market index.

8 Most introductory text books on statistics will show how such a *line of best fit* might be calculated from scatter diagram data.

9 In making such a calculation, the differing capital structures of the companies (i.e., the ratio of equity to fixed interest capital) must be taken into account. This topic will be returned to in a later chapter after the issue of capital structure has been discussed.

10 Indicated by the scatter of the 'plots' on the graph around the regression line. The greater the degree of scatter, the greater the degree of possible error.

FURTHER READING

1 Much of the CAPM literature is mathematically demanding. However, an excellent article which is very readable is the two parts of: F. Modigliani and G.A. Pogue, 'An Introduction to Risk and Return: Concepts and Evidence', *Financial Analysts Journal*, March-April and May-June 1974.
2 On the empirical evidence and testing of the CAPM see F. Black, M.C. Jensen and M. Scholes, 'The CAPM: Some Empirical Tests', in *Studies in the Theory of Capital Markets*, ed. M. Jensen, Prager 1972; S.A. Ross, 'The Current Status of the Capital Asset Pricing Model', *Journal of Finance*, June 1978; R.W. Banz, 'The Relationship Between Return and Market Value of Common Stock', *Journal of Financial Economics*, March 1981; and H. Levy, 'The CAPM: Theory and Empiricism', *The Economic Journal*, March 1983.
3 Roll's criticism of the CAPM tests makes difficult, but worthwhile, reading: R. Roll, 'A Critique of the Asset Pricing Theory's Tests', *Journal of Financial Economics*, March 1977. The article by Ross is also fairly demanding, but it is particularly interesting to see how the APT model is developed in an entirely different way to the CAPM: S.A. Ross, 'The Arbitrage Theory of Capital Asset Pricing', *Journal of Economic Theory*, December 1976.

4 Finally, of direct relevance to the application of the CAPM to investment appraisal, there is a number of good articles, including: S.C. Myers and S. Turnbull, 'Capital Budgeting and the Capital Asset Pricing Model: Good News and Bad News', *Journal of Finance*, May 1977, H. Levy, 'Another Look at the CAPM', *Quarterly Review of Business and Economics*, Summer 1984; D.W. Mullins, 'Does the CAPM Work?', *Harvard Business Review*, January/February 1982; J.C. Van Horne, 'An Application of the CAPM to Divisional Required Returns', *Financial Management*, Spring 1980; and T.E. Conine and M. Tamarkin, 'Divisional Cost of Capital Estimation: Adjusting for Coverage', *Financial Management*, Spring 1985.

QUICKIE QUESTIONS

1 Write down the standard CAPM expression for the expected return on company A shares.
2 What does beta measure?
3 What is unsystematic risk and what are its sources?
4 What determines a share's exposure to systematic risk?
5 Given the following information, what is company B's systematic risk, unsystematic risk and beta value?:

$$\sigma_B = 20\%$$
$$\sigma_M = 10\%$$
$$\rho_{B,M} = +0{\cdot}6$$

6 What is company C's beta value, given the following information?:

$$\text{Cov}\,[r_C, r_M] = +73{\cdot}5$$
$$\sigma_M = 7\%$$

7 Company D has a beta value of 1.2. It is thinking of undertaking a project with a beta value of 1.7. If, when accepted, the project will comprise 10% of the firm's total worth, what will be the subsequent beta value of the company?
8 Does an *over-valued* share lie above or below the CAPM line?
9 What is the principal difference between the CAPM and the arbitrage pricing model?
10 Given the following information, what would be your advice concerning project X:

	Cash flow		
0	−100	r_F	= 8%
1	+60	$E[r_M]$	= 12%
2	+50	β_{industry}	= 1·75

PROBLEMS

1 Vanhal plc is a widely-diversified company listed on The Stock Exchange. As it is not yet involved in the construction industry, the

directors would like to broaden further the company's activities by acquiring all of the issued share capital of a construction company dealt in on the Unlisted Securities Market. Vanhal plc would issue shares with a current market value of £4 million to the shareholders of the company to be acquired. Three construction companies (A, B and C) have been identified as possible target acquisitions, each with a market value of approximately £4 million. Details of the market performance of these three companies are:

Company	Beta factor	Total risk*	Risk specific to the company*	Current gross dividend yield	Price-earnings ratio
A	0·67	30%	28%	11·1%	4·2
B	1·14	36%	31%	9·5%	5·4
C	0·88	50%	48%	12·2%	4·7

*Risk is defined in terms of standard deviation and the unit of measurement is percentage returns.

The directors are unsure which of the three companies to acquire. At present Vanhal plc has a beta factor of 0.67, total risk of 30%, company-specific risk of 28% and a market capitalization of £62 million. The return on the Financial Times All Share Index currently has a standard deviation of 16%.

Required:

(a) Calculate the new market value and the new systematic (or market) risk of Vanhal plc that would occur in each of three independent circumstances:
   (i) if Vanhal plc acquires company A;
   (ii) if Vanhal plc acquires company B; and
   (iii) if Vanhal plc acquires company C.
   You may assume that the stock markets are perfect, that the diversification opportunities of investors are unrestricted and that no synergy is involved.
(b) Explain how diversification can reduce the total risk associated with Vanhal plc's share returns.
(c) Discuss why the directors of Vanhal plc might wish to diversify, and suggest which of the three companies best meets the directors' requirements.
(d) Discuss whether the shareholders of Vanhal plc should welcome the proposed diversification.

2 Mr Swift maintains a well-diversified portfolio containing a large number of different quoted shares. He is considering investing in the quoted ordinary shares of one of two companies, Dove plc and Jay plc, an amount which is small in relation to the total value of his portfolio. He wishes to include those shares which will lead to a reduction in portfolio risk as measured by the variance of portfolio returns. The correlation coefficient of the returns on Dove's shares with the return

on the market portfolio and with the returns on Mr Swift's existing portfolio are expected to be 0.30 and 0.16 respectively over the coming years. The corresponding correlation coefficients for the returns on shares in Jay are 0.25 and 0.21, respectively. The standard deviations of returns for Dove and Jay are expected to be 35% and 30% respectively for the coming year and their expected returns for that period are 9% and 7% respectively.

Required:

(a) Advise Mr Swift on which of the two shares he should select for his portfolio in order to meet his objectives.
(b) Demonstrate why the expected return on an ordinary share in Dove is greater than that for Jay.
(c) Discuss how your advice might change if Mr Swift's portfolio contained shares in only a very small number of listed companies.
(d) Discuss why the relevant measure of risk may vary between a company's shareholders, debt holders and managers.

3 The Government of Trinka is considering how to protect its domestic cement industry. There is only one cement manufacturer in the country – Cemenco Ltd – which is coming in for severe competition from imported cement. Presently the Government are considering banning imports of cement and – because that would leave Cemenco Ltd with a monopoly – impose Government controls on the price of cement.

In this respect the Government wish to be able to compare the systematic riskiness of Cemenco with that of its overseas competitors. With this knowledge, they hope to be able to determine a fair return for the company's shareholders and hence, the price which should be set for cement.

As a result, you have been called in by the Government to try to estimate the company's beta value. Trinka has an active stock exchange and Cemenco are one of the quoted companies. The Government has provided you with the following information:

	Cemenco Ltd		*Trinka Stock Exchange*		*Return*
	Av. share price	*Dividend yield*	*Average TSE Index*	*Average Div. yield*	*Govt. stocks*
	T$				
Current Year	16·42	10%	1983	16%	15%
12 months ago	15·50	12%	1665	16%	16%
24 months ago	12·10	8%	1789	10%	14%
36 months ago	9·50	10%	1490	18%	15%

Required

(a) Estimate the beta value of Cemenco Ltd.
(b) Comment on what effects you think that the Government's action might have on the riskiness of Cemenco Ltd.

4 Note: This question should be attempted only after studying Chapter 13.

(a) A colleague has been taken ill. Your managing director has asked you to take over from the colleague and to provide urgently needed estimates of the discount rate to be used in appraising a large new capital investment. You have been given your colleague's working notes, which you believe to be numerically accurate.

Working notes

Estimates for the next 5 years (annual averages)

Stock market total return on equity	16%
Own company dividend yield	7%
Own company share price rise	14%
Standard deviation of total stock market return on equity	10%
Standard deviation of own company total return on equity	20%
Correlation coefficient between total own company return on equity and total stock market return on equity	0·7
Correlation coefficient between total return on the new capital investment and total market return on equity	0·5
Growth rate of own company earnings	12%
Growth rate of own company dividends	11%
Growth rate of own company sales	13%
Treasury bill yield	12%

The company's gearing level (by market values) is 1:2 debt to equity, and after tax earnings available to ordinary shareholders in the most recent year were £5,400,000 of which £2,140,000 was distributed as ordinary dividends. The company has 10 million issued ordinary shares which are currently trading on the Stock Exchange at 321 pence. Corporate debt may be assumed to be risk free. The company pays tax at 35% and personal taxation may be ignored.

Required:

Estimate the company's weighted average cost of capital using:

(i) The dividend valuation model.

(ii) The capital asset pricing model.

State clearly any assumptions that you make.

Under what circumstances would these models be expected to produce similar values for the weighted average cost of capital?

(b) Discuss the practical problems of using the capital asset pricing model in investment appraisal.

11
Traditional approaches to risk

Chapter Contents

EXPECTED NET PRESENT VALUE

In the previous chapter we developed an argument as to how companies should allow for risk in capital investment decision making by generating a risk-adjusted discount rate using the capital asset pricing model. To contrast against that approach, in this chapter we examine some of the more 'traditional' approaches that management have used to help with the problem of risk in investment decision making.

ENPV

In an uncertain world, even assuming the presence of perfect capital markets, use of the NPV method of investment appraisal cannot be said necessarily to lead to optimal investment decisions or to the maximization of shareholder wealth. All it can do is to lead to the *expected* maximization of wealth. Hindsight, that is knowledge about the actual outcome of past events, may suggest different advice from that given by the NPV appraisal rule, because the latter is based only upon estimates of the future.

When we examined the rationale and operation of the NPV appraisal method, we paid very little attention to how the estimates of a project's future net cash flows were derived. In practice, management is *unlikely* to produce a series of 'point' (i.e., single figure) estimates of each year's net cash flow but instead is likely to construct a *range* of estimates.

For example, a project may have an initial cost of £1,000 and a life of three years, but the level of the net cash flows may be uncertain, depending, say, on the general state of the industry in which the company operates. Example 11.1 shows a simple example of the estimated annual net cash flows based on three economic states: boom, normal and depressed conditions. From these data the project's NPV is calculated in each state and a figure is attached expressing the probability or likelihood of each state actually occurring. These NPVs are combined to produce

Example 11.1

Paraiso PLC is considering whether to purchase a machine to produce glue for ceramic tiles. The machine costs £1,000 and is expected to have a productive life of three years. However, the estimate of the annual net revenue from the machine is uncertain and depends on the state of the house-building industry. The company's management have produced the following estimates:

	State of Industry	*0*	*1*	*2*	*3*
(I)	Boom	−1,000	+500	+700	+980
(II)	Normal	−1,000	+500	+600	+700
(III)	Depressed	−1,000	+300	+300	+250

Paraiso normally use a 10% discount rate in project appraisal, believing that this correctly reflects the risk of the project. (They derive the figure from the CAPM using the house-building industry beta.) On this basis, the project NPVs have been calculated as follows:

State	*NPV*
I	+769
II	+477
III	−291

Latest figures from the Building Trades Research Institute suggest the following probabilities for the industry's future prospects:

State	*Probability*
Boom	0·20
Normal	0·60
Depressed	0·20

On this basis, Paraiso PLC estimate the project's *expected* (i.e., arithmetic mean) NPV:

State	*Prob.*		*NPV*		
I	0·20	×	+769	=	+153·8
II	0·60	×	+477	=	+286·2
III	0·20	×	−291	=	− 52·2
					+387·8 ENPV

As the project has a positive *expected* net present value (ENPV) it is accepted.

the arithmetic mean (i.e., average) NPV of the project: the *expected* NPV of the project, given the different estimates and their probabilities of occurrence. It is upon the value (and more importantly, the sign) of this expected net present value (ENPV) that the normal investment appraisal decision rule is applied.

It is important to notice that, as this example shows, management not only has the task of estimating the project's annual net cash flow in each of the different states of the industry, but must also estimate the probability of the occurrence of each state. (Strictly, these are *subjective* probabilities, because they are based upon management's subjective judgement rather than on past observations of similar events.)

In addition, it is also assumed in the example that, whichever state of the industry occurs, the industry will remain fixed in that state over the duration of the project. If this assumption is unrealistic, further adjustments will need to be made to the ENPV calculation. Example 11.2 illustrates this more complex type of situation.

Example 11.2

Maravista PLC design and manufacture clothes for the 13–15 years segment of the fashion industry. The success or otherwise of their products depends upon whether they are in fashion in any particular year.

The company's management are considering investing £40,000 to produce a range of leather belts which, they believe, will have a two-year fashion life. However, the outcome of the project is dependent upon whether the belt design turns out to be in fashion and hence, *successful* (State I) or out of fashion and so, a *relative failure* (State II), or a *marketing disaster* (State III).

Maravista's marketing analysts have studied the situation carefully and have estimated the following net revenue figures for the project (£000s):

Year 1 State	*Prob.*	*Net Rev.*	*Year 2 State*	*Prob.*	*Net Rev.*
			I	0·6	+100
I	0·5	+80	II	0·3	+ 80
			III	0·1	+ 20
			I	0·4	+ 80
II	0·3	+30	II	0·3	+ 40
			III	0·3	+ 10
			I	0·1	+ 70
III	0·2	+10	II	0·4	+ 40
			III	0·5	+ 5

For example, as Maravista's marketing analyst explained to the chief executive, we believe that in the first year of the product's life it has a 50% chance of being in fashion and, hence, a success. Given it is successful in the first year, then there is a 60% chance of being similarly successful in its second year, a 30% chance of it then being a relative failure and, finally, a 10% chance of turning into a marketing disaster.

On this basis, the analysis can be simplified by estimating the *expected* (i.e., arithmetic mean) revenue in the second year, for each possible first year state:

Year 1 State	*Year 2 Rev.*		*Prob.*		
	+100	×	0·6	=	+60
I	+ 80	×	0·3	=	+24
	+ 20	×	0·1	=	+ 2
					+86 Expected Yr 2 Net Revenue
	+ 80	×	0·4	=	+32
II	+ 40	×	0·3	=	+12
	+ 10	×	0·3	=	+ 3
					+47 Expected Yr 2 Net Revenue
	+ 70	×	0·1	=	+ 7
III	+ 40	×	0·4	=	+16
	+ 5	×	0·5	=	+ 2·5
					+25·5 Expected Yr 2 Net Revenue

Now, the project's expected cash flows have been simplified to:

Year 1 State	*Prob.*	*Year 0 Outlay*	*Year 1 Net Rev.*	*Year 2 Expected Rev.*
I	0·5	−40	+80	+86
II	0·3	−40	+30	+47
III	0·2	−40	+10	+25·5

Maravista usually uses a 20% discount rate to reflect the high-risk nature of the fashion industry and, on this basis, the project's expected NPV can be calculated:

Year 1 State	*Prob.*		*NPV*		
I	0·5	×	+86·4	=	+43·2
II	0·3	×	+17·6	=	+ 5·3
III	0·2	×	−14·0	=	− 2·8
					+45·7 ENPV

As the project has a positive expected net present value of £45,700 approximately, Maravista PLC decides to proceed with production.

Limitations of ENPV

The concept of *expected* NPV (indeed an expected IRR could be similarly calculated) has been found by management to be useful for project appraisal in an uncertain world because it provides an average value of the proposed project's performance. However, it is important to realize that it *cannot* be said to take account of risk because all that the ENPV calculation provides is a measure of the investment's *expected* performance, whereas risk – as we have seen – is concerned with the likelihood that the *actual* performance may diverge from what is expected.

Example 11.3 illustrates this point very simply. Two mutually exclusive projects have identical expected NPVs. Therefore on the basis of the ENPV decision rule, the management should be indifferent between them – they are both expected to make a positive NPV of £8·5m.

However, almost certainly, the management of Armacao PLC will *not* be indifferent, but instead will strongly prefer the 'silicon chip' project. The reason for this is that this project is likely to be viewed as being less risky than the 'semi-conductor' project.

Risk is to do with the fact that the project's actual outcome can vary from what is expected. In this respect the actual outcome can either be better (the *up-side potential*) or worse (the *down-side risk*) than the

Example 11.3

Armacao PLC wants to enter the electronics industry and is considering two possible projects. Both projects require the same outlay of £10m and both have the same expected net present value. However, because this is a venture into a new area of business, Armacao only want to undertake *one* of the projects. The figures are as follows (£ms):

State of World	*Prob.*	*Semi-conductor Project NPV*	*Silicon chip Project NPV*
Strong growth	0·20	+30·6	+13·0
Slow growth	0·60	+ 8·5	+ 8·5
Recession	0·20	−13·6	+ 4·0

Semi-conductor project:

$$0{\cdot}2 \times +30{\cdot}6 = +6{\cdot}12$$
$$0{\cdot}6 \times +\ 8{\cdot}5 = +5{\cdot}10$$
$$0{\cdot}2 \times -13{\cdot}6 = -2{\cdot}72$$
$$+8{\cdot}5 \text{ ENPV}$$

Silicon chip project:

$$0{\cdot}2 \times +13{\cdot}0 = +2{\cdot}6$$
$$0{\cdot}6 \times +\ 8{\cdot}5 = +5{\cdot}1$$
$$0{\cdot}2 \times +\ 4{\cdot}0 = +0{\cdot}8$$
$$+8{\cdot}5 \text{ ENPV}$$

expected outcome. A *gambling* investor will focus most of his attention on the up-side potential, but a *risk averse* investor will be more concerned with looking at the expected outcome and the down-side risk.

Given our assumption (which is generally correct) of risk-averse investors, the managers of Armacao PLC are likely to view the silicon chip project as less risky because, even in the *worst* state of the world, it is still expected to produce a small positive NPV. In contrast, the semi-conductor project will produce a large negative NPV of £13·6m if the economy moves into recession.

There is however one set of circumstances in which the ENPV approach does 'allow' for risk. That is to say, there is one set of circumstances when, if faced by the two alternative projects in Example 11.3, it would be correct to conclude that the company would be indifferent between them because they produce the same ENPV.

Those circumstances would be where the company intended to undertake a *large number* of similar or identical projects. In that case the ENPV indicates (quite correctly) the average outcome of each individual investment. Thus if the company were to undertake (say) *100* semi-conductor projects, then 20% of them would produce an NPV of +£30·6m, 60% would produce an NPV of +£8·5m and the remaining 20 (i.e., 20%) would produce negative NPVs of £13·6m. Thus the *average* outcome *per project* would be a positive NPV of £8·5m.

Similarly, the average outcome of 100 silicon chip projects would be a +£8·5m NPV *per project.* Twenty of the projects would produce an NPV of +£13m, and so on. Therefore, in these circumstances, the company would be *truly* indifferent between the two projects given they have the same ENPV.

Unfortunately, most capital investment projects are *not* undertaken a great number of times, but are unique one-off investments. It therefore follows that the idea of ENPV remains as an inadequate way of 'allowing for' or 'indicating' a project's risk.

Value of additional information

One interesting use of the ENPV technique is that it can help to indicate the value of additional information. Example 11.4 illustrates such a situation.

Example 11.4

Alvor PLC has developed a new product and has now reached the stage of making a decision whether or not to undertake manufacture. The manufacturing machinery would cost £90,000 and the project is expected to have a life of 6 years. However, the performance of the product in the market place is uncertain.

Alvor's marketing director has indicated that there are four possible outcomes (states: I, II, III and IV): very successful, moderately successful, disappointing and complete failure. On this basis, the company's management accountants have estimated the possible NPVs and the project's overall expected NPV (£000s):

State of World	*Prob.*		*NPV*		
I	0·2	×	+110	=	+22
II	0·5	×	+ 70	=	+35
III	0·2	×	+ 5	=	+ 1
IV	0·1	×	− 25	=	− 2·5
				ENPV	+55·5

As the ENPV is positive, the company decides to go ahead with production but, just before this decision is implemented, Carvalho Intelligence PLC, a market research company, offers to undertake a survey of the new product which will indicate, *in advance of production*, what outcome is likely to occur. The cost of the survey would be £2,000 and the management of Alvor PLC are now trying to decide what should be done.

The approach to take is to examine what action the company would take in response to the various possible outcomes of the market research. Clearly, if the market research indicated that either states I, II or III would occur, the company would undertake manufacture as to do so would generate a positive NPV. However, if the market research indicated that state IV would occur, the company would *not* proceed with manufacture, as manufacture would lead to a negative NPV of £25,000:

Survey indicates: State	*Company's Investment Decision*	*Prob. of Survey Result*		*NPV Outcome of Decision*		
I	Accept	0·2	×	+110	=	+22
II	Accept	0·5	×	+ 70	=	+35
III	Accept	0·2	×	+ 5	=	+ 1
IV	Reject	0·1	×	0	=	0
					ENPV	+58

Therefore:

	£
ENPV of project *with* market research survey	58,000
ENPV of project *without* market research survey	55,500
Maximum worth of survey	2,500
Cost of survey	2,000
Net benefit of survey to Alvor PLC	£ +500

On the basis of this analysis, the survey is worthwhile. The company should undertake the survey *prior* to manufacture and only proceed to manufacture if the survey indicates that either states I, II or III will occur.

Example 11.5
Centianes PLC is considering undertaking a project as follows:

Outcome	*Prob.*		*NPV*		
Success	0·6	×	+100	=	+60
Failure	0·4	×	− 40	=	−16
			ENPV		+44

A market research survey will indicate, with *90% accuracy*, which outcome will actually occur. The maximum worth of the survey can be estimated as follows:

There are *four* possible states of the world:

State
A: Survey indicates 'success' and is correct.
B: Survey indicates 'success' and is wrong.
C: Survey indicates 'failure' and is correct.
D: Survey indicates 'failure' and is wrong.

There is a 60% chance the survey will indicate 'success' and a 40% that it will indicate 'failure'. There is a 90% chance that the survey result will be correct and a 10% chance that it will be wrong. The probabilities of each of the four 'states of the world' will be given by the *product* of the individual probabilities:

State		*Prob.*
A	0·6 × 0·9 =	0·54
B	0·6 × 0·1 =	0·06
C	0·4 × 0·9 =	0·36
D	0·4 × 0·1 =	0·04

Therefore:

State	*Decision*	*Prob.*		*Outcome*		
A	Accept	0·54	×	+100 NPV	=	+54
B	Accept	0·06	×	− 40 NPV	=	− 2·4
C	Reject	0·36	×	0 NPV	=	0
D	Reject	0·04	×	−100 NPV*	=	4·0
				ENPV	=	+47·6

ENPV with survey	:	+47·6
ENPV without survey	:	+44·0
Max worth of survey	:	+ 3·6

* Notice that this is an *opportunity cost.* If the survey incorrectly forecasts 'failure' and we act on the survey's advice, we forego the opportunity of gaining an NPV of +100.

In Example 11.4 the additional information was always correct. A more complex analysis involving the opportunity cost concept is required if the additional information may be incorrect. This situation is illustrated in Example 11.5.

The abandonment decision

Another 'special case' of the ENPV decision is the evaluation of an option to abandon a project before it reaches the end of its life. Such an analysis is illustrated in Example 11.6.

However, the limitations of the abandonment analysis should be noted. The first is that when *multiple* abandonment points are available – such as at the end of Years 1, 2 and 3 of a project with a life of 4 years – there is a real world information problem as to how reliable future abandonment values are to be estimated. The second problem is that the analysis of a multiple abandonment point decision is much more complex than that of Example 11.6. A dynamic programming analysis is required. The problem here is that the more complex the analysis required, often the more reluctant are management to accept its advice as they lack an understanding as to how the advice was generated.

Example 11.6

Irmaos PLC operates a series of photocopier shops in which customers can walk off the street and have their photocopying done immediately. The company normally only keeps its machines for two years before disposing of them on the second-hand market.

They have recently been approached by a photocopier manufacturer who is trying to break into the UK market. Each machine will cost £10,000.

Irmaos believe that the crucial factor is the reliability of the new photocopiers. On past experience they believe that there is only a 60% chance that they will prove to be reliable. On this basis they have estimated the net cash flows produced by an individual photocopier:

Photocopier	*Yr 1*	*Yr 2*	*Scrap*
Reliable	+8,000	+6,000	+400
Unreliable	+4,000	+3,000	+200

A 15% discount rate is used to reflect the risk of the photocopying business and, on this basis, the project's NPV and ENPV is calculated:

				NPV	*Prob.*	
Reliable:	−10,000	$+8,000\ (1{\cdot}15)^{-1}$	$+6,400\ (1{\cdot}15)^{-2}$ =	+1,796	×0·6 =	+1,078
Unreliable:	−10,000	$+4,000\ (1{\cdot}15)^{-1}$	$+3,200\ (1{\cdot}15)^{-2}$ =	−4,102	×0·4 =	−1,641
					ENPV	− 563

On this basis, Irmaos declines to purchase the machines. However, in order to try to get the company to change their mind, the photocopier manufacturer offers to buy back the machines at the end of the first year for 50% of their purchase cost. In other words, Irmaos are being offered an abandonment option. This decision can be analysed as follows:

Assuming that the company purchases a photocopy machine and then, at the end of the first year, decides *not* to abandon, the resulting NPVs of the decision are as follows:

Photocopier	*Yr 1*	*Yr 2*	*NPV*	*Decision Taken*
Reliable	$-5{,}000\,(1{\cdot}15)^{-1}$	$+6{,}400\,(1{\cdot}15)^{-2}$	= + 491	Don't abandon
Unreliable	$-5{,}000\,(1{\cdot}15)^{-1}$	$+3{,}200\,(1{\cdot}15)^{-2}$	= −1,928	Abandon

In each case, the negative cash outflow at Year 1 is an opportunity cost. If the photocopier is *not* abandoned, the company forego the opportunity to sell it back to the manufacturer for £5,000.

This analysis allows the abandonment decision (at Year 1) to be made. If the photocopier turns out to be reliable, the machine should *not* be abandoned as this generates a positive NPV outcome. However, if the photocopier turns out to be unreliable then the company *should* abandon the project at the end of Year 1, because not to do so would incur a negative NPV of £1,928.

Having made the *abandonment* decision, the overall *investment* decision can then be made:

Photocopier reliable:

Outlay	: −10,000			
Net revs	:	+8,000	+6,000	
Scrap	:		+ 400	
Net cash flow	: −10,000	$+8{,}000\,(1{\cdot}15)^{-1}$	$+6{,}400\,(1{\cdot}15)^{-2}$	= +1,796 NPV

Photocopier unreliable:

Outlay	: −10,000		
Net revs	:	+4,000	
Abandon value	:	+5,000	
Net cash flow	: −10,000	$+9{,}000\,(1.15)^{-1}$	= −2,174 NPV

Photocopier	*Prob.*		*NPV*		
Reliable	0·6	×	+1,796	=	+1,078
Unreliable	0·4	×	−2,174	=	− 870
				ENPV	+ 208

As the project has a positive ENPV, Irmaos should go ahead and purchase the photocopiers, but should abandon the project by selling them back to the manufacturer at the end of the first year if they prove to be unreliable.

A final example

Example 11.7 works through a more complex expected net present value question (which includes a little inflation for added interest!). It is designed to illustrate how the basic principles outlined in some of the earlier, simple examples may be applied in a more complex situation.

Example 11.7

The directors of Starlite PLC are considering the purchase and exploitation of a disused tin mine which is being offered for sale for £50,000. A review of the mine's history shows that the total amount of pure tin that can be extracted depends upon the type of rock formations in the area and that only the following three possibilities exist:

Rock type	*Total tin output*	*Probability*
A	240 tonnes	0·4
B	120 tonnes	0·4
C	72 tonnes	0·2

If Starlite purchases the mine, the first year of ownership will be spent in making the mine and associated smelting plants operational, at a cost of £95,000 payable at the end of the year. Production will start at the beginning of the second year of ownership, when the output of pure tin will be 2 tonnes per month, whatever the type of rock formation. This production rate will remain unchanged until the mine is exhausted. During the first year of production, the directors expect that the resale value of the tin will be £9,900 per tonne and that labour and other production costs will be £187,000. These revenues and costs are expected to rise by 10% per annum in subsequent years. These cash flows can be assumed to occur at the end of the year in which they arise.

Special mining equipment will also be purchased at the beginning of the first year of production at a cost of £48,000. This equipment will be sold immediately on the cessation of production, at an amount expected to equal its purchase price, less £200 for every tonne of tin produced during its life. Other revenues from the sale of the mine at the end of production are expected to equal the closure costs exactly.

The company has received permission from the present owners of the mine to carry out a geological survey of the area. The survey would cost £10,000 and would reveal for certain the type of rock formations in the area and hence how much tin could be produced from the mine.

Starlite PLC has a money discount take of 21% per annum for this type of project.

The ENPV of the project – without the geological survey – can be calculated as follows.

If the output of tin per month is constant, whatever the rock type, then the different rock types simply affect the *life* of the mining operation:

Annual rate of production: 2 tonnes × 12 = 24 tonnes

Life of mine:

$$\text{Rock Type A:} \quad \frac{240}{24} = 10 \text{ years}$$

$$\text{Rock Type B:} \quad \frac{120}{24} = 5 \text{ years}$$

$$\text{Rock Type C:} \quad \frac{72}{24} = 3 \text{ years}$$

Whatever the rock type, the following cash flows will be incurred:

t_0	− £50,000		purchase cost	
t_1	− £95,000		plant purchase	
t_1	− £48,000		equipment purchase	
t_2	24 × £9,900	=	+237,600	1st year's revenue
			−187,000	1st year's costs
			+£50,600	1st year's net revenue

The net revenue increases 10% per year.

Disposal value of mining equipment:

Rock Type A: £48,000 − (240 × 200) = £ 0
Rock Type B: £48,000 − (120 × 200) = £24,000
Rock Type C: £48,000 − (72 × 200) = £33,600

The discount factor is $(1{\cdot}21)^{-n} \equiv (1{\cdot}1)^{-n}\,(1{\cdot}1)^{-n}$

Rock Type A

PV of mine, plant and equipment purchase costs:

		£
t_0 − £ 50,000 × 1	=	− 50,000
t_1 − £143,000 × $(1{\cdot}21)^{-1}$	=	−118,182
		£−168,182

PV of net revenue flows: (£000)

$$\underset{t_2}{\frac{50{\cdot}6}{(1{\cdot}1)^2(1{\cdot}1)^2}} \quad \underset{t_3}{\frac{50{\cdot}6\cancel{(1{\cdot}1)}}{(1{\cdot}1)^3(1{\cdot}1)^{\cancel{3}2}}} \quad \underset{t_4}{\frac{50{\cdot}6\cancel{(1{\cdot}1)^2}}{(1{\cdot}1)^4(1{\cdot}1)^{\cancel{4}2}}} \quad \cdots\cdots \quad \underset{t_{11}}{\frac{50{\cdot}6\cancel{(1{\cdot}1)^9}}{(1{\cdot}1)^{11}(1{\cdot}1)^{\cancel{11}2}}}$$

$$50{\cdot}6(1{\cdot}1)^{-2}\,A_{10\urcorner 0{\cdot}10} \times (1{\cdot}1)^{-1}$$
$$50{\cdot}6 \times 0{\cdot}83 \times 6{\cdot}14 \times 0{\cdot}91 = \text{£}+234{,}660$$

Net present value: £+66,478

Rock Type B

PV of mine, plant and equipment purchase costs:

$$\underline{\underline{£-168{,}182}}$$

PV of net revenue flows: (£000)

$$50{\cdot}6(1{\cdot}1)^{-2}\,A_{\overline{5}|0{\cdot}10} \times (1{\cdot}1)^{-1}$$
$$50{\cdot}6 \times 0{\cdot}83 \times 3{\cdot}79 \times 0{\cdot}91 = \underline{\underline{£+144{,}847}}$$

PV of disposal of mining equipment:

$$24{,}000(1{\cdot}21)^{-6} = 24{,}000(1{\cdot}1)^{-6}(1{\cdot}1)^{-6}$$
$$= 24{,}000 \times 0{\cdot}56 \times 0{\cdot}56 = \underline{\underline{£+7{,}526}}$$

Net present value: £−15,809

Rock Type C

PV of mine, plant and equipment purchase costs:

$$\underline{\underline{£-168{,}182}}$$

PV of net revenue flows: (£000)

$$50{\cdot}6(1{\cdot}1)^{-2}\,A_{\overline{3}|0{\cdot}10} \times (1{\cdot}1)^{-1}$$
$$50{\cdot}6 \times 0{\cdot}83 \times 2{\cdot}49 \times 0{\cdot}91 = \underline{\underline{£+95{,}163}}$$

PV of disposal of mining equipment:

$$33{,}600(1.21)^{-4} = 33{,}600(1.1)^{-4}(1.1)^{-4}$$
$$= 33{,}600 \times 0{\cdot}68 \times 0{\cdot}68 = \underline{\underline{£+15{,}537}}$$

Net present value: £−57,482

Expected net present value:

		£
+66,478 × 0·4	=	+26,591
−15,809 × 0·4	=	− 6,324
−57,482 × 0·2	=	−11,496
ENPV	=	£+8,771

Hence, on the basis of the expected NPV, the project is worthwhile undertaking without the survey.

We can now move on to examine whether or not the survey is worthwhile. From the previous set of calculations, it can be seen that the project would not go ahead if the company knew, ex ante, that either rock type B or rock type C existed. This is because both would involve negative net present values. Thus the company would only go ahead with the mine if rock type A was indicated. Hence, assuming a survey is undertaken, the expected value of the outcome would be:

Rock Type	*NPV*		*Probability*		£
A	+66,478	×	0·4	=	+26,591
B	0	×	0·4	=	0
C	0	×	0·2	=	0
					£+26,591

The expected net present value of the mine project, without the survey is approximately +£8,800; whilst if the survey is undertaken, this rises to +£16,500[1] approximately. Therefore, on this basis, it would suggest that the survey is worthwhile undertaking. Although the expected net present value approach is a rather unsatisfactory method of selecting between alternative financial opportunities as it takes no account of the risk involved, inspection of the alternative NPVs that might occur under the two options does support the initial advice that the survey should be undertaken:

	Survey *NPV*	*No Survey* *NPV*
Rock Type A	+£56,478	+£66,478
Rock Type B	−£10,000	−£15,809
Rock Type C	−£10,000	−£57,482

SENSITIVITY ANALYSIS

The appraisal of almost any investment project in the real world will involve the making of a great number of estimates. For example, the outlay required to undertake the project, its life, the annual cash inflows and outflows it will generate, the scrap value it will have, and even the correct rate of discount to reduce the cash flows to present values. Estimates will be made for all these factors and the project will then be appraised by calculating an expected net present value.

If this NPV is positive then the appraisal is in favour of acceptance. But, in terms of down-side risk, the decision maker is also interested in how sensitive the advice is to the estimates made about the project. In other words, he is likely to be interested in the *margin of error* that there can be in the estimates made about the individual components of the project (i.e., outlay, life, etc.) before the advice that the appraisal gives (in this case to accept) becomes incorrect.

The decision pivot point

The decision whether to accept or reject a particular project *pivots* around the zero NPV. If the NPV's greater then zero, then the advice is to accept. On the other hand, if the NPV is below zero (i.e., is negative), then the advice is to reject. Thus a *zero* NPV becomes the decision *pivot point.*

Sensitivity analysis is the term used to describe the process where each estimated element of a project's cash flow is taken in turn (with a *ceteris paribus* assumption holding all other estimates constant) to see the extent to which it can vary before the project's positive NPV is reduced to a zero value. Therefore if the estimated element varies by *more* than this amount, then the decision advice given by the original estimate of the project's NPV will be incorrect. These sensitivity calculations are illustrated in Example 11.8.

Example 11.8

Suppose the following estimates have been made about an investment proposal:

Outlay	£1,000
Life	3 years
Annual revenues	£2,000
Annual costs	£1,500
Appropriate discount rate	10%

On the basis of these estimates, the NPV can be calculated as follows:

	Year 0	1	2	3
Capital outlay	−£1,000			
Revenues		+£2,000	+£2,000	+£2,000
Costs		−£1,500	−£1,500	−£1,500
Net expected Cash flows	−£1,000	+£ 500	+£ 500	+£ 500

$$\text{ENPV} = -1{,}000 + 500A_{3\urcorner 0{\cdot}10} = +£243$$

Taking each of the five estimated factors in turn (and holding all the others constant at their initial estimated values), we shall examine the degree of variation necessary to reduce the +£243 NPV to zero.

Outlay: Let the outlay value be x.

$$-x + 500A_{3\urcorner 0{\cdot}10} = 0$$
$$\therefore\ x = 500A_{3\urcorner 0{\cdot}10} = 1{,}243$$

The outlay can be as high as £1,243 before the appraisal advice to invest (i.e., + NPV) becomes incorrect; in other words the original estimate can increase by £243 or by (243/1,000) = 0·243 or 24·3%

Life: Let the life be x years.

$$-1{,}000 + 500A_{x\urcorner 0{\cdot}10} = 0$$

Using linear interpolation, we know that when $x = 3$ the NPV equals +£243. Trying when $x = 2$:

$$-1{,}000 + 500A_{2\urcorner 0{\cdot}10} = -132\ \text{NPV}$$

Thus the value for x that produces a zero NPV lies between 2 and 3:

$$x = 2 + \left[\frac{132}{243 + 132} \times (3 - 2)\right] = 2.35 \text{ years}$$

The project life can be as short as 2·35 years before the advice of the original investment appraisal is incorrect; i.e. the original estimate can decrease by 0·65 year or by 0.65/3 = 0·217 or 21·7%.

Revenues: Let the annual revenues be x.

$$-1{,}000 + xA_{\overline{3}|0\cdot10} - 1{,}500A_{\overline{3}|0\cdot10} = 0$$

$$x = \frac{1{,}000 + 1{,}500A_{\overline{3}|0\cdot10}}{A_{\overline{3}|0\cdot10}} = \underline{\underline{£1{,}902}}$$

Thus the annual revenues can be as low as £1,902, over the three years, before the original advice is incorrect; i.e., the original estimate can decrease by £98 per year or 98/2,000 = 0·049 or 4·9%.

Costs: Let the annual costs be x.

$$-1{,}000 + 2{,}000A_{\overline{3}|0\cdot10} - xA_{\overline{3}|0\cdot10} = 0$$

$$x = \frac{1{,}000 - 2{,}000A_{\overline{3}|0\cdot10}}{A_{\overline{3}|0\cdot10}} = \underline{\underline{-£1{,}598}}$$

The annual costs can be as high as £1,598 in each of the three years before the original investment advice is incorrect; i.e., the original estimate can increase by £98 per year or 98/1,500 = 0·065 or 6.5%.

Discount rate: Let the discount rate be x (i.e. the project's IRR)

$$-1{,}000 + 500A_{\overline{3}|x} = 0$$

$$A_{\overline{3}|x} = \frac{1{,}000}{500} = 2\cdot0$$

Using linear interpolation, $A_{\overline{3}|0\cdot20} = 2\cdot11$ and $A_{\overline{3}|0\cdot25} = 1\cdot95$

$$x = 0\cdot20 + \left[\frac{2\cdot11 - 2\cdot0}{2\cdot11 - 1\cdot95} \times (0\cdot25 - 0\cdot20)\right] = \underline{\underline{0\cdot234}}$$

Thus the estimate for the discount rate can be as high as 23·4% before the original investment advice is incorrect; i.e., the original estimate can be increased by 13·4% or 0·134/0·10 = 1·34 or 134%

Sensitivity Table

Variable	*Original Estimate*	*Maximum Value*	*Maximum Change*	*% Change*
Outlay	1,000	1,243	+243	+24·3%
Life	3	2·35	−0·65	−21·7%
Revenues	2,000	1,902	−98	−4·9%
Costs	1,500	1,598	+98	+6·5%
Discount Rate	10%	23·4%	+13·4%	+134%

The sensitivity table in Example 11.8 shows that the decision to invest is most sensitive to the estimates of annual cash inflows (where an actual outcome of only 4·9% below estimate would cause the NPV decision advice to be incorrect) and the annual cash outflows (a decision sensitivity of 6·5%). The decision advice is fairly insensitive to all the other estimates. We would conclude from this that management should review both of these decision-sensitive estimates to ensure that they are as accurate as possible.

Example 11.8 outlines the general approach of the sensitivity analysis technique, which is a good working tool in that it makes the decision maker more aware of the possible effects of uncertainty on his investment decisions. In addition, it can also help to direct attention to those particular estimates which require a special forecasting effort on account of their effect on the decision's sensitivity.

Non-annuity cash flows

However, Example 11.8 is rather unrealistic because most of its cash flows are annuities. It was this characteristic that allowed us to take the approach that we did. Example 11.9 illustrates the approach to be taken when there are only non-annuity cash flows.

Example 11.9

Benagil PLC is considering undertaking a project and has made the following estimates:

Outlay: £2,300
Life: 3 years
Discount rate: 10%

Revenues:	Yr 1 : +£2,000	Costs:	Yr 1 : −£900
	2 : +£2,400		2 : −£1,100
	3 : +£1,600		3 : −£800

On this basis, the project's NPV has been estimated at +£375.

The management of Benagil now wish to analyse how sensitive is the NPV's decision advice to accept, to changes in the estimates:

Outlay: Let outlay $= x$

$$-x + 1{,}100(1{\cdot}10)^{-1} + 1{,}300(1{\cdot}10)^{-2} + 800(1{\cdot}10)^{-3} = 0 \text{ NPV}$$

$$-x + 2{,}675 = 0$$

$$x = 2{,}675$$

Therefore the outlay can increase by as much as £375 (or 375 ÷ 2,300 = 16.3%) before the original decision advice is changed.

Life: Let life $= x$

when $x = 3$, the project's NPV is +375

when $x = 2$, the project's NPV is:

$$-2{,}300 + 1{,}100(1{\cdot}10)^{-1} + 1{,}300(1{\cdot}10)^{-2} = -226$$

Using linear interpolation to estimate a value for x that gives a zero NPV:

$$x = 2 + \left[\frac{226}{375 + 226}(3 - 2)\right] = 2{\cdot}38 \text{ years}$$

Therefore the project's life can be shortened by up to 0·62 year (approximately 7·5 months) or 0·62 ÷ 3 = 20·7% before the original decision advice is incorrect.

Discount rate

Let the discount rate = x

When x = 10%, the project's NPV is +375.

When x = 20%, the project's NPV is:

$-2{,}300 + 1{,}100(1{\cdot}20)^{-1} + 1{,}300(1{\cdot}20)^{-2} + 800(1{\cdot}20)^{-3} = -18$

Using linear interpolation to estimate a value for x that gives a zero NPV:

$$x = 10\% + \left[\frac{375}{375 + 18}(20\% - 10\%)\right] = 19{\cdot}5\%$$

Thus the correct discount rate for the project can be as high as 19.5%, an increase of 9.5% (or 9.5% ÷ 10% = 95% on the original estimate), before the NPV's decision advice to accept is incorrect.

Revenues

If the revenues were to *decrease by 5% per year*, they would become:

Yr 1	+1,900
2	+2,280
3	+1,520

and the NPV would become:

$-2{,}300 + 1{,}000(1{\cdot}10)^{-1} + 1{,}180(1{\cdot}10)^{-2} + 720(1{\cdot}10)^{-3} = \underline{+125}$

If the revenues were to *decrease by 10% per year*, then the project's NPV would become:

$-2{,}300 + 900(1{\cdot}10)^{-1} + 1{,}060(1{\cdot}10)^{-2} + 640(1{\cdot}10)^{-3} = \underline{-125}$

Costs

If the costs were to *increase by 5% per year*, they would become:

Yr 1	−945
2	−1,155
3	−840

and the NPV would become:

$-2{,}300 + 1{,}055(1{\cdot}10)^{-1} + 1{,}245(1{\cdot}10)^{-2} + 760(1{\cdot}10)^{-3} = \underline{+259}$

If the costs were to *increase by 10% per year*, then the project's NPV would become:

$-2{,}300 + 1{,}010(1{\cdot}10)^{-1} + 1{,}190(1{\cdot}10)^{-2} + 720(1{\cdot}10)^{-3} = \underline{+142}$

Sensitivity Table

Variable	*Original Estimate*	*Maximum Value*	*Maximum Change*	*% Change*
Outlay	2,300	2,675	+375	+16·3%
Life	3	2·38	−0·62	−20·7%
Discount Rate	10%	19·5%	+9·5%	+95%

Revenues : Decision advice *not* sensitive at the 5% level, but *is* sensitive at the 10% level.

Costs : Decision advice *not* sensitive at either the 5% or the 10% level.

Therefore, the advice to management is that the decision given by the NPV calculation is insensitive to changes in most of the estimated variables. However, if the revenues were to fall by 10% of their estimated value the original decision advice would turn out to be incorrect. Hence it may be worth while to re-examine the estimates of annual revenues to see if the company's confidence in their accuracy can be improved.

Limitations of sensitivity analysis

The technique suffers, in particular, from an obvious and important drawback: the fact that each estimated component is varied *in turn* whilst all the others are held constant. Thus, in Example 11.9, the discount rate can be as high as 19·5% (approximately) before the NPV calculation advises rejection of the project, but this degree of sensitivity *only* holds (except through a chance ordering of factors) if all the other estimates turn out to be accurate. In other words, the technique ignores the possible effects on the decision of two or more of the estimated components varying simultaneously.[2]

Even if this problem with sensitivity analysis is set to one side, it can also be criticised on the basis that it makes no attempt to analyse risk in any formal way. Nor does it give any indication as to what the decision maker's reaction should be to the data presented in a sensitivity table.

In the examples used above, the original NPV calculations indicated a decision to accept. Sensitivity analysis provides no rules to guide the decision maker as to whether the initial appraisal advice should or should not be amended in the light of the sensitivity data. With these limitations in mind let us now look at other approaches which may be used to deal with the problem of uncertainty in investment appraisal.

THE RISK-ADJUSTED DISCOUNT RATE

The approach

The risk-adjusted discount rate approach attempts to handle the problem of risk in a more direct and thoughtful way. In fact, we know from our analysis of the CAPM that it is, essentially, a *correct* approach. However, the great distinction between the idea of the CAPM and the idea discussed here is that whereas the CAPM approach to a risk-adjusted discount rate is the outcome of an analytical and carefully-specified model, the approach dealt with here handles the issue on a more casual and intuitive basis.

To use a risk-adjusted discount rate for investment appraisal, the company simply adds to the current risk-free rate an additional premium, the size of which is determined by the estimated riskiness of the project being appraised. On the assumption that investors are risk-averse, the greater the perceived risk of a project the greater will be the risk premium and therefore the greater will be the resulting discount rate used to appraise the project. Thus the risk-adjusted discount rate takes the commonsense approach to handling risk in investment appraisal of adjusting the 'height' of the 'acceptance hurdle' to correspond to the project's risk level.

For example, a company's management may judge that the current rate of return on government long-term bonds is an adequate reflection of the risk-free interest/discount rate. Suppose this rate is 8%. Management may also decide to classify investment proposals into three broad categories, low, medium and high risk, and assign risk premiums of 3%,

5% and 9% respectively. Therefore the cash flows of low-risk projects would be discounted to present value using a discount rate of 8% + 3% = 11%, whilst projects of medium or high risk would be evaluated by discounting their cash flows to present value using 13% and 17% discount rates respectively.

In one very important way, the risk-adjusted discount rate approach to the problem of uncertainty is much more useful to the decision maker than sensitivity analysis in that it does actually produce decision *advice*, in the form of a risk-adjusted net present value. In addition, the method is easily understandable and appears to be intuitively correct: investors *do* require a higher expected return on riskier investments. However our CAPM analysis helps us to identify several drawbacks in this essentially correct (but too casual) analysis.

The problems

The two main problems are the allocation of projects into risk classes and the identification of the risk premiums. In terms of the first of these problems we know that projects should be allocated on the basis of their systematic risk. In this rather casual and judgemental approach the allocation of projects to risk classes is much more likely to be made on a project's *total* variability (its total risk) as it is this that management would perceive to be the risk of the project, if they did not have the insights into risk that the CAPM gives. The second point here is that the allocation of particular projects to particular risk classes will also be at the mercy of the individual managements' personal attitudes towards risk and, in particular, be viewed in relation to how a particular project will affect the *firm's* risk (as opposed to the risk of the shareholders' own investment portfolios).

The second problem concerns the allocation of the risk premium. Once again, this is likely to be unsatisfactory because it is done on the basis of a personalized analysis and without any more knowledge of the market's actual risk-return trade-off than that of casual observation.

Further there may well be a temptation for management to determine risk premiums on the basis of *achieved* rates of return, by projects in particular risk categories. The obvious danger here is that there are likely to be differences (and considerable differences when more risky projects are concerned) between *expected* rates of return and *achieved* rates of return. Hence the achieved rates of return on a firm's investment projects may act as a poor guide to what should be the looked-for returns from future projects.

USE OF THE NORMAL DISTRIBUTION

Another attempt to take a more analytical approach to the problem of risk makes use of the properties of Normal probability distributions. The approach starts from the premise that if a project's risk can be defined as the degree of possible variability between its expected outcome and its actual outcome, then what is of prime importance to the risk-averse decision maker (or more correctly, the risk-averse owner on whose behalf the decision is being made) is just one side of this variability: the risk of project underperformance. Therefore, what would be of interest to the decision maker is the probability of the project actually producing a negative NPV, even though the *expected* result was a positive NPV. On the assumption that the range of possible outcomes for the project are normally distributed, then the properties of the Normal Curve can be used to provide the required probability.

The discount rate

A problem arises, however, in the choice of the discount rate to be used to calculate the possible NPVs of the project being appraised. One possibility is to use the risk-free discount rate. The investment decision advice is then based on whether or not the probability of a negative NPV exceeds some maximum acceptable probability, in much the same way as a risk-premium is utilized when using the risk-adjusted discount rate. If the probability of a negative NPV were sufficiently small, the project would be acceptable.

Example 11.10

A project under evaluation is thought to involve a medium degree of risk. The risk-free discount rate is 4% and the appropriate risk premium is believed to be 6%. The project has the following estimated cash flows:

Cash outlay (year 0): £1,000

Cash inflows:

		Year: 1	2	3	Prob.
Market conditions:	Good	+1,000	+1,000	+1,000	0·10
	Med./good	+800	+800	+800	0·20
	Medium	+600	+600	+600	0·40
	Med./poor	+400	+400	+400	0·20
	Poor	+200	+200	+200	0·10

(a) Using the risk-free discount rate of 4%:

Market Conditions	*NPV*	*Prob.*		*(NPV − ENPV)²*	*× Prob.*	
Good	+1,775	× 0·10	= +177·5	(1,775 − 665)²	× 0·10	= 123,210
Medium Good	+1,220	× 0·20	= +244·0	(1,220 − 665)²	× 0·20	= 61,605
Medium	+ 665	× 0·40	= +266·0	(665 − 665)²	× 0·40	= 0
Medium Poor	+ 110	× 0·20	= + 22·0	(110 − 665)²	× 0·20	= 61,605
Poor	− 445	× 0·10	= − 45·5	(−445 − 665)²	× 0·10	= 123,210
		ENPV	+665·0		Var.	= 369,630

Whilst the ENPV = +665, the standard deviation = $\sqrt{369{,}630}$ = 608 NPV

(Notice that an alternative approach is being used here to calculate the variance and standard deviation, than the approach used earlier with portfolio theory. This is just for convenience because of the size of the numbers. The variance could have been calculated on the basis of $E(NPV^2) - ENPV^2$.)

Probability of a negative NPV: $\frac{0 - 665}{608} = \underline{1 \cdot 094 \text{ Std. units}}$

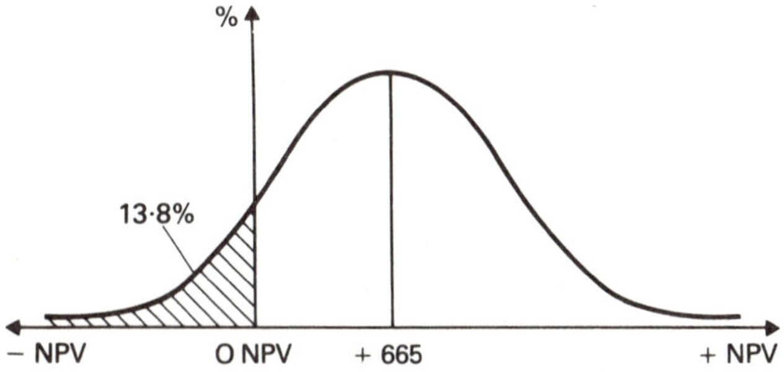

Using area under the Normal curve tables this gives a value for the shaded area (– NPV) of: 0·1379

Therefore there is a 13·8% probability that the project will produce less than the risk-free return of 4%.

(b) Using the risk-adjusted discount rate of 4% + 6% = 10%:

Market Conditions	*NPV*		*Prob.*			*(NPV – ENPV)²*	*× Prob.*		
Good	+1,487	×	0·10	=	+148·7	(1,487 – 492)²	× 0·10	=	99,002·4
Medium Good	+ 989	×	0·20	=	+197·8	(989 – 492)²	× 0·20	=	49,401·8
Medium	+ 492	×	0·40	=	+196·8	(492 – 492)²	× 0·40	=	0
Medium Poor	– 5	×	0·20	=	– 1·0	(–5 – 492)²	× 0·20	=	49,401·8
Poor	– 503	×	0·10	=	– 50·3	(–503 – 492)²	× 0·10	=	49,002·4
			ENPV		+492·0		Var.	=	296,808.4

ENPV = +492

Standard Deviation = $\sqrt{296808 \cdot 4}$ = 545 NPV

Probability of a negative NPV:

$$\frac{0 - 492}{545} = 0 \cdot 903 \text{ Std. units}$$

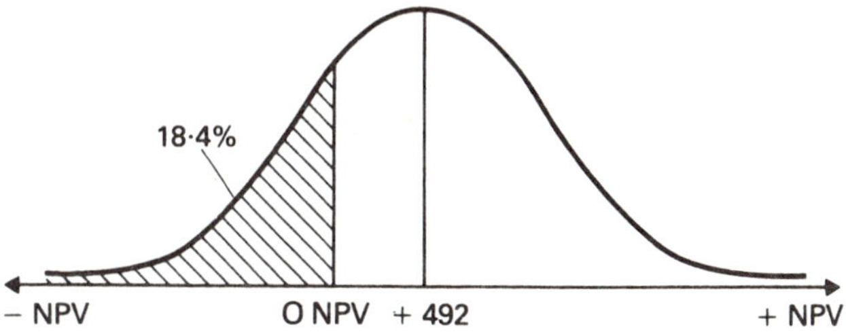

Using area under the Normal curve tables this gives a value for the shaded area (–NPV) of: 0·1841.

Therefore there is an 18·4% probability that the project will produce less than the required return of 10%.

An alternative approach is to discount the project cash flows using an appropriate *risk-adjusted* discount rate in order to calculate the expected NPV and then use the properties of the Normal Curve to estimate the probability of a negative NPV. This latter approach uses the probability of a negative NPV as an *additional* piece of decision information, almost as an extension of the sensitivity analysis concept. By contrast, the former approach attempts to use the properties of the Normal Curve to allow directly for risk in investment decision making. In doing so it avoids the element of 'double-counting' risk which occurs when using a risk-adjusted discount rate to calculate the range of possible NPVs.

A simple illustration, such as that set out in Example 11.10, can be used to explain the mechanics of both approaches. From the results of this example it can be seen that when using a risk free discount rate, the decision advice is based on whether a 13·8% probability of the project actually producing a return below the riskless return is acceptable for the perceived level of risk of the project concerned. Alternatively, the second approach informs the decision maker that the project can be expected to produce a positive NPV of £492 when discounted at a rate thought appropriate for its degree of risk, but that if a decision is made to accept the project there is a 18·4% probability that this decision will turn out to be incorrect (i.e., the project actually produces a negative NPV).

SUMMARY

This chapter has looked at some of the more simple approaches to the problem of risk in capital investment appraisal. None of these can be said really to tackle the issue except in a rather intuitive, rule of thumb way. However, it could be argued that their use in practice is better than ignoring the presence of risk completely. The major points made were as follows:

- The expected net present value (ENPV) approach examines the *average* outcome of a project. However, because of this it fails to capture what is the essence of risk by ignoring *variability* of outcome.
- However, the analysis can be useful for examining the value of additional information to a company.
- The abandonment decision analysis can help to evaluate investment appraisal situations where an option to abandon the project before it reaches the end of its life is available.
- The abandonment decision analysis suffers from the difficulty of obtaining reliable abandonment value data and requires a complex mathematical analysis in all but the simplest problems.
- Sensitivity analysis examines the degree to which the various estimates made about a project can change, before the decision advice given by NPV is overturned.

- There are two main advantages. The first is that it highlights those estimates to which the decision advice is most sensitive. Management can then go back and take more time and trouble to ensure those particular estimates are as accurate as possible. The second advantage is that it gives the decision maker more information to use in deciding whether or not to accept the advice of the original NPV analysis.
- There are two disadvantages of sensitivity analysis. The first is the more serious: it only looks at the effect of changing one estimate at a time. It doesn't examine the effects of simultaneous changes in two or more estimates. The second disadvantage is it gives no indication as to *how* the decision maker should evaluate and make use of the sensitivity data.
- The risk-adjusted discount rate approach described in this chapter represents an intuitive attempt to recognize the relationship between risk and return.
- It can be faulted on a number of grounds. Firstly on the basis of how the risk premiums are derived and secondly – and more importantly – it can be faulted on the basis that risk is likely to be seen more in *total* rather than *systematic* terms.
- Finally, the use of the normal probability distribution was examined. This is an interesting approach to the handling of risk in decision-making, although little used in practice. The most sensible approach is to obtain a probability that the investment project will produce a return that is less than the *risk-free* return. The alternative approach, looking at the probability of a negative NPV calculated on the basis of a discounted rate assumed to reflect the project's risk, is simply a variation on sensitivity analysis.

NOTES

1 £26,591 minus the cost of the survey.

2 In theory this problem can be overcome by use of the Operational Research technique of simulation; but in practice this does little to enhance or clarify the decision maker's view of the effects of uncertainty on a project's desirability.

FURTHER READING

1 The articles in this general area of the more traditional approaches to handling risk are not particularly rewarding. However, two interesting pieces are: G.J. Grayson, 'The Use of Statistical Techniques in Capital Budgeting', in *Financial Research and Management Decisions*, ed. A.A. Robicheck, 1967, which looks at the use of sensitivity analysis; and A.A. Robicheck and S.C. Myers, 'Conceptual Problems in the Use of the Risk Adjusted Discount Rate', *Journal of Finance*, December 1966.

2 Other articles of interest are: D.B. Hertz, 'Risk Analysis in Capital Investment', *Harvard Business Review*, January–February 1964; J.F. Magee, 'How to Use Decision Trees in Capital Investment', *Harvard Business Review*, September–October 1964; A. Rappaport, 'Sensitivity Analysis in Decision Making', *Accounting Review*, July 1967; and E.F. Brigham, D.F. Shome and S.R. Vinson, 'The Risk Premium Approach to Measuring a Utilities Cost of Equity', *Financial Management*, Spring 1985.

QUICKIE QUESTIONS

1 A machine costs £1,000 and has a life of 3 years. It can either be a success or a failure. If it is successful – and it has a probability of 45% – then it will produce an annual net cash flow of £500. If it is a failure, the annual net cash flow will be only £350. The discount rate is 10%. What is its ENPV?

2 What is the maximum worth of a survey that would tell you, in advance of the decision, whether the machine in question 1 would be a success or failure?

3 What would be the maximum worth of the survey in question 2 if it was only 75% accurate?

4 Given the following information:

State	*Prob.*	*£NPV*
I	0·3	+100
II	0·5	+ 50
III	0·2	−300

What would be the maximum worth of a survey which could tell you, in advance, which state of the world would occur?

5 A machine costs £140. It has a two-year life and a 15% discount rate correctly reflects its risk. Its performance depends upon the state of the world:

State	*Yr 1*	*Yr 2*	*Prob.*
I	+100	+100	0·70
II	+ 60	+ 60	0·10
III	+ 40	+ 40	0·20

The company can sell the machine at the end of Yr 1 for £60. At the end of Yr 2 the machine will be worthless. Advise the company.

6 Given the following information about a project:

Outlay	£1,000
Life	5 years
Net cash flow	+£280 per year
Discount rate	10%

How sensitive is the decision advice to changes in the estimate of the life and the annual net cash flow?

PROBLEMS

1 The directors of Linnet Oil plc are considering whether to make an immediate payment of £20 million for a licence to drill oil in a particular geographical area. Having acquired the licence, the company would commission a *seismic survey* to determine whether the area is a suitable prospect, i.e. whether there are any geological structures present which could contain oil. If the area is a suitable prospect, *exploration wells* would be drilled to discover if oil is in fact present. If oil is present, *appraisal wells* would be drilled to ascertain the size and characteristics of the potential field.

The company's development expert has produced the following data about the licence area based upon the results from adjoining areas. If oil is discovered by the exploration wells, the appraisal wells will indicate one of the three following types of oil field:

Type	*Probability of occurrence*	*Millions of barrels*	*Expected life (years)*
I	60%	negligible	zero
II	32%	42	4
III	8%	2250	10

The annual oil production will decline over the life of the field. To approximate the decline, the expert argues that a sensible approach would be to assume that the annual production of the field during the first half of its life is twice the annual production during the second half. For example, for a type II field the first two years' annual production rate would be 14 million barrels per annum and the second two years' annual production rate would be 7 million barrels per annum.

During the entire life of the field, a barrel of oil is expected to sell for \$26·4 and the \$/£ rate is expected to be 1·2\$/£. The annual operating cash surplus is expected to be 45% of sales revenue. The combined tax costs for the company are usually 77% of the operating cash surplus and these tax cash flows can be assumed to arise one year after the cash flows relating to sales and other costs. Production of oil would start in one year's time and the first annual net revenues would arise at the end of the first year of production.

The cost of the appraisal well drilling will be £100 million and the exploration well drilling will cost £10 million. Both costs will be paid in one year's time. The seismic survey costs of £2 million will be paid immediately. All three of the costs, together with the cost of the licence to drill oil, will give rise to tax relief equal to 50% of the cost, receivable one year after the cost is paid.

It is expected that there will be a 50% chance that the seismic survey will indicate the prospect of oil and a 30% chance that the exploration drilling will find oil. The company's after-tax cost of capital for this type of project is 15% per annum.

Required:
(a) Calculate the expected net present value of the venture.
(b) Calculate the maximum price the company should pay for an alternative type of seismic survey which will reduce the probability of indicating a positive prospect from 50% to 30% and so increase from 30% to 50% the chance that the exploration drilling will find oil.

2 Southgate Ltd. is investigating the introduction of a new alcoholic drink to be called Mildmay. Extensive market research by an outside agency, at a cost of £10,000 has suggested that a price of £5 per bottle to the retail trade would be acceptable.

Production of Mildmay will require specialized distilling and flavouring equipment which, it is estimated, would cost £200,000. As with most distilling equipment, this installation is likely to have a long production life but, due to its rather specialized nature, when production of Mildmay ceases it will only be able to be sold for scrap for around £2,000 (net of dismantling costs). Variable costs of production are estimated at £3 per bottle and overheads are estimated at £25,000 per year, avoidable only if production ceases.

At the proposed selling price, the drink trade is expected to demand 50,000 bottles per year, well within the capacity of the production equipment, but after four years interest is expected to decline and so production will cease. However, the company believes that it may well be able to extend product life for a further two years by either running a small trade advertizing campaign at the start of years 5 *and* 6 at a cost of £10,000 per year, or alternatively by reducing the price per bottle by 40p in these two years. The market research company believes that the two alternatives would achieve similar sales results, but just what these sales would be is uncertain. If the campaign is successful in year 5 then sales of 35,000 bottles could be expected in that year, with sales of 28,000 or only 9,000 bottles being equally likely in year 6, or alternatively the year 5 promotion may be relatively unsuccessful with sales of only 7,000 bottles in that year and an equal likelihood of either 12,000 or 5,000 bottles in the following year. The market research agency believes that the campaign has only a 60% chance of being successful in year 5.

All expenses and revenues will be paid or received in cash at the end of the year in which they arise, with the exception of the production equipment for which payment is due at the start of the first year of manufacture and the advertising expenditure which must be paid for at the start of *each* year in which a campaign is mounted. The company normally uses a 10% discount rate for project evaluation purposes.

Required:
(a) Evaluate the financial feasibility of the proposed new drink, in respect of its normal expected life of 4 years, including in your presentation details about the sensitivity of the decision advice to

changes in all the estimates made, except the scrap value and discount rate.

(b) Briefly advise management on the results of the sensitivity analysis.

(c) Evaluate which of the two alternative methods (if any) should be used to extend the product life.

3 A small company in the house building industry has £201,000 cash which is surplus to current requirements. The cash will eventually be used to help finance the construction of a small housing development. The housing development depends upon obtaining permission to build the houses from the local government planning department. It is believed that this permission will be given in two years' time.

The £201,000 can be invested in the money market to yield a return of 10% per year. The money market is considered to be an efficient market.

Alternatively an opportunity exists for the funds to be invested on a temporary basis in Goer, a family owned car hire business which wishes to expand its car hire fleet by thirty cars costing £6,700 each. Goer is temporarily short of funds because of recent inheritance tax payments. If the funds are invested with Goer they will produce an annual net cash inflow to the building company, but the size of this cash flow is not known with certainty, and the cash flow at the end of the second year is dependent upon the cash flow at the end of the first year. Estimates of the net cash inflows to the building company are detailed below.

End of Year 1		*End of Year 2*	
Probability	*Cash inflow* £	*Probability*	*Cash inflow* £
0·6	80,000	0·6	80,000
		0·4	90,000
0·4	100,000	0·6	100,000
		0·4	110,000

In addition Goer will make a payment to the building company at the end of the first year of £141,000 *or* at the end of the second year of £81,000. The building company has to choose at the end of the first year whether to receive payment of £141,000 then or £81,000 a year later. If the payment of £141,000 is received by the building company at the end of the first year the investment will be terminated and there will be no further cash flows to the building company from Goer.

18% per year is considered to be an appropriate discount rate for investments in the car hire business.

Required:

(a) Prepare a report recommending whether the building company should invest in the car hire business or in the money market. All relevant calculations must be included in your report.

Ignore taxation. State clearly any assumptions that you make.

(b) Discuss the practical problems of incorporating abandonment opportunities into the capital investment decision-making process.

Suggest possible reasons why a company might decide to abandon an investment project part way through its expected economic life.

4 The management of Haydn Ltd is planning the launch of a new micro-computer, the SQ. The market for micro-computers is very competitive and the anticipated product life of the SQ is only three years. The marketing director of Haydn Ltd has produced the following table showing three different estimates of likely demand for the SQ during each year of its life.

Demand Predictions	*Probability*	*Year 1*	*Year 2*	*Year 3*
		Units	*Units*	*Units*
Most optimistic	0·2	32,000	16,000	12,000
Best guess	0·5	16,000	8,000	6,000
Most pessimistic	0·3	4,000	2,000	1,500

The above estimates assume a constant selling price of £500 over the three years. The variable production cost per unit of an SQ is £400.

The production director has indicated that the factory is in a position to produce 32,000, 16,000 or 4,000 units per annum, but, once decided, the chosen production level could not be increased until the start of the following year. The total cost of setting up the production line would consist of fixed costs of £1 million, and variable costs of £50 for each unit of production capacity. These costs would be paid at the start of the year's production.

A market research firm has offered, for a fee of £300,000, to carry out a detailed survey which would determine precisely the level of demand for the SQ. The management of Haydn Ltd wishes to know whether the market survey is likely to be worthwhile.

In order to assess whether the survey is worth undertaking, the directors of Haydn Ltd have asked that the following simplifying assumptions be made:

(i) cash flows relating both to sales and variable production costs are to be deemed to arise at the end of the year in which they are incurred;

(ii) demand can be represented by only one of the three sets of possibilities envisaged by the marketing director;

(iii) the level of demand in the first year will determine the levels demanded in the second and third years;

(iv) the appropriate discount rate for the venture is 10% per annum; and

(v) stock levels will remain unchanged.

Required:

(a) Determine the *initial* production capacity that Haydn Ltd should choose, and compute the resulting expected net present value of producing and selling *at that level*

(b) Calculate whether the market survey should be commissioned, and comment on any reservations you might have relating to the use of expected values as an aid in decision making

(c) Discuss the advantages to the company of conducting a market survey of this kind

12
The cost of company capital

Chapter Contents

THE FINANCING DECISION

Up to this stage our analysis has been confined to an evaluation of project investment appraisal. We have not considered how any particular project should be financed – or indeed, whether the method of finance makes any difference.

This exclusion of any consideration about the financing method has been assisted by the assumption of a perfect capital market, which implies that if a company can identify a project that has a non-negative NPV, when discounted at a rate that reflects its level of systematic risk, then the required finance will be made available by the capital market.[1] Thus the question of financing has appeared to be irrelevant.

In this chapter, and in the three that follow, we start to examine whether the question of project financing is irrelevant and if it is not, then what factors should be considered when evaluating different methods or sources of finance. But it is perhaps wise (at this point) to make very much the same sort of observation that was made at the outset of our analysis of the handling of risk in decision making. Therefore just as our knowledge of how we should take account of risk is still incomplete, it is also the case in terms of the financing decision and especially in terms of the decision concerning the 'optimal' capital structure of companies.

In this chapter, we examine much the same area as we did in the chapter on the CAPM – the rate of return on financial securities (e.g., the shares of companies) but, in one sense, from the other side of the coin. This is the area of the cost of company capital. We do this first, in order to begin to examine the financial decision itself. We shall see in the following chapter that the cost of capital concept can also provide us (under certain restrictive circumstances) with a capital investment appraisal discount rate.

Chapters 14 and 15 look directly at the implications for the firm and its owners of the financing decision itself. Then Chapter 16 examines how capital investment decisions and financing decisions interact and how such interactions may be analysed.

Types of long-term finance

Generally speaking capital investment projects are financed from three alternative (but not necessarily mutually exclusive) sources: finance directly supplied by the capital markets in the form of ordinary share capital, finance directly supplied by the capital markets in the form of interest-bearing medium and long-term loans and finance internally generated by the firm in the form of retained profits. There are other sources of long-term finance – one important one may be Government grants[2] – but in the main the three sources of finance mentioned do predominate.

These different types of finance are 'different' in several ways. They differ in how they are issued, the obligations that they impose on a firm's management, and how they are affected by the tax system. However, not the least of their differences is in terms of risk. Our analysis of the CAPM showed that the return required on any investment should reflect the systematic risk involved, and hence if these different types of capital have different levels of systematic risk, then we can expect their returns to reflect these differences.

There is an important difference however, between the CAPM analysis of returns on securities and the analysis which follows. That difference is that whereas the CAPM analysis was undertaken within a *single* time period framework, the following analysis is undertaken within a *multi-time* period framework.

Apart from that one fact the two approaches are entirely compatible. Just as the CAPM was a share valuation model (shares were valued so as to provide the required expected return), so in this current chapter we shall be making extensive use of another (different, but compatible) share valuation model: the *dividend valuation model.*

Finally, although we shall be examining what are the expected returns required by the *suppliers* of corporate finance, because we are interested in what these returns are from the viewpoint of management, they will be referred to as the *costs* of the various types of capital.

THE COST OF EQUITY CAPITAL

Physical and financial investments

In our analysis using the single period investment–consumption model we distinguished between physical investment decisions and financial investment decisions. In fact the distinction between financial and physical investments is almost entirely artificial, as far as decision making is concerned.

A physical (or real) investment could be defined as involving cash (i.e., consumption power) being spent in order to combine and operate productive resources (the factors of production) so as to generate a saleable output (of either goods or services), which can be exchanged for cash. A financial investment still involves an outlay of cash – it is lent on the financial markets – but now a *third party* undertakes the physical investment.

Individuals or companies borrow money through the medium of the financial markets in order to undertake physical investments, with the hope that the investment will produce a sufficient cash return in the future, to allow a surplus to remain once the borrowed funds (capital plus interest) have been repaid. Obviously, this is a highly simplified view of the distinction between physical and financial investments, but it is essentially correct.

The required return on equity capital

There are many ways in which investors can lend money on the capital market. One is to buy the ordinary shares issued by a company (either directly from the company or from a third party in the form of an existing shareholder) so that the *company*, rather than the investor personally, undertakes the physical investments.

An essential characteristic of an investment in ordinary shares or *equity capital*, which differentiates if from most other forms of capital market lending, is that the loan never comes to maturity, i.e. the loan is permanent and is never repaid.[3] (However, ordinary shares are *negotiable*: the permanent loan to a company can be sold on to another investor. These transactions form the bulk of stock exchange dealings.) Because of this characteristic of equity capital, the investors making such loans to a company are held to be the legal owners of the company.

To find what is the expected return required by ordinary shareholders on their capital, we shall return to our earlier discussion on the objective of financial management decision making. The objective, we said, could be stated as the maximization of the (current) market value of the company's ordinary share capital. This was a surrogate for maximizing the dividend flow to shareholders through time (which in itself was a surrogate for wealth maximization), because it is this *dividend flow* which gives a share its market value.

However, we also know that cash flows are uncertain and that cash flows which arise at different points in time cannot be directly compared but must first be converted to values at one point in time (usually, the present time is chosen). Thus the market value of an ordinary share represents the sum of its *expected* future dividend flow, *discounted* to present value.

This particular line of reasoning leads to the share valuation model known as the *dividend valuation* model: the market price of a company's shares equals the sum of its future expected dividend flow, to infinity, discounted to present value. In this model what is of particular interest to us is the *discount rate* implied by a particular stock market share price. The discount rate represents the return an investor can expect to obtain on the shares.

An example

Suppose that an ordinary share in a particular company is generally expected by all investors to produce a 10p dividend at the end of each year, for ever (i.e., in perpetuity). If the share has a market value of 80p, this represents the sum of the expected future discounted dividend stream:

$$80\text{p} = 10\text{p}(1 + i)^{-1} + 10\text{p}(1 + i)^{-2} \cdots + 10\text{p}(1 + i)^{-\infty}$$

as this is a perpetuity, the sum reduces to:

$$80\text{p} = \frac{10\text{p}}{i} \text{ and so } i = \frac{10\text{p}}{80\text{p}} = 0{\cdot}125 \text{ or } 12{\cdot}5\%$$

Therefore i, the rate of discount implied, given the share's market value, is $12\frac{1}{2}\%$. It is this interest or discount rate that reduces the sum of the future expected dividend flow to a present value of 80p.[4]

Therefore $12\frac{1}{2}\%$ must be the expected return that is required by ordinary shareholders in this company, taking into consideration the systematic riskiness of the future expected dividend flow. (This, in turn, depends upon the systematic riskiness of the expected returns from the physical investments which the company has undertaken.) In other words if an investor bought a share in the company for 80p and *did* receive a 10p dividend each year, then he would be getting a $12\frac{1}{2}\%$ annual return on his money.

The cost of equity capital

If equity capital were to be the only source of investment funds used by this company – and the shareholders require an expected return of $12\frac{1}{2}\%$ on their investment, then $12\frac{1}{2}\%$ could be taken by management as representing the discount rate to be used in the company's project appraisal NPV calculations.

The reasoning behind this is that investors have implicitly specified a $12\frac{1}{2}\%$ return through the price set on the shares in the market place. The shares are priced at 80p because, on this basis, investors can expect a $12\frac{1}{2}\%$ return. Why is an expected $12\frac{1}{2}\%$ return required? Because this must be the going rate of return elsewhere on the stock market, for investments of the same level of systematic risk.

If shareholders can obtain a return of $12\frac{1}{2}$% elsewhere on the stock market for a similar level of risk, the inference is that the company's management must earn *at least* this rate of return on any physical investments they wish to undertake with shareholders' funds. If they cannot find projects yielding at least such expected returns (given the risk level) then they should not invest. They should give the money back to shareholders – perhaps in the form of a dividend – because shareholders *can* invest that money to yield a $12\frac{1}{2}$% expected return. Thus $12\frac{1}{2}$% becomes – from the perspective of management – the *cost* of using equity capital to invest in projects. (Notice that this cost is, in fact, an *opportunity cost.*)

Therefore the discount rate that reduces the sum of a share's expected future dividend flow to a present value equal to its market price is called the *cost of equity capital.* It is the minimum expected return required by shareholders from the investment of their funds by the company's management. However, the cost of equity capital is an appropriate discount rate to use in NPV calculations *only* in circumstances where the project being appraised has the same level of systematic risk (i.e., the same beta value) as the systematic risk of the company's *existing* cash flows (i.e., those cash flows generated by capital investment projects that have already been undertaken).

This is a very important (and limiting) proviso, but it is obvious from our previous analysis. Any rate of return is only relative to a given risk level, and so a company's cost of equity capital is a required rate of return relative to its *existing* level of risk. Therefore, this will be appropriate to use as a discount rate for project evaluation only if the project has a similar level of risk as the existing company.

If the project has a *different* level of risk, then the company's existing cost of capital is *not* the appropriate discount rate. In these circumstances, we would have to rely upon a CAPM/beta type of analysis as discussed in Chapter 10, in order to identify the correct rate of discount.

EXPECTED RETURN, DIVIDENDS, MARKET PRICE

Workings of the stock market

Before proceeding to consider further how the required expected return on equity is to be estimated, let us examine the nature of the relationship between expected return, dividends and market price. In order to do so we shall be taking a simplified but generally correct view of the workings of stock markets.

With the company used in the example above, shareholders required an expected return (or yield) of $12\frac{1}{2}$%. On the basis of an expected annual dividend per share of 10p in perpetuity, this produced a market value of 80p per share. Now, in the following analysis, the *riskiness* of the expected future dividend flow will remain unchanged.

Suppose something happens which leads investors, in general, to believe that the company will now pay an annual dividend per share in future of 12p, instead of 10p. At the market price of 80p the share now yields a return of 12p/80p = 0·15. This 15% return is above the required return (of $12\frac{1}{2}$%) for this level of risk, and so investors will start to buy the company's shares because they represent a 'bargain' priced at only 80p.

Stock exchanges work through a supply and demand market mechanism, and therefore this increased demand for the company's ordinary shares will force up the market price. Suppose, in response to this increased demand, the market price rises to 85p per share. It is still yielding an excessively high return: 12p/85p = 0·141, and so demand will continue. In fact the price of the share should rise until its yield equates with the required yield of $12\frac{1}{2}$%. So the market price will settle at 12p/0·125 = 96p per share. (Any *further* increase in share price will cause the share to have too low an expected return, investors will wish to sell, and so the reverse process will start, with the share price falling until it produces the required yield of $12\frac{1}{2}$%.)

A changing required return

The foregoing example illustrates the positive relationship between the dividend expectations of a share and its market price. Increases or decreases in the expected dividend flow will cause a respective rise or fall in market value, with the lynch-pin of the mechanism being the required expected return.

Similarly, if an event occurs which causes investors to change the level of a share's required rate of return. For example, because a company's expected future dividend flow is viewed, for some reason, as becoming more or less risky than before; or because *alternative* investments have become more or less attractive in terms of their risk-return. Then a consequent change in market price will occur until the *revised* required yield has established itself. There is an *inverse* relationship between required return and market price.

As an example, suppose that we return to the original situation of a market price of 80p per share, a constant annual expected dividend of 10p and hence an expected return of $12\frac{1}{2}$%. Suppose that, for some reason, rates of return throughout the economy rise. (One possible reason might be that the Government has increased the return it gives on government stock and so this has pushed up *all* rates of return in the economy.) As a result, investments with a similar level of systematic risk to that of our company whose share price we are considering rise to (say) 15%.

This means that our shares are no longer giving a sufficient return at $12\frac{1}{2}$%. In consequence, investors will start to sell the shares, and this selling pressure will cause the share price to fall. How *far* the share price will fall is determined by what is the new level of required expected return. In this case, the shares will fall in price until they reach $66\frac{2}{3}$p, at which point they too now produce a return of 15% – as do comparable risk investments. Hence the share price has *fallen*, but the expected return has *risen*.

The shareholder and the market

The individual investor has to decide whether to buy, hold or sell a particular share. It is not the individual shareholder's actions, but those of the market as a whole (i.e., all investors collectively) that determines a share's expected yield. Therefore the individual investor has to estimate a share's future expected dividend flow and from this, together with the share's market price, he will be able to derive its expected yield or return.

What action he then takes (buy, sell or hold) depends upon his own personal attitude to risk and the return he requires for bearing varying amounts of it. If he believes that the share's expected yield is *at least* sufficient compensation for the risk that owning the share involves he will buy; if *just* sufficient he will hold; if *less* than sufficient he will sell. The individual shareholder's actions will not have much *direct* effect on the market price. However, if investors in general have a similar attitude to the required 'risk – expected return' trade-off, then they are *all*[5] likely to undertake similar action and the share's market price will adjust accordingly. Hence the position of market equilibrium is achieved, which was referred to in our discussion of the market portfolio and the CML.

APPLYING THE DIVIDEND VALUATION MODEL

Introduction

At first sight, the dividend valuation model may appear to be a rather naive and incomplete model of share price behaviour. It implies that share prices are only determined by the expected level of dividends and systematic risk of the future dividend flow.[6]

However, in essence, it is likely to be valid and it fits in well with the general assertion made earlier in this book: values are applied to objects (including shares) in order to allow decisions to be made about them, and an object's current value, on the assumption of a rational, economic man, is based on the net stream of future benefits it will produce (or, rather more correctly, that it is *expected* to produce). In addition, we have already recognized the importance of cash and cash flow in economic wealth-maximizing decisions, and the dividend valuation model, being a cash flow valuation model, is therefore in close accord with this reasoning.

The model

If we make use of the following notation:

P_E = Market price per share.
V_E = Total market value of equity = $P_E \times$ Number of shares in issue.
d_t = Dividend per share paid in time t.
D_t = Total dividend paid to equity holders at time $t = d_t \times$ number of shares in issue.
K_E = Cost of equity capital (expected return on equity).

then the dividend valuation model can be expressed in general terms as:

$$\text{either } V_E = \sum_{t=1}^{\infty} \frac{D_t}{(1+K_E)^t} \quad \text{or} \quad P_E = \sum_{t=1}^{\infty} \frac{d_t}{(1+K_E)^t}$$

The only difference between the two expressions is that the first displays the model in *total* market value of the equity terms, whereas the second displays the model in terms of the market value *per share.*

If we assume that the future expected dividend flow will remain at a *constant* level for all future time periods (i.e., a level perpetuity), then the model can be simplified into the form we used in the earlier example that explained the relationship between expected return, dividend flow and market price:

$$V_E = \frac{D}{K_E} \quad \text{or} \quad P_E = \frac{d}{K_E}$$

Bid and offer prices

There are several additional points to be made in connection with this model. The first concerns the value of P_E (and consequently V_E) that is to be used.

Shares are normally given *two* prices: a bid (selling) price and an offer (buying) price. The former will be greater than the latter, with the difference being known as the 'jobber's turn'.[7] However, we are retaining the assumption of a perfect capital market, and one of the sub-assumptions of this is that there are no transaction costs involved in buying and selling shares. As the jobber's turn is a type of transaction cost, this assumption allows us neatly to side-step the problem and instead assume that there is no difference between the bid and offer price. Therefore we will use what is referred to as the share's *middle price.* This is usually the price seen quoted in the pages of the financial press.

Cum div and ex div

The second point to be made concerns the fact that market prices of ordinary shares can sometimes be quoted either 'cum div', or 'ex div'. A 'cum div' market price applies to a share just *prior* to its dividend being paid, whilst an 'ex div' price applies to a share just *after* its dividend has been paid.

Suppose a company is generally expected to pay a 10p per share dividend in perpetuity and shareholders require an expected return of 10%. The dividend valuation model can be used to estimate the equity's market value: $P_E = 10\text{p}/0{\cdot}10 = 100\text{p}$. This is the *ex div* market value of the equity (i.e., it is the market value of the share at that point in the company's year when the *next* 10p dividend is due to be paid in approximately 12 months' time), because this simplified version of the model which assumes a constant annual dividend is based on the arithmetic of an *immediate* annuity.[8]

Assuming that there are no changes in investors' expectations and that all expectations are fulfilled, a share's market price will follow a 'saw-tooth' pattern over time. Using the example above, the share's market price will rise steadily over the year from the ex div market price of 100p until, just prior to the payment of the next dividend, it will have a price of 110p (100p plus the forthcoming dividend of 10p). This latter figure is the share's *cum div* price. Once the dividend has been paid the market price falls back to the ex div price of 100p and so restarts the slow rise over the year to its cum div value.

Figure 12.1 illustrates this highly simplified, but basically correct, account of a share's market price movements over time in a perfect market with unchanging and fulfilled expectations about the future:

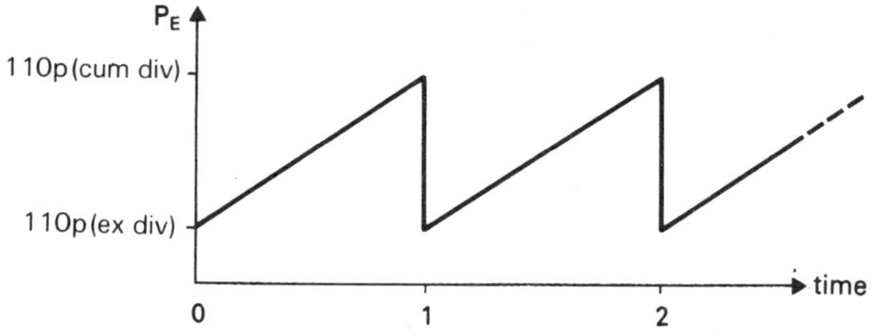

Figure 12.1

As the simplified dividend valuation model employs ex div market prices, so cum div prices have to be adjusted accordingly. For example, if a share was expected to yield a constant annual dividend of 22p and it had a current market price of £$1\cdot59\frac{1}{2}$ cum div, then its equivalent ex div price would be the cum div price, less the expected forthcoming dividend: $159\frac{1}{2}\text{p} - 22\text{p} = 137\frac{1}{2}\text{p}$. The share's required return would thus be: $22\text{p}/137\frac{1}{2}\text{p} = 0\cdot16$. From now on we shall use P_E (and, consequently, V_E) to represent the *ex div* market price of equity.[9]

The dividend growth model

Up to this point we have made use of a simplified version of the dividend valuation model which assumes a constant, level flow of expected dividends through time. This may well be quite realistic.[10] There are several examples of companies that have been observed to pay (approximately) constant dividends per share over relatively long periods of time. However, it is important to realize that such an assumption is *not* an assumption of the general dividend valuation model, but of just the simplified version of it, that we have been using as an example.

If it is believed that a company's flow of future dividends is likely to be a more complex pattern than what we have assumed, then that more complex pattern can be taken account of within the more general model. We are using the simplified model purely for reasons of arithmetic convenience.

An alternative simplifying assumption about the future pattern of a share's dividends is not that they are constant, but that they *grow* at a constant annual rate, in perpetuity. Table 12.1 shows how this 'dividend growth' model can be derived as:[11]

$$P_E = \frac{d_1}{K_E - g} \qquad \text{or as:} \qquad P_E = \frac{d_0(1+g)}{K_E - g}$$

where d_0 = current dividend per share (i.e. at t_0)
d_1 = expected dividend per share in twelve months' time (i.e. t_1)
K_E = cost of equity capital
P_E = ex div market price per share
and g = constant annual growth rate of dividends

Notice that *both* versions of the model are equivalent because $d_1 = d_0(1 + g)$. In other words, next year's dividend equals this year's dividend, times one plus the growth rate.

Just as the constant dividend model can be re-arranged to give the cost of equity capital:

$$K_E = \frac{d}{P_E}$$

Table 12.1

$$P_E = \frac{d_1}{(1+K_E)} + \frac{d_1(1+g)}{(1+K_E)^2} + \frac{d_1(1+g)^2}{(1+K_E)^3} \cdots + \frac{d_1(1+g)^{N-1}}{(1+K_E)^N} \tag{1}$$

multiplying each side by $(1 + g)/(1 + K_E)$ gives,

$$\frac{P_E(1+g)}{(1+K_E)} = \frac{d_1(1+g)}{(1+K_E)^2} + \frac{d_1(1+g^2)}{(1+K_E)^3} \cdots + \frac{d_1(1+g)^N}{(1+K_E)^{N+1}} \tag{2}$$

subtracting equation (2) from equation (1) gives,

$$P_E - \frac{P_E(1+g)}{(1+K_E)} = \frac{d_1}{(1+K_E)} - \frac{d_1(1+g)^N}{(1+K_E)^{N+1}} \tag{3}$$

as long as $K_E > g$ then, as N approaches infinity so $d_1(1 + g)^N/(1 + K_E)^{N+1}$ approaches zero and therefore,

$$P_E - \frac{P_E(1+g)}{(1+K_E)} = \frac{d_1}{(1+K_E)} \tag{4}$$

multiplying equation (4) by $(1 + K_E)$ gives,

$$P_E(1+K_E) - P_E(1+g) = d_1 \tag{5}$$

$$P_E(K_E - g) = d_1$$

$$\therefore P_E = \frac{d_1}{K_E - g} \tag{6}$$

so too can the dividend growth model:

$$K_E = \frac{d_1}{P_E} + g \qquad \text{or} \qquad K_E = \frac{d_0(1+g)}{P_E} + g$$

Therefore if a company's equity has an ex dividend market price per share of 70p and a constant expected annual dividend growth rate of 5%, and a dividend of 10p *has just been paid*, the cost of equity capital or expected return on equity would be:

$$K_E = \frac{10\text{p}(1 + 0{\cdot}05)}{70\text{p}} + 0{\cdot}05 = \frac{10{\cdot}5\text{p}}{70\text{p}} + 0{\cdot}05 = \underline{\underline{0{\cdot}20}} \text{ or } 20\%$$

The dividend growth rate

There are two main approaches to estimating g – the constant expected dividend growth rate – in practice. One is to take the average *past* rate of growth of dividends and assume that this rate will continue unchanged in the future. If need be, this rate can be adjusted to take account of any additional information that leads to the belief that the past growth rate will not be approximately reflected in the future growth rate.

As an example, suppose the past patterns of dividends per share is given by:

Year	*Dividends per share*
t_{-4}	8·0p
t_{-3}	9·0p
t_{-2}	9·5p
t_{-1}	10·5p
t_0	12·0p

The dividends per share have grown over a *four* year period (i.e. five items of data produce four years of growth), from 8p to 12p. This represents an average annual rate of growth (g) of:

$$8\text{p}(1+g)^4 = 12\text{p}$$

$$1 + g = \left(\frac{12\text{p}}{8\text{p}}\right)^{1/4} = 1{\cdot}1067$$

$$g = 1{\cdot}1067 - 1 = \underline{\underline{0{\cdot}1067}} \text{ or } 10\tfrac{2}{3}\% \text{ (approx.)}$$

The other approach, originally put forward by the American economist Myron Gordon, examines the basis of dividend growth and attempts to *derive* a future growth rate rather than just to extrapolate a past growth rate. Gordon started from the idea that a growing stream of future dividends arises from a growing level of investment by the company in profitable projects, and it will therefore be this rate of investment which will partially determine the rate of dividend growth. The other determinant of dividend growth must be the rate of return yielded by these projects. On this basis, and by making a number of limiting assumptions, a simple model can be constructed for deriving the value of the dividend growth rate. The necessary assumptions are as follows:

1 An all-equity company.
2 Retained profits (earnings) are the only source of additional investment capital.
3 A constant proportion of net profits is retained each year for reinvestment.
4 Projects financed through retained profits produce a constant annual return.

On this basis, if b is the constant proportion of earnings retained each year and r is the average rate of return produced by the projects undertaken by the firm, then the future dividend growth rate can be estimated as rb. The derivation of this is given in Table 12.2.

Table 12.2

$$g = rb$$

Assuming a constant proportion (b) of each year's earnings (E_t) are reinvested to earn a constant annual rate of return (r), then the annual earnings pattern is:

$$\begin{aligned}
&E_1 \\
&E_2 = E_1 + rbE_1 = E_1(1 + rb) \\
&E_3 = E_2 + rbE_2 = E_1(1 + rb) + rbE_1(1 + rb) \\
&\vdots \qquad\qquad\quad = E_1(1 + rb)(1 + rb) \\
&\vdots \qquad\qquad\quad = E_1(1 + rb)^2 \\
&\vdots \qquad\qquad\qquad \vdots \\
&E_N \qquad\qquad\; = E_1(1 + rb)^{N-1}
\end{aligned}$$

The annual dividend pattern is therefore:

$$\begin{aligned}
D_1 &= (1 - b)E_1 \\
D_2 &= (1 - b)E_2 = (1 - b)E_1(1 + rb) \\
D_3 &= (1 - b)E_3 = (1 - b)E_1(1 + rb)^2 \\
&\vdots \\
D_N &= (1 - b)E_N = (1 - b)E_1(1 + rb)^{N-1}
\end{aligned}$$

Therefore each year the annual dividends grow by an amount equal to $(1 + rb)$ times the previous year's dividends: an annual rate of dividend growth of rb. In practice, given the validity of the assumptions, b and r would be estimated as follows:

$$b = \frac{\text{Earnings} - \text{Dividends}}{\text{Earnings}}$$

$$r = \frac{\text{Earnings}}{\text{Book value of capital employed}}$$

and the dividend growth model (which is often known as the Gordon Growth model in this form) becomes:

$$P_E = \frac{d_0(1 + rb)}{K_E - rb}$$

Notice that this particular version of the dividend valuation model is only applicable to companies which have an all-equity capital structure, because if debt capital is involved (a case examined in the next section), then it causes problems in keeping r and b, and hence g, constant. Obviously Gordon's variant of the dividend growth model is very naive, but it may well be a self-fulfilling predictor of share market values if investors generally believe that g can be estimated as rb and so partly base their market actions on such calculations.

Taxation and the calculation of K_E

Up to this point we have ignored the part played by taxation. However, from the viewpoint of the minimum acceptable return that management must achieve from their physical investments, tax effects on dividends *may* play an important part.

There are two possible effects which must be taken into account. First of all, tax may actually reduce the amount of cash dividend received by the shareholder (in much the same way as tax reduces a gross salary). In such circumstances, from the company's cost of capital viewpoint, what is of importance is the quantity of cash paid out as dividends, rather than the quantity of cash dividends (after tax) actually received by the shareholders. Secondly, if the company can arrange its affairs (principally in relation to its dividend policy) so as to reduce the amount of tax paid by shareholders, then company management should evaluate the net effects of doing so on shareholder wealth.

The latter point is examined directly in the chapter on dividend policy (Chapter 18), but the former is of immediate interest in the present context if the cost of equity capital is to be used in an NPV appraisal (where it would be applied to the after-corporation tax cash flows of the project). However, the exact effect of tax on the cost of equity capital may well depend upon the intricacy of the actual tax regime.

The UK has what is referred to as an *imputation system* operating as far as corporation tax is concerned. Dividends are not an allowable expense against corporation tax, and their only effect in terms of K_E is to bring forward in time the payment of part of the corporation tax liability. This portion of the company's overall tax liability is known as 'advance corporation tax' (ACT).

With a *constant* annual dividend (not greater than the taxable profit) and an unchanging tax rate in perpetuity, the net effect of such a tax regime on the value of K_E from the company's viewpoint is zero. Each year's constant amount of ACT liability is exactly offset against the allowance for the amount of ACT paid in the previous year. So, in such circumstances, the 'before tax' K_E is the same as the 'after tax' K_E. As a result, the dividend valuation model, and hence the cost of equity capital calculation, remains unaffected except that the dividend (either d_T or D_T) becomes the dividend *net of ACT*.

With dividends expected to *grow* at a constant rate in perpetuity, and assuming that the mainstream corporation tax liability (i.e., total tax liability, minus ACT) is paid twelve months in arrears, the dividend growth model requires the following adjustment:

$$K_E = \frac{d_0(1+g) + (ACT_0 \times g)}{P_E} + g$$

where d_0 represents the current (i.e., t_0) *net* dividend per share, (i.e., net of ACT — the actual cash dividend paid over to shareholders), and ACT_0 represents the advanced corporation tax payable on the d_0 net dividend.

This adjustment is required because, through dividends being increased at an expected annual rate of g, the payment of a small proportion of corporation tax is permanently brought forward in time. An appendix to this chapter gives further details of the imputation system, together with a small numerical example to illustrate the mechanics of the adjustment.

However, as can be seen from the example given, the effect of ACT on the cost of equity capital can be expected to be very small. Example 12.1 shows just how small an effect ACT has on the calculation of K_E. The estimation of K_E should avoid the impression of a false degree of accuracy. Therefore for our purposes, when dealing with the dividend growth model, we will use the version *unadjusted* for ACT, as in the first case of Example 12.1.

Example 12.1

Given the following information about a company's shares:

$$P_E = 120\text{p ex div.}$$
$$g = 5\%$$
$$d_0 = 4\text{p (net of ACT)}$$
$$ACT_0 = 1\tfrac{1}{3}\text{p}$$

$$K_E = \frac{d_0(1+g)}{P_E} + g = \frac{4(1+0{\cdot}05)}{120} + 0{\cdot}05 = \underline{0{\cdot}085} \text{ or } \underline{8{\cdot}5\%}$$

$$K_E = \frac{d_0(1+g) + (ACT_0 \times g)}{P_E} + g = \frac{4(1+0{\cdot}05) + (1\tfrac{1}{3} \times 0{\cdot}05)}{120} + 0{\cdot}05$$
$$= \underline{0{\cdot}0856} \text{ or } \underline{8{\cdot}56\%}$$

The cost of retained earnings

One of the most important sources of corporate long-term investment capital is retained earnings, i.e., that part of net cash flow generated by a company's past investment projects which, at the time it arises, is retained within the firm rather than being distributed to shareholders as part of the dividend flow. Because retained earnings arise from sources internal to the company, rather than externally (such as a new equity issue), there is a temptation to believe that this source of capital is somehow 'costless'.

In fact, both from a legal and an economic standpoint, retained earnings belong to the ordinary shareholders of a company and so the 'cost' of retained earnings, or the minimum expected return that their use in investment projects should generate, is exactly the same as the expected return required by shareholders on new equity: the cost of equity capital. Retained earnings form part of the equity capital of a company and their cost is therefore a reflection of this fact.

This has already been implicitly taken into account in that the *market* value of equity was used in the specification of K_E, and the market value reflects *both* the nominal value of a company's equity capital *and* the value of the retained earnings. (In practice retained earnings are a slightly cheaper source of capital than a new issue of equity because of the issue costs incurred with the latter, but this rather minor point will be dealt with in Chapter 16.)

The dividend valuation model and the CAPM

Finally, before moving on to other sources of investment capital it is worth reiterating a point that was made earlier about the compatibility of the two share valuation models: the dividend valuation model and the CAPM. Although the two models are different, they are also compatible. In other words, given an equilibrium stock market, the cost of equity capital of company j (K_{E_j}) should be (approximately) the same as the expected return on the equity capital of company j [$E(r_j)$].[13]

There are two main differences between the models. The first is that CAPM provides a single period return whereas the dividend valuation model provides a multi-period average return. The second is that the CAPM is a *normative* model in that it indicates what should be the expected return. In constrast, the dividend valuation model can be viewed as being a *positive* model in that it indicates what *is* the expected return. However, given equilibrium stock market prices and correctly specified inputs into both models, they should produce similar results and indeed, they are often seen to do so in practice.

A worked example

Before moving on to examine the cost of debt capital, it might be helpful to work through an example of a cost of equity capital calculation. Example 12.2 provides the data and the calculations.

Example 12.2

Portimao PLC is a long-established, stock exchanged quoted, ship repairing company. Its current balance sheet, in summarized form, is as follows:

		£m
	Fixed assets (net)	40
	Net current assets	25
	Total assets	65
Financed by:		
	Share capital	35
	Reserves	30
	Total liabilities	65

The company's shares currently stand at 130p cum. div. on the stock market. In the current year the company produced earnings after tax of £10m from which the stock market is expecting a total net dividend pay-out of £6m or 12p net per share.

The dividend per share record of the company, over the last six years, is as follows:

	Year	*Div./Share (pence)*
	t_{-5}	9·0
	t_{-4}	9·5
	t_{-3}	10·0
	t_{-2}	10·5
	t_{-1}	11·0
(expected)	t_0	12·0

The current after-tax return on Government stock is 10%, the market excess return is around 8% and Portimao PLC has an equity beta of 0·90.

The company wishes to estimate its cost of equity capital. Given the available information, this can be found both from using the capital asset pricing model *and* from using the dividend valuation model:

Using the CAPM:

$$E[r_{\text{Portimao}}] = 10\% + 8\% \times 0{\cdot}90 = \underline{\underline{17{\cdot}2\%}}$$

Using the Dividend Valuation Model:
From the information on the historical dividend record, it would appear that the dividend growth version of the model is most appropriate. There are two possible approaches to estimating the *future* dividend growth rate:

i) On the basis of the *past* dividend growth rate.
ii) On the basis of the Gordon model: $r \times b$

(i) Past dividend growth rate:

$$\begin{aligned} 9\text{p}\,(1+g)^5 &= 12\text{p} \\ (1+g)^5 &= 12 \div 9 \\ 1+g &= (1\tfrac{1}{3})^{1/5} \\ g &= (1\tfrac{1}{3})^{1/5} - 1 = \underline{0{\cdot}059} \text{ or } \underline{5{\cdot}9\%} \end{aligned}$$

(ii) Gordon $b \times r$

$$b = \frac{£10\text{m} - £6\text{m}}{£10\text{m}} = 0{\cdot}40$$

$$r = \frac{£10\text{m}}{£65\text{m}} = 0{\cdot}154$$

$$g = 0{\cdot}40 \times 0{\cdot}154 = 0{\cdot}062 \text{ or } \underline{6{\cdot}2\%}$$

As both give an estimate of the dividend growth rate of *approximately* 6%, that figure will be used in the dividend valuation model:

$$d_0 = 12\text{p}$$
$$P_E = 130\text{p} - 12\text{p} = 118\text{p}$$
$$g = 0{\cdot}06$$
$$K_E = \frac{12\,(1 + 0{\cdot}06)}{118} + 0{\cdot}06 = 0{\cdot}168 \text{ or } \underline{\underline{16{\cdot}8\%}}$$

Therefore given the estimates of the two share valuation models of 17·2% and 16·8%, Portimao PLC should use *17%* as its estimated cost of equity capital.

THE COST OF DEBT CAPITAL

Debt versus equity capital

So far we have examined the cost of equity capital from the standpoint of the dividend valuation model. We now turn our attention to the other[14] major source of long-term capital: interest-bearing long-term loans. These come in a great variety of forms, and so we will assign them the generic term of 'debt capital'.

Debt capital can be defined as a *loan* made to a company which is normally secured against the assets of the company. Debt capital differs from ordinary share capital in two fundamental ways.

Firstly, subscribers to debt capital do not become part-owners of the company but are merely (secured) creditors, because they are only lending money to the company for a fixed period.[15] On the elapse of this period, the loan is repaid: the debt capital is said to be redeemed. In contrast, equity capital represents a permanent loan which is never repaid except in very special circumstances (such as company liquidation).

Secondly, the holders or suppliers of debt capital receive a contractually *fixed* annual percentage return on their loan, which is specified when the debt capital is issued and is known as the *coupon rate.* Again, this contrasts with the situation of the suppliers of equity capital whose annual return – the dividend – is *not* contractually fixed and the exact level is set at the discretion of the directors.

In addition to these two fundamental differences between debt and equity capital, debt capital is ranked ahead of equity for payment of the annual return. In other words, legally, interest on debt capital *must* be paid in full before any dividend may be paid to the suppliers of equity. Thus, if there is any shortfall in company earnings in any year, it is the ordinary shareholders who are more likely to suffer than the debt holders.

Debt capital therefore represents a loan with a contractually fixed rate of return, a contractually fixed time of repayment and preferential payment treatment over equity capital. In an uncertain world, all three factors combine to make the debt capital of any given company a substantially *less risky* investment for a supplier of capital than that company's ordinary share capital.

As debt can be viewed as less risky than ordinary shares, it follows that the required expected return on a company's debt[16] will be *less than* that required on its equity capital. In a *certain* world, debt and equity capital would logically require the same return from any given company; but in an uncertain world the required returns differ.

The interest valuation model

We know that sometimes shares are *quoted* (they are traded on a stock market), and sometimes they are *unquoted.* The point was made in the introductory chapter that, for convenience, we shall normally be dealing with a stock exchange quoted company in our development of the theory of financial management.

Debt capital is similar to equity capital in that some debt capital is quoted whilst other debt capital (in fact, the majority) is unquoted. Again, for convenience we shall deal initially with *quoted* debt capital, although we will return later to the problem with *unquoted* debt.

In order to examine the cost of debt capital we shall use the principles upon which the dividend valuation model was based in order to develop a *debt valuation model.* Therefore we shall postulate that the market value of debt capital is determined by the summation of the future cash flows it will produce, discounted to present value. These future cash flows consist of the expected future interest flow and (if it is redeemable debt) its redemption value.

In the UK debt capital is normally issued in blocks of £100, and attached to each such unit (which is usually drawn up in the form of a trust deed) are details of its coupon rate, the date of redemption and the value at which it will be redeemed. Normally debt is redeemed at its *par* value, i.e. £100, but sometimes a redemption value above par will be promised as an additional inducement to investors to subscribe to the issue.

As debt capital is traded in supply and demand markets, its market price will depend upon its level of demand in the market. In turn, this level of demand will largely depend upon the difference between the current *market* interest rate for an investment with a similar level of risk and the debt capital's own *coupon* rate. Thus, if a unit of debt has a coupon rate which is below the current market interest rate, then its market value will be below its £100 par value, and vice versa.

For example, let us consider an issue of *irredeemable* debt whose coupon rate is 5%, whilst the current market rate of interest (at the debt's risk level) is 8%. A £100 unit of the debt capital would be expected to produce a flow of interest payments of £5 per year, in perpetuity. When this stream is discounted at the current market rate of interest and summed, its present value is £5 ÷ 0·08 = £62·50. This represents the debt's current *market* value.

Its market value is only £62·50, against a par value of £100, because this is the amount that would currently be needed to purchase other debt producing £5 of interest per year: £62·50 × 0·08 = £5. On a similar analysis, if the market rate of interest fell to 4%, then the market value of the 5% debt would rise to £5 ÷ 0·04 = £125.

The opportunity cost of debt capital

It is at this point that an important fact emerges. We are concerned with finding the 'cost' to a company of the various types of capital it might use to finance an investment project, in order to use this cost as a possible discount or cut-off rate in the appraisal process. For such a use we might easily believe that the debt capital's *coupon rate*, rather than the current market interest rate (assuming they differ), reflects the cost to the firm of using this source of capital. However, such a belief would be incorrect.

This possible misunderstanding really arises from an incorrect interpretation of the word *cost*. Cost of capital does not refer to *how much* the capital costs the firm to buy – in other words, the interest rate – but refers to the best available return, at that risk level, available elsewhere that the firm foregoes when it applies the capital to a particular project: the *opportunity* cost of debt capital is the thing that matters.

Therefore, as far as investment appraisal and the cost of debt capital is concerned, it is the *current* market interest rate that is important; *not* the debt's coupon rate. An example can easily show the logic behind this statement. Suppose a company undertook an issue of debt capital some years ago at a coupon rate of 5%. (At the time of issue 5% would have been the current market interest rate for debt capital of that risk level.) Now the current market interest rate (for a similar risk level) is 8%.

The company has discounted the flows of an investment opportunity which requires an outlay of £1,000 and which produces cash inflows as shown in Table 12.3. It proposes to use part of the proceeds of the 5% debenture issue to finance the investment and so discounts the project's cash flows at 5%. This produces a positive NPV of £28·34 and therefore the company undertakes the investment.

Table 12.3

Project cash flows

Year	*0*	*1*	*2*	*3*	*4*
	−1,000	+290	+290	+290	+290

At a 5% discount rate:

$$\text{NPV} = -1{,}000 + 290A_{\overline{4}|0\cdot05} = \underline{+£28\cdot34}$$

At an 8% discount rate:

$$\text{NPV} = -1{,}000 + 290A_{\overline{4}|0\cdot08} = \underline{-£39\cdot48}$$

As the project has a negative NPV at the current market rate of discount, it should not be undertaken. The £1,000 required outlay could be better employed deposited on the money market at 8% where it could, for example, produce the following flows:

Year	*0*	*1*	*2*	*3*	*4*
	−1,000	+301·92	+301·92	+301·92	+301·92

Compare this flow with that expected from the project. (In other words, given an 8% interest rate, £1,000 now can produce an annuity of £301·92 a year for four years.)

However, if we recall our analysis of the logic of the NPV decision rule, we can see why such a discount rate is incorrect. In discounting a project's cash flows to produce a positive or negative NPV, an implicit comparison is automatically being made between the returns from investing in the project and the returns that could be achieved by investing the project's outlay on the capital market. Hence we use the market interest rate as the discount rate. Therefore, discounting the project in Table 12.3 by 5% means that an *incorrect* comparison is being carried out: in fact, as an alternative to the project, an interest rate of 8% can be earned for the same level of risk. We can see that when discounting the project at 8% it yields a negative NPV, indicating rejection – a better return could be earned by investing the £1,000 on the capital markets.

The cost of irredeemable debt capital

We will now turn to look systematically at how to go about estimating the company's (*opportunity*) cost of debt capital. To start, we will examine the simplest type of debt capital: irredeemable or undated debt. This is debt capital which is not expected to be repaid and whose interest payments form a *perpetuity* cash flow.

We will make use of the following notation:

P_D = market price per unit of debt capital, ex interest[17]
V_D = total market value of debt capital = $P_D \times$ number of units of debt capital issued
i = annual interest per unit of debt capital
I = total annual interest = $i \times$ number of units of debt capital issued

then the general debt valuation model for irredeemable debt capital is:

$$V_D = \frac{I}{K_D} \qquad \text{or, on a per unit basis, } P_D = \frac{i}{K_D}$$

The model can be switched around to provide the cost of irredeemable debentures:

$$K_D = \frac{I}{V_D} \qquad \text{or, similarly, } K_D = \frac{i}{P_D}$$

For example, a company has issued irredeemable debt at a coupon rate of $7\frac{1}{2}$% and each unit of debt currently has a market value of £93·75, ex-int. The company's cost of debt capital can then be estimated as: K_D = £7·50 ÷ £93·75 = 0·08 or 8%. We can conclude from this that, for an investment of the debt's risk level, the current market interest rate is also 8%.

Because we are dealing with an uncertain world, just as we talked in terms of K_E being the minimum required *expected* return to equity, so we should talk in terms of the *expected* return to debt holders. Although a company's debt is less risky than their ordinary shares, it is not riskless.[18] Sometimes debt can be a very risky investment, for instance in cases where there is a substantial probability that the issuing company will be unable to meet the future interest and redemption payments (if the debt is redeemable).

In calculating the cost of debt capital by means of the formula $K_D = I/V_D$ (or i/P_D) we are calculating what is called the debt's *yield to maturity*. This is the maximum yield (as opposed to the expected yield) that the debt will produce at its current market price, as it assumes that all future contractual payments attached to the debt will be met by the issuing company.

However, working on the normal assumption of viewing companies as *going concerns*, then K_D, or the yield to maturity, is likely to be a fairly accurate estimate of the cost of debt capital for investment appraisal purposes. If the going concern concept is *not* thought applicable to a particular company, its marginal cost of debt capital should be based on the alternative cash flow which its debt is *expected* to yield.

The cost of redeemable debt

The cost, of redeemable debt is found by estimating the internal rate of return of the debt cash flow. This can be found by using the linear interpolation method that was used in the earlier discussion about the IRR.

Example 12.3 illustrates the approach.[19]

Example 12.3

Lagoa PLC issued £10m of 5% debt seven years ago. It is due to be redeemed at par in three years' time. The debt has a current market price of £101 *per cent* (i.e. per £100 unit), cum interest.

The company's cost of debt capital can be estimated as follows. First, the equivalent ex interest price of the debt would be: £101 − £5 (i.e. the annual amount of interest payable) = £96. Then, if the company were to issue an identical debenture *now*, its cash flow would be:

0	1	2	3
+£96	−£5	−£5	−£105

The company would be able to sell the debt for £96 but it would then have to pay out £5 of interest at the end of each of the next three years. In addition, in three years' time, the debt would have to be repaid at its £100 per value.

Using linear interpolation to find the IRR of this cash flow:

At a 5% discount rate:

$$+96 - 5A_{\overline{3}|0\cdot05} - 100\,(1\cdot05)^{-3} = \underline{-4\cdot0 \text{ NPV}}$$

At a 15% discount rate:

$$+96 - 5A_{\overline{3}|0\cdot15} - 100\,(1\cdot15)^{-3} = \underline{+18\cdot83 \text{ NPV}}$$

Therefore K_D, the IRR, can be estimated as:

$$K_D = 5\% + \left[\frac{4\cdot0}{18\cdot83 + 4\cdot0} \times (15\% - 5\%)\right] = 6\cdot75\%$$

(Notice that when calculating the IRR we obtained a *negative* NPV at the low discount rate and a *positive* NPV at the higher discount rate. This is the opposite of our previous experience with project IRRs. This is because the debenture cash flow – an *inflow* followed by a series of *outflows* – is the opposite of a normal project's cash flow.)

Furthermore, the total market value, ex. int., of the company's debt capital can be calculated as:

$$V_D = £10\text{m} \times \frac{£96}{£100} = £10\text{m} \times 0{\cdot}96 = \underline{\underline{£9{\cdot}6\text{m}}}$$

Finally, notice that a very rough approximation to the cost of redeemable debt can be obtained as follows:

$$K_D = \text{coupon rate} + \text{average annual capital gain.}$$

The debt issued by Lagoa has a 5% coupon. As the current ex int. price is £96 and they are redeemable at £100, then the capital gain is approximately 4%. As this capital gain is made when the debentures are redeemed in three years' time, the average annual capital gain is: $4\% \div 3 = 1\frac{1}{3}\%$. Thus Lagoa's cost of debt capital can be roughly approximated as:

$$= 5\% + 1\tfrac{1}{3}\% = \underline{6\tfrac{1}{3}\%}$$

The impact of corporation taxation

The company requires knowledge of its cost of debt capital for investment appraisal purposes and so, from this viewpoint, the expected return which the *supplier* of debt capital receives is not the main focus of attention. The point of importance is the cash flow which the *company* must secure in order to service the debt.

In this respect, taxation has an important effect when the tax regime (as most tax regimes, including the UK's, usually do) allows companies to offset debt interest (but *not* redemption payments) against corporation tax liability. Therefore, as far as company investment appraisal is concerned, it is the *after* corporation tax cost of debt capital which is important.

So far, we have ignored taxation in the calculation of K_D, and so we have, in effect, been calculating a before-tax cost of debt capital: $K_{D_{BT}}$. If T represents the current rate of corporation tax – and assuming it is expected to remain a constant over the life of the debt – then the after-tax cost of *irredeemable* debentures can be found as:

$$K_{D_{AT}} = \frac{i(1 - T)}{P_D} \text{ or } K_{D_{AT}} = K_{D_{BT}}(1 - T)$$

For redeemable debentures, their after-tax cost can be found by solving the internal rate of return of the following cash flow:

$$P_D - i(1 - T)A_{\overline{n|}K_{D_{AT}}} - R(1 + K_D)^{-n} = 0$$

where n equals the number of years to redemption and R represents the redemption value of the debt capital. Example 12.4 illustrates the calculations.

Example 12.4

Cinta PLC has issued £25m of 15% irredeemable debt. The current market price is £116.50 ex int. Corporation tax is charged at 35%. Therefore the company's after-tax cost of debt capital is:

$$K_{DAT} = \frac{£15(1 - 0{\cdot}35)}{£116{\cdot}50} = \underline{0{\cdot}084} \text{ or } 8{\cdot}4\%$$

The total market value of the debt capital is:

$$V_D = £25\text{m} \times 1{\cdot}1650 = \underline{£29{\cdot}125\text{m}}$$

Luvas PLC has issued £5m of 13% debentures. They are due to be redeemed in four years' time at par. Their current market value is £104 ex int. Corporation tax is charged at 35%. The company's current cost of debt capital is found by solving the IRR of the following cash flow:

$$+£104 - £13\,(1 - 0{\cdot}35)\,A_{4\urcorner K_{DAT}} - £100\,(1 + K_{DAT})^{-4} = 0 \text{ NPV}$$

At 5%, the cash flow's NPV is: $\underline{-8{\cdot}23 \text{ NPV}}$

At 15%, the cash flow's NPV is: $\underline{+43{\cdot}21 \text{ NPV}}$

Using linear interpolation, the after-tax cost of debt capital can be estimated as:

$$K_{DAT} = 5\% + \left[\frac{8{\cdot}23}{43{\cdot}21 + 8{\cdot}23} \times (15\% - 5\%)\right] = \underline{6{\cdot}6\%}$$

And the total market value of the debt capital would be:

$$V_D = £5\text{m} \times 1{\cdot}04 = \underline{£5{\cdot}2\text{m}}$$

Notice that, again, the after-tax cost of debt could be *very* roughly approximated as:

Coupon rate $(1 - T)$ + Average annual capital gain

So: Coupon rate $(1 - T) = 13\%\,(1 - 0{\cdot}35) = 8{\cdot}45\%$
and: Average annual capital loss $= -4\% \div 4 = -1\%$

Therefore $K_{DAT} = \underline{7{\cdot}45\%}$

This adjustment to take account of tax must be made, as the following example shows. If a company issues debt with a 10% coupon rate and pays corporation tax at 35%, then the company does not actually pay £10 interest per unit of debt per year (although the debt holder actually receives £10 of interest per year). As debt interest is allowable against corporation tax, the company only pays £10(1 − 0·35) = £6·50. The balance of interest of £3·50 can be viewed as being paid by the tax authorities. This obviously causes the *effective* cost of debt (to the company) to fall substantially below the before-tax rate.

There are two further points worth noting. First, the after-tax K_D is only applicable on the assumption that a company has sufficient tax liability to take advantage of tax relief on debt interest. Secondly, the K_{DAT} computations in the examples are an approximation because corporation tax (and hence the reduction in corporation tax which comes about through offsetting debt interest) is paid approximately 12 months in arrears. This fact has not been taken into account in the discounting calculations. The calculation *could* be adjusted to allow for this, but such exactness is probably not really justified, especially as K_D is, in itself, only an estimate of the *expected* K_D.

Other types of debt capital

So far we have only considered *quoted* debt capital. It is possible to estimate the cost of *unquoted* debt capital, but only if the cost of *similar-risk* quoted debt is also known. Example 12.5 illustrates such a situation.

Example 12.5

Lagosta PLC has issued £12m of 8% irredeemable debt capital which currently has a market price of £92 ex interest. In addition, they have issued £6m of 14% irredeemable debt which is unquoted. As both the quoted and unquoted debt rank equally for payment purposes they can be assumed to be of similar risk.

The cost of the quoted debt capital is therefore:

$$K_{DQ} = \frac{£8}{£92} = 0{\cdot}087 \text{ or } \underline{8{\cdot}7\%}$$

and $V_{DQ} = £12\text{m} \times 0{\cdot}92 = \underline{£11{\cdot}04\text{m}}$

As the unquoted debt is of similar risk to the quoted debt, it can be assumed to have a similar cost, therefore:

$$K_{DUQ} = K_{DQ} = 8{\cdot}7\%$$

Given this estimate, an estimate can also be made of the implied 'market' value of the unquoted debt:

$$P_{DUQ} = \frac{£14}{0{\cdot}087} = \underline{£160{\cdot}92} \text{ per unit}$$

$$V_{DUQ} = £6\text{m} \times 1{\cdot}6092 = \underline{£9{\cdot}655\text{m}}$$

Furthermore, all the examples of debt capital used so far have involved *fixed* coupon rates. The situation with debt capital which has a coupon rate which *varies* with current market interest rates is very much easier to handle.

In such circumstances, K_D is simply the current interest rate payable on the debt. The total market value of the debt will always equal its *nominal* value. (It is only the fact that, with fixed coupon debt, the coupon rate can vary from the current market interest rate that causes the market price to vary from the nominal value.) Example 12.6 illustrates this situation with the most common type of variable-rate debt: a bank loan.

Example 12.6

Podia PLC has a £10m bank loan, repayable in seven years' time. The interest rate payable is 3% over bank base rate. The company pays corporation tax at 35%. Bank base rate is currently 11%. It wishes to calculate its after-tax cost of the bank loan. This can be done as follows:

The company currently pays an interest rate of: 11% + 3% = 14%
Therefore: $K_{D_{AT}} = 14\% (1 - 0{\cdot}35) = \underline{9{\cdot}1\%}$.
The 'market value' of the bank loan is equal to its nominal value of £10m.

Implicit and explicit costs of debenture capital

It is important to remember that financial decisions are principally made on behalf of and for the benefit of ordinary shareholders, the legal owners of a company. As far as debt holders are concerned, management's only wish is to fulfil their contractual obligations to them of interest and redemption payments.

In this respect, we have only considered here the *explicit* cost of debt capital, but there is also an *implicit* opportunity cost which company management must taken into account. This implicit cost of debt arises from risk considerations that directly affect the ordinary shareholders. We shall examine this aspect in detail later, in the chapter on capital structure, but it is as well to be aware at this stage that debt capital does have a cost which is additional to its explicit cost.

Cost of miscellaneous long-term capital

There are a wide variety of sources of long-term investment capital, the costs of which we have not mentioned. Examples include preference shares and convertible debt. The costs of all of these can be found using the principles of valuation derived earlier.

The cost of preference share capital can be calculated in a way analogous to debt, except that preference share dividends are not usually allowable against corporation tax. The cost of convertible debt is slightly more difficult.

Essentially, the holder of convertible debt capital acquires debt capital (i.e. paying a fixed rate of interest), with an option – at a later date – to convert the debt capital into ordinary shares or to have the debt redeemed. The option to convert into ordinary shares is usually at a specified, predetermined price per share, and the owners of such convertibles are allowed to choose the time of conversion, within limits set down by the issuing company. It is these variable elements – the time of conversion, the proportion of investors converting into ordinary shares and the subsequent dividend flow received by these shares – which make the calculation of the cost more difficult. Example 12.7 illustrates a simple situation.

Example 12.7

Amarra PLC has issued £5m of 6% debt which is either repayable at par value in three years' time, or is convertible into shares at a fixed price of 250p per share. The debt is currently priced at £102·97 ex interest.

The company's shares have a market price of 220p ex div, this year's dividend of 10 pence having just been paid. Dividends are expected to grow in the future at 10% per year.

Taxation is to be ignored. What is the cost of the convertible debt capital?

The first point is to decide whether debt holders are likely to redeem or convert in three years' time. In order to proceed we need to estimate the worth of the company's shares in three years' time:

$$K_E = \frac{10\,(1 + 0{\cdot}10)}{220} + 0{\cdot}10 = 0{\cdot}15 \text{ or } 15\%$$

If dividends are to grow at 10% per year, then the dividend in three years' time will be: 10p $(1{\cdot}10)^3$ = 13·31p and so the estimated market price of the shares in three years' time will be:

$$P_{E_{t3}} = \frac{13{\cdot}31\,(1 + 0{\cdot}10)}{0{\cdot}15 - 0{\cdot}10} = 292{\cdot}82\text{p}$$

As debt holders have an option to convert to equity at a price per share of only 250p, conversion will be preferred to redemption in three years' time. Each £100 unit of debt will convert into £100 ÷ 250p = 40 shares which will have a value of: 40 × 292·82p = £117·13 (which, of course, would be preferred to a cash redemption figure of only £100). The cost of the convertible debt can now be estimated from the IRR of the following cash flow:

$$+\pounds 102{\cdot}97 - \pounds 6A_{\overline{3}|K_D} - \pounds 117{\cdot}13\,(1 + K_D)^{-3} = 0 \text{ NPV}$$

At 5%, the cash flow has an NPV of: $\underline{-14{\cdot}55}$.
At 15%, the cash flow has an NPV of: $\underline{+12{\cdot}26}$

Using linear interpolation:

$$K_D = 5\% + \left[\frac{14{\cdot}55}{12{\cdot}26 + 14{\cdot}55} \times (15\% - 5\%)\right] = \underline{\underline{10{\cdot}4\%}}$$

THE EFFICIENT MARKETS HYPOTHESIS

Implications of market efficiency

If the market prices of shares (and other financial securities, such as debt capital) can be said to be efficient, this means that the share price rapidly reflects the effects of all information which is relevant to their value. This concept of stock market efficiency is of prime importance to the financial manager for a number of reasons.

The first and most obvious reason why the market efficiency concept is of importance is that it implies that a company's share price correctly values the shares. The cost of capital calculations undertaken earlier in this chapter would be of little use if we suspected that the share price did *not* correctly value the company's shares, given all the available information.

The second reason why market efficiency is an important concept for financial managers relates back to our discussion on objectives. We stated that the objective of financial decision making was to maximize shareholder wealth. Furthermore, in order to make this objective operationally meaningful to financial managers, it was translated into maximizing the worth of the company's shares. From this aspect it is therefore important that the stock market is efficient and the company's shares are correctly valued: the financial manager wants to ensure that the *effects* of his decisions, once communicated to the stock market, are then rapidly reflected in the share price.

There are a number of other reasons why financial managers should view the concept of efficient stock market prices as being important. One is to do with the *timing* of the raising of new capital. Often it is thought, for example, that new equity capital should only be raised when the share price is high (and K_E low). If new equity was issued when the share price was low, the shares would be issued too 'cheaply' and the cost of capital (K_E) would be too high.

If stock markets are efficient at pricing shares, this would imply that there is no such thing as shares being *cheap* or *expensive.* At all times, shares would be *correctly* priced, based on all the relevant information available and known about at that time. As a result there is no *right* or *wrong* time to issue shares in the sense that they can be viewed as neither cheap or expensive.

A further important implication of market efficiency concerns take-overs. A take-over of one company by another can best be viewed as nothing more than a large capital expenditure decision. Just like any other capital expenditure decision, companies are looking for *positive* NPV 'projects' and will want to avoid *negative* NPV 'projects'.

Put simply, a positive NPV project is a project which costs less than its worth. If the stock market is efficient at pricing shares this implies that a take-over of a stock market quoted company can never be *expected* to represent a positive NPV investment. The share price will reflect the company's true worth – given all the available information – and a take-over bid for less than the company is expected to be worth would not be successful.

This implication for take-overs does not apply to *unquoted* company take-overs. The market for unquoted companies, just like the 'market' for ordinary projects, is not likely to be efficient, and so the possibility of identifying *positive* NPV investments remains.

Finally, an important implication of the market efficiency concept for financial managers concerns the *disclosure* of information. The market can only be expected to value a company's shares on the basis of the relevant information of which it is aware. Therefore if financial managers want the market to *correctly* value their company's shares, they must ensure that they communicate sufficient information to the market to allow it to do so.

Levels of market efficiency

Having discussed why the concept of market efficiency is important for financial managers, we now reach a crucial question. Is the stock market efficient in the pricing of shares? Do share prices quickly and correctly reflect the impact of new, relevant information? In order to answer this question it is usual to divide the idea of efficiency into three different *degrees* or *levels*:

(1) Weak efficiency.
(2) Semi-strong efficiency.
(3) Strong efficiency.

Weak efficiency is the lowest level of efficiency. It implies no more than that share prices reflect all information that could be obtained from studying and analysing *past* movements in the share price.

Semi-strong efficiency is the next level up of efficiency. Therefore if the market is semi-strong efficient, it will also be weakly efficient. Semi-strong efficiency implies that share prices reflect all the relevant, *publicly* available information that is known about the company and its circumstances.

Finally, there is strong efficiency, which is the most extreme form of market efficiency. If the stock market is strongly efficient this implies that share prices reflect *all* relevant information about their value, even though some of that information may *not* be available to investors in general.

Market efficiency and share dealing

Many stock market investors, if not most, try to *beat* the stock market. What they try to do is to identify under-valued shares and buy them before their price rises, and similarly they also look for over-valued shares in order to sell them before their prices fall. In other words such investors are backing their *own* judgement about what the shares are worth, against the *collective* judgement of the stock market as seen in the current price of the shares.

There are basically three forms of *analysis* (as opposed to *hunch*) that investors use to help them identify over or under-valued shares: technical analysis, fundamental analysis and the use of 'inside' information.

Technical analysts study charts of share price movements (and hence are often referred to as *chartists*), with the intention of discovering particular patterns of share price movements which appear to re-occur. Once these patterns have been identified, then, in following the share price movements of a particular company, if they see one of these patterns *starting* to develop, they are then able to predict the shares' *future* course of movement and so give buy or sell investment advice.

Therefore technical analysts do not know why, nor do they particularly want to know why, a particular share's price is predicted to rise or fall. All they know is that, that is the movement implied by the developing pattern.

Fundamental analysis takes a completely different approach. Fundamental analysts tend to specialize in particular sectors of the stock market, about which they become *extremely* knowledgeable. They cast very wide information-capture nets and then, on the basis of this information and with the use of a share valuation model (such as the dividend valuation model or the price-earnings model[20]), they derive a value for the shares. This value is then compared with the current market price of the shares and, if the analyst thinks the shares are worth more than the current market price, 'buy' advice is given. Conversely, if the analyst believes the shares to be over-valued on the market, then 'sell' advice is given.

The third approach to stock exchange investment is of course in *some* forms illegal. But in many forms it is not. All investors are, in a sense, looking for 'inside information'. In other words they are looking for information, insights or connections which they believe are *not* yet fully reflected in the market price. It is in this sense – rather than in the illegal sense – that we refer to the use of inside information as the third approach to formulating stock exchange investment advice.

The efficient markets hypothesis [EMH] has implications for all three approaches. Quite simply, if the market is weakly efficient, technical analysis is worthless. If there is any information to be gained from looking at past share price movements, that information – according to the weak efficiency definition – is *already* impounded in the current share price. You would be *unable* to predict future share price movements on the basis of past share price movements.

If the market is semi-strong efficient, not only is technical analysis worthless but so too is fundamental analysis. The implication of semi-strong efficiency is that however wide is the fundamental analyst's trawl for information and however good his input of that information into his share valuation model, that information's implications are *already* impounded in the share's market price. Thus if the fundamental analyst believes the shares are over- or under-priced it is likely that it is the *analyst's* valuation, rather than the *market's* valuation, which is incorrect.

Finally, in a world of strong stock market efficiency, you would not even be able to expect to profit from inside information. This is because, with strong efficiency, the share price reflects *all* relevant information about the company, whether or not that information is in the public domain.

The empirical evidence of EMH

In short, the empirical evidence overwhelmingly suggests that most of the world's stock markets are efficient in the weak sense. Furthermore the evidence for semi-strong efficiency is very substantial, although there are some anomalies. The evidence for strong efficiency is much more mixed and unclear – mainly because of difficulties in testing. However, even so, there is evidence to suggest that stock markets are, to some extent, even strongly efficient.

As far as weak efficiency is concerned, many empirical studies have shown that share prices tend to follow a *random walk*. By that, what is *not* meant is that share prices move without any reason. In fact, quite the opposite happens. Share prices move in response to new relevant information becoming available. New information arises at *random* intervals of time, and could be either good news or bad news and, as a result, share price movements themselves occur randomly both in terms of timing and direction.

In such a random walk, the best estimate of *tomorrow's* share price is *today's*. It goes without saying that you cannot predict *random* movements by looking at charts of past movements in share prices. The Readings gives references to a selection of the work which has shown stock market share prices to be following such a random walk. In addition to the overwhelming bulk of evidence on this, no technical analyst has been able to show that technical analyst does provide superior returns to a simple 'buy and hold' stock market investment strategy.

Semi-strong efficiency

A large number of rather ingenious tests have been carried out to examine semi-strong efficiency. One of the first tests was carried out by Fama, Fisher, Jensen and Roll and was published in 1969. They examined the price behaviour of shares where *bonus* or *scrip* issues were made. (Referred to as *stock split*, in the USA.)

In a, say, one-for-one bonus issue, one new share is issued free of charge for every existing share. Thus the number of shares in issue is doubled. In such an exercise nothing has happened to alter the total worth of the company but, as the number of shares has doubled, the price *per share* can be expected to be halved.

Fama *et al.* looked at the 'abnormal returns' on the shares of such companies over the thirty months *prior* to the bonus issue and over the thirty months *after* the bonus issue. By 'abnormal return' what is meant is the return on the shares is greater (a positive abnormal return) or less than (a negative abnormal return) the return expected given the share's beta value.

What they found was that in the thirty months prior to the bonus issue announcement the shares gave a strong positive abnormal return (i.e. the price of the shares rose). Subsequent to the announcement, there was virtually no movement, on average, in the shares' return. Figure 12.2 illustrates the situation.

The implications of this finding are as follows. A bonus issue should

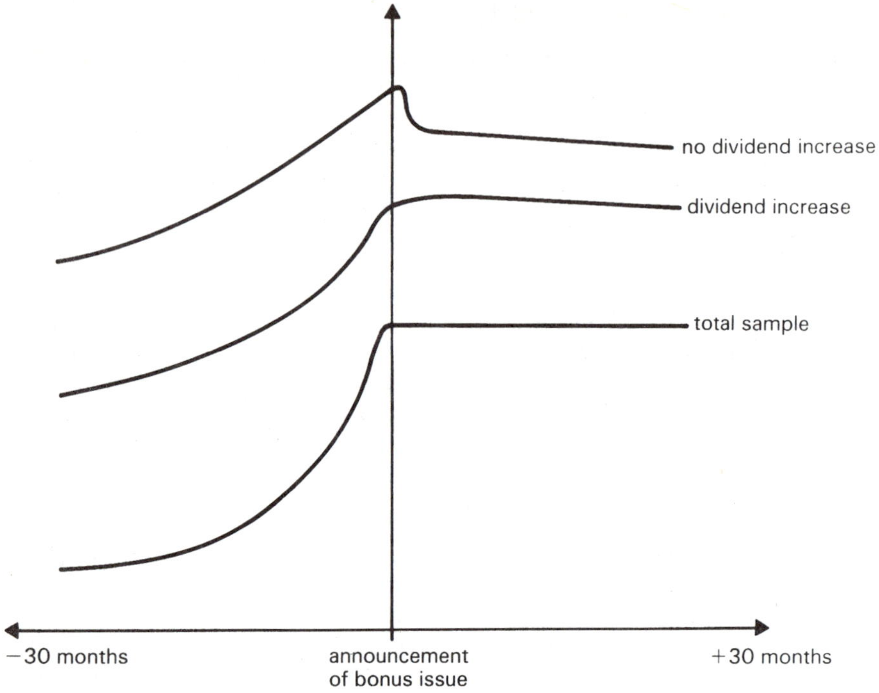

Figure 12.2

not really have any effect on the wealth of shareholders. The company remains exactly the same as before and all that happens is that the number of shares in issue is increased, but nothing has happened to change the value of those shares in aggregate. Therefore why should a share's price tend to rise prior to a bonus issue?

The answer to this question is that with bonus issues there is often an effective increase in dividends. For example, in our one-for-one bonus issue the dividend *per share* might have been maintained – thereby effectively doubling the level of dividends paid out. And, of course, an increase in dividends *would* cause an increase in shareholder wealth. Thus it would be reasonable to imply that a share's price tends to rise prior to an announcement of a bonus issue *in anticipation* that this event would be accompanied by an effective increase in dividends.

Now not all bonus issues are accompanied by an increase in dividends. Fama *et al.* divided their sample of bonus-issuing companies into those who did and did not increase dividends at the time of the bonus issue. They then found that for those companies that *did* increase dividends there was, on average, no significant change in their returns *after* the bonus issue. In other words, the shares had risen in anticipation of the dividend increase and, once the increase had been announced, they maintained their new level.

Notice therefore the efficiency of the stock market. The share price rose in anticipation of the information and, once the information was publicly disclosed, the share price *already* reflected the impact of that information.

On the other hand, those companies making a bonus issue and *not* increasing dividends suffered, on average, *negative* abnormal returns after the bonus issue: again, evidence that the shares had originally risen in anticipation of new information (about a dividend increase) but, when that information subsequently didn't arise, the price then fell back. Again, this situation is illustrated in Figure 12.2.

Strong efficiency evidence

As was mentioned earlier, the evidence for or against strong efficiency is much less clear, the reason being that strong efficiency involves 'inside information' and researchers have difficulty of getting prior knowledge of such information to use in testing.

However, a number of tests have been carried out on the performance of *unit trusts* (known as mutual funds in the USA). The idea here is that unit trust managers often have semi-private conversations with the top executives of the major companies in which they invest. In these meetings they are likely to gain insights and information about the company which is unlikely to be available to investors generally.

If the market is *not* efficient in the strong sense, then unit trust managers should be able to profit from this additional information. The empirical evidence suggests that they cannot so do. For example, in another early study (1969) by Jensen which looked at the performance of 115 unit trusts, no evidence was found of superior performance or, where there was a positive abnormal return, it was so small as to be eliminated in the unit trust's management charges.

Conclusion

The evidence on market efficiency should not really be seen as surprising. It appears to indicate that new information divides itself up into that which is capable of being anticipated by the market (such as the level of profits for the year) and that which is *not* capable of being anticipated (such as a major factory fire).

The market appears to be very good at anticipating new information and the share price progressively reacts as these market 'guesses' become more confidently held. It is not surprising that this is the case, given the number of highly paid, intelligent people who are consistently striving to anticipate movements in share prices. It is equally unsurprising that no single analyst has been able to show that they can consistently act ahead of the rest.

In respect of that much smaller class of information, the information that is *not* capable of anticipation, the situation is different. Inside knowledge of this type of information (which is *not* the type likely to be obtained by unit trust managers) is likely to lead to an ability to 'beat' the stock market; though, of couse, it is likely to be illegal to use the information in that way. In other words, it would appear logical that the market is not strongly efficient in the strictest sense of the definition.

On the other hand, the evidence also points to the fact that when unanticipated information does become publicly disclosed, share prices tend to react very rapidly as a result; again, too rapidly for most investors to react quickly enough to beat the share price movement. In this respect, the study by Neiderhoffer and Osborne (1973) is of particular interest.

As far as financial managers are concerned, it is the evidence on semi-strong market efficiency which is important. Here the evidence is very substantially (but not *completely*) in favour of semi-strong efficiency. Therefore managers should be aware of, in particular, the fact that the results of their decisions will be reflected in the company's share price, once those decisions have been communicated to the stock market.

SUMMARY

This chapter has examined the costs of equity and debt capital and then explored the efficient markets hypothesis and its implications. The main points covered were:

- The dividend valuation model states that the share price is equal to the present value sum of the future expected dividends, discounted to present value.
- The discount rate in such an analysis reflects the *current* rate of return on similar systematic risk investments. This rate of return is known as the cost of equity capital and represents the opportunity cost, to management, of using shareholders' funds to undertake capital investment projects.
- Normally two, alternative, simplifying assumptions are used about the future flow of dividends represented in the model: either dividends per share are assumed to remain at a constant level in the future, or they are expected to grow at a constant annual rate.
- Assuming dividend growth, the growth rate can either be estimated on the basis of the *past* rate of growth of dividends; or by using the Gordon approach. This states that the dividend growth rate – under certain assumptions – is the product of the earnings retention rate and the company's return on capital.
- In a similar way to shares, debt capital is also valued on the present value sum of the future expected interest and redemption cash flow.
- The discount rate in such an analysis reflects the *current* rate of return on similar risk investments. As such, it again represents the opportunity cost, to management, of using debt capital to finance projects.
- In other words, if managers wish to maximize shareholder wealth they should not invest debt capital to earn a lower rate of return than could be earned elsewhere in the capital market from a similar risk investment.

- The efficient markets hypothesis examines the degree to which the stock market is efficient in reflecting relevant information in share prices.
- Weak efficiency occurs when market prices follow a random walk and thereby limiting the usefulness of technical analysis.
- Semi-strong efficiency occurs when share prices quickly and correctly relect any relevant information as it arises in the public domain. Its occurrence limits the usefulness of fundamental analysis of share prices.
- Strong efficiency occurs when share prices reflect *all* relevant information, whether or not it is in the public domain. In such circumstances investors could not even expect to profit from the possession of inside information.
- The empirical evidence overwhelmingly supports weak efficiency, and substantially supports semi-strong efficiency. On strong efficiency, the empirical evidence is less clear.
- The implications for financial managers of semi-strong efficiency in particular, are important. It implies project NPVs will be reflected in share prices; the timing of capital-raising exercises is unimportant from the viewpoint of whether the company's shares are currently 'cheap' or 'expensive' and it casts doubt on the take-over of a publicly-quoted company ever being expected to produce a positive NPV.

NOTES

1 The exception to this was our discussion as to how our DCF appraisal techniques coped with the problem of capital rationing.

2 Another one is lease-finance. This will be explicitly considered at a later stage.

3 Except under very exceptional circumstances, such as liquidation.

4 This is assuming that the rate of discount remains a constant at $12\frac{1}{2}$% in perpetuity. Alternatively, we could view the $12\frac{1}{2}$% as the (weighted) *average* rate of discount over this time period.

5 Or, if not all, at least a sufficient number to move the market price.

6 It should be pointed out that the dividend valuation model does not, *itself,* make any distinction between systematic and unsystematic risk. However, from our knowledge of portfolio theory and the CAPM we can infer that the dividend valuation model *implies* a consideration of systematic rather than total risk.

7 The middleman who makes the market for shares on the London Stock Exchange is called a jobber or market maker. The difference between the bid and offer price represents his profit or 'turn'.

8 For a detailed explanation of immediate annuities, see the earlier appendix on compounding and discounting.

9 We have only examined the situation where a single annual dividend is paid. Where, say, dividends are paid twice a year (an interim and a final dividend) there are, in effect, two ex/cum dividend situations. For example, suppose a 5p per share dividend is paid half-yearly on a share with an ex div market value of 100p. We cannot say that $K_E = 10/100 = 0{\cdot}10$ as this only represents the share's nominal annual return. The effective annual return would be given by:

$$100 = \frac{5}{K_E} + \frac{5(1 + K_E)}{K_E}$$

so that $K_E = 10/95 \approx 0{\cdot}105$ or $10\frac{1}{2}\%$.

10 This assumption could be relaxed so that dividends through time, *on average*, are assumed to be a constant, but to do so can lead to problems where the discount rate changes over time.

11 Obviously the model can also be presented in terms of *total* market values: $V_E = D_1/(K_E - g)$

12 Sometimes referred to as the 'Gordon Growth Model' when presented in this form.

13 In fact, for the two models to give the same expected return on equity we need to assume that both the risk-free return and the expected return on the market portfolio will remain constant and – obviously – that the market does price securities in the way that CAPM postulates.

14 The reader should remember that in analysing the cost of equity capital we have covered the 'cost' both of directly raised equity capital and the 'cost' of retained earnings.

15 Irredeemable or undated debentures do exist, where the loan is never repaid (except in liquidation), but are very rare.

16 Just like ordinary shares, debentures are not homogeneous in terms of risk. The riskiness of any particular debenture depends upon a number of factors including the riskiness of the company issuing debentures, the security (if any) attached to the debenture and how it ranks for payment with other fixed-interest capital issued by the company.

17 Debt market values follow a saw-tooth pattern similar to those of equity market values. Just as we only dealt with ex div equity market values – adjusting a cum div value if necessary onto an equivalent ex-dividend basis – so similarly the debt valuation model only deals with ex interest debt market values.

18 Although the amount of risk they involve may be *very* small.

19 It is worthwhile noting that if redeemable debentures have an ex int. market price of £100 and they are redeemable at par value, then their cost of debt capital *does* equal their coupon rate.

20 The price-earnings model is not of much interest to us, but it is a widely used share valuation model. In many ways it has a similar *logic* to the dividend valuation model but the reason why we are uninterested in it is because it is based on *accounting* numbers rather than *cash* flow. The model holds that a share price is determined by a multiple of the (accounting) earnings per share. The multiple itself is determined by two principal factors: the *quality* (or riskiness) of the

expected earnings and the prospects for future *growth* in earnings. To see the P − E model's similarity with the dividend valuation model, consider the dividend growth version and the determinants of the share price: the dividend growth rate and the riskiness of the future expected dividend flow.

APPENDIX

With the current imputation system in the UK, for the basic rate taxpayer who receives relatively little income in the form of dividends (unearned income) there is *effectively* no tax on dividends (although basic rate tax is *imputed* to have been paid). However, from the company's viewpoint, dividend payments have the effect of bringing forward (by one year under the assumption below) the payment of part of the total corporation tax liability. This advanced corporation tax is calculated as the amount of tax that would have been payable on the dividends paid, if they were taxed at the basic rate of income tax.

As an example, suppose a company has a constant annual taxable profit of 100. Corporation tax is levied at 35%, assumed payable 12 months in arrears. The company propose to pay a net dividend this year of 10, increasing at a compound annual rate of 10%. Income tax is at 25% and there is an imputation system. The current market value of the company's equity is 550 ex div.

Unadjusted to allow for the effects of corporation tax, the dividend growth model yields:

$$K_E = \frac{10(1 + 0{\cdot}1)}{550} + 0{\cdot}1 = 0{\cdot}12$$

However, this is only an approximation. Taking account of tax the ACT payable on the net dividend of 10p is: 10p × $\frac{25}{75}$ = 3·33p and K_E is:

$$K_{E_{AT}} = \frac{10(1 + 0{\cdot}1) + (0{\cdot}10 \times 3{\cdot}33)}{550} + 0{\cdot}1 = 0{\cdot}1206$$

Hence the management must earn a return on equity slightly over 12% (12·067%) in order to provide the 12% return expected by shareholders.

Calculations are shown in the tables below. As a result of a policy of increasing dividends by 10%, a small proportion of corporation tax is brought forward in time and this also increases at 10% per annum; but in terms of the required expected return, this is raised slightly to allow for this tax effect.

Year	0	1	2	3
Net dividend (10% growth rate)	10	11	12·10	13·31
ACT ($\frac{25}{75}$ of div.)	3·33	3·67	4·03	4·44
Gross dividend	13·33	14·67	16·13	17·75

Therefore, as a result of a policy of increasing dividends by 10%, a small proportion of corporation tax is brought forward in time and this also increases at 10% per annum; but in terms of the required expected return, this is raised slightly to allow for this tax effect.

Year	0	1	2	3
Corporation tax liability	35	35	35	35
− ACT paid in previous year	3·03[a]	3·33[b]	3·67	4·44
Corporation tax payable	31·97	31·67	31·33	30·97
+ ACT payable	3·33	3·67	4·03	4·44
Total CT payable	35·30	35·34	35·36	35·41
Extra CT payable (i.e., > 35)	0·30	0·34	0·36	0·41
Dividend	10·00	11·00	12·10	13·31
Cash out-flow from dividends	10·30	11·34	12·46	13·72

[a]This is calculated on the assumption that the dividend at time − 1 was:

$$\frac{100}{110} \times 10 = 9{\cdot}1 \text{ (approx).}$$

[b]The ACT payable on the dividend of 10 is given by: $10 \times \frac{25}{75} = 3{\cdot}33$

FURTHER READING

1 The two most interesting original articles on cost of capital are: D. Durand, 'Growth Stocks and the St. Petersburg Paradox', *Journal of Finance*, September 1957, and M.J. Gordon, 'Dividends, Earnings and Stock Prices', *Review of Economics and Statistics*, May 1959.

2 Some more recent contributions of interest are: M.J. Gordon and L.I. Gould, 'The Cost of Equity Capital: a Reconsideration', *Journal of Finance*, June 1978; A. Chen, 'Recent Developments in the Cost of Debt Capital', *Journal of Finance*, June 1978; R.S. Pindyck, 'Risk, Inflation and the Stock Market', *American Economic Review*, June 1984; L.J. Gitman and V.A. Mercurio, 'Cost of Capital Techniques Used by Major US Firms', *Financial Management*, Winter 1982; and J.J. Siegal, 'The Application of the DCF Methodology for Determining the Cost of Equity Capital', *Financial Management*, Spring 1985.

3 On the EMH there is a wealth of articles to select from. However, a good starting point is: E.F. Fama, 'Efficient Capital Markets: A Review of Theory and Empirical Work', *Journal of Finance*, May 1970.

4 For an interesting article on weak efficiency in a range of stock markets see: B.H. Solnik, 'Note on the Validity of Random Walk for European Stock Prices', *Journal of Finance*, December 1973. The articles referred to in the text are: E.F. Fama, *et al.*, 'The Adjustment of Stock Prices to New Information', *International Economic Review*, February 1969, M.C. Jensen, 'Risk, the Pricing of Capital Assets and the Evaluation of Investment Portfolios', *Journal of Business*, April 1969, and V. Neiderhoffer and V. Osborne, 'Market Making and Reversal on the Stock Exchange', *Journal of American Statistical Association*, December 1973. Finally, for a discussion of EMH within

a UK context, see: P.R. Marsh, 'Equity Rights Issues and the Efficiency of the UK Stock Market', *Journal of Finance*, December 1979.

5 Finally, of obvious interest, there is: T.B. O'Keefe and S.Y. Soloman, 'Do Managers Believe the EMH?: Additional Evidence', *Accounting and Business Research*, Spring 1985.

QUICKIE QUESTIONS

1 Given the following information, estimate the company's cost of equity capital:

P_E = £1·47 cum div	Div/Share record	t_{-3}	$11\frac{1}{4}$p
d_0= 13p net		t_{-2}	12p
		t_{-1}	$12\frac{1}{2}$p
		t_0	13p

2 What are the assumptions behind the $g = b \times r$ model?

3 Estimate the company's after-tax cost of capital and the total market value of the debt capital ex int.:

£12m 15% debt capital. Redeemable in four years at £110 per cent. Current market price is £128 cum interest. Corporation tax is at 35%.

4 If a company had issued £10m of 12% unquoted debt, redeemable in 3 years at par and similar in risk to those in question 3, estimate their total market worth.

5 What is the after tax cost of debt capital of an issue of 18% debt which is redeemable at par in 7 years' time and whose current market price is £118 cum interest? Corporation tax is charged at 35%.

6 What are the three levels of market efficiency?

7 What are the implications of semi-strong market efficiency for financial managers?

8 What are the implications of stock market efficiency for stock exchange investment analysis?

9 Why do share prices follow a random walk?

10 What does a technical analyst attempt to do?

PROBLEMS

1 Thamos plc is a successful food retailing company. Over the last five years it has increased its share of the UK food retail market by 30%. Thamos plc makes no use of debt and has financed its operations entirely from retained earnings. Thamos plc has a current price/earnings ratio of 28 compared with the food retailing sector average of 19. Other financial data over the last five years are shown below.

	t_{-4}	t_{-3}	t_{-2}	t_{-1}	*Current Year*
Earnings per share (p)	16·1	19·3	24·7	30·5	35·8
Net dividend per share (p)	4·86	5·86	7·5	9·0	11·0
Book value of equity per share (p)	103	124	142	165	190

Required:

(a) Estimate the cost of equity capital for Thamos plc using the following:
   (i) dividend growth model;
   (ii) Gordon model;
   (iii) capital asset pricing model (you should assume a risk-free rate of interest of 10%, a beta of 0·8 and a market premium for risk of 9%).

(b) Discuss whether the assumptions underlying the models used in part (a) are realistic and explain how the effects of using these assumptions are reflected in the results obtained.

(c) Explain why managers need to know the cost of the equity capital of their companies.

2 You are given the following information about six companies, all of which are financed entirely by equity capital:

	Black Snake	*Black Stump*	*White Turkey*	*White Eyes*	*Red Eagle*	*Red Fox*
Number of ordinary shares of £1 (000s)	150,000	500,000	2,000	10,000	100,000	60,000
Market value per share, *ex div*, (£)	3·42	0·65	2·20	1·12	1·49	2·57
Current earnings (Total) (£000s)	62,858	63,952	989	2,454	21,996	21,362
Current dividend (Total) (£000s)	6,158	48,130	599	1,033	11,466	4,932
Balance sheet value of capital employed (£000s)	315,000	293,000	3,800	9,800	117,000	106,000
Dividend five years ago (Total) (£000s)	2,473	37,600	372	514	7,122	2,454
Estimated cost of capital (%)	–	20·0	–	24·0	–	18·5

Red Eagle and Red Fox are diversified companies; the other four companies are all brewers with a similar mix of products. There have been no changes in the share capital of any of the companies over the last five years.

Required:

(a) Estimate the cost of capital for Black Snake, White Turkey and Red Eagle.

(b) Discuss the reasons for the variations in cost of capital from company to company.

(c) Describe, giving your reasons, any additional evidence to which you would refer in order to increase your confidence in the estimates of the cost of capital in practice.

Ignore taxation.

3 Berenice plc is a large UK listed retailing company with a current equity market capitalization of £1,012 million. Its directors have recently decided to manufacture a greater proportion of the goods sold in the company's retail stores. As part of this strategy, they are currently contemplating the acquisition of one of their suppliers, Clorinda plc, a small listed company based in Lancashire which produces a complete range of bedroom textiles, e.g. sheets, pillow-cases, duvets and blankets. At present, 30% of Clorinda plc's sales are purchased by Berenice plc.

The current equity market value of Clorinda plc is £7·3 million, representing a price-earnings ratio of 8·2 (the average for the sector being 14·1). Its shareholders are believed to be as follows:

	%
Berenice plc	4
Individual private investors	25
Directors of Clorinda plc	27
Institutional investors	44
	100

The directors of Berenice plc regard the Clorinda plc management as being sleepy, inefficient and old-fashioned. They believe that with a new management team, the work practices of Clorinda plc could be revolutionized. They believe that if the old weaving machines were to be replaced by new models the employee wages bill could be cut, and annual profits after tax could be increased by 60%. As part of the rationalization of work practices, two textile mills would no longer be required. These mills are situated in prime residential areas and if they were demolished and replaced by an executive housing development, it is estimated that a profit after tax of £1·2 million would be realized. Obtaining planning permission is not expected to be a problem, because of the shortage of new housing in the area.

The directors of Berenice plc are keen to proceed with the take-over as soon as possible, especially as the price of Clorinda plc's shares has started to rise for no apparent reason.

Required:
Discuss whether the 'true worth' of a company is necessarily reflected by its market capitalization, illustrating your answer by reference to the information concerning Clorinda plc.

13
The weighted average cost of capital

Chapter Contents

THE PROJECT DISCOUNT RATE

At the outset of the previous chapter it was stated that – apart from other uses principally concerned with the capital structure decision – the cost of capital analysis could possibly provide another way (as an alternative to the CAPM) of identifying a discount rate/cut-off rate for DCF investment appraisal. It is to this that we now turn our attention.

The (long-term) capital structures of companies can be separated into two types. Companies can have either a capital structure which consists entirely of equity capital, or a *mixed* capital structure where debt capital and equity capital are held in varying proportions. The latter structure is the more common in practice (especially amongst stock exchange quoted companies) but the former provides us with a much less complex situation, and so initially we shall examine the question of the investment appraisal discount rate in terms of an all-equity company.

All-equity companies

Suppose that a company has an all-equity capital structure and intends to remain as such (at least up to the horizon of its current planning). *Under a number of limiting assumptions*, we can state that its current cost of equity capital could properly be used as the discount rate for investment appraisal.

This rate, the expected return required by the ordinary shareholders, could be used because it represents the minimum acceptable return for a project undertaken by the company, in opportunity cost terms. The cost of equity capital represents the opportunity cost of the shareholders' capital, in that it reflects the return that they could earn elsewhere (for a similar level of risk). Therefore their capital should be applied to a particular capital investment project undertaken by the company's management, *only* if it is expected to yield this return, as a minimum.

This condition applies whether the project is being financed by a new equity issue, or by funds from an equity issue made in the past, or by using retained net earnings. In all cases, the investment capital represents shareholders' funds, and the company should only use such funds if each project to which they are applied earns at least this minimum return. Use of the NPV decision rule, with the cost of equity capital as the discount rate, will ensure that this is the case.

There are two important limiting assumptions to this advice. The first is that the company is assumed to be evaluating projects which, if they were accepted, would not cause any significant change in the company's overall level of risk. That is, the acceptance of the project would not cause investors generally to view the company's expected future cash flows as having changed in their level of uncertainty. The reason for this assumption is obvious. The market-derived cost of equity capital is the required return relevant *only* to the company's existing level of risk and so would be an inappropriate rate to apply to a project which had a different level of risk.

The second limiting assumption is that the project being appraised is small, relative to the overall size of all company, i.e., the project represents a marginal investment. The reason for this assumption is as follows. The company's cost of equity capital is a marginal cost; it refers to the minimum expected return required from a relatively small (i.e., marginal) investment in the shares of the company. This is so because the current share price that is used in the cost of equity calculation is the price at which a relatively small quantity of the company's shares can be currently bought or sold – if a large quantity of shares were involved, then a separate price would have to be negotiated. Therefore, the cost of equity capital is only appropriate for the evaluation of a project which represents a marginal change in the company's total investment. If either of these assumptions is violated, then the company's cost of equity capital does *not* provide an appropriate rate of discount for project investment appraisal.

Mixed capital structure companies

Where a company's capital structure is composed of both debt and equity capital, with their differing opportunity costs, what discount rate should be used for investment appraisal purposes? The short answer to this question, which we shall expand upon and attempt to justify, is that a weighted average of the costs of all the individual components of the capital structure should be used.

On the surface this can appear to be strange advice. For example, assume a company possess a capital structure of which (measured in current stock market values) half is equity with a cost of (say) 20% and half is debt with a cost of (say) 10%. Using the proportion of each type of capital in the overall structure as the weights, we find that the company's weighted average cost of capital (which we shall call K_0) is given by: $(0{\cdot}5 \times 20\%) + (0{\cdot}5 \times 10\%) = 15\%$.

Now, suppose an investment opportunity is perceived by the company which requires a cash outlay of £1m and the company proposes to raise the capital through a debt issue at the current market rate of interest of 10%. The cost – in the everyday sense of the word – of the capital put into the project would be 10% and so it would appear logical to use this as the discount rate: if the project yields a return greater than 10% (i.e., it has a positive NPV at a 10% discount rate), the company must find the project beneficial.

In contrast to this, we have stated that the company's weighted average cost of capital should be the discount rate used for project evaluation: 15%.[1] But why should the company require a minimum return of 15%, when it appears that the project would be worth while as long as it yields a return in excess of 10%?

For instance, if the project were found to have a yield (i.e., an IRR) of 14%, evaluating it using K_0 as the discount rate would lead to its rejection even though it appears to produce a return 4% above its cost. To use K_0 as the discount rate looks nonsensical.

For another view of things, suppose the same company later has another investment opportunity which it is proposed to finance through an issue of equity capital (where cost is 20%). If the project yields a return of 17% (say), it would have a positive NPV when discounted by K_0 and so would be accepted. Once again, the use of K_0 appears to lead to a nonsensical decision: acceptance of a project which does not even generate sufficient return to cover the cost of the capital outlay required.

A constant capital structure

The reason for these apparent anomalies arises principally because we are *assuming* that the company intends to retain its existing capital structure mix of fixed interest and equity capital. (Just *why* a company should wish to do so will be dealt with in the following chapter on the capital structure decision. However, for the moment, let us accept that management believe that the company's existing capital structure is somehow *ideal* and so wish to retain it.)

This means therefore that, in the case of the example used above, because the company's current capital structure is composed of a 50:50 mix of debt and equity, the advice to use K_0 as the discount rate assumes that the company will finance the project in such a way as not to change the ratio of this mix. It follows that the cost of this mix is equal to the company's weighted average cost of capital and hence it is this figure that should be used as the NPV discount rate.

However, although we have so far ignored them, there are relatively substantial issue costs attached to the raising of (external) capital. These exhibit considerable economies of scale (i.e., the greater the amount of capital raised from a single source, the lower will be the percentage of issue costs). In order to take advantage of these scale economies, the capital structure mix of companies, in practice, is likely, in the short run, to fluctuate *around* the existing or desired structure, as first (say) debt capital is raised for one project and then equity capital for the next. So the somewhat more pragmatic assumption underlying the use of the weighted average cost of capital is that, although there will be minor fluctuations in the short run, in the medium to longer term a company's capital structure will remain stable.

'Pool' of funds concept

A further reason can also be given for *not* appraising projects using the cost of a particular source of funds, but instead using a weighted average cost of capital. That reason is as follows. It is neither practical nor especially sensible, to try to identify a particular source of investment cash, physically, with a particular project. Once cash enters a company, it enters the general *pool* of capital within that company, and it is out of this pool that investment funds are drawn, in order to be applied to particular investment projects.

Not unnaturally, the cost involved in using funds out of this pool of capital is the weighted average of all the individual capital inputs. Therefore, on the assumption that a company's capital structure (and hence the make-up of its capital pool) remains stable in the medium to longer term, it is the weighted average of these capital costs that must be the minimum acceptable return from any investment project. Neither the cost of what appears to be the individual source of capital used, nor the K_0 of the *short-term* capital structure fluctuation are appropriate for designating a minimum acceptable return in opportunity cost terms.

The arguments for the use of the weighted average cost of capital as the investment appraisal discount rate are not perfect, and they are made under a number of assumptions which may or may not be borne out in practice. We have already noted these when examining the all-equity company case: unchanging capital structure, unchanging company risk, marginal projects. But if we return to the example we used previously, we can see that using K_0 does produce the most *sensible* long-term investment decision advice. The first project (yielding a 14% return) *should* be rejected as it cannot generate the expected return required by the company in the medium to longer term, whereas it is correct to accept the second project (yielding 17%) because it can meet this requirement.

THE CALCULATION OF K_0

Let us now turn to examine how the weighted average cost of capital (WACC) is calculated and how a company's capital structure is *measured*. The two questions are to some extent interlinked, but we shall start with the calculation of K_0.

The formal derivation

A company's WACC is derived (or imputed) in a way that is analogous to other costs of company capital. It is the lynch-pin of the relationship between the expected *total* future net cash flow of the company (i.e., dividends plus interest) and the current *total* market value of the company (i.e., debt capital plus equity).

In other words, using as a basis the logic which underpins the dividend valuation model, a company's *total* market value must be based on the sum of the expected future *total* net cash flow, discounted to present value. This cash flow can be split into two separate streams: interest payments (and loan capital repayments) and dividend payments. Assuming that a company has not issued *redeemable* debt capital, then the WACC could be found by solving the following equation for K_0 (i.e. K_0 is given by the internal rate of return of the cash flow):

$$V_E + V_D - \sum_{t=1}^{\infty} \frac{D_t}{(1+K_0)^t} - \sum_{t=1}^{\infty} \frac{I_t}{(1+K_0)^t} = 0$$

where V_E and V_D are the current total market values of equity and debt and D_t *and* I_t are the total dividend and interest payments made at time t.

If the assumption of only irredeemable debentures is joined by an assumption of a constant annual dividend flow in perpetuity,[2] then the expression for K_0 simplifies to:

$$V_E + V_D - \frac{D}{K_0} - \frac{I}{K_0} = 0$$

Multiplying both sides by K_0 and re-arranging, gives:

$$V_E K_0 + V_D K_0 - D - I = 0$$

$$K_0(V_E + V_D) = D + I$$

$$K_0 = \frac{D + I}{V_E + V_D}$$

On the basis that, under the cash flow assumptions made, $V_E = D/K_E$ and so $D = V_E \times K_E$ and similarly $I = V_D \times K_D$:

$$K_0 = \frac{(V_E \times K_E) + (V_D \times K_D)}{V_E + V_D} \quad \text{or}$$

$$K_0 = K_E \times \left(\frac{V_E}{V_E + V_D}\right) + K_D \times \left(\frac{V_D}{V_E + V_D}\right)$$

So here we can see why the discount rate to be used in project appraisal is the WACC and that the weights to be applied to the individual costs of capital are the market values of each capital source, as a proportion of the company's total market value.

In the example used, taxation was ignored. If tax is to be included – as indeed it should be given that we require the *after tax* discount rate to be applied to the *after tax* project cash flows – then the *after tax* cost of debt capital should be used in the calculation of K_0.

The assumptions behind the use of the WACC

Given the formal derivation of the weighted average cost of capital, we can now see that there are in fact *four* assumptions that have to be complied with if it is to be used as an NPV discount rate:

(1) The project should be marginal. That is, the project should be small relative to the size of the firm.
(2) The project should be financed in such a way as not to change the company's existing capital structure.
(3) The project should have the same degree of systematic risk as the existing average systematic risk level of the company.

and now (4) All cash flows (i.e. dividends, interest *and* project cash flows) should be level perpetuities.

The first assumption is required because both K_E and K_D represent marginal costs of capital: That is they represent the return available on relatively small investments in the equity and debt securities of the company. Therefore K_0, in turn, also represents a marginal cost of capital: the *overall* return on a relatively small investment in the company. It therefore follows that, strictly speaking, the WACC should only be used as an NPV discount rate on projects which are themselves relatively small.

The second assumption is required because, if the project is financed in such a way that the capital structure of the company is changed, then obviously the *weights* in the WACC calculation will change. This, we would expect, would lead to a change in the value of K_0.

There is also a second reason why K_0 might be expected to change in these circumstances. It was pointed out in the previous chapter that a company's debt capital is a less risky investment than a company's equity capital. This is because, legally, a company *must* pay its debt interest in full before equity dividends can be paid. Thus, in bad years, there is a greater chance that equity holders will miss out on their dividends than debt holders missing out on their interest. The equity holders stand behind the debt holders in the year-end *pay-out queue.*

As a result of equity being more risky than debt, the expected return on a company's equity capital is *greater*, than is the expected return on its debt. This extra return that equity holders receive is compensation for the risk that arises from being at the back of the pay-out queue, and is termed the *financial risk* premium.

Obviously, the more debt interest the company has to pay, the greater is the risk for equity holders that the firm will have insufficient cash flow to pay them their dividend. All the cash flow having gone to paying interest charges. Therefore, the more debt interest the company has to pay out, the greater will be the financial risk premium demanded by equity holders – that is, the greater will be K_E. Therefore, unless projects are financed so as not to change the capital structure, K_0 would also be expected to change because of the resulting change in K_E.

In these circumstances the question would then appear to be: which K_0 should be used: the company's *existing* K_0 or the *new* K_0 that applies once the capital structure is changed? The answer, in fact, is that *neither* would be correct. Why this is so will be explained more fully in Chapter 16. For now, all we will say is that if the company is thinking of undertaking a project and wants to finance it in such a way as to change the capital structure, then *two* decisions are involved.

The company is making a capital investment decision *and* a capital structure decision. The NPV technique is a capital investment appraisal technique *only*. It cannot cope with a simultaneous capital structure decision as well. Hence the assumption that the capital structure will remain unchanged.

The third assumption is required because the NPV discount rate should reflect the systematic risk of the project. The company's WACC is its *overall* rate of return. Like any other market-derived rate of return it reflects the systematic risk involved in the overall company. Therefore K_0 would only be a suitable NPV discount rate if the project had a similar level of systematic risk.

Finally, there is the fourth assumption. From the formal derivation of the WACC calculation it can be seen that, strictly speaking, the WACC model is a level perpetuity cash flow model. Therefore the company's K_0, calculated on the basis of the model, should really only be applied to projects which themselves have perpetuity cash flows.

How realistic are these assumptions? The first and last assumptions cause little difficulty in practice. Most projects evaluated *are* relatively small when compared to the size of the company. Even if they were not, the violation of the first assumption is unlikely to lead to a serious distortion of the investment appraisal.

A similar conclusion can be reached over the last of these four assumptions. The fact that the company may have *redeemable* debt (and so a non-perpetuity interest flow) and *growing* dividends (and so a non-perpetuity dividend flow) is likely to make little difference in practice. The WACC can still be calculated as an average of the costs of equity and debt, weighted by their market value proportions. Similarly, the fact that the project is almost certainly *not* going to have perpetuity cash flows is not likely to bias the investment appraisal unduly, using K_0 as the discount rate.

The second assumption does cause problems. These are normally avoided, as we have seen, by accepting that the capital structure *may* change in the short run, but is likely to be maintained in the medium to long term. However if financing the project does cause a *significant* change in capital structure then an NPV-WACC approach to the investment appraisal is not appropriate. What *is* an appropriate approach will be discussed in Chapter 16.

That leaves the third assumption about risk. It is here that we run into real difficulties.

The WACC and project risk

If the company is a single-product company (such as a cement manufacturer), and the project under consideration is a general expansion of its existing business then it may well be safe to assume that the project *does* have the same degree of systematic risk as the existing risk of the company. However, if the project represents a move into a *new* area of business, then the existing WACC would *not* be an appropriate discount rate to use.

However, very few companies are single-product companies. Most companies are, to some extent, diversified. In such circumstances the company's WACC does not reflect the systematic risk of *any one* particular area of its business. It reflects its *average* level of systematic risk throughout all its areas of business.

Therefore, for a diversified company, its WACC is going to be an unsuitable discount rate for project appraisal purposes. Its WACC is unlikely to reflect the systematic risk of any particular project, except by chance. Example 13.1 illustrates this situation, making use of the CAPM.

With Example 13.1 it can be seen that the company's WACC reflects the *average* level of the company's systematic risk ($\beta = 1{\cdot}36$). Therefore its K_0 of $17\frac{1}{2}$% would be *too low* a required rate of return to evaluate projects in its high risk ($\beta = 1{\cdot}92$) office furniture manufacturing division. Therefore, given its high risk, projects should produce a minimum expected return of 21·4%.

At the same time, the company's K_0 of $17\frac{1}{2}$% is *too high* a required rate of return for its low risk ($\beta = 0{\cdot}80$) supermarket division. In that division, the minimum required return for projects should be only 13·6%.

This example highlights the dangers of companies using a single required rate of return for all projects. Yet many companies do exactly that. For example, a survey in the USA by Brigham, carried out in 1975, found that nearly 50% of the companies used a *single* required rate of return to evaluate *all* projects.

Example 13.1

Rocha PLC has two main divisions. One operates a chain of supermarkets while the other manufactures office furniture. The company is financed by both debt and equity capital.

The total market value of the company's equity is £30·3m ex dividend. The company has recently paid this year's dividend which totalled £4m. This was in line with the company's policy of increasing dividends by 6% per year. In addition, Rocha has issued £12·625m of 8% irredeemable debt. This is currently quoted at £80 per cent, ex interest.

The company's equity has a beta value of 1·72 and its debt beta[3] is estimated at 0·29. The supermarket industry has an average beta of 0·80 while office furniture manufacturers have an average beta of 1·92. Rocha's business is roughly divided equally between its two divisions.

The risk-free return is 8% and the FTSE stock market index is 15%.

Rocha currently uses its weighted average cost of capital to evaluate *all* projects, but is now thinking of using a different discount rate for each one of its divisions.

WACC calculation

This can be arrived at through three different routes:

1 Cost of equity capital: $K_E = \dfrac{£4m\,(1\cdot06)}{£30\cdot3m} + 0\cdot06 = 0\cdot20$ or $\underline{20\%}$

Total market value of equity $= V_E = \underline{£30\cdot3m}$

Cost of debt capital: $K_D = \dfrac{£8}{£80} = 0\cdot10$ or $\underline{10\%}$

Total market value of debt: $V_D = £12\cdot625m \times 0\cdot80 = \underline{£10\cdot1m}$
Total market value of company: $V_0 = V_E + V_D = \underline{£40\cdot4m}$
Weighted average cost of capital:

$$K_0 = \left(20\% \times \frac{30\cdot3}{40\cdot4}\right) + \left(10\% \times \frac{10\cdot1}{40\cdot4}\right) = \underline{\underline{17\tfrac{1}{2}\%}}$$

2 Cost of equity capital:

$$K_E = 8\% + [15\% - 8\%] \times 1\cdot72 = \underline{20\%} \text{ (approx.)}$$

Cost of debt capital:

$$K_D = 8\% + [15\% - 8\%] \times 0\cdot29 = \underline{10\%} \text{ (approx.)}$$

Weighted average cost of capital:

$$K_0 = \left(20\% \times \frac{30\cdot3}{40\cdot4}\right) + \left(10\% \times \frac{10\cdot1}{40\cdot4}\right) = \underline{\underline{17\tfrac{1}{2}\%}}$$

3 Rocha's *overall* beta value:

$$\beta_{Rocha} = [0\cdot50 \times \beta_{supermarkets}] + [0\cdot50 \times \beta_{office\ furn.\ mfg.}]$$
$$\beta_{Rocha} = [0\cdot50 \times 0\cdot80] + [0\cdot50 \times 1\cdot92] = \underline{1\cdot36}$$

Weighted average cost of capital:

$$K_0 = 8\% + [15\% - 8\%] \times 1\cdot36 = \underline{\underline{17\tfrac{1}{2}\%}} \text{ (approx.)}$$

Divisional discount rates

1 Supermarket division
Required return $= 8\% + [15\% - 8\%] \times 0\cdot80 = \underline{\underline{13\cdot6\%}}$
2 Office Furniture manufacture division
Required return $= 8\% + [15\% - 8\%] \times 1\cdot92 = \underline{\underline{21\cdot4\%}}$

(Notice that: $(21\cdot4\% \times 0\cdot50) + (13\cdot6\% \times 0\cdot50) = 17\tfrac{1}{2}\%$)

Diagrammatically, the problem is illustrated in Figure 13.1. If the company simply applies its WACC to all projects, then it will incorrectly *accept* the high risk projects whose risk and expected return characteristics locate in shaded area A. Conversely, it will incorrectly *reject* low risk projects whose risk and return characteristics locate in shaded area B.

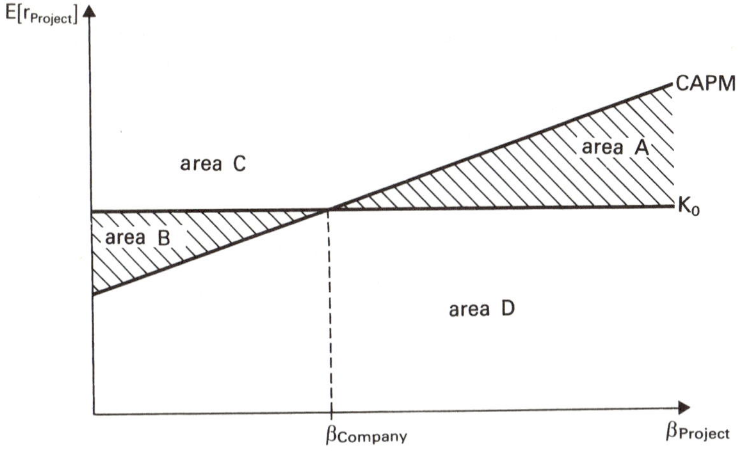

Figure 13.1

With projects whose risk and return characteristics locate in either areas C or D, there is no problem. Area C projects will be correctly accepted by the WACC. Area D projects will be correctly rejected. However, the danger lies with area A and B projects.

Therefore, returning to Example 13.1, the company's supermarket division could be quite needlessly rejecting what are perfectly acceptable (area B) projects because too high a minimum return is being specified. But, even worse, the furniture manufacturing division may be accepting projects thinking they will produce a positive NPV when, in reality, they can be expected to generate negative NPVs. The mistake arises because too *low* a discount rate is being used for the risk involved.

For project appraisal purposes, what is always required is an NPV discount rate which is *tailor-made* to reflect the individual systematic risk level of that particular project. The company's WACC does *not* provide this, but the CAPM *can* provide it.

The absence of tax

We will pick up on this analysis in Chapter 16. However, it is *very* important to note that Example 13.1 did not include tax. Tax makes a significant difference to the analysis, as we shall see.

Difficulties in calculating the WACC

The evidence of practice (see Brigham, 1975) is that many companies experience so many difficulties in actually calculating their WACC that they don't bother. Instead they substitute a *management-determined* figure as an estimate. These difficulties include both the cost of equity capital and of debt capital.

As far as equity capital is concerned the initial problem is to decide which share valuation model to utilize: the dividend valuation model or the capital asset pricing model. Apart from *conceptual* difficulties about the choice, each model suffers from data input difficulties.

With the CAPM there are obviously the difficulties associated with the fact that it is a *single-period* model, and so doubt must be cast on the sense in using it to generate a number to be used in a *multi-period* NPV analysis. In addition there is also the fact that the model may be *incomplete* in that the beta measure of systematic risk might not capture the whole story about what determines expected return.

There are also data input problems, to some extent, with all three of the CAPM's variables: r_F, $E[r_M]$ and β. As far as the risk-free return is concerned, there are two difficulties. One is that, although the return on government stock is risk-free in *money* terms, it is not genuinely risk-free in consumption or *purchasing power* terms. The other problem is to do with tax. The risk-free return should be specified after personal tax, using the personal tax rate of the marginal investor. As always, in practice, the marginal investor and his personal tax rate are hard to identify with confidence.

There are also two problems with the identity of the excess market return ($E[r_M] - r_F$). The first is, once again, to do with identifying the correct adjustment for taxation. The second is that, in practice, the excess market return tends to be rather volatile. (See Ibbotson and Sinquefield, 1982.) Therefore we have to settle for the rather unhappy compromise of using a long-run average excess market return.

Finally, as far as beta is concerned, there is the estimation problem. Betas, in practice, are normally estimated on the basis of the *past* relationship between a company's return and the market's return. However, we really require an estimate of the *future* value of beta. Thus this approach is only a reliable estimation method if it can be assumed that betas are stable over time. The evidence on this point is somewhat unclear.

As far as the alternative share valuation model is concerned – the dividend valuation model – there are also data input difficulties. The first is again concerned with tax – this time with the tax impact on dividends. Although we stated earlier that the *net of ACT* dividend is usually used in the model, this is on the implied assumption that the marginal investor is a basic rate tax-payer, which may not be the case in practice.

Difficulties can also arise with the input of the ex dividend market price per share. Shares are quoted 'ex dividend' for about four weeks and if, during that time, the share price is volatile, then there is the problem of having to derive some sort of *average* price per share. The other problem here is the need to assume that the market share price is in equilibrium. Despite efficient markets considerations, doubts may be cast on this, especially if there are take-over rumours in the stock market.

Finally, the major problem with using the dividend valuation model is to derive a reliable estimate for the future rate of growth of dividends. Estimating the future on the basis of the past is never a reliable forecasting technique, unless there are *positive* reasons to believe that the past will be replicated in the future. On the other hand, we also know that the Gordon approach to estimating '*g*' is so hedged with unrealistic assumptions as to cast great doubt on its real-world validity.

However, despite all the foregoing, the major stumbling block to the calculation of a company's weighted average cost of capital lies with debt, and not with equity. There are two particular problems which are then compounded with a third.

The first problem, once again, concerns tax. Tax regimes in the real world are so complex that it often proves very difficult to estimate accurately the tax impacts on debt capital. Secondly, most debt capital in the real world is unquoted and, unlike our earlier examples, similar-risk quoted debt is usually not readily available to assist us in estimating the cost of debt.

Finally, with debt, a great deal of debt capital is issued in highly complex, exotic forms. (We saw one slightly exotic type of debt – convertible debt – but in practice debt issues can be *far* more complex in construction.) This just compounds the difficulties of allowing adequately for the impact of tax and of imputing values for unquoted debt.

The gearing ratio

Turning briefly to the second question posed in this section, how a company's capital structure is to be measured, it should be clear from the foregoing analysis that market values of capital should be utilized in measuring or expressing a company's capital structure because they are the relevant factor.

We shall describe a company's capital structure by the term *gearing ratio*,[4] and we shall normally define it as the ratio of the total market value of a company's debt capital to the total market value of its equity: V_D/V_E. We shall now turn to start to examine the significance of a company's gearing ratio.

DIFFERING CORPORATE AND PRIVATE COSTS OF DEBT

Financing via debt capital

Through the single-period investment–consumption model, we developed the important Hirshleifer Separation Theorem. The essence of the theorem is that investment and consumption decisions can be effectively separated and analysed in isolation. Thus company managements can make decisions about physical investment opportunities without reference to the indifference curve maps of individual owners/shareholders.

On receipt of the dividend from the company, each shareholder can decide, with reference to his own indifference map, whether or not to use the capital market to borrow or lend money. In this way, the theory of investment decision making is able neatly to side-step one of the great stumbling-blocks of the practical application of economic theory: the identification of individuals' indifference maps and the need to make an interpersonal comparison of utility, when the preferences of individuals differ.

The reader may well have wondered at the ease with which the Separation Theorem conclusion gave way to a seemingly different analysis. The theorem would appear to suggest that companies need be financed only by equity share capital and retained cash earnings, and that money market borrowing and lending at fixed interest rates can be left to individual shareholders, in their personal manipulation of the pattern of their received dividend flows.

But, having dealt with the conclusion of this theorem, the analysis turned later to examine the costs of a *variety* of sources of company finance and the way in which these costs may be combined into a weighted average, and possibly then be used as a discount rate for investment appraisal.

Therefore, the idea of using debt capital to finance a company was introduced without either giving any reason *why* a company should raise debt capital (when the Separation Theorem implies that this decision can be left to the individual shareholder), or analysing the alterations it makes, if any, to the conclusions of the investment–consumption model. In fact, under the initial assumptions of the single-period model, the answers to both questions are relatively straightforward.

Introducing tax

There is really *no* reason why a company should borrow money on a perfect capital market (i.e., raise debt capital), because individual shareholders are perfectly capable of taking such action if they wish. But, even where a company does raise debt capital, it does not really disturb the conclusions of the model. The debt can be viewed as just another investment undertaken by management, which can be fitted into the logic of the physical investment line with little difficulty.

However, in the real world, companies raise debt capital as well as equity capital for many reasons. Principal among these is the disturbance in the capital market caused by taxation: *companies* can offset interest payments against taxation whereas individuals normally cannot.

Therefore, assuming that a company and an individual are seen as equally risky by the capital markets, the company can effectively borrow at a lower rate of interest (after tax) than can individual shareholders. So let us now analyse this situation, in terms of the single-period investment–consumption model, where the company's effective cost of borrowing on the capital market is less than that of the individual shareholder.

Debt capital in the perfect market case

First of all, assuming the existence of a perfect capital market in which individuals and companies borrow at effectively the *same* rate of interest, let us examine in what circumstances a company may raise debt capital, i.e., borrow.

Figure 13.2A shows the physical investment opportunities discovered by a company which have been ranked in order of decreasing rate of return. Under our previous analysis, we know that in order to help maximize shareholder wealth, the company will move along its physical investment line (PIL) until a point of tangency is reached with the financial investment line (FIL). This tangency occurs at point Q.

Moving to Figure 13.2 B, where the vertical axis is superimposed on the previous figure, this shows that the shareholders' current resources in the company, OA, are not sufficient to achieve the point of optimality on the physical investment line. *Additional* cash resources, to the value of OB, are required.

To reach the point of physical investment optimality, the company is faced with two possible alternatives. It can either request its shareholders to subscribe additional equity capital (thus causing the vertical axis to shift to the left so as to intersect the horizontal axis at point B, rather than at point O). Alternatively, the company can itself borrow amount OB on the capital market and repay CD (capital plus interest) at time t_1.

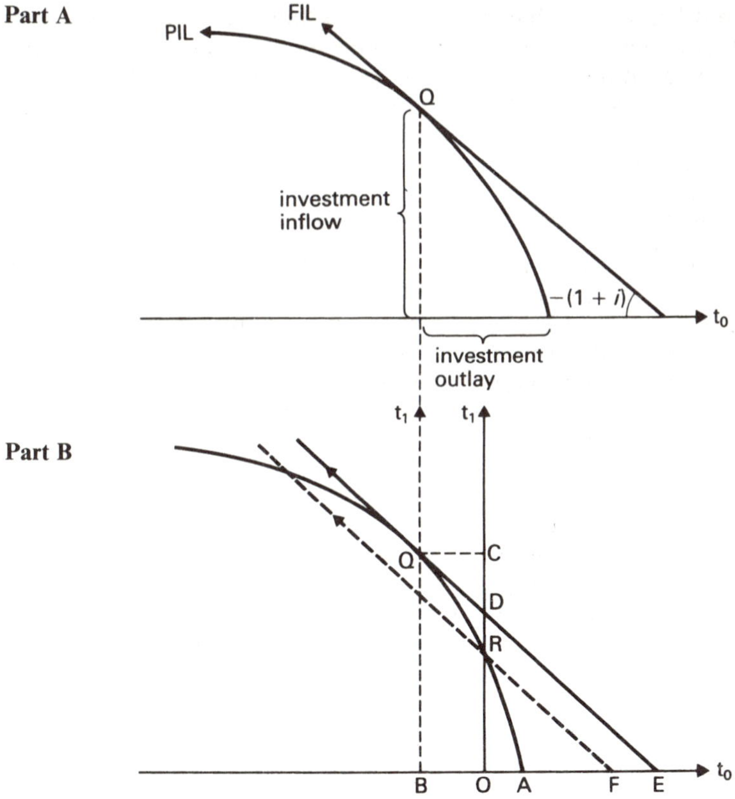

Figure 13.2

With this latter course of action, the present value of the company's equity capital would be OE, and the gain in shareholders' wealth arising out of the physical capital investments would be AE. If instead, the company had simply invested the existing cash resources of shareholders up to point R on the physical investment line, then the current value of the equity would only be OF and the gain in shareholders' wealth would also have been smaller at AF.

That *additional* gain in shareholders' wealth of EF would also arise if, instead, the company undertook the former course of action and asked its shareholders to subscribe an amount OB of new equity. The resulting present value of the equity would now be even greater at BE, but the *gain* in shareholder *wealth* would be the same as previously: AE. In other words the *gain* in wealth is found from the current value of the equity (BE), less the newly subscribed equity (OB) and less the original equity (OA).

The important result which follows from this analysis is that, in a perfect capital market, a company that wishes to maximize its shareholders' wealth should make physical investments until the return on the marginal investment becomes equal to the market interest rate; and it makes no difference to shareholders' wealth how these investments are financed, whether it be by equity capital or debt capital or by some combination of equity and debt. In the example used above, the company can maximize its shareholders' wealth either by using all equity investment capital (i.e. raise OB of additional equity) or by a mixture of both equity and debt (i.e., raise OB on the debt capital market).

Debt capital in the imperfect market case

So much for the perfect market case. Let us now examine the effects of debt capital financing when we have the particular type of capital market imperfection described earlier, which enables companies to borrow on the capital market at lower *effective* interest rates than can shareholders. In this analysis we shall assume that the company's interest rate and the individual shareholder's interest rate, represent both the borrowing and the lending rate for each.

Figure 13.3 sets up a situation similar to that of the previous analysis, except that there are now two points of tangency between the physical investment line and the *two* financial investment lines (one reflecting the company's interest rate and the other the shareholders' interest rate). These two points of tangency are at Y and Z respectively. Just as in the previous analysis, we shall assume that both points represent a capital investment requirement which is in excess of the company's existing resources. Thus both tangency points occur in the graph's north-west quadrant.

In this situation, the company is faced with a number of alternative courses of action, of which we shall initially specify and examine the effects of four:

1 Raise no additional capital.
2 Raise equity capital only.

3 Raise both debt and equity capital.
4 Raise debt capital only.

With the first of these four alternatives, the company would invest the whole of its capital resources (OA) available in time t_0 in physical investments, so as to reach point D on the physical investment line. The effect of this would be to give the company's equity capital a present value of OM.

Taking the second alternative of raising additional equity capital only, the maximum amount which the company could raise would be ON, thus allowing the company to move around the physical investment line to point Z. At this point, any further investment – which would necessitate raising further amounts of equity capital – would reduce the gain in the equity's current value; as it is, moving to point Z would cause the current total value of the equity to increase from OM to NB, which represents a gain in shareholder wealth – over the previous alternative course of action – of MB.

It is important to notice that with the first alternative (where no additional cash is raised), it would not matter which cost of capital (i.e., the company's interest rate or the shareholders' interest rate) was used to evaluate investment opportunities, because both would effectively move the company to point D. However, with the second alternative, the company must use the *shareholders'* cost of capital as the evaluation rate to ensure its location at point Z (which in Figure 13.3 equals shareholders' market interest rate).

The third alternative would be for the company to raise amount ON in new equity capital and amount NE in debt capital. In order to do so, in-

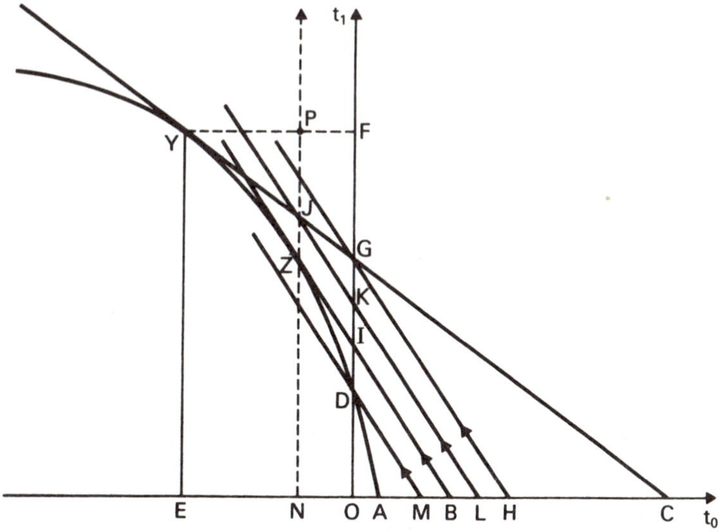

Figure 13.3

vestment opportunities would first be appraised with the shareholders' cost of capital as the discount rate. The total investment capital required for acceptable projects at this discount rate would specify the amount required to be raised in the form of new equity.

Those investment opportunities which remained unaccepted would then be appraised by the *company's* cost of capital. The total capital outlay required for the acceptable projects at this lower rate would then specify the amount of debt capital to be raised.

The overall effect of raising capital from these two sources and investing it in the accepted opportunities would locate the company at point Y on the physical investment line. This level of investment allows the company to generate cash of amount NP at time t_1, of which PJ represents interest and debt capital repayment and the remainder, NJ, is available for payment of dividend at t_1, which, at the shareholders' cost of capital, has a present value of NL. Thus this third alternative raises shareholders' wealth by a *further* amount: BL.

The fourth alternative requires that all investment opportunities are appraised with the *company's* cost of capital as the discount rate. The total amount of capital required to undertake the investments appraised as acceptable at this rate (AE), less the existing capital resources of the company (AO), specifies the amount of debt capital to be raised (OE). Once again, the combined effect is to move the company around its physical investment line to point Y and so generate a cash inflow of NP at time t_1. Of this cash inflow, amount FG represents the interest and capital repayment, and the remainder, amount OG, is available for dividends. The present value of this dividend (and hence of the company's equity) is OH. Thus this fourth alternative has resulted in yet a further increase in the shareholders' wealth by amount LH.

The extreme use of debt capital

The logical conclusion of the foregoing analysis is fairly obvious. It is fully developed in Figure 13.4, where it is assumed that at time t_0 the company has available capital resources (all equity) of amount OA.

Facing the physical investment line of AF and using the shareholders' cost of capital as the investment appraisal discount rate, the company would move to point Z, producing a time t_0 dividend of OD and a time t_1 dividend of OG. The present value of this dividend pattern represents the company's current value of OH.

If the company then appraises all the unaccepted projects at the *corporate* discount rate and borrows amount CD to undertake those which are acceptable, the company is moved further around the physical investment line to point Y. This would result in a revised amount of the market value of the equity of OJ, and an increase in shareholder wealth of HJ.

However, to *maximize* the increase in the company's equity value from its existing level of OA and hence bring greatest benefit to the shareholders, the company should pay a dividend at time t_0 of virtually *all* of OA (this dividend amount is labelled on Figure 13.4 as OB, where AB represents a minute fraction of the existing equity[5]) and borrow amount BC.

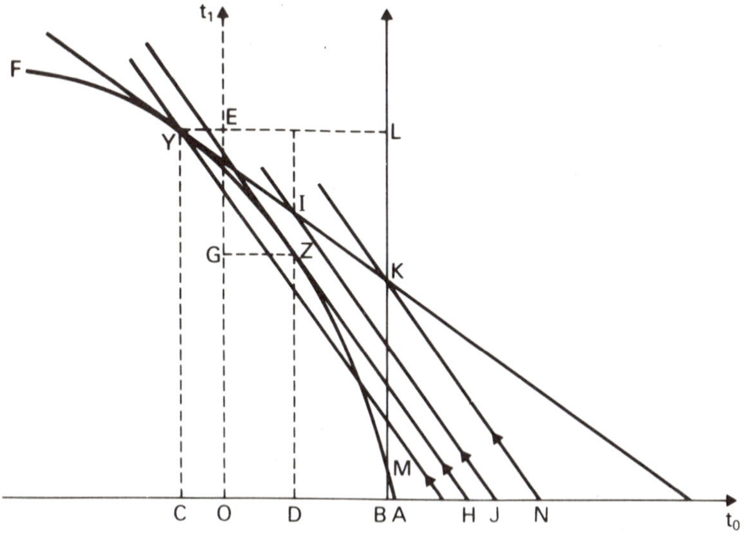

Figure 13.4

This would result in paying lenders an amount in time t_1 of KL, which represents interest and capital repayment, whilst leaving BK as dividend. The combined dividend flow of OB in time t_0 and KB in time t_1 has the effect of maximizing the current value of the company (given the investment opportunities available and the market interest rates) from its existing value of OA to that of ON, which represents an increase in shareholders' wealth of AN.

Therefore, when faced with an ability to borrow money at a rate *below* that charged to individual shareholders, because of the corporate tax relief on debt interest, the company should evaluate its physical investment opportunities using the *corporate* interest rate as the NPV discount rate, and should raise as much as possible of the resulting required investment capital in the form of debt rather than equity (i.e., the company's capital structure should be composed of 99·99% debt capital and 0·01% equity capital).

This rather surprising result is extremely important. It will be further developed in the following chapter.

The role of the WACC

The foregoing analysis has led us to conclude that, in order to locate correctly on the physical investment line, a company should use its own borrowing and lending interest rate as the discount rate for investment appraisal. In the model used, this rate had the appearance of being the company's after-tax cost of debt capital (K_{DAT}), and so how can this be reconciled with our earlier conclusion that a company should use a weighted average of its own (K_D) and its shareholders' (K_E) interest rate: the weighted average cost of capital K_0?

The conclusion that a company's WACC was the appropriate rate to use for investment appraisal was made on the important assumption that the company intended to retain (at least in the medium to longer term) a given capital structure mix of debt and equity. On this basis therefore, the company's financial investment line is not determined by the cost of debt capital but by the weighted average cost of all the types or sources of capital contained within its existing capital structure. Thus, in concluding that the company should use its own market interest rate for investment appraisal purposes, this rate is really its weighted average cost of capital.

But, of course, the Hirshleifer single-period investment-consumption analysis ignores risk. In particular, it ignores different *levels* of risk. Therefore we know just how suspect this conclusion is on the use of the WACC.

However, of more interest is the conclusion of the analysis as far as capital structure is concerned. It appears to be saying that, in a taxed world where *companies* get tax relief on debt interest, but individual investors do not, then companies should use as much debt capital as possible, if they wish to maximize shareholder wealth.

Therefore, up until this point, we have only considered financial managers improving shareholder wealth through good *capital investment* decisions. This analysis now tends to suggest that financial managers can also improve shareholder wealth through good *financing* or *capital structure* decisions. This is the subject of the next two chapters.

SUMMARY

The main points made are as follows:

- A company's *overall* cost of capital can be calculated on the basis of an average of the costs of the individual sources of capital, weighted by the market-valued proportions of those individual sources of capital: the WACC.
- The cost of a *specific* source of capital should not be used as an NPV discount rate. Instead, the company's overall weighted average cost of capital should be used.
- The WACC provides a suitable discount rate, given the validity of four assumptions: the project is marginal; no change in capital structure; no change in systematic risk level and all level-perpetuity cash flows.
- Of the four assumptions, the second and third are crucial. If a project is financed so as to cause a change in capital structure then an NPV/WACC analysis appears inappropriate. NPV is an investment appraisal technique and it cannot adequately handle a simultaneous capital structure decision.
- The third assumption is crucial because of the logic of NPV: the discount rate reflects the return available elsewhere on an investment with similar systematic risk to the project under appraisal.

- A company's WACC reflects its existing systematic risk level. Therefore to provide a suitable discount rate the project must have that level of risk also. In the real world such an assumption is likely to be very suspect.
- It was concluded that, in most circumstances it was likely to be safer to generate a discount rate from CAPM which was tailor-made to the project's systematic risk level, rather than to use WACC.
- Finally, returning to the Hirshleifer single-period investment-consumption analysis, this appeared to indicate that given the real-world situation where the effective after-corporation tax cost of company debt capital was *less* than the cost of capital market borrowing, companies should use as much debt capital as possible if shareholder wealth was to be maximised.

NOTES

1 We are deliberately ignoring the fact here that the issue of debenture capital affects the company's capital structure and so affects the weights and hence the value of K_0. The effect of this change, and whether or not the company's existing K_0 or new K_0 should be used as the discount rate, will be dealt with later.

2 Therefore both the interest cash flow and the dividend cash flow are level perpetuity cash flows.

3 Although so far we have only talked about the beta value of shares, debt capital also possesses systematic risk and so will have a beta value.

4 The word 'leverage' is used in the United States.

5 It is necessary to leave a minute amount so as not to liquidate the company totally.

FURTHER READING

1 There are a number of interesting articles which are, in the main, critical of the use of the WACC as an NPV discount rate. For example, see: F.D. Arditti, 'The Weighted Average Cost of Capital: Some Questions on its Definition, Interpretation and Use', *Journal of Finance*, September 1973, and M.J. Brennan, 'A New Look at the Weighted Average Cost of Capital', *Journal of Business Finance*, Summer 1973.

2 Particularly good, in this context, are: S.M. Keane, 'The Cost of Capital as a Financial Decision Tool', *Journal of Business Finance and Accounting*, Autumn 1978; H.P. Lanser, 'Valuation, Gains from Leverage and the Weighted Average Cost of Capital as a Cut-off Rate', *Engineering Economist*, Fall 1983; and E.F. Brigham and T.C. Tapley, 'Financial Leverage and the Use of the NPV Criterion: A Re-examination', *Financial Management*, Summer 1985.

3 Reference was also made to the fact that, in practice, a single

company-wide discount or hurdle rate is common practice (although it's not always the WACC because of computational difficulties). The article referred to was: E.F. Brigham, 'Hurdle Rates for Screening Capital Expenditure Proposals', *Financial Management*, Autumn 1975.

4 Finally, reference was made to problems with the volatility of the excess market return. See: R.G. Ibbotson and R.A. Sinquefield, 'Stocks, Bonds, Bills and Inflation: The Past and the Future', Financial Analysis Foundation, 1982.

QUICKIE QUESTIONS

1 Given the following information, what is the company's weighted average cost of capital?

$d_0 = 5\text{p}$ $P_E = 88\text{p}$ cum. div.
$g = 0{\cdot}07$ 24m shares in issue.
£25m 15% irredeemable debt. $P_D = £110$ ex. int.
£10m 12% irredeemable debt, unquoted.
£3m 7-year term loan at 4% over base.
Bank base rate = 10%.
Corporation tax = 35%.

2 What is the argument for why the cost of a *specific* source of capital should not be used as the NPV discount rate?
3 What are the assumptions behind the use of the WACC as an NPV discount rate?
4 What is the problem faced by a diversified company wishing to use its WACC as an NPV discount rate?
5 Why is the CAPM likely to produce a superior NPV discount rate than WACC?
6 Why is the company's *effective* cost of debt capital likely to be less than the rate available to investors, given similar risk?
7 If the company can borrow more cheaply than can investors, what implications does this have for the company's capital structure?
8 How is a company's capital structure measured?

PROBLEMS

1 The directors of Osmin plc are considering opening a factory to manufacture a new product. Detailed forecasts of the product's expected cash flows have been made, and it is estimated that an initial capital investment of £2·5 million is required. The company's current (t_0) authorized share capital consists of 4 million ordinary shares, each with a nominal value of 25p. During the last five years the number of shares in issue has remained constant at 3 million, and the market price per share is 135p ex div. The dividends for the last five years have been as follows:

Year	t_{-4}	t_{-3}	t_{-2}	t_{-1}	t_0
Dividend per share (pence)	10·0	10·8	11·6	13·6	13·6

Osmin plc currently has in issue 800,000 8% debentures redeemable in 4 years' time. The current market price of these debentures is £82·5 ex interest. The company also has outstanding a £900,000 bank loan repayable in 8 years' time. The rate of interest on this loan is variable, being fixed at 1½% above the bank's base rate which is currently 15%.

Required:

(a) Calculate the weighted average cost of capital (WACC) for Osmin plc.

(b) Explain briefly to the directors of Osmin plc what assumptions they are making if the WACC calculated in (a) above is used to discount the expected cash flows of the project.

(c) Describe the practical problems that might be encountered when attempting to compute the WACC for a large UK listed company.

Ignore taxation.

2 Redskins plc is a holding company owning shares in various subsidiary companies. Its directors are currently considering several projects which will increase the range of the business activities undertaken by Redskins plc and its subsidiaries. The directors would like to use discounted cash flow techniques in their evaluation of these projects but as yet no weighted average cost of capital has been calculated.

Redskins plc has an authorized share capital of 10 million 25p ordinary shares, of which 8 million have been issued. The current *ex div* market price per ordinary share is £1·10, a dividend of 10p per share having been paid recently. The company's project analyst has calculated that 18% is the most appropriate after-tax cost of equity capital. Extracts from the latest balance sheets for both the group and the holding company are given below:

	Redskins plc and subsidiaries	*Redskins plc*
	£000s	*£000s*
Issued share capital	2,000	2,000
Share premium	1,960	1,960
Reserves	3,745	708
Shareholders' funds	7,705	4,668
Minority interests	895	–
3% Irredeemable debentures	1,400	–
9% Redeemable debentures	1,500	1,500
6% Loan stock	2,000	2,000
Bank loans	1,540	600
Total long term liabilities	6,440	4,100

All debt interest is payable annually and all the current year's payments will be made shortly. The current *cum interest* market prices for £100 nominal value stock are £31·60 and £103·26 for the 3% and 9% debentures respectively. Both the 9% debentures and the 6% loan stock are redeemable at par in ten years' time. The 6% loan stock is not traded on the open market, but the analyst estimates that its effective pre-tax cost is 10% per annum. The bank loans bear interest at 2% above base rate (which is currently 11%) and are repayable in six years. The effective corporation tax rate of Redskins plc is 35%.

Required:
(a) Calculate the effective after-tax weighted average cost of capital as required by the directors.
(b) Discuss the problems that are encountered in the estimation of a company's weighted average cost of capital when the following are used as sources of long term finance:
  (i) bank overdraft
  (ii) convertible loan stock.
(c) Outline the fundamental assumptions that are made whenever the weighted average cost of capital of a company is used as the discount rate in net present value calculations.

3 Bonzo plc is a divisionalized company, quoted on the Lodon Stock Exchange. Two of its divisions are currently evaluating investment proposals and have submitted them to Head Office for approval.

The project cash flows are as follows:

Cement division	*£000s*	*Timber division*	*£000s*
Year: 0	−200	Year: 0	−150
1	+100	1	+ 75
2	+100	2	+ 48·36
3	+ 79·3	3	+ 75

The following information about the company is available:

Current Balance Sheet (summarized)

		£000s
Assets:	Net fixed assets	7,500
	Net current assets	2,460
		9,960
Finance:	30m 10p Ordinary shares	3,000
	Reserves	6,960
		9,960

Dividend/share and Earnings/share record

Year	*Dividend (p)*	*Earnings (p)*
t_{-4}	5·12	6·19
t_{-3}	5·32	6·44
t_{-2}	5·53	6·69
t_{-1}	5·76	6·90
t_0 (current year)	5·99	7·31

The current total market value of the company's shares is £13·35 million, ex div. Bonzo plc has a beta of 1·16. The cement industry has a beta of 1·50 and the timber industry has a beta of 0·66. The annual return on 3-year Government Stock is currently 11% and the expected return on the F.T. All-Share Index is 17%. Ignore tax.

Required:

(a) The company usually evaluate all investment proposals with NPV, using the cost of company capital as the discount rate. Estimate this discount rate and evaluate both projects.

(b) Advise the company as to why they should evaluate projects using risk-adjusted discount rates. Estimate an appropriate rate for each project and re-evaluate them both.

(c) Comment and explain, with the help of a diagram, the implications of your answers to parts (a) and (b).

Use discount rates to *two places of decimal only* in all calculations. Assume all-equity financing throughout.

14
The capital structure decision

Chapter Contents

THE MODIGLIANI AND MILLER CAPITAL STRUCTURE HYPOTHESIS

The analysis in the previous chapter led us to an interesting provisional conclusion. Management who wish to maximize their company's shareholders' wealth should gear the company up to such an extent that its capital structure would consist almost entirely (99%+) of debt capital, with the very minimum of equity capital. This conclusion does not seem to match with practice,[1] where companies' capital structures rarely contain more than 50% debt capital and the average level of gearing is around 25% debt capital and 75% equity capital.

An optimal capital structure

To take a closer look at the problem, let us begin by posing the question: Can any particular ratio of debt to equity in a company's capital structure be said to be optimal in terms of helping to increase the wealth of ordinary shareholders? This is an important question for several reasons.

First, and most important, up to this stage we have assumed that management could increase the wealth of ordinary shareholders *only* by the decisions they made about physical investment projects. If, however, an optimal gearing ratio exists, then it would appear that management could also increase shareholder wealth by manipulating the company's capital structure through the selection of particular types (e.g., debt and equity) of project finance. In other words, not only can the *investment* decision enhance shareholders' wealth, but so too can the *financing* decision.

A second reason for the importance of the question about the existence of an optimal capital structure is the implications that it has for the approach which we have developed to investment decision making. Hitherto, we have assumed that the question of *how* a particular investment project is to be financed (the financing decision) can be taken separately from the investment decision itself (as a direct result of the Separation Theorem). The investment decision has therefore been examined in isolation. If the financing decision can be shown to be important for the company – in terms of the desired capital structure – then we may have to revise our approach to investment appraisal.

A third reason could also be proposed. In suggesting the possible use of the weighted average cost of capital for discounting and appraisal purposes we assumed that a company's capital structure would remain constant. This assumption would obviously gain support if it could be shown that an optimal capital structure does exist for a company. Because, then, management would wish to attain and *remain* at that particular gearing ratio.

The capital structure decision was first rigorously analysed by two Americans, Modigliani and Miller (universally known in the abbreviated form of M and M), in a justly famous article that first appeared in 1958. Much of our analysis in this section will be based upon the approach that they took. Initially we will assume that there is *no tax*.

The total market value model

We introduced the term 'gearing' or 'leverage' when examining the costs of the various sources of capital which are available to a company. We defined the term as the ratio of the market value of a company's debt capital to the market value of its equity capital.[2] The distinction between debt and equity was important because each type of capital bore a different level of risk: debt capital was a less risky investment in a company than an equity capital investment in that same company.

This risk differential resulted from the fact that debt capital interest had first claim on a company's annual net earnings, ahead of equity capital dividends. In addition, debt capital had repayment preference over equity capital in circumstances of company liquidation. As a result of this risk differential, the suppliers of debt capital to a company would require a lower return than the suppliers of equity, because they bore less risk.

In order to calculate the costs of the different capital sources, two valuation models were constructed both based on the premise that an object's value is determined by the flow of future net benefits which it produces. Therefore, a company's equity capital derived its value from the future (discounted) flow of dividends which it was expected to produce. Similarly, debt capital was valued on the basis of the summation of the future expected (discounted) interest flow and the redemption payment.

From these two valuation models, it follows that the total market value of a company (debt plus equity), V_0, must be derived from its expected future (discounted) net cash flow – which consists of its future dividend flow and its future interest and redemption flow. It will be helpful, for later analysis, to restate this in terms of the notation used earlier when analysing a company's cost of capital.

Table 14.1 gives this restatement (ignoring taxation for the present), under the assumption of constant annual dividends in perpetuity and irredeemable debentures. If we let $V_E K_E + V_D K_D = Y$, and if we assume that none of a company's net cash flow is retained but is paid out in full each year as dividends and interest, then Y is a constant and so a company's total market value is given by:

$$V_0 = \frac{Y}{K_0}$$

Table 14.1

If Y is the company's total annual cash flow which is assumed to be a level perpetuity that is paid out each year as dividends and interest:

$$V_E = \frac{Y - V_D \times K_D}{K_E} \qquad (1)$$

$$V_E \times K_E = Y - V_D \times K_D \qquad (2)$$

Taking expression (2) and factoring out V_0:

$$\frac{V_0 \times V_E \times K_E}{V_0} = Y - \frac{V_D \times K_D \times V_0}{V_0} \qquad (3)$$

$$\frac{V_0 \times V_E \times K_E}{V_0} + \frac{V_D \times K_D \times V_0}{V_0} = Y \qquad (4)$$

$$V_0\left[\frac{V_E \times K_E}{V_0} + \frac{V_D \times K_D}{V_0}\right] = Y \qquad (5)$$

$$V_0 = \frac{Y}{\dfrac{V_E \times K_E}{V_0} + \dfrac{V_D \times K_D}{V_0}} = \frac{Y}{K_0} \qquad (6)$$

where $\mathrm{V_E} \times \mathrm{K_E} = D$ and $\mathrm{V_D} \times \mathrm{K_D} = \mathrm{I}$.

Gearing and V_0 in a no-tax world

The question that we wish to examine is whether or not a company's gearing ratio (i.e., its capital structure) can affect its total market value.[3] From the above it should be clear that changing a company's gearing ratio will affect its total market value (V_0) *only* if it causes a change in either the company's annual net cash flow (Y) or its weighted average cost of capital (K_0). We can argue that changing the gearing ratio of a company will *not* affect either of these factors, as follows.

Changing the gearing ratio cannot have any effect on the company's annual cash flow (Y) as that is determined by the assets in which the company has invested and not by how those assets are financed. The only effect that changing the gearing has on the firm's annual cash flow is that it changes the *proportions* of the cash flow that are paid out as dividends and interest. The more highly geared the firm, the greater is the proportion of its annual cash flow paid out as interest and the smaller the proportion paid out as dividends. However, changing the level of gearing will *not* change the level of the annual cash flow, just its destination (between debt and equity holders).

Changing the gearing ratio will also not affect the value of K_0. The company's weighted average cost of capital reflects the average return required by the suppliers of the capital. Its level if determined (as in any rate of return) by the degree of systematic risk in the *company's* overall cash flow. There is no reason why changing the gearing ratio should affect the systematic risk of the cash flow being generated by the company's assets, and hence changing the gearing ratio will not affect K_0.[4]

From this analysis we can draw two important conclusions. The first is that simply changing a company's capital structure cannot (by itself) change the company's total market value. Thus companies can only enhance their shareholders' wealth by making good *investment* decisions. The *financing* decision (through which a company's capital structure or gearing ratio can be changed) *cannot* affect shareholder wealth.

The second conclusion is that companies whose *assets* display the same degree of systematic risk can be expected to have the same weighted average cost of capital, *even though* they may have entirely different gearing ratios. This is because it is the systematic risk of the company's collection of assets which determines its overall return of K_0.

The assumptions

However, before proceeding further with this analysis, we should first make explicit the very important assumptions upon which it is based. These are:

1. At any given level of risk, individuals and companies can all borrow at the same rate of interest, which remains constant regardless of the gearing.
2. There are no costs attached to market transactions, the supply of information or the process of bankruptcy.[5]
3. There is no difference between corporate borrowing and personal borrowing in terms of risk (e.g., there is no limited liability advantage for companies).
4. There is no taxation.

An example

Suppose we are considering the setting up of a company which would operate a set of machines that would cost £100,000 in total. These machines involve a given level of systematic risk which requires the

Table 14.2

	Option 1	Option 2	Option 3
Machine annual cash flow	15,000	15,000	15,000
Less interest payments	–	5,000	8,000
Dividend payments	15,000	10,000	7,000
Return on equity (D/V_E)	15%	20%	35%
Return on debt (I/V_D)	–	10%	10%
WACC (Y/V_0)	15%	15%	15%
Total value of company (Y/K_0)	100,000	100,000	100,000

expectation of an annual return of 15%. Therefore they are expected to produce an annual net cash flow of £15,000 in perpetuity. This cash flow will be paid out in its entirety each year, to the suppliers of capital.

Three different financing packages are being considered:

1 The machines are financed entirely by equity capital.
2 £50,000 of 10% debt (the current market cost of debt capital) is raised with the remaining £50,000 supplied via equity capital.
3 £80,000 of 10% debt is raised, with the balance provided by equity capital.

Table 14·2 illustrates the returns to equity and debt, and the weighted average cost of capital that would result from each of these three financing options.

It should be noted that this example does nothing to prove or disprove the relationship between a company's gearing ratio and its weighted average cost of capital that was argued in the previous section. Rather, it is *based* upon that relationship, in that it assumes that K_0 remains unchanged, despite the different gearing ratios. As a result of that assumption (and the four assumptions listed above), the rest follows.

However, this example does serve a very useful purpose in that it highlights the fact that although K_0 remains unchanged as gearing changes, the cost of equity capital *does* change. It is the relationship between gearing and K_E that is now examined.

Business and financial risk

In the earlier discussion of portfolio theory and the CAPM we saw that total risk could be split up into two components: systematic (or undiversifiable) risk and unsystematic (or diversifiable) risk. Further, we saw that it was only an investment's systematic risk that determined its expected return. We can now split a *company's* systematic risk into two components: *business* risk and *financial* risk.

The business risk of a company refers to the systematic risk of the *operating* cash flows. In other words, business risk relates to the systematic risk of the net cash flows that result from the operation of the company's *assets.* Both the equity and the debt holders in a company bear this risk.

However, financial risk refers to some *additional* systematic risk which is borne only by the equity holders of a geared company.[6]

In Chapter 12, when we discussed the cost of debt capital, it was pointed out that K_D was only the *explicit* cost of debt capital and that there was another cost, an *implicit* (or hidden) cost. This implicit cost is caused by the presence of financial risk.

Financial risk arises directly out of the gearing process and is borne by the equity shareholders in a geared company. It is caused through debt capital having priority over equity capital in both the distribution of the company's annual net cash flow (as interest and dividends) and in any final liquidation distribution. As interest payments to debt holders must legally be paid in full by the company before any dividend payments can be made, the greater the proportion of debt capital within a company's capital structure, the greater the probability that the company will have no cash remaining with which to pay a dividend. This risk of a reduced or zero dividend, which is borne by ordinary shareholders, is termed financial risk, and its severity is likely to increase as a company increases its level of gearing.

Diagrammatically, a company's expected annual net operating cash flow can be portrayed as a probability distribution. In an all-equity company (on the assumption of no retention by the company of this net cash flow), the probability distribution of the net operating cash flow also represents the probability distribution of the dividend flow. Gearing up has the effect of imposing a fixed annual charge on this distribution (the interest payments), so shifting the *dividend payment* probability distribution to the left. (See Figure 14.1.) The greater the proportion of debt in the capital structure, the further will be the leftward movement and the greater will be the proportion of the dividend probability distribution falling within the negative portion of the horizontal axis. Thus the greater is the risk of a reduced or zero dividend as gearing is increased.

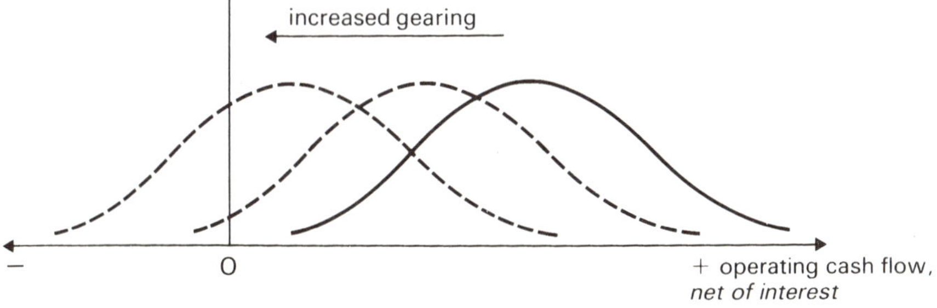

Figure 14.1

Thus financial risk arises from the fact that equity holders are always at the back of the annual 'pay-out queue'. The more highly geared the company, the greater amount of interest that has to be paid before dividends can be paid (i.e., the longer the queue in front of the equity holders), and hence the greater amount of financial risk borne by ordinary shareholders.

This financial risk is *systematic risk* in that it cannot be diversified away. As a result, shareholders will require a higher expected return on their capital for bearing increased amounts of financial risk. Therefore as a company increases its gearing, the amount of financial risk borne by ordinary shareholders increases and, in consequence, the cost of equity capital rises.

This effect is seen in the example in Table 14.2. As the gearing ratio increases, the return on equity rises from 15% to 35%. In option 1, the 15% return on equity simply reflects the business risk of the assets. However, the 20% return in option 2 reflects a 15% return for holding the business risk of the assets, *plus* a 5% return for holding the financial risk represented by the level of gearing involved. Further, it is important to note that the shareholders have *not* gained in moving (say) from option 1 to option 2. The higher return on equity simply reflects the higher risks involved in holding equity capital.

Asset betas and gearing

Given that beta values are used as an index of systematic risk, it follows from the above that we can distinguish between the beta value of a *geared* company's equity and the beta value of its assets. The reason for this is that the assets will only contain '*business*' systematic risk, whereas the equity will contain both '*business*' and '*financial*' systematic risk.

We know from our discussion of the CAPM in Chapter 10 that the beta value of a *collection* of securities is a weighted average of the beta values of the individual securities. This allows us to conclude therefore that the beta value of an *asset* is a weighted average of the beta values of the collection of *securities* that finance that asset. (In reality this relationship is determined the other way around. The betas of the financing securities will be determined by the systematic risk of the asset they are financing.)

Hence:

$$\beta_{\text{company assets}} = \beta_{\text{equity}} \times \frac{V_E}{V_0} + \beta_{\text{debt}} \times \frac{V_D}{V_0}$$

Further, if we assume that a company's debt capital is virtually riskless, then $\beta_{\text{debt}} \approx 0$ and so the relationship reduces to:

$$\beta_{\text{company assets}} = \beta_{\text{equity}} \times \frac{V_E}{V_0}$$

and

$$\beta_{\text{equity}} = \beta_{\text{company assets}} \times \frac{V_0}{V_E}$$

Thus, for an all-equity company, the asset beta and the equity beta will be identical, but for a geared company the equity beta will be *greater than*

Table 14.3

Company
Balance Sheet

£ Liabilities = £ Assets

↓ ↓

Systematic risk of liabilities = Systematic risk of assets

↓ ↓ ↓

Equity Debt

↓ ↓

$$\beta_{\text{equity}} \times \frac{V_E}{V_0} + \beta_{\text{debt}} \times \frac{V_D}{V_0} = \beta_{\text{assets}}$$

↓ ↓ ↓

$$K_E \times \frac{V_E}{V_0} + K_D \times \frac{V_D}{V_0} = K_0$$

the asset beta. The equity capital contains more systematic risk than the assets because it involves both business *and* financial risk.

This distinction between asset betas and equity betas is important in relation to the use of beta values in determining a project discount rate. We shall return to examine this in the following chapter. Table 14.3 develops the relationship further.

Gearing and K_E

We shall turn now to examine the exact nature of the relationship between gearing and the cost of equity capital, but all the while retaining our set of specified assumptions. The relationship can be derived from the dividend valuation model as is shown in Table 14·4.

Table 14·4

Given the relationship:

$$V_0 = \frac{Y}{K_0} \qquad (1)$$

then

$$Y = V_0 K_0 \equiv V_E K_0 + V_D K_0 \qquad (2)$$

The dividend valuation model can be expressed as

$$K_E = \frac{D}{V_E} \equiv \frac{Y - V_D K_D}{V_E} \qquad (3)$$

Substituting the definition of Y given in (2):

$$K_E = \frac{V_E K_0}{V_E} + \frac{V_D K_0}{V_E} - \frac{V_D K_D}{V_E} \qquad (4)$$

Cancelling and simplifying:

$$K_E = K_0 + (K_0 - K_D)\frac{V_D}{V_E}$$

From Table 14·4 it can be seen that the cost of equity capital of a company consists of two elements, K_0 (which reflects the expected return required for the business risk of the company's assets), plus $(K_0 - K_D)\ V_D/V_E$. This latter element represents the *financial risk premium* and it is a *positive* linear function of the gearing ratio.

Therefore, returning to the example used in Table 14·2. Option 3 (say) involved the following data:

$$K_0 = 15\%$$
$$K_D = 10\%$$
$$V_D = £80{,}000$$
$$V_E = £20{,}000$$

Hence

$$K_E = 15\% + (15\% - 10\%) \times \frac{80{,}000}{20{,}000} = \underline{\underline{35\%}}$$

Earlier, we concluded that companies with assets that had the same degree of business risk (the same asset betas) would have the same weighted average costs of capital, whatever their gearing ratios. Therefore a slightly different (but equivalent) way of expressing the relationship between gearing and the cost of equity capital can be given:

$$K_{E_g} = K_{E_{ug}} + (K_{E_{ug}} - K_D)\frac{V_D}{V_E}$$

where K_{E_g} = Cost of equity capital of a geared company
and $K_{E_{ug}}$ = Cost of equity capital of a *similar business risk*, but *all-equity financed* company.

The graphical relationship

The relationship between a company's gearing ratio and the costs of its various types of capital is shown in Figure 14.2. The lower diagram illustrates the fact that the total worth of a company's assets (and hence the total worth of the company) remains constant, however the assets are financed. Although, once again, it should be pointed out that this set of relationships – often referred to as the *M and M No Tax Case* – was developed under the four sets of assumptions specified earlier.

THE ARBITRAGE PROOF

All the conclusions that we have drawn from the foregoing analysis are based on the initial premise that a company's gearing ratio does not itself determine or affect either its WACC or its total market value; but what reason do we have for believing this initial premise to be correct? Modigliani and Miller showed that if this was found *not* to hold true in practice (for example, if two companies with the same degree of business risk were found to have different WACCs) then that would represent a short-run *disequilibrium* situation.

In such circumstances, *arbitragers* would move into the market, *selling*

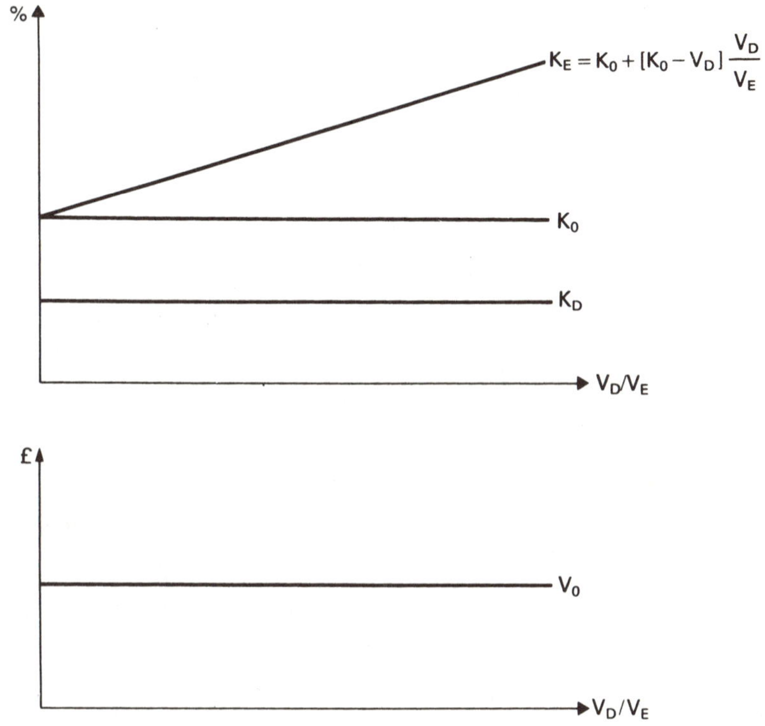

Figure 14.2

shares in the company with the lower valued K_0 and *buying* shares in the company with the higher valued K_0. They would do so because they could profit from such transactions.

Investors would continue to trade until the WACCs of the two companies equated. This equating of the weighted average costs of capital would be brought about through normal market supply and demand forces (selling shares causing the price to fall and vice versa). Once this position was reached, no further gains could be made, and equilibrium would have been restored.

The word *arbitrage* is a technical term meaning that two identical goods cannot be sold in the same market for different prices. But if such a situation does arise, then it will not persist for long as dealers will start to buy at the lower price and sell at the higher price, thereby making a profit. Buying pressure (increased demand) will force up the price of the lower priced goods and selling pressure (increased supply) will force down the price of the higher priced goods.

Although stockbrokers do not often refer to this process in the share market by the term arbitrage, many of their transactions are arbitrage deals. The same is true of many commodity transactions on the commodity exchanges – but there they *do* refer to them by the technical name of arbitrage, as do foreign exchange dealers. In fact arbitrage is a very common form of transaction in many different markets.

An arbitrage example

As an example, suppose that there are two companies, A and B, with identical levels of business risk, although their annual net cash flows are of different magnitudes. Data on the two companies are given in Table 14·5.

Because these two companies have identical levels of business risk, their WACCs should be the same. As they are not, an arbitrage opportunity exists: specifically for shareholders in company B (the company with the lower K_0) to move out of B and into company A.

Consider an investor who owns shares in B that have a current market value of £30,000. Those shares can be expected to produce an annual dividend of £30,000 × 0·166 = £5000. For this expected annual dividend flow the shareholder is bearing two types of risk: he holds the business risk of the company, plus he holds financial risk as company B is geared.

Table 14·5

	Company	
	A	*B*
Year	1 → ∞ £000s	1 → ∞ £000s
Annual dividends (D)	1,000	2,000
Annual interest (I)		400
Annual cash flow (Y)	1,000	2,400
Equity market value (V_E)	6,250	12,000
Debt market value (V_D)		4,000
Total market value (V_0)	6,250	16,000
Equity cost of capital ($K_E = D/V_E$)	0·16	0·166
Debt cost of capital ($K_D = I/V_D$)	–	0·10
Weighted average cost of capital ($K_0 = Y/V_0$)	0·16	0·15
Number of shares in issue	6·5m	10m
Market price per share (P_E)	50p	120p

If he were to sell his £30,000 shareholding and simply invest the proceeds in the shares of company A, the two investments (shares in A, compared with shares in B) would *not* be comparable as company A has an all-equity capital structure; thus although the business risk of the two investments would be the same, the shareholding in A would result in no financial risk being held.

To be able to compare like with like requires the investor to maintain the *same* level of financial risk in company A as that held as a shareholder in company B. To do so, he substitutes home-made gearing (or home-made financial risk) for the corporate gearing that was borne as a shareholder in B.

Company B has borrowed (at the market rate of interest, K_D) £1 for every £3 of its shareholders' capital (i.e., the debt–equity ratio is 1:3), and so the investor should similarly borrow £1 (at the perfect capital market interest rate of 10%) for every £3 of his own cash. Hence he borrows £10,000 and, by so doing, maintains his existing financial risk level.

The investor has now amassed a total of £40,000 (£10,000 borrowed and £30,000 of his own) and *all* of this is now invested in the shares of company A. He thereby maintains both the business and the financial risk levels he held as a shareholder in company B. This shareholding in A can be expected to produce an annual dividend of £40,000 × 0·16 = £6,400. Out of this he has to pay an annual interest charge on his loan of £10,000 × 0·10 = £1,000, leaving him a net annual expected cash flow of £5,400. Thus the investor – through an arbitrage transaction – has increased his annual income by £400 *with no change in either of the risk levels borne.*

Other shareholders in company B will also see this opportunity to make an arbitrage gain and will undertake similar transactions. The net result will be that selling pressure on B's shares will force the market price down to a point at which the WACCs of the two companies equate. Once this point is reached, there will be no further gains to be made from arbitrage dealings and so the price will stabilize: equilibrium will have been attained.

If the (not too unreasonable) assumption is made that the market correctly prices company A's equity and company B's debt, then the foregoing analysis suggests that the market value of B's equity will fall sufficiently far to raise the company's WACC to 16% (i.e., equal to that of company A). The equilibrium value of B's equity can then be calculated, as is shown in Table 14.6.

Thus the market value of company B's equity capital will fall from £12m to £11m. In other words the shares will fall in price from 120p each to 110p each.

Table 14.6

In equilibrium the WACC of company B will be 16% (that is, equal to the WACC of company A). Therefore the equilibrium total market value of company B is (£000s):

$$V_0 = \frac{2{,}400}{0{\cdot}16} = 15{,}000$$

Given that company B's debt is correctly valued at 4,000, then the equilibrium value of company B's equity will be:

$$V_E = 15{,}000 - 4{,}000 = \underline{11{,}000}$$

At which point $K_E = \dfrac{2{,}000}{11{,}000} = 0{\cdot}182$ (approx.) which is exactly what is predicted by our M and M expression for the cost of equity capital:

$$K_E = 0{\cdot}16 + [0{\cdot}16 - 0{\cdot}10]\frac{4{,}000}{11{,}000} = 0{\cdot}182 \text{ (approx.)}$$

However notice that this expression will only provide K_E when *equilibrium* values of K_0 (or $K_{E_{ug}}$), K_D, V_E and V_D are used.

Reverse arbitrage

However, suppose that the stock-market got things slightly wrong and overreacted to the arbitrage transactions taking place, with the result that company B's shares fell in price to 104p per share. The situation would be as follows (figures in £'000s):

$$\text{Company B:}\quad \begin{aligned} K_E &= £2{,}000/£10{,}400 = 0{\cdot}1923 \\ K_D &= £400/£4{,}000 \quad\;\; = 0{\cdot}10 \\ K_0 &= £2{,}400/£14{,}400 = 0{\cdot}166 \end{aligned}$$

As the company's WACC is now *above* that of company A, there would be an arbitrage opportunity in a move from the shares in company A into company B. However, notice that such a move, unlike the previous example, would involve going *from* an all-equity company *to* a geared company. This situation is sometimes referred to as *reverse* arbitrage, but it is rather misleading to do so as it is simply another arbitrage transaction, but now the *mechanics* of the move differ.

For example, suppose that there is an investor who holds £5,000 worth of shares in company A. He presently expects to receive an annual dividend of £5,000 × 0·16 = £800. This is in exchange for holding just the business risk of company A. As the company is all-equity, the shareholder bears no financial risk. Thus the problem now is how does the shareholder sell his shares in A and move into B – to take advantage of the temporary disequilibrium price of B's equity – while maintaining his current level of *zero* financial risk?

One approach is to buy *both* the debt and equity of company B in the same proportion as B's debt–equity ratio. Therefore the shareholder would sell his shares in A for £5,000 and buy £4 of B's debt for every £10·40 of B's equity that was bought (B's debt–equity ratio is now £4m:£10·4m). Thus he would buy £3,611·11 of B's equity and £1,388·89 of B's debt.

This process by which the investor maintains his zero financial risk level can be explained in several ways. Perhaps the most intuitively appealing is that although he takes on a *positive* amount of financial risk through his equity holding in B, he also takes on a *negative* amount of financial risk through his debt holding. The net effect of holding both securities, in a combination equal to the gearing ratio, is that the financial risk is cancelled out.[7]

The effect of this reverse arbitrage transaction would be to give the investor an annual expected dividend of £3,611·11 × 0·1923 =£694·42 and annual interest of £1,388·89 × 0·1 = £138·89. Thus a total annual income of £833·31 would be expected, which represents a gain of £33·31 over his original investment in company A, with no change in the risk borne.

Once again, other investors are likely to spot the opportunity to make this arbitrage gain and will act in a similar fashion. Their combined effect will be to bring about an equilibrium position and the equating of the WACCs of the two companies.

Two further points

In both the example of 'normal arbitrage' and of 'reverse arbitrage' there has been a concern to maintain a particular level of financial risk in order to allow investment returns to be comparable. However, in both cases, this was done on the basis of B's gearing ratio when in *disequilibrium.* Company B's equilibrium debt–equity ratio is 4:11. Therefore a more precise approach to holding financial risk at a given level would be to utilize this equilibrium ratio.

Thus in the normal arbitrage example, the investor would have substituted home-made for corporate gearing by borrowing £10,909·09 and the resulting arbitrage gain would have been slightly higher at £454·54. Similarly, in the reverse arbitrage example, the investor would have bought £1,333·33 of company B's debt and £3,666·67 of its equity. This again would result in a slightly increased arbitrage gain of £838·43.

Finally, what if an investor identifies the possibility for gain by arbitraging between two geared companies? In these circumstances *both* mechanisms have to be employed. For example suppose company C had a debt–equity ratio of 1:3 whereas company D had a debt–equity ratio of 2:1. A shareholder in C wishes to move to D in order to take an arbitrage gain but also wishes to maintain his existing level of financial risk. This can be achieved by selling his shareholding in C, borrowing £1 for every £3 of sale proceeds and then applying the whole amount (borrowings plus own cash) to buying both the debt and equity of D in the proportion of £2 of debt for every £1 of equity.

Conclusions

The analysis *up to this point* allows three important conclusions to be made. The first is that companies with this same level of business risk will, in equilibrium, have the same weighted average expected cost of capital. Secondly, changes in a company's gearing ratio should leave its WACC unchanged. The increased return required by ordinary shareholders that arises out of an increase in gearing represents the compensation required for bearing additional financial risk. It is determined by the expression: $K_E = K_0 + (K_0 - K_D)\,V_D/V_E$. Finally, and perhaps most important, the analysis leads us to conclude that the financing decision is relatively unimportant. It can have no bearing on the value of the company and so does not affect the wealth of ordinary shareholders.

In respect of the second of these three conclusions, the Modigliani and Miller analysis can be couched in very simple terms:

As a company increases its gearing, *two* effects occur. The first is that the company gains an *advantage* in that debt capital is cheaper than equity capital. The reason for this is that debt is a lower risk security than equity as debt holders get preferential 'pay-out' treatment, hence debt requires a lower expected return.

The second effect is that the company incurs a *disadvantage* in that the expected return required by equity capital increases. This is because increasing the gearing increases the financial risk held by equity and so forces up the required expected return, by way of compensation.

These two effects – the advantage and the disadvantage – are two sides of the same coin. They both arise through the same phenomenon: debt holders are paid before equity holders. Therefore it is not surprising that the two effects exactly cancel each other out, so that the net effect is zero: changing the gearing leaves the company's total market value and its WACC unaltered.

The assumptions

Having outlined the basic M and M capital structure hypothesis, and before proceeding to examine alternative theories about the relationship between a company's gearing ratio and the cost of its equity capital, let us now take a closer look at the many assumptions upon which the hypothesis is based. In particular, we shall look at the assumptions underlying the arbitrage process which helps to restore the M and M equilibrium position to short-run disequilibrium stock market prices and which is held up as proof of their capital structure theory.

Arbitrage, as we know, is a technical term to describe a supply and demand market process which prevents perfect substitutes from selling at different prices in the same market. The key phrase here is *perfect substitutes* and so, for the arbitrage process to act as a proof of the M and M hypothesis, ordinary shares in an all-equity company must be seen as (or must be able to be made) a perfect substitute for shares in a geared company.

We know from the valuation principles, which were defined originally, that value results from the future flow of net benefits and the certainty (or otherwise) attached to that future flow. Therefore, if we take two companies with the same expected annual cash flow and the same level of business risk, it follows that they should have identical total market values. However, we also know that if one company is all-equity and one company is geared, their ordinary shares are not perfect substitutes for each other, because the shares in the geared company include an additional risk element: financial risk.

In order to make the ordinary shares in the two companies perfect substitutes in terms of the risk borne in holding them, the investors in the geared company must be able to substitute home-made gearing (i.e., personally gear themselves) for corporate gearing. (We saw this process being undertaken in the first example used above.) To be able to do so, there must be no difference between the cost and risk of corporate borrowing (and hence gearing) and individual borrowing (gearing). This requires two assumptions of highly questionable real-world validity: individuals and companies must be able to borrow at the same rate of interest and the facility of limited liability for companies either must not exist, or must also extend to individuals.

In practice, individuals almost invariably have to pay a higher rate of interest on borrowed money than do companies, and in that borrowing their liability is unlimited, whereas companies have the protection of limited liability. Therefore, quite plainly, corporate and individual borrowing differs both in terms of cost and of risk, and so this requirement of the arbitrage process, as far as share dealings are concerned, appears to be unfulfilled.

However, the discrepancy between theory and practice can be resolved to some extent by the fact that for share prices to regain an equilibrium position, not *all* investors have to arbitrage in order to cause the necessary price changes through the supply and demand market mechanism. Just sufficient share transactions are required to 'move the market'. There are many limited liability companies with substantial holdings of shares in other companies, who could themselves undertake arbitrage transactions (and thereby avoid the problems outlined above), and so bring about market equilibrium.

This counter-argument, against the real-world invalidity of the two assumptions required for effective stock market arbitraging, appears reasonably sound – at least in theory – although it should be pointed out that there is some evidence to suggest that many institutional investors do not readily indulge in arbitrage transactions. However, there is another assumption involved in the arbitrage process which in practice does not hold, and so causes frictional problems: the assumption that all market transactions are undertaken at no cost (i.e., no stockbrokers' fees or commissions).

In practice, market transaction costs can be *relatively* expensive. Such a cost is likely to interfere with the smooth and efficient operation of arbitraging (e.g., the gain that might accrue to an investor from arbitraging may be completely offset by the transaction costs involved, and so these costs could be expected to interfere with the equilibrium producing mechanism). However, it could be claimed that transaction costs will only out-weigh arbitrage gains either in very small share transactions or at the 'fine-tuning' stage, when the amount of disequilibrium remaining (and hence the level of arbitrage gains) is small.

Thus, although transaction costs will (as always) interfere with the economic mechanism, the degree of interference may well be relatively unimportant. We shall return to this assumption later, for it contains another, implicit assumption, that bankruptcy costs are zero. But before doing so, we shall examine the effects of two other assumptions within the hypothesis: that the cost of debt capital remains constant whatever the level of gearing, and that there is no taxation.

A rising cost of debt

No really satisfactory reconciliation with the conclusions of the M and M theory exists, once the more realistic view is taken that the cost of debt capital to a company rises as gearing (and hence risk to the suppliers of debt) rises. Logically, as a company gears up, the cost of debt should increase, so that K_D approaches what would have been the cost of equity capital, if the company had remained ungeared. Because, at the extreme of 99·99% gearing, the risks borne by the suppliers of debt capital would be virtually the same as the risks borne by equity capital if the company were ungeared.

The problem with a rising cost of debt capital is that, for the company's weighted average cost of capital to remain a constant, its cost of equity capital must start to *decline* as the company reaches very high levels of gearing. Figure 14·3 illustrates this rather unlikely situation.

To explain this phenomenon, Modigliani and Miller rather ingeniously reasoned that as a company gears up to very high ratios, ordinary shares become exceptionally risky – so risky that they attract *gambler* investors who are risk *seekers.* To these investors the shares become increasingly attractive as their riskiness rises: hence the expected return on equity (K_E) required by shareholders starts to fall. This explanation for the behaviour of the cost of equity capital at high gearing levels, which is necessary for the M and M hypothesis to be sustained at extreme levels of gearing, is often viewed with considerable scepticism; but their suggestion *may* sometimes hold.

Although the risks involved with ordinary shares ownership become substantial at high gearing levels, there is also the chance that shareholders will receive an extremely high level of dividend, and the possible size of this dividend (per share) is likely to increase as the gearing level increases: a typical 'gamble' situation.

Nevertheless, we are probably safe in concluding that the problem is likely to become important only at high levels of gearing. As companies rarely venture into such regions, then the case for the M and M hypothesis can still be said to hold for most *normal* levels of company gearing. We shall consider reasons why companies do *not* gear up to high levels in practice at a later stage.

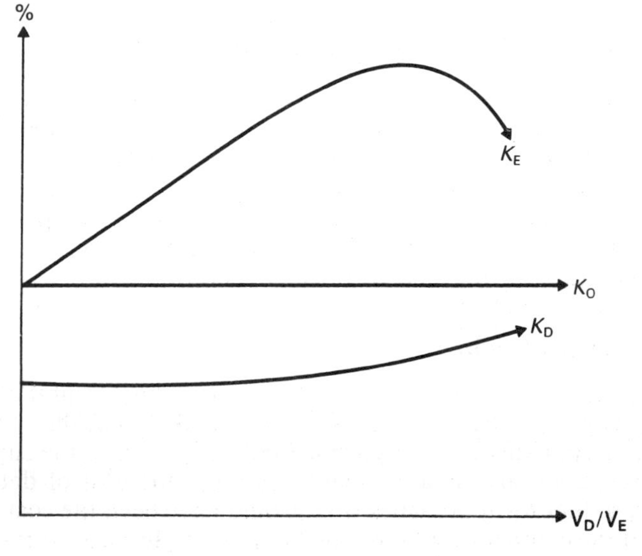

Figure 14.3

SUMMARY

- This chapter has developed the M and M *no-tax* capital structure hypothesis. Its basic conclusion is that the capital structure decision cannot affect shareholder wealth and so is irrelevant.
- The analysis is presented in two stages. The first concerns the firm valuation model: $V_0 = Y \div K_0$ and the fact that K_0 is determined by the risk of Y. Gearing determines how Y is divided up between dividends and interest, but has no effect on the *risk* of Y and so has no effect on K_0. It is from this analysis that the basic conclusion follows.
- Further, assuming K_D remains a constant, then it is shown that K_E is a positive, linear function of the gearing ratio, given by the expression:

  $$K_E = K_0 + [K_0 - K_D]\frac{V_D}{V_E}$$

- Thus the first stage of the analysis gives a constant K_0 at all levels of gearing and the second stage gives a constant K_D and a linearly increasing K_E. Finally, given the overall firm valuation model, as neither Y or K_0 changes with gearing, nor will V_0. Graphically this is seen in Figure 14.2.
- A secondary conclusion of the M and M analysis is that what determines a company's *overall* return (K_0) is its business risk – that is, the general uncertainty surrounding its net operating cash flow. As this is unaffected by gearing it therefore follows that companies with the same degree of business risk (that is, the same *asset* betas) will all have the same K_0, even though they might have different capital structures.
- Finally, M and M show that this conclusion *must* hold in an equilibrium capital market. If not, and companies in the same business risk class had different WACCs, then this would represent an arbitrage opportunity.
- If such arbitrage opportunities arise then investors will move in quickly to take advantage – and so make a profit – and the effect will be to re-establish the market equilibrium position.

NOTES

1 A not entirely surprising result, in view of the rather unrealistic assumptions made in order to reach the conclusions of the analysis.

2 There are numerous definitions of gearing in use, perhaps the most common of which is the ratio of the market value of debt capital to *total* market value (i.e. debt plus equity). In those circumstances, the proportion of debt can be quoted as a percentage of a firm's *total* capital.

3 In fact, remembering the objective function we have assigned to management decision making, we really want to know whether the gearing ratio can affect the market value of a company's *equity* capital. We shall later reconcile changes in total market value and equity market value.

4 As a result, the assumption of an unchanging capital structure as a condition for the use of the weighted average cost of capital as an investment appraisal discount rate would appear to be no longer necessary.

5 In other words, it is assumed that if the company becomes bankrupt it will be possible to liquidate its assets and distribute them amongst the various claimants without cost.

6 The equity holders of an all-equity financed company *only* hold business risk. They do *not* hold any financial risk.

7 It should be noticed that this cancelling out process does not mean that the financial risk has been eliminated in a diversification sense. Financial risk is systematic and therefore non-diversifiable.

FURTHER READING

At the end of this chapter we have only really reached the half-way point in our analysis of the capital structure decision. However, obviously M and M's original article, together with some contemporary observations, are well worthwhile: F. Modigliani and M. Miller, 'The Cost of Capital, Corporation Finance and the Theory of Investment', *American Economic Review*, June 1958; J.F. Weston, 'A Test of Cost of Capital Propositions', *Southern Economic Journal*, October 1963, and R.F. Wippern, 'Financial Structure and the Value of the Firm', *Journal of Finance*, December 1966.

QUICKIE QUESTIONS

1 If a company had a cost of equity capital of 20% and a cost of debt of 10% and a 1:4 debt/equity ratio, what would the company's cost of capital be if it was *all equity* financed?
2 Given the information in question 1, if the company was to change its gearing ratio from 1:4 to 3:5 what would be the change in its K_E and its K_0?
3 Two companies A and B are in the same business risk class. A is all-equity and B has a gearing ratio of 1:3. You have £100 worth of shares in company A. Show how you would arbitrage into company B.
4 In an arbitrage transaction, what is the purpose of home-made gearing?
5 What is financial risk and who bears it?
6 A company has a gearing ratio of 1:2. Its cost of equity capital is 20% and its cost of debt is 10%. If $E[r_M] = 15\%$ and $r_F = 10\%$ what is the company's asset beta?
7 Given the information in question 6, if the company were to change its gearing from 1:2 to 2:5, what would be the company's revised equity beta? (Assume K_D remains at 10%.)

8 Given the information in question 6, another company also has a cost of equity of 20% and a cost of debt of 10%. However it has a debt/equity ratio of 2:5. Are they in the same business risk class?

PROBLEMS

1 Alpha plc and Beta plc are two publicly quoted companies whose assets have the same level of systematic risk. Each has a constant annual earnings flow (before dividends and interest) of £5 million. This level of earnings is expected to be maintained by both companies in the future.

Alpha has issued £8 million of 9% irredeemable debentures; each £100 debenture is currently quoted at £50, ex int. Beta has no debt. Each of Alpha's 17·2 million ordinary shares is currently quoted at £1, ex div.; while Beta has issued 46·4 million shares each of which has a market price of 50p, ex div. Both companies pay out the entire earnings flow each year as dividends and interest.

Jill Gamma holds 464,000 shares in Beta as part of her well-diversified investment portfolio. Her market analysis leads her to believe that Alpha shares are currently under-priced, because of a temporary disequilibrium in the market. As a result, she is considering selling her Beta holding and investing in Alpha instead.

Required:
(a) Suggest how Ms Gamma could undertake the arbitrage deal so as to maintain her current level of financial risk. Explain briefly why you think your suggested approach will maintain her financial risk level. What would be her resulting gains?
(b) What would be the equilibrium share price of Alpha's equity if other investors also undertook arbitrage deals?

Assume that the market prices of Alpha's debentures and Beta's shares are in equilibrium. Assume no taxation.

2 Cabernet plc and Chardonnay Ltd, are two companies in the same business risk class. Cabernet is a quoted company with a debt: equity ratio of 1:3. The company's equity has a beta of 1·6 and the debt capital can be assumed to be riskless. Chardonnay is an unquoted, all-equity financed company.

The expected return on the F.T. All-Share Index is 16%. The return on Government stock (and also the return on Cabernet's debt) is 10%.

Assume that both Cabernet anu Chardonnay pay out constant annual dividends. Cabernet's debt is irredeemable. Ignore taxation.

Required:
(a) Explain precisely what is meant by the term 'same business risk class'. Estimate the beta value of Chardonnay's equity.

(b) Estimate the weighted average cost of capital of each company and comment briefly on the significance of your figures in respect of the Modigliani and Miller (no-tax) capital structure hypothesis.

(c) A small shareholder in Chardonnay has just received his regular dividend of £150. The shareholder has now been offered £1,000 for his shareholding. However, he does not know whether or not to sell his shares as he relies heavily on his annual dividend from the company.

Explain how the shareholder can make himself better-off with no change in risk by selling his shares in Chardonnay and investing in Cabernet. What would be his resulting gain?

(d) Assuming Cabernet's debt and equity capital are at their equilibrium value, estimate the equilibrium value of the investor's shareholding in Chardonnay.

3 Ekwitty Ltd has an all-equity capital structure. Geer Ltd is very highly geared. Both companies come within the same business risk class. You are given the following information:

	Geer Ltd *Yrs 1 – ∞*	*Ekwitty Ltd* *Yrs 1 – ∞*
Annual dividends	100,000	180,000
Annual interest	80,000	–
Total annual cash earnings	180,000	180,000
Total market value of equity	400,000	1,800,000
Total market value of debt	1,000,000	–

There is a perfect capital market, no taxation, no transaction costs and no difference between corporate and private gearing.

Required:

(a) What would you conclude from the above information?

(b) Draw a diagram, or diagrams (not to scale), to illustrate the current situation and to show what would happen if arbitragers entered the market.

(c) Illustrate the gain to be made from arbitrage by an individual currently holding £1,000 worth of shares in one of the above companies (i.e. there are only arbitrage gains to be made from trading one way; therefore you have to specify initially the direction of arbitrage).

Assume: the ordinary shares of Ekwitty Ltd and the debentures of Geer Ltd are in equilibrium.

15
Capital structure in the real world

Chapter Contents

MODIGLIANI AND MILLER IN A TAXED WORLD

Taxation and capital structure

The M and M capital structure hypothesis relies heavily on the assumption of a tax-free world, and the conclusions of their analysis change radically once this assumption is relaxed. In the initial analysis of the capital structure problem (under the set of simplifying assumptions used) we stated that the total market value of a company could be defined as: $V_0 = Y/K_0$. Therefore, a company's gearing ratio could only affect its total market value (V_0) if it affected either the company's expected annual net cash flow (Y) or its weighted average cost of capital (K_0). With the introduction of a taxation regime which allows debt capital interest to be set off against tax liability, a company *will* be able to increase its expected annual net *after-tax* cash flow by gearing up.

This is effectively the same situation as was examined by means of the single-period investment–consumption model in the last section of Chapter 13. Table 15.1 shows that a geared company's total *after tax* cash flow can now be split into two elements: the after-tax cash flow that would arise if it were all equity financed, *plus* the tax relief it receives on the debt interest payments[1]. Therefore the total after tax cash flow of the company will increase as it increases its gearing. This is because the more

Table 15.1

The dividend and interest valuation models indicate that the total value of a company is equal to the present value sum of the future expected dividend and interest cash flow streams. Still assuming all level perpetuity cash flow streams, where X represents the annual operating net cash flow before interest and taxes:

$$V_E = \frac{(X - V_D K_D)(1 - T)}{K_{E_g}} \tag{1}$$

$$V_D = \frac{D K_D}{K_D} \tag{2}$$

$$V_0 = \frac{(X - V_D K_D)(1 - T)}{K_{E_g}} + \frac{V_D K_D}{K_D} \tag{3}$$

Looking at the total cash flow:

$$(X - V_D K_D)(1 - T) + V_D K_D$$

and expanding the terms:

$$X - XT - V_D K_D + V_D K_D T + V_D K_D$$

Cancelling and simplifying:

$$X(1 - T) + V_D K_D T$$

Thus the company's after tax cash flow is what it would be if it were all equity financed $[X(1 - T)]$, plus the value of the interest tax relief $(V_D K_D T)$. The total value of the company is found by discounting these annual cash flows to present value. The discount rate to be applied to $X(1 - T)$ is the cost of equity capital that *would* apply to the company *if* it were all equity financed $(K_{E_{ug}})$. The discount rate to be applied to $V_D K_D T$ (i.e., the interest rate that reflects the risk involved) is K_D. Thus:

$$V_0 = \frac{X(1 - T)}{K_{E_{ug}}} + \frac{V_D K_D T}{K_D} \tag{4}$$

$$V_0 = \frac{X(1 - T)}{K_{E_{ug}}} + V_D T \tag{5}$$

Hence, the more highly geared the company becomes, the larger becomes the second term (the first term remains unchanged) and so the greater becomes the value of the company.

---

highly geared the company becomes, the more debt interest it pays, the greater the amount of tax relief it obtains and hence the smaller is the amount of tax paid. In such circumstances, the company would theoretically maximize its total market value by gearing up so that its capital structure consists of virtually all debt and just a token amount of equity to determine ownership.

In other words, taking the final expression for V_0 in Table 15.1:

$$V_0 = \frac{X(1-T)}{K_{E_{ug}}} + V_D T \qquad (5)$$

this can be interpreted as follows: The total market value of a geared company (V_0) is equal to what it *would be worth* if it was all-equity financed $\left[\frac{X(1-T)}{K_{E_{ug}}}\right]$, plus the present value of tax relief on debt interest ($V_D T$).

Therefore, expression (5) can be re-written as:

$$V_{0_g} = V_{E_{ug}} + V_D T$$

where V_{0_g} is the total market value of a geared company and $V_{E_{ug}}$ represents what the company would be worth if it was all-equity financed. $V_D T$ represents the present value worth of the tax relief on debt interest and is often referred to as the *tax shield.*

Therefore under the assumption of tax relief being available on debt interest, the total market value of the company is an increasing function of the level of gearing. What effect does gearing now have on both a company's cost of equity capital and its weighted average cost of capital? To answer that question we must once again examine the relationships involved.

Taxation and the WACC

The revised relationship between the gearing ratio and WACC can be derived both intuitively and analytically. Let us start with the intuitive explanation.

We saw in a world *without tax* that there was both an advantage ($K_D < K_E$) and a disadvantage (financial risk → increased K_E) to gearing up. However, these two effects exactly offset each other and so the net effect was zero: K_0 remained unaffected by gearing changes.

With the introduction of tax, there is now an additional *advantage* to gearing-up: the tax relief obtained on the debt interest. Further, this advantage is *cumulative* – the more highly geared a company becomes, the more tax relief it obtains and the smaller its tax liability becomes. Thus we could intuitively argue that in a world where there was tax relief on debt interest, we would expect a company's *after-tax* WACC to be progressively lowered as it increased its level of gearing.

Indeed, this conclusion can also be inferred from the WACC expression. In this expression, the cost of debt capital is *after tax* and as a company gears-up, a progressively greater weight is given to this 'cheap' capital:

$$K_0 = K_E \times \frac{V_E}{V_0} + K_D(1-T) \times \frac{V_D}{V_0}$$

Table 15.2

Starting with the company valuation expression derived in Table 14.7:

$$V_0 = \frac{X(1 - T)}{K_{E_{ug}}} + V_D T \qquad (1)$$

Multiplying through by $K_{E_{ug}}$

$$V_0 K_{E_{ug}} = X(1 - T) + V_D T K_{E_{ug}} \qquad (2)$$

Re-arranging and factoring out V_0:

$$V_0 K_{E_{ug}} - V_D T K_{E_{ug}} = X(1 - T) \qquad (3)$$

$$V_0 K_{E_{ug}} - \frac{V_0 V_D T K_{E_{ug}}}{V_0} = X(1 - T) \qquad (4)$$

$$V_0 \left(K_{E_{ug}} - \frac{V_D T K_{E_{ug}}}{V_0} \right) = X(1 - T) \qquad (5)$$

$$V_0 = \frac{X(1 - T)}{K_{E_{ug}}[1 - (V_D T / V_0)]} \qquad (6)$$

Given that

$$V_0 = Y / K_0$$

Then

$$K_0 = K_{E_{ug}}[1 - (V_D T / V_0)] \qquad (7)$$

A more analytical derivation of the relationship between the WACC and gearing can be given as shown in Table 15.2 (where $K_{E_{ug}}$ represents the cost of equity capital of a similar business risk, but all equity financed company).

The derivation of the WACC in Table 15.2 shows (as we intuitively reasoned) that as a company increases the proportion of debt in its capital structure, so the WACC declines. In fact, the WACC is a negative *linear* function of the ratio V_D / V_0.

The cost of equity capital

The cost of equity capital's relationship with the gearing ratio can also be intuitively derived. We know that the expected return required by equity rises (in a world of no taxes) as gearing is increased, because of the increasing burden of financial risk. The financial risk arises because debt interest has to be paid in full, before any dividends can be paid.

In a taxed world, debt interest payments are, effectively, subsidized by the tax authorities. Thus if the company had interest of £100 to pay and corporation tax was at 35%, then £35 out of the £100 of interest payable would be provided for through a reduced tax liability. Therefore, in a taxed world, although the cost of equity capital would still be expected to increase with increased gearing because of the presence of financial risk, it would do so at a slower rate than in a tax-free world. The presence of subsidized interest payments effectively *reduces* gearing ratios from the

Table 15.3

The WACC can be calculated either as:

$$K_0 = \frac{V_E}{V_0} \times K_{E_g} + \frac{V_D}{V_0} \times K_D(1 - T)$$

or

$$K_0 = K_{E_{ug}}\left(1 - \frac{V_D T}{V_0}\right)$$

Therefore:

$$\frac{V_E}{V_0} \times K_{E_g} + \frac{V_D}{V_0} \times K_D(1 - T) = K_{E_{ug}}\left(1 - \frac{V_D T}{V_0}\right) \quad (1)$$

Multiplying through by V_0 and re-arranging:

$$K_{E_g} = \frac{K_{E_{ug}}(V_0 - TV_D)}{V_E} - \frac{V_D K_D}{V_E} + \frac{V_D K_D T}{V_E} \quad (2)$$

$$= \frac{K_{E_{ug}} V_E}{V_E} + \frac{K_{E_{ug}} V_D}{V_E} - \frac{K_{E_{ug}} T V_D}{V_E} - \frac{V_D K_D}{V_E} + \frac{V_D K_D T}{V_E}$$

$$= K_{E_{ug}} + \frac{K_{E_{ug}} V_D}{V_E}(1 - T) - \frac{K_D V_D}{V_E}(1 - T)$$

$$K_{E_g} = K_{E_{ug}} + (K_{E_{ug}} - K_D)\frac{V_D(1 - T)}{V_E} \quad (3)$$

viewpoint of shareholders and their financial risk.

Once again, this intutitive argument can be shown, analytically, to hold good. Table 15.3 illustrates the relationship. What we derive is an expression that is very similar to the cost of equity capital function in an untaxed world, except that the effect of the gearing ratio is *dampened* by the presence of taxation. As a result, the amount of debt in the gearing ratio is recorded as $V_D(1 - T)$, rather than by V_D.

The graphical relationship

The relationship between the various costs of capital and the gearing ratio are shown graphically in Figure 15.1. (Note that although the WACC is a *linear* function of V_D/V_0, it is an *asymptotic* function of V_D/V_E.)

Therefore we can reiterate the conclusion of the M and M with-tax capital structure hypothesis. Companies should try to gear themselves up (by issuing debt capital) as high as possible. The more highly geared the company, the lower will be K_0, the higher will be V_0 and the greater will be shareholder wealth. This increase in shareholder wealth comes about through the *tax shield*, for it is the shareholders who gain the benefit by the company receiving tax relief on debt interest and so paying less tax.

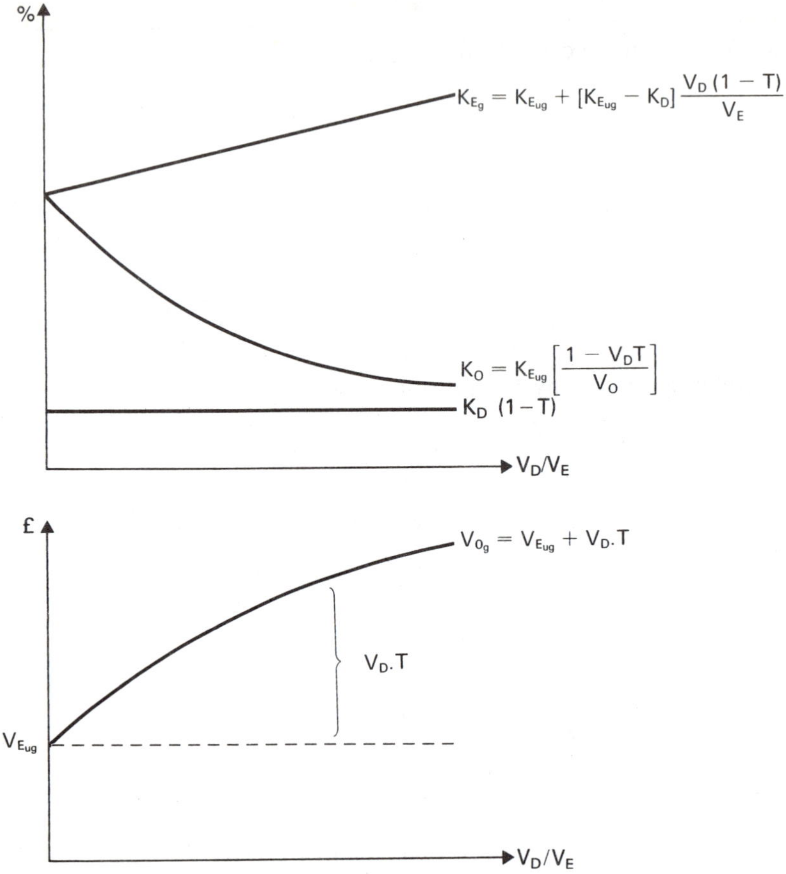

Figure 15.1

CAPITAL STRUCTURE AND THE REAL WORLD

Introduction

The previous analysis suggests that companies should gear themselves up to the maximum possible extent. However, in the real world companies only undertake a modest amount of gearing – the average for all companies in the UK is for debt capital to represent about 25% of total market value. This fact suggests that our model is too simple – it must be excluding some important facts about the financing decision and its effects.

Agency costs

One possible reason why we do not find companies gearing up to the high levels suggested by the previous analysis is that there are some 'hidden' costs of debt capital that we have so far ignored. One particular group of these is referred to as agency costs.

Agency costs arise out of what is known as the principal–agent problem. This problem is concerned with how the instructions or objectives, and the rewards, given to agents (i.e., management) can be formulated so that the agents, acting in their own interests, also act in the interests of the principals (i.e., the suppliers of company capital). In other words, the principal–agent problem is the problem of external financial control of managements by the suppliers of company finance.

In respect of debt finance, the suppliers of debt finance are concerned that they are not fooled or misled by a company's management. For example, a situation could occur where a management raise finance for a supposed investment in a low-risk project but, once the debt is issued, they use the money to invest in a high-risk project. In such circumstances the debt holders are likely to suffer in that their expected rate of return does not properly reflect the risk of their investment.

In order to try to avoid this sort of situation we find that debt suppliers often impose very restrictive conditions (or covenants) in loan agreements that constrain management's freedom of action. For example, debt covenants may restrict the level of dividends that may be paid (to prevent shareholders stripping the firm of cash, to the detriment of debt holders), or they may restrict the level of additional debt finance that can be raised (in order to maintain a given degree of security); or they may restrict management from disposing of major fixed assets without the debt holders' agreement.

All of the examples mentioned above represent *constraints* on management – they constrain their freedom of action – and are known as *agency costs.* All agents realize that they are going to be controlled or constrained by their principals, but that does not mean that agents actually *like* these costs they are forced to bear. They do not, and will often try to minimize them.

The more money the suppliers of debt capital lend to a company – that is the more highly geared the company becomes – then the more constraints they are likely to impose on the management in order to secure their investment. Hence it could be argued that management may well limit the level of a company's gearing in order to avoid the more onerous of these agency costs. As a result we do not find, in practice, companies gearing up to the high levels suggested by the M and M analysis.

Bankruptcy costs

Another cost which may be viewed as a part of the general agency costs, is that of bankruptcy. In the previous analysis it was always assumed, implicitly, that companies could go bankrupt costlessly, but what happens when the possibility and the associated costs of corporate bankruptcy are introduced?

The probability of bankruptcy is likely to be (amongst other things) an increasing function of a company's gearing ratio but, as far as the capital structure problem is concerned, the important factor is the substantial cost which may be involved in a company's liquidation or bankruptcy. If a company that was forced into bankruptcy could be liquidated costlessly (i.e., if its assets could be sold off at their 'correct' market values and if there were no legal or administrative costs), then the fact that the probability of bankruptcy is an increasing function of the gearing ratio would not have any adverse effect on the total market value of a company.

Unfortunately, in the real world, the costs of bankruptcy are considerable. As well as very substantial administrative and legal costs, the company's specialized assets may have to be disposed of at less than their operational values, because they have lost their going-concern/synergy value and because their sale has to take place hurriedly in an imperfect market. These costs (in whole or in part) will come out of the liquidated pool of funds which is destined to be returned to shareholders. Therefore, bankruptcy involves a company's shareholders in a cost they would otherwise have not incurred and so it is effectively responsible for causing a reduction in their level of wealth.

All shareholders, whether they be shareholders in geared or all-equity companies, face the (hopefully small) probability that their company may be forced into bankruptcy. This fact is just one component of the concept of business risk and, as such, is allowed for in the expected value of the future dividend flow and the required expected return on equity capital. However, the act of gearing up by a company has the effect of positively adding to the probability of its bankruptcy, due to the fact that if a company is unable to meet its fixed debt interest payments, then the debt holders have the legal right to liquidate the company in order to repossess their capital and unpaid interest.

Therefore, as a company increases its level of gearing, an increasing proportion of its expected annual cash flow is likely to be paid out as interest. But, as the future is uncertain, these annual cash flows are variable while debt interest represents a fixed, contractual obligation, and so there is also an increasing chance that the company's cash flows will not be sufficient to meet these debt interest payments. A succession of such years for a geared company will almost certainly lead to bankruptcy and the incursion of its associated costs.

Thus, as gearing increases so too does the probability of bankruptcy and hence the *expected* cost of bankruptcy. (Expected cost of bankruptcy = cost of bankruptcy × probability of bankruptcy.) Given this analysis, the M and M expression for the total market value of a geared company might be altered to:

$$V_{0_g} = V_{E_{ug}} + V_D T - E[b/c]$$

where $E[b/c]$ represents the expected cost of bankruptcy. As a result, it could be argued that management restrict the company's level of gearing

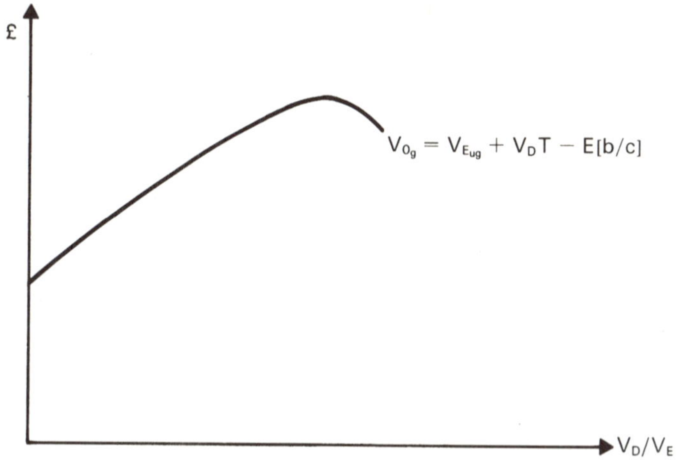

Figure 15.2

because V_{0_g} – and so shareholder wealth – *reduces* at very high levels of gearing. Figure 15.2 illustrates the possible situation.

Therefore bankruptcy costs would appear to provide yet another reason why we do not find companies with very high gearing ratios: there is this additional implicit cost which is borne by shareholders. However, these expected costs may not be the most important element in the role that the possibility of bankruptcy plays in limiting gearing ratios.

Shareholders can generally be expected to hold well diversified portfolios. Therefore, if one particular company within an investment portfolio goes into liquidation, the associated costs will be incurred by the investor, but they are likely to be relatively small. In contrast the management of a company hold *undiversified* portfolios as fas as their *labour* is concerned (i.e., they only work for the one company) and so, to them, the cost of bankruptcy is *very* substantial – they lose their employment. Therefore we can conclude that management – for their *own* reasons – are also likely to want to restrict the level of gearing, in order to restrict the *probability* of bankruptcy and hence avoid the very substantial *personal* costs involved.

Debt capacity

A further reason for explaining why companies do not gear up to high levels to take advantage of debt interest tax relief is debt capacity. In fact it could be argued that debt capacity may play the most important role in the determination of real world capital structures.

Most debt capital lent to companies by banks and other debt suppliers is *secured* against the assets of the company. Very little debt capital is unsecured. The idea behind securing a loan against the company's assets is obvious. If the company defaults on the loan agreement, the bank can step in, seize the assets against which the loan was secured, sell them off and recover their loan (and any unpaid interest) out of the sale proceeds.

From the foregoing, it will be clear that some assets provide better security for a loan than other assets. Perhaps the two most important characteristics of an asset in determining its suitability to act as security against a loan are:

1 The 'quality' of the second-hand market in the asset.
2 The asset's rate of depreciation.

The quality of the second-hand market refers to the ease (or otherwise) with which a seized asset could be sold. Thus the better the quality of the second-hand market, the more suitable is the asset as loan security. Similarly an asset which depreciates rapidly is going to offer poor security. The value of the asset may then be worth significantly less than the outstanding value of the loan – particularly in the latter years of a loan's term.

Therefore it's not surprising that if a company wished to acquire a piece of property costing £1m, the bank may be willing to loan £900,000 against the security of the asset. The property would be said to have a 90% *debt capacity*. However, if a company wished to purchase £1m worth of specialized industrial equipment, the bank may only be willing to lend, say, £300,000 against the security of that asset. The asset only has a debt capacity of 30%.

Property could be expected to have a high debt capacity because of its very active second-hand market and its slow rate of depreciation (or even, appreciation). Specialized industrial machinery, on the other hand, is likely to have a relatively low debt capacity because it probably has a poor second-hand market and a high rate of depreciation.

Therefore, from this discussion on debt capacity, we may conclude that high levels of corporate gearing are unusual, not because of a positive management decision to limit the gearing level, but simply because the company has run out of debt capacity. In other words the capital structure decision may be determined more by the *suppliers* of debt capital, rather than by the managers of the company.

Tax exhaustion

A final reason that we will mention for observed gearing levels is tax exhaustion. Debt financing gained its attractions from the tax relief allowable on the interest payments. As a company increases its gearing, so it increases its annual interest payments and it also increases the amount of tax *relief* that it gains. The term 'tax exhaustion' refers to the situation where a company does not not have a sufficient tax *liability* to be able to take advantage of all the tax *relief* that it has available.

At the point of tax exhaustion the *effective* cost of debt capital rises significantly from $K_D(1 - T)$ to simply K_D. Therefore, once this position is reached, debt capital loses its attraction for the company, and so we have a fourth possible reason for the observed levels of corporate gearing.

FURTHER VIEWS ON CAPITAL STRUCTURE

Introduction

The Modigliani and Miller analysis of the capital structure problem, whether in a taxed or a tax-free world, is based upon a number of assumptions about the environment and the working of the capital markets. On the basis of these assumptions, their analysis produces rigorous conclusions about the nature of the trade-off between financial risk and gearing and about the behaviour of a company's cost of equity capital, its weighted average cost of capital and also its total market value, as the gearing ratio changes.

In addition, an important conclusion arising from the discussion, as far as company managements and shareholders are concerned, is that gearing up (i.e., increasing the proportion of debt in a company's capital structure) enhances the total market value of the company – and hence increases shareholders' wealth – through the tax relief that is allowable on corporate debt interest.

However, when we examine the real world we find that companies do not follow this conclusion to its logical extreme and gear-up so that 99% + of capital is debt. We then concluded that there must be some relevant factors that were missing from the analysis, of which we considered four possibilities: agency costs, bankruptcy costs, debt capacity and tax exhaustion. What can we conclude from this discussion? Perhaps the safest conclusion that we can make is that the capital structure decision (and hence the financing decision) is both complex and difficult. In particular the costs of increased gearing cause identification problems that prevent any general decision advise being formulated.

In this section we will examine two further views of the capital structure decision faced by companies. The first is referred to as the "traditional view" as it is a view that is often casually subscribed to, without much rigorous analysis being applied. The second is a more recent development by Miller (of M and M) who had some further thoughts on the matter.

The traditional view of capital structure

It is often held that the generally accepted wisdom of investors, analysts and company managements alike (hence called the 'traditional' view) is that there are both advantages and disadvantages, as far as the maximization of shareholders' wealth is concerned, to corporate gearing. It is believed that at relatively low levels of gearing the advantages outweigh the disadvantages and so the market value of the company gradually rises but that, after a while, the relationship reverses and the disadvantages start to outweigh the advantages, so that further increases in gearing cause the company's market value to decline. Figure 15.3 sketches the various relationships involved in this traditional view of capital structure.

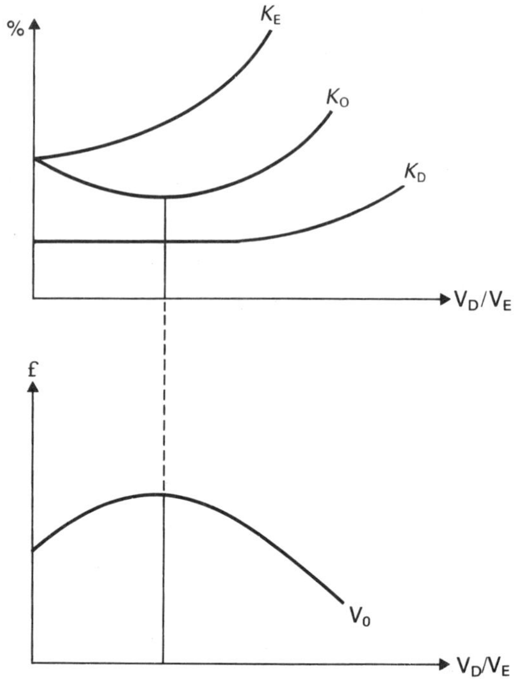

Figure 15.3

The main advantage of gearing is seen to be that, because corporate debt interest is allowable against taxation, a company is able to raise capital at an effective cost which is substantially below the market rate (i.e., debt capital is held to be 'cheap' capital because of tax relief). The main disadvantage arises from the fact that increased gearing results in an increased level of financial risk being borne by the company's shareholders. This, in turn, leads the shareholders to require a higher expected return on their capital (i.e., an increased K_E), by way of compensation.

A further disadvantage is also postulated. This is that, at very high gearing ratios, debt holders also start to bear their own version of financial risk – due to the quantity of debt issued and so the amount of interest required to be paid out of cash flow. As a result, K_D starts to rise in order to provide compensation for this additional risk.

In contrast to this traditional view of capital structure, the M and M hypothesis was that, in a tax-free environment, the advantages and disadvantages of gearing exactly offset each other at all gearing ratios; whereas in a taxed world, the advantages consistently outweigh the disadvantages at all levels of gearing. However, the real point of difference between the M and M and traditional views is the exact nature of the relationship between the cost of equity capital and the gearing ratio.

Whereas in the M and M hypothesis the increased return required by equity capital as compensation for bearing financial risk rises at a *constant* rate as the gearing level increases, the traditional view is that this required expected return rises at an *increasing* rate, i.e., at a rate which is, at relatively low levels of gearing, below that hypothesized by M and M, but which increases above the return required by equity in the M and M model, at higher gearing ratios.

In this respect it is interesting to note that as financial risk is systematic, the CAPM analysis would probably lead us to expect a positive *linear* relationship between the cost of equity and the gearing ratio (if it is nonly financial risk that is causing the cost of equity to rise). Thus CAPM would support the M and M hypothesis.

As far as the rising cost of debt argument is concerned, the M and M analysis simply assumes that K_D remains a constant at all gearing levels. Whether K_D would actually *rise* at a high gearing level is debatable. Our discussion on debt capacity would suggest that as long as the company can provide suitable security for any debt, then debt holders are not likely to bear their own version of financial risk as gearing increases. Thus the assumption of a constant K_D may well be realistic – up to the level of gearing at which the firm's overall debt capacity is reached.

The traditional view of capital structure is just that: a view or reflection of what is traditionally believed to be the relationship between a company's various costs of capital and the gearing ratio, and it has never rested on a rigorous theoretical model as does the M and M hypothesis. Several writers have expressed the traditional view of capital structure in algebraic form, but none has been able to show satisfactorily, in the way in which M and M used the existence of arbitrage transactions, *why* the cost of equity capital should have a non-linear relationship with the gearing ratio, as argued by the traditionalist view.

However, the most notable feature about the traditionalist view of capital structure (which follows on from the assumed nature of the K_E function) is the U-shaped weighted average cost of capital curve and the corresponding inverted-U total market value curve. At low gearing levels, the advantages outweigh the disadvantages, and so K_0 is pulled down; and as a result V_0 rises. But, as the company continues to gear up, the advantages now start to become out-weighed by the disadvantages, K_0 rises and consequently V_0 falls.

This leads firmly to the conclusion that each company has an optimal capital structure which minimizes its weighted average cost of capital and so maximizes its total market value. Company managements must search for this particular gearing ratio (which is likely to vary from company to company and may well vary over time for any one particular company) and so the financing decision is elevated to a position of importance almost on a par with the investment decision itself.

Corporate and personal taxes

The Modigliani and Miller analysis of the capital structure decision in a taxed world implies that tax relief on debt interest would encourage companies to gear up to as high a level as possible. The greater the level of gearing, the greater would be the tax subsidy on debt financing accruing to the company. However M and M only considered *corporate* taxes. It was left to a subsequent analysis by Miller (1977) to include the effects of *personal* as well as corporate taxes. Miller's arguments, although they can be developed intuitively, are complex and they are briefly outlined below.

Miller showed that when personal as well as corporate taxes are taken into account then the expression for the value of the tax shield (the present value of the tax relief on corporate debt) changes. Thus the M and M expression:

$$V_{0_g} = V_{E_{ug}} + V_D T$$

changes to:

$$V_{0_g} = V_{E_{ug}} + V_D\left[1 - \frac{(1 - T_C)(1 - T_E)}{1 - T_D}\right]$$

where T_C = Corporate tax rate
T_E = Personal tax rate on equity income
T_D = Personal tax rate on debt income

In a *homogeneous* personal tax regime where all personal income is taxed at the same rate, then $T_E = T_D$ and so Miller's expression for V_{0_g} reduces back to:

$$V_{0_g} = V_{E_{ug}} + V_D T_C$$

In other words, homogeneous personal taxes were an implicit assumption of the M and M with tax analysis.

However, in the real world the personal tax regime is heterogeneous where $T_E \neq T_D$. Here Miller argued that, effectively, $T_E = 0$ as shareholders can avoid taxes on dividends by taking dividends as capital gains (i.e. selling cum div. and repurchasing at ex. div.) for which there is a large annual tax-free allowance. In addition he put forward a macro-economic argument that, in an equilibrium market for corporate debt $T_D = T_C$.

It is this latter argument that lies as the heart of Miller's analysis and it is the most controversial part of his thesis. He argued that the existence of tax relief on debt interest – but not on equity dividends – would make debt capital more attractive than equity capital to companies. However, given that the market for corporate debt capital operates under the laws of supply and demand, companies would have to offer a higher return on debt (K_D) in order to generate a greater supply of debt.

Assuming a certain world in which investors hold either debt or equity, to persuade an equity supplier to switch over to become a *debt* supplier (because the company would prefer debt), the company must offer an after-personal tax return on debt at least as equal to the after-personal tax return on equity. Then, remembering that $T_E = 0$, the after-personal tax return on debt must, at a *minimum*, be:

$$K_D(1 - T_D) = K_E$$

Therefore, the minimum interest rate the company must pay on debt capital is:

$$K_D = \frac{K_E}{1 - T_D}$$

If the previous expression gives the *minimum* debt interest rate the company must offer to persuade equity investors to switch to debt, what then is the *maximum* interest rate the company would be willing to pay? This would be where the after-corporate tax cost of debt equalled the cost of equity:

$$K_D(1 - T_C) = K_E$$

At that point, the company would be indifferent between equity and debt finance as the effective cost of each would be the same. In other words, the highest interest rate they would be willing to pay would be:

$$K_D = \frac{K_E}{1 - T_C}$$

Given a supply and demand market for corporate debt, as long as the interest rate: $K_D < K_E/(1 - T_C)$ companies would want to issue debt. And as long as $K_D \geqslant K_E/(1 - T_D)$, investors would be willing to supply debt. Thus an equilibrium position in the corporate debt market – where supply and demand equated – would occur where:

$$\frac{K_E}{1 - T_C} = K_D = \frac{K_E}{1 - T_D}$$

In other words, equilibrium would occur where $T_C = T_D$; where the corporate tax rate equals the personal tax rate of the marginal (or incremental) investor in debt capital. This is shown graphically in Figure 15.4.

From this analysis, the conclusion can be drawn that, from the viewpoint of an individual company, it will be indifferent between raising debt or equity as the effective cost of each will be the same. (Obviously a non-tax paying company would strongly prefer equity finance because $K_D > K_E$.) All the advantages of the tax relief on debt interest will go to the suppliers of debt capital whose own personal T_D is less than T_C. This is represented by the shaded area on Figure 15.4.

This conclusion can be seen from the fact that Miller's expression for V_{0_g}:

$$V_{0_g} = V_{E_{ug}} + V_D\left[1 - \frac{(1 - T_C)(1 - T_E)}{1 - T_D}\right]$$

reduces, when $T_E = 0$ and $T_D = T_C$, to:

$$V_{0_g} = V_{E_{ug}}$$

The value of the tax shield now becomes zero. There is no advantage to gearing and one capital structure is therefore as good as another. (Notice that this conclusion is, rather ironically, identical to that of the original M

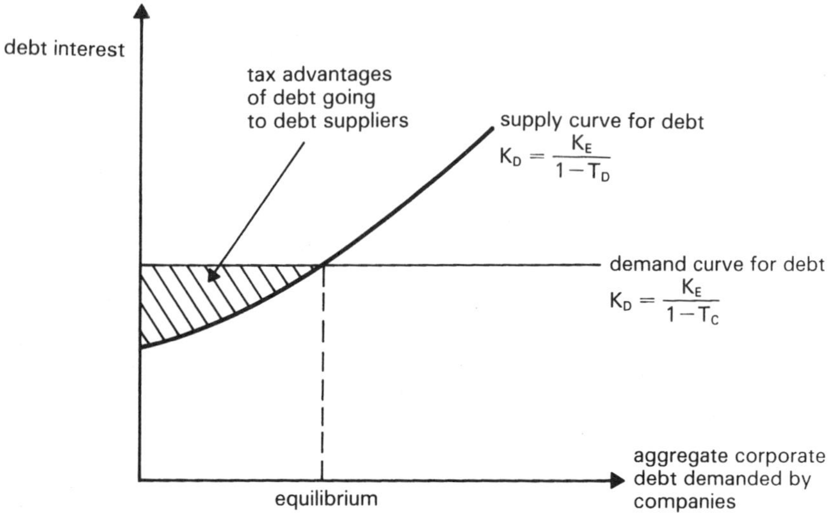

Figure 15.4

and M *no tax* capital structure hypothesis.) Hence the financing/capital structure decision is relegated to being a matter of little importance for corporate financial management.

Whether Miller's argument holds true in practice is unclear. As supportive evidence he draws attention to the fact that if debt *does* possess a net advantage due to tax relief on interest, then companies would be *expected* to move to higher gearing ratios at times of high rates of corporation tax and vice versa. (In other words, the higher the rate of corporation tax, the greater the tax advantage of debt.) However, he claims that there is little evidence to suggest that this does occur, which therefore supports his argument. Miller's evidence has been subject to criticism and hence there are some doubts about the empirical validity of his hypothesis. Nevertheless, his argument does caution against over-exaggerating the tax advantages of debt capital, and it provides another way of explaining observed gearing ratios: companies do not gear up to high levels not only because there are hidden costs involved in doing so, but also because the gains are themselves rather small.

In conclusion

In concluding our examination of the capital structure problem, all we can say is that it would appear that the financing decision may be of some importance, in so far as a company's capital structure can have both beneficial and detrimental effects on its total market value and, consequently, on the market value of the ordinary shares. However, the exact nature of the relationship in real life between a company's gearing level, its total market value and the costs of its various types of capital, remains unclear. What we have seen is that gearing can be a double-edged sword and hence should always be treated with caution.

SUMMARY

- This chapter has discussed the M and M with-tax capital structure hypothesis, the traditional view of capital structure, Miller's 1977 analysis of debt and taxes and the 'real world' determinants of capital structure.
- The M and M with tax analysis shows that as a company increases its gearing there are three effects: the advantage that debt costs less than equity ($K_D < K_E$); the disadvantage that gearing increases financial risk and so the cost of equity rises and the advantage that gearing brings further tax relief and so reduces the tax liability of the firm.
- The M and M no tax analysis shows how the first two effects exactly offset each other (not surprisingly, because they both arise from the same source: the ordering of the 'pay-out queue' of debt and equity holders). This leaves a net advantage. As gearing increases, the after-tax WACC declines and V_0 rises.
- Assuming a constant cost of debt, then it follows that K_{E_g} is a positive linear function of the gearing ratio.
- Therefore the conclusion of the analysis is that companies should attempt to gear-up as much as possible: the higher the gearing, the lower is K_0, the higher is V_0 and the greater is the increase in shareholder wealth.
- However, against this view is the traditional view which, like the M and M analysis, sees that there are both advantages and disadvantages to gearing. However, the traditional view holds that at low gearing levels the advantages outweigh the disadvantages and so the WACC is lowered. However at high gearing the reverse relationship holds and so the WACC rises.
- As a result, the company's WACC is U-shaped and the optimal gearing ratio is located where K_0 is minimized and V_0 is maximized. At that point shareholder wealth is also maximized.
- The empirical evidence does very little to solve the conflict between the two approaches because of a lack of company data for high gearing levels, which is where the two theories seriously diverge.
- However, empirically we find that companies tend *not* to gear-up to the high levels the M and M analysis would lead us to expect suggesting either that the WACC curve *is* U-shaped or the M and M analysis excludes some important variables.
- There is *no* reason – either of an analytical or of an empirical nature – to suggest that the WACC function is *really* U-shaped. Therefore this leads us to conclude that the M and M analysis excludes some important factors in the real world capital structure decision.
- These important real-world determinants are thought to be: bankruptcy costs, agency costs, debt capacity and tax exhaustion.
- Finally, the Miller analysis suggests that when personal taxes are included in the analysis and given two somewhat contentious arguments about personal tax rates, then it can be shown that the value of

the tax shield on corporate debt interest reduces to zero. That is not to say that companies do not get tax relief on debt interest. Rather it implies that even allowing for tax relief on debt interest, the use of debt capital confers no benefits on shareholder wealth.

NOTE

1 From this point on, K_D will refer to the before tax cost of debt capital. References to the after tax cost of debt will be designated K_{DAT}, as before, or $K_D(1 - T)$, where T is the rate of corporation tax.

FURTHER READING

1 There are many articles on this area that are of interest. The basic ones of course are the two by M and M: F. Modigliani and M. Miller, 'The Cost of Capital, Corporation Finance and the Theory of Investment', *American Economic Review*, June 1958, and 'Corporation Income Taxes and the Cost of Capital', *American Economic Review*, June 1963, and, in addition, the later analysis by Miller: M.H. Miller, 'Debt and Taxes', *Journal of Finance*, May 1977.

2 A good overview is provided in: S.C. Myers, 'The Capital Structure Puzzle', *Journal of Finance*, July 1984, and this is extended in J. Rutterford, 'An International Perspective on the Capital Structure Puzzle', *Midland Corporate Finance Journal*, Autumn 1985. Another, more demanding, overview is to be found in: A.H. Chan and E.H. Kim, 'Theories of Corporate Debt Policy: A Synthesis', *Journal of Finance*, May 1979.

3 In terms of Miller's analysis there have been some good recent articles: H. de Angelo and R.W. Mausulis, 'Leverage and Dividend Irrelevancy under Corporate and Personal Taxation', *Journal of Finance*, May 1980; V.A. Aivazain and J.L. Callen, 'Miller's Irrelevance Mechanism', *Journal of Finance,* March 1987; J. Cordes and S. Sheffrin, 'Estimating the Tax Advantage of Corporate Debt', *Journal of Finance*, March 1983; and A. Kane, A.J. Marcus and R.L. McDonald, 'How Big is the Tax Advantage of Debt?', *Journal of Finance*, July 1984.

4 On the real-world factors behind the capital structure decision, articles of interest include: A. Barnea, R.A. Haugen and L.W. Senbet, 'Market Imperfections, Agency Problems and Capital Structure: A Review', *Financial Management*, Summer 1981; J.S. Ang and J.H. Chua, 'Corporate Bankruptcy and Job Losses Among Top Level Managers', *Financial Management*, Winter 1981; S.G. Rhee and F.L. McCarthy, 'Corporate Debt Capacity and Capital Budgeting Analysis', *Financial Management*, Summer 1982; and A. Agrawal and G.N. Mandelher, 'Managerial Incentives and Corporate Investment and Financing Decisions', *Journal of Finance*, September 1987.

5 Finally, there has been some interesting empirical work published: C.S. Patterson, 'The Financing Objectives of large US Electric Utilities', *Financial Management,* Summer 1984; P. Marsh, 'The Choice Between Equity and Debt: An Empirical Study', *Journal of Finance*, March 1982; M. Bradley, G.A. Jarrell and E.H. Kim, 'On the Existence of an Optimal Capital Structure: Theory and Evidence', *Journal of Finance*, July 1984; and M. Long and I. Malitz, 'The Investment-Financing Nexus: Some Empirical Evidence', *Midland Corporate Finance Journal*, Autumn 1985.

QUICKIE QUESTIONS

1 Given the following facts about a company:

$$K_E = 25\%$$
$$K_D = 10\% \text{ pre-tax}$$
$$V_D : V_E = 1{:}3$$
$$T_C = 35\%$$

What is the cost of equity capital of a similar business risk, all-equity financed, company?

2 Given the information in question 1, what would be its K_0 if it moved its gearing ratio from 1:3 to 1:2?

3 An all-equity financed company is presently worth £40m. It is thinking of issuing £10m of 14% irredeemable debt to repurchase £10m of equity. Given a corporate tax rate of 35%, what would be the effect on shareholder wealth?

4 What is the M and M expression for K_0 in a taxed world?

5 What does the 'tax shield' represent?

6 What is meant by debt capacity?

7 Given a company which has issued £10m of debt (i.e. its current market value), a gearing ratio of 1:3, a probability of going bankrupt of 5% and estimated bankruptcy costs of £1m; what would the company be worth if it was all-equity financed assuming a corporate tax rate of 35%?

8 What is Miller's expression for the total market value of a geared company?

PROBLEMS

1 Mandina plc and Clarice plc are two companies operating in different industries. Mandina plc operates in an industry for which the average asset beta (i.e. the ungeared beta after *removing* the impact of financial risk) is 0·5; the corresponding beta is 1·5 for the industry of Clarice plc. Both industries are homogeneous, and the industry asset betas are appropriate to the degree of business risk experienced by both companies. The current earnings before interest and tax for

Mandina plc are £500,000 and for Clarice plc £1,200,000. These levels of earnings are expected to be maintained for the indefinite future, as neither company retains any earnings. The rate of return on riskless lending and borrowing opportunities is 7% per annum, and the return on the market portfolio is 15%. Both rates are expected to remain constant indefinitely.

Mandina plc and Clarice plc each have 8% irredeemable debentures with a market value of £1,000,000 in their capital structures. At these levels of gearing there is an 8% chance of Mandina plc becoming bankrupt, and a 10% chance of Clarice plc becoming bankrupt. In both cases, the present value of the associated after-tax costs of bankruptcy will be £500,000.

The rate of corporation tax will be 35% for the foreseeable future and all debenture interest is expected to be tax deductible. You may assume that markets are perfect apart from the existence of corporate taxes and bankruptcy costs.

Required:

(a) Calculate the total market values and debt/equity ratios of Mandina plc and Clarice plc.

(b) Discuss why the directors of some UK listed companies may choose high gearing ratios, whereas others may choose to have negligible debt in their capital structures.

2 Given below are extracts from the annual accounts of four UK listed companies, together with information concerning their stock market performance. Companies A and B are from the brewing sector and have as their principal business activities: brewing beer, wholesale and retail selling of beers, wines, spirits and soft drinks and the ownership and management of public houses. The principal activities of companies C and D are the distribution and service of electronic components, microprocessor systems and related equipment. Company D is also involved in the manufacture of steel products such as partitions and lintels.

	Company			
	A	*B*	*C*	*D*
Latest Annual Report extracts:				
Ordinary shareholders' funds (£m)	90·4	65·4	5·9	33·3
Long term loans (£m)	1·1	0·2	–	0·4
Bank overdraft (£m)	1·7	5·6	1·1	0·7
Net dividend per share (p)	4·3	8·2	2·4	9·9
Annual dividend growth since 1980	12%	10%	19%	22%
Current Stock market details:				
Equity market value (£m)	68·0	63·2	68·8	123·4
Market value of long term loans (£m)	0·6	0·1	–	0·3
Beta value	0·75	0·88	1·24	1·26
Share price (£)	1·64	2·80	3·03	4·70

You should assume that the return on short-dated government securities is 11% and that the equivalent return on all long-term loans is 12%. The market premium for risk (i.e. the difference between the return on the Financial Times All-Share Index and the return on short-dated government securities) should be assumed to be 9%.

Required:

(a) Calculate the weighted average cost of capital for each of the four companies, assuming a corporation tax rate of 35% and ignoring bank overdrafts.

(b) Using both the information given in the question, and the results of your calculations in part (a), explain why the weighted average costs of capital differ between the four companies.

(c) Discuss the proposition that under the present UK system of personal and corporate taxation, a company's capital structure does not affect its total market value.

3 The Government of Despina has used a number of different corporation tax systems in recent years. In t_{-3} corporate profits were not taxable; however, in t_{-2} a corporate income tax at 50% of taxable profits was introduced. Under this tax regime debt interest was not allowed as a charge against taxable profits. In t_{-1} the Government modified the tax system, allowing interest on corporate borrowings as a charge against taxable profits. Finally, in t_0, capital allowances and debt interest were allowed as charges against taxable profits. The magnitudes of these allowances were such as to shield fully earnings before interest from corporate taxes for all companies in Despina.

The market capitalization of the equity of two companies, Dora and Bella and the market capitalization of the debentures in Bella at the end of each of the four years are:

		t_{-3} ($000)	t_{-2} ($000)	t_{-1} ($000)	t_0 ($000)
Dora	Equity	1,000	510	520	980
Bella	Equity	800	370	440	790
	Debentures	200	140	160	190

Both companies were believed to have had identical earnings streams over the four-year period; to have had identical business risk characteristics; and to have paid out all their earnings as dividends at the end of each year. Neither company was expected to exhibit any growth during the four-year period, although the levels of earnings expectations and the rates of return on corporate shares varied between years.

You are required to explain the relative values of Dora and Bella in the light of the differing tax systems in Despina over the past four years.

16
Investment and financing decision interactions

Chapter Contents

COMPANY VALUATION AND INVESTMENT APPRAISAL

The Hirshleifer Separation Theorem that was developed in Chapter 3 led to the conclusion that managements could appraise capital investment opportunities *without* reference to how they are to be financed. However, that model was developed under a very restrictive set of assumptions, including that of a perfect capital market.

In the last chapter we saw that when we allow for some real world capital market imperfections (in particular, the fact that tax relief is available on debt interest, but not on equity dividends) the separation theorem starts to break down. As a result, there arise significant interactions between capital investment and financing decisions.

The question of concern in this chapter is how are we to take account of such interactions? As a starting point, we are going to examine the relationship between different company valuation models and alternative approaches to investment appraisal. Before doing so, however, we must set out the assumptions upon which the analysis is based. There are five in total:

1 All cash flows represent level perpetuities.

2 Investors are rational, risk-averse and base decisions on expected return and variance of returns.
3 Capital markets are perfect and in equilibrium.
4 Bankruptcy is costless.
5 Companies are each located at a 'target' gearing ratio at which they wish to remain.

Dividend and interest valuation models

The dividend valuation model states that the total market value of a company's equity reflects the sum of the future expected dividend flow, discounted to present value. A similar statement can be made about the total market value of debt capital. Thus – using our usual notation – the total market value of the firm is given by the sum of the equity and the debt market values:

$$V_0 = \frac{(X - V_D K_D)(1 - T)}{K_{E_g}} + \frac{V_D K_D}{K_D}$$

If the company's annual cash flow is taken as its dividend plus interest flow:

$$(X - V_D K_D)(1 - T) = \text{Annual dividend flow}$$
$$V_D K_D = \text{Annual interest flow}$$

then the total annual cash flow can be expressed as follows:

$$\begin{aligned}(X - V_D K_D)(1 - T) + V_D K_D &= X - XT - V_D K_D \\ &\quad + V_D K_D T + V_D K_D \\ &= X(1 - T) + V_D K_D T\end{aligned}$$

where $X(1 - T)$ represents the annual after tax cash flow that *would* occur *if* the company had been all-equity financed, and where $V_D K_D T$ represents the annual amount of tax relief the company gains from having to pay debt interest.

Adjusted present value model

Taking the two annual cash flow streams as given above, and discounting each to present value, we arrive at an alternative expression for valuing the total market value of the company:

$$V_0 = \frac{X(1 - T)}{K_{E_{ug}}} + \frac{V_D K_D T}{K_D} = \frac{X(1 - T)}{K_{E_{ug}}} + V_D T$$

Notice that each cash flow is discounted at a rate that best reflects its risk. Thus $X(1 - T)$ is discounted by what would have been the company's cost of equity capital if it were all equity financed and $V_D K_D T$ is discounted at the cost of debt capital.

This company valuation model could be called the *adjusted* present value (APV) model as the company is *first* valued as if it were all-equity financed, and then this value is *adjusted* to allow for the tax relief on debt capital.

The M and M valuation model

If the APV model is multiplied through by $K_{E_{ug}}$ and V_0 is factored out, then a third valuation model is arrived at:

$$K_{E_{ug}} V_0 - V_D T K_{E_{ug}} = X(1 - T)$$

$$K_{E_{ug}} V_0 - \frac{V_0 V_D T K_{E_{ug}}}{V_0} = X(1 - T)$$

$$V_0 = \frac{X(1 - T)}{K_{E_{ug}}[1 - (T V_D / V_0)]}$$

This values the firm as the present value of the future expected after tax cash flow. Here the discount rate is the M and M weighted average cost of capital, and this implicitly takes the tax relief on debt interest into account. Hence it is applied simply to the after tax-cash flows that would arise if the firm were all equity financed.

The traditional valuation model

Finally, returning to the dividend valuation model, but now factoring out V_0, a fourth company valuation model is derived:

$$V_E = \frac{(X - V_D K_D)(1 - T)}{K_{E_g}}$$

$$V_E K_{E_g} = X(1 - T) - K_D V_D (1 - T)$$

$$\frac{V_0 V_E K_{E_g}}{V_0} + \frac{K_D V_D V_0 (1 - T)}{V_0} = X(1 - T)$$

$$V_0 = \frac{X(1 - T)}{\frac{V_E}{V_0} K_{E_g} + \frac{V_D}{V_0} K_D (1 - T)}$$

Here the numerator is the same as with the previous model, but now the denominator is the traditional expression for the WACC. Once again, the effect of the tax relief on debt interest is implicitly allowed for in the discount rate.

APPROACHES TO INVESTMENT APPRAISAL

All four models of company valuation are equivalent, as long as the set of five assumptions specified initially, all hold good. However, it should be noted that each model implicitly reflects a different approach to investment appraisal. The dividend and interest valuation model reflects a dividend flow approach; the APV valuation model reflects an APV approach and the M and M and traditional valuation models each reflect the standard net present value approach.

Maintaining the gearing ratio

An example may help to illustrate these different approaches. Suppose we have the following data about a company (remember that we have the assumption of all level perpetuity cash flows):

$$\begin{aligned} V_E &= £400{,}000 \\ V_D &= £100{,}000 \\ D &= £\ 73{,}500 \\ I &= £\ 10{,}000 \\ T &= 35\% \end{aligned} \qquad \text{therefore} \qquad \begin{aligned} K_E &= 18{\cdot}375\% \\ K_D &= 10\% \\ K_0 &= 16\% \end{aligned}$$

The company is considering a project requiring an outlay of £100,000, which is expected to produce an annual after-tax net cash flow of £28,000 in perpetuity (£43,077 per year, pre-tax). It would not involve any change in risk.

Given that the company wishes to remain at its current (target) gearing ratio of 1:4 (debt–equity), how is the investment to be financed? It would not be correct to simply finance the project with £20,000 of debt and £80,000 of equity, as this ignores the project's NPV which would accrue to the equity holders. Instead a somewhat more lengthy analysis is required.

If the company is going to maintain its current gearing ratio (and there is no change in risk caused by the project's acceptance), then K_0 will remain at 16%. Hence the project's annual net cash inflows will have a present value of:

$$\frac{£28{,}000}{0{\cdot}16} = £175{,}000$$

If there is to be no change in the gearing ratio, this increase in company value must be split between debt and equity in the ratio 1:4. Therefore, as a result of the project the market value of the debt should increase by £35,000 and the market value of the equity should rise by £140,000.

The increase in the market value of the debt issued by the company implies that £35,000 of *new* debt is raised in order to undertake the project. The remaining £65,000 of the £100,000 required outlay would therefore come from the equity holders.

The total value of the company's equity would rise by £140,000 because the equity holders have subscribed an extra £65,000 and, in addition, they will receive the benefit of the project's NPV:

$$-£100{,}000 + \frac{28{,}000}{0{\cdot}16} = +£75{,}000 \text{ NPV}$$

Thus the total market value of the equity capital will rise by: £65,000 + £75,000 = £140,000.

Having decided that the project will be financed by £35,000 of debt capital (at a K_D of 10%) and £65,000 of equity capital, in order to maintain the existing gearing ratio, let us now turn to examine the application of each of the possible approaches to investment appraisal.

Dividend flow approach

This approach evaluates the project on the basis of examining the total market value of the equity *before* (V_E) and *after* (V_E^*) the investment is undertaken. The decision rule is to accept the project as long as it does not cause a reduction in shareholder wealth:

$$V_E^* - (V_E + \text{newly issued equity}) \geq 0$$

where $V_E^* = D^*/K_E^*$ (the asterisk refers to the situation post-investment).

As there is to be no change in the gearing ratio (and hence no change in financial risk: $K_E^* = K_E = 18{\cdot}375\%$. But what about the post-investment annual dividend flow? This can be found as follows:

		£
Project cash flow	=	43,077
less Interest payable on new debt	=	3,500
Taxable cash flow	=	39,577
less Tax at 35%	=	13,852
Additional dividends	=	25,725
Existing dividends	=	73,500
Post-investment dividends = D^*	=	99,225

$$\text{Hence } V_E^* = \frac{£99{,}225}{0{\cdot}18375} = £540{,}000$$

$$\text{and } £540{,}000 - (£400{,}000 + £65{,}000) = +75{,}000$$

The project should be accepted as it will increase shareholder wealth by £75,000.

APV approach

The second approach uses the APV. Here, the project's net cash flow is evaluated as if it were all equity financed and then the benefits of the tax relief from the new debt capital are added on. The decision rule is to accept the project as long as its total worth is greater than the outlay required:

$$(V_{\text{project}} - \text{Outlay}) \geq 0$$

where
$$V_{\text{project}} = \frac{X(1-T)}{K_{E_{ug}}} + V_D T$$

The first task here is to identify what *would be* the discount rate if all equity financing where involved. For this, use can be made of the M and M expression:

$$K_{E_g} = K_{E_{ug}} + (K_{E_{ug}} - K_D)\frac{V_D(1-T)}{V_E}$$

This can be switched around to solve for $K_{E_{ug}}$:

$$K_{E_{ug}} = \frac{V_E K_{E_g} + V_D K_D (1-T)}{V_E + V_D(1-T)}$$

which in the case of the present example gives a value for $K_{E_{ug}}$ of:

$$\frac{(£400{,}000 \times 0{\cdot}18375) + (£100{,}000 \times 0{\cdot}10)(1 - 0{\cdot}35)}{£400{,}000 + £100{,}000(1 - 0{\cdot}35)} = 0{\cdot}172$$

or 17·2% approx.

Therefore the value of the investment opportunity can now be found:

$$V_{\text{project}} = \frac{£28{,}000}{0{\cdot}172} + £35{,}000 \times 0{\cdot}35$$

$$= £162{,}750 + £12{,}250 = £175{,}000$$

As the value of the project is £75,000 more than the required outlay, it should be accepted.

NPV approach

With this approach either the M and M or traditional expressions can be used for calculating the company's weighted average cost of capital of 16%. The decision rule is to accept the project as long as it has a non-negative NPV:

$$-£100{,}000 + \frac{£28{,}000}{0{\cdot}16} = +£75{,}000 \text{ NPV}$$

Therefore the project should be accepted. It will increase shareholders' wealth by £75,000.

A changing capital structure

The equivalence of all three approaches (and all four company valuation models) is obvious from the above example. However, it should also be noted that in order to determine how the project should be financed in order to maintain the existing gearing ratio, *the project's worth had first to be found.* In other words the whole analysis smacks of a 'cart-before-the-horse' approach.

To highlight this problem and the difficulties it causes we now examine a situation where the company finances the investment in such a way that it does *not* maintain the existing gearing ratio. For example, suppose the company intended to finance the project with an £80,000 issue of 10% debt capital and £20,000 of equity.

In order to utilise the dividend flow approach, we need to find V_E^*. This is given by $V_E^* = D^*/K_E^*$.

The post-investment dividend flow is easy enough to find (£96,300), but we *cannot* identify what will be the post-investment cost of equity capital. This can only be found by first knowing what will be the post-investment gearing ratio which, in turn, we cannot identify until we know the worth of the project.

If we are prevented from using the dividend flow approach, what about the NPV/WACC approach? Again we face a difficulty. We cannot use the *existing* WACC for obvious reasons: it reflects the existing capital structure, which will change if the project is accepted. Further – even if we wished to use it – we could not identify the post-investment WACC for the same reasons as we could not use the dividend flow approach.

One possible way around the difficulty is as follows. The M and M capital structure analysis shows that there are three effects directly arising from an increase in corporate gearing. Two of these, the advantage of debt being 'cheaper' than equity and the disadvantage of the cost of equity rising because of increased financial risk, exactly off-set each other. This leaves one net advantage: the tax relief on debt interest.

We know that behind the use of the WACC as the NPV discount rate is the assumption of an unchanging capital structure. In using the WACC, the net advantage of debt capital is taken into account by using the *after tax* cost of debt capital. Thus if the project were appraised using the company's *existing* WACC, the implicit assumption would be that it was being financed with £35,000 of debt (because it is this amount of debt that will maintain the existing gearing).

In this example, it is proposed to finance the project using £80,000 of debt. The advantage to the company that accrues from using the £45,000 *extra* debt (i.e., £80,000 − £35,000) is given by the present value of the tax relief.

$$V_D T = £45{,}000 \times 0{\cdot}35 = £15{,}750$$

If the project were to be financed with the existing gearing ratio, then K_0 would remain unchanged at 16% and the NPV of the project would be:

$$-£100{,}000 + \frac{£28{,}000}{0{\cdot}16} = +£75{,}000$$

Hence the *total* benefits of the project are given by its worth if there was no change in capital structure (£75,000), *plus* the worth of the change in capital structure (£15,750). This represents a total of £90,750. However, once more notice the cart-before-the-horse element of the analysis. It can *only* be accurate if we know how the project should be financed in order to maintain the existing gearing ratio (i.e. £35,000:£65,000 debt:equity ratio).

That brings us around to the APV approach. Given the company's existing gearing ratio and its existing cost of equity capital, we have previously calculated that – if the company were all-equity financed – its cost of equity capital would be 17·2% approx. Hence the 'pure' value of the investment opportunity under consideration – which can be referred to as the *Base-case PV* – is (as before):

$$-£100{,}000 + \frac{£28{,}000}{0{\cdot}172} = \underline{£62{,}750}\text{ NPV}$$

The present value of the tax relief on the £80,000 of debt used to finance the investment is:

$$£80{,}000 \times 0{\cdot}35 = \underline{£28{,}000}$$

Therefore the *adjusted* present value of the investment proposal is given by:

$$£62,750 + £28,000 = \underline{£90,750}$$

THE ADJUSTED PRESENT VALUE

Of all three approaches to the appraisal of the project used in the example above, *only* the adjusted present value (APV) approach was capable of handling the situation where the company's existing gearing ratio was *not* being maintained. Furthermore, in that example, we also saw that it is not as straightforward as it might initially appear for a company to finance a project in such a way as not to change the existing capital structure. (Where we had a gearing ratio of 1:4 the £100,000 project in question had to be financed by a 35:65 debt:equity mix and not simply 1:4.)

From that example we must conclude that, unless a project *is* going to be financed in such a way as to leave the capital structure unchanged (or if we have an M and M *no-tax* world where capital structure is irrelevant), APV is the only safe way of assuming that all the effects of a project – together with its financing method – are going to be captured in the appraisal.

However, before we examine the use of the APV technique in greater detail, let us first clarify the basic approach. Adjusted present value essentially uses a *divide and conquer* approach to capital investment appraisal. As we saw in the previous example, it first evaluates the project, *assuming* that it is all-equity financed. This is referred to as the project's base-case present value. Then this figure is adjusted to take into account any *side-effects* that arise through the financing method used. Although these side-effects can be numerous, the principal one, again as we saw in the example, is likely to be the tax relief on the interest paid on the debt capital used.

The base-case discount rate

In the example used to illustrate the basic mechanics of the APV technique the base-case discount rate was calculated by taking the geared *company's* K_E and then using a re-arranged version of the M and M expression for the cost of equity capital in a taxed world:

$$K_{E_g} = K_{E_{ug}} + [K_{E_{ug}} - K_D]\frac{V_D(1-T)}{V_E}$$

was re-arranged to find $K_{E_{ug}}$, the all-equity cost of equity capital:

$$K_{E_{ug}} = \frac{V_E K_{E_g} + V_D K_D(1-T)}{V_E + V_D(1-T)}$$

Now this approach is a perfectly acceptable means of identifying the base-case discount rate ($K_{E_{ug}}$), but *only* in one set of circumstances.

In the example used in the previous section, we assumed that the project had the same degree of systematic risk as the company's existing average systematic risk level. Given this assumption, the approach used for calculating the base-case discount rate is satisfactory. However, as we have already discussed at an earlier stage when criticising the use of the WACC as an NPV discount rate, such an assumption is likely to be highly unrealistic in practice.

Therefore, if we wish to use the APV technique, but feel that we cannot legitimately assume that the project's systematic risk reflects the company's average systematic risk, how are we to go about calculating a suitable base-case discount rate? The answer is – at it was before in our discussion about the use of the WACC – to use the capital asset pricing model.

Asset betas and gearing

In Chapter 10 we discussed the possible use of the CAPM to generate an NPV discount rate that was *tailor-made* to reflect the systematic risk level of the project under evaluation. This could be achieved by using as a surrogate for the project's beta, the beta value of the project's *industry* group. The industry beta would simply be the average equity beta value of all the quoted companies within that industry.

Example 16.1

For simplicity, assume that debt betas equal zero. Therefore[1]

$$\beta_{\text{assets}} = \beta_{\text{equity}} \times \frac{V_E}{V_0}$$

Suppose a project is to be financed using a 1:3 gearing ratio (i.e. debt:equity) and the project's industry group has an equity beta of 1·2 and an average gearing ratio of 1:4. The industry's equity beta could be *ungeared* and then *re-geared* to reflect how the project is financed as follows:

$$\beta_{\text{industry assets}} = 1{\cdot}2 \times \frac{4}{5} = 0{\cdot}96$$

$$\beta_{\text{industry assets + project gearing}} = 0{\cdot}96 \times \frac{4}{3} = 1{\cdot}28$$

The beta value of 1·28 could then be put into the CAPM to provide a value for the *project's* cost of equity capital. This, together with the cost of debt used to finance the project and the project's gearing ratio, could then be used to calculate a 'weighted average cost of capital' for the project and used as an NPV discount rate.

Later, in Chapter 14, we saw how capital structure caused financial risk and that financial risk formed part of the total systematic risk borne by the equity capital in a company. This therefore implies that if we are to use an *industry* beta to act as a surrogate for a *project's* beta, then account must be taken of any difference between the industry's gearing ratio and the gearing ratio used to finance the project.

This could be done through the expression we developed in Chapter 14:

$$\beta_{\text{assets}} = \beta_{\text{equity}} \times \frac{V_E}{V_0} + \beta_{\text{debt}} \times \frac{V_D}{V_0}$$

where the industry's *asset* beta could be re-geared to reflect how the project is financed. Example 16.1 illustrates a possible situation.

However, we must be careful with Example 16.1, because it is only applicable in a *no-tax* situation.[2] This is because the expression used for identifying the asset beta does not take into account the fact that tax relief on debt capital effectively *reduces* the financial risk borne by equity at any particular gearing level.

Asset betas and tax

Let us now look at the identification of an asset beta in a taxed world. We know from the M and M expression for the total market value of a geared company in a taxed world:

$$V_{0_g} = V_{E_{ug}} + V_{D_g}T$$

where V_{0_g} = total market value of a geared company
$V_{E_{ug}}$ = what the company would be worth if it was all equity financed
$V_{D_g}T$ = present value of the tax relief on debt interest

This expression can be restated as follows:

$$\begin{aligned} V_{E_g} + V_{D_g} &= V_{E_{ug}} + V_{D_g}T \\ V_{E_{ug}} &= V_{E_g} + V_{D_g} - V_{D_g}T \\ V_{E_{ug}} &= V_{E_g} + V_{D_g}[1 - T] \end{aligned}$$

And, on the basis that the beta value of a company's assets reflects a weighted averaged of the beta values of the securities that finance those assets, then we can formulate the expression in terms of beta values:

$$\beta_{\text{assets}} = \beta_{\text{equity}} \times \frac{V_E}{V_E + V_D[1 - T]} + \beta_{\text{debt}} \times \frac{V_D[1 - T]}{V_E + V_D[1 - T]}$$

This is therefore our revised expression for calculating asset betas in a *taxed* world.

However, before we now start to apply this expression, one word of caution has to be sounded. One assumption that has been maintained throughout this analysis is of perpetuity cash flows. This is *not* a *necessary* assumption of the APV technique, but it *is* an assumption of the expression we have developed for estimating an asset beta in a taxed world.

Therefore if this expression is used in a situation where the cash flows are *not* perpetuities, then it should be recognized that there will be some degree of error. However, when estimating an industry's asset beta, this assumption's lack of validity may not be substantial and so the error would be relatively minor.

Applying the APV technique

Example 16.2 illustrates the use of the APV technique in a relatively simple situation. However, it should be noted that, even here, a traditional NPV/WACC approach would have great difficulty at arriving at a satisfactory evaluation of the project.

Two further points

There are two further points to be made about Example 16.2. The first concerns the reference to debt capacity.

As can be seen from the analysis used in the example, debt capacity is

Example 16.2: The Problem

Tento PLC is an industrial holding company. It is currently considering diversifying into the construction industry. The particular project under evaluation would require capital expenditure of £100,000 and would have a zero scrap value at the end of its three-year life. It is estimated that the project would generate an annual net cash flow (revenues less operating cash costs) of £50,000.

The proposal is to finance the project with an £80,000 three-year term loan from Tento's bank. The project would have sufficient debt capacity to support such a loan and the annual interest rate would be 14%. There would be an arrangement fee on the loan of £1,500. In addition, the company would utilise £20,000 of retained earnings.

The construction industry has an average equity beta of 2·43 and its debt capital can be considered to be virtually risk-free and so can be assumed to have a zero beta value. The average gearing (debt:equity) ratio in the industry is 3:4.

Tento PLC pays corporation tax at 35%, twelve months after year-end. Capital expenditure attracts a 25% writing-down allowance calculated on the reducing balance and tax relief is available on debt interest. The project would be bought on the first day of the company's financial year and the loan taken out accordingly.

The after-tax return on Government stock with a three year maturity is 10·2% per annum. The excess market return is 6% per annum, after tax.

The company wishes to evaluate the proposed investment using an Adjusted Present Value Analysis.

Example 16.2: The Solution

The starting point is to identify the NPV of the project as if it was all-equity financed – that is the base-case present value:

1 *Base-Case Discount Rate*

$$\beta_{\text{industry assets}} = 2{\cdot}43 \times \frac{4}{4 + 3(1 - 0{\cdot}35)} = \underline{1{\cdot}634}$$

Using CAPM: $10{\cdot}2\% + 6\% \times 1{\cdot}634 = \underline{20\%}$ = Base-case discount rate.

This is the return required from the project due to its systematic business risk (principally, its revenue sensitivity and its proportion of fixed to variable operating costs).

2 *Writing-Down Allowances*

£	*W.D.A.*	*Tax Relief*	*Timing*
100,000 × 0·25 =	£25,000 × 0·35 =	£8,750	Yr 2
−25,000			
= 75,000 × 0·25 =	18,750 × 0·35 =	6,562	Yr 3
−18,750			
= 56,250 − 0 =	56,250 × 0·35 =	19,688	Yr 4

3 *Base-Case Present Value*

Year	0	1	2	3	4
Outlay	(100,000)				
WDA tax relief			8,750	6,562	19,688
Net cash flow		50,000	50,000	50,000	
Tax on cash flow			(17,500)	(17,500)	(17,500)
After-tax cash flow	(100,000)	50,000	41,250	39,062	2,188
20% discount factor	×1	×·8333	×·6944	×·5787	×·4823
P.V. cash flow	(100,000)	41,665	28,644	22,605	1,055

Base-case present value: (£6,031)

4 *Present Value of the Financing Side Effects*

(i) *Present Value of the Tax Shield*

Annual interest: £80,000 × 0·14 = £11,200

Annual tax relief: £11,200 × 0·35 = £ 3,920

P.V. of tax relief: $£3{,}920\ A_{3\urcorner 0{\cdot}14}(1{\cdot}14)^{-1} = \underline{£8{,}009}$

Notice that the pre-tax cost of debt capital is used as the discount rate. This rate is used as the best rate to reflect the low risk nature of the tax relief cash flow. (The *after-tax* cost of debt is not used as this would represent 'double counting' of the debt interest tax relief.)

(ii) *Present Value of Capital Issue Costs*

Arrangement fee: (£1,500)

Tax relief on arrangement fee: £1,500 × 0·35 = £525

P.V. of the tax relief: $£525(1{\cdot}14)^{-2} = \underline{£404}$

5 *Adjusted Present Value*

		£
Base-case present value	:	(6,031)
Present value of tax shield	:	8,009
Arrangement fee	:	(1,500)
P.V. of arrangement fee tax relief	:	404
Adjusted Present Value	:	+£ 882

Although the project would have been rejected if it had been all-equity financed (NPV: − £6,031), it *is* worthwhile accepting the project because of its proposed financing method: its overall APV is positive. Therefore, if the project is accepted it will increase shareholder wealth by £882.

valuable. A project's debt capacity indicates its ability to act as security for a loan. It is the tax relief available from such a loan which gives debt capacity its value.

This then raises a problem. Some projects may be undertaken where the amount of debt finance used effectively *undergears* the project, leaving spare debt capacity. Alternatively, a project might be financed by more debt capital than the project itself can support. In other words, the project might be overgeared because of *unused* debt capacity elsewhere in the company.

The problem here concerns how the project should be evaluated via APV. Should the P.V. of the tax shield be based on the *actual* amount of debt financing used, or on the *theoretical* amount of debt financing the project's own debt capacity would allow it to raise? The answer is that the tax shield should be based on the *theoretical* level of financing as to do otherwise would lead to the danger of *cross-subsidisation.* Example 16.3 shows two possible situations.

Example 16.3

Suppose a company is considering Project A. It costs £100,000 and has an infinitely long life. It has a debt capacity of 80%. The management decide to finance the project with £50,000 of equity and £50,000 of irredeemable debentures at 10% interest. The corporation tax is 35% and there are no other costs involved.

Project A's base-case PV is negative: −£25,000. If the PV of the tax shield is based on the *actual* level of debt financing its value is:

$$\frac{£50{,}000 \times 0{\cdot}10 \times 0{\cdot}35}{0{\cdot}10}(1{\cdot}10)^{-1} = \underline{£15{,}909}$$

However, based on the *theoretical* amount of debt the project could support, the tax shield is then valued at:

$$\frac{£80{,}000 \times 0{\cdot}10 \times 0{\cdot}35}{0{\cdot}10}(1{\cdot}10)^{-1} = \underline{£25{,}455}$$

Therefore, in the former case the APV would be negative and the project – incorrectly – rejected. While in the latter case the project should, quite properly, be accepted because of its positive APV. This latter analysis is correct because although the project is *not* utilizing the whole of its debt capacity, the company has got the ability to raise debt finance in the future, secured against this project's unused debt capacity. Hence, its value should be credited to the project.

Suppose the company decided to undertake Project A. Some time later Project Z was discovered. This requires £80,000 of capital expenditure and it has a 50% debt capacity. However, instead of just using £40,000 of 10% debt, the company proposes to use £60,000 of 10% debt – £40,000 of which is secured against the project's own assets, in line with its debt capacity, and £20,000 secured against the *unused* debt capacity arising from the earlier acceptance of Project A.

If Project Z has a negative base-case present value of £18,000 and it could be financed with irredeemable debt (for simplicity), then its APV might be either positive or negative, depending on the tax shield chosen.

On the basis of debt financing of £60,000, the PV of the tax shield is:

$$\frac{\pounds 60{,}000 \times 0{\cdot}10 \times 0{\cdot}035}{0{\cdot}10}(1{\cdot}10)^{-1} = \pounds 19{,}091$$

Thus the project would be accepted with an APV of: $-$£18,000 + £19,091 = +£1,091

However, on the basis of the debt financing which the project can support in its own right – £40,000 – the PV of the tax shield is:

$$\frac{\pounds 40{,}000 \times 0{\cdot}10 \times 0{\cdot}35}{0{\cdot}10}(1{\cdot}10)^{-1} = \pounds 12{,}727$$

In this case the project's APV is negative: $-$£18,000 + £12,727 = $-$£5,273 and so should be rejected.

The *latter* analysis is, of course, correct. In the former analysis, the PV of the tax shield contains a *subsidy* from project A equal to the value of A's unused debt capacity:

$$\frac{\pounds 20{,}000 \times 0{\cdot}10 \times 0{\cdot}35}{0{\cdot}10}(1{\cdot}10)^{-1} = \pounds 6{,}364$$

Quite simply, to be acceptable, a project should be capable of generating a positive APV in its own right. Logically, we should not cross-subsidize between projects in the evaluation process.

The second point to be made is as follows. The logic behind the APV technique is simple: different risk cash flows should be evaluated separately using discount rates which specifically reflect the systematic risk level involved. For this reason, the technique is sometimes referred to as the *Valuation of Components Rule* (VCR).

In a more sophisticated analysis of a large project more than one discount rate may be used to calculate the base-case PV. For example, it may be thought that a project's *revenues* are significantly more (systematic) risky than its *cost* cash flows. Therefore the present value of the revenues may be calculated separately from the present value of its costs, using a different discount rate in each case. Alternatively, it could be legitimately argued that the WDA tax relief cash flows are particularly low risk and so should have a separate discount rate applied to them which specifically reflects their low risk nature.

A more complex example

A more complex problem is illustrated in Example 16.4. Here the APV analysis takes account not only of the tax relief on debt interest, but also of a cheap loan and capital issue costs. Any number of side-effects can be included in the analysis by just adding them on to the base-case present value.

Example 16.4: The Problem

The project that a company is considering consists of the purchase and operation of two machines A and B. Machine A costs £60,000 and Machine B £40,000. The project is expected to produce a net annual revenue, before tax, of £66,000 and is expected to have a life of 3 years. At the end of its life the two machines will be worthless.

For this type of asset the company would normally expect to finance 75% of the capital expenditure with debt capital with a maturity equal to that of the project's life. Thus they expect to raise £45,000 of debt to purchase Machine A and £30,000 of debt to purchase Machine B. The balance, in each case, would be met from an issue of equity. Issue costs are expected to be $7\frac{1}{2}$% of the amount raised in the case of equity, but can be assumed to be zero in the case of debt.

Because the Government wishes to promote the purchase and operation of Machine B, they will make a loan available (repayable at the end of three years) for 100% of Machine B's cost, at a subsidized rate of interest of only 6%. This is in contrast to the current market cost of debt of 10%. However, as a result of this facility, the company will only raise £35,000 of debt to finance Machine A, so that the overall debt ratio of the project remains at around 75%.

The project falls within an industry category having a beta value of 1·363 and an average debt–equity ratio of 1:3. The risk-free return and excess market return are 6% and $7\frac{1}{2}$%, respectively – both after tax. Corporation tax is 35%. For simplicity, assume that tax is paid at each year-end without delay and that there is no tax relief available on either capital expenditure or issue costs.

Example 16.4: The Solution

Base PV of project

$$\beta_{project} = 1{\cdot}363 \times \frac{3}{3 + 1(1 - 0{\cdot}35)} = 1{\cdot}12$$

$$E(r_{project}) = 6\% + 7\tfrac{1}{2}\% \times 1{\cdot}12 = 15\%$$

$$-£100{,}000 + £66{,}000(1 - 0{\cdot}35)A_{\overline{3}|0{\cdot}15} = -£2{,}038$$

Financing side-effects

PV of tax relief on debt interest

Machine A
$£35{,}000 \times 0{\cdot}10 \times 0{\cdot}35 A_{\overline{3}|0{\cdot}10} = £3{,}046$
Machine B
$£40{,}000 \times 0{\cdot}06 \times 0{\cdot}35 A_{\overline{3}|0{\cdot}10} = £2{,}089$
+£5,135

PV of cheap loan

Interest saving after tax
$£40{,}000 \times (0{\cdot}10 - 0{\cdot}06)(1 - 0{\cdot}35)A_{\overline{3}|0{\cdot}10}$ £3,979

Issue costs: $£25{,}000 \times 0{\cdot}075$ −£1,875

Base PV of project	−£2,038
plus PV of tax relief on interest	+£5,135
plus PV of cheap loan	+£2,586
less issue costs	−£1,875
APV	+£3,808

Therefore the project should be accepted; it has a positive APV of +£3,808

In conclusion

In conclusion, what can be said about investment and financing interactions? It should be noted that, in most cases (except for such situations as found in Example 16.4), the major financing side effect arises from the tax shield. However, in this respect, we should not ignore the conclusion of Miller's 1977 analysis that the worth of the tax shield is zero.

Whether or not Miller's analysis holds good in the real world is still subject to empirical testing. However, it may well be realistic to suggest that the value of the tax shield, even if it is not zero, is substantially less than the value placed upon it by the M and M with-tax analysis.

In such a case, an APV analysis – although technically more correct in nost circumstances than a 'traditional' WACC/NPV analysis – may add very little to the project evaluation. In other words, given all the general uncertainties surrounding any investment appraisal, an NPV/WACC analysis may be thought to be sufficiently accurate.

However, in contrast to the above comment, it should also be pointed out that in *very* major projects (sometimes referred to as *giant* projects) the financing package attached to the project plays a crucial role. In such circumstances an APV analysis would be strongly desirable.

LEASE OR PURCHASE DECISION

Financial and operating leases

In recent years leasing has become an important method of obtaining the services of an asset, as an alternative to outright purchase. Therefore it can be seen as a source of finance and hence the 'lease or purchase' decision can be classed as a financing decision.[3]

The evaluation of the lease or purchase decision has been problematical mainly because it cannot really be viewed as a *pure* financing decision, as it also involves interactions with the investment decision.[4] In this section, we will examine how the lease or purchase decision should be evaluated, in the light of our development of the APV technique.

The process of leasing involves one party (the lessor) purchasing an asset and renting out the use of that asset to another party (the lessee). Thus the lessee is able to operate the asset without actually being the legal owner.

It is usual for lease contracts to be classified into either financial or operating leases. The main characteristics of a financial lease are as follows. The lessor will lease the machine to the lessee, with the intention of receiving the full purchase price of the leased asset, plus a rate of return on capital, through the lease payments. For this reason, a financial lease cannot usually be cancelled or terminated by either party. Therefore with this type of lease, the lessee – although not the legal owner – holds all the risks of asset ownership (e.g., the risk of technological obsolescence and the risk that the demand for the asset's services will be below expectations). The lessor holds no risk, other than the risk of the lessee's default on the lease payments. Hence a financial lease is virtually indistinguishable from more normal debt capital – both in theory and in practice.

An operating lease is almost the opposite of a financial lease. With this type of lease, it is possible to terminate the contract at short notice. Hence the lessor does *not* necessarily expect to recover the full cost of the asset, plus a return on capital, out of the lease payments, but will also take account of the expected second-hand value of the asset at the termination of the leasing agreement. Therefore, with an operating lease, the lessee does not bear any of the risks of ownership – these are borne instead by the lessor – because of the option to cancel the agreement at short notice. Such a lease can be viewed, not so much as a form of finance (although that is what it is), but more of a marketing device. In other words the *manufacturer* of an asset may offer the asset's services through an operating lease as a marketing device to encourage 'sales' (e.g., photocopiers are often 'sold' on operating leases).

The evaluation of an operating lease is relatively straightforward. Because the lease is terminable at short notice, the lease payments are treated as just another operating cost of the asset involved. Hence a straightforward NPV analysis can be used, where the (after tax) lease payment cash flows are included along with all the other cash flows involved, and which are then discounted to present value by a discount rate that reflects the asset's systematic risk.

Evaluating a financial lease

We stated earlier that a financial lease is effectively the equivalent of debt capital in that, from a gearing viewpoint, the present value of a lease contract liability would be seen in the same terms as the liability on straightforward debt finance. However, the APV analysis of lease finance differs somewhat from that involving debt finance.

Example 16.5 illustrates the APV technique being applied to a 'lease versus loan-purchase' decision. This can then be contrasted with the evaluation of the same project in Example 16.6, but which is done along the lines of a more *traditional* lease versus purchase analysis. The anomalies in this second example should be fairly obvious – given what we know about risk and return relationships. (The fact that the two analyses produce the same conclusion is, of course, fortuitous.)

Example 16.5: The Problem

A company is considering undertaking a project which consists of the acquisition and operation of a machine. The machine would cost £1,000 and would have a zero scrap value at the end of its 3-year life.

It is expected to produce the following net cash flows (i.e. revenues less operating costs), pre-tax:

Year	*Cash Flow*
1	+600
2	+500
3	+200

The machine could either be bought outright or acquired via a financial lease. Purchase would be made through a £600 3-year term loan at 14% interest, secured against the machine (which has a 60% debt capacity), together with £400 of retained earnings. The lease agreement requires three payments of £320, paid annually in advance.

Assume that all initial transactions are made on the last day of the previous accounting year and the company expects to have a corporate tax liability throughout the next three years.

It is thought that the project is required to produce an after-tax return of at least 20% to make it acceptable. This can be assumed to represent an adequate base-case discount rate.

Corporation tax is charged at 35%, payable 12 months in arrears. Writing down allowances of 25% on the reducing balance are available on capital expenditure.

Example 16.5: The Analysis

In this type of situation, an APV analysis has to be undertaken on the basis of a pair of mutually exclusive alternatives: the project purchased and the project leased.

(a) *Project purchased*

Base-case PV:

Year	0	1	2	3	4
Outlay	(1,000)				
Net cash flow		600	500	200	
Tax charge			(210)	(175)	(70)
After-tax c/f	(1,000)	600	290	25	(70)
20% discount	×1	×·8333	×·6944	×·5787	×·4823
	(1,000)	499·98	201·38	14·47	(33·76)

Base-case PV: −£317·93

PV of financing side-effects

(i) PV of WDA tax relief

Tax relief:

	WDA		*Tax relief*	*Timing*
1,000 × 0·25 =	250	× 0·35 =	87·50	Yr 1
−250				
=750 × 0·25 =	187·5	× 0·35 =	65·63	Yr 2
−187·5				
=562·5 × 0·25 =	140·63	× 0·35 =	49·22	Yr 3
−140·63				
=421·87 − 0 =	421·87	× 0·35 =	147·65	Yr 4

PV calculations using K_D (14%) to reflect the low-risk nature of the cash flow:

Year	*Tax relief*	*14% discount*	
1	+ 87·50 ×	0·8772	= + 76·76
2	+ 65·63 ×	0·7695	= + 50·50
3	+ 49·22 ×	0·6750	= + 33·22
4	+147·65 ×	0·5921	= + 87·42
			+247·90 PV of tax relief

(ii) PV of tax shield

Annual interest : £600 × 0·14 = £84

Annual tax relief : £84 × 0·35 = £29·40

PV of tax relief : $£29.40 A_{\overline{3}|0\cdot14}(1\cdot14)^{-1} = +£59\cdot87$

Adjusted present value

Base-case PV :	−£317·93
PV of WDA tax relief :	+£247·90
PV of tax shield :	+£ 59·87
APV	−£ 10·16

Therefore the project is *not* worthwhile if loan-purchased.

(b) *Project leased*

Base-case PV: −£317·93

PV of financing side effects

(i) PV of lease payments: $-320 - 320A_{\overline{2}|0\cdot14} = -£846\cdot94$

(ii) PV of tax relief on lease payments:
$(+320 \times 0\cdot35)A_{\overline{3}|0\cdot14} = +£260\cdot02$

(iii) PV of capital expenditure saved = +£1000

Adjusted present value

Base-case PV	:	−£317·93
PV of lease payments	:	−£846·94
PV of tax relief	:	+260·02
PV of saved capital expenditure	:	+£1,000
APV		+£ 95·15

Therefore the project *is* worthwhile if leased.

Example 16.6

A more traditional approach to 'lease versus purchase' decisions (although there are many variations) is to treat it as a two-stage decision. The first is to compare the PV cost of leasing against purchase. The second is to then evaluate the project using the least-cost method of acquisition as the 'outlay'. In the first stage of the decision the *after-tax* cost of debt is used to reflect the low-risk nature of the cash flows *and* to take into account the tax-deductibility of debt. In the second stage, a discount rate is used which reflects the project's own systematic risk level.

Stage One

After tax cost of debt: 14%(1 − 0·35) = 9·1% = discount factor

P.V. of lease cash flows:

Year	*Lease*	*Tax relief*		*Discount factor*	
0	−320		×	1	= −320
1	−320	+112	×	0·9166	= −190·65
2	−320	+112	×	0·8401	= −174·74
3		+112	×	0·7701	= + 86·25
				PV of lease payments	= £−599·14

PV of purchase cash flows

Year	*Outlay*	*WDA*		*Discount factor*	
0	−100		×	1	= −1000
1		+87·50	×	0·9166	= + 80·20
2		+65·63	×	0·8401	= + 55·14
3		49·22	×	0·7701	= + 37·90
4		147·65	×	0·7058	= + 104·21
				PV of purchase	= −£722·55

Therefore, it is cheaper to acquire the machine with a lease rather than purchase.

Stage Two
Project's NPV analysis

Year	*PV Cost*	*Net cash flow*	*Tax charge*		*20% discount factor*		
0	−599·14			×	1	=	−599·14
1		+600		×	0·8333	=	+499·98
2		+500	−210	×	0·6944	=	+201·38
3		+200	−175	×	0·5787	=	+ 14·47
4			− 70	×	0·4823	=	− 33·76
						NPV =	£+82·93

Therefore the project is worth undertaking via a financial lease agreement.

SUMMARY

- This chapter has investigated the investment and financing decision interactions.
- Four different valuation models were analysed. All four were found to be equivalent, given a set of restrictive assumptions which included a fixed or unchanging gearing ratio.
- Given these assumptions, all four valuations models were capable of correctly evaluating a capital investment proposal.
- However, when the assumption of an unchanging gearing ratio is relaxed, all become, effectively, unworkable – with the exception of the adjusted present value model.
- The APV model is a very general model and, because it takes a divide and conquer approach – evaluating each different risk cash flow separately – it can handle highly complex capital investment appraisals, *together* with the associated financing implications.
- Finally, the lease versus purchase decision was analysed using an APV/Valuation by Components Rule approach. Here it was seen that the analysis had to be conducted on the basis of a mutually exclusive investment decision.

NOTES

1 An alternative, equivalent expression, after Hamada (1972), which is widely used is:

$$\beta_{\text{assets}} = \beta_{\text{equity}} \Big/ \left(1 + \frac{V_D}{V_E}\right)$$

but notice this expression assumes $\beta_{\text{debt}} = 0$.

2 Because of this, in Example 16.1, there is really no need to re-gear the industry's asset beta of 0·96. This could be used in CAPM to generate a suitable discount rate for the project, which would be equal to the project's WACC. This is because, in a no tax world, capital structure – although it does affect K_E – does *not* affect the overall return required.

3 Some approaches treat the decision as an *investment* decision.

4 For a survey of the different approaches, see Bower (1973).

FURTHER READING

1 Two excellent articles which look at the whole area of investment and financing decisions, their interactions and the use of CAPM are: M.E. Rubinstein, 'A Mean-Variance Synthesis of Corporate Financial Theory', *Journal of Finance*, March 1973, and R.S. Hamada, 'The Effect of the Firm's Capital Structure on the Systematic Risks of Common Stocks', *Journal of Finance*, May 1972. In addition, a worthwhile reference on debt betas is: M. Weinstein, 'The Systematic Risk of Corporate Bonds', *Journal of Financial and Quantitative Analysis*, September 1981.

2 In addition, the following articles are of interest in providing a general overview: A.K. Makhaya and H.E. Thompson, 'Comparison of Alternative Models for Estimating the Cost of Equity Capital for Electric Utilities', *Journal of Economics and Business*, February 1984; and I.E. Brick and D.G. Weaver, 'A Comparison of Capital Budgeting Techniques in Identifying Profitable Investments', *Financial Management*, Winter 1984.

3 As far as APV is concerned, the original article is: S.C. Myers, 'Interactions of Corporate Financing and Investment Decisions – Implications for Capital Budgeting', *Journal of Finance*, March 1974. However, a good introductory article is to be found in R. Taggart, 'Capital Budgeting and the Financing Decision: An Exposition', *Financial Management*, Summer 1977.

4 Other articles of interest include: D.R. Chamber, R.S. Harris and J.J. Pringle, 'Treatment of Financing Mix in Analysing Investment Opportunities', *Financial Management*, Summer 1982; R.C. Greenfield, M.R. Randall and J.D. Woods, 'Financial Leverage and the Use of the NPV Investment Criterion', *Financial Management*, Autumn 1983; and I. Cooper and J.R. Franks, 'The Interaction of Investment and Financing Decisions when a Firm has Unused Tax Credits', *Journal of Finance*, May 1983.

5 A good introductory article on the lease decision is R.S. Bower, 'Issues in Lease Financing', *Financial Management*, Winter 1973. In addition, three other articles worth reading are: L.D. Schall, 'Evaluation of Lease Financing Contracts', *Midland Corporate Finance Journal*, Spring 1985; J. Ang and P.P. Peterson, 'The Leasing Puzzle', *Journal of Finance*, September 1984; and H.H. Weingartner, 'Leasing, Asset Lives and Uncertainty: Guide to Decision Making', *Financial Management*, Summer 1987.

QUICKIE QUESTIONS

1 If a company has a gearing ratio of 1:3 why will financing a £1,000 project with £250 of debt and £750 of equity not necessarily maintain the firm's existing capital structure?
2 What does the base-case discount rate represent?
3 What does the base-case present value of a project represent?
4 Distinguish between an operating lease and a financial lease.
5 If an industry's equity beta is 1·45 and its debt beta is 0·25 with an average gearing rate of 2:5, what is its assets beta, given a 35% corporate tax rate?
6 Given the information in question 5, estimate the beta value for the industry's average level of *financial* risk.
7 What is debt capacity?
8 A project costs £5,000. It will be financed with a £3,000 5-year loan at 10% interest. The corporation tax rate is 35%, paid 12 months in arrears and the project has a 50% debt capacity. What is the PV of its tax shield?

PROBLEMS

1 Arthur PLC, an industrial conglomorate, is currently evaluating a project to produce a new electronic lock mechanism recently developed by the company. The project will require an immediate outlay of £10,000 on production machinery. This would have a zero scrap value at all times and would not be an allowable expense against tax. The project is expected to have a three year life and produce a net annual cash flow of £6,650 in each year. This amount would be subject to corporation tax.

Although the project only has a debt capacity of 30% of cost, the company has unused debt capacity elsewhere and so proposes to finance the project with a £4,000 three-year loan, with an annual interest charge of 14%, together with a £3,000 rights issue of equity and £3,000 of retained earnings. The rights issue will incur issue costs amounting to 2% of the money raised and the debt capital will incur issue costs of 1%. Both sets of issue costs are allowable against tax.

The Electronics Sector has an equity beta of 1·26 and an average gearing ratio of 1:3 (debt:equity). The industry's debt can be assumed to have a beta of 0·10. The after-tax return on Government stock is 7% and the after-tax return on the FT Index is 15%. Corporation tax is charged at a rate of 35% at each year-end without delay.

Required:

(a) Evaluate the project for the management of Arthur PLC.
(b) How would your evaluation change if the manufacturer of the production machinery offered you a three year £10,000 interest-free loan (with an issue cost of 1%)?

2 Alpacca Products PLC is a widely diversified industrial company. It has recently acquired the rights to manufacture a special type of mechanical folding widget patented by a German company. The rights – which last for five years – were bought by Alpacca's marketing director shortly before he was dismissed for incompetence.

The company's production director has now been given the task of assessing whether manufacture is likely to be a worthwhile investment for Alpacca. His decision, already presented to the Board, is to reject the project on the basis of an indicated negative NPV.

However, the chairman of Alpacca Products is uneasy about the production director's analysis and has called you in as a consultant for advice. From the production director's report, you establish the following facts:

Cash flows

	Capital £000	*Sales* £000	*Operating expenses* £000	*Tax* £000	*Net Cash flow* £000
Immediately	(1,300)				(1,300)
End year 1–5		1,800	(1,450)	(140)	210
End year 5	600				600

NPV calculation:

	Net Cash flow £000	*Discount Factor* (10%)	*Present value* £000
Immediately	(1,300)	1	(1,300)
End year 1–5	210	3·9708	834
End year 5	600	0·6209	372
Total NPV			(94)

The production director's analysis is based on the following:

(a) The company's market research department have estimated sales of 100,000 units per annum at £18 per unit.

(b) The estimate of annual operating expenses consists of the following:

	£000
Direct materials @ £2·50 per unit	250
Direct labour @ £3·20 per unit	320
Production overhead @ £3·80 per unit	380
Interest @ 10%	120
Administration, selling and distribution expenses	380
Total	1,450

The labour rate is based on a time allocation of workers on a fixed rate. Each worker costs the company £15,000 per annum, and this contract would necessitate employing 11 new ones. The company would need to spend £35,000 training these new employees in the first year, but this is not included specifically above as such costs are incorporated in production overhead expenses.

Production overhead is calculated on an allocated rate per labour hour of which 20% relates to variable overhead. Specific items of fixed overhead incurred as a result of this contract are:

Depreciation	£80,000 per annum
Supervisory labour	£56,000 per annum
Rent of additional property	£12,000 per annum

Interest is based on the latest interest rate information, and it is the company's intention to finance this project with a £1·2m, 5-year term loan at 10% interest, plus £0·1m. of retained earnings.

Administration, selling and distribution expenses are charged on the basis of a fixed rate on sales, 25% of these expenses are variable.

(c) The tax charge is based on a rate of 40%, which is the company's current marginal rate of corporation tax.

(d) The project is discounted at the anticipated interest rate.

(e) The capital cost of £1·3m represents £1m for plant and machinery, and £300,000 for working capital. It is anticipated that the plant and machinery will have a resale value of £600,000 at the end of five years.

In addition to the above you ascertain the following:

(i) The company's marginal tax rate will fall to 35% after year 1.

(ii) The company will claim capital allowances at the rate of 25% on the reducing balance.

(iii) On average, tax is payable one year after the relevant profits arise.

(iv) The production machinery is estimated to have a 50% debt capacity. Working capital only has a 10% debt capacity. However, the company is, at present, all-equity financed and so has a considerable amount of unused debt capacity.

(v) Manufacturing companies with similar characteristics to the proposed project have average equity and debt betas of 2·29 and 0·15 respectively. Their average gearing ratio is 2:3 and their average marginal rate of corporation tax is 35%.

(vi) The current after-tax risk free return on Government Stock is estimated at 8·5%. The average return on the FTSE stock market index is 15·5%.

(vii) The capital expenditure on the machinery would take place (at year 0) on the last day of the company's previous financial year for maximum tax efficiency.

Required:

Draft a report to the chairman of Alpacca Products PLC:

(a) presenting a revised assessment to assist them in their decision making;

(b) discussing any differences between your assessment and that of the production director;

(c) briefly discussing the basis of Adjusted Present Value as a decision making criterion.

3 Louise is the financial controller of a division of a large manufacturing company listed on the London Stock Exchange. She is currently evaluating whether to lease or buy a specialised machine. If the machine were to be purchased on 1st January the cash price of £92,000 would be financed by a loan of £100,000 on which interest would be payable at 16% per annum in six-monthly instalments *in advance*. The capital element of the loan would be repaid in two equal annual instalments in 12 and 24 months' time. The two interest payments in each calendar year would be based on the amount of the loan outstanding at the beginning of that year. The machine would be used for two years, when it would be transferred to another division within the company at its tax written down value.

If a lease were to be taken out, four rentals of £16,000 would be paid at six-monthly intervals starting on 1st January. The machine would be returned to the lessor at the end of two years.

The company has an accounting reference date of 30th June and corporation tax is payable twelve months later. Louise expects that the corporation tax rate of 35% will continue and that the machine will be eligible for an annual writing down allowance of 25%. She has calculated that the effective six-monthly after-tax cost of the loan is 6%. Louise expects that the company will have sufficient tax liabilities to absorb allowances generated by either the lease or buy option.

Required:

(a) Show whether Louise is correct in her calculation of the effective six-monthly after-tax cost of the loan as 6%.

(b) Using the after-tax cost of the loan of 6%, determine whether the machine should be leased or purchased using the cash raised from the loan.

(c) Determine whether the machine should be leased or purchased if the company were to have no tax liabilities in the foreseeable future (assuming the transfer value of the machine remains unchanged).

(d) Discuss the factors which management should consider when deciding between finance leases and operating leases.

17
Overseas capital investments

Chapter Contents

INTRODUCTION

Domestic versus foreign projects

The appraisal of capital investments in foreign countries involves several difficulties not present in domestic project appraisal. Principal among these difficulties are the following.

1 Foreign exchange (FX) rates fluctuate over time in an essentially unpredictable way. Therefore an overseas project's cash flows are exposed to the risk of adverse FX movements.
2 There are a variety of ways in which an overseas government (the *host* government) might take action which adversely discriminates against an overseas project once the investment has been undertaken. Such actions might range from the imposition of penalty rates of taxation, and restrictions on the remittance of project net cash flows back to the parent, to confiscation of the project's assets without compensation. These possibilities are referred to as *country risk*.
3 There is the problem of correctly evaluating the systematic risk and required expected rate of return on the project within an international, rather than domestic, context.

4 Finally, there is the problem of the correct project appraisal procedure. In particular, should the analysis be undertaken from the viewpoint of the project itself, or from the viewpoint of the parent company? This problem arises because of differences that can occur between a project's net cash flows, and a project's net cash flows *which are available for repatriation* back to the parent company.

This chapter examines these difficulties and the way in which they might be overcome. However, before proceeding further, it is necessary first to look at the FX markets.

FOREIGN EXCHANGE MARKETS

The historical background

Foreign exchange (FX) rates are simply the price of one country's money expressed in terms of another country's money. For example, if the exchange rate between US dollars and pounds sterling ($/£) was $2 = £1, then this would mean either that pounds cost two dollars each, or that dollars cost fifty pence each.

Between 1944 and 1973, international trade within the Western World operated on the basis of *fixed* FX rates. The system was set up in 1944 following international negotiations that took place in Bretton Woods in the USA. Although it remained in force for nearly thirty years, it came under increasing pressure throughout the 1960s as capital markets – both national and international – began to expand and develop.

The system of fixed FX rates was finally abandoned in 1973 and was replaced by a system of floating (or variable) exchange rates. It is this system of floating or variable exchange rates that remains in force today.

Although the current system of floating FX rates is, to some extent, *managed* by governments and their central banks, their ability to do so is somewhat limited; the reason being that any individual government – or capable of countering the world-wide forces of supply and demand except in the very short run. It is these forces, fundamentally, that cause FX rates to move: an increased demand for the dollar by people holding pounds sterling will push up the price of the dollar relative to pounds sterling – and vice versa. These forces, and their causes, we shall return to shortly.

The spot and forward market

The FX market is a world-wide market with no single centralized location. Instead the market consists of the FX *dealing rooms* of the large international banks which are linked together, 24 hours a day, through a sophisticated communications system.

The FX market is divided up into two distinct segments – the *spot* market and the *forward* market. In the spot market, currency deals (to buy or sell one currency in exchange for another), are made for *immediate* (i.e. 'on the spot') exchange of currencies.[1]

In the forward market, currency deals are agreed *now* for the *future* delivery (i.e. exchange) of currencies. Such deals are made for a specific amount of currency, at a specific rate of exchange (the *forward rate*) and for delivery on a specific future date.

The futures and options markets

In addition to the spot and forward markets, there are two additional markets: the currency futures market and the currency options market.[2] Within the context of this chapter, neither one is as important as the spot and forward markets, but they are briefly covered here in order to try to give as full a picture as possible of the FX markets.

The currency futures market is similar to the forward market, but has been set up much more recently.[3] It differs from the forward market in that the forward market deals in *tailor-made* currency deals while the futures market deals in *off-the-peg*, packaged currency deals.

In other words, in the forward market you can deal in almost any currency, for any amount and for any period of time forward.[4] Thus a company could, for example, arrange to buy $1,345,500 in exchange for Pounds Sterling for delivery in 147 days' time. In contrast the futures market only deals in a restricted range of currencies, for a restricted number of standard forward periods and for standardized amounts of currency. Typically futures are only available in the very major trading currencies of the world and for forward periods of 3, 6 or 9 months. Each futures *contract* is for a standardized quantity of currency, so that a DM/$ futures contract (i.e. German marks/US dollars) comes in DM 125,000 units only.

The futures market has some important advantages over the forward market. One is that dealing costs for relatively small amounts of currency are much lower because of the standardized nature of the contracts. But the restricted range of currencies, the relatively small size of individual contracts and the restrictive range of forward dates makes it more suitable for a small importing or exporting company. In particular, as far as overseas capital investments are concerned, it is the forward market that will be of greater relevance.

One characteristic of both futures and forward currency markets is that the deal *must* be completed (i.e. *closed out*). Thus with the illustration of the forward purchase of $1,345,500 for £, once the contract has been entered into, exchange of currencies must take place on the appointed date. A similar requirement (although the mechanics are different) applies to futures contracts.

In contrast, currency options contracts do not necessarily result in a currency exchange taking place. Suppose a company buys an *option* to forward purchase $1,345,500, at a specific exchange rate, on a specific future date. Then it is up to the purchaser of the option to decide whether, on that future date, they *exercise* the option and exchange the currencies, or allow the option to *lapse* and so not go through with the deal. Quite simply, they can take whatever course of action best suits them at the time.

Option contracts come in two forms. Over-the-counter currency options provide a tailor-made deal in a similar way to a forward deal. Traded currency options provide a packaged deal similar to currency futures. Obviously currency options cost more than the equivalent forward or futures contracts because of the additional feature that they have – the option purchaser's ability to walk away from delivery if it suits them at the time. As a result, they are normally only used when that additional feature is particularly desirable.

Such a situation exists where a company does not have a *certain* need to buy or sell a particular foreign currency, but has a *possible* need (usually, contingent upon some other event). For example, if a company sells some goods to a US customer and invoices them for $1m, on three months' credit, then they may well want to fix up a *forward contract* to sell those $1m in exchange for pounds sterling in three months' time. A forward contract is suitable here because they know for certain that they will have $1m in three months' time.

However, suppose a potential US customer asks a company to provide a *quotation* for the supply of particular goods in competition with another company. The company quotes a price of $1m on three months' credit. They would not then fix a forward deal to sell the $1m because they may not be awarded the contract, and so may not receive $1m. Instead, in such circumstances, they may decide to buy an *option* to sell $1m forward. If they win the contract, then they can – if they wish – go through with the agreed currency exchange. But, if they lose the contract to a competitor, then they can simply allow the option to lapse.

CAUSES OF FX MOVEMENTS

Introduction

Returning to the spot and forward markets, it was stated earlier that what caused FX rates to move in a floating rate system were the forces of supply and demand. We now turn to examine the *causes* that lie behind movements in supply and demand.

However, it should be pointed out, that our understanding of these forces and their impact on FX rates is not wholly understood. It is believed that we know the main individual determinants of FX rates, but what is much less clear is how they interact together in the real world.

The terminology of the market

Before examining the causes of movements in FX rates, we must first look at the terminology of the market. We will use, as an example, the exchange rate between $ and £.

The $/£ spot and (say) three-month forward rates[7] may be quoted as:

Spot:	1·8050
Forward:	1·8120

In other words, for immediate exchange of currencies, the FX rate is \$1·8050 = £1. Whereas, for exchange of currencies in 3 months' time, the FX rate is \$1·8120 = £1. Notice that, typically, FX rates are given to four decimal places: 1·8050 would read – one dollar, eighty cents and 50 *basis points.*

The rates given in the example above would be the *middle-rates* which would represent a convenient simplification of the real world. In practice, there would be two spot and two 3-month forward rates: a buying rate and a selling rate. For example:

Spot \$/£:	1·8045 – 1·8055
3 Mth. Fwd. \$/£:	1·8110 – 1·8130

In each case the *first* rate is the rate at which the financial manager can *buy* \$ (and so sell £), and the second rate is the one at which he or she can *sell* \$ (and so buy £).[6]

For simplicity, we shall just make use of middle rates. We shall also assume that the forward rate represents the market's best estimate *currently*, of what *will be* the spot rate at that future point in time. So, in our initial example, the forward rate indicates that currently the market estimates that the spot \$/£ exchange rate will move to 1·8120 in 3 months' time. That is why therefore, the FX market is willing to enter a contract *now*, to exchange \$ and £ in 3 months' time at a rate of 1·8120.[7]

Again, returning to our initial example:

\$/£ Spot:	1·8050
Forward:	1·8120

This means that for immediate delivery each \$ costs 55·40 pence (i.e. the inverse of 1·8050). Similarly, for delivery in 3 months' time, each \$ costs 55·19 pence. Therefore the \$ is getting *cheaper* relative to £. As the forward rate is taken to represent the market's best estimate of the future spot rate, this particular forward rate indicates that the \$ is expected to lose value, or *depreciate* against £.

In this example, the exchange rates *could* have been given as:

\$/£ Spot:	1·8050
Forward:	0·70 cent discount

Where the forward rate is quoted at a *discount* on the spot rate, the actual forward rate can be found by *adding* the discount to the spot rate, and it indicates that the currency is expected to *depreciate.*

Conversely, if the forward rate was quoted as a *premium* to the spot rate, then the actual forward rate can be found by *subtracting* the premium from the spot rate, and it indicates that the currency is expected to *appreciate.* For example:

\$/£ Spot:	1·8050
Forward:	1·35 cent premium

The actual forward rate can be calculated as: \$1·8050 minus 1·35 cents = 1·7915. We know that the current spot rate of 1·8050 values the \$ at 55·40 pence approximately. The inverse of the forward rate indicates that the cost of a \$ is expected to increase to 55·82 pence. Hence, in this example, the \$ is expected to appreciate against £.[8]

Finally, given an expected annual rate of appreciation or depreciation of one currency against another, then future exchange rates may be estimated as follows:

$$\text{Spot rate } (1 + \text{Annual rate of depreciation})^N = \text{Estimated exchange rate in } N \text{ years' time}$$
$$\text{Spot rate } (1 - \text{Annual rate of appreciation})^N = \text{Estimated exchange rate in } N \text{ years' time.}$$

Therefore, if the current \$/£ spot rate is 1·8050, and the \$ is expected to depreciate by 5% per year against £ in the foreseeable future, we could, for example, estimate the \$/£ expected exchange rate in one, two and three years' time:

$$1{\cdot}8050\,(1{\cdot}05)^1 = 1{\cdot}8952 : \text{Year 1}$$
$$1{\cdot}8050\,(1{\cdot}05)^2 = 1{\cdot}9900 : \text{Year 2}$$
$$1{\cdot}8050\,(1{\cdot}05)^3 = 2{\cdot}0895 : \text{Year 3}$$

The balance of international trade

One of the main determinants of movements in FX rates is the *imbalances* in international trade between countries. Let us take the case of Japan and the US as an example.

Japan exports goods and services to the US. These Japanese exporters wish to be paid in yen (¥).[9] Therefore the American importers of Japanese goods have to *sell* \$ in order to *buy* ¥ to pay for the goods that they import.

Similarly, the US exports to Japan and these US exporters require to be paid in \$. Therefore the Japanese importers of American goods have to *sell* ¥ in order to *buy* \$ and so pay for the goods.

If there was a *balance* of trade between Japan and the US then the quantities of ¥ that US importers would want to buy would equal the quantity of ¥ Japanese importers would want to sell. A similar balance between supply and demand for the \$ would also hold. As a result, the FX rate between the currencies would be fairly stable.[10] However, in practice, Japan exports more to the US than the US exports to Japan. As a result, US importers want to buy a greater quantity of ¥ than Japanese importers want to sell; and also Japanese importers want to buy a smaller quantity of \$ than US importers want to sell.

Therefore, there is a shortage of ¥ and an excess of supply of \$ and so the forces of supply and demand push *up* the price of the ¥ and push *down* the price of the \$. The ¥ therefore appreciates against the \$. The \$/¥ FX rate is moving through the operation of supply and demand market forces.

The Interest Rate Parity Theorem

A second major cause of movements in exchange rate is differences in interest rates, for comparable risk investments, between countries. The interest rate parity theorem (IRPT) states that FX rates can be expected to move to take up differences in interest rates and thereby bring about effective interest rate parity between countries.

For example, suppose you have savings of £1,000 that you wish to place on risk-free deposit for a year by investing in Government stocks. You find that the return offered by UK Government stocks is 7% while the return offered by US Government stocks is 11%.

Under such circumstances, you might be tempted to place your savings on \$ deposit to yield 11%, rather than £ deposit which only yields 7%. However, the IRPT suggests that what you *gain* from the higher \$ interest rate you can be expected to *lose* through a depreciating \$ FX rate. In other words, FX rates can be expected to move so as to make you effectively indifferent between £ deposits and \$ deposits.

In \$/£ terms, the IRPT relationship is given by:

$$\frac{1 + i_{\$}}{1 + i_{£}} = \frac{\text{Forward rate}}{\text{Spot rate}}$$

where: $i_{\$}$ is the \$ interest rate per time period
$i_{£}$ is the £ interest rate per time period for a comparable systematic risk investment
and where the forward rate is forward FX rate for the same time period as the interest rate.

In the example used above, therefore:

$$\frac{1 + 0{\cdot}11}{1 + 0{\cdot}07} = \frac{\text{12 mth. Fwd. rate}}{\text{Spot rate}}$$

and if the current spot rate is 1·8050, then in 12 months' time the market will expect the FX rate to move to:

$$\text{12 mth. Fwd rate} = \frac{(1 + 0{\cdot}11) \times 1{\cdot}8050}{(1 + 0{\cdot}07)} = \underline{1{\cdot}8725}$$

and, at this rate we would be indifferent between a \$ deposit and a £ deposit for our £1000 of savings as Table 17.1 illustrates.

Table 17.1

£1,000 deposit in £ will yield: £1,000 (1·07) = £1,070.
£1,000 deposit in \$ will yield:
(i) Convert £1,000 to \$ at spot: £1,000 × 1·8050 = \$1,805
(ii) Place on \$ deposit to produce: \$1,805 (1·11) = \$2,003·55
(iii) Reconvert back to £ in 12 months' time at the then expected spot rate yields: \$2,003·55 ÷ 1·8725 = £1,070.[11]

The immediate lesson to be learnt from the IRPT is that one cause of movement in FX rates is differences in interest rates. A second lesson, and one of some importance to financial managers, is that we should not be fooled by seemingly attractive interest rates in another currency: if interest rates are higher in the US than in the UK, we might be tempted to place money on \$ deposit and raise £ loans. The IRPT states that such apparent advantages are illusions. FX rates can be expected to move to bring about parity in interest rates between different countries.

Does the IRPT operate in the real world? The answer is that it generally does, especially where there are no exchange control restrictions; the reason being that, if it did *not* hold, then arbitrage opportunities would open up, enabling profits to be made by raising loans in one currency and placing them on deposit in another currency. As with all arbitrage opportunities, their existence would create supply and demand forces which would quickly bring the FX market back into equilibrium where the IRPT does hold.

The Purchasing Power Parity Theorem

The third major cause behind FX rate movements is differences in inflation rates between different countries. This has its basis in the Law of One Price which states, with regard to goods and services which are capable of being *traded internationally*, that (in \$/£ terms):

$$\text{£ price of a good} \times \text{\$/£ spot rate} = \text{\$ price of a good}$$

Again, if this did not hold then it would present an arbitrage opportunity where the good could be bought in the cheaper country and sold in the more expensive country.[12] Therefore, suppose a particular good sells for £1,000 in the UK and the \$/£ spot rate is 1·8050, the Law of One Price indicates that the \$ price of the good should be:

$$\text{£}1{,}000 \times 1{\cdot}8050 = \underline{\$1{,}805}$$

Now suppose prices inflate up in the UK at 4% per year, whilst they increase by 6% per year in the US. This means that in 12 months' time the £ price of the good can be expected to have risen to: £1,000 (1·04) = £1,040 and the \$ price to: \$1,805 (1·06) = \$1,913·30.

As a result, to enable the Law of One Price to continue to hold, this implies that the \$/£ FX rate can be expected to move over this period to:

$$\frac{1{,}913{\cdot}30}{1{,}040} = \underline{1{\cdot}8397}$$

and so:

$$\text{£}1{,}040 \times 1{\cdot}8397 = \$1{,}913{\cdot}30$$ [13]

Thus the purchasing power parity theorem (PPPT) holds that FX rates can be expected to move so as to take up differences in inflation rates and therefore maintain the Law of One Price:

$$\frac{1 + \text{inflation}_{\$}}{1 + \text{inflation}_{£}} = \frac{\text{Forward rate}}{\text{Spot rate}}$$

where the forward rate is for the same period of time as the inflation rate. (For instance, in our example we used *annual* rates of inflation and so the 12 month forward rate would be 1·8397.)

Does the PPPT work in practice? The answer is that it does, to some extent. The Law of One Price obviously will not work with goods (such as property) which cannot be physically traded internationally. For example, you could not buy a factory in New York, ship it across the Atlantic and sell it in London. In addition, where transportation costs form a significant proportion of the good's total value, then the Law again will not really operate. Therefore it probably does not work in respect of cornflakes or toothpaste.

However, where goods can be freely traded internationally and where transportation costs do not represent a significant part of the good's total value, then the Law of One Price will *tend* to operate. For example, in things such as precious metals, commodities, cars and even industrial machinery, there will tend to be a link between price inflation and exchange rate movements.

Therefore, we are probably safe to conclude that the idea of the PPPT will probably operate over the longer term. But, because of the various imperfections in the operation of the Law of One Price, there are likely to be significant deviations from PPPT in the shorter term.

The International Fisher Effect

It can be seen from the IRPT and the PPPT that both can be combined, in a perfect international world, to suggest:

$$\frac{1 + i_{\$}}{1 + i_{£}} = \frac{1 + \text{inflation}_{\$}}{1 + \text{inflation}_{£}} = \frac{\text{Forward rate}}{\text{Spot rate}}$$

Recalling the earlier chapter on inflation and the Fisher Effect of:

(1 + real int. rate) (1 + average inflation rate) = (1 + mkt. interest rate)

the International Fisher Effect implies that all countries have the same underlying *real* interest rate. What causes differences in market interest rates is differences in average inflation rates. The IRPT and the PPPT therefore combine to bring about both interest rate and purchasing power parity.

FOREIGN PROJECT APPRAISAL

The basic approach

A project in a foreign country generates a stream of net cash flows in the currency of its host country. How is the parent to evaluate those cash flows in an NPV analysis? We can formulate *two* possible approaches to the problem which should provide exactly the same expected result.

Using as an example a UK company investing in the US, the two alternative approaches are:

(i) *The project's \$ cash flows* are discounted at the \$ discount rate to generate a \$ NPV. This can then be converted at the \$/£ spot rate to give a *£NPV*.
(ii) *The project's \$ cash flows* are converted to £ cash flows. These £ cash flows are then discounted at the £ discount rate to generate a *£NPV*.

Notice how each approach starts off at exactly the same point (the project's \$ cash flows), and ends up at exactly the same point (the £NPV). Both approaches are illustrated in Example 17.1.

As both approaches provide exactly the same result, given our estimates and given that the IRPT holds, which approach should be used in practice is likely to depend on what information is available, and how difficult it might be to forecast the information that may *not* be available. Generally, it may be assumed that management might be more uneasy about forecasting future FX rates than they would be about forecasting the required \$ return. Therefore approach (i) may be the more likely one to be found in practice. There is, however, a lack of empirical evidence on the matter.

Example 17.1

	Year	*\$m*
US project's net cash flows:	0	−10
	1	+ 5
	2	+ 6
	3	+ 4

The \$/£ spot rate is 1·8050 and the \$ is expected to depreciate by 5% per year. A similar-risk UK-based project would be expected to earn a minimum return of 20%.

Calculations:
Given the spot rate and the expected rate of annual depreciation, the future exchange rates can be estimated:

$$1{\cdot}8050\,(1{\cdot}05)^1 = 1{\cdot}8952 : \text{Year 1}$$
$$1{\cdot}8050\,(1{\cdot}05)^2 = 1{\cdot}9900 : \text{Year 2}$$
$$1{\cdot}8050\,(1{\cdot}05)^3 = 2{\cdot}0895 : \text{Year 3}$$

Using the IRPT, the \$ discount rate can be estimated:

$$\frac{1 + \text{annual discount rate}_\$}{1 + \text{annual discount rate}_£} = \frac{\text{FX rate in 12 months' time}^{14}}{\text{Spot FX rate}}$$

$$\$ \text{ discount rate} = \frac{(1 + 0{\cdot}20) \times 1{\cdot}8952}{1{\cdot}8050} - 1 = \underline{0{\cdot}26 \text{ or } 26\%}$$

Approach (i)

Year	*\$m*	*26% discount factors*		*\$P.V. c/fs*
0	−10	1	=	−10
1	+ 5	0·7936	=	+ 3·968
2	+ 6	0·6299	=	+ 3·779
3	+ 4	0·4999	=	+ 2·000
				\$− 0·253m NPV

−\$0·253m ÷ 1·8050 = −£0·14m NPV

Approach (ii)

Year	*\$m*		*\$/£ rate*		*£m*		*20% discount factors*		*£P.V. c/fs*
0	−10	÷	1·8050	=	−5·540	×	1	=	−5·540
1	+ 5	÷	1·8952	=	+2·638	×	0·8333	=	+2·198
2	+ 6	÷	1·9900	=	+3·015	×	0·6944	=	+2·094
3	+ 4	÷	2·0895	=	+1·914	×	0·5787	=	+1·108
									£−0·14m NPV

The project cash flows

Whichever approach to the appraisal of overseas projects is used, both take as their starting point the project's net cash flows denominated in the host country's currency. It is here that some controversy is found.

The point of dispute is whether the project's net cash flows should be viewed from the standpoint of the project itself, or from the standpoint of the parent. In other words should the year-by-year net operating cash flows of the project be evaluated, or should the project's net cash flows *available to be remitted back to the parent* be evaluated?

With foreign country projects these two cash flows can often be significantly different because of host country restrictions on the repatriation of project net cash flows. Example 17.2 shows how crucial the difference might be.

Example 17.2

Rush PLC is thinking of undertaking a capital investment in an overseas country whose currency is the dollar. The project's net cash flows are:

Year	*\$m*
0	−10
1	+ 8
2	+ 4
3	+ 3·5

At the current \$/£ spot rate of 2·50, the project will require an outlay of £4m. The company intends to finance the whole of this out of retained earnings. Given the systematic risk involved, it is thought that 20% is a suitable required rate of return in \$ terms. The company follows a policy of paying out all of each year's net cash flow as a dividend.

The host country's laws permit foreign projects to remit back to their parents a maximum annual cash flow equal to 10% of the project's cost. Any surplus (or blocked) cash flows have to be placed on special deposit at an interest rate of 5%. All blocked funds can be remitted back to the parent at the end of the project's life.

From the viewpoint of the project, it produces a positive NPV and so is acceptable:

Year	*\$m*	× *20% discount*		
0	−10	× 1	=	−10
1	+ 8	× 0·8333	=	+ 6·67
2	+ 4	× 0·6944	=	+ 2·78
3	+ 3·5	× 0·5787	=	+ 2·02
				\$+ 1·47m NPV

+\$1·47m ÷ 2·50 = +£0·588m NPV

However, from the viewpoint of the parent the project is undesirable as it has a *negative* NPV:

Year	*1*	*2*	*3*
Blocked funds		7	10.35
+ interest		+0·35	+0·52
+ project cash flow	+8	+4	+3·5
Total cash flow	+8	+11·35	+14·37
Repatriated c/f	−1	−1	−14·37
Blocked funds	+7	+10·35	–

Year	*\$m*	× *20% disc.*		
0	−10	× 1	=	−10
1	+ 1	× 0·8333	=	+ 0·83
2	+ 1	× 0·6944	=	+ 0·69
3	+14·37	× 0·5787	=	+ 8·32
				\$− 0·16m NPV

−\$0·16m ÷ 2·50 = −£64,000 NPV

Although there has been some controversy over this matter, it is difficult to understand why. It should appear obvious that, as it is the parent which is investing in the project, the project *must* be evaluated from the *parent's* viewpoint.

That is to say, what is important is the NPV of the project's cash flows that are available to be remitted back to the parent. The fact that the project used in Example 17.2 has a positive NPV when viewed in its own right must be irrelevant. However good an investment might appear to be, there is little point in undertaking that investment if the investor cannot enjoy its benefits. Thus Rush PLC, acting on its shareholders' behalf, are not going to be interested in undertaking the project if it does not represent a positive NPV investment *from their point of view*.

Overseas currency finance

The conclusion reached above then raises an interesting point as far as financing is concerned. One of the fundamental principles of capital investment appraisal is that the financing decision can be kept separate from the investment decision. This then leads us always to exclude *financing* cash flows in calculating a project's NPV. (Notice that this approach even held in an APV analysis. The base case present value did not include any financing cash flows.)

The reason for this is *not* that the financing cash flows are being *ignored*, but that their present value is always *equal* to the amount of finance involved. Therefore the outlay on a project at 'Year 0' reflects the

Example 17.3

A company wishes to buy a machine for £1,000. It has a net operating cash flow of £450 per year for each of the three years of its life and a zero scrap value. Given the systematic risk of the project, a 15% discount rate is thought suitable for evaluation purposes.

The machine is to be financed by a 3-year £1,000 term loan at 10% interest.

Ignoring tax (which would just be a complication, but which would not change the conclusions drawn), the approach used is to calculate the project's NPV, without *apparently* taking either the loan interest payments or loan repayment into account:

$$-1{,}000 + 450A_{\overline{3}|0{\cdot}15} = \underline{+27{\cdot}44 \text{ NPV}}$$

However, the loan cash flows are *not* being ignored. They involve the following cash flows.

Year	*£*
0	
1	− 100
2	− 100
3	−1,100

Applying the principle that the discount rate should always reflect the risk of the cash flow, the discount rate that would best reflect the risk of the loan cash flow would be the loan interest rate itself; and so

Year	*£*	*10% discount*	
0			
1	−100	× 0·9091 =	− 90·91
2	−100	× 0·8264 =	− 82·64
3	−1,100	× 0·7513 =	− 836·43
			PV −1,000[15]

Therefore, in entering the project's outlay of £1,000 in the NPV analysis we are implicitly entering the *present value* of the financing cash flows involved with the project.

present value of the financing cash flows involved with the outlay. Example 17.3 simply illustrates this point, which has been made in earlier chapters, but which is of particular importance as far as overseas project appraisal is concerned.

However, problems can arise as far as this principle is concerned when part or all of a foreign project's finance is raised in the foreign currency rather than – what has been implicitly assumed so far – via the *export* of £. This is because the foreign financing can affect the amount of the project's cash flows available to be remitted back to the parent. To illustrate this, let us return to Rush PLC and the project dealt with in Example 17.2, but *now* involve some foreign currency financing. Example 17.4 gives the details.

In Example 17.4 it can be seen that because of the change in the *source* of the finance ($ rather than £ for 50% of the financing requirement) the resulting impact on the cash flows available to the parent now makes this particular project worthwhile.

Example 17.4

Rush PLC now propose to finance the foreign project (referred to in Example 17.2) as a joint venture with investors in the host country. Foreign investors will buy $5m of equity and Rush PLC will export £2m for the remaining 50% of the equity. The company plans to follow its normal policy of paying out each year's entire net cash flow as dividends.

Under these circumstances, from the *project's* viewpoint, its NPV remains at +£0·588m. However, from the *parent's* viewpoint, the revised financing plans alter their analysis:

Year	*1*	*2*	*3*
Project cash flows	+8	+4	+3·5
− foreign dividends	−4	−2	−1·75
+ blocked funds		+3	+4·15
+ interest		+0·15	+0·21
Total cash flow	+4	+5·15	+6·11
Repatriated c/f	−1	−1	−6·11
Blocked funds	+3	+4·15	–

Year	*$m*		*20% discount*		
0	−5[16]	×	1	=	−5
1	+1	×	0·8333	=	+0·83
2	+1	×	0·6944	=	+0·69
3	+6·11	×	0·5787	=	+3·54
					$+0·06m

+$0·06m ÷ 2·50 = +£24,000 NPV

As a result the foreign project which *did* produce a negative NPV now produces a *positive* NPV.

Example 17.5

Rush PLC *had* decided to use a 20% discount rate in \$ terms because they had identified the project's asset beta to be 1·6. In the US, the current return on Government stocks is 12% and the return on the New York Stock Exchange index is 17%. Therefore, using the CAPM:

$$20\% = 12\% + [17\% - 12\%] \times 1{\cdot}6$$

The company *now* propose to finance the \$10m project by exporting £ to finance half the project and then raise a 3-year \$5m term loan for the remainder. The interest rate on the loan would be 12% as it would be viewed in the US as being virtually risk-free.

$$\text{Given the relationship: } \beta_{\text{assets}} = \beta_{\text{equity}} \times \frac{V_E}{V_0}$$

$$\text{then } \beta_{\text{equity}} = \beta_{\text{assets}} \times \frac{V_0}{V_E} = 1{\cdot}6 \times \frac{2}{1} = 3{\cdot}2$$

and the \$ return required on the project, from the *equity's* viewpoint, can be estimated via the CAPM:

$$\underline{28\%} = 12\% + [17\% - 12\%] \times 3{\cdot}2$$

The project appraisal analysis is now as follows:

Year	*1*	*2*	*3*
Project cash flows	+8	+ 4	+3·5
− interest payments	−0·6	− 0·6	−0·6
− loan			−5·0
+ blocked funds		+ 6·4	+9·12
+ interest		+ 0·32	+0·46
Total cash flow	+7·4	+10·12	+7·48
Repatriated c/f	−1	− 1	−7·48
Blocked funds	+6·4	+ 9·12	–

Year	*\$m*	*× 28% discount rate*		
0	−5	×	1	= −5
1	+1	×	0·7812	= +0·78
2	+1	×	0·6103	= +0·61
3	+7·48	×	0·4768	= +3·57
				\$−0·04m

−\$0·04m ÷ 2·50 = −£16,000 NPV

From the parent company's viewpoint, the project is not worthwhile.

Therefore Example 17.4 contains a very important conclusion as far as foreign project appraisal is concerned: the cash flows of any finance raised in the host country *must* be included in the NPV evaluation of the project, if there are restrictions imposed on the repatriation of the project's cash flows back to the parent. If there are no restrictions on net cash flow remittance back to the parent, then the project should be appraised on the same as any domestic project – excluding all the financing cash flows.

The project discount rate

The conclusion reached in the above section then leads on to the problem about identifying the correct discount rate to use (whether Approach (i) is applied and a $ discount rate is required, or Approach (ii) is applied and a £ discount rate is needed). With the Rush PLC example used in Examples 17.2 and 17.4 the problem was deliberately avoided by using all-equity financing. In such a case the discount rate simply has to reflect the systematic *business* risk of the project.

The all-equity financing used in the two Rush PLC examples also helped avoid having to make a distinction between taxed and no-tax cases. Therefore the analysis to date applies equally to both situations. However, we know from previous chapters that as soon as we start to look seriously at the choice and identification of the discount rate, we *must* distinguish between taxed and no-tax situations. For the moment, we will proceed on the assumption that there are *no* taxes.

What would happen in the Rush PLC example if the company had originally intended to finance the project by exporting £4m, of which £2m would be in the form of retained earnings and the other £2m would be raised via a 3-year term loan? In these circumstances, the £ discount rate would have been the project's weighted average cost of capital.

However, what if Rush then decided to raise the 3-year term loan in $? In these circumstances, as far as the project appraisal from the parent's viewpoint is concerned, what would be evaluated would be the project's cash flows available for repatriation back to the parent. The point here is that these cash flows would be the ones that were available for *equity* only (the debt interest having been paid in $). As a result, the discount rate to apply to these cash flows would be one which reflected the project's business risk *plus* the financial risk that arises from the gearing – in other words the cost of equity capital. Example 17.5 illustrates the situation, making use of the Rush PLC data.

Foreign projects in a taxed world

Just as with domestic projects, so it is that with overseas projects: the only really satisfactory approach to use in a taxed world is an APV analysis. But with such an analysis, because of the importance of having to look at the project's cash flows from the parent's viewpoint, a greater *decomposition* of the various elements is required than we have so far used with APV. As a result, the analysis becomes more complex. Example 17.6 illustrates an application.

Example 17.6

Visa PLC is a highly profitable UK conglomerate. It is thinking of undertaking a capital investment in an overseas country whose currency is the dollar. The following information is available:

Project	Cost: \$12m Life: 3 years Scrap value: \$3·4m Operating cash flow £8m/year, pre-tax
Finance	\$4m 3-year term loan at 15% £3m 3-year term loan at 9·5% £1m retained earnings These financing arrangements fully utilize the project's debt capacity.
Risk:	The project is in an area that the company know well as far as UK investment is concerned and an asset beta of 1·40 is usually applied.
Market Data:	In the UK, the risk-free rate of return is 6% after tax and the return on the FTSE market index is 16% after tax.
Tax and Other Data:	The UK corporate tax rate is 35%, paid 12 months in arrears. The corporate tax rate of the host country is 40%, payable at each year-end without delay. In the host country, straight-line depreciation on cost, and interest charges, are both allowable expenses against tax. Overseas investors are allowed only to remit 50% of each year's pre-tax, but after interest, accounting profits back to the parent. All blocked funds earn 5% tax free in a special Government account and can only be repatriated at the end of the project's life. The project is not expected to attract any UK tax on the remitted cash flow. The current spot exchange rate is \$2·00 = £1. The \$ is expected to depreciate against £ by 5% per year, for the foreseeable future.

Calculations:

The estimated FX rate in 12 months' time is: $2{\cdot}00\,(1{\cdot}05)^1 = \underline{2{\cdot}10}$.

The £ base-case discount rate can be found from the CAPM:

$$6\% + [16\% - 6\%] \times 1{\cdot}40 = \underline{20\%}.$$

Using the IRPT, the \$ base-case discount rate can now be estimated:

$$\$ \text{ required return} = 2{\cdot}10 \times \frac{(1 + 0{\cdot}20)}{2{\cdot}00} - 1 = 0{\cdot}26 \text{ or } \underline{26\%}$$

The project can now be evaluated, as if it were all equity financed:

	$m
Annual operating cash flow	+8
less depreciation	−4
Annual accounting profit	+4

Tax charge: $4m × 0·40 = $1·6m/year
Remittable cash flow: $4m × 0·50 = $2m/year.

Parent cash flow analysis:

		$m	
Year	*1*	*2*	*3*
Blocked Funds :		+ 4·4	+ 9·02
Interest at 5% :		+ 0·22	+ 0·45
Operating cash flow :	+8	+ 8	+ 8
Tax charge :	−1·6	− 1·6	− 1·6
Scrap value :			+ 3·4
Tax charge on scrap :			− 1·36
Net cash flow :	+6·4	+11·02	+17·91
Remittable cash flow :	−2·0	− 2·0	−17·91
Blocked cash flow :	+4·4	+ 9·2	–

Base case PV calculation:

Year	*$m*	*26% discount*[17]	
0	−12	× 1 =	−12
1	+ 2	× 0·7936 =	+ 1·59
2	+ 2	× 0·6299 =	+ 1·26
3	+17·91	× 0·4999 =	+ 8·95
			$− 0·20m

−$0·2m ÷ 2·00 = <u>−£0·1m Base-case present value</u>

Present value of the financing side-effects:

(i) *Tax relief on $ loan*
$4m × 0·15 = $0·6m/year interest
$0·6m × 0·40 = $0·24m/year tax relief

None of this tax relief can be remitted back to the parent until Year 3 and will be reinvested up to that time at 5% interest. Thus the PV of the additional Year 3 cash flow is:

$$\left.\begin{array}{l}\$0{\cdot}24\text{m} \times S_{\overline{3}|0{\cdot}05}(1{\cdot}15)^{-3} \\ \$0{\cdot}24\text{m} \times 3{\cdot}1525 \times 0{\cdot}6575\end{array}\right\} = +\$0{\cdot}50\text{m} \div 2{\cdot}00 = \underline{+£0{\cdot}25\text{m}}$$

(ii) *PV of Increase in blocked funds:*
The debt interest charges will reduce the company's accounting profit, and so will reduce the level of remittable cash flows:

\$0·6m/year interest = reduction in accounting profit
\$0·6m × 0·50 = \$0·3m/year increase in blocked funds

$$\left.\begin{array}{l}\$0{\cdot}3\text{m } A_{\overline{3}|0{\cdot}15} \\ \$0{\cdot}3\text{m} \times 2{\cdot}2832\end{array}\right\} = -\$0{\cdot}68\text{m} \div 2{\cdot}00 = \underline{-£0{\cdot}34\text{m}}$$

(iii) *PV of the increased terminal cash flow to parent*
The additional blocked funds are invested to yield 5% and are remitted at Year 3:

$$\left.\begin{array}{l}\$0{\cdot}3\text{m } S_{\overline{3}|0{\cdot}05}(1{\cdot}15)^{-3} \\ \$0{\cdot}3\text{m} \times 3{\cdot}1525 \times 0{\cdot}6575\end{array}\right\} = +\$0{\cdot}62\text{m} \div 2{\cdot}00 = \underline{+£0{\cdot}31\text{m}}$$

(iv) *Tax relief on £ loan*
£3m ×0·095 = £0·285m/year interest
£0·285m × 0·35 = £0·1m/year tax relief

$$\left.\begin{array}{l}£0{\cdot}1\text{m } A_{\overline{3}|0{\cdot}095}(1 + 0{\cdot}095)^{-1} \\ £0{\cdot}1\text{m} \times 2{\cdot}5089 \times 0{\cdot}9132\end{array}\right\} = \underline{+£0{\cdot}23\text{m}}$$

Adjusted Present Value:

		£m
Base-case P.V.	:	−0·10
PV \$ loan tax shield	:	+0·25
PV of increase in blocked funds	:	−0·34
PV of increase in terminal c/f	:	+0·31
PV £ loan tax shield	:	+0·23
	APV :	£+0·35m

The project is worthwhile. From the parent company's viewpoint it is expected to have a positive APV of £350,000 approximately.

A simpler approach

A simpler approach to that of Example 17.6, which should still produce an analysis with an acceptable degree of accuracy, can be suggested. This would involve using the approach used in Example 17.5 to produce a modified base-case present value and then allowing for just the UK-based financing side effects.

In this approach, the base-case cash flows would be the project cash flows remittable to the parent and the base-case discount rate would, effectively, be the cost of equity capital which reflected the combined business and financial risk of this cash flow. Example 17.7 take the same Visa PLC problem as used in 17.6, but applies this simpler analysis.

Example 17.7
Accounting profit:

		$m
Annual operating cash flow	:	+8
less depreciation	:	−4
less interest	:	−0·6
Accounting profit		−3·4

Annual tax charge: $3·4m × 0·40 = $1·36m

Annual remittable cash flow: $3·4m × 0·50 = $1·7m

Project's remittable cash flows to parent:

		$m	
Year	*1*	*2*	*3*
Blocked funds		+ 4·34	+ 8·9
Interest at 5%		+ 0·22	+ 0·44
Operating cash flow	+8	+ 8	+ 8
Tax charge	−1·36	− 1·36	− 1·36
Interest payments	−0·6	− 0·6	− 0·6
Loan repayment			− 4·0
Scrap value			+ 3·4
Scrap tax charge			− 1·36
Net cash flow	+6·04	+10·6	+13·42
Remittable c/f	−1·7	− 1·7	−13·42
Blocked funds	+4·34	+ 8·9	–

Thus the revised 'base-case cash flow' is:

Year	*$m*
0	− 8
1	+ 1·7
2	+ 1·7
3	+13·42

The 'base-case discount rate' can be calculated via the *equity* beta found from the following expression:

$$\beta_{\text{assets}} = \beta_{\text{equity}} \times \frac{V_E}{V_E + V_D(1 - T_C)} + \beta_{\text{debt}} \times \frac{V_D(1 - T_C)}{V_E + V_D(1 - T_C)}$$

Assuming (for convenience) that the debt beta is zero, then:

$$\beta_{\text{equity}} = \beta_{\text{assets}} \times \frac{V_E + V_D(1 - T_C)}{V_E}$$

where β_{assets} = 1·40 (given)
V_E = £4m (exported £: loan plus retained earnings)
V_D = £2m (overseas currency loan)
T_C = overseas corporate tax rate

$$\beta_{\text{equity}} = 1{\cdot}40 \times \frac{4 + 2(1 - 0{\cdot}40)}{4} = 1{\cdot}82$$

and using the CAPM, a £ discount rate can be generated:

$$6\% + [16\% - 6\%] \times 1{\cdot}82 = \underline{24{\cdot}2\%}$$

Using the IRPT, a $ discount rate can then be calculated:

$$\frac{2{\cdot}10 \times (1 + 0{\cdot}242)}{2{\cdot}00} - 1 = 0{\cdot}304 \text{ or } \underline{30{\cdot}4\%}$$

'Base-case present value':

Year	*$m*	*30.4% disc.*	
0	− 8	× 1 =	−8
1	+ 1·7	× 0·7669 =	+1·30
2	+ 1·7	× 0·5881 =	+1·00
3	+13·42	× 0·4510 =	+6·05
			$+0·35m ÷ 2·00
			= +£0·17m

Present value of the financing side effects:

£ loan tax shield:

£3m × 0·095 = £0·285m/year interest
£0·285m × 0·35 = £0·1m/year tax relief

$$\left.\begin{array}{l} £0{\cdot}1\text{m } A_{3\urcorner 0{\cdot}095}(1 + 0{\cdot}095)^{-1} \\ £0{\cdot}1\text{m} \times 2{\cdot}5089 \times 0{\cdot}9132 \end{array}\right\} = \underline{+£0{\cdot}23\text{m}}$$

Adjusted Present Value:

	$m
Base-case present value	+0·17
PV of £ loan tax shield	+0·23
	£+0.40m

This analysis also indicates acceptance: the project is expected to have a positive APV of £400,000.

FINANCING FOREIGN PROJECTS

Translation risk

Translation risk can be defined as the risk a company is exposed to through movements in FX rates when it holds medium-to-long term assets and liabilities in an overseas currency. The concept specifically refers to the fact that, with such assets and liabilities, at each year-end their values have to be *translated* into £ terms for inclusion in the parent company's balance sheet. Table 17.2 illustrates the problems that might arise.

Table 17.2

A UK company undertakes a project in the US, costing $10m. It is financed through the export of £ via a £5m loan. The $/£ exchange rate is 2·00.

The parent company's opening balance sheet will show:

Balance Sheet

£ Loan: £5m	$ Assets: £5m

Suppose 12 months go by and the $/£ exchange rate has now moved to 3·00. The company's balance sheet now shows up a FX loss:[18]

Balance Sheet

£ Loan: £5m	$ Assets: £3·33m
less FX Loss: (£1·67m)	
£3·33m	

The reason for the loss is that the $10m-worth of assets are now only worth £3·33m in £ terms because the $ has depreciated against £.[19]

Overcoming the firm's exposure to translation risk is quite simple – if it is possible. The solution is to finance the project through a *$ loan* rather than a £ loan. In such circumstances, the company is protected against FX risk through the *matching* principle: the foreign currency asset is matched with a foreign currency liability. Therefore a fall in the value of one – through a movement in the FX rate – will be countered (or matched) through a corresponding fall in the other. Table 17.3 illustrates the situation.

Table 17.3

Using the data from Table 17.2, if the UK company financed the project with a $10m loan, then the opening balance sheet would show:

Balance Sheet

$ Loan: £5m	$ Assets: £5m

while, 12 months later when the FX rate has moved to $3·00, the balance sheet now becomes:

Balance Sheet

$ Loan: £3·33m	$ Assets: £3.33m

Although the £ value of the assets has declined, this decline has been matched by the £ worth of $ loan. As a result there is no net FX loss.

The problem with the solution to the problem of translation risk as advocated in Table 17.3 is that such a financing method is usually unavailable or unadvisable. For example, many Governments insist that a minimum proportion of a project's outlay is financed directly by the parent company. Even where such a requirement is not legally stipulated, it is probably not a very good idea, from a public relations viewpoint, for the parent not to put in any of its *own* money into the project.

Indeed, there is a third reason why 100% foreign currency financing might not be possible. Quite simply the host country's capital market may not be sufficiently developed to provide the financing levels required.

Given, therefore, it is unrealistic to suppose that 100% foreign currency financing is possible, the standard financing advice for overseas projects is:

(i) The project's *property* fixed assets: finance with a foreign currency loan;
(ii) The project's *non-property* fixed assets: finance via the export of £;
(iii) The project's *working capital* requirements: finance with a foreign currency loan.

This advice means that the firm will be protected from FX risk as far as property fixed assets and working capital are concerned through the *matching* principle. But what about the non-property fixed assets?

It is with the non-property fixed assets that the Law of One Price (referred to in an earlier section of this chapter) comes to the rescue. The idea here is that non-property fixed assets (such as industrial machinery) obey, to some extent, the workings of the Law of One Price because they are capable of being traded internationally. Neither property fixed assets nor working capital are capable of being physically traded internationally, and so do not follow the law and need to be protected against FX risk through matching.

We will use what appears to be a highly specific example to illustrate how the Law of One Price can give protection against FX risk. However, the example is only as specific as it appears to ease the explanation. It will *tend* to hold generally, whatever the circumstances, given that the assets in question can be traded internationally (and that the transportation costs do not form too significant an element in its total value). Table 17.4 gives the details.

It is not suggested that the Law of One Price will work as *perfectly* in practice as it did in Table 17.4. But, given that the $ depreciates against £ and given that industrial machinery is traded internationally, then there will be a definite *tendency* for the $ worth of the machine to rise as the value of the $ declines. Thus, at the very least, companies can expect to get *some* protection (if not perfect protection) against FX risk through the workings of the law.

In summary therefore, the general principle behind financing foreign projects is to raise as much finance as possible in the overseas currency so as to get the maximum protection from translation risk through matching. Where 100% foreign currency financing is not possible, then

Table 17.4

Suppose that the $10m US project referred to in Table 17.2 was composed of the following elements:

Property:	$2m
Machinery:	$7m
Working Capital:	$1m

The suggested financing scheme would be a $3m loan and $7m-worth of exported £.

The fall in the $/£ FX rate from 2·00 to 3·00 from one year-end to the next will cause the £ worth of the US property and working capital to decline, but this will be matched by a corresponding decline in the £ worth of the $ loan. But in these circumstances what happens as far as the US machinery is concerned?

Suppose (for the purpose of easing the explanation) that the machinery in question is manufactured in the UK and is normally sold for £3·5m. At an opening $/£ FX rate of 2·00, this is why it cost $7m to purchase it for the US project.

After an elapse of 12 months, the machinery still costs £3·5m but, because the $ has depreciated against £, the US cost of the machinery now becomes: £3·5m × 3·00 = $10·5m. (What is seen here is the working-through of the Law of One Price: the £ price of a good × $/£ FX rate = $ price of the good.)

Therefore (ignoring the problem of depreciation which is just a complication and does not change the basis of the argument), we would be justified in valuing the machinery of our US project at the end of the first year at $10·5m rather than $7m on a *replacement cost* basis. (And the company's UK auditors are likely to accept such an argument.)

As a result the company's balance sheets would appear as follows:

Opening balance sheet: $/£ = 2·00

$ loan	: £1·5m	$2m property	: £1m
£ funding	: £3·5m	$7m machinery	: £3·5m
	£5·0m	$1m work. capt.	: £0·5m
			£5·0m

Balance sheet at Year 1: $/£ = 3·00

$ loan	: £1m	$2m property	: £0·67m
£ funding	: £3·5m	$10·5m machinery	: £3·5m
	£4·5m	$1m work. capt.	: £0·33m
			£4·5m

The company has managed to hedge its exposure to FX translation risk through a combination of the matching principle and the operation of the Law of One Price.

the company should try to ensure that at least those assets which are not going to be responsive to the operation of the Law of One Price are financed in the overseas currency.

OTHER RISKS

Economic risk

The previous discussion on translation risk also touches upon another FX risk of foreign investments which could be called *economic* risk. This is the risk of *unexpected* changes in FX rates.

For example, a proper investment appraisal evaluation might have been undertaken which had indicated that a project would bring about an increase in parent shareholders' wealth. The project then performs *perfectly* to plan but, because of unexpected and adverse FX movements, in hindsight, it leads to a *reduction* in parent company shareholders' wealth.

The possible presence of this risk causes real difficulties. The first question it raises is whether the risk is systematic or unsystematic. The second is, if it is systematic, how should it be taken into account in the appraisal process? There is, of course, an even more fundamental question here: does this type of risk exist at all? Example 17.8 illustrates what is behind this latter question.

Example 17.8

A US project costs $1m. It has a life of three years and results in an annual production output of 1,000 units. The net after-tax cash flow resulting from the production is expected to be $0·5m in *current* terms. This cash amount is expected to increase in line with the average US inflation rate which is expected to remain constant at 8% per year.

The project will be entirely financed with £ and there are no restrictions on net cash flow remittance to the UK parent. A similar risk UK project would be expected to produce a minimum annual return of 16%.

The current $/£ spot exchange rate is 1·9000 and UK general inflation rate is expected to remain constant at 5% per year.

On the basis of this information, the $ discount rate can be estimated via the IRPT. First though, the $/£ FX rate has to be estimated for 12 months' time. This can be done through the PPPT:

$$\text{\$/£ rate in 12 months: } \frac{(1 + 0{\cdot}08) \times 1{\cdot}9000}{(1 + 0{\cdot}05)} = 1{\cdot}9543$$

and so, using the IRPT:

$$\text{\$ discount rate} = \frac{1{\cdot}9543 \times (1 + 0{\cdot}16)}{1{\cdot}9000} - 1 = 0{\cdot}193 \text{ or } \underline{19{\cdot}3\%}$$

The project can now be evaluated:

Year	\$m	× 19·3% discount		
0	−1·0 ×	1	=	−1·0
1	+0·54 ×	0·8382	=	+0·453
2	+0·583 ×	0·7026	=	+0·410
3	+0·630 ×	0·5889	=	+0·371
				\$+0·234m

\$+0·234m ÷ 1·90 = +£0·123m NPV

The project is worthwhile and should be accepted.

If the firm then undertakes the project, the \$/£ FX rates that they are expecting over the next 3 years can be found from the PPPT:

Spot: 1·9000 (given)
Year 1: 1·9543 (already calculated)

Year 2: $\frac{(1 + 0{\cdot}08)^2 \times 1{\cdot}9000}{(1 + 0{\cdot}05)^2} = 2{\cdot}0101$

Year 3: $\frac{(1 + 0{\cdot}08)^3 \times 1{\cdot}9000}{(1 + 0{\cdot}05)^3} = 2{\cdot}0675$

Therefore, they are expecting the following £ cash flow from the project:

Year	*\$m*	÷ *\$/£*	=	*£m*
0	−1	÷ 1·9000	=	−0·526
1	+0·54	÷ 1·9543	=	+0·276
2	+0·583	÷ 2·0101	=	+0·290
3	+0·630	÷ 2·0675	=	+0·304

(And this £ cash flow will, of course, have a +NPV of £123,000 when discounted at 16% [ignoring rounding errors].)

However, suppose that US inflation turns out to be higher than expected, say 12% rather than 8%. It means that the future exchange rates will also differ:

Year 1: $\frac{(1{\cdot}12) \times 1{\cdot}90}{(1{\cdot}05)} = 2{\cdot}0267$

Year 2: $\frac{(1{\cdot}12)^2 \times 1{\cdot}90}{(1{\cdot}05)^2} = 2{\cdot}1618$

Year 3: $\frac{(1{\cdot}12)^3 \times 1{\cdot}90}{(1{\cdot}05)^3} = 2{\cdot}3059$

Will the UK parent suffer as a result of this unexpected, adverse movement in the \$/£ FX rates? They should not, if the project performs as expected and produces 1,000 units per year; the reason being that the increased US inflation rate *should* result in increased

$ cash flows from the project which will now inflate up at 12% rather than 8%:

Year	*$m*	÷	*$/£*	=	*£m*
0	−1	÷	1·9000	=	−0·526
1	+0·56	÷	2·0267	=	+0·276
2	+0·627	÷	2·1618	=	+0·290
3	+0·702	÷	2·3059	=	+0·304

Therefore the parent will receive exactly the same £ cash flow whose NPV will remain at +£123,000.

The problem with Example 17.8 is that life does not work quite so perfectly. Remember, although the IRPT tends to work well, the PPPT tends to be more approximate because of the imperfections in the workings of the Law of One Price. Therefore the FX rates may not turn out as predicted at a 12% inflation level and, indeed, the project's net after-tax cash flow may not respond, in the perfect way illustrated, to the rise in US inflation. Thus it is fairly safe to conclude that, in the real world, the risk of unexpected FX movements *does* exist for firms investing overseas.

This then brings us back to the first question posed: is this risk wholly systematic or unsystematic or partly both? The answer is highly uncertain, but probably some of it is capable of being diversified away through international diversification.

The uncertainty arises because economists cannot agree whether individual country capital markets are segmented (and so largely independent of each other) or integrated. But, despite this, there is a relatively simple solution (although this is not always possible to apply and it is far from a perfect answer). That solution is to eliminate the risk of unexpected FX rate movements by using the forward markets to sell forward a project's expected foreign currency net cash flow.

This solution may not be possible to apply in practice because forward markets only extend substantial periods of time forward in the world's *major* currencies. If the project was in Egypt, for example, we would have difficulties trying to apply this solution. Even when suitably extended forward markets do exist (such as with $/£), forward contracts are for *certain* amounts of currency, while the project's cash flow is only *expected*. Thus a perfect hedge against the FX risk is unlikely to be achieved.

Alternatives to the forward sale of currencies also exist through the matching principle. For example an overseas currency loan extending over the life of the project could be raised. The loan could be converted immediately into £ and capital and interest could be repaid out of the project's net cash flow. Again, this would not give a perfect hedge, but it would provide a significant degree of protection. A further alternative would be to use the overseas project's net cash flow to purchase exportable goods from the host country; thereby converting the project's FX risk-exposed *cash* flow into a non-exposed (or, less exposed) *goods* flow.

Country risk

The final risk attached to foreign projects is *country risk*. This is the risk that, once the project has been undertaken, then the host government may adversely change the 'rules of the game'.

The most common instance of country risk concerns changes to the rules on project net cash flow repatriation, but other possibilities are the unexpected imposition of penalty rates of taxation or even expropriation of the project's assets without proper compensation. Such moves may come about through a change in the host government's political complexion or through macro-economic problems.

As far as the risks of restrictions being imposed unexpectedly on net cash flow repatriation, the simple rule is to try and minimize its possible impact by using as many different remittance channels as are available. Thus a project's net cash flows may be remitted back to the parent in the form of dividend payments or interest payments. If the overseas project undertakes any process for which the parent has royalty rights, then royalty payments may be another possible channel.

Although an overseas project's lower and middle management are drawn from the host country itself, the top management are normally seconded from the parent. The parent might then charge the foreign project for the services of these top management, effectively using the *management charge* as a further means of remitting back the project's net cash flow.

Finally, if there is any transfer of goods between the parent and the overseas project, then the transfer pricing mechanism can be employed as yet another channel for remitting back the project's net cash flows.

Obviously, national governments are aware of all these different possible channels and so if they *really* want to restrict the repatriation of a project's net cash flows to an overseas parent, then they are perfectly capable of doing so. However, sometimes a government might want to be *seen* to be doing something about restricting foreign project cash flows without wanting to restrict them absolutely. Thus they might enforce restrictions on, for example, dividends as this is seen as a politically sensitive area linked directly to profits. At the same time, however, such things as interest and royalty payments may be seen as much more legitimate business expenses and so remain unrestricted.

As far as the other elements of country risk are concerned there are two main possible courses of action that can be taken to reduce them. The first would be to tie-in host country investors or even the host government, through such things as joint ventures. This sort of arrangement is likely to discourage any host government from taking such adverse action against the project that the overseas parent pulls out, if this would then cause the project to fail. Such action would not only hurt the overseas parent, but would also hurt host country investors.

The second course of action is insurance. It is possible to insure an overseas project against the more extreme forms of country risk such as expropriation. In such circumstances, the cost of the insurance should be included as part of the overall cost of undertaking the project in any financial appraisal.

SUMMARY

This chapter has provided a fairly brief overview of a highly complex area that contains many still unresolved difficulties. The main points covered were as follows:

- Four FX markets can be identified: spot; forward; futures and options. As far as overseas capital investments are concerned the most important ones are likely to be the spot and forward markets.
- Three principal causes of FX movements were identified: imbalances in international trade; differences in interest rates and differences in inflation rates. However, in the real world, we have difficulties in understanding how they interact with each other although, in theory, they are all clearly interconnected.
- As far as foreign project appraisal is concerned, there are two equivalent approaches: the project's overseas currency cash flows can be converted to £ cash flows and a £ discount rate applied; alternatively, the project's overseas currency cash flows can be discounted at the overseas currency discount rate to produce an NPV. This can then be converted at spot into a £NPV.
- A major difference between domestic and foreign project evaluation arises when the latter suffers from cash flow remittance restrictions. In such circumstances the project must be evaluated from the viewpoint of the cash flows that are available to be remitted back to the parent. In particular, this means including in the project's cash flows any foreign currency *financing* cash flows.
- Once taxation is brought into consideration, then an APV analysis becomes appropriate. However, such an approach can be complex and a simplified approach can be utilized by modifying APV.
- Foreign project financing can play a significant role in reducing the parent's exposure to translation risk. Here, the standard advice is to finance the project requirement for property and working capital in the overseas currency, while the non-property fixed assets can be financed via the export of £.
- Finally both economic and country risk were examined and ways by which exposure to both may be reduced were discussed.

NOTES

1 In fact, delivery of the currencies takes place with a delay of two working days to allow the administrative process to run its course.

2 There are futures and options markets in other things besides currencies. For

example there are *interest rate* futures and there are *share* options. Obviously our discussion in this chapter is confined purely to the currency markets.

3 The original market – the Chicago International Money Market – was set up in 1971. New York followed in the late 1970s and the London International Financial Futures Exchange (LIFFE) was set up in 1984.

4 This statement needs to be modified slightly. The forward market – like any other market – exists because there is a demand for its services. Therefore a forward market may not exist where there is very little trade between two currencies, say between the Mauritian Rupee and the Peruvian Sol. Nor will a forward market exist (in the meaning of our discussion) where such trade in the currency is illegal (that is, a currency is non-convertible). This is the case with most Eastern-bloc countries.

5 A forward rate can be easily quoted for *any* period of time forward up to 12 months. Indeed forward deals in major currencies such as \$/£ can be arranged for periods ahead of as much as 5 or 10 *years* in the future.

6 Of course from the bank's viewpoint – which is the financial intermediary through which a company wishing to buy or sell foreign exchange would deal – the first rate is the selling rate (the rate at which the bank will sell \$ to the customer) and the second rate is the buying rate (the rate at which the bank will buy \$ from the customer).

7 This is the so-called Expectations Theory. It may not always hold good because of imperfections in the FX markets.

8 Notice that if buying and selling spot rates were given, then there would be two discounts or premiums given for the forward rate. For example:

\$/£ Spot	1·9540 – 1·9550
1 mth. Forward	0·10 – 0·12 discount

9 If, for no other reason, all their costs of production are incurred in yen and their dividends to shareholders and interest payments to debt holders have also to be paid in yen.

10 Other factors, that is, being equal.

11 We can be excused a 1 pence rounding error.

12 Transportation costs between countries can cause problems for the Law of One Price and we shall return to this later.

13 Again, a 1 pence rounding error can be excused.

14 Notice that an *annual* discount rate is being calculated, so the estimated exchange rate in *12 months'* time is used.

15 The rounding error is just two pence.

16 Notice, the parent only has to contribute \$5m to the project in terms of £.

17 These discount factors are not included in the tables supplied and have been calculated separately.

18 For simplicity, these examples ignore depreciation on loan repayments. The conclusions of the analysis remain unchanged in a more realistic setting.

19 The $ *could* have appreciated and a FX gain would have been made.

FURTHER READING

1 International aspects of investment appraisal and financing decisions are complex and form the subject matter of specialist books. Two good books which examine the problems from a UK perspective are: A. Buckley, *Multi-national Finance*, Philip Allan, 1986, and J.B. Holland, *International Financial Management*, Blackwell 1986.
2 Good introductory articles on the subject matter include: A.C. Shapiro, 'Capital Budgeting for the Multinational Corporation', *Financial Management*, Spring 1978, and, by the same author, 'International Capital Budgeting,' *Midland Corporate Finance Journal*, Spring 1983, and A. Buckley, 'Evaluating Overseas Projects', *Accountancy*, May 1987.
3 On the use of APV in an international context, see: D.R. Lessard, 'Evaluating Foreign Projects – an Adjusted Present Value Approach', in D. Lessard (ed.), *International Financial Management,* Warren, Gorham and Lamont, 1979.
4 On the financing problem see: M.R. Eaher, 'Denomination Decision for Multinational Transactions', *Financial Management*, Autumn 1980 and A. Buckley, 'Financing Overseas Subsidiaries', *Accountancy*, August 1987.
5 Other articles of interest include: R.C. Hechman, 'Foreign Exchange Exposure: Accounting Measures and Economic Reality', *Journal of Cash Management*, February-March 1983; S.H. Goodman, 'Foreign Exchange Rate Forecasting Techniques', *Journal of Finance*, May 1979; and D.J. Oblack and R.J. Helm, 'Survey and Analysis of Capital Budgeting Methods Used by Multinationals', *Financial Management*, Winter 1980.

QUICKIE QUESTIONS

1 What is the PPPT formula?
2 If a project requires at 25% return in the UK and the $/£ exchange rate is: 1·9050 spot and 1·8420 twelve-months forward, what is the project's $ required return?
3 The current $/£ spot rate is 1·9280. The $ is expected to appreciate against £ by 7% per year. Estimate the $/£ FX rate in 3 years' time.
4 The $/£ spot rate is 1·7940, the 2 month forward rate is at 1·50 cent premium. What is the forward rate?
5 What are the two basic approaches by which a UK company can evaluate a US project?
6 Why should foreign financing flows be included in an overseas project's appraisal?

7 What is the standard advice for financing overseas projects?
8 What possible channels might a company use to remit back a foreign project's cash flows?
9 What is country risk?
10 What is economic risk?

PROBLEMS

1 The management of Alcandro plc is currently considering whether to establish a subsidiary company in Betulia, a country whose currency is the Bandl. The management of Alcandro plc believes that the market for its products in Betulia is expanding and that by producing locally Alcandro plc will be able to sell into what has traditionally been a very difficult export market.

The subsidiary company will require plant and equipment costing 4,000 million Bandls and land and buildings costing 600 million Bandls, to be paid for at the start of the first year of production. Initial working capital of 400 million Bandls will also be required. The subsidiary company will be all equity financed, 60% being provided by Alcandro plc and 40% by investors in Betulia. At the end of four years, the Betulian investors will be offered all Alcandro plc's shares in the subsidiary at a price based upon the subsidiary's fourth year's profit after tax (but before royalty fees), capitalized at a price/earnings ratio of 11.

Sales in Betulia are expected to be 5,000 units in the first year of production rising by 500 units in each of the next three years. The selling price of one unit will be 400,000 Bandls in the first year increasing by 15% per annum, rounded to the nearest 1,000 Bandls. Production costs excluding depreciation in Betulia are estimated to be 30% of sales value. Alcandro plc will supply its Betulian subsidiary with specialized parts. These will be invoiced in Bandls at 80,000 Bandls per unit of finished product, rising by 15% per annum (rounded to the nearest 1,000 Bandls). Alcandro plc's profit margin on these sales is estimated to be 40%. It is expected that the Betulian company will purchase these specialized parts from other suppliers when Alcandro plc relinquishes control. The working capital requirements of the subsidiary at the beginning of each year are expected to be equal to 20% of that year's sales revenues.

In Betulia, companies are taxed at a rate of 20% on accounting profits. Depreciation is an allowable expense, provided it is calculated in the income statement on a straight line basis over five years. Land and buildings are not regarded as depreciable assets. Tax is paid one year after the accounting period to which it relates and tax losses can be carried forward.

The Betulian subsidiary will sign a royalty agreement entitling Alcandro plc to 15% of the subsidiary's sales revenues payable at the end of each year. The royalty agreement expires at the end of four years, after which time royalties will cease. Royalty payments are not an allowable expense for tax purposes, but are to be included in the calculation of accounting profit.

In its share prospectus to Betulian investors, Alcandro plc has stated that it will not levy any management charges other than the royalty fee, and the Betulian subsidiary will distribute by way of dividends all profit attributable to its shareholders. In Betulia, a company cannot pay a dividend until all past accounting losses have been extinguished.

The following rates of exchange are expected to occur (0 represents the start of the first year of production and sales):

Year	*Rate (Bandl/£)*
0	500
1	550
2	605
3	666
4	732
5	805

Alcandro plc's cost of capital for this type of investment is 20% per annum.

Required:

(a) Determine whether Alcandro plc should proceed with its proposed investment in Betulia.

(b) Suggest other ways in which Alcandro plc could finance its operations in Betulia, and compare your suggestions with the proposed financing method.

Ignore UK taxation.

2 Blue Grass Distillery Inc, a North Carolina based manufacturer of rye whiskey, is evaluating its position with respect to the United Kingdom market.

The EEC has just announced a five-year 25% common external tariff on rye whiskey, to protect Scottish and Irish distillers. Blue Grass believes that this tariff will reduce the profits on its exports to the UK to negligible levels. The company is therefore considering whether to establish a subsidiary in a Welsh Development Area in order to avoid the tariff, or to pull out of the UK market completely.

If the company immediately stops exporting to the UK market some production could be diverted to the non-EEC Scandinavian market, yielding an annual after-tax net cash flow of $1·5 million for the foreseeable future. The company is currently working at full capacity and has no plans to expand production in the USA.

The proposed UK subsidiary would cost £15 million to establish, 20% of which would be met by a grant from the EEC. A suitable factory has already been located in South Wales and production could commence quickly. The company's marketing department forecast possible sales of 20,000 gallons in the first year and 50,000 gallons a year for the following four years. Blue Grass evaluate all projects on the basis of a five-year planning horizon.

The rye whiskey would be sold to off-licences at a price of £300 per gallon in the first year. Subsequently this price is expected to rise in line with the rate of UK inflation. The distilling and bottling costs in the UK have been estimated at £140 per gallon plus £2 million of fixed costs in the first year. These too are expected to rise in line with inflation. In addition a royalty of $50 per gallon will be charged by Blue Grass. The realisable value of the factory at the end of five years is expected to be £10 million.

It is the company policy of Blue Grass Distillery to remit to the United States all possible funds from its foreign subsidiaries at the end of each year. Corporate taxes, payable one year in arrears, are levied at a rate of 30% in the USA and 35% in the UK. A bilateral tax agreement exists between the two countries.

A 25% writing-down allowance is available on the whole of the £15 million outlay.

Exchange Rates ($/£)	Spot	$1·5500
	12 Mths. Fwd.	$1·4725

Sterling is expected to depreciate against the dollar by 5% per year.

UK inflation rate forecasts for the next five years have been published by the UK Treasury, as follows:

Year	*RPI Increase*
1	4%
2	4%
3	3%
4	3%
5	4%
6	5%

After-tax return on UK Government Stock (5 year maturity): 7%
After-tax UK excess market return: 5%
Standard Deviation of returns on the UK market portfolio: 0·48
Standard Deviation of returns on the proposed investment: 0·65
Correlation Coefficient of returns between the UK market portfolio and the proposed investment: +0·885

Required:

(a) Evaluate the project and advise management on the proposal to set up a UK subsidiary.

(b) How would you advise the management of Blue Grass Distilleries Inc. about the financing of the UK subsidiary?

3 Polycalc plc is an internationally diversified company. It is presently considering undertaking a capital investment in Australia to manufacture agricultural fertilizers. The project would require immediate capital expenditure of A$ 15m, plus A$ 5m of working capital which would be recovered at the end of the project's four year life. It is estimated that an annual revenue of A$ 18m would be generated by

the project, with annual operating costs of A$ 5m. Straight-line depreciation over the life of the project is an allowable expense against company tax in Australia which is charged at a rate of 50%, payable at each year-end without delay. The project can be assumed to have a zero scrap value.

Polycalc plans to finance the project with a £5m 4-year loan at 10% from the Euro-sterling market, plus £5m of retained earnings. The proposed financing scheme reflects the belief that the project would have a debt capacity of two-thirds of *capital* cost. Issue costs on the Euro debt will be $2\frac{1}{2}$% and are tax deductible.

In the UK the fertilizer industry has an equity beta of 1.40 and an average debt : equity gearing ratio of 1:4. Debt capital can be assumed to be virtually risk-free. The current return on UK Government Stock is 10% pre-tax and the excess market return is 10·75% post tax.

Corporate tax in the UK is at 35% and can be assumed to be payable at each year-end without delay. The marginal rate of personal tax is 29%. Because of a double-taxation agreement, Polycalc will not have to pay any UK tax on the project. The company is expected to have a substantial UK tax liability from its other operations for the foreseeable future.

The current A$/£ spot rate is 2·0000 and the A$ is expected to depreciate against the £ at an annual rate of 10%.

Required:

(a) Using the Adjusted Present Value technique, advise the management of Polycalc on the project's desirability.

(b) Comment briefly on the company's intended financing plans for the Australian project. Suggest, with reasons, a more sensible alternative.

4 The directors of Eibl plc are considering whether to set up a subsidiary in Heina, a country whose currency is the Croll. The Heina subsidiary would assemble and market a sophisticated tractor. Survey data indicate that the Heina subsidiary could expect to sell 500 tractors in the first year of operations, increasing by 10 tractors in each of the next 5 years.

In the first year, the unit selling price of a tractor would be 3 million Crolls, increasing at an annual rate of 10% (rounded to the nearest 100,000 Crolls), and each tractor would require components costing £5000. This cost of the components would increase by 6% per annum in subsequent years. Eibl plc would provide the components to be assembled and would invoice its Heina subsidiary for these with no profit mark-up. The unit cost would be calculated to the nearest £100.

Annual production, administration and selling costs in Heina are expected to be 45% of the sales value of the tractors sold in that year.

At the start of its operations the Heina subsidiary would require working capital of 160 million Crolls. At the end of each year of production the required level of working capital would be approximately equal to 10% of that year's sales. Assembly equipment costing 1200 million Crolls would be installed and paid for immediately.

Annual profits of companies in Heina are subject to a business tax of 40%. Working capital movements are excluded from the computation of taxable profit, but companies are entitled to include a deduction representing 20% of the cost of equipment for each of the first five years of the equipment's life. Business tax is paid at the end of the year to which the assessment relates.

Eibl plc would usually evaluate this type of investment over a 5 year period. At the end of the fifth year a notional market value of the subsidiary would be calculated by applying a price-earnings ratio of 6 to the profit after tax arising in the fifth year (as pre-tax accounting profit equals taxable profit, no deferred tax liabilities can arise). If Eibl plc were to sell its subsidiary after 5 years the sale proceeds would be taxed in Heina at a rate of 30%.

The initial finance of 1360 million Crolls would be provided in the form of equity capital from the existing cash resources of Eibl plc. The cost of capital used by Eibl plc for this type of venture is 25%, but investors based in Heina would require a return of only 20% when investing in an equivalent venture. At present the Croll/£ exchange rate is 150 Croll/£, although predictions of the relative interest and inflation rates of the UK and Heina suggest that the Croll will depreciate against the £ by 4% per annum. In the project appraisals of Eibl plc the exchange rate is rounded to the nearest whole number.

Apart from the initial investment, revenues, costs and working capital changes can be assumed to arise at the end of the year in which they occur.

Required:

(a) Prepare a statement showing to the nearest 100,000 Crolls the net cash flow that would arise in each year of the venture and hence determine whether the investment would be acceptable to investors based in Heina (assuming details of the venture remain as outlined).

(b) Calculate whether Eibl plc should set up the Heina subsidiary, assuming cash surpluses are remitted to the UK at the end of each year.

(c) Discuss what improvements could be made by Eibl plc to the proposed financial arrangements with the Heina subsidiary.

Ignore UK Taxation.

18
The dividend decision

Chapter Contents

DIVIDEND POLICY IN PERFECT CAPITAL MARKETS

The dividend decision is the third major category of corporate long-term financial decisions that we shall investigate. In a similar vein to both the capital investment decision and the capital structure decision, we shall pursue the question: can management affect shareholder wealth through the dividend decision?

The dividend decision is, perhaps, the least analysed and most elusive and controversial of the three areas of financial decision making. Indeed, one of the most celebrated academic articles on the area was entitled 'The Dividend Puzzle' (Black, 1976).

Consequently, the theory in this area is the least evolved and least complete. The complications and confusions surrounding the dividend decision arise principally because it is the lynch-pin to both the investment and financing decisions. As such, it therefore becomes difficult to abstract it from these influences so that it may be examined, initially at least, in isolation.

The problem of the dividend decision can be stated in the form of two questions: Does the *pattern* of the dividend flow through time to shareholders affect the market value of the equity capital? If it does, can one *particular* pattern of dividends then be identified which would maximize the equity's market value? However, the meaning of these two questions can appear ambiguous, and so we shall start by clarifying the nature of our enquiry into the dividend decision.

The fundamental valuation model that we have used tells us that the market value of a company's equity capital is given by the summation of the expected future dividend stream, discounted to present value. In this sense, dividends can clearly be said to affect the market value of a company's ordinary shares – in fact, they are the major determinant. However, the question that we shall explore is whether or not the *pattern* of the expected dividend flow is a determinant of equity market value, rather than the *magnitude* of the summated present value of the expected flow.

As far as a company's management is concerned, the dividend decision problem is one of *allocation.* How, at the end of each accounting period (for simplicity we shall assume this to be a twelve-month period, although in practice the dividend decision is usually made twice-yearly in the UK and quarterly in the USA), should the company's net after-tax cash flow be allocated amongst the competing ends?

There is a possible three-way split to be made: interest payments to the suppliers of debt capital,[1] dividend payments to shareholders, and retention within the company for application to investment opportunities. As it is the capital structure decision which largely determines the level of interest payments, we are left with the question as to how the annual net of tax and interest cash flow (we could call it the distributable cash earnings) should be divided up between dividend payments and retention within the company for reinvestment.

Dividends as a residual

We can start the analysis by recalling the basic single-period investment–consumption model which existed in a world of perfect capital markets and no taxation. We shall also assume that there are no sources of capital available to management which are external to the company. Figure 18.1 illustrates the model.

In terms of the dividend decision, the company management must decide at time t_0 what proportion of the company's wealth OA (this could be viewed as being equivalent to the distributable cash earnings referred to above) should be invested and what proportion should be paid out as a dividend. We know that for optimality (i.e., for the maximization of shareholder wealth) the company should retain amount AB and distribute amount OB.

Therefore, notice that the decision on the division of amount OA was taken *only* with reference to the physical investment opportunities available and the perfect capital market rate of interest. The amount OB distributed as dividend to the company owners at time t_0 was purely the cash *residual* that was left after the investment decision had been made.

From this, we can derive a rather obvious dividend decision rule, which states that the distributable cash earnings should be retained within the company for reinvestment, as long as there are investment opportunities available which satisfy the NPV decision rule. Once this supply of investment opportunities has been exhausted (i.e. the company has moved to point C in Figure 18.1) any distributable cash earnings remaining uninvested should be paid out to shareholders as a dividend.

This is the so-called *dividend irrelevancy* hypothesis which was first

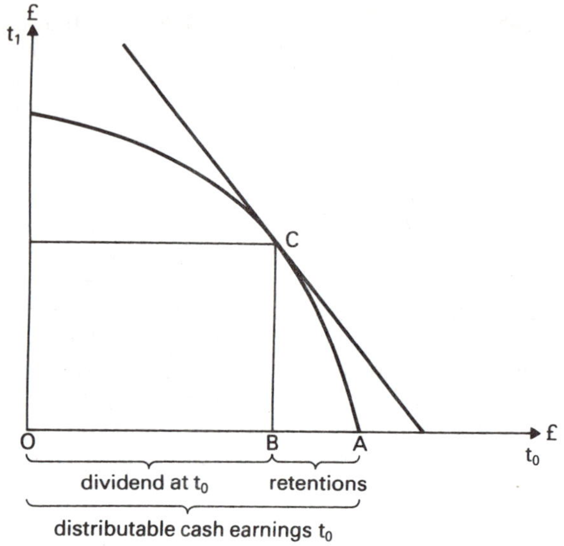

Figure 18.1

explicitly formulated by Modigliani and Miller, but the name of the hypothesis – at this stage – is somewhat misleading: dividends themselves are not irrelevant (as we know from the dividend valuation model), but it is the *pattern* of dividends which is irrelevant. They should be treated purely as a residual which arises once the investment decision is made.

In reaching this conclusion, M and M approached the problem of the dividend decision from a different, but equivalent, viewpoint. We shall illustrate this by means of an example, the data for which is illustrated in Table 18.1.

Suppose an all-equity financed company normally pays out its entire net cash flow each year as dividend. The company has previously undertaken investments which will generate an annual perpetuity net cash flow of £1,000. The current market value of the company would be given by the present value sum of this future expected dividend flow (V_E).

The management have now discovered a project which they wish to undertake at t_1. The project costs £1,000 and, rather than raise an extra £1,000 from shareholders (by selling them some new shares), they decide to retain the dividend that was due to be paid at t_1. The project will produce a net cash inflow of £1300 at t_2 and the management propose to pay this out as *additional* dividend at that time.

Thus the *new* market value of the equity (V_E^*) would be given by the present value sum of the *revised* expected dividend flow. This revised flow can be seen as consisting of two components: the original dividend flow (V_E) plus the project's cash flow (NPV_p).

The company would only undertake the proposed investment if the revised market value of the equity was greater than (or at least equal to) the existing market value of the equity: $V_E^* > V_E$. To ensure this, the NPV of the project must be greater than or equal to zero. The conclusion that can be drawn from this is that, what has enhanced shareholder wealth was the investment decision alone. The decision on dividend policy was irrelevant. The dividend decision was purely a *residual* of the investment decision.[2]

However, it must be remembered that the M and M argument is set in the perfect no-tax world of their initial capital structure hypothesis. As a counter to this view, we now turn to examine the more traditional view of dividend irrelevancy which holds that the pattern of dividend flow *is* relevant and *does* affect the market value of the ordinary shares.

Table 18.1

	t_1	t_2	t_3	t_n
$V_E = \sum_{t=1}^{n} \frac{D_t}{(1+K_E)^t} =$	+1,000	+1,000	+1,000 ...	+1,000
$NPV_p = \sum_{t=1}^{2} \frac{A_t}{(1+K_E)^t} =$	−1,000	+1,500		
$V_E^* = \sum_{t=1}^{n} \frac{D_t^*}{(1+K_E)^t} =$	0	+2,500	+1,000 ...	+1,000

Where V_E = current market value of the equity.
D_t = existing dividend flow.
V_E^* = post-investment market value of the equity.
D_t^* = post-investment dividend flow.
NPV_p = net present value of the proposed investment.

$$V_E^* = V_E + NPV_p$$

or

$$\sum_{t=1}^{n} \frac{D_t^*}{(1+K_E)^t} = \sum_{t=1}^{n} \frac{D_t}{(1+K_E)^t} + \sum_{t=1}^{2} \frac{A_t}{(1+K_E)^t}$$

To undertake the proposed investment: $V_E^* \geq V_E$
therefore: $NPV_p > 0$

Dividend patterns and the valuation model

Suppose that a company with an all-equity capital structure has made sufficient investments in the past to generate an annual net cash inflow of Y, in perpetuity. A constant proportion, b, of this cash flow is reinvested each year in projects which yield an average rate of return of r, whilst the remainder of each year's cash flow is paid out as dividends. As a result, Gordon's version of the basic dividend valuation growth model[3] can be applied to estimate the current market value of the company's equity capital:

$$V_E = \frac{Y(1-b)(1+rb)}{K_E - rb}$$

Assuming a given value for Y and for K_E, we can see that the value for V_E produced by the model is dependent on the values given to r and b. It is the effect of different values of b that is of interest, because it is this that reflects the dividend decision: different values of b produce different dividend flow patterns over time.

The effect of the retention proportion on the market value of the equity depends upon the value of r relative to K_E. Where $r > K_E$, then V_E increases as b increases: where $r < K_E$, the reverse relationship holds, and where $r = K_E$, then V_E is unaffected by changes in b.

(But notice that what remains unaffected in such a situation is the *wealth* of ordinary shareholders. For example, if $Y = £100$ and $K_E = r = 0{\cdot}20$ then, when $b = 0$, $V_E = £500$ and when $b = 0{\cdot}1$, $V_E = £510$. Shareholder wealth can be seen to be unaffected by changes in b by the fact that when $b = 0$, they received a dividend of £100 and their shares had a market value of £500. Total wealth was therefore £600. When $b = 0{\cdot}1$, they received a dividend of £90, £10 being reinvested, and their shares had a market value of £510. Total wealth is unchanged at £90 + £510 = £600.)

At first sight therefore, it may well appear that the dividend decision can affect the market value of the equity (because it determines b), but *how* the dividend decision affects V_E depends upon the relationship of r to K_E. But really, it is not the dividend decision which is causing the market value of the equity to change, but the investment decisions which follow, i.e., it is the investment of the retained earnings which causes fluctuations in the equity market value.

We are seeing here, once again, confirmation of the NPV investment appraisal rule: increasing b will lead to an enhancement of equity market value only if the retained cash flows are being invested in projects yielding positive NPVs when discounted by K_E (i.e., when the project's yield or IRR $> K_E$). Retention of distributable cash flow for investment in projects yielding negative NPVs (i.e. $r < K_E$) serves merely to reduce the current market value of the company's equity capital.

Traditional view of the dividend decision

Not withstanding the foregoing analysis, the traditional[4] view of the dividend decision is that at any particular point of time £1 of dividends (i.e., distributed cash flow) is somehow more valuable than £1 of retained cash flow – even though the cash flow may have been retained for investment in a project yielding a substantial positive NPV. This is sometimes referred to as the 'bird in the hand' argument.

Proponents of this traditional view use the dividend growth model to support their argument in the following way. So far in this analysis, in using the dividend growth model, we have held K_E constant as b was varied. The traditionalists argue that this cannot be done, because K_E is partly a function of the value of b, because of the presence of risk. The cost of equity capital, as we have calculated it, is really no more than an average of a whole family of discount rates, each of which is related to a cash flow in a specific period. Therefore a company, by retaining a part of its current period cash flow, is replacing a *certain* cash flow 'now' with an *uncertain* future cash flow (i.e., the future dividends generated by the investment financed by the cash retention). This increased uncertainty will effectively raise the discount rate used against these future flows and so will cause K_E (the average discount rate) also to rise.

Thus, increasing the value of b is likely to lead to an increase in the value of K_E and so equity market values can be said to be affected by dividend policy itself and not simply through the effects of the investment undertaken with the retention, because dividend policy can alter the riskiness of the expected dividend flow. The optimal dividend-retention policy must be that which trades off the beneficial effects of retention and profitable re-investment (i.e., an increased value for b on the assumption that $r > K_E$), against the detrimental effects of increased risk, so as to maximize the market value of the equity.

The traditional view can be put in an alternative and simpler way. The early payment of dividends may not actually change a company's business risk level, but it can favourably alter an investor's *perception* of the level of risk. Thus current dividends are viewed as more valuable than retained earnings because the investor's perception of risk is imperfect and this may lead him to undervalue the future dividend stream that the retained earnings will generate.

An arbitrage criticism

The arguments of the traditionalists do not really stand up to a close theoretical examination, if the existence of a perfect capital market is assumed. The main counter-argument that can be put forward is that if two companies are identical in every respect except that their dividend-retention ratios differ, and if the market values retained earnings differently from dividends, the market prices of the two companies will be in disequilibrium (i.e., two identical goods will be selling at different prices in the same market). This will allow investors to undertake profitable arbitrage transactions, substituting home-made dividends for corporate dividends by selling part of their shareholding.

The following analysis illustrates this substitution in showing the irrelevance of dividend pattern and the opportunities which exist for arbitraging if a traditional view of dividend retention persists in the stock market.

Assuming that we have a perfect capital market in which there are no taxes or transaction costs and that the market interest rate of return is 10%. An all-equity company has made previous investments which are sufficient, in total, to generate an annual cash flow of £1,000 in perpetuity. All this cash flow is paid out each year as dividends. Thus the company has a total market value of £1,000/0·10 = £10,000. Each of the company's 1,000 ordinary shares therefore has a market value of £10 and receives an annual dividend of £1.

An investor owns 100 of the company's shares. Thus the market value of his shareholding is £1,000, from which he receives an annual dividend of £100.

The company has just paid the current year's dividend and has informed shareholders that next year's dividend (at time t_1) will be withheld so as to invest in a project that will yield a net cash inflow of £2,000 at time t_2. The project's cash inflow will be paid out, at that time, as an additional dividend. The company's revised dividend flow, and hence its revised market value, at t_0 is as follows:

	t_1	t_2	t_3 ...
Existing cash flow	+1,000	+1,000	+1,000
Project cash flow	−1,000	+2,000	
Revised dividend flow	0	+3,000	+1,000

$$V_E \qquad V_E = \sum_{t=0}^{\infty} \frac{D_t}{(1 + 0{\cdot}1)^t} = £10{,}743{\cdot}80$$

As a result of its intentions, the company's market value has risen by £743·80: the NPV of the project. Our investor's shareholding will have risen in value by £74·38 to £1,074·38.

However, suppose he relies upon his £100 per year dividend from the company for consumption purposes and is therefore alarmed at the news that he will receive no dividend next year (t_1). There are two main alternative courses of action he may take to replace the withheld dividend, neither of which will reduce the current level of his wealth of £1,074·38:[5] he can either sell part of his shareholding to generate sufficient cash to replace the dividend missed at t_1 (i.e. £100), or he can borrow the money at the perfect market rate of interest of 10%. Let us examine the mechanics of this first alternative.

At time t_1, the company's total market value is the sum of the discounted future dividend flow:

	t_1	t_2	t_3	t_4 ...
Dividend flow	0	+3,000	+1,000	+1,000 ...

$$V_{E_{t_1}} = \sum_{t=1}^{\infty} \frac{D_t}{(1 + 0{\cdot}1)^t} = £11{,}818{\cdot}18$$

Therefore each share has an approximate market value of £11·82, and our investor's shareholding is worth £1,181·82. If he now sells sufficient shares to produce £100 in cash as a substitute for his foregone dividend, he will sell £100/£11·82 = 8·46 shares.[6] He now only holds 91·54 shares in the company.

At time t_2 the company has £3,000 to be distributed as dividend so each share receives a dividend of £3 and our investor receives a total dividend of: 91·54 × £3 = £274·62. Of this, £100 is required for consumption, leaving a balance of £174·62 available to repurchase shares in the company and so recover his original shareholding position. The ex div. market value of the company at time t_2 will be £10,000 (the discounted sum of the future dividend flow) and so the individual share price is £10. Our investor can now buy back the 8·46 shares he previously sold at a cost of £84·60, leaving him with additional cash at time t_2 of £174·62 − £84·60 = £90·02. Thus our shareholder has effectively used 'home-made' dividends as a substitute for the company dividends which the management decided to retain. In doing so, his wealth position remains unchanged as the present value (i.e., at time t_0) of £90·02 at t_2 is £74·38 – the amount by which his shareholding increased in value at time t_0 when the company's decision was announced.

A similar analysis could be undertaken where the investor borrows £100 at t_1 (at the market interest rate), and repays capital and interest at t_2, using his increased dividend payment at that time. The net outcome will be exactly the same as before.

It should be clear from this example that if stock markets valued retained earnings less favourably than dividends, there would be opportunities for profitable arbitrage transactions to take place (with investors either buying shares in companies which are increasing their cash flow retention proportions – as they will be undervalued – or selling shares in companies which are reducing their retention proportions – as they are likely to be overvalued). These transactions should rapidly force out correct market valuations. Such an exercise is left to the reader to undertake.

The possibility of external finance

Up to this point in our consideration of the dividend decision, we have only considered situations in which the sole source of investment capital has been retained earnings. If we now widen the analysis to include the opportunity for companies to raise external finance for investment, what now becomes of the dividend decision?

When the possibility of external finance was excluded, the decision rule for company managements wishing to maximize shareholder wealth was to apply each year's cash earnings to investment in projects with positive NPVs. If the source of such projects dried up before all the net cash earnings had been allocated, then the remaining earnings could be paid out as a dividend. Thus the dividend 'policy' was to treat dividends as a residual to the investment decision.

Dividends cannot be said to be *irrelevant* in such circumstances. They are very relevant because, unless they are treated as a residual of the investment decision, they will be preventing 'profitable' investment from being undertaken and so will result in the shareholders' wealth failing to achieve the maximum.

Once the possibility of raising external finance is allowed, dividends no longer need to act as a residual but become truly irrelevant. This is because the payment of a dividend can no longer be held to *prevent* profitable investment from being undertaken, because the required finance can always be raised externally.

However, the raising of external finance in such circumstances – be it either debt or equity – is also likely (but not necessarily) to change a company's gearing ratio, and so the dividend decision can be said to be truly irrelevant only if, at the same time, it is accepted that changes in a company's gearing ratio leave its market value unaffected. If not, then dividend policy may well indirectly affect equity market values. As we are in a tax-free world of perfect capital markets, we can fairly safely assume that the conclusions of the initial M and M capital structure hypothesis also hold.

It is worthwhile noticing that this interdependence of the two M and M hypotheses works in both directions: not only does dividend irrelevancy depend on the capital structure hypothesis, but in turn the capital structure hypothesis holds true only if a company's dividend-retention ratio leaves its market value unaffected. For example, suppose that the greater the proportion of cash earnings paid out as dividends, the higher would be the market value of a company's equity capital. In such circumstances capital structure could not be said to be independent of market values because, other things being equal, the smaller the proportion of retained earnings the higher would be the company's market value, and vice versa.

The introduction of the possibility of external finance also leaves the traditional view largely unaffected. Dividend policy still retains its importance on the basis that current dividends are more highly valued than future dividends generated by retained earnings. But in addition, just as the two M and M hypotheses are in tandem, so too are the traditional views of dividends and capital structure. Therefore a company's dividend policy also gains importance from the fact that it is a partial determinant of the level of retained earnings and so can affect the company's market value through changing the gearing ratio. The exact effects of a company's dividend policy through such influences are not certain, but are dependent on its location on the U-shaped weighted average cost of capital curve.

DIVIDEND POLICY IN AN IMPERFECT MARKET

'Clientele' effect

Once we move away from the assumption of a perfect capital market and a tax-free world, the dividend decision becomes much more problematical. In particular, there are a number of different capital market imperfections which are likely to interfere seriously with the hypothesis of dividend irrelevancy.

The dividend irrelevancy argument has been founded on the perfect capital market approach/separation theorem of our initial single-period investment–consumption analysis. The pattern of cash flows that the company provides the shareholders with through the dividend policy is irrelevant because, each individual shareholder can adjust this dividend pattern to fit his desired consumption pattern by use of the capital market. It was this characteristic which allowed company managements to avoid the problem of having to identify the indifference curves of individual shareholders, when making investment decisions on their behalf.

However, capital market imperfections such as transaction costs (which in practice can be very substantial, especially at the individual shareholder level), differential interest rates, and the presence of absolute capital rationing for the individual shareholder, all interfere with this process.

Quite simply, these capital market imperfections mean that an individual cannot *costlessly* adjust his dividend pattern to fit his preferred consumption pattern; indeed the cost of doing so may be relatively high. (In the case of absolute capital rationing for the individual, the cost of some consumption patterns can be seen as infinitely high.) In such circumstances, simple wealth maximization (i.e., in terms of the current market value of the equity) may not be a unique desire of shareholders, as the *pattern* of wealth receipt also becomes important.

In these circumstances, the company's dividend policy takes on a new dimension. Shareholders may positively prefer companies to supply them with a dividend pattern which matches fairly closely with their desired consumption pattern, thereby relieving them of having to adjust this cash flow themselves.

In practice companies often do this by following a stable and easily identifiable dividend policy, but whether it is done explicitly for these reasons is open to argument. As an example, many companies strongly follow a policy in which dividend reduction is anathema and an increased dividend will be declared only if management are convinced that the new dividend level can be at least sustained, if not improved upon, in future years. In this way, shareholders whose own consumption pattern closely follows the dividend pattern of the company will be attracted by the knowledge that they are unlikely to need to resort to the imperfect capital market in order to make dividend/consumption pattern adjustments.

Unfortunately, the fact that an easily identifiable dividend pattern may mean that shareholders avoid the costs of adjustment, does not mean that such advantage is necessarily gained costlessly. Indeed, the cost which is directly saved by the shareholder may be more than offset by the consequential cost to the company (which will, in turn, rebound on to the shareholders).

This consequential cost may come about in that, by paying a dividend, the company is left with insufficient finance to undertake a profitable investment (i.e., one with a positive NPV) and so the investment opportunity is missed. Alternatively, because a dividend has been paid, the company has to raise finance for an investment from an external source which involves the incurrence of issue costs.

It may be thought that the dividend decision in this situation resolves into a straightforward cost minimization trade-off, but a problem arises with the identification and quantification of the costs incurred or avoided by the shareholders and the fact that they are unlikely to be the same for each individual shareholder. So we are reduced to concluding that in an imperfect capital market, probably the best approach that a company can hope to take is to follow a consistent dividend policy[7] and hope that the particular policy chosen does not incur too heavy cost penalties, relative to the transaction and opportunity cost savings made by shareholders. Such a policy is often referred to as arising from the 'clientele' effect. By following a consistent dividend policy, the company attracts to it a clientele of shareholders whose consumption pattern accords with the dividend pattern.

Dividends as signals

Another capital market imperfection which bears on the dividend decision concerns the need for information in an uncertain world. Capital markets are imperfect in the sense that information is neither costless nor universally available, and so decisions have often to be made by stock market investors on the basis of imperfect and incomplete information.

In such circumstances, a company's dividend declaration – a free and universally available piece of data – is often thought to signal information about its future performance. In fact, given that information about a company's future performance prospects is fairly sparse – especially to the individual investor – *any* information that becomes available is seized upon and embodied with a measure of importance which may often be in excess of its real value.

In these terms, the dividend decision once again gains in importance. If the stock market places such an (albeit maybe unjustified) informational content on the dividend declaration, then a company will not be acting so as to maximize its shareholders' wealth if it ignores this fact. It is most likely for this reason that many publicly quoted companies follow the dividend policy referred to earlier, where a dividend is reduced or passed completely only in the most dire financial circumstances.

This signalling effect of the dividend declaration is an important issue for companies. Several studies have shown that an increase or decrease over the *expected* level of dividends does precipitate a rise or fall (respectively) in the market share price. Hence the dividend declaration effect on the share price may be a major (if not *the* major) consideration in the decision.

Tax considerations

Taxation and especially differential rates of personal income tax, a taxation distinction between income and capital gains, and the fact that a company might have both private and corporate shareholders who are taxed under different tax regimes, form a serious capital market imperfection which interferes with the dividend irrelevancy approach. The major problem with the presence of taxation is that it can interfere with the value equivalence between dividends and retained earnings. As a result, some shareholders may prefer 'home-made' dividends (generated through selling part of their shareholding) because the rate of capital gains tax may be lower than their marginal income tax rate, which would be imposed upon company-distributed dividends. In contrast, other shareholders may prefer company-distributed dividends because their marginal tax rate results in less tax being paid than the combined effect of capital gains tax and transactions costs incurred in the process of providing home-made dividends.

Once again, in the face of different taxation rates and different taxation regimes, we must conclude by saying that if a company follows a widely recognized, consistent dividend policy, then it can be expected to attract that class of shareholders on whom the particular dividend policy chosen has the most favourable (or least harmful) taxation effects.

In reaching this conclusion, there still remains the problem of what action the company should take in the face of significant changes in the taxation regime, as far as dividends are concerned. Should it try to adjust its dividend policy so as to bring about the most favourable outcome to its existing shareholders, or should it continue with its existing policy in the hope that new shareholders, to whom the company's dividend policy is now favourable in terms of taxation, will be attracted and so replace some of the existing share-holders?

The optimal decision in such circumstances requires an accurate evaluation of the cost trade-off concerned (on the basis that the objective of financial management is to benefit *existing* shareholders) between the cost to the company of changing its dividend policy[8] and the cost to its shareholders of *not* changing its policy. Both costs will be difficult to quantify in precise terms, but both may possibly be substantial and so should not be ignored.

The empirical evidence

Much of the empirical work on dividend policy has been carried out in the United States. Therefore some of these results must be interpreted with care as they may well reflect the specifics of the US personal tax system. However, the empirical evidence does appear to confirm the view that companies believe that the dividend decision is important and cannot be treated simply as a by-product of investment and financing decisions. For example Lintner (1956) in a survey of companies found that many did try to pay out an approximately constant proportion of earnings each year. At the same time there was a reluctance to match dividend growth with earnings growth and as a result dividend growth lagged behind earnings growth. These results were confirmed in a later study by Fama and Babiak (1968) which estimated that dividend growth lagged two to three years behind earnings growth.

This evidence does seem to support the signalling effect of dividends. Management appear to go to some lengths to ensure that dividends are only raised when they are fairly certain that they will be able to maintain at least that new level of dividends in the future. The fear is that, if they were forced to *lower* dividends after an over-optimistic increase in the previous year, the market would read into the dividend decision unfavourable information.

If dividends are really seen by investors as a means of sending signals then we would expect share prices to react to *unexpected* changes in dividend policy. Pettit's 1972 study found exactly this reaction and these results were confirmed by two later studies: Aharony and Swary (1980) and Asquith and Mullins (1983). Indeed the Asquith and Mullins study seemed to suggest that, if anything, the information content effect of dividends was even stronger than that shown up in Pettit's original analysis.

As far as clienteles are concerned, the most well-known empirical evidence is that of Elton and Gruber (1970). They were particularly concerned about tax clienteles and the fact that some investors would strongly prefer to receive their returns in the form of capital gains rather than dividends, whilst other investors would prefer the reverse. Their evidence suggests that tax clienteles do exist: that shareholders in high dividend paying companies have lower tax rates than shareholders in low dividend paying companies.

However, more recently work by Miller and Scholes (1982) has cast doubt on Elton and Gruber's evidence. They essentially use an arbitrage argument based on earlier work by Brennan (1970). If tax clienteles do really exist, as evidenced by Elton and Gruber's results, this should present arbitrage opportunities: low rate taxpayers should be able to profit from the higher rate taxpayer's preference for capital gains and vice versa.

Conclusion

In truth, we really do not know whether dividend policy can affect shareholders' wealth. However the bulk of the empirical evidence does tend to suggest that either dividend policy *is* important, or is *seen to be* important.

In either case, therefore, it does seem that the dividend decision should be taken with care, given the imperfections of the real-world capital market. However, the identity of the correct dividend decision depends to a great extent upon how the individual shareholders are personally affected by the various market imperfections. It is likely, given a random selection of stock market investors, that the market imperfections with respect to dividends will affect individual shareholders in a number of conflicting ways, thus making a consensus dividend policy an unlikely possibility. The only escape from this dilemma for a company that intends to maximize the wealth of its shareholders is to follow a consistent dividend policy, which then allows the individual shareholder to judge its desirability in relation to his own personal circumstances.

SUMMARY

- This chapter has looked at the dividend decision. However, it is difficult to reach any firm conclusions.
- In a perfect capital market world of no taxes, the dividend decision can be seen to be irrelevant. A shareholder receives his annual return in two elements: the dividend and the capital gain. The decision about what proportion of a firm's net distributable cash flow to retain and what proportion to pay out as dividends is therefore simply a decision as to

how the overall return on the shares should be packaged. How large should be the capital gain package and how large should be the dividend package? However, the overall return itself is left unaffected by the decision.

- When capital market imperfections such as taxes, transaction costs and imperfect information are introduced, then it is possible for the dividend decision to begin to take on importance.
- Where dividends and capital gains are treated differently from the viewpoint of personal taxes and capital gains cannot be costlessly converted into income (nor dividends reinvested) without incurring transaction costs, it can be argued that companies should follow a stable and consistent dividend policy so as to attract to them a clientele of investors whose own personal tax position, and need (or otherwise) for income, suits that particular dividend policy.
- In addition to the clientele effect, the dividend decision may also be held to have an information content which it signals to the market. If this is so, then dividend policy is important in that management should ensure that their company's dividend decision does not give the *wrong* signal to the market.
- Although the empirical evidence is mixed and although some findings have been disputed, it does appear that the evidence points to the dividend decision being important both from a clientele and a signalling effect viewpoint.

NOTES

1 Including preference share capital.

2 The reader may find it worth while to reflect how the M and M dividend irrelevancy hypothesis is also just a natural continuation of their capital structure hypothesis.

3 The model's numerator is slightly more fully defined than when it was first introduced.

4 So-called because it is one which is widely held amongst both stock market investors and analysts.

5 A third possible alternative is a combination of the two courses of action.

6 For simplicity, we are assuming here that shares are divisible. The fact that this is not true in practice can be viewed as a slight market imperfection.

7 It is important to notice that constant dividends are not being advocated, but a constant *policy*. This policy may be to treat dividends as a residual of the investment decision and hence may result in a highly erratic dividend *flow*, but a constant policy.

8 A cost which will ultimately be felt by the shareholders.

FURTHER READING

1 The basic reading on dividend policy must be: M.H. Miller and F. Modigliani, 'Dividend Policy, Growth and the Valuation of Shares', *Journal of Business*, October 1961, and F. Black, 'The Dividend Puzzle', *Journal of Portfolio Management*, Winter 1976. For general empirical evidence on dividend policy, see J. Lintner, 'Distribution of Incomes of Corporations among Dividends, Retained Earnings and Taxes', *American Economic Review*, May 1956, and E.F. Fama and H. Babiak, 'Dividend Policy: An Empirical Analysis', *Journal of the American Statistical Association*, December 1968.

2 In addition, an interesting recent test of dividend irrelevancy is: G. Richardson, S.E. Sefcik and R. Thompson, 'A Test of Dividend Irrelevancy using Volume Reactions to a Change in Dividend Policy', *Journal of Financial Economics*, December 1986.

3 For evidence on the information content of dividends, see T.W. Foster and D. Vickrey, 'The Information Content of Stock Dividend Announcements', *Accounting Review*, April 1978; R.R. Pettit, 'Dividend Announcements, Security Performance and Capital Market Efficiency', *Journal of Finance*, December 1972; J. Aharony and I. Swary, 'Quarterly Dividends and Earnings Announcements and Stockholders Returns', *Journal of Finance*, March 1980; P. Asquith and D.W. Mullins, 'The Impact of Initiating Dividend Payments on Shareholder Wealth', *Journal of Business*, January 1983; J.R. Woolridge and C. Gosh, 'Dividend Cuts: Do They Always Signal Bad News?', *Midland Corporate Finance Journal*, Summer 1985; and A.R. Ofer and D.R. Siegal, 'Corporate Financial Policy, Information and Market Expectations: An Empirical Investigation of Dividends', *Journal of Finance*, September 1987.

4 On dividend policy, taxes and the clientele effect see: E.J. Elton and M.J. Gruber, 'Marginal Stockholders Tax Rates and the Clientele Effect', *Review of Economics and Statistics*, February 1970; D. Farrar and L. Selwyn, 'Taxes, Corporate Financial Policy and Returns to Investors', *National Tax Journal (US)*, December 1967; M. Brennan, 'Taxes, market Valuation and Corporate, Finanical Policy', *National Tax Journal*, December 1970; M. Miller and M. Scholes, 'Dividends and Taxes: Some Empirical Evidence', *Journal of Financial Economics*, December 1978: R.H. Litzenberger and K. Ramaswamy, 'The Effects on Dividends on Common Stock Prices: Tax Effects or Information Effects?', *Journal of Finance*, May 1982; and J.R. Woolridge, 'Dividend Changes and Security Prices', *Journal of Finance*, December 1983.

5 Finally, two further, interesting articles are: H.K. Barker, G.E. Farrelly and R.B. Edelman, 'A Survey of Management Views on Dividend Policy', *Financial Management*, Autumn 1985; and M.H. Miller, 'Behaviour Rationality in Finance: The Case of Dividends', *Journal of Business*, October 1986.

QUICKIE QUESTIONS

1 Why might the dividend decision be said to be irrelevant?
2 What is the argument about dividends being a residual to the investment decision?
3 What is the link between dividend irrelevancy and capital structure irrelevancy?
4 What is the bird-in-the-hand argument?
5 Which investors prefer capital gains to dividends?
6 If a clientele effect exists, what does it imply for dividend policy?
7 What empirical evidence is there to support the signalling effect of dividends?
8 In the real world, would it be wise for a company to retain a dividend which shareholders were expecting, in order to invest in a positive NPV project?

PROBLEMS

1 Pulini plc is currently financed entirely by 1 million ordinary shares with a nominal value of 75p per share which were issued at par. The dividends paid by Pulini plc have remained constant at £150,000 per annum and the market generally believes that dividends will continue at this level indefinitely, given the information presently available. The current dividend of Pulini plc is about to be declared and the current market price per share is £1·40.

The company has recently signed a contract to service factory equipment for an annual fee of £80,000, receivable in advance. The first annual fee has just been received. The contract, which is to commence immediately, will entail the annual purchase of specialised materials costing £22,400 payable at the end of each year, and will incur no other incremental costs. The contract will continue indefinitely and will have the same risk as the existing operations of Pulini plc. No details of the contract have been communicated or leaked to the stock market.

You may assume, for calculation purposes only, that there is no time delay between the dates of declaration and payment of the dividend.

Required:

(a) Estimate the cum-div market value of Pulini plc in each of the three following situations:

(i) the details of the contract are not communicated to the market, and the dividends are declared to be £150,000;

(ii) the details of the contract are communicated and believed by the market, but the dividends declared remain at £150,000; and

(iii) the details of the contract are not communicated to the market, but the dividends declared fully reflect the incremental annual cash flows from the contract

(b) Discuss whether a company can affect its market price by altering its dividend policy

(c) Outline the factors which might influence company management when deciding on the level of dividends to be declared.

Ignore taxation in part (a), but not in parts (b) and (c).

2 In the early 1980s Chartwell Leasing plc ran into severe financial difficulties due to mistakes its management had made in the computer leasing business in which it operated. Between 1981 and 1985 it made large operating losses and had to stop paying dividends. However, late in 1985 a new management team was installed in the company – at the instigation of the institutional shareholders and non-executive directors. This new management turned the company around by restructuring its business and focusing on the international leasing of construction equipment and the company is once again profitable.

As a result, at the board meeting held recently at the end of the company's financial year – which had seen a further increase in profits – the directors discussed whether or not the company should re-start paying dividends. However opinions were divided. The chairman thought that a stable dividend policy should be introduced as quickly as possible. The finance director thought that dividend policy was unimportant as he remembered quite clearly from his MBA finance course that dividends are irrelevant. Finally, the treasurer (who also acted as the chief accountant) was of the opinion that the company should only pay an annual dividend if there were not sufficient profitable projects available to absorb all the company's earnings. Thus the amount paid out in dividends should purely be this residual.

Required:
Discuss dividend policy with special reference to the comments made by the board members of Chartwell Leasing plc.

3 Charles and Lupin Pooter each own 50% of the issued ordinary share capital of Charles Pooter (Contractors) Ltd, but neither plays any part in its management. The company presently has £3,000 available on bank current account which it is proposing to invest in a project which is expected to produce cash inflows of £800 in Year 1, £1,000 in Year 2, and £1,700 after three years. No other cash flows are expected to be associated with the project. If the £3,000 is not used on this project it will be paid out as a dividend to Charles and Lupin. If the project is accepted the cash inflows it produces will be paid out in full as dividends as they arise.

Lupin is in agreement with the company investing in the proposed project, but Charles wishes to take his wife, Carrie, on a world cruise and claims that the company is not acting in his best interests if it fails to pay the money as dividend to enable him to do so. Charles Pooter (Contractors) Ltd is able both to lend and borrow funds freely at 5%.

Required:
(a) Calculate the net present value of the proposed project to Charles Pooter (Contractors) Ltd.
(b) Explain whether the company is acting in the best interests of *both* its shareholders by accepting the project if:
 (i) Charles and Lupin may both borrow freely at 5%;
 (ii) Charles and Lupin may both borrow freely at 10%.
(c) Comment briefly on the implications of your answers to (a) and (b) above for capital investment theory.

Ignore taxation.

19
Financial decision making in practice

Chapter Contents

THEORY AND PRACTICE

Speed of change

At the outset of this book we stated that the objective was to develop a *normative* theory of financial management decision making. In other words, our concern was primarily with how financial decisions *should be* made, rather than how they *are* made. However, in this final chapter attention is turned to look at how financial managements do actually make some of the decisions we have analysed in the previous eighteen chapters.

In developing a normative theory, it is important that practice should not be ignored. Certainly it cannot be said that where theory and practice diverge, it is necessarily good theory and bad practice. Financial managers are, generally speaking, both intelligent and thoughtful. Therefore when faced with a significant difference between theory and practice, our first reaction should be an attempt to reason out *why* the difference occurs. Indeed the usefulness of this approach was no more clearly seen than in analysing the capital structure decision. Our theory led us to one conclusion, whereas practice indicated a completely different result. In consequence, we then started to consider what other elements of importance to the decision were being excluded from the initial theoretical model.

Notwithstanding the above comments, there is little doubt that bad or incorrect practice exists, just as much as bad or incorrect theory exists. Our understanding of the theory of financial decision making has developed over time – often in rather sudden and rapid surges – but the practical application of the theory sometimes (but not always) lags a considerable way behind. However, this is understandable as there is bound to be some inertia to change in decision making practices. We have been talking about the *major* financial decisions that are undertaken by management. Often the financial numbers involved are very large indeed and the decision outcomes are of crucial importance to the firms' future health. It is not therefore surprising that some managements show a reluctance to throw out tried and trusted decision analysis techniques in favour of more recent theoretical developments.

Another factor that affects the rate at which new developments in the theory are taken up by decision makers in practice is the way in which theoretical developments are disseminated. Many of the more recent theoretical developments are somewhat analytically terse and inaccessible and there is often a substantial time lag before they get written up in a more 'user-friendly' format. Further, there is some evidence to suggest that when managements do try to apply the more sophisticated decision analysis techniques, there is a considerable lack of understanding and misunderstanding. For example, in one study (Gitman and Mercurio, 1982), whereas the majority (69·5%) of the survey respondents claimed familiarity with such terms as 'beta' and the 'capital asset pricing model', only about 30% were familiar with the terms from the *underlying* theory (e.g., 'systematic risk' and 'capital market line').

SURVEYS OF PRACTICE

There have been a great many surveys undertaken, both in the UK and the USA, concerned with financial management practices. Most consist of postal questionnaires sent to large companies (e.g., Fortune Top 1000 Companies or Times Top 1000 companies). The problem is that this type of survey – although often the only feasible approach – does suffer from several potential difficulties. The response rate is often very low (25% to 30%), there is some uncertainty about whether the questionnaire is completed by the most suitable person within a company and there must also be some doubt about the completeness and honesty of the responses received. In addition, it is often difficult to eliminate all ambiguity in the questions posed (and in the answers received), which makes the interpretation of the survey results somewhat problematical. However, perhaps the main drawback to many of the surveys that have been conducted is that they have tended to over-emphasize the '*what* do you do?' question, and to neglect the '*why* do you do it?' question. From the viewpoint of theory development, it is this latter question that holds the real interest, especially when theory and practice diverge.

In this chapter, no attempt will be made to give a detailed break-down of the survey evidence of financial decision making. A comprehensive bibliography is given so that individual surveys can be followed up in detail. Instead, the objective is to provide the reader with a more general, overall impression of how closely practice accords with theory.

We shall examine five commonly surveyed areas of practice: the investment appraisal techniques used; how the DCF discount rate/hurdle rate is specified; how capital rationing is handled; how inflation is accounted for in investment appraisal and, finally, how risk and uncertainty is allowed for in investment appraisal.

Quantitative vs qualitative appraisal

When we start to enquire of management how they appraise capital investment decisions, we find their approaches fall into two distinct categories:

(1) Qualitative or judgemental approaches.
(2) Quantitative or analytical approaches.

The studies that have enquired into this aspect (e.g., Carsberg and Hope, 1976; Petty, Scott and Bird, 1975) show considerable consistency. Both in the UK and in the US about 75% of surveyed managements believed that *quantitative* or analytical analysis of capital investment decisions was important. However, the other 25% thought that (at best) quantitative analysis should only be used to lend support to *qualitative* judgement. Klammer in an earlier (1972) US study found that 50% of companies required a quantitative analysis for at least 75% of the projects that were appraised and most of the other companies undertook a quantitative analysis for between 25% and 75% of all investment projects.

Therefore we can conclude that although quantitative analysis is thought to be important, qualitative analysis also plays a substantial role. This raises two questions: how *effective* is quantitative analysis? (i.e., how much reliance is placed on analytical appraisal techniques) and why do managements indulge in qualitative appraisal?

There is some doubt about the effectiveness of the analytical appraisal advice. When the investment appraisal *rejection* rate is examined a typical survey result would be that in two-thirds of companies, over 75% of appraised projects are accepted, whereas in a quarter of companies, the acceptance rate is in excess of 90%. This high level of project acceptance is rather suspicious and it opens up three possible explanations: either there are a great number of acceptable (i.e., + NPV) projects available to companies; or some appraisals are being 'fudged' so that acceptance is indicated when a rejection is really merited; or companies operate an informal appraisal system, underneath the formal system, that filters out most unacceptable projects before they reach the formal appraisal stage.

Casual observation may lead us to reject the first of these possibilities, but accept the likelihood of the other two. Given the degree of competitiveness in most areas of industry and commerce, it would be surprising to find large numbers of easily identifiable, profitable projects. Most managers would agree that profitable investment opportunities are usually few and far between. That leaves the possibility that the analytical appraisal techniques are sometimes being 'fiddled' to give the desired decision advice. Human nature tells us that this may well be likely. The identification of an investment opportunity, together with the work required to produce the cash flow forecasts and estimates of likely risk requires considerable effort. Therefore, by the time a project reaches the formal appraisal stage, there may be many people within a company who have a personal interest in seeing the project being accepted and their efforts therefore bearing fruit. Hence the temptation to fudge the figures in order that the appraisal techniques produce the desired advice.

The final possibility that was put forward was of an informal appraisal system. Again, casual reasoning would lead us to suspect that these may well exist in situations where management would be unwilling to 'lose face' by having an investment proposal, which was *personally* sponsored or supported, rejected at the formal appraisal stage. In such circumstances an informal appraisal mechanism may well filter out many of the poorer projects. Many survey authors allude to this possibility, especially Scapens, Sale and Tikkas (1982).

Turning to the second question concerning the use of qualitative judgement, there is considerable evidence that it does play an important role. Fremgen (1973) in a US survey found that 97% of his respondent companies admitted having approved investment projects for which the analytical appraisal techniques had advised rejection. Carsberg and Hope (1976) found that one-third of their sample companies ranked *judgement* as the most important appraisal method. The authors proposed two possible reasons for this emphasis. One was that the use of managerial judgement fitted in with the concept of managerial 'flair' and entrepreneurship. (Indeed, Pike, 1982, asked some managers why they did not take risk into account formally, in investment appraisal: one reply was that such an analytical approach was undesirable as it went against true entrepreneurism.) The other possible reason proposed by Carsberg and Hope was that management were guarding against ex-post criticism. The reasoning here was that if an investment decision was taken purely on the basis of an analytical appraisal, then ex-post, the soundness of the judgement could be tested by comparing expected and actual outcomes. However, if management claimed that several qualitative factors were taken into account in reaching an investment decision, the soundness of that judgement would be much more difficult to judge, post investment.

Investment appraisal techniques

Most companies use more than one analytical technique to appraise investment opportunities. UK studies (such as Pike, 1982) show that roughly one-quarter of companies just use one technique with pay-back and return on capital employed (ROCE) being, respectively, first and second most popular, and NPV being most unpopular. Where multiple methods are used, payback and ROCE are still very widely employed, but most companies will also use a DCF technique. However, the IRR technique is consistently more popular than NPV, by a substantial margin.

The Pike survey also asked firms why they used the methods they did and why they did not use other methods. Payback was used because it was thought to be simple, comprehensive, allowed for risk (*sic*) and was suitable for ranking in the face of capital rationing (*sic*). Non-users referred to the fact that it did not allow for the time value of money and it ignored cash flows that arose outside the payback time period.

The IRR was thought to be a good device for ranking projects, especially where they involved different outlays or time scales (*sic*), it was easy to understand as it gave a percentage rate of return and to operate, the technique did not require the specification – at the outset – of a discount rate.

Where the IRR was specifically rejected – usually for the possible presence of multiple IRRs – NPV was usually used instead. However, the NPV technique came in for considerable adverse comment. There was a substantial range of reasons for its non-use including: it was difficult to understand, it was unnecessary for short-lived projects, it was difficult to use because of constantly changing hurdle rates (*sic*), it was too hypothetical and it was a questionable technique to use in periods of high inflation (*sic*).

Several surveys, including Carsberg and Hope (1976), Pike (1982) and Westwick and Shohet (1978) enquired whether the choice of method of appraisal was determined by a particular characteristic such as type or size of project, firm size or firm activity. There was little conclusive evidence, except that DCF techniques tended to be used with larger projects and that larger companies were more likely to use DCF techniques generally.

The situation in the US is slightly different. As in the UK, payback is still very popular and NPV very unpopular. The Fremgen (1973) survey, for example, found that two-thirds of companies used pay-back, but only 4% used NPV. However, the ROCE was considerably *less* popular and the IRR was considerably *more* popular than in the UK. The Scapens, Sale and Tikkas (1982) survey – which was a comparative study of UK and US practice – confirms the overall impression that DCF techniques generally were in more widespread use in the US. They found that, in their sample, 84% of US companies used DCF techniques, as against only 54% in the UK.

The discount rate

There are various different approaches to the choice of the discount rate for use in the DCF analysis. However, it does appear that both in the UK and in the US one of the most widely used determinants is management judgement. For example, both Carsberg and Hope (1976) and Petty, Scott and Bird (1975) found between 40% and 55% of respondents claimed to use a *management-determined* target rate of return that was not directly related to market factors.

The bank overdraft rate and the rate of interest on some other specific sources of funds drew support from between 10% and 20% of sample funds in both countries. However, in the US there appeared to be much greater support for *some* type of WACC, with 46% of firms in the Schall, Sundem and Geijsbeek (1978) study and 88% of firms in the Gitman and

Mercurio (1982) study claiming some type of WACC application.

Of those firms that did use some type of WACC, considerable differences were found in the degree of sophistication employed in the calculations involved. For example, Gitman and Mercurio found some very odd adjustments being made to allow for tax, as well as finding that 40% of their sample used *nominal* coupon rates in the calculation of the cost of debt capital.

Finally, both US and UK studies suggest that once firms settle on project hurdle rates (e.g., the company's WACC), a substantial period of time elapses between revisions; these eventually being prompted by major changes in market conditions.

Capital rationing

Most surveys report that between 60% and 90% of firms experience capital rationing in that they have found it necessary to reject some acceptable projects. When asked for the cause of the capital rationing, various reasons are reported. Fremgen (1973) found acceptable projects were sometimes rejected in order to maintain earnings per share or a particular dividend policy, as well as a constraint being imposed by management (or a 'higher authority') on the amount of borrowings. Gitman and Forrester (1977) and Gitman and Mercurio (1982) found similar responses, but with a greater emphasis on debt-raising limitations.

In terms of how firms dealt with capital rationing, the Fremgen (1973) study again is typical. About one-fifth of companies admitted to using linear programming, at some time, but none used it on a regular basis. Most firms ranked projects in terms of their usual appraisal technique (mainly IRR or pay-back), but the most widespread method of selection was via management's own subjective judgement as to an investment's importance.

Inflation

With inflation, companies generally made a poor job of correctly taking it into account in investment appraisal. Carsberg and Hope (1976) found that the most popular – but incorrect – approach was to adjust the discount rate to take out effects of general inflation (correct) and then to apply this to cash flows expressed in current prices[1] (incorrect). In fact, only 15% of Carsberg and Hope's sample of large companies took *correct* account of inflation in their investment appraisal calculations.

Westwick and Shohet (1978) found that 77% of their sample attempted to take inflation into account, with the most popular – but incorrect – adjustment being to raise cash flows in line with expected, *specific* rates of inflation and then also raising the discount – hurdle rate. Finally, Pike's survey indicated that 89% of companies considered inflation in investment appraisal (whereas only 70% did in 1975), but now the most popular method was to adjust project cash flows to take account of *general* inflation (again, incorrect). However, there was also a tendency for larger companies to adjust cash flows by specific inflation rates, or to use current prices and apply a real rate of discount.

Risk

Pike, in his UK survey, found that only 37% of companies formally analysed risk. Amongst these both sensitivity analysis and use of a risk-adjusted discount rate (RADR) were equally popular, and three times as popular as the two other most common methods: reducing the pay-back time period and probability analysis. In terms of firm size, larger firms tended to use sensitivity analysis, medium sized firms used a RADR and small firms tended to reduce the pay-back time period.

When the 67% of the sample firms which did *not* use risk analysis were asked why they did not, a range of confused answers were given. Pike provides some examples such as: 'risk was impossible to quantify and very subjective and so a formal risk analysis is a contradiction in terms' (*sic*), 'too time-consuming', 'too complex' and 'such an analysis brought undesirable negative pressure on decision makers and went against the true entrepreneurial approach'.

Of those that did use a formal risk analysis, half were very wary, untrusting and sceptical of the results, whereas the other half were very enthusiastic. This latter group commented that it was an excellent discipline, was useful in assessing the sensitivity of a project to unforeseen changes and forced project sponsors 'to think about how wrong they could be'.

The US surveys showed roughly similar results with between 30% and 40% of companies making use of a formal risk analysis. Klammer (1972) and Mao (1970) both found the RADR to be the most popular, as did Gitman and Forrester (1977). However, Petty, Scott and Bird (1975), Fremgen (1973) and Schall, Sundem and Geijsbeek (1978) all found that around 60% of firms used a shortened payback, as against 35% using a RADR. Interestingly in contrast to the UK, sensitivity analysis found little general support.

Conclusion

Although one recent study (Moore and Reichert, 1983) claims that their US survey results 'are consistent with the hypothesis that strong emphasis is being placed upon rigorous financial analysis . . . there appears to be a high degree of compatibility between financial techniques employed by practitioners and those advocated by academics', and that 'fairly sophisticated capital budgeting procedures are currently being used by 86% of all respondents', we must conclude that the overall picture is somewhat discouraging.

We know that some companies *are* correctly applying extremely sophisticated techniques (such as APV) to financial decision making and that they are keeping abreast with theoretical developments as they occur. However, by and large, there seems to be a substantial gap between industry practice and normative theory. The application of even the most elementary techniques of DCF to problems involving inflation, risk and capital rationing leaves a considerable amount of room for improvement.

Despite the foregoing, we should avoid jumping to any hasty conclusions on the evidence available to date. In particular, a great deal more work is required, along the lines of the Pike study, enquiring into why firms 'do what they do'. Further work is also required along the lines of Klammer's study, to investigate the relationship (if any) that exists between firm performance and the use of sophisticated financial decision appraisal techniques.

SUMMARY

- This final chapter has looked at the results of a number of empirical surveys that have investigated practice both in the UK and the US.
- Although difficult to reach specific conclusions, the following general remarks can be made.
- Much capital investment is undertaken without any formal appraisal at all. Instead it is accepted on the basis of being 'necessary' or because it fits in with the firm's corporate plan.
- Of those companies that do use formal appraisal techniques, by far and away the *most* popular technique is payback and by far and away the *least* popular is NPV. However, it should also be noted that payback usually includes discounted payback (which is a truncated version of NPV). In addition, most companies do not usually use just one technique but multiple investment appraisal techniques.
- The evidence on the discount rate suggests that many companies cannot identify their WACC and so use some type of management-determined rate. This is then used company-wide for considerable periods of time before revision.
- Capital rationing was found to be a very common experience and there was some evidence of being externally imposed on firms by the capital market. Generally speaking, management abandoned formal attempts to solve the capital rationing problem and employed subjective judgement to decide which projects should be accepted.
- Inflation is generally poorly handled by companies. For example, Carsberg and Hope (1976) found that companies did almost anything but handle the problem correctly.
- Risk was also poorly handled. The Pike (1982) survey found that two-thirds of companies didn't allow for risk differences and those that did, did not go further than using some sort of management-determined RADR or sensitivity analysis.
- The conclusion of the survey data is that there is a wide disparity between firms. Some firms do undoubtedly use very sophisticated appraisal techniques such as APV. But, on the other hand, some companies appear to be hopelessly out of their depth in terms of understanding how the techniques should be applied, their advantages and their limitations.

NOTE

1 Incorrect, unless it is assumed that *all* the individual elements of the project's cash flow will inflate in line with the *general* rate of inflation.

FURTHER READING

In this chapter, reference was made to the following surveys of which Pike (1982) is the most comprehensive of the UK surveys, and Scapens, Sale and Tikkas (1982) provides an interesting contrast between the UK and the USA:

R.S. Bower and D.R. Lessard, 'Capital Management and Capital Theory: An Operational Approach to Risk Screening', *Journal of Finance,* May 1973.

B.V. Carsberg and A. Hope, *Business Investment Decisions Under Inflation: Theory and Practice,* London, Institute of Chartered Accountants in England and Wales, 1976.

F.J. Fabozzi, 'The Use of Operational Research Techniques for Capital Budgeting Decisions – A Sample Survey', *Journal of the Operational Research Society,* Spring 1978.

J.M. Fremgen, 'Capital Budgeting Practices: A Survey', *Management Accounting (N.Y.),* May 1973.

L.J. Gitman and J.R. Forrester, 'A Survey of Capital Budgeting Techniques Used by Major US Firms', *Financial Management,* Autumn 1977.

L.J. Gitman and V.A. Mercurio, 'Cost of Capital Techniques Used by Major U.S. Firms: Survey and Analysis of Fortune's 1000', *Financial Management,* Winter 1982.

C. Gurnami, 'Capital Budgeting Theory and Practice', *Engineering Economist,* Fall 1984.

T.D. Klammer, 'Empirical Evidence of the Adoption of Sophisticated Capital Budgeting Techniques' *Journal of Business,* July 1972.

J.C.T. Mao, 'Survey of Capital Budgeting – Theory and Practice', *Journal of Finance,* May 1970.

J.S. Moore and A.K. Reichert, 'An Analysis of the Financial Management Techniques Currently Employed by Large U.S. Corporations', *Journal of Business Finance and Accounting,* Winter 1983.

J.W. Petty, D.F. Scott and M.M. Bird, 'The Capital Expenditure Decision-Making Process of Large Corporations', *Engineering Economist,* Spring 1975.

R.H. Pike, *Capital Budgeting in the 1980's*, London, Institute of Cost and Management Accountants, 1982.

M. Ross, 'Capital Budgeting Practice of Twelve Large Manufacturers', *Financial Management*, Winter 1986.

R.W. Scapens, T.J. Sale and P.A. Tikkas, *Financial Control of Divisional Capital Investment,* London Institute of Cost and Management Accountants, 1982.

L.D. Schall, G.L. Sundem and W.R. Geijsbeek, 'Survey and Analysis of Capital Budgeting Methods', *Journal of Finance,* March 1978.

C.A. Westwick and P.S.D. Shohet, 'Investment Appraisal and Inflation', *Research Committee Occasional Paper No.* 7, London, Institute of Chartered Accountants in England and Wales, 1978.

Compounding and discounting tables

Table A Compound interest factor $(1 + i)^N$

i		0·04	0·06	0·08	0·10	0·12	0·14	0·16	0·18	0·20
N	1	1·0400	1·0600	1·0800	1·1000	1·1200	1·1400	1·1600	1·1800	1·2000
	2	1·0816	1·1236	1·1664	1·2100	1·2544	1·2996	1·3456	1·3924	1·4400
	3	1·1249	1·1910	1·2597	1·3310	1·4049	1·4815	1·5609	1·6430	1·7280
	4	1·1699	1·2625	1·3605	1·4641	1·5735	1·6890	1·8106	1·9338	2·0736
	5	1·2167	1·3382	1·4693	1·6105	1·7623	1·9254	2·1003	2·2878	2·4883
	6	1·2653	1·4185	1·5869	1·7716	1·9738	2·1950	2·4364	2·6996	2·9860
	7	1·3159	1·5036	1·7138	1·9487	2·2107	2·5023	2·8262	3·1855	3·5832
	8	1·3686	1·5939	1·8509	2·1436	2·4760	2·8526	3·2784	3·7589	4·2998
	9	1·4233	1·6895	1·9990	2·3580	2·7731	3·2519	3·8030	4·4335	5·1598
	10	1·4802	1·7909	2·1589	2·5937	3·1058	3·7072	4·4114	5·2338	6·1917
	11	1·5395	1·8983	2·3316	2·8531	3·4785	4·2262	5·1173	6·1759	7·4301
	12	1·6010	2·0122	2·5182	3·1384	3·8960	4·8179	5·9360	7·2876	8·9161
	13	1·6651	2·1329	2·7196	3·4523	4·3635	5·4924	6·8858	8·5994	10·6993
	14	1·7317	2·2609	2·9372	3·7975	4·8871	6·2613	7·9875	10·1472	12·8392
	15	1·8009	2·3966	3·1722	4·1773	5·4736	7·1379	9·2655	11·9737	15·4070

Table B Present value factor $(1 + i)^{-N}$

i		0·04	0·06	0·08	0·10	0·12	0·14	0·16	0·18	0·20
N	1	0·9615	0·9434	0·9259	0·9091	0·8929	0·8772	0·8621	0·8475	0·8333
	2	0·9246	0·8900	0·8573	0·8264	0·7972	0·7695	0·7432	0·7182	0·6944
	3	0·8890	0·8396	0·7938	0·7513	0·7118	0·6750	0·6407	0·6086	0·5787
	4	0·8548	0·7921	0·7350	0·6830	0·6355	0·5921	0·5523	0·5158	0·4823
	5	0·8219	0·7473	0·6806	0·6209	0·5674	0·5194	0·4761	0·4371	0·4019
	6	0·7903	0·7050	0·6302	0·5645	0·5066	0·4556	0·4014	0·3704	0·3349
	7	0·7599	0·6651	0·5835	0·5132	0·4532	0·3996	0·3538	0·3139	0·2791
	8	0·7307	0·6274	0·5403	0·4665	0·4039	0·3506	0·3050	0·2660	0·2326
	9	0·7026	0·5919	0·5002	0·4241	0·3606	0·3075	0·2630	0·2255	0·1938
	10	0·6756	0·5584	0·4632	0·3855	0·3220	0·2697	0·2267	0·1911	0·1615
	11	0·6496	0·5268	0·4289	0·3505	0·2875	0·2366	0·1954	0·1619	0·1346
	12	0·6246	0·4970	0·3971	0·3186	0·2567	0·2076	0·1685	0·1372	0·1122
	13	0·6006	0·4686	0·3677	0·2897	0·2292	0·1821	0·1452	0·1163	0·0935
	14	0·5775	0·4423	0·3405	0·2633	0·2046	0·1597	0·1252	0·0985	0·0779
	15	0·5553	0·4173	0·3152	0·2394	0·1827	0·1401	0·1079	0·0835	0·0649

Table C Present value of an annuity $A_{N\neg i}$

i	0·04	0·06	0·08	0·10	0·12	0·14	0·16	0·18	0·20
N 1	0·9615	0·9434	0·9259	0·9091	0·8929	0·8772	0·8621	0·8475	0·8333
2	1·8861	1·8334	1·7833	1·7355	1·6901	1·6467	1·6052	1·5656	1·5278
3	2·7751	2·6730	2·5771	2·4869	2·4018	2·3216	2·2459	2·1743	2·1065
4	3·6299	3·4651	3·3121	3·1699	3·0373	2·9137	2·7982	2·6901	2·5887
5	4·4518	4·2124	3·9927	3·7908	3·6048	3·4331	3·2743	3·1272	2·9906
6	5·2421	4·9173	4·6229	4·3553	4·1114	3·8887	3·6847	3·4976	3·3255
7	6·0021	5·5824	5·2064	4·8684	4·5638	4·2883	4·0386	3·8115	3·6046
8	6·7327	6·2098	5·7466	5·3349	4·9676	4·6389	4·3436	4·0776	3·8372
9	7·4353	6·8017	6·2469	5·7590	5·3282	4·9464	4·6065	4·3030	4·0310
10	8·1109	7·3601	6·7101	6·1446	5·6502	5·2161	4·8332	4·4941	4·1925
11	8·7605	7·8869	7·1390	6·4951	5·9377	5·4527	5·0286	4·6560	4·3271
12	9·3851	8·3838	7·5361	6·8137	6·1944	5·6603	5·1971	4·7932	4·4392
13	9·9856	8·8527	7·9038	7·1034	6·4235	5·8424	5·3423	4·9095	4·5327
14	10·5631	9·2950	8·2442	7·3667	6·6282	6·0021	5·4675	5·0081	4·6106
15	11·1184	9·7122	8·5595	7·6061	6·8109	6·1422	5·5755	5·0916	4·6755

Table D Terminal value of an annuity $S_{N\neg i}$

i	0·04	0·06	0·08	0·10	0·12	0·14	0·16	0·18	0·20
N 1	1·0000	1·0000	1·0000	1·0000	1·0000	1·0000	1·0000	1·0000	1·0000
2	2·0400	2·0600	2·0800	2·1000	2·1200	2·1400	2·1600	2·1800	2·2000
3	3·1216	3·1836	3·2464	3·3100	3·3744	3·4396	3·5056	3·5724	3·6400
4	4·2465	4·3746	4·5061	4·6410	4·7793	4·9211	5·0665	5·2154	5·3680
5	5·4163	5·6371	5·8666	6·1051	6·3528	6·6101	6·8771	7·1542	7·4416
6	6·6330	6·9753	7·3359	7·7156	8·1152	8·5355	8·9775	9·4420	9·9299
7	7·8983	8·3938	8·9228	9·4872	10·0890	10·7305	11·4139	12·1415	12·9159
8	9·2142	9·8975	10·6366	11·4359	12·2997	13·2328	14·2401	15·3270	16·4991
9	10·5828	11·4913	12·4876	13·5795	14·7757	16·0853	17·5185	19·0859	20·7989
10	12·0061	13·1808	14·4866	15·9374	17·5487	19·3373	21·3215	23·5213	25·9587
11	13·4864	14·9716	16·6455	18·5312	20·6546	23·0445	25·7329	28·7551	32·1504
12	15·0258	16·8699	18·9771	21·3843	24·1331	27·2707	30·8502	34·9311	39·5805
13	16·6268	18·8821	21·4953	24·5227	28·0291	32·0887	36·7862	42·2187	48·4966
14	18·2919	21·0151	24·2149	27·9750	32·3926	37·5811	43·6720	50·8180	59·1959
15	20·0236	23·2760	27·1521	31·7725	37·2797	43·8424	51·6595	60·9653	72·0351

Table E Annual equivalent factor $A_{\overline{N}|i}^{-1}$

i	0·04	0·06	0·08	0·10	0·12	0·14	0·16	0·18	0·20
N 1	1·0400	1·0600	1·0800	1·1000	1·1200	1·1400	1·1600	1·1800	1·2000
2	0·5302	0·5454	0·5608	0·5762	0·5917	0·6073	0·6230	0·6387	0·6545
3	0·3603	0·3741	0·3880	0·4021	0·4163	0·4307	0·4453	0·4599	0·4747
4	0·2755	0·2886	0·3019	0·3155	0·3292	0·3432	0·3574	0·3717	0·3863
5	0·2246	0·2374	0·2505	0·2638	0·2774	0·2913	0·3054	0·3198	0·3344
6	0·1908	0·2034	0·2163	0·2296	0·2432	0·2572	0·2714	0·2859	0·3007
7	0·1666	0·1791	0·1921	0·2054	0·2191	0·2332	0·2476	0·2624	0·2774
8	0·1485	0·1610	0·1740	0·1874	0·2013	0·2156	0·2302	0·2452	0·2606
9	0·1345	0·1470	0·1601	0·1736	0·1877	0·2022	0·2171	0·2324	0·2481
10	0·1233	0·1359	0·1490	0·1627	0·1770	0·1917	0·2069	0·2225	0·2385
11	0·1141	0·1268	0·1401	0·1540	0·1684	0·1834	0·1989	0·2148	0·2311
12	0·1066	0·1193	0·1327	0·1468	0·1614	0·1767	0·1924	0·2086	0·2253
13	0·1001	0·1130	0·1265	0·1408	0·1557	0·1712	0·1872	0·2037	0·2206
14	0·0947	0·1076	0·1213	0·1357	0·1509	0·1666	0·1829	0·1997	0·2169
15	0·0899	0·1030	0·1168	0·1315	0·1468	0·1628	0·1794	0·1964	0·2139

Table F Sinking fund factor $S_{\overline{N}|i}^{-1}$

i	0·04	0·06	0·08	0·10	0·12	0·14	0·16	0·18	0·20
N 1	1·0000	1·0000	1·0000	1·0000	1·0000	1·0000	1·0000	1·0000	1·0000
2	0·4902	0·4854	0·4808	0·4762	0·4717	0·4673	0·4630	0·4587	0·4545
3	0·3203	0·3141	0·3080	0·3021	0·2963	0·2907	0·2853	0·2799	0·2747
4	0·2355	0·2286	0·2219	0·2155	0·2092	0·2032	0·1974	0·1917	0·1863
5	0·1846	0·1774	0·1705	0·1638	0·1574	0·1513	0·1454	0·1398	0·1344
6	0·1508	0·1343	0·1363	0·1296	0·1232	0·1172	0·1114	0·1059	0·1007
7	0·1266	0·1191	0·1121	0·1054	0·0991	0·0932	0·0876	0·0824	0·0774
8	0·1085	0·1010	0·0940	0·0874	0·0813	0·0756	0·0702	0·0652	0·0606
9	0·0945	0·0870	0·0801	0·0736	0·0677	0·0622	0·0571	0·0524	0·0481
10	0·0833	0·0759	0·0690	0·0627	0·0570	0·0517	0·0469	0·0425	0·0385
11	0·0741	0·0668	0·0601	0·0540	0·0484	0·0434	0·0389	0·0348	0·0311
12	0·0666	0·0593	0·0527	0·0468	0·0414	0·0367	0·0324	0·0286	0·0253
13	0·0601	0·0530	0·0465	0·0408	0·0357	0·0312	0·0272	0·0237	0·0206
14	0·0547	0·0476	0·0413	0·0357	0·0309	0·0266	0·0229	0·0197	0·0169
15	0·0499	0·0430	0·0368	0·0315	0·0268	0·0228	0·0194	0·0164	0·0139

Answers to quickie questions

CHAPTER 1

1 (a) The capital investment decision.
  (b) The financing and capital structure decision.
  (c) The dividend decision.
2 The process by which the company seeks out alternative courses of action, alternative projects, etc.
3 The maximization of shareholder wealth.
4 It is a *reporting* concept, not a decision-making concept. Its use is to report on the success or failure of decisions taken. It has only a secondary role in the decision-making process itself.
5 On the basis of the expected flow of dividends they will generate in the future.
6 The problem is one of control. How does the principal control the agent to ensure that the agent acts in the principal's best interests?
7 (a) Corporate planning.
  (b) Budget setting.
  (c) Variance analysis.
  (d) Investment appraisal.
  (e) Pricing decisions.
  (f) Internal audit.
  (g) Financial accounts.
  (h) Taxation services.
  (i) Management information systems.
8 See Figure 1.2.
9 It allows highly *illiquid* securities (e.g. shares) that are issued by companies to be held as highly *liquid* investments by investors, as it provides a market place where such investments can be easily bought and sold.
10 Investors are generally assumed to be risk-averse. This dislike of risk does not mean that investors will not take on risky investments, but that they have to be rewarded for doing so. The reward is given in terms of a higher expected return on the investment: the higher the risk, the higher must be its expected return.

CHAPTER 2

1 Stage One: The best of the alternative projects has the shortest payback.
  Stage Two: Accept the best project as long as its return meets the decision criterion.
2 Working capital is excluded from the analysis. Net cash flow:

0	−11,000	
1	+ 4,000	Payback = 2·75 years
2	+ 4,000	
3	+ 4,000	
4	+ 3,000	
5	+ 3,000	(i.e. +2,000 +1,000)

3 (i) Quick and simple to calculate.
(ii) Thought to automatically select less-risky projects in mutually exclusive decision situations.
(iii) Saves management the trouble of having to estimate project cash flows beyond the maximum payback time-period.
(iv) Convenient method to use in capital rationing.

4 The payback criterion is reduced until total capital expenditure equates with the amount of finance available.

5 (i) Management's experience of successful projects within the firm.
(ii) Industry practice.
(iii) Reflects the limit of management's forecasting skills.

6 The payback decision rule, adjusted to take account of the time value of money.

7 Ignores cash flows outside the payback time period. (The fact that 'normal' payback ignores the time value of money is equally important but this criticism can, of course, be easily overcome through the use of discounted payback.)

8 Money has a time value because it can earn a rate of interest/a rate of return.

9 The question does not specify which ARR/ROCE to calculate, so *both* are given:

Annual depreciation: (£11,000 − £1,000) ÷ 5 = £2,000

Profit: £4,000 − £2,000 = £2,000 Yr 1
4,000 − 2,000 = 2,000 Yr 2
4,000 − 2,000 = 2,000 Yr 3
3,000 − 2,000 = 1,000 Yr 4
2,000 − 2,000 = 0 Yr 5
Total profit = £7,000 ÷ 5 = £1,400 = Av. Ann. Profit

Average Capital Employed:

$$\frac{£11{,}000 - £1{,}000}{2} + £1{,}000 + £4{,}000 = £10{,}000$$

Return on Initial Capital Employed = £1,400 ÷ £15,000 = 0·093 or $9\frac{1}{3}$%
Return on Average Capital Employed = £1,400 ÷ £10,000 = 0·14 or 14%

10 (i) Evaluates via a percentage rate of return.
(ii) Evaluates on the basis of profitability.
(iii) Appears logical to evaluate projects on the same basis as management have their own performance evaluated by shareholders.

11 (i) Ignores the time value of money.
(ii) Evaluates on the basis of profit, not cash, flow.

CHAPTER 3

1 This is an example of the economic concept of diminishing marginal utility. Each additional £1 of t_0 consumption foregone, through investment, is likely

to be of increasing value in terms of consumption benefits foregone. Each additional £1 of future consumption gained is likely to be of decreasing value. Hence, the time value of money rises.

2 The complete range of maximum consumption combinations that the firm owner can obtain at t_0 and t_1.

3 The marginal return on the investment opportunity at any particular point.

4 A curve of constant utility. All combinations of consumption at t_0 and t_1 that lie along a single indifference curve would provide the same level of utility or satisfaction.

5 It invests until the return on the marginal investment equates with the owner's marginal time value of money.

6 Lending at t_0 would reduce the amount of money available for consumption at t_0 and increase the amount available at t_1, hence the move would be *up* the financial investment line.

7 The firm should continue to invest in projects as long as the marginal rate of return is not less than the market rate of interest. This rule is, of course, obvious. There would be little point in investing money in a project which gave a lower return than what could be obtained by lending the money on the capital market.

The cash (dividend) distribution to shareholders in t_0 and t_1 that arises out of the firm's investment decision can then be re-distributed by shareholders, using the capital markets, to suit their own set of indifference curves.

8 A risky investment is one where the outcome is uncertain.

9 Ensure that any project earns at least the capital market rate of return that is available for investments of equivalent risk to the project.

10 (i) Single time horizon.
(ii) Infinitely divisible projects.
(iii) All independent projects.
(iv) Rational investors.

11 Investors dislike risk: they are said to be risk-averse. Hence they require a reward for taking on risk, which is the expectation (but, of course, not the certainty) of a higher return.

12 In these circumstances, the market rate of return offers you greater compensation than you require to forego current consumption. Therefore you would want to lend money.

CHAPTER 4

1

0	−1,000 × 1	=	−1,000
1	+ 500 × 0·8772	=	+ 438·60
2	+ 600 × 0·7695	=	+ 461·70
3	+ 400 × 0·6750	=	+ 270
			+ 170·30 NPV

2 There are several interpretations:
(i) It produces a return > 10%.
(ii) It produces £120 more (in t_0 terms) than a £1,000 capital market investment of similar risk.
(iii) The project would produce a sufficient cash flow to repay its outlay, pay its financing charges *and* provide an additional £120 in t_0 terms.
(iv) If accepted, shareholder wealth would increase by £120.

3 At 4% discount rate : NPV = +147·48
At 20% discount rate: NPV = − 9·28

$$\text{Therefore IRR} = 4\% + \left[\frac{147{\cdot}48}{147{\cdot}48 - (-9{\cdot}28)} \times (20\% - 4\%)\right]$$
$$= \underline{19{\cdot}05\%} \text{ approx.}$$

4

Year	*Cash flow*		*Discount Factor*	
0	−500	×	1	= −500
1	+200	×	0·9091	= +181·82
2	+300	×	0·8264	= +247·92
3	+200	×	0·7513	= +150·26

500 − 181·82 − 247·92 = 70·26 ÷ 150·26 = 0·47
∴ payback is 2·47 years approx.

5 The return available elsewhere on the capital market on a similar risk investment.
6 For the same project they should be identical. In both cases they are the opportunity cost return referred to in the answer above to question five.

7 $+350\, A_{\overline{4}|0{\cdot}10} = 350 \times 3{\cdot}1699 = \underline{+1{,}109{\cdot}47}$

8 (i) Annuity due.
(ii) Immediate annuity.
(iii) Deferred annuity.

9 Given the PV of a perpetuity is: $\frac{\text{Annual amount}}{\text{Discount rate}}$, then:

$$\text{IRR} = \frac{\pounds 100}{\pounds 1{,}000} = 0{\cdot}10 \text{ or } 10\%$$

$$\text{because: } -\pounds 1{,}000 + \frac{\pounds 100}{0{\cdot}10} = 0 \text{ NPV}$$

10 $-1{,}000 + 200\, A_{\overline{2}|0{\cdot}16} + 500\, A_{\overline{3}|0{\cdot}16}\,(1 + 0{\cdot}16)^{-2} = \text{NPV}$
$-1{,}000 + (200 \times 1{\cdot}6052) + (500 \times 2{\cdot}2459 \times 0{\cdot}7432) = \underline{+\pounds 155{\cdot}62}$

CHAPTER 5

1 The NPV rule is to accept whichever project has the largest positive NPV. Differences in magnitude, duration and risk can be ignored. Hence project A should be accepted.
2 The assumptions made are:
(i) There is a perfect capital market so that the firm can finance the large project just as easily as it can finance the small project.
(ii) The projects represent independent decisions in that they are not part of a continuous replacement chain.
(iii) The discount rates used do correctly reflect the risk of each project.
3 NPV and IRR both make assumptions about the rate of return at which project generated cash flows are reinvested. NPV assumes that the rate is the market discount rate, while IRR assumes that it is equal to the IRR of the project generating those cash flows. Given a perfect capital market, the NPV method is making the correct assumption.
4 Non-conventional cash flows, where there is more than one change in sign. Generally there will be as many IRRs as there are changes in sign. The problem can be avoided by using the extended yield technique.
5 Using the extended yield technique:

Year 3: $-20\,(1 + 0{\cdot}10)^{-3} = -18{\cdot}18$ at Year 0

Therefore the revised cash flow is:

0	−118·18
1	+ 60
2	+ 80

At a 4% discount rate: +13·48 NPV
At a 20% discount rate: −12·63 NPV

$$\therefore \text{ IRR} = 4\% + \left[\frac{13{\cdot}48}{13{\cdot}48 - (-12{\cdot}63)} \times (20\% - 4\%)\right] = \underline{12{\cdot}3\% \text{ approx.}}$$

6

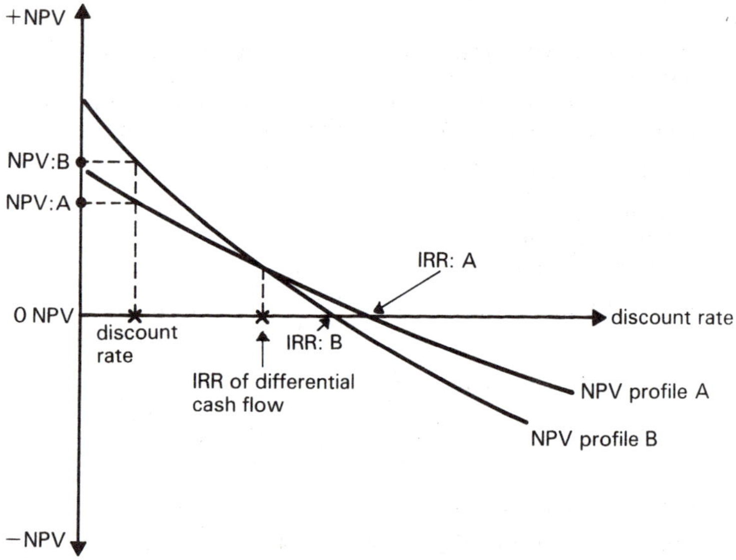

7 If IRR diff. c/f > hurdle rate: accept project smallest IRR.
If IRR diff. c/f < hurdle rate: accept project largest IRR.

CHAPTER 6

1 $\dfrac{(1{\cdot}13)}{(1{\cdot}04)} - 1 = 0{\cdot}086$ or $\underline{8{\cdot}6\%}$

2 Either: Project money cash flows discounted at the market discount rate to NPV.
or: Project money cash flows discounted at the general rate of inflation and then at the real discount rate to NPV.

3 The money cash flow, deflated (discounted) by the *general* rate of inflation.

4 $\dfrac{1{\cdot}155}{1{\cdot}05} - 1 = 0{\cdot}10$ = real discount rate

(a) $£10,000\,(1{\cdot}05)^2 = \underline{£11,025}$
(b) $\underline{£10,000}$
(a) $£11,025\,(1{\cdot}155)^{-2} = £11,025\,(1{\cdot}10)^{-2}(1{\cdot}05)^{-2} = \underline{£8,263{\cdot}73}$
(b) $£10,000\,(1{\cdot}155)^{-2} = £10,000\,(1{\cdot}10)^{-2}(1{\cdot}05)^{-2} = \underline{£7,495{\cdot}45}$

5		*WDA*		*Tax relief*	*Timing*
500	× 0·25 =	+125	× 0·35 =	+43·75	Year 2
125					
375	× 0·25 =	+ 93·75	× 0·35 =	+32·81	Year 3
93·75					
281·25 − 0	=	+281·25	× 0·35 =	+98·44	Year 4

6 Historic cost: £60,000 – irrelevant, sunk cost.
Written down book value: £10,000 – irrelevant non-economic figure.
Scrap now: £3,000
Rent and then scrap: £2,500 + £800 = £3,300.
Therefore, if the machine is used to undertake the project, the best opportunity foregone is the 'rent and then scrap' alternative. So this is the opportunity cost of using the machine on the project: −£3,300.
7 Discount the after-tax cash flows by the after-tax discount rate.
8 They are non-incremental.
9 Market price of factory space: £2 per m^2 (external opportunity cost)
Contribution: £15 per m^2 (internal opportunity cost)
Cost to project: 150 × [£15 + £2] = £2,550.

CHAPTER 7

1 Hard and soft capital rationing.
2 The firm cannot necessarily accept a project just because it has a positive NPV, nor can it necessarily reject a project just because it has a negative NPV. Hence the standard NPV decision rule breaks down.
3 The benefit-cost ratios are:

A:	+60 ÷ 100 = +0·60	(1)
B:	+90 ÷ 200 = +0·45	(3)
C:	+20 ÷ 40 = +0·50	(2)
D:	−10 ÷ 100 = −0·10	(–)

200	available	
−100	invest in A, producing	: + 60 NPV
100		
− 40	invest in C, producing	: + 20 NPV
60		
− 60	invest in 30% B, producing	: + 27 NPV
–		+107 Total NPV

4 The benefit-cost ratios are:

A:	+60 ÷ 50 = +1·20	(1)
B:	+90 ÷ 200 = +0·45	(2)
C:	+20 ÷ 150 = +0·133	(3)
D:	−10 ÷ – = –	

240	available	
− 50	invest in A, producing	: + 60 NPV
190		
−190	invest in 95% of B, producing	: + 85·5 NPV
0		+145·5 Total NPV

As D has a *cost-benefit* ratio of: $-10 \div 20 = -0{\cdot}50$
and B, the marginal project, has a benefit-cost ratio of 0·45, further investment is not worthwhile.

5 Benefit-cost ratios:

A	: 40 ÷ 100	= 0·40	(1)
*B	: 30 ÷ 100	= 0·30	(2)
*C	: 50 ÷ 200	= 0·25	(3)
D	: 10 ÷ 100	= 0·10	(4)
E	: 4 ÷ 50	= 0·08	(5)

300	available	
−100	invest in A, producing	: +40 NPV
200		
−100	invest in B, producing	: +30 NPV
100		
−100	invest in D, producing	: +10 NPV
0		+80 Total NPV

alternatively:

300	available	
−100	invest in A, producing	: +40 NPV
200		
−200	invest in C, producing	: +50 NPV
0		+90 Total NPV

Therefore, the best alternative is to undertake projects A and C.

6
$$\begin{aligned} &40a - 20b + 50c \quad \text{Max} \\ &100a + 150b + 200c \leqslant 190 \\ &200a + 120c \leqslant 110 + 70b \\ &30c \leqslant 50a + 70b \\ &a, b, c \leqslant 1 \\ &a, b, c \geq 0 \end{aligned}$$

7

Dual values	+	*10% discount factor*	=	*Total opportunity cost of cash*	
1·86	+	1	=	2·86	t_0
0·73	+	0·9091	=	1·6391	t_1
0·64	+	0·8264	=	1·4664	t_2
1·21	+	0·7513	=	1·9613	t_3

Gain from an extra £1 at t_1:

$$£1 \times 1{\cdot}6391 = \underline{£1{\cdot}6391}$$

Loss from repayment of £1, plus interest (i) at t_2

$$£(1 + i) \times 1{\cdot}4664 = £\ 1{\cdot}4664 + 1{\cdot}4664i$$

The maximum interest rate would occur at the point where the gain equals the loss:

$$1{\cdot}6391 = 1{\cdot}4664 + 1{\cdot}4664i$$
$$1{\cdot}6391 - 1{\cdot}4664 = 1{\cdot}4664i$$
$$\frac{1{\cdot}6391 - 1{\cdot}4664}{1{\cdot}4664} = i = 0{\cdot}118 \text{ or } \underline{11{\cdot}8\%\ \text{max.}}$$

8 NPV:

$$\begin{aligned} -100 \times 1 &= -100 \\ +\ 40 \times 0{\cdot}9091 &= +\ 36{\cdot}36 \\ +\ 90 \times 0{\cdot}8264 &= \underline{+\ 74{\cdot}38} \\ &\quad \underline{\underline{+\ 10{\cdot}74 \text{ NPV}}} \end{aligned}$$

Internal Opportunity Cost:

$$\begin{aligned} -100 \times 1{\cdot}86 &= -186 \\ +\ 40 \times 0{\cdot}73 &= +\ 29{\cdot}2 \\ +\ 90 \times 0{\cdot}64 &= \underline{+\ 57{\cdot}6} \\ &\quad \underline{\underline{-\ 99{\cdot}2}} \end{aligned}$$

Total opportunity cost:

+10·74	NPV
−99·20	Internal opportunity cost
−88·46	Net total opportunity cost

As this net figure is negative, the additional project will not be a worthwhile investment, reject.

CHAPTER 8

1 (i) How to measure the project's risk.
(ii) How to find the return available on the capital market for that level of risk.
2 Transitivity means that choice between alternatives is consistent: if X is preferred to Y and Y is preferred to Z then X *must* be preferred to Z if the choice is to exhibit transitivity.
3 The *certain* outcome held to be equivalent to an investment with an *uncertain* outcome.

4 $U(+\ 10{,}000) = 1$
$U(-\ 5{,}000) = 0$
$U(C - E) = p\,U(+\ 10{,}000) + (1 - p)\,U(-\ 5{,}000)$
$U(3{,}500) = [0{\cdot}60 \times 1] + [0{\cdot}40 \times 0] = \underline{0{\cdot}60}$

5 Risk aversion.
6 Linear.
7 Certainty equivalent < expected outcome.

8 $$\frac{(\text{Selling price} - \text{Purchase price}) + \text{Dividends received}}{\text{Purchase Price}} = \text{Return}$$

9

State of World	*Prob.*		*Return*		
I	0·20	×	+40%	=	+ 8%
II	0·60	×	+15%	=	+ 9%
III	0·20	×	−10%	=	− 2%
					+15% = $E(r)$

$$\begin{array}{lcl} \textit{(Return)}^2 & \textit{Prob.} & \\ (40\%)^2 \times & 0{\cdot}20 & = 320 \\ (15\%)^2 \times & 0{\cdot}60 & = 135 \\ (-10\%)^2 \times & 0{\cdot}20 & = \underline{\ 20} \\ & & 475 = E(r^2) \end{array}$$

$$\sigma^2 = E(r^2) - E(r)^2 = 475 - (15\%)^2 = 475 - 225 = \underline{250}$$

$$\sigma = \sqrt{\sigma^2} = \sqrt{250} = 15{\cdot}81\%$$

Solution: Expected Return : 15%
Risk (std. dev.) : 15.81%

10 Down-side risk is concerned with the possibility that an investment might do *worse* than expected.

CHAPTER 9

1 The correlation coefficient. The further away it is from + 1, the greater the degree of risk reduction effect.

2 $\sigma_p = \sqrt{[x^2\sigma_A^2 + (1-x)^2\sigma_B^2 + 2x(1-x)\,\text{Cov}\,(r_A, r_B)]}$

or

$\sigma_p = \sqrt{[x^2\sigma_A^2 + (1-x)^2\sigma_B^2 + 2x(1-x)\,\sigma_A\sigma_B\rho_{A,B}]}$

3 A:

$$\begin{aligned} 0{\cdot}3 \times 28\% &= 8{\cdot}4\% \\ 0{\cdot}4 \times 18\% &= 7{\cdot}2\% \\ 0{\cdot}3 \times 6\% &= \underline{1{\cdot}8\%} \\ E(r_A) &= 17{\cdot}4\% \end{aligned}$$

B:

$$\begin{aligned} 0{\cdot}3 \times 35\% &= 10{\cdot}5\% \\ 0{\cdot}4 \times 15\% &= 6\ \% \\ 0{\cdot}3 \times 20\% &= \underline{6\ \%} \\ E(r_B) &= 22{\cdot}5\% \end{aligned}$$

$$\begin{aligned} (28\% - 17{\cdot}4\%) \times (35\% - 22{\cdot}5\%) \times 0{\cdot}3 &= +39{\cdot}75 \\ (18\% - 17{\cdot}4\%) \times (15\% - 22{\cdot}5\%) \times 0{\cdot}4 &= -\ 1{\cdot}80 \\ (6\% - 17{\cdot}4\%) \times (20\% - 22{\cdot}5\%) \times 0{\cdot}3 &= \underline{+\ 8{\cdot}55} \\ \text{Cov}\,[r_A, r_B] &\quad \underline{+46{\cdot}50} \end{aligned}$$

A:

$$\begin{aligned} 0{\cdot}3 \times (28\%)^2 &= 235{\cdot}2 \\ 0{\cdot}4 \times (18\%)^2 &= 129{\cdot}6 \\ 0{\cdot}3 \times (\ 6\%)^2 &= \underline{10{\cdot}8} \\ E(r_A^2) &= \underline{375{\cdot}6} \end{aligned}$$

B:

$$\begin{aligned} 0{\cdot}3 \times (35\%)^2 &= 367{\cdot}5 \\ 0{\cdot}4 \times (15\%)^2 &= 90{\cdot}0 \\ 0{\cdot}3 \times (20\%)^2 &= \underline{120{\cdot}0} \\ E(r_B^2) &= \underline{577{\cdot}5} \end{aligned}$$

$\sigma_A = \sqrt{[E(r_A^2) - E(r_A)^2]}$

$\sigma_A = \sqrt{(375{\cdot}6 - 17{\cdot}4^2)} = \underline{8{\cdot}5\%}$

$\sigma_B = \sqrt{[E(r_B^2) - E(r_B)^2]}$

$\sigma_B = \sqrt{(577{\cdot}5 - 22{\cdot}5^2)} = \underline{8{\cdot}4\%}$

$$\rho_{A,B} = \frac{\text{Cov}\cdot[r_A, r_B]}{\sigma_A \times \sigma_B} = \frac{+46{\cdot}50}{8{\cdot}5 \times 8{\cdot}4} = \underline{\underline{+0{\cdot}65}}$$

4 $E(r_p) = xE(r_A) + (1-x)\,E(r_B)$

$$\begin{aligned} 20\% &= x \times 17{\cdot}4\% + (1-x)\,22{\cdot}5\% \\ 20 &= 17{\cdot}4x + 22{\cdot}5 - 22{\cdot}5x \\ 20 - 22{\cdot}5 &= 17{\cdot}4x - 22{\cdot}5x \\ -2{\cdot}5 &= -5{\cdot}1x \\ \frac{-2{\cdot}5}{-5{\cdot}1} &= x = 0{\cdot}49 \end{aligned}$$

Therefore invest 49% of the funds in investment A, and the remaining 59% in B:

$$20\% = (0{\cdot}49 \times 17{\cdot}4\%) + (0{\cdot}51 \times 22{\cdot}5\%)$$

5 $E(r_i) = \sum_{i=1}^{N} x_i \rho_i$

$$\sigma_p = \sqrt{\sum_{i=1}^{N}\sum_{j=1}^{N} x_i x_j \sigma_i \sigma_j \rho_{ij}}$$

6 A portfolio which lies along the Capital Market Line (CML). It provides either (i) the *maximum* level of expected return for a given level of risk; or (ii) the *minimum* level of risk for a given level of return.

7 $E(r_j) = r_F + \lambda\,\sigma_j$ or $E(r_j) = r_F + \dfrac{E(r_M) - r_F}{\sigma_M}\sigma_j$

8 An efficient portfolio consists of investing in the market portfolio and Government stock (or, borrowing at the risk-free interest rate). Thus, using:

$$\begin{aligned} E(r_p) &= xE(r_M) + (1 - x)r_F \\ 15\% &= x \times 16\% + (1 - x)\ 10\% \\ 15 &= 16x + 10 - 10x \\ 15 - 10 &= 16x - 10x \\ \frac{5}{6} &= x \end{aligned}$$

Therefore *83⅓%* of the funds should be placed in the market portfolio and the balance, *16⅔%*, should be invested in Government stock. The resulting portfolio's risk can be calculated from:

$$E(r_p) = r_F + \frac{E(r_M) - r_F}{\sigma_M}\sigma_p$$

$$15\% = 10\% + \frac{16\% - 10\%}{3\%}\sigma_p$$

$$\frac{15\% - 10\%}{2\%} = \sigma_p = \underline{\underline{2{\cdot}5\%}}$$

9
$$\begin{aligned} 20\% &= x \times 16\% + (1 - x)\ 10\% \\ 20 &= 16x + 10 - 10x \\ 20 - 10 &= 16x - 10x \\ 10 &= 6x \\ \frac{10}{6} &= x = 1{\cdot}6\dot{6} \end{aligned}$$

Therefore borrow 66⅔% of own personal funds at the risk-free interest rate of 10%:

$$\text{Borrow } £1{,}000 \times 0{\cdot}6\dot{6} = £666{\cdot}67.$$

Invest your own funds (£1,000) *plus* the borrowed funds (£666·67) in the market portfolio.

Risk of the portfolio would be:

$$20\% = 10\% + \frac{16\% - 10\%}{3\%}\sigma_p$$

$$\frac{20\% - 10\%}{2\%} = \sigma_p = \underline{\underline{5\%}}$$

10 The market portfolio is the ultimate diversified portfolio and so contains *only* non-diversifiable risk. It consists of shares in *all* companies quoted on the stock exchange, held in proportion to the companies' total market values.

CHAPTER 10

1 $r_A = r_F + [E(r_M) - r_F]\,\beta_A$

2 The *systematic* risk of an investment, *relative* to the risk of the market portfolio.

3 Unsystematic risk is that part of an investment's total risk that can be diversified away. Its sources are those factors that are *specific* to the investment, such as its management's ability and the quality of its research and development activities.

4 There are two principal factors:
(i) the sensitivity of the firm's revenues to the level of economic activity in the economy;
(ii) the proportion of fixed to variable costs.

5 $20\% \times 0{\cdot}6 = 12\% =$ systematic risk
$8\% =$ unsystematic risk
$20\% =$ total risk

$$\beta_B = \frac{20\% \times 0{\cdot}6}{10\%} = \frac{12\%}{10\%} = \underline{1{\cdot}20}$$

6 $$\beta_C = \frac{\text{Cov}\,[r_C, r_M]}{\sigma_M^2} = \frac{73{\cdot}5}{7\% \times 7\%} = \frac{73{\cdot}5}{49} = \underline{1{\cdot}5}$$

7 $\beta_{\text{company + project}} = (1{\cdot}20 \times 0{\cdot}90) + (1{\cdot}70 \times 0{\cdot}10) = \underline{1{\cdot}25}$

8 If a share is over-valued, it is giving an expected return of *less* than it should. Hence, it would lie below the CAPM, similar to X on Figure 10.2.

9 The CAPM is a *single factor* model: expected return is determined by a single factor – systematic risk or beta. The arbitrage pricing model is a *multi-factor* model: expected return is determined by more than a single factor.

10 $E(r_{\text{project}}) = 8\% + [12\% - 8\%] \times 1{\cdot}75 = 15\%$

$$\begin{aligned} -100\,(1{\cdot}15)^{0} &= -100 \\ +\ 60\,(1{\cdot}15)^{-1} &= +\ 52{\cdot}18 \\ +\ 50\,(1{\cdot}15)^{-2} &= \underline{+\ 37{\cdot}80} \\ &\ \ -\ 10{\cdot}02 \text{ NPV} \end{aligned}$$

The project has a negative NPV when discounted at 15%. Thus it produces a return of less than 15%. As the CAPM indicates that the minimum return from an investment with this level of systematic risk (estimated by the beta value of the industry group into which the project can be classified) is 15%, the project should be rejected.

CHAPTER 11

1 Success: $-1000 + 500\,A_{\overline{3}|0{\cdot}10} = +243$ NPV
Failure: $-1000 + 350\,A_{\overline{3}|0{\cdot}10} = -130$ NPV

State	*Prob.*		*NPV*		
I	0·45	×	+243	=	+109
II	0·55	×	−130	=	− 72
					+ 37 ENPV

2

Survey Indicates	*Action*	*Prob.*		*Outcome*		
State I	Accept	0·45	×	+243 NPV	=	+109
State II	Reject	0·55	×	0 NPV	=	0
						+109 ENPV

ENPV with survey	: +109
ENPV without survey	: + 37
Max. worth of survey	: + 72

3

Survey Indicates	*Probability*	*State*
State I correctly	0·45 × 0·75 = 0·3375	A
State I incorrectly	0·45 × 0·25 = 0·1125	B
State II correctly	0·55 × 0·75 = 0·4125	C
State II incorrectly	0·55 × 0·25 = 0·1375	D

State	*Action*	*Prob.*		*Outcome*		
A	Accept	0·3375	×	+243 NPV	=	+82
B	Accept	0·1125	×	− 72 NPV	=	− 8
C	Reject	0·4125	×	0 NPV	=	0
D	Reject	0·1375	×	−243 NPV	=	−33
				ENPV		+41

ENPV with survey	: +41
ENPV without survey	: +37
Max. worth of survey	: + 4

4

State	*Prob.*		*NPV*		
I	0·3	×	+100	=	+30
II	0·5	×	+ 50	=	+25
III	0·2	×	−300	=	−60
			ENPV		− 5

Therefore, without the survey we would *not* accept the project and so incur a *zero NPV.*

Survey Indicates	*Action*	*Prob.*		*Outcome*		
I	Accept	0·3	×	+100	=	+30
II	Accept	0·5	×	+ 50	=	+25
III	Reject	0·2	×	0	=	0
				ENPV		+55

ENPV with survey	: +55
ENPV without survey	: 0
Max. worth of survey	: +55

5 If the machine is bought and, at the end of Yr 1, the decision is taken *not* to abandon the project, then the outcomes will be:

State	*Yr 1*	*Yr 2*	*NPV*	*Decision*
I	−60	+100	+23·43	Don't abandon
II	−60	+ 60	− 6·81	Abandon
III	−60	+ 40	−21·93	Abandon

The investment decision is therefore:

State	*Yr 0*	*Yr 1*	*Yr 2*	*NPV*	*Prob.*	
I	−140	+100	+100	+22·57 ×	0·70	= +15·80
II	−140	+ 60 } + 60		−35·65 ×	0·10	= − 3·56
III	−140	+ 40 } + 60		−53·04 ×	0·20	= −10·61
					ENPV	+ 1·63

The complete decision is that the company should purchase the machine but, if either states II or III occur, then the machine should be sold off at the end of the first year.

6 $-1{,}000 + 280\,A_{\overline{5}|0\cdot10} = +61\cdot42$ NPV

Life = x At 5 year life: $+61\cdot42$ NPV

At 4 year life:

$-1000 + 280\,A_{\overline{4}|0\cdot10} = -112\cdot40$ NPV

Using linear interpolation: $x = 4 + \left[\dfrac{112\cdot40}{61\cdot42 + 112\cdot40} \times (5-4)\right] = \underline{4\cdot65}$ yrs.

Thus the life of the project can be reduced by up to 0·35 of a year (approx $4\frac{1}{4}$ months) before the original decision advice is incorrect. This represents a maximum change of $0\cdot35 \div 5 = 7\%$.

Net cash flow = x

$$-1000 + x\,A_{\overline{5}|0\cdot10} = 0 \text{ NPV}$$
$$x = 1000 \div A_{\overline{5}|0\cdot10} = 264$$

Thus the annual net cash flow can fall by up to 16 per year, or $16 \div 280 = 5\cdot7\%$ before the original decision advice is incorrect.

CHAPTER 12

1 $P_E = 147 - 13 = \underline{130\text{p}}$ ex div.

$$11\tfrac{1}{4}(1+g)^3 = 13$$
$$g = (13 \div 11\tfrac{1}{4})^{\frac{1}{3}} - 1 = \underline{0\cdot049}$$
$$K_E = \frac{13(1+0\cdot049)}{130} + 0\cdot049 = 0\cdot154 \text{ or } 15\cdot4\%$$

2 (i) Both r and b remain constant values.
(ii) All-equity financed company.
(iii) All projects financed out of retained earnings.

3 $P_D = £128 - £15 = £113$ ex int.

$$+113 - 15(1-0\cdot35)A_{\overline{4}|K_{DAT}} + 110(1+K_{DAT})^{-4} = 0 \text{ NPV}$$

At 5%, NPV = −12·07
At 15%, NPV = +22·28

$$K_D = 5\% + \left[\frac{12{\cdot}07}{22{\cdot}28 + 12{\cdot}07} \times (15\% - 5\%)\right] = \underline{8{\cdot}5\%}$$

$$V_D = £12\text{m} \times 1{\cdot}13 = \underline{£13{\cdot}56\text{m}}$$

4 $\left.\begin{array}{l} 12(1 - 0{\cdot}35)A_{\overline{3}|0{\cdot}085} + 100(1{\cdot}085)^{-3} \\ (7{\cdot}8 \times 2{\cdot}5540) + (100 \times 0{\cdot}7216) \end{array}\right\} = £92{\cdot}08 = P_D$

$$£10\text{m} \times 0{\cdot}9208 = \underline{£9{\cdot}208\text{m}} = V_D$$

5 Given note 19 and the fact that:

$$P_D = £118 - £18 = £100 \text{ ex int.}$$

and the debt is redeemable at par then the coupon rate equals K_D and so

$$K_{DAT} = 18\%(1 - 0{\cdot}35) = \underline{11{\cdot}7\%}$$

6 (i) Weak efficiency.
(ii) Semi-strong efficiency.
(iii) Strong efficiency.

7 (i) Share prices will reflect management decisions as long as they are communicated to the Stock Market.
(ii) Shares are never over or under-valued from the point of view of the timing of capital raising.
(iii) A take-over of a quoted company is unlikely to represent a positive NPV investment.

8 With weak efficiency, technical analysis is worthless; with semi-strong efficiency, so too is fundamental analysis and with strong efficiency investors cannot even expect to gain from inside information.

9 Share prices react to the disclosure of new, relevant information. New information arises at random intervals of time and can be randomly either good or bad. Hence share price movements themselves occur at random.

10 A technical analyst tries to identify patterns that recur in past share price movements. Then if one of those patterns is observed starting to develop, the technical analyst hopes that this will provide an ability to predict the future share price movement as the pattern develops more fully.

CHAPTER 13

1 $K_E = \dfrac{5(1{\cdot}07)}{83} + 0{\cdot}07 = \underline{13{\cdot}4\%}$ $\qquad V_E = 24\text{m} \times 83\text{p} = \underline{£19{\cdot}92\text{m}}$

$$K_{DQ} = \frac{15(1 - 0{\cdot}35)}{110} = \underline{8{\cdot}9\%} \qquad V_{DQ} = £25\text{m} \times 1{\cdot}10 = \underline{£27{\cdot}5\text{m}}$$

$$K_{DUQ} = K_{DQ} = \underline{8{\cdot}9\%} \text{ (assuming similar risk).}$$

$$P_{DUQ} = \frac{12(1 - 0{\cdot}35)}{0{\cdot}089} = £87{\cdot}64 \qquad \therefore V_{DUQ} = £10\text{m} \times 0{\cdot}8764 = \underline{£8{\cdot}76\text{m}}$$

$$K_L = 14\%(1 - 0{\cdot}35) = \underline{9{\cdot}1\%} \qquad V_L = \underline{£3\text{m}}$$

$$V_0 = £19{\cdot}92\text{m} + £27{\cdot}5\text{m} + £3\text{m} = \underline{£59{\cdot}18\text{m}}$$

$$K_0 = \left(13{\cdot}4\% \times \frac{19{\cdot}92}{59{\cdot}18}\right) + \left(8{\cdot}9\% \times \frac{27{\cdot}5}{59{\cdot}18}\right) + \left(8{\cdot}9\% \times \frac{8{\cdot}76}{59{\cdot}18}\right)$$

$$+ \left(9{\cdot}1\% \times \frac{3}{59{\cdot}18}\right) = \underline{\underline{10{\cdot}4\%}}$$

2 In the medium to long term the company will maintain a fixed capital structure and it is the overall return on this mix of capital that projects must be able to generate to allow the company to continue in existence.
3 (i) Project is small relative to the size of the company.
(ii) Project will be financed in such a way as not to change the capital structure.
(iii) Project has the same degree of systematic risk as that of the company's existing cash flows.
(iv) All level perpetuity cash flows.
4 Its WACC will reflect its *average* level of systematic risk and not the particular level of systematic risk of any one of its individual business activities. Thus the WACC is an unsuitable NPV discount rate to evaluate projects in any one of the company's areas of activity.
5 The CAPM produces an NPV discount rate which is tailor-made to the level of systematic risk of the individual project. The WACC only reflects the company's existing, *average* systematic risk level.
6 Because companies, but not individual investors, can get tax relief on debt interest.
7 Companies should finance themselves almost entirely with debt capital.
8 The *gearing* or *leverage* ratio is usually measured as $V_D{:}V_E$, although it is sometimes measured, as a percentage, as: $V_D \div V_0$.

CHAPTER 14

1 Given:

$$K_{E_g} = K_{E_{ug}} + [K_{E_{ug}} - K_D]\frac{V_D}{V_E} \quad \text{then}$$

$$20\% = K_{E_{ug}} + [K_{E_{ug}} - 10\%]\frac{1}{4}$$

$$20\% = K_{E_{ug}} + 0{\cdot}25\,K_{E_{ug}} - 2{\cdot}5\%$$

$$20\% + 2{\cdot}5\% = 1{\cdot}25\,K_{E_{ug}}$$

$$\frac{22{\cdot}5\%}{1{\cdot}25} = K_{E_{ug}} = \underline{\underline{18\%}}$$

2 Again using the M and M equation:

$$K_{E_g} = 18\% + [18\% - 10\%]\frac{3}{5} = \underline{\underline{22{\cdot}8\%}}$$

In a no-tax world, the gearing ratio does *not* affect the WACC. So the change in capital structure will leave K_0 unchanged:

$$K_0 = 20\% \times \frac{4}{5} + 10\% \times \frac{1}{5} = \underline{\underline{18\%}}$$

$$K_0 = 22{\cdot}8\% \times \frac{5}{8} + 10\% \times \frac{3}{8} = \underline{\underline{18\%}}$$

3 Sell your shares in company A for £100 cash and buy £25 of debt in company B and £75 of company B's equity.
4 In arbitrage it is necessary to show the *pure* gain that can be made with no

change in either business or financial risk. Business risk does not cause problems as the two companies involved in the arbitrage would be in the same business risk class (same asset betas). However, if a shareholder in a *geared* company wished to arbitrage into another company, care must be taken in order to preserve the existing degree of financial risk held. This is maintained by substituting home-made for corporate gearing.

5 Financial risk is borne by the shareholders in a geared company. It arises out of the fact that, because debt interest has to be paid in full before equity dividends can be paid, then shareholders are at risk that the company may have insufficient cash flow to pay dividends because it has all gone out in interest payments. This is financial risk.

6 As $K_D = r_F = 10\%$, then we can assume $\beta_{debt} = 0$
Using CAPM, $20\% = 10\% + [15\% - 10\%]\beta_{equity}$

therefore $$\frac{20\% - 10\%}{[15\% - 10\%]} = \beta_{equity} = 2{\cdot}0$$

$$\beta_{assets} = 2{\cdot}0 \times \frac{2}{3} + 0 \times \frac{1}{3} = \underline{\underline{1{\cdot}33}}$$

7 $$\beta_{equity} = \beta_{assets} \times \frac{V_0}{V_E} = 1{\cdot}33 \times \frac{7}{5} = \underline{\underline{1{\cdot}87}}$$

8 For two companies to be in the same business risk class, they should have the same asset betas and – in a no tax world – the same WACC. As the WACCs of the two companies are *not* the same, we can conclude that they are not in the same business risk class:

$$K_0 = 20\% \times \frac{2}{3} + 10\% \times \frac{1}{3} = \underline{\underline{16{\cdot}67\%}}$$

$$K_0 = 20\% \times \frac{5}{7} + 10\% \times \frac{2}{7} = \underline{\underline{17{\cdot}14\%}}$$

Alternatively, the asset beta of the question 6 company is $\underline{\underline{1.33}}$

The asset beta of the question 8 company is:

$$\left(2{\cdot}0 \times \frac{5}{7}\right) + \left(0 \times \frac{2}{7}\right) = \beta_{assets} = \underline{\underline{1{\cdot}43}}$$

CHAPTER 15

1 Using: $$K_{E_g} = K_{E_{ug}} + [K_{E_{ug}} + K_D]\frac{V_D(1 - T_C)}{V_E}$$

then: $$25\% = K_{E_{ug}} + [K_{E_{ug}} - 10\%]\frac{1(1 - 0{\cdot}35)}{3}$$

$$25\% = K_{E_{ug}} + 0{\cdot}217K_{E_{ug}} - 2{\cdot}17\%$$

$$25\% + 2{\cdot}17\% = 1{\cdot}217K_{E_{ug}}$$

$$27{\cdot}17\% \div 1{\cdot}217 = K_{E_{ug}} = \underline{\underline{22{\cdot}32\%}}$$

2 $K_{0_g} = K_{E_{ug}}\left(1 - \frac{V_D T_C}{V_0}\right)$, therefore:

$$K_{0_g} = 22{\cdot}32\%\left(1 - \frac{1 \times 0{\cdot}35}{1 + 2}\right)$$

$$K_{0_g} = 22{\cdot}32\% \times 0{\cdot}8833 = \underline{\underline{19{\cdot}7\%}}$$

3 $V_{0_g} = V_{E_{ug}} + V_D T_C$, therefore:

$$V_{0_g} = £40\text{m} + (£10 \times 0{\cdot}35) = \underline{\underline{£43{\cdot}5\text{m}}}$$

Shareholder wealth would have increased by the value of the tax shield:

$$V_D T_C = £10\text{m} \times 0{\cdot}35 = \underline{\underline{£3{\cdot}5\text{m}}}$$

4 $K_{0_g} = K_{E_{ug}}\left(1 - \frac{V_D T_C}{V_0}\right)$

5 The tax shield represents the present value of the tax relief on debt interest. It is the source of the increase in shareholders' wealth that arises from increasing the level of gearing.

6 Debt capacity describes an asset's ability to act as security for a loan. Specifically, an asset's percentage debt capacity indicates the size of loan it would act as security for, expressed as a percentage of the asset's worth.

7 Using: $V_{0_g} = V_{E_{ug}} + V_D T_C - E[b/c]$

then: $£40\text{m} = V_{E_{ug}} + (£10\text{m} \times 0{\cdot}35) - (0{\cdot}05 \times £1\text{m})$

$£40\text{m} - £3{\cdot}5\text{m} + £0{\cdot}05\text{m} = V_{E_{ug}} = \underline{\underline{£36{\cdot}55\text{m}}}$

8 $V_{0_g} = V_{E_{ug}} + V_D\left[1 - \frac{(1 - T_C)(1 - T_E)}{1 - T_D}\right]$

CHAPTER 16

1 Because the project's NPV will *add* to the market value of the equity.

2 The return required from the project which purely reflects its systematic *business* risk (i.e. it assumes the project is all-equity financed).

3 What the NPV of the project would be, if it was all-equity financed.

4 An operating lease is essentially a marketing device to encourage sales and can be viewed as an operating cash flow. A financial lease is a particular method of project financing.

5 $\beta_{\text{assets}} = 1{\cdot}45 \times \frac{5}{5 + 2(1 - 0{\cdot}35)} + 0{\cdot}25 \times \frac{2(1 - 0{\cdot}35)}{5 + 2(1 - 0{\cdot}35)} = \underline{\underline{1{\cdot}20}}$

6 The equity beta reflects both the business *and* financial systematic risk. The asset beta purely reflects the business systematic risk. Therefore the *financial* systematic risk is reflected in a beta value of: $1{\cdot}45 - 1{\cdot}20 = \underline{\underline{0{\cdot}25}}$.

7 Debt capacity concerns an asset's ability to act as security for a loan.

8 The PV of the tax shield is based on debt capacity. Therefore the PV of the tax shield can be calculated as:

$£2500 \times 0{\cdot}10 = £250 \times 0{\cdot}35 = £87{\cdot}50$ = Annual tax relief

PV of tax relief: $£87{\cdot}50 A_{\overline{5}|0{\cdot}10}(1{\cdot}10)^{-1} = \underline{£301{\cdot}54}$

CHAPTER 17

1 $\dfrac{1 + \text{inflation}_{\$}}{1 + \text{inflation}_{£}} = \dfrac{\text{Forward rate}}{\text{Spot rate}}$

2 $\dfrac{1{\cdot}8420 \times 1{\cdot}25}{1{\cdot}9050} - 1 = 0{\cdot}209$ or $\underline{20{\cdot}9\%}$ approx.

3 $1{\cdot}9280(1 - 0{\cdot}07)^3 = \underline{1{\cdot}5508}$

4 \$1·7940
less 150
\$1·7790 = 2 month forward rate

5 (i) Project's \$ cash flows are discounted by \$ discount rate to give a \$ NPV which is then converted at spot to a £ NPV; or
(ii) Project's \$ cash flows are converted into £ cash flows and then discounted at the £ discount rate to give a £ NPV.

6 Because they may well affect the cash flow available to be remitted back to the parent.

7 Property fixed assets and working capital, finance in the overseas currency. Non-property fixed assets, finance via the export of £.

8 (i) Dividends;
(ii) Interest;
(iii) Management charges;
(iv) Royalty payments;
(v) Transfer prices.

9 The risk that the host government might adversely change the 'rules of the game' *after* the company have undertaken the investment.

10 Economic risk describes the risk that a company is exposed to from unexpected FX rate movements and their resulting impact on the £ worth of a foreign project's cash flows.

CHAPTER 18

1 The dividend decision could be said to be irrelevant because it does not affect the overall return on the shares, but simply determines how that return is split up between dividend and capital gain.

2 Given the irrelevancy argument of the dividend decision, a company should invest as much of its retained earnings as possible in positive NPV projects. If all earnings cannot be utilized in this way, then the residual should be paid out as a dividend. In this way, shareholder wealth will be maximized.

3 If dividends are to be truly irrelevant, then companies must be indifferent between financing projects with retained earnings and financing via cash raised externally. For this to be the case, the company's capital structure must also be an irrelevant consideration.

4 The bird-in-the-hand argument is that dividends, because they represent a *certain current* cash flow, are worth more than retained earnings which represent an *uncertain future* cash flow. Hence dividends are preferred to capital gains.

5 Investors with high marginal rates of personal tax are likely to prefer capital gains to dividends. There are two reasons. The first is that the marginal rate of capital gains tax is likely to be less than the marginal rate of tax on dividends. Secondly, the investor can *control* the time at which he takes his capital gains

to give the greatest degree of tax efficiency. In contrast dividends must be taken when the company decides to pay them.

6 The clientele effect implies that companies should follow a consistent dividend policy to attract to them a specific clientele of investors.

7 There are two main classes of evidence. One is that companies seem reluctant to face a situation where they have to reduce dividends from one year to the next. Thus dividend growth lags behind earnings growth. The other evidence suggests that share prices react significantly to unexpected changes in dividends.

8 Given the evidence on signalling, to retain an expected dividend for capital investment purposes might be thought of as unwise. The market might interpret the decision as a signal about an unfavourable financial position.

Index